Communications in Computer and Information Science   1392

More information about this series at http://www.springer.com/series/7899

V. Arunachalam · K. Sivasankaran (Eds.)

Microelectronic Devices, Circuits and Systems

Second International Conference, ICMDCS 2021
Vellore, India, February 11–13, 2021
Revised Selected Papers

Springer

Editors
V. Arunachalam ⓘⒹ
Vellore Institute of Technology
Vellore, India

K. Sivasankaran ⓘⒹ
Vellore Institute of Technology
Vellore, India

ISSN 1865-0929   ISSN 1865-0937 (electronic)
Communications in Computer and Information Science
ISBN 978-981-16-5047-5   ISBN 978-981-16-5048-2 (eBook)
https://doi.org/10.1007/978-981-16-5048-2

This Springer imprint is published by the registered company Springer Nature Singapore Pte Ltd.
The registered company address is: 152 Beach Road, #21-01/04 Gateway East, Singapore 189721, Singapore

Preface

It is our great pleasure to collate the research papers presented at the 2nd International Conference on Microelectronic Devices, Circuits, and Systems (ICMDCS 2021) and publish them in this prestigious Springer conference proceedings series "Communications in Computer and Information Science (CCIS)".

ICMDCS 2021 was organized by the Department of Micro and Nanoelectronics, School of Electronics Engineering (SENSE), at the Vellore Institute of Technology (VIT), India, and took place during February 11–13, 2021. The conference was technically supported by the industry partner GlobalFoundries, India. Due to the COVID-19 pandemic scenario, ICMDCS 2021 was conducted in virtual mode, thanks to video conferencing technology.

The conference received 103 research papers in subject areas including digital integrated circuit (IC) design; analog, radio frequency (RF), and mixed-signal IC design; device modeling and technology; RF communication circuits; embedded systems; and nonlinear circuits and systems. After the plagiarism check and rigorous review process, 38 articles were accepted for presentation in 8 technical sessions.

The conference had 12 keynote talks given by eminent academicians and industry leaders from India, the USA, Germany, France, Japan, and Singapore. Some of the notable speakers were Kaushik Roy, Purdue University, USA; Stuart Parkin, Max Planck Institute of Microstructure Physics, Germany; Saifur Rehman, Virginia Tech, USA; and David Rogers, Nanovation, France.

In addition to the keynote and technical paper presentations, pre-conference industry sponsored tutorial sessions on recent advancements in the abovementioned areas were offered by experts from GlobalFoundries, Intel, and Siemens EDA on February 11, 2021.

Certainly, ICMDCS 2021 was a platform to hear, demonstrate, and witness the growth of microelectronic, embedded and smart systems with more than 63 presenting authors and 45 delegates.

We express our sincere thanks to the Vellore Institute of Technology management for providing encouragement and the facilities to organize this conference. Vipin Madangarli, Director, Design Enablement, GlobalFoundries, India, provided constant support in organizing the event. Also, we are thankful to the faculty and staff of SENSE for their wholehearted contributions from the inception of the conference to the final submission of the papers to CCIS.

Arunachalam V.
Sivasankaran K.

Organization

Chief Patron

G. Viswanathan (Chancellor)   Vellore Institute of Technology, India

Patrons

Sankar Viswanathan   Vellore Institute of Technology, India
(Vice-president)
Sekar Viswanathan   Vellore Institute of Technology, India
(Vice-president)
G. V. Selvam (Vice-president)   Vellore Institute of Technology, India
Kadhambari S. Viswanathan   Vellore Institute of Technology, India
(Assistant Vice-president)
Rambabu Kodali (Vice   Vellore Institute of Technology, India
Chancellor)
S. Narayanan (Pro-vice   Vellore Institute of Technology, India
Chancellor)

General Chair

Kittur Harish Mallikarjun   Vellore Institute of Technology, India

Organizing Chairs

Arunachalam V.   Vellore Institute of Technology, India
Sivasankaran K.   Vellore Institute of Technology, India

Technical Review Chair

Nithish Kumar V.   Vellore Institute of Technology, India

Registration Chairs

Sri Abibhatla Sridevi   Vellore Institute of Technology, Vellore,
India
Aarthy M.   Vellore Institute of Technology, Vellore,
India

Virtual Platform Chairs

Prayline Rajabhai	Vellore Institute of Technology, India
Aarthy M.	Vellore Institute of Technology, India
Sanjay R.	Vellore Institute of Technology, India
Antony Glittas	Vellore Institute of Technology, India

Technical Session Chairs

S. Kumaravel	Vellore Institute of Technology, India
Sri Abibhatla Sridevi	Vellore Institute of Technology, India
R. Sakthivel	Vellore Institute of Technology, India
NIthish Kumar V	Vellore Institute of Technology, India
V. N. Ramakrishnan	Vellore Institute of Technology, India
Rajan Kumar Pandey	Vellore Institute of Technology, India
Jagannadha Naidu K.	Vellore Institute of Technology, India
Vikas Vijayvargiya	Vellore Institute of Technology, India

Tutorial Chairs

Sivanantham S.	Vellore Institute of Technology, India
Sivasankaran K.	Vellore Institute of Technology, India
Vipin Madangarli	GlobalFoundries, India

Technical Program Committee

Aditya Deulkar	Samsung Semiconductor India, India
Abhishek Ramanujam	Analog Devices, Ireland
Xiao-Zhi Gao	Helsinki University of Technology, Finland
Roy Paily	Indian Institute of Technology, Guwahati, India
Parameswaran Ramanathan	University of Wisconsin-Madison, USA
Vignesh Rajamani	Oakland University, USA
Navin Bishnoi	Marvell Semiconductors, Bangalore, India
Sreehari Veeramachaneni	BITS, Hyderabad, India
Debesh K. Das	Jadavpur University, India
Maryam Shojaei Baghini	Indian Institute of Technology, Bombay, India
P. Krishnamoorthi	Philips India Pvt. Ltd., Bangalore, India
P. Sakthivel	Anna University, India
P. Ramesh	Amritha University, Calcutta, India
G. Lakshminarayanan	National Institute of Technology, Tiruchirappalli, India

Sang Hyeon Kim	Korea Advanced Institute of Science and Technology, South Korea
Sudarshan Srinivasan	Intel, Bangalore, India
Tapan K Nayak	CERN, Switzerland
Vanathi P. T.	PSG College of Technology, India
Venkata Vanukuru	GlobalFoundries, Bangalore, India
Venkateswaran	SSN College of Engineering, India
Virendra Singh	Indian Institute of Technology, Bombay, India
Vita Pi-Ho Hu	National Chiao Tung University, Taiwan
Xingsheng Wang	University of Glasgow, UK
Anis Suhaila Mohd Zain	Technical University of Malaysia, Malaysia
Ashok Govindarajan	Zilogic Systems, India
Balamurugan G.	Honeywell, Bangalore, India
V. Chandrasekar	Colorado State University, USA
Changhwan Shin	Sungkyunkwan University, South Korea
Hyungcheol Shin	Seoul National University, South Korea
Jawahar Senthil Kumar V.	Anna University, India
Gaurav Goel	Intel, Bangalore, India
Jayaraman K.	Maxim Integrated, Bangalore, India
Jing Guo	University of Florida, USA
Jongwook Jeon	Konkuk University, South Korea
Yang Hao	Queen Mary University of London, UK
Lavakumar A.	Synopsys, Bangalore, India
Meganathan D.	Anna University, India
Moorthi S.	National Institute of Technology Tiruchirappalli, India
Nirmal Kumar P.	Anna University, India
Pradeep Nair	Texas Instruments, Bangalore, India
N. Balamurugan	Thiagarajar College of Engineering, India
C. P. Ravikumar	Texas Instruments, Bangalore, India
Vipin Madangarli	GlobalFoundries, Bangalore, India
M. Raja	BITS Dubai Campus, UAE
Kewal K. Saluja	University of Winsconsin-Madison, USA
Krishnendu Chakrabarty	Duke University, USA
Xiao-Zhi Ga	Helsinki University of Technology, Finland
Subramaniam Ganesan	Oakland University, USA
Anand Paul	Kyungpook National University, South Korea
K. Bharanitharan	Tainan, Taiwan
Vijaya Samara Rao Pasupureddi	Carinthia University of Applied Sciences, Austria

Vishwani D. Agrawal   Samuel Ginn College of Engineering,
                               Auburn University, Alabama
Balamurugan G.   Honeywell, Bangalore, India
V. Kamakoti   Indian Institute of Technology, Madras,
                               India
Susmita Sur-Kolay   ACM Unit, Indian Statistical Institute,
                               India
M. Sabarimalai Manikandan   Indian Institute of Technology,
                               Bhuvaneshwar, India

Contents

Communication Technologies and Circuits

Technology and Modelling for Micro Electronic Devices

Electronics for Green Technology

Digital Design for Signal, Image and Video Processing

Feature Extraction Techniques for the Classification of Four-Class Motor Imagery Based EEG Data: A Comparison

Rupesh Mahamune$^{(\boxtimes)}$ ⓘ and S. H. Laskar ⓘ

Electronics and Instrumentation Engineering Department,
National Institute of Technology Silchar, Assam, India
rupesh_rs@ei.nits.ac.in

Abstract. In this paper, the four-class classification (Left hand, right hand, feet, and tongue) Motor Imagery (MI) signals is performed using four different feature extraction techniques. First, raw EEG signals are pre-processed using the Multi-Class Common Spatial Pattern (CSP) method (one-versus-rest scheme), which discriminates features in feature space and improves the accuracy of classification. Then, four different features, namely channel FFT energy, mean band power, mean channel energy, and Discrete Wavelet Transform (DWT) based mean band energy features, are extracted from pre-processed EEG signals and compared to find the most suitable feature for the discrimination of four-class MI tasks. Besides, three classifiers, namely Bayesian Network classifier (Naive Bays), Linear discriminant analysis (LDA), and Linear Support Vector Machine (SVM), are compared. Performance evaluation is done on BCI competition IV dataset 2a using classification accuracy along with different performance measures calculated from a confusion matrix. The performance of the LDA classifier is found better than linear SVM and Naive Bays. The presented framework with DWT as a feature extraction technique and LDA classifier has obtained an average test classification accuracy of 80.29% over four subjects out of nine. The less computational cost of this framework makes it suitable for online Motor Imagery based BCI Systems.

Keywords: Electroencephalogram signals (EEG) · Motor imagery (MI) · Brain computer interface (BCI) · Discrete wavelet transform (DWT) · Common spatial pattern (CSP)

1 Introduction

Brain Computer Interface (BCI) set up a communication between computers and humans via the neural information of the brain activity [1]. Motor Imagery(MI) based BCI systems using EEG signals are the most promising applications [2] especially for paralyzed patients and asynchronous BCIs [3]. The prominent issue in the BCI system is the balance between accuracy and speed. Therefore

© Springer Nature Singapore Pte Ltd. 2021
V. Arunachalam and K. Sivasankaran (Eds.): ICMDCS 2021, CCIS 1392, pp. 3–18, 2021.
https://doi.org/10.1007/978-981-16-5048-2_1

the number of features should be minimum to keep the balance between speed and accuracy.

The spatial distribution of the MI signal is different for different imagined movements. As the frequency band of a single trial varies from subject to subject, the classification of MI tasks becomes challenging. Therefore, raw EEG signals were decomposed into spatial patterns with maximum deviation in their variance using CSP [4], which helped discriminate the MI tasks. Later on, in BCI application, information transfer rate was improved using multi-class CSP method (one vs rest scheme) by Dornhege et al. [5].

The feature extraction technique contributes in obtaining better classification accuracy. Different feature extraction techniques were proposed in the literature to enhance MI signals to obtain better classification rates. Vega-Escobar et al. [6], decomposed MI signals using DWT and extracted PSD features to classify two class MI tasks. It was observed that the proposed method gave better classification accuracy than using PSD features of raw MI signals. Marcin et al. [28], used Higher Order Statistics of Wavelet Components for EEG data classification. Xu BG et al. [29], used wavelet coefficient statistics along with 6th order AR coefficients to form the feature sets. Sakhavi et al. [7], extracted temporal features after the application of FBCSP to train CNN to classify MI signals. Yang et al. [8], used augmented CSP (ACSP) features to classify MI signals. This reduces the loss of the important frequency information when fixed bands are selected for feature extraction. Lu et al. [9], used frequency domain features extracted from EEG signals using Fast Fourier Transform (FFT) and wavelet package decomposition (WPD) to train three restricted Boltzmann machine (RBM). It was found that FFT performed better than WPD. Hardik et al. [10], identified and removed artifact present in the data during pre-processing stage using modified common spatial pattern (CSP), which had led to better CSP log variance features and used Self-Regulated Interval Type-2 Neuro-Fuzzy Inference System (SRIT2NFIS) for classification of Motor Imagery tasks. Sakhavi et al. [11], extracted energy-based features using FBCSP and fed to convolution neural networks (CNN). It was found that the proposed method performed better than Support Vector Machine (SVM) with static energy features significantly. Thang et al. [12], selected optimal time slice and components to train CSP filters and discriminated the mental tasks by using Event Related Desynchronization/ Event Related Synchronization (ERD/ERS) effects. Hamedi et al. [13], extracted Root Mean Square (RMS) features and Integrated EEG (IEEG) and compared Multilayer Perceptron and Radial Basis Function Neural Networks for the MI tasks discrimination. Xygonakis et al. [14], extracted CSP variance features from the selected regions of interest (ROIs) using CSP filters and achieved better classification accuracy using LDA for four-class MI signals. Resalet et al. [15], revealed that the alpha Band Pass (alpha-BP) feature using power spectral density (PSD) was the best feature in MI-based applications after comparing with alpha band power fast fourier transform (alpha-BP-FFT), Mean Absolute Value and Auto-Regressive (AR) for 3-class MI data. Mohamed et al. [16], used Continuous Wavelet Transform (CWT) to extract features from MI signals, and the classifiers, namely SVM, RBFN, and Bayes Net, were employed to discriminate left, right-hand movement, and forward imagery tasks. Out of three classifiers, Bayes Net was found better than the other two classifiers. In recent years, deep learning networks have outperformed to discriminate the MI tasks [11,17,18]. But the only drawback with them is the longer training time to train the networks.

Thus, from the literature, it is observed that there is a research scope to employ different combinations of features and classifiers for the multi-class classification of MI signals.

In this paper, four different feature extraction techniques, namely channel FFT energy, mean band power, mean channel energy, and mean band energy features extracted using Discrete Wavelet Transform (DWT), are compared to classify four-class MI signals. Materials and methods are described in Sect. 2 of this paper, while Sect. 3 defines the terms used for performance evaluation. Section 4 explains the results obtained, and at the end, conclusions are drawn from this work in Sect. 5.

2   Materials and Methods

2.1   Data Acquisition and Datasets

In this paper, dataset 2a by Brunner et al. from BCI Competition IV has been used [19]. Nine subjects were involved in the data acquisition process. It includes four MI classes (Right hand, left hand, both feet, and tongue movement imagination). For each subject, two sessions were recorded. Each session has six runs, and each run has 48 trials. Forty-eight trials include 12 trials of each class. So each session consists of 288 trials. Figure 1 (a) shows the data acquisition format of one trial with respect to time. At the beginning of each trial, a short acoustic warning tone was presented. Then a fixation cross appeared on the computer screen for 2 s. After that from $t = 2$ s a cue was displayed during which subject had to do one of the MI task out of four till $t = 6$ s. At the end of a trial, a short break lasted for 1.5–2.5 s, during which the subject was allowed to relax. Fig. 1 (b) shows the location of 22 channels. These 22 channels were sampled 250 Hz and three monopolar EOG channels and filtered between 0.5 100 Hz using a band-pass filter, and a notch filter 50 Hz was also applied. Invalid trials of EEG data were discarded before the experiments using artifact correction method described in [19] by Brunner et al.

2.2   Classification Framework

Block diagram of the classification framework is shown in the Fig. 2 and the overall classification process is detailed in the following sub-sections.

Band-Pass Filtering. First of all, the raw EEG data is filtered 7 Hz and 31 Hz using the 5-th order Butterworth finite impulse response (FIR) band-pass filter as brain activities related to MI lies within this frequency band [2].

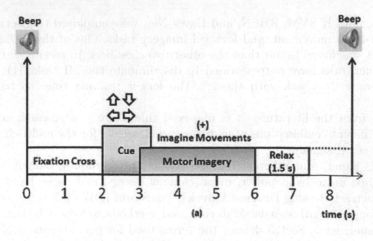

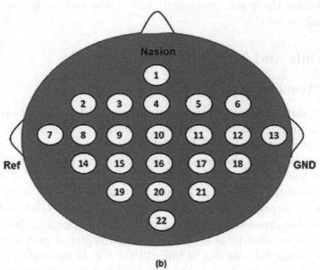

Fig. 1. (a) Data acquisition format of one trial with respect to time for the motor imagery paradigm; (b) Electrode placement according to the international 10–20 system (adapted from [19])

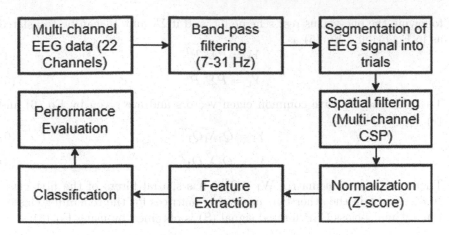

Fig. 2. Block diagram of the classification framework

Segmentation. Trials are separated from each channel using the header structure information (see [19] for details) and data from each trial is selected with the time slot starting from 2.5 s to 5.5 s.

Common Spatial Pattern. Common Spatial Pattern (CSP) method decomposes the raw EEG signals into spatial patterns and these spatial patterns have maximum differences in variance as shown by Naeem et al. [20]. Wang et al. in [21] concluded that this technique discriminated the classification tasks accurately.

1. Multi-class CSP:

   Consider a N*T matrix X_i represents the multi-channel EEG data per trial, where i ∈ {1,2,3,4} corresponding to four MI tasks, N stands for the number of channels and T stands for the number of samples per channel. For each MI task, find average covariance matrix $\sum_i$, i∈ {1,2,3,4}. Equation (1) gives the whitening matrix as follows:

$$P = \lambda^{-1/2}Q_0{}^T \tag{1}$$

   where Q_0 stands for the matrix of eigenvectors and λ stands for diagonal matrix of eigenvalues from Eq. (2):

$$\Sigma = \Sigma_{i=1}^4 \Sigma_i = Q_0\lambda Q_0{}^T \tag{2}$$

   To obtain the spatial filter matrix of first Class, sum of the covariance matrices of rest three classes is calculated using Eq. (3) as follows:

$$\Sigma_1' = \Sigma_{i=2}^4 \Sigma_i \tag{3}$$

following the one-versus-rest scheme [5], and if Σ_1 and Σ_1' can be translated as in Eq. (4) and Eq. (5) as

$$Y_1 = P\Sigma_1 P^T \tag{4}$$

$$Y_1' = P\Sigma_1' P^T \tag{5}$$

Then Y_1 and Y_1' have common eigen vectors and are given by Eq. (6) and Eq. (7) as follows:

$$Y_1 = Q_1 \lambda_1 Q_1{}^T \tag{6}$$

$$Y_1' = Q_1 \lambda_1' Q_1{}^T \tag{7}$$

Then the projection matrix $W_1 = Q_1^T P$ has spatial filters of the first class. similarly obtain the other four projection matrices for the remaining classes. Finally, multi-class CSP filtered signal (S) is obtained by using Eq. (8):

$$S = XW^T \tag{8}$$

where W^T includes spatial filters corresponding to the four classes (W_1, W_2, W_3 and W_4) in its columns. In this work, all available 22 EEG channels are decomposed into 8 channels having maximum differences in variance as shown by [20].

Normalization. After pre-processing by multi-class CSP, all the trials from each channel are normalized because mean and standard deviation (SD) are sensitive to outliers. Normalization enhances features in a dataset and identifies outliers. In this step, z-score normalization [22] is used to normalize each trial as it gives the highest accuracy than other normalization techniques, such as min-max and log normalization. The z-score normalized signal S' is given by the following Eq. (9):

$$S' = \frac{S - \mu}{\sigma} \tag{9}$$

where μ is the mean of the samples of a trial, σ represents the standard deviation of the samples.

Feature Extraction. Eight channels (obtained after decomposition using Multi-class CSP) are used in this step and the classification of MI tasks is carried out using the following feature extraction techniques:

1. DWT based Mean Band Energy (MBE)
   A four-level decomposition of a signal using DWT is shown in the Fig. 3. DWT is a fast, non-redundant transform than Continuous Wavelet Transform [23, 24]. Mother wavelet functions, namely Daubechies 2 (db2), Daubechies 4 (db4), Daubechies 6 (db6), and Daubechies 7 (db7), are compared, and dB7 mother wavelet function is selected as it gives the best feature set. Also, DWT with four-level decomposition and Debauchies 7 (db7) [25] as a mother wavelet is used to decompose each trial from the selected channels to get the approximation and detailed coefficients.

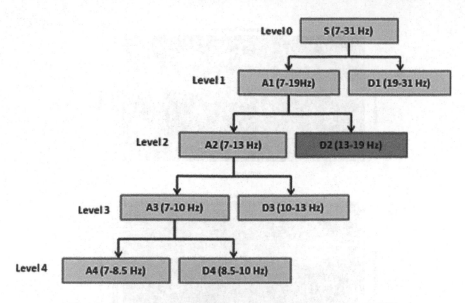

Fig. 3. Four level decomposition of a single trial using DWT

$x(n)$ is a discrete time signal, where n = 0,1,2,..., M-1. DWT coefficients for high pass filters and low pass filters are calculated using Eq. (10) and (11) respectively.

$$W_\phi(j_0, k) = \frac{1}{\sqrt{M}} \Sigma_n x(n) \sqrt{2} \phi_{j_0,k}(n) \tag{10}$$

$$W_\psi(j, k) = \frac{1}{\sqrt{M}} \Sigma_n x(n) \psi_{j,k}(n) \tag{11}$$

where, $j \geq j_0$, W_ϕ and W_ψ are approximation and detailed coefficients respectively, while $\phi_{j_0,k}(n)$ is given by Eq. (12) as

$$\phi_{j_0,k}(n) = \sqrt{2}\phi(2^{j_0}n - k) \tag{12}$$

and $\psi_{j,k}(n)$ is given in Eq. (13):

$$\psi_{j,k}(n) = \Sigma_r h_\psi(r) \sqrt{2}\phi(2^j n - r) \tag{13}$$

where $\phi(x)$ is a scaling function and $\psi_{j,k}(n)$ is a wavelet function

Generally, $j_0 = 0$, $j = 0, 1, 2, ..., J-1$, $M = 2^J$ and k is the shift parameter. In the Fig. 2, $J = 6$ i.e. six level decomposition. Discrete signal $x(n)$ is reconstructed using IDWT as in Eq. (14):

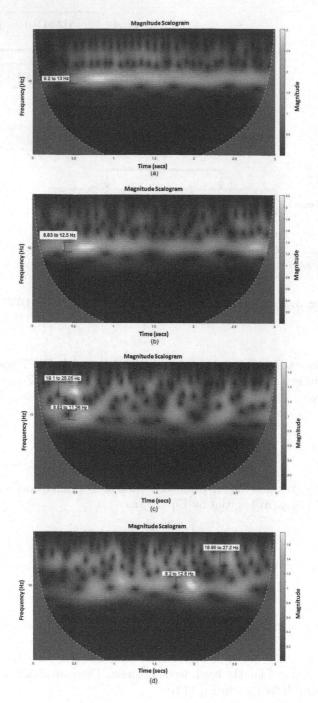

Fig. 4. Magnitude scalogram representation for (a) left hand, (b) right hand, (c) both feet and (d) tongue Motor Imagery

$$x(n) = \frac{1}{\sqrt{M}} \Sigma_k W_\phi(j_0, k)\phi_{j_0,k}(n) + \Sigma_{j=0}^{\infty}\Sigma_k W_\psi(j, k)\psi_{j,k}(n) \qquad (14)$$

where W_ϕ and W_ψ are approximation and detailed coefficients respectively. Also the reconstructed x(n) can be using Eq. (15) (see Fig. 3 for details):

$$x(n) = A_4(n) + D_4(n) + D_3(n) + D_1(n) \qquad (15)$$

where A_n and D_n are approximation and detailed coefficients at level 'n' respectively.

Finally, band-energy of A4, D4, D3, and D1 is calculated (except D2 from 13–19 Hz), and their mean is taken as DWT band energy feature (see Eq. (17)). These four bands are selected as a percentage of energy for the coefficients within these bands is higher for the MI tasks (see Fig. 4). Magnitude scalogram is drawn using Continuous Wavelet Transform (CWT) with Morse wavelet.

The energy of each band is computed as the mean of squared time domain samples using Eq. (16):

$$BP_i = \frac{1}{N}\Sigma_{k=1}^{N} x_i[k]^2, i = 1, 2, \ldots, 4. \qquad (16)$$

where x_i corresponds to the ith band with k = 1,2, ..., N samples and BP_i is the band energy of the ith band of a trial decomposed using DWT. Mean Band energy is calculated using Eq. (17):

$$MBE = \frac{1}{4}\Sigma_{i=1}^{4} BP_i, i = 1, 2, \ldots, 4. \qquad (17)$$

where MBE represents Mean Band Energy and these values are then used as feature vector components.

2. Mean band power (BP)

The power of three major frequency bands: 8–14 Hz, 19–24 Hz and 24–31 Hz of each trial is calculated. The power is obtained by squaring the resulting signal and the signal is filtered using a w-sized smoothing window operation as per Eq. (18).

$$p'[n] = \ln\left(\frac{1}{w}\sum_{k=0}^{w}p[n-k]^2\right) \qquad (18)$$

The mean power values are calculated using Eq. (19):

$$y_i = \frac{1}{N}\sum_{k=1}^{N}p'[k], \overline{1, n} \qquad (19)$$

where y_i is the mean power value of each computed band. These values are then used as feature vector components [26].

3. Channel FFT Energy (CFFT)

As analyzed by Cecotti et al. in [26], this method employs the Fast Fourier Transform (FFT) for computing i-th EEG channel signal energy estimation in the frequency domain. The FFT result is squared and the sum of all elements is computed (20):

$$y_i = \log \left(\sum\nolimits_{k=1}^{N} FFT(x_i)^2 \right) \overline{1,n} \tag{20}$$

Final feature vector components are formed after Box-Cox transformation is applied.

4. Mean Channel Energy (MCE)

The energy of each ith EEG channel is computed as the mean of squared time-domain samples using Eq. (21). The result is then transformed using a Box-Cox [27] transformation (i.e., logarithm) to make the features more normally distributed. Finally, the resulting values are combined into a feature vector.

$$y_i = \log \left(\frac{1}{N} \sum\nolimits_{k=1}^{N} x_i[k]^2 \right) \overline{1,n} \tag{21}$$

where N stands for the number of samples in a channel and n represents the total number of channels.

Classification. In this step, extracted feature sets from nine datasets of session 1 (A01T to A09T) are used to train the classifiers using 10-fold cross-validation. The session two datasets are tested using this trained classifier to obtain session-to-session transfer classification accuracy. Three classifiers, namely Bayesian Network classifier, Linear Support Vector Machine (SVM), and Linear Discriminant Analysis (LDA), are employed to classify four MI tasks.

3 Performance Evaluation Metrics

The performance of the proposed framework is evaluated using the following performance measures.

Confusion Matrix: A confusion matrix is used to evaluate the performance of a classification model.

1. **Classification Accuracy.** Classification accuracy is calculated for the performance evaluation of the classification framework with different feature extraction techniques. It is the percentage of correct decisions made in classifying the total tasks and is defined as:

$$Accuracy = \frac{(TruePositive + TrueNegative)}{(TotalInstances)} \tag{22}$$

2. **Precision**

$$Precision = \frac{TP}{(TP + FP)} \tag{23}$$

3. **Recall**

$$Recall = \frac{TP}{TP + FN} \tag{24}$$

4. **Specificity**

$$Specificity = \frac{TN}{(FP + TN)} \tag{25}$$

5. **Area under curve (AUC)**

$$AUC = 0.5 * (Recall + Specificity) \tag{26}$$

6. **F1 Score**

$$F1Score = \frac{2 * Precision * Recall}{(Precision + Recall)} \tag{27}$$

where True positive (TP) is the number of 'positive' patterns categorised as 'positive', False positive (FP) is the number of 'negative' patterns categorised as 'positive', False negative (FN) is the number of 'positive' instances categorised as 'negative', and True negative (TN) is the number of 'negative' patterns categorised as 'negative'.

Table 1. Session-to-session transfer classification accuracy (%) of all subjects from dataset 2a using four different features using LDA classifier

Subject	BP	MCE	CFFT	MBE
S1	75.15	74.80	74.80	**76.73**
S2	35.74	**43.16**	**43.16**	41.31
S3	77.38	**79.86**	**79.86**	**79.86**
S4	51.63	56.89	56.89	**57.98**
S5	37.04	**32.69**	**32.69**	32.63
S6	43.65	46.90	46.90	**47.91**
S7	81.31	82.03	**82.39**	82.29
S8	49.55	62.83	62.83	**63.88**
S9	77.40	81.57	81.57	**82.29**
Mean	58.76	62.31	62.35	**62.76**

4   Results and Analysis

In this paper, classification of the four-class (Left hand, right hand, feet, and tongue) MI signals is performed using four different feature extraction techniques. The overall classification framework has been designed in Matlab R2018a

Table 2. Classification accuracy of each class for all subjects using MBE features. L, R, F and T represent Left, Right, Feet and Tongue classes. Ovr stands for the overall accuracy.

Subject	LDA					Linear SVM					Naive Bays				
	L	R	F	T	Ovr	L	R	F	T	Ovr	L	R	F	T	Ovr
S1	79.16	**84.72**	**70.83**	72.22	**76.73**	**86.11**	65.27	**70.83**	77.77	75	66.66	80.55	54.16	**86.11**	71.87
S2	**31.94**	45.83	**44.44**	43.05	41.31	**31.94**	58.33	44.44	40.27	**43.75**	19.44	43.05	34.72	**48.61**	36.45
S3	**87.5**	100	51.38	**80.55**	79.86	81.94	100	62.5	66.66	77.77	73.61	100	61.11	66.66	75.34
S4	20.83	**81.94**	61.11	68.05	**57.98**	16.66	80.55	62.5	70.83	57.63	**66.66**	43.05	30.55	**80.55**	55.2
S5	**70.83**	2.77	50	6.94	**32.63**	20.83	4.16	**93.05**	12.5	**32.63**	2.77	**9.72**	76.38	**20.83**	27.43
S6	66.66	25	37.5	**62.5**	47.91	62.5	**30.55**	34.72	58.33	46.52	**70.83**	12.5	**47.22**	40.27	42.7
S7	**72.22**	**98.61**	**90.27**	68.05	**82.29**	62.5	93.05	83.33	**77.77**	79.16	52.77	84.72	80.55	72.22	72.56
S8	**84.72**	29.16	56.94	84.72	**63.88**	83.33	15.27	**61.11**	**93.05**	63.19	65.27	8.33	50	83.33	51.73
S9	**90.27**	**66.66**	**79.16**	93.05	**82.29**	**90.27**	56.94	73.61	97.22	79.51	88.88	31.94	48.61	**98.61**	67.01
Mean	**67.12**	**59.41**	60.18	64.34	62.76	59.56	56.01	**65.12**	**66.04**	61.68	56.32	45.98	53.7	**66.35**	55.58

Table 3. Average confusion matrix of all subjects for four classes (Values in the table are number of trials.)

LDA					Linear SVM					Naive Bays				
Labels	L	R	F	T	Labels	L	R	F	T	Labels	L	R	F	T
L	**48.33**	13.44	5.67	4.56	L	42.89	14.00	10.67	4.44	L	40.56	13.22	10.33	7.89
R	13.22	**42.78**	9.11	6.89	R	11.78	40.33	12.11	7.78	R	12.89	33.11	13.00	13.00
F	8.11	5.33	43.33	15.22	F	5.11	5.22	**46.89**	14.78	F	6.33	6.56	38.67	20.44
T	7.00	6.89	11.78	46.33	T	4.89	5.56	14.00	**47.56**	T	7.78	3.00	13.44	**47.78**

Table 4. Comparison based on performance measures (in %).

Classifiers	Labels	Precision	Recall	Specificity	AUC	F1-score
LDA	L	0.66	0.67	0.87	0.77	0.66
	R	0.57	0.59	0.88	0.74	0.57
	F	0.64	0.60	0.88	0.74	0.61
	T	0.63	0.64	0.88	0.76	0.61
Linear SVM	L	0.64	0.60	0.90	0.75	0.61
	R	0.67	0.56	0.89	0.72	0.54
	F	0.62	0.65	0.83	0.74	0.62
	T	0.62	0.66	0.88	0.77	0.62
Naive Bays	L	0.58	0.56	0.88	0.72	0.56
	R	0.59	0.46	0.89	0.68	0.46
	F	0.60	0.54	0.83	0.68	0.54
	T	0.51	0.66	0.81	0.74	0.58

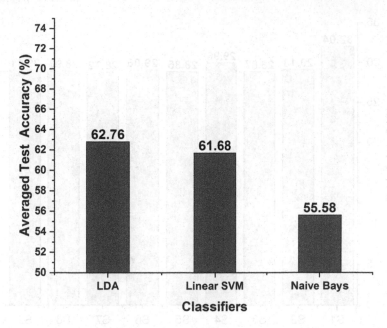

Fig. 5. Comparison between three classifiers showing averaged test classification accuracy (session 2)

on windows 8.1 operating system with 4 Gb RAM and evaluated on dataset 2a of BCI competition IV. Four different features, namely BP, MCE, CFFT, and MBE are calculated and compared. The performance evaluation is carried out by calculating classification accuracy. Results has been detailed in Table 1. It is observed that the framework with MBE features have been giving the best averaged test classification accuracy in comparison with the other three features (see Table 1).

In addition, Fig. 5 shows the comparison of three classifiers, namely Naive Bays, Linear SVM, and LDA, for a given framework. It is found that LDA has been giving the best averaged test classification accuracy of 62.76% for the session 2 dataset. Furthermore, the framework with DWT feature extraction method has obtained an averaged test classification accuracy of 80.29% over four subjects (S1, S3, S7, and S9) out of nine (see Table 1), which makes it suitable for online Motor Imagery based BCI Systems.

Table 2 shows the contribution of the LDA classifier in the overall classification accuracy compared with Linear SVM and Naive Bays classifier. For this, the classification accuracy of each class is calculated for all the subjects using MBE features with three classifiers (see Table 2). The ratio of the correctly classified trials for one class to the total number of trials in that class represents the Class classification accuracy. Also, the average confusion matrix over all subjects is shown in Table 3. Table 2, shows the reliability of the LDA classifier in classifying right hand and left-hand class without compromising the classification of

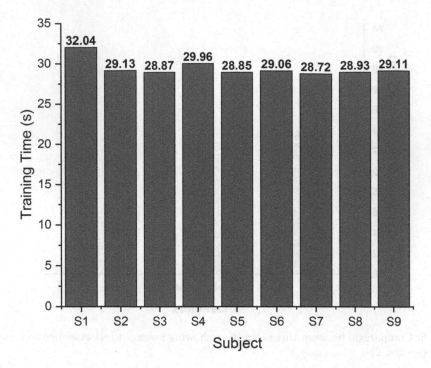

Fig. 6. Time required by the classification framework to train LDA classifier using MBE features for BCI competition IV dataset 2a (session 1)

feet and tongue classes. The confusion has been reduced between left/right and feet/tongue classes (see Table 3).

In order to select the best classifier for the proposed framework, the performance metrics are calculated for LDA, Linear SVM, and Naive Bays classifier (see Table 4). A good model should have higher precision, recall, specificity, Area under Curve (AUC), and F1 score, i.e., it should have low FP and low FN. Results show that LDA has performed better than Linear SVM and Naive Bays.

Furthermore, the time required by the proposed framework to train LDA classifier using DWT based MBE features for each subject (session 1) is shown in Fig. 6. An average time of 29.4 s is required to train the LDA classifier to classify four MI tasks. Such a less computation time of the presented framework makes it suitable for online Motor Imagery based BCI systems.

5   Conclusion

A framework is presented for the discrimination of four-class Motor Imagery signals, and its performance has been evaluated using publicly available BCI Competition IV dataset 2a. This framework with DWT based feature extraction technique has been performed better than the other feature extraction techniques

(BP, MCE, and CFFT). The presented classification framework with LDA classifier with 10-fold cross-validation has achieved an averaged test classification accuracy of 80.29% over four subjects out of nine from BCI Competition IV dataset 2a. In addition, the proposed framework's performance evaluation is carried out using different performance measures calculated using a confusion matrix. Results show that the LDA classifier has been giving better results to discriminate the four MI tasks in comparison with Naive Bays and Linear SVM. Also, the less computational cost of the framework with MBE features makes it suitable for real time applications.

It could be possible to modify the CSP method to get the best results for all nine subjects, which would improve the mean classification accuracy for all subjects; this approach will be extended in the future.

References

1. Wolpaw, J.R., Birbaumer, N., McFarland, D.J., Pfurtscheller, G., Vaughan, T.M.: Brain-computer interfaces for communication and control. Clin. Neurophysiol. **113**(6), 767–791 (2002)
2. Pfurtscheller, G., Neuper, C.: Motor imagery and direct brain-computer communication. Proc. IEEE **89**(7), 1123–1134 (2001)
3. Dharwarkar, G.: Using temporal evidence and fusion of time-frequency features for brain-computer interfacing. Master's thesis, University of Waterloo (2005)
4. Mu, J., Pfurtscheller, G., Flyvbjerg, H.: Designing optimal spatial filters for single-trial EEG classification in a movement task. Clin. Neurophysiol. Official J. Int. Fed. Clin. Neurophysiol. **110**(5), 787–798 (1999)
5. Dornhege, G., Blankertz, B., Curio, G., Muller, K.R.: Boosting bit rates in non-invasive EEG single-trial classifications by feature combination and multiclass paradigms. IEEE Trans. Biomed. Eng. **51**(6), 993–1002 (2004)
6. Vega-Escobar, L., Castro-Ospina, A.E., Duque-Munoz, L.: DWT-based feature extraction for motor imagery classification. In: 6th Latin-American Conference on Networked and Electronic Media (LACNEM 2015), pp. 3–6 (2015)
7. Sakhavi, S., Guan, C., Yan, S.: Learning temporal information for brain-computer interface using convolutional neural networks. IEEE Trans. Neural Netw. Learn. Syst. **29**(11), 5619–5629 (2018)
8. Yang, H., Sakhavi, S., Ang, K.K., Guan, C.: On the use of convolutional neural networks and augmented CSP features for multi-class motor imagery of EEG signals classification. In: 2015 37th Annual International Conference of the IEEE Engineering in Medicine and Biology Society (EMBC), pp. 2620–2623. IEEE (2018)
9. Lu, N., Li, T., Ren, X., Miao, H.: A deep learning scheme for motor imagery classification based on restricted Boltzmann machines. IEEE Trans. Neural Netw. Learn. Syst. **25**(6), 566–576 (2016)
10. Meisheri, H., Ramrao, N., Mitra, S.: Multiclass common spatial pattern for EEG based brain computer interface with adaptive learning classifier. arXiv preprint arXiv:1802.09046 (2018)
11. Sakhavi, S., Guan, C., Yan, S.: Parallel convolutional-linear neural network for motor imagery classification. In: 2015 23rd European Signal Processing Conference (EUSIPCO), pp. 2736–2740. IEEE (2015)

12. Temiyasathit, C.: Increase performance of four-class classification for motor-imagery based brain-computer interface. In 2014 International Conference on Computer, Information and Telecommunication Systems (CITS), pp. 1–5. IEEE (2014)
13. Hamedi, M., Salleh, S.H., Noor, A.M., Mohammad-Rezazadeh, I.: Neural network-based three-class motor imagery classification using time-domain features for BCI applications. In: 2014 IEEE Region 10 Symposium, pp. 204–207. IEEE (2014)
14. Xygonakis, I., Athanasiou, A., Pandria, N., Kugiumtzis, D., Bamidis, P.D.: Decoding motor imagery through common spatial pattern filters at the EEG source space. Comput. Intell. Neurosci. **2018**, Article ID 7957408, 10 p. (2018). https://doi.org/10.1155/2018/7957408
15. Resalat, S.N., Saba, V.: A study of various feature extraction methods on a motor imagery based brain computer interface system. Basic Clin. Neurosci. **7**(1), 13 (2016)
16. Mohamed, E.A., Yusoff, M.Z., Selman, N.K., Malik, A.S.: Enhancing EEG signals in brain computer interface using wavelet transform. Int. J. Inf. Electron. Eng. **4**(3), 234 (2014)
17. Kant, P., Laskar, S.H., Hazarika, J., Mahamune, R.: CWT Based transfer learning for motor imagery classification for brain computer interfaces. J. Neurosci. Methods **345**, 108886 (2020)
18. Uktveris, T., Jusas, V.: Application of convolutional neural networks to four-class motor imagery classification problem. Inf. Technol. Control **46**(2), 260–273 (2017)
19. Brunner, C., Leeb, R., Müller-Putz, G., Schlögl, A., Pfurtscheller, G.: BCI Competition 2008-Graz data set A. Institute for Knowledge Discovery (Laboratory of Brain-Computer Interfaces), Graz University of Technology, 16 (2008)
20. Naeem, M., Brunner, C., Pfurtscheller, G.: Dimensionality reduction and channel selection of motor imagery electroencephalographic data. Comput. Intell. Neurosci. (2009)
21. Wang, Y., Gao, S., Gao, X.: Common spatial pattern method for channel selection in motor imagery based brain-computer interface. In: 2005 IEEE Engineering in Medicine and Biology 27th Annual Conference 2006 Jan 17, pp. 5392–5395. IEEE (2006)
22. Zhang, H., Yang, H., Guan, C.: Bayesian learning for spatial filtering in an EEG-based brain-computer interface. IEEE Trans. Neural Netw. Learn. Syst. **24**(7), 1049–1060 (2013)
23. Samar, V.J., Bopardikar, A., Rao, R., Swartz, K.: Wavelet analysis of neuroelectric waveforms: a conceptual tutorial. Brain Lang. **66**(1), 7–60 (1999)
24. Gorji, H.T., Taheri, H., Koohpayezadeh, A., Haddadnia, J.: Ocular artifact detection and removing from EEG by wavelet families: a comparative study. J. Inf. Eng. Appl. **13**, 39–46 (2013)
25. Zhao, Q., et al.: Automatic identification and removal of ocular artifacts in EEG-improved adaptive predictor filtering for portable applications. IEEE Trans. Nanobiosci. **13**(2), 109–117 (2014)
26. Cecotti, H., Graeser, A.: Convolutional neural network with embedded Fourier transform for EEG classification. In: 2008 19th International Conference on Pattern Recognition, 8 Dec 2008, pp. 1–4. IEEE (2008)
27. Box, G.E., Cox, D.R.: An analysis of transformations. J. Roy. Stat. Soc. Ser. B Methodological **26**(2), 211–243 (1964)
28. Xu, G., et al.: A deep transfer convolutional neural network framework for EEG signal classification. IEEE Access **7**, 112767–112776 (2019)
29. Grosse-Wentrup, M., Buss, M.: Multiclass common spatial patterns and information theoretic feature extraction. IEEE Trans. Biomed. Eng. **55**(8), 1991–2000 (2008)

Performance Analysis of 32-Bit DADDA Multiplier Using 15–4 Compressor

Avinash Gidd, Shivani Ghasti, Snehal Jadhav, and K. Sivasankaran(✉) (iD)

Department of Micro and Nano Electronics, SENSE,
Vellore Institute of Technology, Vellore 632014, Tamil Nadu, India
{avinash.rajendra2020,shivanisunil.ghasti2020,
snehalsanjeev.jadhav2020}@vitstudent.ac.in,
ksivasankaran@vit.ac.in

Abstract. Multiplier is an integral part of computations in digital signal processing and various applications. Many computational problems are targeted to have high speed, less on chip area and reduced power consumption. In a multiplier partial product generation and its compression determines its performance. In this paper we have designed a 32×32 bits Dadda multiplier using 16×16 bits Dadda multiplier which is designed using higher order 15–4 Approximate and exact compressors along with 4–2 low error rate compressors. Use of higher order compressors along with Dadda algorithm improves the speed of multiplier with compromised accuracy. The designed multiplier performs operation with 20.69% pass rate for average case. Simulation results are obtained using ModelSim while timing and power analysis has been performed in Intel Quartus Prime using Time Quest Timing Analyzer and PowerPlay power analyzer.

Keywords: DADDA multiplier · 15–4 compressor · Approximate computation

1 Introduction

Applications such as computer arithmetic operations, computation algorithms like FIR filters, IIR filters and FFT which are used in multimedia functions uses multiplier. Designing high speed multiplier is a critical task since most of the power and processing time is consumed by multiplier. In multiplication addition of partial product is main element which decide performance of multiplier. The process of reduction of partial products makes the multiplier a sluggish element. To speed up the multiplication operation dada multiplier can be used along with compression technique as it is faster than Wallace multiplier, Valid results are achieved using Approximate computation in image processing and multimedia. Therefore, to reduce latency various Approximate compression techniques can be used such as Approximate 4–2 compressor. The Approximate compressor makes a multiplier efficient by reducing its power consumption, number of transistors and delay in comparison to an exact design. As low order compressor is efficient when size of multiplier is small. For larger multiplier 16×16, 32×32 require higher order

V. Arunachalam and K. Sivasankaran (Eds.): ICMDCS 2021, CCIS 1392, pp. 19–30, 2021.
https://doi.org/10.1007/978-981-16-5048-2_2

compressor to provide better performance in power and speed. Higher order compressor is realized using lower order compressor with various design which has lower error rate.

To reduced number of full adders in partial product generation compressors are used. In previously used 4–2 compressors the error ratio is high. To achieve smaller error, and optimize power delay and area two designs are proposed in this paper. As proposed design eliminates Cin and Cout it reduces number of compressors required in partial product reduction. [1, 7] Main goal while using compressors is achieving trade off in area, power and delay. To reduce the error in previous Approximate 4–2 compressor new design is put forward which have improved error rate. Also, the use of multiplexer in designed caused less delay. [3, 6] DADDA multiplier is faster than other multipliers. With use of Exact 4–2 compressor the delay is decreased. 32 × 32-bit multiplier is implemented from 4 × 4 multiplier. The implemented multiplier showed less power consumption and delay. [9] In continuation to their work [9], this paper [5] has proposed an Approximate 4–2 compressor which uses four OR gates for Approximate sum(S), three AND gates and one 3 input OR gate for Approximate first carry and one 5 input AND gate for Approximate second carry. This approximation gives around 80.44% accurate and 19.56% inaccurate values. The conventional 5–3 compressor design has 5 XOR gates. As logical effort of a multiplier is lesser than XOR, to overcome the critical delay while generating the outputs, the conventional circuit is modified by using 4:1MUX. Two partial products are used as select line for MUX and the remaining three partial products are given as inputs. 15–4 compressor designed using the modified compressor as base module which gives 11% improvement in speed and decrease in power by 8.7% [8, 16]. Four different Approximate 5–3 compressors are designed using approximation based on the analysis of the truth table. Out of the four designs, design1 has the lowest error rate of 18.75% and design4 has the lowest delay of 2,664 s [4, 10]. In this paper carry select adder combined with binary to excess-1 converter is used to design Dadda multiplier, this improved the speed and power consumption.

[9] In this paper 32-bit Dadda multiplier is designed using 4–2 compressors. The accuracy and speed depend on the compressor used. Dadda Multiplier power consumption has been reduced and processing speed is increased. In [11] an area efficient Carry Select Adder is utilized to eliminate cells of distributed adders by using the common Boolean logic. The intricacy of lookup table is reduced using this methodology. With latency being the only disadvantage of this circuit, a predictive 4–2 compressor is implemented using this logic which is further used to carry out a 32-bit DADDA multiplier. After designing various 32-bit multipliers using Verilog HDL and further performing their functional simulation in Modelsim, in [12] an overview of performance comparison of these multipliers in various modes was taken. Dadda multiplier exhibited the least delay among all in the area-optimized and auto-optimized mode. [13, 15] proposes a new algorithm for 4–2 compressor used for implementing approximate multiplier. This multiplier's analyses results show that it is 3.19% more area efficient, 53.74 faster and 3.79% more power consumption efficient than traditional multiplier implemented using 4–2 exact compressor. [14, 17] In this paper two approximate compressors with optimized area, reduced delay and improved power consumption with comparable accuracy in comparison with already existing designs are proposed. Using proposed compressors 8 × 8 and 16 × 16 Dadda multipliers implemented.

In this paper we present 32-bit Approximate multiplier using 15–4 compressor we found that by using compressor in the partial product accumulation gives lower error rate, minimized transistor count and improvement in speed. Using only lower order 4–2 compressor in higher order multiplier causes lager error so to reduce error higher order 15–4 compressor is used.

The paper is organized as follow. Design of 4–2 Approximate compressor is explained in Sect. 2. Design of Approximate 5–3 compressor is explained in Sect. 3. 15–4 compressor designed using 5–3 compressor is explained in Sect. 4. 16 × 16 multiplier design is explained in Sect. 5. 32 × 32 multiplier designed using 16 × 16 multiplier is explained in Sect. 6. Simulation Results and Discussionis explained in Sect. 7.

2 Design of 4–2 Approximate Compressor

To achieve trade-off between speed and accuracy the 4–2 Approximate compressor is designed by replacing two full adders in exact 4–2 compressors with two multiplexers. Figure 1 shows the exact 4–2 compressor with 4 inputs I3, I2, I1, I0 and Cin, and Cout.

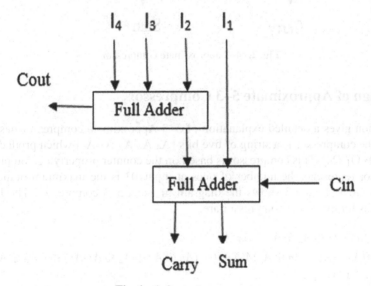

Fig. 1. 4–2 exact compressor

I3, I2, I1 are inputs to the full adder and I4 is select line for multiplexers. Figure 2 shows Approximate 4–2 compressor: Instead of delay of two full adders, delay of only one mux is there whenever there is carry from previous block. Also, both sum and carry generated by full adder are applied parallelly to multiplexers. The carry generated from previous stage is applied as select line for both the multiplexers and considered as MSB bit which reduces the probability of error.

In this design out of total 16 combinations 2 inputs give error in output. i.e., I4 I3 I2 I1 = 1111 and I4 I3 I2 I1 = 1000 give error. The error rate is nearly 12.5%. therefore, error is also reduced significantly as well as speed is improved.

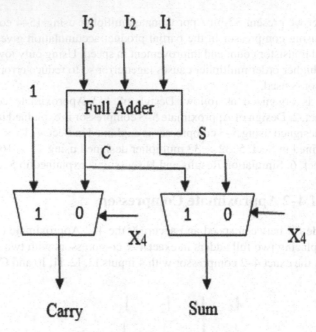

Fig. 2. 4–2 approximate compressor

3   Design of Approximate 5–3 Compressor

This section gives a detailed explanation of 5–3 Approximate compressor design [2]. Input to the compressor is a string of five bits [A_4 A_3 A_2 A_1 A_0] which produces 3-bit output [O_2 O_1 O_0]. This compressor is based on the counter property i.e., output of the compressor represents the number of ones at input101 is the maximum output when all inputs are 1. Figure 3 shows the diagram of exact 5–3 compressor. The Boolean expressions for exact 5–3 compressor are:

$$O_0 = A_0 \oplus A_1 \oplus A_2 \oplus A_3 \oplus A_4$$
$$O_1 = ((A_0 \oplus A_1 \oplus A_2 \oplus A_3)A_4) + (\sim (A_0 \oplus A_1 \oplus A_2 \oplus A_3)A_3) \oplus ((A_0 \oplus A_1)A_2$$
$$+(\sim (A_0 \oplus A_1)A_0))$$
$$O_2 = ((A_0 \oplus A_1 \oplus A_2 \oplus A_3)A_4 + (\sim (A_0 \oplus A_1 \oplus A_2 \oplus A_3)A_3 \times ((A_0 \oplus A_1)A_2$$
$$+(\sim (A_0 \oplus A_1)A_0)$$

It was observed that for 26 input combination out of 32 (2^5) input combinations O_2 can be Approximate by logical ANDing between A_3 and A_2 (Fig. 4). Due to this approximation the computational complexity of O2 reduces which increases the speed of 5–3 compressor. This approximation gives an error rate of 18.75%. Logical expression for Approximate O'_2

$$O_2 = A_2 \times A_3$$

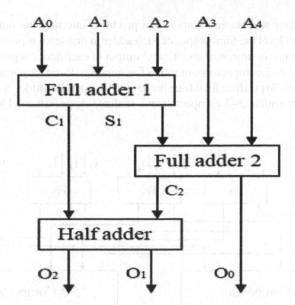

Fig. 3. 5–3 exact compressor

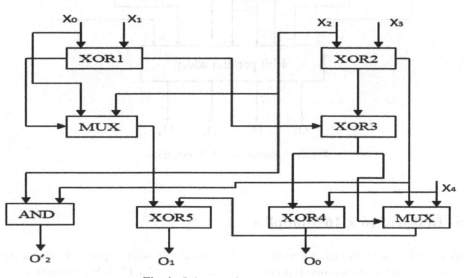

Fig. 4. 5–3 approximate compressor

4 Design of 15–4 Approximate Compressor

This section deals with realization of 15–4 compressor using lower order 5–3 compressor. The 15–4 compressor compress 15 input (I_{14}-I_0) to 4 output (O_3-O_0). Basically 15–4 compressor consist three level. At level one five full adders are required. At level two 5–3 compressor are required and in last stage parallel adder are required. At level one individual full adder accepts three inputs and produces intermediate output 'Sum' and 'Carry'. At second level the Sum output of each adder in first level is provided as input to one 5–3 Approximate compressor and 'Carry' output of each adder is given to second 5–3 compressor. The 5–3 compressor compress five inputs to three output and it is given to 4-bit parallel adder. To produce final four-bit output 4-bit parallel adder is used. In second stage using Approximate 5–3 compressor we realized Approximate 15–4 compressor (Fig. 5).

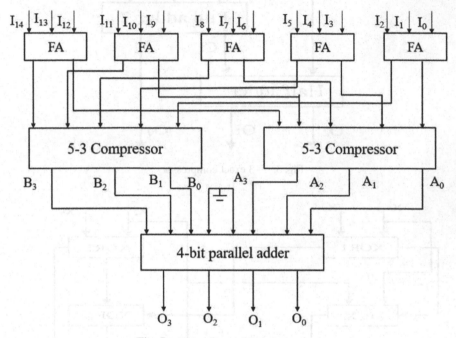

Fig. 5. Approximate 15–4 compressor

5 Design of 16 × 16 Multiplier

16 × 16 Dadda multiplier is designed in three stages. At stage 1 partial products are generated and its compression is performed using higher order 15–4 Approximate compressors and 4–2 compressors. At stage 1, 8 exact and 3 Approximate 15–4 compressors are used while 18 4–2 exact compressors and 2 full adders are used. At stage 2 compressed partial products generated from stage 1 are further compressed using 26 4–2 exact compressors. At stage 3, the partial products are reduced to two row form using 3 4–2 exact compressors and 7 full adders. Finally, the addition of partial products is performed using ripple carry adder and half adder (Fig. 6).

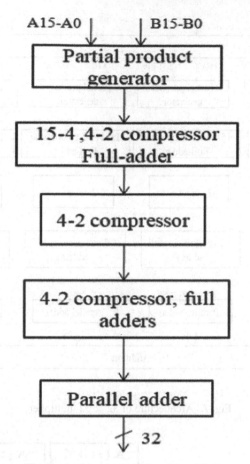

Fig. 6. Architecture of 16 × 16 multiplier

6   Design of 32 × 32 Multiplier Using 16 × 16 Multiplier

32 × 32 multiplier is designed using four 16 × 16 multipliers as shown in Fig. 8.The 32-bit data is divided into two 16-bit data and is multiplied using a lower order 16 × 16 multipliers. Four rows of partial products are generated. The partial products A[31:16] × B[15:0], A[15:0] × B[31:16] are shifted by 16-bits, whereas A[31:16] × B[31:16] is shifted by 32 bits. These shifted partial products are further compressed into row of two using full adders. The 64-bit output is obtained using ripple adder (Fig. 7).

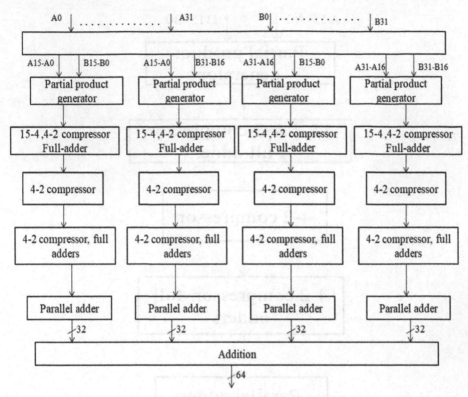

Fig. 7. Architecture of 32 × 32 multiplier

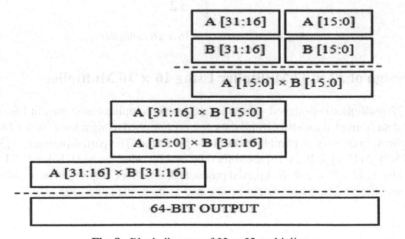

Fig. 8. Block diagram of 32 × 32 multiplier.

7   Simulation Results and Discussion

The functionality of proposed design is verified using Modelsim software. Timing and power analysis have been performed in Intel Quartus Prime using Time Quest Timing Analyzer and PowerPlay power analyzer. The results of 5–3, 15–4 compressors and multipliers are discussed in this section.

7.1   5–3 Compressor

Figure 9 show the simulation waveform of 5–3 Approximate compressor which count the number of occurrences of ones in given input. The approximation gives an error rate of 18.75%. Here for input test pattern 00011, there are two number of one's present. According to the function of compressor it counts the number of ones present in the input which is reflected in the output i.e., 010 for the given test pattern.

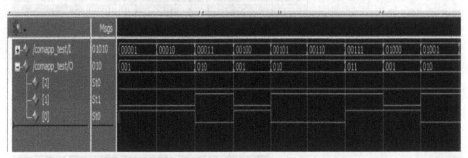

Fig. 9. Waveform of approximate 5–3 compressor

7.2   15–4 Compressor

Figure 10 show the simulation waveform of 15–4 Approximate compressor which count the number of occurrences of ones in given input. The approximation gives an error rate of 30.98%.

7.3   16 × 16 Multiplier

16 × 16 multiplier is implemented using lower order 4–2 Approximate compressor and higher order 15–4 Approximate compressor. After simulation and analysis power, error rate and speed has been calculated and shown in Table 1, Fig. 11 shows the functional simulation waveform of 16 × 16 multiplier.

7.4   32 × 32 Multiplier

32 × 32 multiplier is designed using four 16 × 16 multiplier. Power, speed and error rate are computed after simulation and analysis which are shown in Table 1. Fig. 12 shows the functional simulation waveform of 32 × 32 multiplier.

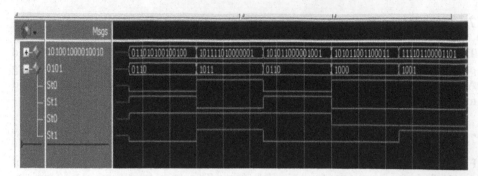

Fig. 10. Waveform of approximate 15–4 compressor

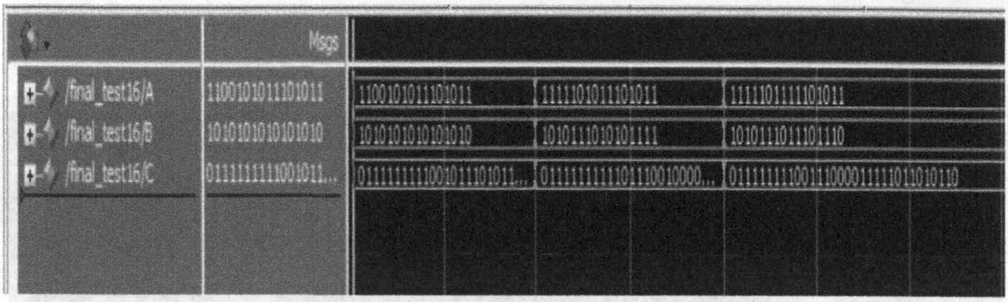

Fig. 11. Waveform of 16 × 16 multiplier

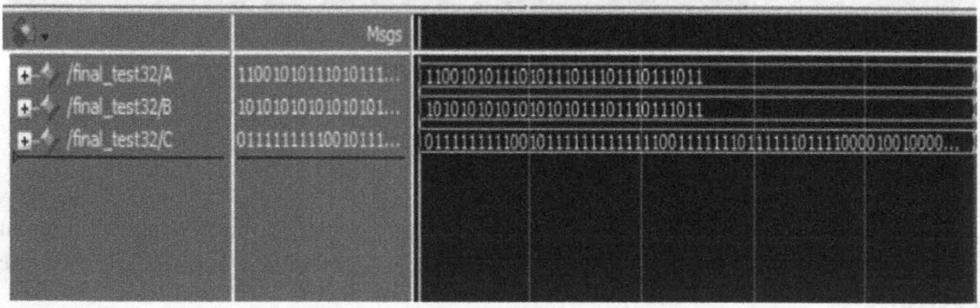

Fig. 12. Waveform of 32 × 32 multiplier

Table 1. Result analysis of different multipliers

Multiplier	Power (mw)	Delay (ns)	Pass rate (%)
16 × 16	92.51	33.305	28.9
32 × 32	364.03	54.01	20.69

8   Conclusion

From this design it can be concluded that higher order multipliers can be effectively designed using lower order multipliers. The use of higher order compressors such as 15–4 compressor along with Dadda algorithm can improve the speed of computation. Due to the Approximate compression techniques used in this design speed improvement is achieved at the expense of accuracy and power consumption.

References

1. Momeni, A., Han, J., Montuschi, P., Lombardi, F.: Design and analysis of approximate compressors for multiplication. IEEE Trans. Comput. **64**(4), 984–994 (2015)
2. Marimuthu, R., Rezinold, Y.E., Mallick, P.S.: Design and analysis of multiplier using approximate 15–4 compressor. IEEE Access **5**, 1027–1036 (2017)
3. Mody, J., Lawand, R., Priyanka, R., Sivanantham, S., Sivasankaran, K.: Study of Approximate compressors for multiplication using FPGA. In: 2015 Online International Conference on Green Engineering and Technologies (IC-GET), Coimbatore, pp. 1–4 (2015)
4. Swathi Krishna, T.U., Riyas, K.S., Premson, Y., Sakthivel, R.: 15–4 Approximate Compressor based multiplier for image processing. In: 2018 2nd International Conference on Trends in Electronics and Informatics (ICOEI), Tirunelveli, pp. 671–675 (2018)
5. Chanda, S., Guha, K., Patra, S., Singh, L.M., Lal Baishnab, K., Kumar Paul, P.: An energy efficient 32 Bit approximate Dadda multiplier. In: 2020 IEEE Calcutta Conference (CALCON), Kolkata, India, pp. 162–165 (2020)
6. Reddy, K.M., Vasantha, M.H., Nithin Kumar, Y.B., Dwivedi, D.: Design and analysis of multiplier using approximate 4-2 compressor. AEU – Int. J. Electron. Commun. **107**, 89–97 (2019)
7. Savithaa, N., Poornima, A.: A High-speed area efficient compression technique of Dadda multiplier for image blending application. In: 2019 Third International Conference on I-SMAC (IoT in Social, Mobile, Analytics and Cloud) (I-SMAC), Palladam, India, pp. 426-430 (2019)
8. Marimuthu, R., Pradeepkumar, M., Bansal, D., Balamurugan, S., Mallick, P.S.: Design of high speed and low power 15–4 compressor. In: 2013 International Conference on Communication and Signal Processing, Melmaruvathur, pp. 533–536 (2013)
9. Chanda, S., Guha, K., Patra, S., Karmakar, A., Singh, L.M., Lal Baishnab, K.: A 32-bit energy efficient exact Dadda multiplier. In: 2019 IEEE 5th International Conference for Convergence in Technology (I2CT), Bombay, India, pp. 1–4 (2019)
10. Munawar, M., et al.: Low power and high speed Dadda multiplier using carry select adder with binary to excess-1 converter. In: 2020 International Conference on Emerging Trends in Smart Technologies (ICETST), Karachi, Pakistan, pp. 1–4 (2020)
11. Nandam, M.V.S., Alluri, S.: High performance 32-bit Dadda multiplier using EDA. In: 2020 7th International Conference on Smart Structures and Systems (ICSSS), Chennai, India, pp. 1–5 (2020)
12. Swee, K.L.S., Hiung, L.H.: Performance comparison review of 32-bit multiplier designs. In: 2012 4th International Conference on Intelligent and Advanced Systems (ICIAS2012), Kuala Lumpur, pp. 836–841 (2012)
13. Varma, K.R., Agrawal, S.: High speed, Low power Approximate Multipliers. In: 2018 International Conference on Advances in Computing, Communications and Informatics (ICACCI), Bangalore, pp. 785–790 (2018)

14. Edavoor, P.J., Raveendran, S., Rahulkar, A.D.: Approximate multiplier design using novel dual-stage 4:2 compressors. IEEE Access **8**, 48337–48351 (2020)
15. Kyaw, K.Y., Goh, W.L., Yeo, K.S.: Low-power high-speed multiplier for error-tolerant application. In: 2010 IEEE International Conference of Electron Devices and Solid-State Circuits (EDSSC), Hong Kong, China, pp. 1–4 (2010)
16. Kulkarni, P., Gupta, P., Ercegovac, M.: Trading accuracy for power with an underdesigned multiplier architecture. In: 2011 24th Internatioal Conference on VLSI Design, Chennai, India, pp. 346–351 (2011)
17. Dominic Savio, M.M., Deepa, T.: Design of higher order multiplier with approximate compressor. In: 2020 IEEE International Conference on Electronics, Computing and Communication Technologies (CONECCT), Bangalore, India, pp. 1–6 (2020)

Rooftop Detection Using Satellite Images for Urban Terrace Farming

Sayon Palit, Aneesh Chopra, P. Balakrishnan, Bessie Amali. D. Geraldine, and K. S. Umadevi(✉)

Vellore Institute of Technology, Vellore, India
umadeviks@vit.ac.in

Abstract. Terrace or Rooftop farming is becoming popular in cities because they protect the roofs, provides green environment, as well as there is a dearth of space for farming. Identification of rooftops will also be beneficial for governments and corporations in foreseeing the implementations of their projects to meet day to day essentials. Geospatial applications like designing and planning urban cities, Agriculture, and Natural Resource Management, etc., needs the extraction of geographical parameters for a particular location. This article aims aim to segment the rooftops obtained using satellite images and extract their polygonal/simple rooftop areas and further work on finding optimal area for terrace farming. The objective of the proposed work is to calculate the total surface area of extracted rooftops and suggest multilayer terrace farming. The insights from this work can be used by policy-makers, architects and urban planners to accommodate rooftop cultivation in their designs, thus reducing the carbon footprint of the building and moving towards a more sustainable urban habitat.

Keywords: Urban terrace farming · Satellite images · Rooftop detection · Multilayer farming

1 Introduction

1.1 Need for Urban Farming

In recent years, as green spaces are replaced by solid structures, the ecological quality in metropolitan regions is becoming horrible. Urban communities and towns would struggle mitigating the metropolitan warmth island wonder without abundant verdant regions, decreasing air and commotion contamination. The need to control the negative impacts of advancement has pushed newly spawning manufacturers, landscape engineers, and metropolitan organizers to think of answers for save the ideal nature of the climate and they suggest that building a housetop nursery or rooftop garden. Also, these verdant regions help improve a building's aesthetics.

© Springer Nature Singapore Pte Ltd. 2021
V. Arunachalam and K. Sivasankaran (Eds.): ICMDCS 2021, CCIS 1392, pp. 31–42, 2021.
https://doi.org/10.1007/978-981-16-5048-2_3

A rooftop garden is basically a garden on the roof of structure involving man-made green spaces on the highest degree of private and business structures having various plants. The individuals of antiquated Mesopotamia have developed trees and bushes on ziggurats. Some Ancient days, European homes had rooftops made with turf and the Hanging Gardens of Babylon, one of the Seven Wonders of the Ancient World, are known to have layered nurseries with loads of vegetation. Until the twentieth century, having a roof garden likened to oddity and abundance. By 1970s, the principal green rooftops were made and introduced in homes just as business foundations. Because of blockage and less green space in the present metropolitan scenes, more private proprietors and building engineers pick to create roof gardens.

Rooftop or Terrace planting is getting progressively mainstream in urban areas, on account of both the lack of space just as the residents' requirement for greener conditions. It is just common, at that point, for open roofs in urban communities to fill in as sound, elective spaces to grow a nursery.

– Temperature control: Exposed roofs in urban areas add to the increment in surface warmth. Cultivating on your roofs can bring down the general temperature of house by 7%.
– Encouraging Eco-accommodating works on: Encouraging practices, for example, home-fertilizing the soil significantly helps in lessening the waste stacked every day onto city trash dumps. Cultivating own food may likewise bring down the general water utilization and utilize gathered water from rain.
– Pesticide food: While various urban areas need to adjust their cultivating endeavors as per their climate, the metropolitan cultivating pattern has gotten on universally, incited by the dread of pesticides in industrially developed produce.
– Sustainable food: It diminishes your food miles (the distance food is shipped from the hour of its creation until it arrives at the purchaser) to zero.
– In a group of four or five, cauliflowers would give enough to as numerous dinners; four or five tomato plants, when they begin fruiting, can supply tomatoes for regular use all through their developing season.
– More green spaces: The advantage of getting a charge out of a green space in clogged urban areas is an uncommon one. By changing over our housetops and terraces into natural food gardens, we add to making a greener, better city.

Selection of Crops. One can grow most of the plants including ornamental and flowering plants on roof top, but to make it more useful vegetables and fruit plants can be cultivated. Choosing the right vegetable and fruits needs a common sense and often preferences are to vegetables commonly used in kitchen. Leafy vegetables, climbers, perennial fruits are some of the options for cultivators. The selection of these also depends on factors like interest, spacing for climbers, availability of light, shadow due to adjacent buildings etc. In order to have an effective policy in promoting terrace garden, robust method of identification of empty roof tops on a massive scale is challenging. Satellite imaging is best

Table 1. Research contributions on rooftop detection.

Author	Algorithms used	Dataset used	Limitations (Gap identified)	Scope for future work
Baluyan, Hayk, et al. [1]	Support vector machine	Google maps images	Poor performance with rooftops	Improve the classification process to discover more informative features and use of alternative classifiers, such as the unbalanced SVM
Kumar, A. [2]	Canny contouring, thresholding	Sentinel-2-satellite images	Specific resolution	Feature embedding and multiclass classification using branched network is proposed
Ghanea et al. [3]	Unsupervised clustering and binary filtering	Region growing GeoEye satellite data	Constructions using similar material could not be segmented	Using Infrared band to segment greenery as well
Ghanea et al. [4]	Region selection and growing	Quickbird satellite imagery	Can't extract buildings with similar spectra as other objects like parking lots	Multi scale segmentation for better extraction
Shi et al. [5]	MeanShift algorithm feature selection	Aerial imagery	Small changes in illumination tend to be insensitive when using the normalized chromaticity in detection of object	To robust track the object rooftop region and select appropriate key frame in multiple aerial views
Jochem et al. [6]	Solar potential analysis, seed point selection and region growing	Laser scanned data from Federal State of Vorarlberg	Unable to solve all 3D shapes	Method cannot be used to perform solar potential assessment of roof planes
Xu et al. [7]	Hierarchical segmentation in three levels	Budapest Szada Bodenzee Normandy	The adapted shadows and vegetation extraction method fails to capture all of the shadows and vegetation correctly in several cases	A dark channel-based depth is effective and robust for most aerial scenes
Collins et al. [8]	Ascender system Boldt algorithm	Model board 1 dataset	There has to be improvements to the Ascender system in order to increase the overall detection rates	To develop more general and flexible building reconstruction systems
Song et al. [9]	LogitBoost algorithm	Google map imagery	The algorithm is very complex and having multiple levels	The increase of the training set and the introduction of the complex building model
Boz et al. [10]	Tilt analysis, Azimuth analysis	Residential commercial institutions datasets	Computational time is a limitation of this study, which is compounded with higher volumes of input data	Usage of this model in customized research using different radiation models

opted and the common challenge is to identify the edges because of varying degree of the polygonal slope of the terrace. In this work, using satellite images identification of cultivatable area and suitable multi-layer cropping method is proposed in this work.

2 Literature Survey

Extraction of structures' mathematical data from satellite pictures has become a vital component in numerous geo-spatial applications, for example metropolitan city plan and arranging, military re-enactment, and site observing of a specific geographic area. Distinguishing proof of roofs will likewise be valuable for governments and organizations in anticipating the usage of their tasks identified with family units. For instance, in numerous Western Countries, roofs having a territory over 250 sqft are needed to cover it with manors. To comprehend the impact of its usage in different nations, for example, India will assist with distinguishing the qualified housetops under the plan and afterward finish if the undertaking is practical in their territory.

The issue with roof is having shifting levels of polygonal shape and hard to arrange using straightforward model as satellite pictures are generally making it hard to distinguish the edges. This work plans to section our housetops got from satellite pictures and concentrate their polygonal/basic roof zones and further chipping away at ideal position of sun oriented boards. As an extra item we will endeavor to compute the all-out surface region of separated housetops. The experiences from this task can be utilized by strategy producers, engineers and metropolitan organizers to oblige housetop development just as sun based energy age into their plans, hence lessening the carbon impression of the structure and moving towards a more supportable metropolitan environment.

The advancements and contributions of the researchers in field of satellite image processing gathered to give a brief overview of the basics, algorithms and dataset used, performance measures, their limitations and scope for future work are tabulated and given Table 1. The aim of the proposed work is to use an appropriate technology to identify the roof top area and effectively utilizes the roof space thus enabling self-sustained agricultural practices. Hence, to identify the roof top free space Otsu Thresholding method is used.

The aim of the proposed work is to use an appropriate technology to identify the rooftop area and effectively utilises the roof space thus enabling self-sustained agricultural practices. Hence, to identify the rooftop free space we decided upon using a variety of image processing techniques to fit our requirements. Firstly most satellite imagery of Indian subcontinent tends to be of comparatively lower resolution than Western nations. To address this we need to apply sharpening and smoothing techniques to ensure image quality is up to the standards required for further steps. Next from the enhanced image we need to extract the rooftop which can be done only by finding its edges so an edge detection algorithm is required. Post edge detection the contouring of the rooftop area is done by utilising the fact that most roofs are planar surfaces which are usually designed to reflect sunlight in order to maintain stable indoor temperatures and thus are brighter than surrounding non-roof elements.

The Otsu Adaptive thresholding algorithm comes into play here to help create the contour of the roof area by separating the image elements into roof and non-roof via an adaptive threshold value by performing a Bitwise AND operation between the edge contoured image and the adaptive threshold image will provide a clear demarcation of roof area which can be further simplified via binary thresholding which results in a clear binary form of roof and non-roof elements.

In many of the alternative and modern techniques of rooftop detection algorithms, such as roof detection using SVM, preservation of colors added with the machine-learning based prediction adds an unnecessary amount of processing power for a minute task which is often required to be done at large scale and thus, increasing costs for it to become a viable option. Additionally, they require a lot of data to be trained on before being able to be deployed for real-time/actual use. Further, it focuses on segment classification via k-means rather than pixel-wise classification to detect roofs which can add in additional noise and result in less accurate predictions. For evaluating the SVM approaches performance, methods commonly used with machine learning approaches like Precision and Recall are used.

In comparison to Rooftop extraction via Hierarchical RGB-D Priors, they require good quality and color satellite images of rooftops to be able to extract the subjects. This is a hassle since many of the developing nations do not have access to good quality satellite images of their area which will stagnant their process in this field. Additionally, using a hierarchical structure to the process may parallelize to a large scale if needed.

3   Rooftop Free Space Detection

A combination of image processing techniques and creating an ultimate pipeline which takes in a rooftop image as input at the start of pipeline and gives us extracted rooftop area, optimum space for terrace gardening on the extracted area as well as an estimate for the area covered by rooftop in reality (in sqm). The various image processing techniques used in the proposed work includes Otsu Thresholding (Adaptive Thresholding), Bilateral Filtering, Canny Edge Detection and several Bitwise operators (see Fig. 1).

Steps Involved in Processing the Satellite Images

1. The images must be in grayscale already whilst remaining images must be colored, in order to handle them all in a similar manner. So the color images are converted into grayscale images. It helps to reduce processing load since the true colors are not necessarily required for edge extraction and can be done alone on the basis of grayscale as extraction is done on the basis of difference in intensities.
2. Next step in the pipeline is Bilateral Sharpening/Filtering. This is done to preserves the edges in the image while also reducing the noise in it. Intuitively, it replaces all the pixels with the weighted average of its surrounding/neighborhood pixels.

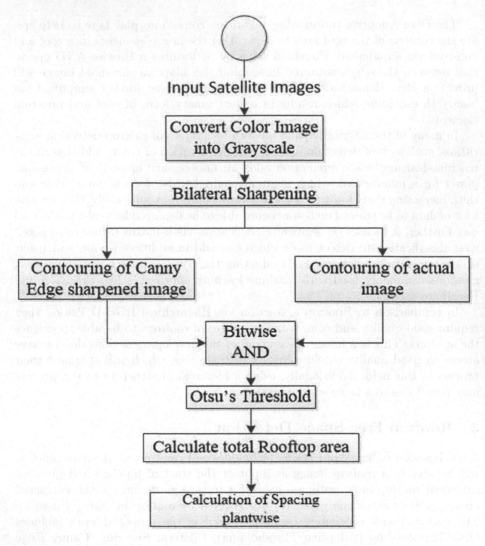

Input Satellite Images

Convert Color Image
into Grayscale

Bilateral Sharpening

Contouring of Canny
Edge sharpened image

Contouring of actual
image

Bitwise
AND

Otsu's Threshold

Calculate total Rooftop area

Calculation of Spacing
plantwise

Fig. 1. Rooftop detection technique

3. After Bilateral Sharpening, we split the pipeline to work on two images and perform contouring i.e. forming boundaries. First, Canny edge detection is applied on the original image, which is a multi-step algorithm that can detect edges with noise. Edges candidates which are not dominant in their neighborhood aren't considered to be edges. Then on the resulting, Otsu thresholding is applied which is used to perform automatic thresholding. It Returns single intensity threshold that classifies images into foreground and background (in the proposed case it is modified for roof and non-roof)

4. To find the rooftop area bitwise AND operation is performed between Canny Contour image and Threshold Contour image. This threshold is again using Binary Threshold which results in getting the rooftop area contour as seen in image.

5. The actual area of the roof is found by multiplying number of white pixels by the area covered per pixel. Area covered per pixel can be calculated using following formula:-

$$metersPerPixel = \frac{156543.03392 * \cos(\frac{latitude*\pi}{180})}{2^x} \qquad (1)$$

where x represents the zoom ratio.

6. Finally, the rooftop gardening area is calculated by using the white area inside the rooftop and checking its mean intensity.

4   Experiment and Research

Dataset. The dataset comprises over 3000 images of rooftops obtained from both, high resolution and low resolution satellite images. There are not many high resolution images present capturing Asian countries, thus we also focused on other alternatives. These high resolution images are satellite images of the European Landscape, primarily France. The dataset is further extrapolated via data augmentation to be able to train our neural network better. Every image is flipped vertically as well as horizontal while retaining all information it holds. The data are processed using Python 3.5.x and above, Google Maps and OpenCV and the results observed are

- The input image (Fig. 2a) which has been converted to grayscale (see Fig. 2b).
- The image sharpening is done using following sharpening mask [11, 12] (see Table 2).
- Bilateral filtering is done to retain the edges and remove noises (Fig. 2c).
- Canny Edge Detection algorithm is executed on the filtered image to detect edges with noise reduction (Fig. 2d).
- Parallelly, Otsu Thresholding is also applied on the original image to separate foreground and background (Fig. 2e).
- The segments the roof area and calculates the area of the roof as well as places maximize the area at an optimum angle (Fig. 2f).

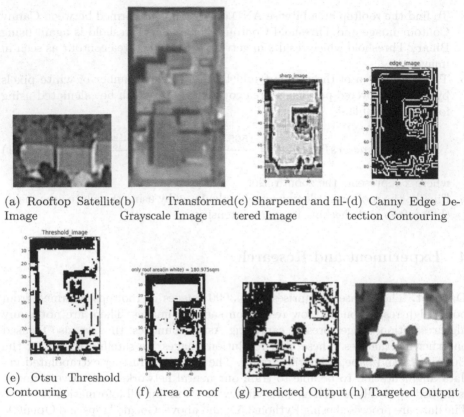

(a) Rooftop Satellite Image (b) Transformed Grayscale Image (c) Sharpened and fil-tered Image (d) Canny Edge Detection Contouring

(e) Otsu Threshold Contouring (f) Area of roof (g) Predicted Output (h) Targeted Output

Fig. 2. Results obtained

Table 2. Sharpening mask

-2	-2	-2
-2	17	-2
-2	-2	-2

A deterministic performance measure for the work can be to compare the area of roof found by the pipeline with ground truth value which can be obtained from local municipal corporations.

Evaluation. For the evaluation, we had a subset of images for which we had formed our very own ground truth and the basis of which our algorithm's performance (Fig. 2g) could be measured. For creating the ground truths, simply filled the rooftop area with white color via Photoshop (Fig. 2h). Since, r pipeline does the same as well and thus, it would be easier to compare if the colors in both the case were same.

Fig. 3. Intersection over Union

Intersection over Union (IoU) metric used for evaluation (Fig. 3), also referred to as the Jaccard index, is essentially a method to quantify the percentage of overlapping between the target mask and our prediction output. This metric is closely related to the Dice coefficient which is often used as a loss function during training. Quite simply, the IoU metric measures the number of pixels common between the target and prediction masks divided by the total number of pixels present across both masks. In the figure below, we have plotted the IOU-score for a subset of images, so that you're able to understand the scoring, alongside with the overall average IoU-score in red i.e. *0.81943* (Fig. 4).

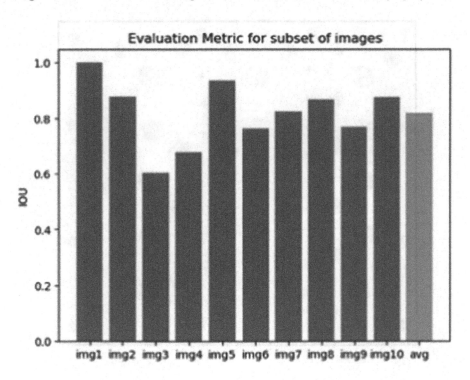

Fig. 4. Evaluation of subset of images

5   Proposal for Multilayer Farming in Rooftop

Multilayer farming is an unconventional, as different types of vegetables, pulses and fruits are grown, they complement each other in many ways such as providing shade canopy, litter, increasing moisture holding capacity of the soil while nurturing microflora. A Five layer method is the most popular model in multilayer farming. The layer 1 comprises underground root vegetables such as carrot, beetroot, Ginger, yam, etc. Most of these plants require less direct sunlight or have good growth in shadowed environment. In the second layer, leafy vegetables such as spinach, coriander etc., which grows close to the surface of the soil, can be cultivated. Midcover fruit bearing plants like tomato, eggplant, chilli, sprouts, cauliflower, and peas can be grown at the third level. A climber normally forms a canopy and hence they can form the fourth layer. The common climbers, Vines, all types of guards, cucumber and so on can be part of this layer. Tall canopy vegetables like Drumstick, Curry leaves, etc. will form the layer five.

As there are crops with different lifecycles, some will die off and need to be replaced. Some act as trap crops and prevent pest attacks. This kind of farming

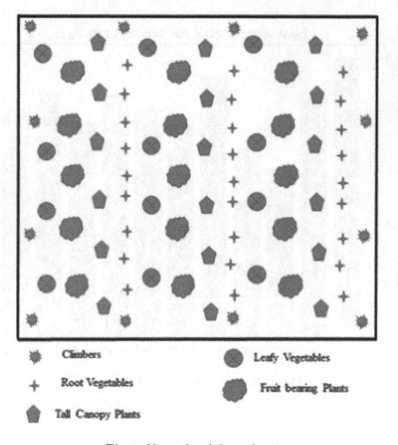

Fig. 5. View of multilayer farming

helps people holding small area of land to grow various seasonal vegetables and horticultural crops throughout the year.

In the proposed work, the active area that can be farmed is determined by Otsu threshold algorithm; to deploy multilayer farming, the rooftop area can be analysed based on the geographical location, total amount of light falling on that area and the wind pattern. The spacing and the choice of plants are based on the canopy that will be formed and life cycle of the plants (Fig. 5).

Land Preparation, Spacing and Planting. Land is set up by furrowing and beds until evenly spreaded. Also, Lumps and stubbles ought to be eliminated from the seedbed. Spacing guidance for various crop types are enlisted below:

- *Leafy Vegetables:* Methi seeds are sowed in the bed and raking the surface to cover the seeds is regularly followed. Yet, Seeds are sowed in lines at a space from 20 to 25 cm to encourage the intercultural tasks.
- *Fruit bearing plants:* Spacing for Tomato is suggested during the Fall/ Winter crop is 75 × 60 cm and for the Spring/Summer crop 75 × 45 cm. The Seedbed 60 cm breadth ought to be ideal, 5 cm to 6 cm lengthy and 20–25 high.
- *Shrubs:* On bed, plant rose in pit of 30 cm × 75 cm distance. Distance between plant to plant relies on the type of the sampling.
- *Climbers:* To plant snake gourd, plough the primary field to a fine and burrow pits of size 30 × 30 × 30 cm at 2.5 m × 2 m dividing and structure bowls. Spread the cylinders sidelong on the raised beds of 120 cm wide at 150 cm dispersing. Water the beds by working the trickle framework persistently for 8–12 h. Plant the seedlings in the openings made at 60 cm dividing.
- *Tropical Trees:* For planting guava, use dividing of 6 × 5 m. Utilization of planting distance of 7 m, at that point in square framework.

6   Conclusion and Future Work

The proposed work is able to segment rooftops to a great extent, and this model can be used efficiently as part of a bigger pipeline where understanding the neighbourhoods of the city is important. The model can be further tweaked by using Pixel2Pixel ML Framework to let Machine Learning models do pixel-wise segmentation of the rooftop. Future work involves determining rooftop types in order to figure out if solar panels can be placed on top of them or not, as well as being able to calculate rooftop area at photos taken from various depths. We propose a system for Indian locality with a frame of 6 feet width. In this four layers of crops are suggested. Since the cultivation on the roof top and mostly from edge to edge of the building, Creepers are the good option to be at the edges of the frame. Since many times these are planted in pots, it can be easily shifted to different places in order to avoid the congestions that may be arrived at the later stage of the cultivation.

References

1. Baluyan, H., Joshi, B., Al Hinai, A., Woon, W.L.: Novel approach for rooftop detection using support vector machine. International Scholarly Research Notices (2013)
2. Kumar, A.: Solar potential analysis of rooftops using satellite imagery. arXiv preprint arXiv:1812.11606 (2018)
3. Ghanea, M., Moallem, P., Momeni, M.: Automatic building extraction in dense urban areas through GeoEye multispectral imagery. Int. J. Remote Sens. 35(13), 5094–5119 (2014)
4. Ghanea, M., Moallem, P., Momeni, M.: An automatic region-based segmentation algorithm for building extraction from high resolution satellite images. In: International Conference on Sensors and Models in Photogrammetry and Remote Sensing, Open Journal of Photogrammetry and Remote Sensing, Tehran, pp. 18–19 (2011)
5. Shi, F., Xi, Y., Li, X., Duan, Y.: An automation system of rooftop detection and 3D building modeling from aerial images. J. Intell. Robot. Syst. 62(3), 383–396 (2011)
6. Jochem, A., Höfle, B., Rutzinger, M., Pfeifer, N.: Automatic roof plane detection and analysis in airborne lidar point clouds for solar potential assessment. Sensors 9(7), 5241–5262 (2009)
7. Xu, S., et al.: Automatic building rooftop extraction from aerial images via hierarchical RGB-D priors. IEEE Trans. Geosci. Remote Sens. 56(12), 7369–7387 (2018)
8. Collins, R.T., et al.: The ascender system: automated site modeling from multiple aerial images. Comput. Vis. Image Underst. 72(2), 143–162 (1998)
9. Song, Z., Pan, C., Yang, Q., Li, F., Li, W.: Building roof detection from a single high-resolution satellite image in dense urban area. In: Proceedings of International Society for Photogrammetry and Remote Sensing, Open Journal of Photogrammetry and Remote Sensing, Beijing, China, pp. 271–277 (2008)
10. Boz, M.B., Calvert, K., Brownson, J.R.: An automated model for rooftop PV systems assessment in ArcGIS using LIDAR. Aims Energy 3(3), 401–420 (2015)
11. Albert, A., Kaur, J., Gonzalez, M.C.: Using convolutional networks and satellite imagery to identify patterns in urban environments at a large scale. In: Proceedings of the 23rd ACM International Conference on Knowledge Discovery and Data Mining, pp. 1357–1366. Association for Computing Machinery, New York (2017)
12. He, K., Zhang, X., Ren, S., Sun, J.: Deep residual learning for image recognition. In: Proceedings of IEEE Conference on Computer Vision and Pattern Recognition, pp. 770–778. IEEE, Las Vegas (2016)

High-Frequency Noise Removal on Corrupted ECG Signal Using Exponential Averagers

R. Mohan Raj[1], P. Thanapal[2], S. Saravanan[3], M. Sundar Prakash Balaji[4], and V. Elamaran[5(✉)]

[1] Department of ECE, PSNA College of Engineering and Technology, Dindigul, Tamilnadu, India
[2] School of Information Technology and Engineering, Vellore Institute of Technology, Vellore 632014, India
thanapal.p@vit.ac.in
[3] Department of ECE, Srinivasa Ramanujan Centre, SASTRA Deemed University, Kumbakonam, Tamilnadu, India
[4] Department of EEE, RVS College of Engineering and Technology, Coimbatore, India
[5] Department of ECE, School of EEE, SASTRA Deemed University, Thanjavur 613401, India
elamaran@ece.sastra.edu

Abstract. An significant aspect of modern medical research, technology, and engineering is the study and processing of bio-signals and the interpretation of clinical images. There are more and more resources available with the growth of computer and information technology that make it easy for professionals to evaluate, analyze, and manipulate any area of science and engineering. Many real-time applications need the input data to be processed rapidly, which is the more challenging part of the filter design. In the FIR filter, for instance, while removing high-frequency components (noise) from an ECG signal, the critical path delay becomes enormous as the duration of the filter increases. In contrast with the simple moving average filters, this study demonstrated exponential averager techniques to suppress noise. Apart from the conventional approaches, the look-ahead and clustered look-ahead with pipelining mechanisms, to improve performance, are analyzed in detail. The exponential averagers (conventional and proposed) were synthesized on an Altera Cyclone IV FPGA EP4CE115F29C7 device using Quartus II software v13.1 tool.

Keywords: Clustered look-ahead · Digital filtering · Exponential averager · FPGA design · Look-ahead · Pipelining · Quartus II

1 Introduction

In these days, signal and image processing holds fast and furious development in academia, research institutes, and industries. The analysis and processing of bio-signals and the interpretation of clinical images is an important part of current medical science, technology, and engineering. With the growth of computer and information technology,

© Springer Nature Singapore Pte Ltd. 2021
V. Arunachalam and K. Sivasankaran (Eds.): ICMDCS 2021, CCIS 1392, pp. 43–54, 2021.
https://doi.org/10.1007/978-981-16-5048-2_4

there are more and more tools made available that make it easy for professionals to probe, examine, and exploit any field of science and engineering [1–3].

Bio-signals such as the Electrocardiogram (ECG), the Electroencephalogram (EEG), the Electromyogram (EMG), the Electroneurogram (ENG), the Electrogastrogram (EGG), the Phonocardiogram (PCG), the Electrooculogram (EOG), the Carotid Pulse (CP), and the Evoked Potential (EP) are essential tools used by a medical practitioner in diagnosing a wide range of health issues [4]. The ability to detect physiological responses, early recognition, quick treatment, diagnosis, subject understanding, and finding of both clinical and pre-clinical scenarios is critical. Detection, classification, source separation, and feature extraction on the physiological signals of disease can diagnose such associated diseases [5].

The function of the heart, which is measured by electrocardiography, is determined by the results of the signal obtained. Physicians have recognized cardiovascular epidemic comprised of a class of diseases that have a high fatality rate. Cardiovascular diseases are caused by the formation of coronary artery disease. The collapse of heart muscles, leading to premature cardiac arrest, is the heart attack. By appropriate analysis and treatment within an hour of the onset of a probable heart attack, the survival rate of patients may be increased [6].

A common ECG waveform is shown in Fig. 1. Each portion of the ECG signal provides different types of information for the physician determining the patient's heart health. The role of digital data processing is to work quickly and accurately in order to meet a needs as quickly as possible. Special remarks may be made here regarding the need to study the QRS complex as it exists in different forms [7, 8].

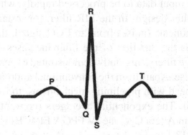

Fig. 1. A common ECG wavefor.

The outcome of the recording is often polluted by either the background noise or the intrinsic interference in the recordings while physiological is recorded. Generally, the signal is indicated by a low amplitude. To obtain vital information from ECG signals for better diagnosis of heart diseases, denoising must be done. ECG signal processing includes research in various fields, including data acquisition and instrumentation systems, signal amplification and control, noise reduction filtering techniques, and extraction of morphological and statistical features [9, 10].

2   Materials and Methods

2.1   High-Frequencey Noise Removal Using an Exponential Averager

An Exponential Averager. The exponential average can be deployed with reduced hardware structures, compared with an 8-tap moving average filter to suppress high-frequency components (noise). Using exponential smoothing, the filter achieves the noise reduction mechanism,

$$y(n) = \alpha x(n) + (1 - \alpha)y(n - 1) \tag{1}$$

where $x(n)$ is the input sample, $y(n-1)$ is the previous sample of output, $y(n)$ is the sample of output, and is the weighting factor, a constant between zero and one. For example, with $\alpha = 1/8$, a better smoothing effect (filtering high-frequency noise) will be created by the filter.

The Motivation. The motivation for using the exponential averager is that it has the following attractive properties for the need for noise-reduction filtering:

- Important control over the frequency response of its size, i.e. greater control over noise-reduction activity than non-recursive moving averages
- Needs only less per output sample computations than the traditional moving averages
- Only one delay factor (reduced memory requirements) for smoothing is included.
- Due to higher expectations for more recent samples, the dynamic changes in a system respond more quickly than the moving averages.

More specifically, during the averaging process, the speed and stability and how the averaging scheme affects the input samples with the variable response over time are critical parts.

High-Freqeuncy Noise Removal. Because of the equal weight for both the old and new samples, the unweighted moving average is not quicker to react to the dynamic changes in a system. Also, higher computations per output sample and more delay elements based on the tap size are needed for the traditional moving average filter. The moving averager also leads to more power dissipation due to greater size and more calculations. There is also a need for lower hardware architectures such as an exponential averager to eliminate high-frequency components from an ECG signal. It is also important to adjust the amount of noise reduction by changing the value of the weighting factor, like "alpha" in an exponential averager (see Eq. 1).

Matlab Simulations. A typical effect of high-frequency noise removal from an ECG that was sampled at 1000 Hz is shown in Fig. 2. The exponential averager was used to perform this ECG filtering experiment as follows:

$$y(n) = \frac{1}{8}x(n) + \frac{7}{8}y(n - 1) \tag{2}$$

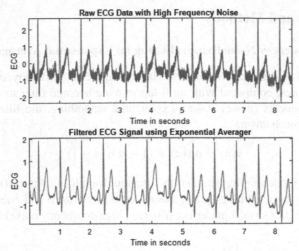

Fig. 2. High-frequency noise reduction diagram from an ECG. (a) Initial signal from ECG. (b) Removed high-frequency noise by an exponential averager.

Need for High-Performance Exponential Averager. The main objective of this study is to shape efficient exponential averages of reduced or high-performance hardware and implement them on an FPGA device. The Exponential Averager is an IIR filter, unlike the traditional moving average filter. On an Altera DE2-115 FPGA (EP4CE115F29C7) device using very high-speed integrated circuit hardware description language (VHDL), the performance of the exponential averagers was assessed. A real-time filter's primary demands are as follows:

- Lesser area
- Lower power consumption
- Reduced delay (higher perormance)

2.2 Conventional Exponential Averager Designs

Conventional. For obvious reasons, based on Eq. 2, the schematic of the conventional exponential averager is shown in Fig. 3. At the beginning, the multiply is placed by 1/8, thus called "*conv_divb*". In the hardware, 60 logic elements, 15 registers, 138.68 mW (power dissipation), and 151.90 MHz (speed) are required for this traditional approach. This design requires more crucial delay in the path (6.583 ns). Therefore, by exploring various methods, this study attempted to enhance the design with attention to reducing critical path latency.

Division by Eight After the Feedback Network. The multiplying by portion (1/8) can be put after the feedback, as seen in Fig. 4 and hence it is named as "*conv_dive*". It needs lower LEs (45) and better speed (361.66 MHz), lower power dissipation (135.86 mW) than the '*conv-divb*' because the division occurs at the end, for obvious reasons.

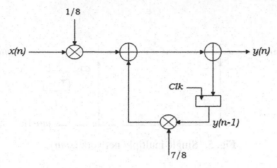

Fig. 3. The conventional exponential moving averager (*conv_divb*).

Single Multiply Network. Also, Eq. (1) can be expressed as [11],

$$y(n) = \alpha x(n) + y(n-1) - \alpha y(n-1)$$

$$= \frac{1}{8}x(n) + y(n-1) - \frac{1}{8}y(n-1)$$

$$= \left(\frac{1}{8}(x(n) - y(n-1))\right) + y(n-1) \tag{3}$$

Equation (3) obviously needs only one multiplier, which is better from a hardware perspective. Figure 5 reveals the schematic of the single multiply network, called "*smn*". Only fewer logic elements (47 LEs), 15 registers are needed for this design with a performance of 146.19 MHz. More significantly, this involves lower dissipation of power (132.53 mW) than the traditional method.

It needs more critical path delay (6.840 ns) due to the decreased hardware arrangements in a single multiply network, although it is appropriate for the area and power dissipation wise. Therefore, there is a poor performance in this approach.

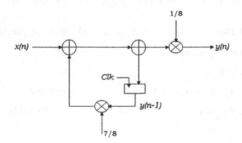

Fig. 4. *Conv_dive*: The "alpha" term after the feedback network.

Pipelined Exponential Averager. Since the architecture (*conv_dive*) obtains better results (fewer LEs, higher performance), the pipelining technique is incorporated into it, and named as "*conv_dive_pipe*". Figure 6 shows the "conv_dive with pipelining

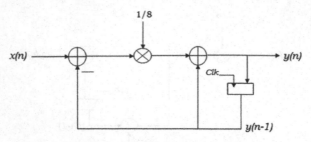

Fig. 5. Single multiply network (*smn*).

structure" for an exponential averager. These findings are compared in Table 1 with the "*conv_dive*" architecture. The motive behind the use of the pipelining method is to maximize performance. As predicted, Table 1 shows better pipeline design performance (408.83 MHz). Moreover, the pipelined design achieves a speed-up of about 13%, compared without pipelining. In this context, there may be other viable mechanisms also for better results.

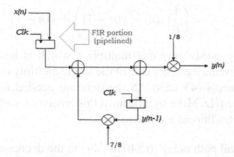

Fig. 6. Exponential moving averager with pipelining mechanism (*conv_dive_pipe*).

Table 1. Simulation results (Pipelined vs. *conv_dive*).

Metrics	Without pipelined	With pipelined
Logic elements	45	52
Registers	15	30
Dynamic power	0.88 mW	0.93 mW
Performance	361.66 MHz	408.83 MHz

2.3 Proposed Exponential Averager Designs

Pipelined Exponential Averager Using Look-Ahead. In this section, an exponential averager is adopted with the look-ahead scheme. The location of the multiplying operation "alpha" at the front and at the end is also examined in depth.

The look-ahead using pipeling technqiue with multiplying by (1/8) before the feed-back network is called as "*la_pipe_divb*". The look-ahead theory can be explicitly implemented as follows, since the exponential averager falls into the IIR filter category [12]:

$$y(n) = \frac{1}{8}x(n) + \frac{7}{8}y(n-1)$$

$$y(n+1) = \frac{1}{8}x(n+1) + \frac{7}{8}y(n)$$

$$y(n+2) = \frac{1}{8}x(n+2) + \frac{7}{8}y(n+1)$$

$$= \frac{1}{8}x(n+2) + \frac{7}{8}\left(\frac{1}{8}x(n+1) + \frac{7}{8}y(n)\right)$$

$$= \frac{1}{8}x(n+2) + \frac{7}{64}x(n+1) + \frac{49}{64}y(n) \tag{4}$$

From Eq. (4), the output y(n) can therefore be expressed as,

$$y(n) = \frac{1}{8}x(n) + \frac{7}{64}x(n-1) + \frac{49}{64}y(n-2) \tag{5}$$

Obviously, in the FIR section of Eq. (5), the pipelining registers can be inserted. Figure 7 shows the schematics of the pipelined look-ahead exponential averager.

The difference equation is expressed as, for the multiply by "alpha" operation at the end (*div_e*),

$$y(n) = \left(x(n) + \frac{7}{8}y(n-1)\right) \times \frac{1}{8} \tag{6}$$

Now by applying the look-ahead principle to it (*la_pipe_dive*), as follows [12]:

$$y(n+1) = x(n+1) + \frac{7}{8}y(n)$$

$$y(n+2) = x(n+2) + \frac{7}{8}y(n+1)$$

$$= x(n+2) + \frac{7}{8}\left(x(n+1) + \frac{7}{8}y(n)\right)$$

$$= x(n+2) + \frac{7}{8}x(n+1) + \frac{49}{64}y(n) \tag{7}$$

From Eq. (7), the output y(n) can therefore be expressed as,

$$y(n) = x(n) + \frac{7}{8}x(n-1) + \frac{49}{64}y(n-2) \tag{8}$$

In the FIR portion of Eq. (8), the pipeline registers can easily be inserted, and the corresponding schematic can be seen in Fig. 8.

Obviously, in the FIR scction of Eq. (5), the pipelining registers can be inserted. Figure 8 shows the schematics of the pipelined look-ahead exponential averager.

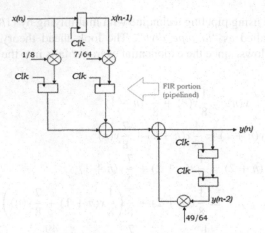

Fig. 7. Pipelined exponential moving averager with look-ahead approach (*la_pipe_divb*)

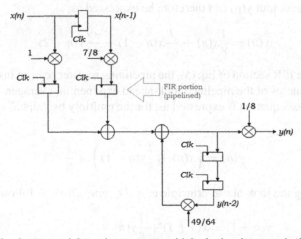

Fig. 8. Pipelined exponential moving averager with look-ahead approach (*la_pipe_dive*).

Pipelined Exponential Averager Using Clustered Look-Ahead. The clustered look-ahead using the pipelining technique with division by eight after the feedback network (end) is named as "*cla_pipe_dive*". The clustered look-ahead technique can be applied to (5) by using Z-transformation as follows [12]:

$$Y(z) = X(z) + \frac{7}{8}X(z)z^{-1} + \frac{49}{64}Y(z)z^{-2}$$

$$H(z) = \frac{Y(z)}{X(z)}$$

$$= \frac{1 + \frac{7}{8}z^{-1}}{1 - \frac{49}{64}z^{-2}}$$

$$= \frac{1 + \frac{7}{8}z^{-1}}{1 - \frac{49}{64}z^{-2}} \times \frac{1 + \frac{49}{64}z^{-2}}{1 + \frac{49}{64}z^{-2}}$$

$$= \frac{1 + \frac{7}{8}z^{-1} + \frac{49}{64}z^{-2} + \frac{343}{512}z^{-3}}{1 - \frac{2401}{4096}z^{-4}} \tag{9}$$

From Eq. (9), the output y(n) can therefore be expressed as,

$$y(n) = x(n) + \frac{7}{8}x(n-1) + \frac{49}{64}x(n-2) + \frac{343}{512}x(n-3) + \frac{2401}{4096}y(n-4) \tag{10}$$

Clearly, to the FIR portion of Eq. (10), the pipelining registers can be added. Figure 9 shows the "cla_pipe_dive" structure.

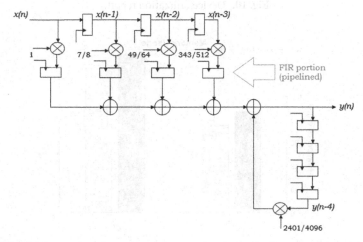

Fig. 9. Pipelined exponential moving averager using look-ahead approach (*cla_pipe_dive*).

3 Simulation Results

The suggested exponential averager is detailed here using look-ahead with pipelining and clustered look-ahead with pipelining. The "*dive*" design styles provide lower logic elements in both systems compared to the "*divb*" method (139 in "*la_pipe_dive*" and 433 in "*cla_pipe_dive*"), which can be seen in Fig. 10. They need more logical elements because of more flexibility in the clustered look-ahead pipelining scheme; they also need more egisters than the forms of "*la-pipe*" (see Fig. 11). 45 memory bits are needed for the "*cla_pipe*" design types, while the "*la_pipe*" design types need no memory bits. Figure 12 displays the performance results; the "*la_pipe_dive*" system provides better performance (519.48 MHz) than all of them.

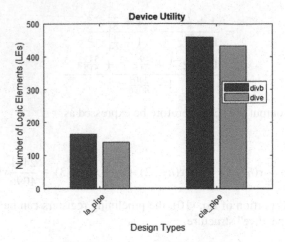

Fig. 10. Device utilization report.

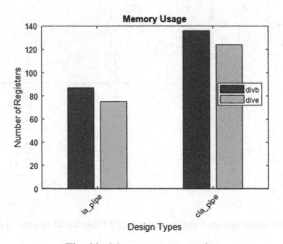

Fig. 11. Memory usage results.

Figure 13 shows the total power dissipation effects, which include dynamic power, static power, and I/O power. There are almost no major variations between the two designs in overall energy consumption. We can note from the graph that the "cla-pipe-dive" configuration absorbs lower power than others.

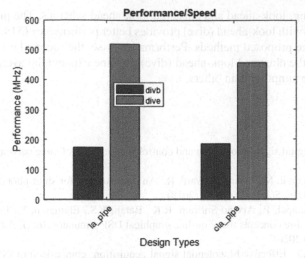

Fig. 12. Performance reults.

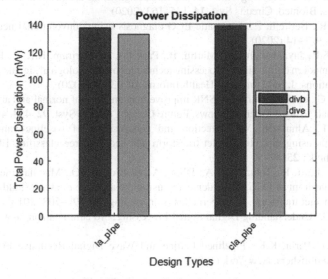

Fig. 13. Power dissipation results.

4 Conclusion

The various design structures of the exponential averager, both traditional and proposed, are studied, analyzed and synthesized using Quartus II software on Altera EP4CE115F29C7 FPGA device. Among conventional approaches, the performance-wise, the pipelined structure (*pipe_div_e*) is best found with the 408.83 MHz speed. For further research, common techniques are used to minimize delay (increase performance), such as pipelining, look-ahead and clustered look-ahead schemes. The pipelined exponential averager with look-ahead (dive) provides better performance (519.48 MHz) than others, one of the proposed methods. Performance-wise, the second best configuration (456.82 MHz), the clustered look-ahead (dive) pipeline exponential averager, achieves lower power consumption than others.

References

1. Shin, Y.J.: Digital signal processing and control for the study of gene networks. Sci. Rep. **6**, 1–18 (2016)
2. Liang, Y., Elgendi, M., Chen, Z., Ward, R.: An optimal filter for short photoplethysmogram signals. Sci. Data **5**(180076), 1–12 (2018)
3. Sasi, G., Thanapal, P., Arvind Shriram, R.K., Balaji, V.S., Elamaran, V.: Exploring digital signal processing concepts using on-line graphical DSP simulator. Int. J. Adv. Sci. Technol. **29**, 410–421 (2020)
4. Jiang, Y., et al.: Effective biopotential signal acquisition: comparison of different shielded drive technologies. Appl. Sci. **8**, 1–19 (2018)
5. Wei, Y., et al.: A review of algorithm & hardware design for AI-based biomedical applications. IEEE Trans. Biomed. Circuits Syst. **14**, 145–163 (2020)
6. Avanzato, R., Beritelli, F.: Automatic ECG diagnosis using convolutional neural network. Electronics **9**, 1–14 (2020)
7. Balaji, M.S.P., Jayabharathy, R., Martin, B., Parvathy, A., Shriram, R.K.A., Elamaran, V.: Exploring modern digital signal processing techniques on physiological signals in day-to-day life applications. J. Med. Imaging Health Inform. **10**, 93–98 (2020)
8. Rajkumar, G., et al.: Spectral and SNR improvement analysis of normal and abnormal heart sound signals using different windows. Future Gener. Comput. Syst. **92**, 438–443 (2019)
9. Haider, S.I., Alhussein, M.: Detection and classification of baseline-wander noise in ECG signals using discrete wavelet transform and decision tree classifier. Electronika IR Elektrotechnika **25**, 47–57 (2019)
10. Jenkal, W., Latif, R., Toumanari, A., Dliou, A., El B'charri, O., Maoulainine, F.M.R.: An efficient algorithm of ECG signal denoising using the adaptive dual threshold filter and the discrete wavelet transform. Biocybernetics Biomed. Eng. **36**, 499–508 (2016)
11. Lyons, R.G.: Understanding Digital Signal Processing, 3rd edn. Pearson New International Edition (2013)
12. Chung, J.G., Parhi, K.K.: Pipelined Lattice and Wave Digital Recursive Filters. Kluwer Academic Publishers, New York (1996)

Baseline Wandering Noise Removal Using High-Speed IIR Filters with an FPGA Implementation

R. Mohan Raj[1], Vemula Rajesh[2], S. Saravanan[3], M. Sundar Prakash Balaji[4], and V. Elamaran[5(✉)]

[1] Department of ECE, PSNA College of Engineering and Technology, Dindigul, Tamilnadu, India
[2] Department of ECE, School of EET, Kalasalingam Academy of Research and Education, Anand Nagar, Krishnankoil 626126, India
[3] Department of ECE, Srinivasa Ramanujan Centre, SASTRA Deemed University, Kumbakonam, Tamilnadu, India
[4] Department of EEE, RVS College of Engineering and Technology, Coimbatore, India
[5] Department of ECE, School of EEE, SASTRA Deemed University, Thanjavur 613401, India
elamaran@ece.sastra.edu

Abstract. Biomedical engineering and technology are currently undergoing vast transformation due to rapid growing of automation and artificial intelligence. The outcome of the recording is often polluted by either the background noise or the intrinsic interference in the recordings while physiological is recorded. The powerline interface and baseline wandering noise tend to appear in each obtained electrocardiogram (ECG) data and can affect the intelligence of the signal. The primary objective of this study is to apply various filtering techniques to remove the unnecessary noise (baseline wandering), although it is not possible to misinterpret the necessary details more than defined in standard guidance. Using a DC bias elimination filter with various design structures such as conventional, pipelined, look-ahead, and clustered look-ahead to eliminate the baseline wandering effect from an ECG signal to give better output (clock speed). The filters were implemented in an Altera FPGA DE2115 device. The description of resource usage, efficiency (speed) and total results of power dissipation are analyzed in detail.

Keywords: Clustered look-ahead · DC bias removal · Digital filtering · FPGA design · Look-ahead · Pipelining · Quartus II

1 Introduction

In each obtained electrocardiogram (ECG) data, the powerline interface and baseline wandering noise tend to appear and can impair the signal intelligence. They must be removed from the simplification of the patient's true diagnosis. Substandard power supplies, transformers, or electromagnetic disturbance induced by a frequency of 60-Hz and its harmonics can inject power-line interference (hum noise). For example, due to this

© Springer Nature Singapore Pte Ltd. 2021
V. Arunachalam and K. Sivasankaran (Eds.): ICMDCS 2021, CCIS 1392, pp. 55–65, 2021.
https://doi.org/10.1007/978-981-16-5048-2_5

hum noise, the desired signal, an ECG signal, might be corrupted [1–3]. The notch filter with a 60-Hz cut-off frequency and the comb filter with a 60-Hz multiple sample rate are the most possible solutions to eliminate the noise from the hum. Adaptive digital filters can also provide the remedy for hum noise reduction [4–6].

A low-frequency noise of about 0.5 to 0.6 Hz is the second, i.e. the baseline wander (closer to a dc). This baseline wandering is practically due to inadequate skin sensitivity to electrodes, i.e. due to relaxed interaction with electrodes or poor positioning or even tightly positioned electrodes. This can also happen during respiration due to the contraction of the chest wall and the function of the muscle. The observed ECG would comprise the baseline wandering effect if the patient breathes deeply. Usually, soon after the application of electrodes, the baseline wander is recognized. The baseline wandering may occur during the recording of an ECG signal due to patient motion and poor skin preparation [7, 8].

Figure 1 shows one such pattern of baseline wandering. The corresponding wandering ECG baseline signal may look like a curly, irregular, or shaky signal. All the intelligence of an ECG signal is available but not stationary in baseline wandering. For sure, a high-pass filter may be used since the frequency range of the interference is nearer to the zero frequency (DC), to minimize the baseline wandering impact [9].

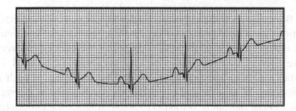

Fig. 1. Wandering baseline in the ECG signal.

Naturally, baseline wander noise will appear due to body gestures, electrode impedance effects, and breathing effects; thus, filtering is important to remove the knowledge from an ECG signal. For example, filtering muscle noise will be extremely challenging as its content occurs concurrently with an ECG signal during the patient's data collection, but there are more difficulties in such applications [10].

A DC bias removal filter (see Fig. 2) could yield the expected infinite attenuation at zero frequency to remove the DC offset. This filter can then be used to nullify the ECG signal's baseline wandering. This filtered is described as follows [11]:

$$H(z) = \frac{1 - z^{-1}}{1 - Az^{-1}} \tag{1}$$

The input-output relationship of Eq. (1) is expressed as,

$$y(n) = x(n) - x(n-1) + A y(n-1) \tag{2}$$

where $x(n)$ is the input sample, $x(n-1)$ is the previous input sample, $y(n-1)$ is the previous output sample, $y(n)$ is the output sample, and for the better removal of a DC

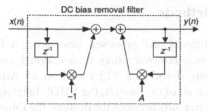

Fig. 2. A simple filter to suppress DC bias.

variable, A is a positive value a bit nearer to the unit. A is the weighting factor in the range from zero to one, a constant. For example, a greater removal of any DC bias (suppressing the 0 Hz) will be achieved by the filter with $A = 0.875$. Equation (2) thus becomes

$$y(n) = x(n) - x(n - 1) + \frac{7}{8} y(n - 1) \qquad (3)$$

A typical result of DC bias elimination from an ECG which was sampled at 250 Hz is shown in Fig. 3.

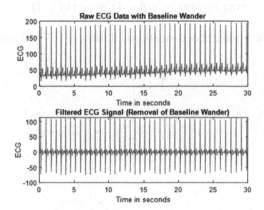

Fig. 3. A simple filter to suppress DC bias.

The primary intention of this study is to develop and realize efficient hardware-reduced or high-performance DC bias removal filters on an FPGA system. The DC bias reduction filter, unlike the traditional moving average filter, is an IIR filter [12, 13]. It will also help to improve efficiency by implementing pipelining processes, look-ahead and clustered look-ahead procedures. On an Altera DE2-115 FPGA (EP4CE115F29C7) device using very high-speed integrated circuits hardware description language (VHDL), the performance of the exponential averagers was assessed. A real-time filter's primary demands are as follows [14]:

- Lower in size
- Lower power dissipation
- Reduced delay (higher performance)

2   Materials and Methods

In this section, the traditional and proposed designs of a DC bias removal filter are addressed. The DC bias removal filters (conventional and proposed) were synthesized using the Quartus II software v13.1 tool on an Altera Cyclone IV FPGA EP4CE115F29C7 unit. For all of the models, the VHDL language is used. For the study (comparison) of simulation results between the designs, the following three performance metrics were adopted (existing and proposed).

- Use of logic elements (LEs)
- Performance (clock speed)
- Power dissipation

2.1   Conventional Approaches

The traditional DC bias removal filter, i.e., Eq. (3) is exposed again for the demonstrable reason as,

$$y(n) = x(n) - x(n-1) + \frac{7}{8} y(n-1)$$

The schematic view of the above equation is illustrated in Fig. 4 and named as "*conv*".

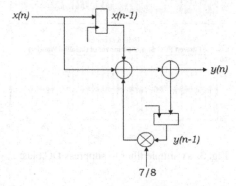

Fig. 4. The typical filter for DC bias elimination (*conv*).

It is observed that 60 logic components, 30 registers, 144.51 mW (power dissipation), and 154.82 MHz (performance) are required for the traditional DC bias removal filter. This appraoch demands more critical path delay (6.459 ns), and we will therefore concentrate more on reducing the delay of the critical path for higher results.

Pipelined DC Bias Removal Filter. Pipeline registers can be connected directly to the FIR portion of the traditional DC bias removal filter [15]. The resulting schematic is shown in Fig. 5 and named as "*conv_pipe*" structure. In Fig. 5.10, a section of the VHDL code for this structure is shown. As anticipated, this structure provides better performance (476.87 MHz) due to pipelining, requires more registers (45), and needs

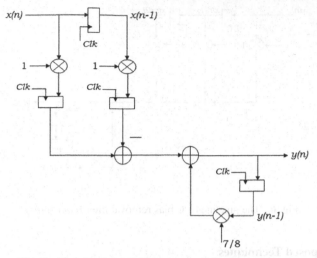

Fig. 5. The pipelined DC bias removal filter (*conv_pipe*).

slightly more logic components (63 LEs) than traditional ones. In this context, there may be other potential mechanisms for enhanced efficiency.

DC Bias Removal Filter Using Look-Ahead Technique. It is possible to apply the look-ahead approach to a DC bias reduction filter as follows [15]:

$$y(n) = x(n) - x(n-1) + \frac{7}{8}y(n-1)$$

$$y(n+1) = x(n+1) - x(n) + \frac{7}{8}y(n)$$

$$y(n+2) = x(n+2) - x(n+1) + \frac{7}{8}y(n+1) \tag{4}$$

$$= x(n+2) - x(n+1) + \frac{7}{8}\left(x(n+1) - x(n) + \frac{7}{8}y(n)\right)$$

$$= x(n+2) - \frac{1}{8}x(n+1) - \frac{7}{8}x(n) + \frac{49}{64}y(n)$$

From Eq. (4), the output y(n) can thus be represented as,

$$y(n) = x(n) - \frac{1}{8}x(n-1) - \frac{7}{8}x(n-2) + \frac{49}{64}y(n-2) \tag{5}$$

Figure 6 shows the schematic of the traditional DC bias elimination filter using a look-ahead strategy, thus called "*conv_la*". The goal behind using the look-ahead strategy is to reduce the delay in the critical latency. The performance is stronger (236.29 MHz) than the conventional (154.82 MHz) but lower than the approach to the "*conv_pipe*" (476.87 MHz). This architecture requires more logic elements (135 LEs) and registers (75) because of the look-ahead complexity.

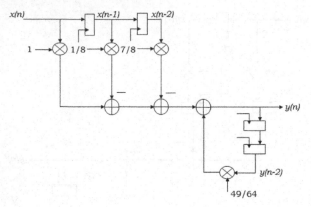

Fig. 6. The pipelined DC bias removal filter (*conv_pipe*).

2.2 The Proposed Techniques

Pipelined DC Bias Removal Filter Using Look-Ahead Technique. Pipelining registers can be given successfully to the FIR portion of Eq. (5); "*la_pipe*" is the subsequent configuration (see Fig. 7). This design provides better efficiency (528.54 MHz) than all previous designs at the expense of more logic elements (150 LEs) and registers (88) due to pipelining with a look-ahead approach [15].

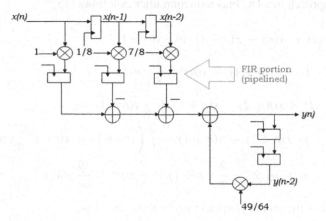

Fig. 7. Pipelined DC bias removal filter using a look-ahead approach (*la_pipe*).

Pipelined DC Bias Removal Filter Using Clustered Look-Ahead. The clustered look-ahead technique is exhibited in the DC bias removal filter in this section [15]. The clustered look-ahead is named "*cla_pipe*" using the pipelining method. The clustered look-ahead technique can be applied to Eq. (5) by using Z-transformation as follows:

$$Y(z) = X(z) - \frac{1}{8}z^{-1}X(z) - \frac{7}{8}z^{-2}X(z) + \frac{49}{64}z^{-2}Y(z)$$

$$H(z) = \frac{Y(z)}{X(z)}$$

$$= \frac{1 - \frac{1}{8}z^{-1} - \frac{7}{8}z^{-2}}{1 - \frac{49}{64}z^{-2}} = \frac{1 - \frac{1}{8}z^{-1} - \frac{7}{8}z^{-2}}{1 - \frac{49}{64}z^{-2}} \times \frac{1 + \frac{49}{64}z^{-2}}{1 + \frac{49}{64}z^{-2}}$$

(6)

From Eq. (6), the output y(n) can thus be represented as,

$$y(n) = x(n) - \frac{1}{8}x(n-1) - \frac{7}{64}x(n-2) - \frac{49}{512}x(n-3) - \frac{343}{512}x(n-4) + \frac{2401}{4096}y(n-4)$$

(7)

Clearly, it is possible to add pipeline registers to the FIR section of Eq. (7). Figure 8 shows the schematic of the pipelined DC bias elimination filter using a clustered look-ahead method, and named as "cla_pipe". Owing to the difficulty in the architecture, the "cla_pipe" approach needs more logic elements (467 LEs) and registers (151). This design also provides lower performance (394.78 MHz) than the "la_pipe" approach because of the wide FIR section used for the pipeline (528.54 MHz). This structure dissipates more dynamic power (2.59 mW) than all others, for the same cause (complexity).

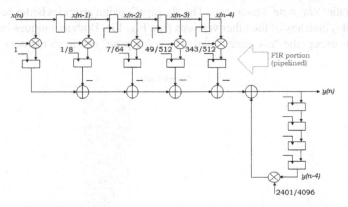

Fig. 8. Pipelined DC bias removal filter using clustered look-ahead approach (cla_pipe).

3 Simulation Results

The simulation results on current and suggested methods of a DC bias removal filter are summarized in this section.

Results on Existing Methods (without Pipelined). For the traditional (existing) designs, Table 1 records the simulation performance. The "*conv_la*" solution needs more logic elements (135) and registers (75) than the standard one because of the difficulty. For sure, the "*conv_la*" provides better efficiency (236.29 MHz) than the other one because of the pipelining.

Table 1. Simulation results on conventional designs (without pipelined).

Metrics	Conventional	Conventional using look-ahead (*cla*)
Logic elements	60	135
Registers	30	75
Power dissipation	144.51 mW	136.25 mW
Performance	154.82 MHz	236.29 MHz

Results on Pipelined Designs. This describes the suggested DC bias reduction filter using look-ahead with pipelining and clustered look-ahead with pipelining outcomes. Also, the simulation results of a DC bias elimination filter using the "conv pipe" method are provided for comparison. In Fig. 9, the system utilization report is presented. For example, the "*cla_pipe*" needs 467 logic elements. The more complicated designs need more logic elements. The effects of the number of registers used by the systems can be seen in Fig. 10. The more complex designs obviously need more registers, such as 151 registers for the "*cla_pipe*" statements. The "la-pipe" design provides better performance (528.54 MHz) than any of the other versions (see Fig. 11). Both techniques involve zero memory bits except the "*cla_pipe*," while the "*clas_pipe*" needs 45 memory bits.

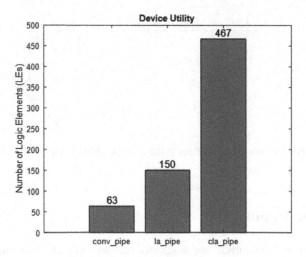

Fig. 9. Device utilization summary.

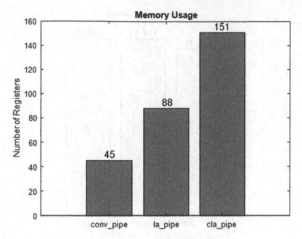

Fig. 10. Results on memory usage.

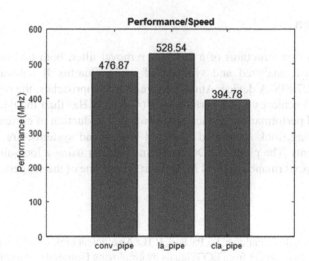

Fig. 11. Results on clock speed.

In Fig. 12, the total power dissipation outcomes, including dynamic power, static power, and I/O power, are shown. For obvious reasons, the "*conv_pipe*" dissipates lower power (136.31 mW) than others due to less complexity.

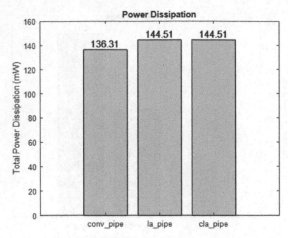

Fig. 12. Power dissipation results.

4 Conclusion

The different design structures of a DC bias removal filter, both traditional and proposed, are tested, analyzed and synthesized using Quartus II software on Altera EP4CE115F29C7 FPGA device. Among conventional approaches, the pipelined structure (*conv_pipe*) achieves better performance (476.87 MHz) than the typical one. The commonly used performance enhancement strategies (reduction of critical path delay), such as pipelining, look-ahead and clustered look-ahead systems, are used for further improvements. The pipelined DC bias removal filter using a look-ahead approach provides better performance (528.54 MHz) than others, one of the suggested techniques.

References

1. Singhal, A., Singh, P., Fatimah, B., Pachori, R.B.: An efficient removal of power-line interference and baseline wander from ECG signals by employing Fourier decomposition technique. Biomed. Signal Process. Control **57**(101741), 1–8 (2020)
2. Bahaz, M., Benzid, R.: Efficient algorithm for baseline wander and powerline noise removal from ECG signals based on discrete Fourier series. Australas. Phys. Eng. Sci. Med. **41**(1), 143–160 (2018). https://doi.org/10.1007/s13246-018-0623-1
3. Mateo, J., Sanchez-Morla, E.M., Santos, J.L.: A new method for removal of powerline interference in ECG and EEG recordings. Comput. Electr. Eng. **45**, 235–248 (2015)
4. Pinto, J.R., Cardoso, J.S., Lourenco, A.: Evolution, current challenges, and future possibilities in ECG biometrics. IEEE Access **6**, 34746–34776 (2018)
5. Balaji, M.S.P., Jayabharathy, R., Martın, B., Parvathy, A., Shriram, R.K.A., Elamaran, V.: Exploring modern digital signal processing techniques on physiological signals in day-to-day life applications. J. Med. Imaging Health Inform. **10**, 93–98 (2020)
6. Sasi, G., Thanapal, P., Arvind Shriram, R.K., Balaji, V.S., Elamaran, V.: Exploring digital signal processing concepts using on-line graphical DSP simulator. Int. J. Adv. Sci. Technol. **29**, 410–421 (2020)

7. Daqrouq, K., Ajour, M., AI-Qawasmi, A.R., Alkhateeb, A.: The discrete wavelet transform based electrocardiographic baseline wander reduction method for better signal diagnosis. J. Med. Imaging Health Inform. **8**, 1590–1597 (2018)

8. Sharma, R.R., Pachori, R.B.: Baseline wander and power line interference removal from ECG signals using eigenvalue decomposition. Biomed. Signal Process. Control **45**, 33–49 (2018)

9. Patel, R., Gireesan, K., Sengottuvel, S., Janawadkar, M.P., Radhakrishnan, T.S.: Suppression of baseline wander artifact in magnetocardiogram using breathing sensor. J. Med. Biol. Eng. **37**, 554–560 (2017)

10. Kozumplik, J., Provaznik, I.: Fast time-varying linear filters for suppression of baseline drift in electrocardiographic signals. Biomed. Eng. Online **16**(24), 1–16 (2017)

11. Lyons, R.G.: Understanding Digital Signal Processing, 3rd edn. Pearson New International Edition, New York (2013)

12. Hui, W., et al.: Revisiting FPGA implementation of digital filters and exploring approximate computing on biomedical signals. J. Med. Imaging Health Inform. **10**, 2000–2004 (2020)

13. Balaji, M.S.P., et al.: Analysis of energy concentration of the speech, EEG, and ECG signals in healthcare applications – a survey. J. Med. Imaging Health Inform. **10**, 49–53 (2020)

14. Mallavarapu, P., Upadhyay, H.N., Rajkumar, G., Elamaran, V.: Fault-tolerant digital filters on FPGA using hardware redundancy techniques. In: Proceedings of the 2017 International Conference of Electronics, Communication and Aerosspace Technology (ICECA), pp. 256–259 (2017)

15. Chung, J.G., Parhi, K.K.: Pipelined Lattice and Wave Digital Recursive Filters. Kluwer Academic Publishers, New York (1996)

VLSI Testing and Verification

Design for Trust Using Transition Probability

G. Arunachalam[✉]

Amrita Vishwa Vidhyapeetham University, Coimbatore, Tamil Nadu, India
cb.en.u4ece17111@cb.students.amrita.edu

Abstract. With the evolution of Internet, systems are moving towards a digital era. But there occurs a problem of security and safety, where the adversaries can attack our systems with viruses and malwares to extract the data from our system. To identify and to prevent the hacking, in particular, Trojan insertion we can design hardware based detection system. As the hardware based solutions are faster than software based solutions, the design of trust based obfuscation systems will give lesser time for an attacker to attack a victim's system. Thus the overall damage in a victim's system can be reduced. We propose in this paper a method by which we can identify the vulnerable nodes in a circuit using Transition Probability concepts to enhance the security of an IC. The authorization of the designed system will happen only when the correct input patterns are given. This probabilistic approach ensures that an attacker cannot extract net list and decode the circuit.

Keywords: Hardware security · Transition probability · Trojans · Net list · Trust based obfuscation system

1 Introduction

In the modern world, Integrated Circuits (IC's) are designed and manufactured in a planetary environment. They often lead to hardware related security issues which include piracy, overproduction and insertion of malicious circuits. The malware can be due to viruses and Trojans. Viruses are self-replicating programs that can damage the computer's hardware, software and operating system. Viruses can hamper and corrupt the files of a system. A Trojan is a malicious code that looks appropriate which can take control of our computer. The difference between the Trojans and Virus are that Virus can execute and replicate them. A user has to execute the Trojans.

Trojans are generally of two types: Software Trojans and Hardware Trojans. In general, software Trojans are concealed inside a software code and enabled when certain conditions are met during program execution. Software Trojans can spread from one user to user and infect the files of a computer. For e.g., A Trojan can be activated from one user to another by an USB, where Trojans are activated when the USB is infected with a Trojan and the receiver end of the user's computer is also infected with a Trojan and corrupts the computer. Hardware Trojans are concealed within physical hardware and triggered during some hardware operations. Hardware Trojans also can spread from one

---

G. Arunachalam—B.Tech – Final Year ECE Student.

© Springer Nature Singapore Pte Ltd. 2021
V. Arunachalam and K. Sivasankaran (Eds.): ICMDCS 2021, CCIS 1392, pp. 69–79, 2021.
https://doi.org/10.1007/978-981-16-5048-2_6

user to another user or from one attacker to another attacker via physical insertion of Trojans into the circuits. For e.g., an infected IC Hardware Trojans can be implanted in weak parts of an IC to steal the information or modify the functionality of an IC. There are different techniques and methods to combat the threat of hardware security. The Hardware Trojans are the modification of IC's by an attacker, which could steal, disable or destroy the information and also leak the information of a chip [1].

In Register Transfer Level (RTL), or during masking or during layout design, hardware Trojans could be inserted. Trojans can be defined on the basis of characteristics based primarily on physical characteristics, activation characteristics and features of action. Physical characteristics of a Trojan are classified based on the structure, size, distribution and type of Trojan. A Trojan is said to be functional if an attacker adds gates or transistors to the chip, whereas a parametric Trojans is said to modify the circuit. The activation characteristics are those in which a Trojan could be internally activated or externally activated. The action characteristics include transmission of information/modification of specification/modifications of functions. Thus in essence, the Trojans can disable or change the functions of the circuit. In order to combat the threat of Hardware security there are several design based trust techniques which can enhance the security of an IC.

This paper is organized as follows: In Sect. 2, we discuss the literature survey. In Sect. 4 we talk about the transition probability algorithm and calculation of probability for each logic gate. In the subsequent Sect. 5 we elucidate about the Verilog code and the extraction of net list for ISCAS circuits. In Sect. 6 we present a pseudo code for the calculation of Transition Probability. The next Sect. 7 is devoted to our results and analysis. Finally in the last Sect. 8 we give our conclusions and future work.

2 Literature Survey

Pramod Subramanian et al. [2] in their paper on "Evaluating the security of logic encryption algorithms" explain about the insertion of key gates into the original circuit based on the insertion of obfuscation cell. But in their work they use encryption techniques using satisfy ability checking. This adds on overhead for the user. In our present work, we do not introduce any such logic encryption techniques.

Jayesh Popat et al. [3] in their paper on "Transition Probabilistic Approach for Detection and Diagnosis of Hardware Trojan in Combinational Circuits" have given details about the detection of Trojans using transition probability algorithm. Their paper also gives details about the probability calculation of each logic gate. But they have not concentrated in the identification of rare nodes. But in our present paper we have modified their algorithm and we also determine the rare node using the transition probability algorithm.

A paper on "A Novel Hardware Logic Encryption Technique for thwarting Illegal Overproduction and hardware Trojans" by Sophie Dupuis et al. [4] uses random insertion of obfuscation cell. In the case of complex circuit, we will get a large number of node insertion points and how to choose the relevant node for insertion is not addressed by them. In our present work, we use a systematic approach for the insertion of logic gates.

Md. Imran Khan and Md. Ahasan Kabir [5] have reviewed the various designs for security techniques and also addressed the various challenges faced in the design for trust techniques and their limitations. However their paper doesn't give any analysis or results in support of combating the threat of Hardware Trojans.

Muhammad Yasin et al. [15] have reviewed about the locking of the design by randomly inserting additional gates and on adding the gates only a correct key makes the design to produce correct outputs.

3 Design for Trust Techniques

There are various kinds of design for trust techniques are available. We enumerate some of them.

Logic Obfuscation: Obfuscation conceals the original design's functionality and structure by adding extra gates into the original design [6]. Logic obfuscations are the key gates for an obfuscation cell. E.g., XOR, XNOR as shown in Fig. 1. For instance if XOR gate is an obfuscation cell and if the input is 0 then the output acts as a buffer [7]. If 1 is given as an input it acts as an inverter so that the output will be obfuscated. The extra gates added are generally small in number so that the adversaries may require more time to determine the input pattern for a given circuit.

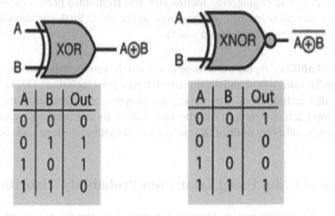

Fig. 1. EXOR and EXNOR as obfuscation cells.

Controllability and Observability of Hardware Trojan Detection: In this method one can determine whether a Trojan is inserted or not in the given circuit [8, 9]. Controllability establishes a specific signal at each and every node of the circuit from setting values at the input. Controllability can also be interpreted as the difference between setting a logic signal to 0 or 1. On the other hand observability is able to predict the signal value at any node by controlling the input and observing the output of a circuit. In other words observability is defined as observing the difference of logic signal.

Split Manufacturing: The Front End of Line Layer (FEOL) and the Back End of Line Layer (BEOL) are fabricated separately to enhance the security of an IC [9]. To improve the security partition pins are rearranged to deceive an attacker. But this approach has to be used while fabricating the IC itself.

IC Camouflaging: In this technique, one has to duplicate or mimic the cells to customize the gate function. However an attacker can reverse engineer the IC by depackaging, delayering and extracting the net list. Here reverse engineering refers to the abstraction of information or design elements from physical components which can be further broken into individual components to understand the flow of the design.

Physical Unclonable Function: Physical Unclonable Function (PUF) has a unique feature due to the micro structure present in it. With the introduction of some physical factors to the PUF it is also said to be unstable and undisciplined. The PUF also generates random keys to enhance the security of the device. Some of the features of the PUF are given below:

- The PUF can be used as analog PUFs, digital PUFs and memory PUFs.
- PUF are used in net list extraction of the original circuit.
- When using any two PUF they should not generate the same key.
- The PUF module can be demonstrated by adding the obfuscation cell for the benchmark circuits.
- With area and power reduction, the obfuscation technique can be implemented for preventing the reverse engineering techniques and from third parties as well.
- PUF may be damaged because of its noisy aggression. With the damaged PUF it makes the attackers to identify them easily.

Transition Probability: Apart from these common design for trust techniques one can also look at the Transition probability algorithm based trust technique [3]. In our present work we use this technique. In this paper, we propose an effective method of using probabilistic approach and finding out the rare nodes. In this method we compute the probability at each and every node of the circuit and determine the rare node occurrences.

4   Insertion of Gates Using Transition Probability Algorithm

In Fig. 2 below we explain how to identify the node location for the insertion of logic gates to avoid Trojan attacks using Transition Probability concepts.

Algorithm

1. Start and set the original circuit as current design.
2. Assign the probability of 0.5 for the Logic level 0 and Logic level 1.
3. After calculating the transition probability at every node/net of the circuit, sort the transition probability and store them in an array. Compute the Transition Probability as:

$$\text{Transition Probability} : (\text{Logic 0 probability} * \text{Logic 1 probability}) \quad (1)$$

4. Choose the lowest transition probability net as the target net, which is the rare node in the net list due to low transition probability.

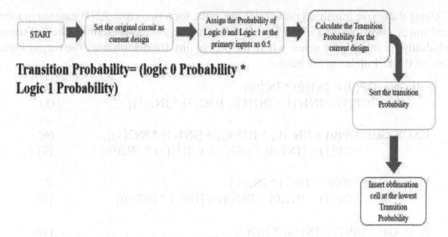

Transition Probability= (logic 0 Probability * Logic 1 Probability)

Fig. 2. Block diagram for identifying the node location for inserting the gates

5. The obfuscation cell is inserted in the rare node position of the net list.

Thus the low probability nets are chosen to be the insertion point for gates. Once the rare nodes are identified based on the transition probability values on the nets, we can decide the location of obfuscation cell insertion.

Probability Calculation for Various Logic Gates

In Fig 3, for a two input AND gate, we find the probability for the levels of OP(1) and OP(0). According to the transition probability algorithm, we assign the primary inputs as 0.5 for logic levels 0 and 1. Eqs. (2) and (3) below show the formulas for determining the probabilities for basic logic gates [3].

$$OP(1) = IN1(1) * IN2(1) = 0.5 * 0.5 = 0.25, \tag{2}$$

$$OP(0) = IN1(0) + IN2(0) - [IN1(0) * IN2(0)] = 0.5 + 0.5 - [0.5 * 0.5] = 0.75 \tag{3}$$

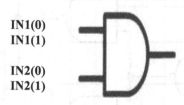

IN1(0)
IN1(1)

IN2(0)
IN2(1)

Fig. 3. Two input and one output AND Gate

Using the above transition probability formula, for a two input AND gate we get the transition probability as 0.25 * 0.75 = 0.1875. Similarly, we can determine the transition probability for other logic gates, where the probability for determining the output logic levels of 0 and 1 are as given below:

OR Gate: OP(0) = IN1(0) * IN2(0)   (4)
$\quad\quad$ OP(1) = IN1(1) + IN2(1) − [IN1(1) * IN2(1)]   (5)

EXOR Gate: OP(0) = [IN1(0) * IN2(0)] + [IN1(1) * IN2(1)]   (6)
$\quad\quad$ OP(1) = [IN1(0) + IN2(1)] + [IN1(1) * IN2(0)]   (7)

NAND Gate: OP(0) = IN(1) * IN2(1)   (8)
$\quad\quad$ OP(1) = IN1(0) + IN2(0) − [IN(1) * IN2(0)]   (9)

NOR Gate: OP(1) = IN1(0) * IN2(0)   (10)
$\quad\quad$ OP(0) = IN1(1) + IN2(1) − [IN1(1) * IN2(1)]   (11)

EXNOR Gate: OP(1) = [IN1(0) * IN2(0)] + [IN1(1) * IN2(1)]   (12)
$\quad\quad$ OP(0) = [IN1(0) * IN2(0)] + [IN1(1) * IN2(1)]   (13)

NOT Gate: OP(0) = IN1(1)   (14)
$\quad\quad$ OP(1) = IN1(0)   (15)

5 Verilog Code and Net List

Here, we consider the standard benchmark circuit namely ISCAS'85 C17 as shown in Fig. 4 below. This circuit is a combination circuit with 17 nodes in it [3, 10]. Now, in order to determine the Transition probability for a circuit, we first need to write the Verilog code for the given circuit and extract the net list in excel format using synopsis compiler [11].

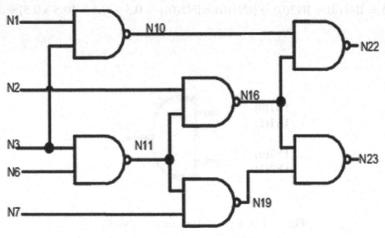

Fig. 4. The benchmark ISCAS'85 C17 circuit

The Verilog code for the above circuit is given below [14]: The circuit consists of five inputs, NAND gates and two outputs.

```
CODE:
    module c17 (N1,N2,N3,N6,N7,N22,N23);
    input N1,N2,N3,N6,N7;
    output N22,N23;
    wire N10,N11,N16,N19;
    nand NAND2_1 (N10, N1, N3);
    nand NAND2_2 (N11, N3, N6);
    nand NAND2_3 (N16, N2, N11);
    nand NAND2_4 (N19, N11, N7);
    nand NAND2_5 (N22, N10, N16);
    nand NAND2_6 (N23, N16, N19);
    endmodule
```

After executing the code using a synopsis compiler, we obtain the net list in an excel format as shown below in Table 1:

Table 1. Extraction of net list for ISCAS'85 C17 circuit

	A	B	C	D	E
1	Input	Outputs			
2	N1,N2,N3,N22,N23				
3					
4	nand	NAND2_1	N10	N1	N3
5	nand	NAND2_2	N11	N3	N6
6	nand	NAND2_3	N16	N2	N11
7	nand	NAND2_4	N19	N11	N7
8	nand	NAND2_5	N22	N10	N16
9	nand	NAND2_6	N23	N16	N19

Now, after obtaining the net list we determine the transition probability using the net list given in Table 1. Based on the above procedure, we can obtain the net list for all circuits and determine the transition probability for the chosen circuit and identify the rare nodes which have got the lowest transition probability.

6 Pseudo Code

The pseudo code for determining the transition probability of a given circuit is:

Read the excel file of netlist of the circuit
Store Primary input nets name in list named as **PI**
Store Primary output nets name in list named as **PO**
Create a multidimensional list named **netlist** with 5 entries (gate_type, gate_name, output_net_name, input1_net_name, input2_net_name)
Store net_names from **netlist** into the **net_name** of list type
Create an empty multidimensional list named **netlist_tp** with 3 entries (net_name, probability of 0, probability of 1)
Assign k as length of **net_name**
Assign i=0
For(i=0, i < k, i=i+1){
If **net_name** ith element in **PI**
   Append to **netlist_tp** net_name and probabilities as 0.5
   else
   continue}
Assign n as length of **netlist**
For(i=0, i < n , i=i+1){
If gate_type is AND
   probability of 0 is pr1(0) + pr2(0)-[pr1(0) * pr2(0)]
   probability of 1 is pr1(1) * pr2(1)
   Append output_net_name and probabilities to **netlist_tp** net_name and probabilities
else If gate_type is OR
   probability of 0 is pr1(0) * pr2(0)
   probability of 1 is pr1(1) + pr2(1)-[pr1(1) * pr2(1)]
   Append output_net_name and probabilities to **netlist_tp** net_name and probabilities
else if gate_type is XOR
   probability of 0 is [pr1(0) * pr2(0)] + [pr1(1) * pr2(1)]
   probability of 1 is [pr1(0) + pr2(1)] + [pr1(1) * pr2(0)]
   Append output_net_name and probabilities to **netlist_tp** net_name and probabilities
else if gate_type is NAND
   probability of 0 is pr1(1) * pr2(1)
   probability of 1 is pr1(0) + pr2(0)-[pr1(0) * pr2(0)]
   Append output_net_name andprobabilities to **netlist_tp** net_name and probabilities
else if gate_type is NOR
   probability of 0 is pr1(1) + pr2(1)-[pr1(1) * pr2(1)]
   probability of 1 is pr1(0) * pr2(0)
   Append output_net_name and probabilities to **netlist_tp** net_name and probabilities
else if gate_type is XNOR
   probability of 0 is [pr1(0) +pr2(1)] + [pr1(1) * pr2(0)]
   probability of 1 is [pr1(0) * pr2(0)]-[pr1(1) * pr2(1)]
   Append output_net_name and probabilities to **netlist_tp** net_name and probabilities
else if gate_type is NOT
   probability of 0 is pr1(1)
   probability of 1 is pr1(0)
   Append output_net_name and probabilities to **netlist_tp** net_name and probabilities
   }
Sort **netlist_tp**
Create a 2d list **Transition_Prob (net_name, Probability)** and append net_name and (probability of 0 * probability of 1) from **netlist_tp**

7 Results and Analysis

After implementing the above pseudo code in python software, we have obtained the results for ISCAS'85 C17 Benchmark circuits as shown in Table 2.

Table 2. Probability calculation of logic levels 0 and 1.

	Input	Output	Unnamed: 2	Unnamed: 3	Unnamed: 4
0	N1,N2,N3,N6,N7	N22,N23	NaN	NaN	NaN
1		NaN	NaN	NaN	NaN	NaN
2		nand	NAND2_1	N10	N1	N3
3		nand	NAND2_2	N11	N3	N6
4		nand	NAND2_3	N16	N2	N11
5		nand	NAND2_4	N19	N11	N7
6		nand	NAND2_5	N22	N10	N16
7		nand	NAND2_6	N23	N16	N19

Netnames= ['N1', 'N10', 'N11', 'N16', 'N19', 'N2', 'N22', 'N23', 'N3', 'N6', 'N7']

	Netname	Probability of 0	Probability of 1
0	N1	0.500000	0.500000
1	N2	0.500000	0.500000
2	N3	0.500000	0.500000
3	N6	0.500000	0.500000
4	N7	0.500000	0.500000
5	N10	0.250000	0.750000
6	N11	0.250000	0.750000
7	N16	0.375000	0.625000
8	N19	0.375000	0.625000
9	N22	0.468750	0.531250
10	N23	0.390625	0.609375

Using the above Table 2, we have determined the probability for ISCAS'85 C17 benchmark circuit. In Table 2, N1, N2, N3…N10 represent the Net name i.e., the number of nets present in the circuit. Inputs in the circuit are the N1, N2, N3, N6, N7 and the outputs are N22, N23. The NAND2_1upto NAND2_6 is the gates present in the circuit. In the NAND2_1 the net N10 represent the output net while N1 and N3 represent the input gates of the NAND2_1 gate. Similarly for all other gates transition probability is calculated up to NAND2_6 as shown in Table 2. Then we determine the probability for nets N1, N2, N3, N6, N7, N10, N11, N16, N19, N22, N23 with each net consisting the probability of Logic 0 and probability of Logic 1 respectively.

After determining the probability for each net, with individual probability of logic 0 and logic 1, we next determine the transition probability using the formula (**LOGIC 0 PROBABILITY * LOGIC 1 PROBABILTIY**) as shown in Table 3, we see that after determining the individual transition probability at each nets, we compare the probabilities having least probability and we find that nets N10, N11 as the least transition probability nets and these are the rare nets which can be used to insert the obfuscation cell to enhance the security of an IC.

Table 3. Transition probability calculation for ISCAS'85 C17 circuit

	Netname	Probability of 0	Probability of 1
0	N1	0.500000	0.500000
1	N2	0.500000	0.500000
2	N3	0.500000	0.500000
3	N6	0.500000	0.500000
4	N7	0.500000	0.500000
5	N10	0.250000	0.750000
6	N11	0.250000	0.750000
7	N16	0.375000	0.625000
8	N19	0.375000	0.625000
9	N22	0.468750	0.531250
10	N23	0.390625	0.609375

	Netname	Transition Probability
0	N1	0.250000
1	N2	0.250000
2	N3	0.250000
3	N6	0.250000
4	N7	0.250000
5	N10	0.187500
6	N11	0.187500
7	N16	0.234375
8	N19	0.234375
9	N22	0.249023
10	N23	0.238037

8   Conclusions and Future Work

In this paper, we have implemented the standard ISCAS'85 benchmark circuits and obtained the transition probability using the transition probability concepts. From this analysis we determine the least occurrence node in a circuit to insert the obfuscation cell. We have also mentioned the procedures how to extract a net list using the ISCAS'85 C17 circuits. We have also developed a pseudo code and implemented the same using necessary Python code for all other logic circuits. We will introduce the relevant obfuscation cell at the chosen node and demonstrate how Trojan attack can be prevented [12] in our future work. We are also planning to implement the proposed technique for other ISCAS circuits which are complex in nature [13].

Acknowledgements. I would like to thank Prof. M. Priyatharishini for her invaluable contributions in not only suggesting this problem but also providing the necessary guidance, hardware and software support in successfully carrying out this work.

References

1. Zhang, J.: A practical logic obfuscation technique for hardware security. IEEE Trans. Very Large Scale Integr. (VLSI) Syst. **24**(3), 1193–1197 (2016)
2. Subramanyan, P., Ray, S., Malik, S.: Evaluating the security of logic encryption algorithms. In: IEEE International Symposium on Hardware Oriented Security and Trust (HOST), May 2015 (2015)
3. Popat, J., Mehta, U.: Transition probabilistic approach for detection and diagnosis of hardware Trojan in combinational circuits. In: IEEE Annual India Conference, December 2016 (2016)

4. Dupuis, S., Ba, P.-S., Di Natale, G., Flottes, M.-L., Rouzeyre, B.: A novel hardware logic encryption technique for thwarting illegal overproduction and hardware Trojans. In: International On-Line Testing Symposium, July 2014 (2014)
5. Imran Khan, M., Ahasan Kabir, M.: Review of design for security techniques: advancement and challenges. In: International Conference on Electrical, Computer and Communication Engineering (ECCE), Cox's Bazar, Bangladesh, 16–18 February 2017 (2017)
6. Rajendran, J., Pino, Y., Sinanoglu, O., Karri, R.: Security analysis of logic obfuscation. In: Proceedings of the 49th ACM/EDAC/IEEE Design Automation Conference, June 2012, pp. 83–89 (2012)
7. Yasin, M., Sinanoglu, O.: Evolution of logic locking. In: 2017 IFIP/IEEE International Conference on Very Large-Scale Integration (VLSI-SoC), October 2017 (2017)
8. Tehranipoor, M., Wang, C. (eds.): Introduction to Hardware Security and Trust. Springer, New York (2012). https://doi.org/10.1007/978-1-4419-8080-9
9. Li, H., Liu, Q., Zhang, J.: A survey of hardware Trojan threat and defense. Integration **55**, 426–437 (2016)
10. Jha, S., Jha, S.K.: Randomization based probabilistic approachto detect Trojan circuits. In: HASE, p. 117124 (2008)
11. Wolff, F., Papachristou, C., Bhunia, S., Chakraborty, R.S.: Towards Trojan-free trusted ICs: problem analysis and detection scheme. In: Design, Automation and Test in Europe, March 2008, pp. 1362–1365 (2008)
12. Wu, T.F., Ganesan, K., Hu, Y.A., Wong, H.S.P., Wong, S., Mitra, S.: TPAD: hardware Trojan prevention and detection for trusted integrated circuits. IEEE Trans. Comput. Aided Des. Integr. Circ. Syst. **35**(4), 521–534 (2016)
13. Abramovici, M., Bradley, P.: Integrated circuit security - new threats and solutions. In: CSIIR Workshop (2009)
14. Khatri, A.R., Hayek, A., Borcsok, J.: ATPG method with a hybrid compaction technique for combinational digital systems. In: 2016 SAI Computing Conference (SAI) (2016)
15. Yasin, M., Rajendran, J., Sinanoglu, O.: On improving the security of logic locking. In: IEEE Transactions on Computer-Aided Design of Integrated Circuits and Systems, January 2015 (2015)

A Comparative Analysis of Open Loop and PI Controlled Buck Converter

Tohfa Haque$^{(\boxtimes)}$ ⓘ, Md. Sarwar Islam ⓘ, and Md. Ariful Islam ⓘ

United International University, Dhaka, Bangladesh

Abstract. In this paper, we have shown a study of a DC-DC buck converter based on the open-loop and closed-loop concept. The DC-DC buck converter is widely used to convert a high level of dc voltage to a low level of dc voltage. We have carried out a comparative study between the uncompensated buck converter and proportional-integral (PI) controlled buck converter with respect to voltage regulation. Showed evidence that PI controlled buck converter has better voltage regulation for wide load variation. For experimental set up designed a buck converter that converts 12 V dc voltage to a 5 V dc voltage, simulated in LTspice and demonstrated in hardware.

Keywords: DC-DC converter · Buck converter · PI controller · Voltage regulation

1 Introduction

The need for power electronics is increasing more and more, so the attention for more efficient power supply is getting highlighted. For efficient power supply, switch mode power supply (SMPS) comes first [1]. Because of its wide application, SMPS always has high demand. Most of the applications are, such as charging devices, electric vehicles, renewable energy system, solar PV, uninterrupted power supply (UPS) and many more [2]. The uses of portable device are increasing so the need for charging devices is highly interested topic. Many factors need to be considered in order to design an efficient battery charger. Convention battery charger comes with some drawbacks, such as poor voltage regulation, low power density. Whereas SMPS devices offer high power density, lightweight, and better voltage regulation [3]. Recently, many new topologies have been originated; buck converter, boost converter, buck-boost converter and cuk converter are the most established ones [9]. Buck converter is used to step down the input dc voltage based on the pulse-width modulation (PWM) signal. Buck converter is widely used in computer system, battery charger. It produces a regulated dc signal and can stand by for long period [5, 6]. Despite having lots of advantage, buck converter shows poor voltage regulation when the load changes widely. These non-linear characteristic is shown because of its parasitic resistance in inductor, capacitor, diode and power MOSFET [2]. To overcome these drawbacks, a buck needs a feedback loop that will change the on time of power MOSFET according the load demand.

V. Arunachalam and K. Sivasankaran (Eds.): ICMDCS 2021, CCIS 1392, pp. 80–88, 2021.
https://doi.org/10.1007/978-981-16-5048-2_7

2 Methodology

2.1 Operations of Buck Converter

Main purpose of this paper is to design a better regulated buck converter and comparison of a basic buck voltage regulation with the buck converter with proportional controller.

To convert a dc voltage level to another level of dc voltage, a dc-dc converter is needed. In this paper, buck converter methodology with and without controller will be explained. For high level of DC level to low level of DC level conversion buck converter is needed.

Basically, a buck converter consists of power switches, diode and LC filter. A power switch is for the voltage regulation; by turning off and on it produces a low level DC voltage from the input DC voltage.

The full buck operation is combined with two modes: buck on and buck off. At buck on stage, Fig. 1b, when MOSFET is closed, the freewheeling diode is turned off. The inductor energies and the load side is connected directly to the supply side. Figure 1c, at the buck off stage, the freewheeling diode turns on, the inductor discharges through the load. The capacitor is used for making the output DC voltage smooth [4].

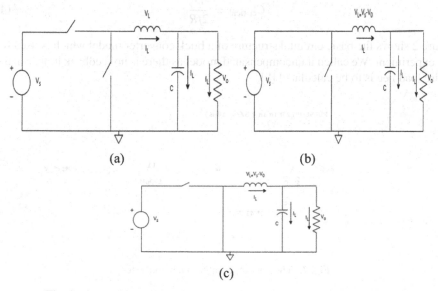

Fig. 1. (a) Buck converter circuit, (b) Buck on mode, (c) Buck off mode.

The duty cycle D is less than 1 $(0 < D < 1)$. The output voltage level is $Vo = DVs$. The operating period of the buck converter is T, the switch is on for DT time and off for (1-D) T time. For higher voltage 'Vs, the output voltage of buck converter will always be lower. The minimum inductance for maintaining the continuous current the value of inductor is L_{min}.

$$L_{min} = \frac{(1-D)R}{2f} \qquad (1)$$

The Uncompensated Buck Converter

Without controller, the buck converter output voltage regulation falls if the load exceeds the desire value. Figure 2 shows the basic implementation of DC-DC buck converter. In this uncompensated circuit, it has fixed duty cycle and fixed load to obtain desire output voltage and current level. The power switch will be closed for on time DT and inductor current remains positive. The diode stays at the reverse bias.

$$v_L = V_S - V_o \tag{2}$$

When power MOSFET is open, the stored energy of inductor dissipates through the load. In this period of cycle, the freewheeling diode gets sufficient voltage to turn on. The voltage equation of inductor is following:

$$v_L = -V_o \tag{3}$$

Inductor places a crucial role to smoothing the output current and maintains it to the desire level for the total period. The capacitor of LC filter is used to keep the output voltage constant. The critical value of capacitor is following:

$$C_{\text{critical}} = \frac{D}{2fR} \tag{4}$$

Figure 2 shows the basic circuital structure of a buck converter model which is used for this experiment. We called it uncompensated model as there is no feedback loop. So, the desire load needs to be calculated [8].

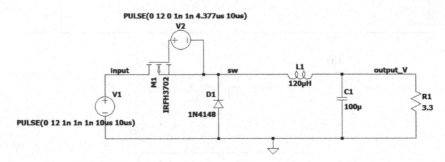

Fig. 2. The uncompensated buck converter.

The Compensated Buck Converter

In this experiment a buck converter is implemented with proportional–integral (PI) controller which has a better voltage regulation. In Fig. 3, the basic block is shown for controlled buck converter. This design has a feedback loop that will sense the output voltage with the reference voltage level and will generate the error [2]. The proportional controller block multiples the error with a gain K_P. The integral control unit adds up another control parameter by multiplying with the integration of error with K_i. Then it

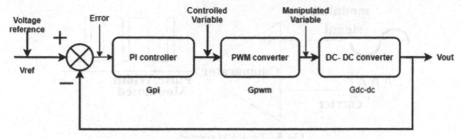

Fig. 3. The basic block of controlled DC-DC converter.

produces the controlled signal that will be feeded to the gate of power MOSFET, after PWM conversion.

The PI controller is implemented using an operational amplifier. It provides the whole system a better regulation as it compensated the load changes effect by comparing the output voltage with the reference voltage. The basic block diagram for PI controller seems as Fig. 4. This whole block takes the error as an input for the previous state and determines the adjusted PWM signal for current state. The block generates a modulation signal based on the previous signal output [7]. To get the previous state output, we have used a voltage divider circuit as a voltage sensor.

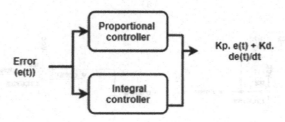

Fig. 4. The basic block of PI controller.

$$Error, \ e(t) = Actual - Reference \tag{5}$$

$$Controlled \ Variable = K_P. \ e(t) + K_i \int e(t)dt \tag{6}$$

When the load demands higher t_{on}, this block will produce higher duty cycle. When the load decreases, duty cycle will decline as it originates by comparing a reference voltage.

The PWM converter is simply a comparator which has a saw tooth wave as reference and gives a PWM signal using the modulated signal information. The circuital design of a PWM converter is shown in Fig. 5.

The blocks described previously has been joined together and simulated in LTspice. The whole circuit of PI controlled DC-DC converter is shown in Fig. 6.

In this paper, we have simulated a buck converter in LTspice. The operating frequency and details of circuital parameter is given in Table 1.

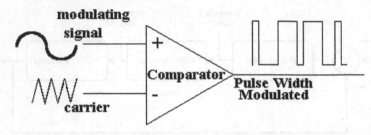

Fig. 5. The PWM converter.

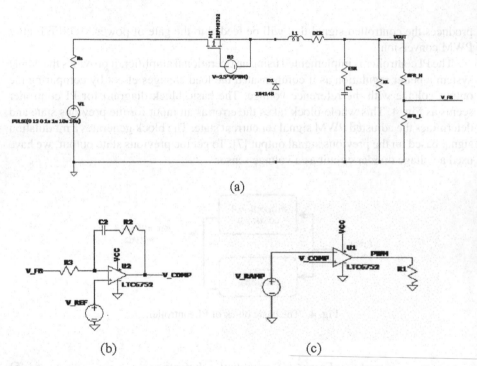

Fig. 6. (a) The compensated DC-DC converter (b) PI controller unit (c) PWM controller unit.

3   Results

3.1   Simulated Results

The uncompensated and compensated circuits have been simulated in LTspice. We have varied the load and observed the output voltage and current. The data has been collected. The resistive desired load is calculated, as the output voltage is 5 V and output current is 1.2 A. So, the value of R is as following.

$$R = \frac{V}{I} = \frac{5\,V}{1.2\,A} = 3.3\,\Omega \tag{7}$$

Table 1. Circuit parameters.

Parameter	Value
Operating frequency	10 kHz
Input voltage (V_S)	12 V
Output voltage (V_o)	5 V
Output current	1.2 A
Inductor (L)	120 μH
Capacitor (C)	100 μF

If the load increases, current demand increases and voltage level drops. So, if we increase the load for this DC-DC buck converter, the output current and voltage level will change. So, the output voltage desired load for uncompensated buck converter is shown in Fig. 7.

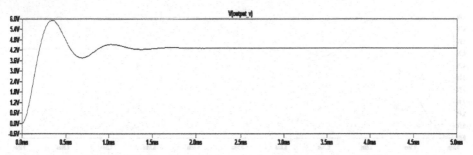

Fig. 7. The V_o of an open loop buck converter for R = 3.3 Ω.

For an open loop buck converter, if load is increased, the output voltage and current will not be the same level as before (Fig. 8).

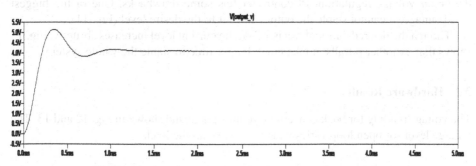

Fig. 8. The V_o of an open loop buck converter for R = 2 Ω.

The wave shape of the output voltage for R = 2 Ω evident that the load increment decreases the voltage regulation.

In order to observe the effect of PI control, the circuit has simulated for the same load. In Fig. 9 and 10, the output voltage of a compensated DC-DC converter circuit is shown.

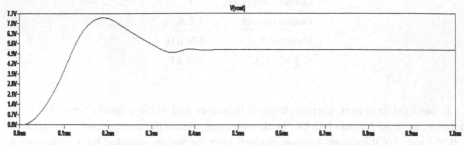

Fig. 9. The V_o of a close loop buck converter for R = 3.3 Ω.

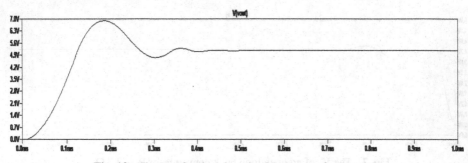

Fig. 10. The V_o of a close loop buck converter for R = 2 Ω.

Using a PI converter, the output voltage does not change much, Fig. 9 and 10 are the evidence. PI controller increases the voltage regulation of a DC-DC converter. Enabling the better voltage regulation, PI controller has some drawbacks. One of the biggest disadvantage, it cannot stable the output current to the desire level (Fig. 11).

Though the desired current level is 1.2 A, the current level increases abruptly, Fig. 13 shows that. Another pitfalls, it take much longer time to stable the whole system.

3.2   Hardware Results

The voltage reading for buck converter circuit is taken and shown in Fig. 12 and 13. The voltage level for open loop varies widely for varying the load.

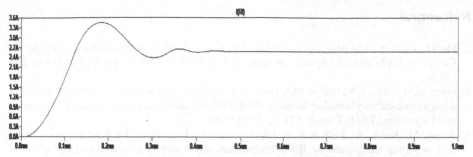

Fig. 11. The I_o of a close loop buck converter for R = 2 Ω.

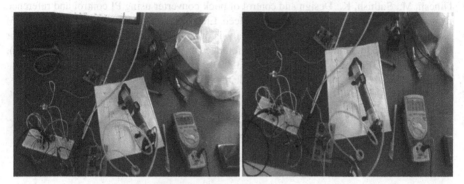

Fig. 12. The output voltage of uncompensated buck converter for various loads.

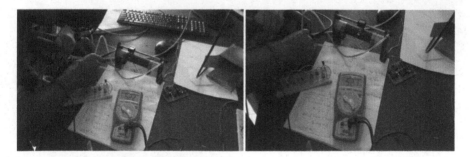

Fig. 13. The output voltage of compensated buck converter for various loads.

4 Conclusion

In this paper, the PI controller for the dc-dc converter is designed to take the processed output voltage as the input of the controller. By sensing the output voltage and comparing it with a reference level of voltage, a PWM signal is generated. If any changes in voltage on the load side occur, it senses the change in voltage and generates the duty cycle accordingly. Whereas, for the open-loop buck converter, the output voltage varies widely for the varying load.

References

1. He, Q., Zhao, Y.: The design of controller of buck converter. In: International Conference on Computer Application and System Modeling, ICCASM 2010, Taiyuan, pp. V15-251–V15-255 (2010)
2. Garg, M.M., Hote, Y.V., Pathak, M.K., Behera, L.: An approach for buck converter PI controller design using stability boundary locus. In: IEEE/PES Transmission and Distribution Conference and Exposition (T&D), Denver, CO, pp. 1–5 (2018)
3. Salem, M., Jusoh, A., Idris, N.R.N.: Implementing buck converter for battery charger using soft switching techniques. In: IEEE 7th International Power Engineering and Optimization Conference (PEOCO), Langkawi, pp. 188–192 (2013)
4. Hart, D.W.: Introduction to Power Electronics. McGraw Hill (2011)
5. Dinesh, M., Sathish, K.: Design and control of buck converter using PI control and reference regulator technique. Int. J. Recent Technol. Mech. Electr. Eng. (IJRMEE) 2(3), 046–049 (2015)
6. Kiran, B.R., Ezhilarasi, G.A.: Design and analysis of soft-switched Buck-Boost Converter for PV applications. In: Annual IEEE India Conference (INDICON), New Delhi, pp. 1–5 (2015). https://doi.org/10.1109/INDICON.2015.7443509
7. Lacoste, R.: Robert Lacoste's the Darker Side, pp. 285–304. Newnes (2010)
8. Rashid, M.H.: Power Electronics Handbook: Devices, Circuits, and Applications, pp. 211–224. Academic, Burlington, MA (2006)
9. Lopa, S.A., Hossain, S., Hasan, M.K., Chakraborty, T.K.: Design and simulation of DC-DC converters. Int. Res. J. Eng. Technol. (IRJET) 9(1), 63–70 (2016)

Low Power Hardware Design for N-Bit Fixed Point Division Algorithm Using GDI Logic

Sudheer Raja Venishetty[1](✉) ⓘ, Anil Kumar Chidra[1] ⓘ, B Sai Likhitha[1], Merigu Deepak[1], and Kumaravel Sundaram[2] ⓘ

[1] Vaagdevi College of Engineering, Warangal 506005, Telangana, India
sudheerraja_v@vaagdevi.edu.in
[2] Vellore Institute of Technology, Vellore 632014, Tamilnadu, India
https://www.vaagdevi.edu.in/electronics-communication-engineering/

Abstract. Considering the increase in the computational complexity of computer applications within the recent years concerning area, speed and power, this paper presents a novel approach to hardware realization of a fixed-point binary division operation. Various steps involved in the development of hardware required for performing fixed-point binary division with low power, low area and high speed are discussed. Restoring division algorithm supported subtraction and shifting is considered here because it is found to be one among the efficient and accurate among the state of art algorithms from digit recurrence group and may be easily extended to signed numbers also. So as to realize better trade-off between power, delay and area, the hardware designed for implementing the division algorithm is simulated using Gate Diffusion Input (GDI) logic. Simulations are carried out using UMC 180 nm Process technology under Cadence Spectre environment. The hardware architecture developed during this paper is additionally implemented using conventional CMOS logic for the aim of comparison.

Keywords: Binary division · Restoring division algorithm · Gate diffusion input (GDI) logic · CMOS logic · Area · Speed · Power

1 Introduction

The advancements in the development of contemporary electronic applications like real-time digital signal processors, microcontroller based systems etc. demands arithmetic and logic operations that should be processed at very high speeds with low power. Binary division is one such ALU operation that has wide applications in the digital signal processing, computer graphics and image processing fields. Computational complexity involved in implementing the division operation made the researchers to propose different algorithms for the accurate and efficient execution of this operation, like digit recurrence method, multiplicative method, approximation methods, and Coordinate Rotation Digital Computer (CORDIC) method etc. The designing of hardware required for division

© Springer Nature Singapore Pte Ltd. 2021
V. Arunachalam and K. Sivasankaran (Eds.): ICMDCS 2021, CCIS 1392, pp. 89–100, 2021.
https://doi.org/10.1007/978-981-16-5048-2_8

operation using deep sub-micron VLSI technology for achieving better performance metrics like high speeds at smaller chip sizes has resulted in a serious problem of power consumption by digital circuits techniques.

In comparison to the other arithmetic operations, division of binary numbers is more complicated as precision of digits is very important for effective division. Division algorithm based on pre-scaling technique for faster division is described in [1,2]. Division algorithm for achieving longer pipeline latency based on series approximation method is discussed in [3]. [4] describes a multiplicative division algorithm for reducing the latency difference between division and multiplication without introducing excessive hardware, thus the same hardware used for multiplication can be utilized with minor changes for division. Digit recurrence algorithms with reduced logical depth and low latency are discussed in [5,6]. The major advantages of digit recurrence algorithm include Simplicity of the implementation and availability of the exact remainder with convergence rate linear with operand size. The most conventional methods for implementing division using multiplication include Newton-Raphson (N-R) and Goldschmidt (GdS) [7–9]. Quadratic convergence of producing double accuracy bits in every iteration is the common characteristic among all the multiplication based division algorithms. Self-correction ability from iteration to iteration is the key strength of N-R method. However the performance of N-R method is limited by two dependent multiplications compared to GdS algorithm, in which multiplication can be implemented in a parallel manner but without self correcting ability. Both the algorithms need efficient fixed point multiplication techniques with initial approximation to reduce the number of iterations and to achieve the high speed operation. Reciprocal computation can be treated as a special type of division where dividend has a fixed value of 1. This reciprocal unit plays an important role for the implementation of N-R algorithm. [10] Describes various fixed point signed and unsigned number division based on digit recurrence and multiplicative division algorithms and the performance comparison with respect to area, power and speed is made.

In this paper, a novel approach of hardware realization of fixed point binary division operation based on restoring algorithm taken from digit recurrence group is discussed. The hardware required for executing the various steps involved in restoring binary division algorithm is designed. Low power Gate diffusion input (GDI) logic technique is used to implement the designed hardware and the same is simulated in UMC 180 nm process under cadence spectre environment. To study the efficacy of proposed architecture, hardware is also implemented using conventional CMOS logic technique and the comparisons are made.

Restoring division algorithm based on digit recurrence technique is discussed in Sect. 2. Section 3 and Sect. 4 describes the proposed architecture and the low power transistor level implementations of various elements associated using GDI and CMOS logic. While Sect. 5 and Sect. 6 present's simulation results and the conclusions respectively.

2 Restoring Algorithm

A perfect blueprint is mandatory for a perfect building, the same way an algorithm holds major role in development of digital circuit architecture for any complex mathematical operation. Digit recurrence method [7–9] is considered to be an apt technique for the perfect implementation of fixed point division of binary numbers. Restoring division algorithm from the digit recurrence group discussed in [10] is reproduced here for the sake of clarity in Fig. 1. The various steps involved in executing the restoring algorithm are illustrated in the flow chart and is labeled as, Steps 1–5.

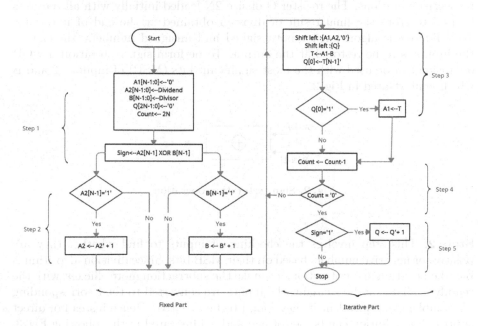

Fig. 1. Flow chart for restoring algorithm [10].

The basic principle involved in restoring division algorithm is continuous and iterative use of basic subtraction and shifting operations which can be easily implemented with the state of art algorithms. The number of iterations in the algorithm depends on the size of the inputs dividend and divisor. Since, every successive iteration of digit recurrence method produces one single digit of output, the number of iterations will be double the size of inputs.

3 Proposed Block Level Architecture

The main objective of the proposed work is to design a hardware architecture required for the implementation of binary division using restoring algorithm. The architectural development is done in two levels. At first, block level description is made for evaluating each step associated in the flow chart and later the blocks proposed are designed using low power GDI and Conventional CMOS digital techniques. For ease of implementation, the entire flow of algorithm is divided into two parts fixed and iterative with five steps labeled as Steps 1–5 as shown in Fig. 1.

Fixed Part Implementation

Step 1: At first, the inputs dividend, divisor is stored into arbitrary registers A2 and B of size N bit respectively. Another N-bit register A1 initially loaded with all zero bits is used for storing the shift as well operated values from the respective iterations. The register Q of size 2N loaded initially with all zero bits is used to store the final result of division obtained at the end of iterations. To validate the algorithm for both signed and unsigned numbers, the sign of the inputs is to be restored at the output. To perform sign restoration, Ex-OR operation can be used with the most significant bits (MSB) of inputs A2 and B which is illustrated in Fig. 2.

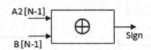

Fig. 2. Sign restoration operation.

Step 2: This step involves the checking of inputs to find whether they are positive or negative numbers based on their MSB bits. Since division algorithm is based on continuous subtraction. To make the subtraction more efficient with the readily available adder's circuit, the inputs are converted to their corresponding 2's complement equivalent if they found to be negative. Hence instead of direct subtraction, addition can be performed and is illustrated in the following Fig. 3. The same architecture can be used for both the inputs A2 and B.

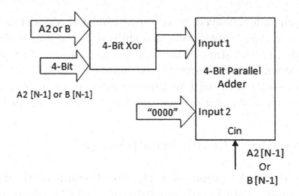

Fig. 3. 2's complement generator.

Iterative Part Implementation

Step 3: The step 3 is the heart of complete algorithm. This step is comprised of shifting and subtraction operations with bit restoring option. One step arithmetic left shift operation is performed on concatenated bits of A1 and A2 inputs. Similarly the arithmetic left shift for one step is performed on the contents of the arbitrary register Q. Subtraction is performed on the contents of A1 and B registers, storing the result to another arbitrary register T of length N. The MSB bit of T is loaded into LSB of Q representing final result. The LSB of Q is checked for logic 1 and is used to restore the contents of A1. To provide novelty and to make the complete hardware to be combinational, the sequential shifting operation is simply performed by suitable circuit connections. The complete block of shifting, subtraction and bit restoration is shown in Fig. 4.

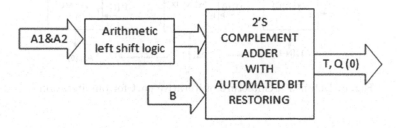

Fig. 4. Block diagram of iterative part for one iteration.

In Fig. 4, arithmetic left shift operations are performed simply by proper connections of respective inputs to each iterative stage. This type of connection logic will avoid additional sequential circuitry required for performing shift operations, resulting in novelty of the proposed hardware. However this type of connection logic is not suitable for large length inputs (for example inputs greater than 16 bit) which can be overcome by including the additional circuitry required for shifting. 2's complement adder is implemented using the 2's complement generator hardware described in Fig. 3 in conjunction with a N-bit parallel adder. As described in Fig. 4, bit restoring logic for A1 register is performed with the help of N-2x1 multiplexers, with one input from the output of adder performing the operation T = A1-B, and another input directly from the register A1. The least significant bit of the register Q i.e., Q (0) is applied as select line. Hence Fig. 4 can be elaborated as shown in Fig. 5.

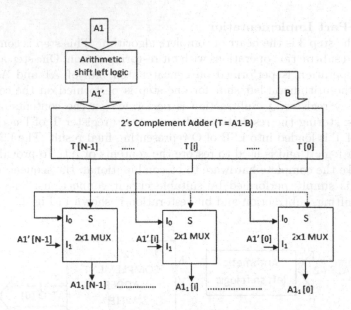

Fig. 5. Detailed architecture of iterative part for one iteration.

Step 4: The complete shifting and subtraction operation of step 3 is repeated for 2N number of times. Hence the hardware architecture required for a N bit input point division is shown in Fig. 6.

Step 5: The final step of algorithm involves the finding of whether the result obtained after 2N iterations in register Q is in 2's complement form or not. This is done with the help of sign bit obtained from step 1.

4   Low Power Implementation of Proposed Hardware Architecture

The hardware required for the implementation of fixed point division algorithm in Fig. 1 is proposed and discussed in Sect. 3. To make the ease of implementation, the proposed hardware shown in Fig. 6 is designed for 4-bit inputs and is illustrated in Fig. 7. The transistor level circuitry for the various blocks shown in Fig. 7 can be designed by using various digital logic techniques of state of art literature.

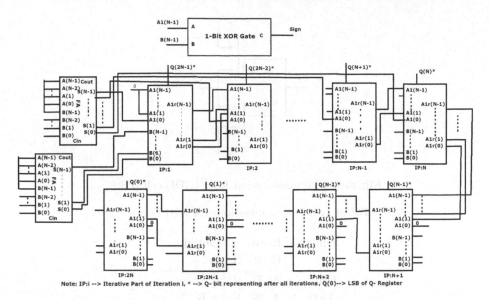

Fig. 6. Hardware architecture for a N-bit input fixed point division.

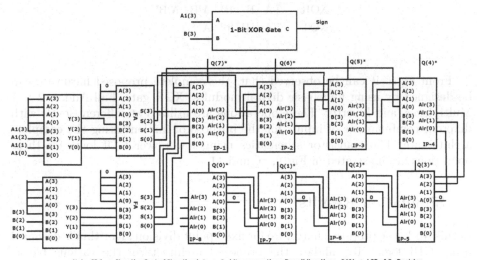

Note: IP:i --> Iterative Part of Iteration i, * --> Q- bit representing after all iterations, Q(0)--> LSB of Q- Register

Fig. 7. Hardware architecture for a 4-bit input fixed point division.

To take the advantage of low power and area, the various blocks of the architecture developed for 4-bit fixed point division algorithm illustrated in Fig. 7 is designed using GDI logic [11,12]. For the sake of clarity, basic GDI cell and its function table is reproduced in Fig. 8 and Table 1 respectively.

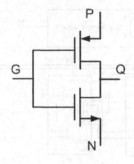

Fig. 8. Gate diffusion input logic (GDI) cell [12].

Table 1. Input combinations for GDI Logic.

Function	Inputs			Outputs
	G	P	N	Q
OR	A	B	'1'	A+B
AND	A	'0'	B	A.B
MUX	A	B	C	A'B+A.C
XOR	A	B	B'	A'B+A.B'
NOT	A	'1'	'0'	A'

From Fig. 6 it can be observed that, the complete proposed hardware can be designed by using four basic digital modules, XOR gate, Full Adder, 2 × 1 Multiplexer, and Inverter. These operations are utilized at different levels with different combinations of inputs for the purpose of implementing the complete architecture. The transistor schematics using low power GDI logic for these operations are illustrated in Fig. 9, 10 and 11.

5   Simulation Results

In this work, the proposed hardware for fixed point division algorithm is designed using GDI logic. To validate the proposed architecture, the various blocks involved are simulated using UMC 180 nm process in cadence spectre environment with a supply voltage of 1.8 V. For the purpose of simulation and for the ease of implementation for achieving optimized pull-up to pull-down ratios, the length and width of all the NMOS transistors are fixed at 500 nm and 1 μm respectively and 500 nm and 2.5 μm for PMOS respectively [13–16].

Table 2 shows the count of transistors for implementing the basic modules in designing the proposed architecture using GDI logic. Table 3depicts the total number of transistors required to develop complete hardware for the purpose of 4 bit input fixed point division shown in Fig. 7 using GDI logic in comparison with CMOS logic. It can be perceived from Table 3, that GDI logic requires a

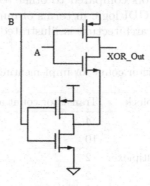

Fig. 9. XOR using gate diffusion input logic (GDI).

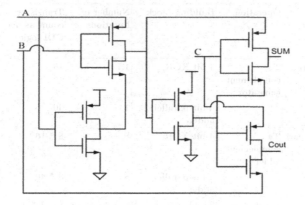

Fig. 10. Full adder using GDI.

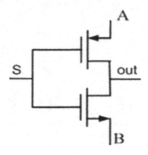

Fig. 11. 2 × 1 Multiplexer using GDI.

very less number of transistors compared to other techniques. The comparison of conventional CMOS and GDI logic in terms of number of transistors for the different blocks of proposed architecture is illustrated in Fig. 12.

Table 2. Transistor count for implementing basic blocks.

Sr. No.	Building block	Transistor count as per GDI Logic
1	XOR gate	4
2	Full adder	10
3	2 × 1 Multiplexer	2
4	Inverter	2

Table 3. Transistor count for implementing 4-bit fixed point division.

Sr. No	Part of algorithm	Operation	Building block	Number of iterations	Transistor count as per GDI logic	Transistor count as per standard CMOS logic
1.	Fixed part	2's complement generator	4-bit XOR	1	16	56
			4-bit parallel adder	1	40	184
2.	Iterative part	2's complement adder	4-bit XOR	8	8 * 16	8 * 56
			4-bit parallel adder	8	8 * 40	8 * 184
		2 × 1 Multiplexer	2 × 1 Multiplexer	8	8 * 4 * 2	8 * 4 * 12

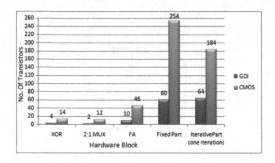

Fig. 12. Bargraph showing performance in terms of area for various blocks.

6 Conclusion

In this paper, novel hardware architecture is proposed for the purpose of N-Bit fixed point division algorithm based on restoring techniques. The proposed algorithm is developed using the standard restoring algorithm from the state of art literature. The technique used here for the development of architecture includes the principle of modularity and hence different steps involved are designed using basic modules like XOR gate, Full adder, Multiplexer, and Inverter. The logic involved in developing repetitive architectures is purely combinational. For the efficacy of architecture, the proposed structures are implemented in GDI logic and have been simulated using UMC 180 nm CMOS process in Cadence Spectre Environment. From the simulation results, it is observed that, the proposed architecture is well suited for the purpose of calculating fixed point division for a length of input up to 16 bits with less power and area. It may also be extended for more sized inputs but at the cost of complexity. Hence the proposed hardware architecture is well suited for developing fixed point division modules in any low power ALUs at optimized speeds with lesser area.

References

1. Ercegovac, M.D., Lang, T.: Simple radix-4 division with operands scaling. IEEE Trans. Comput. **39**(9), 1204–1208 (1990)
2. Ercegovac, M.D., Lang, T., Montuschi, P.: Very-high radix division with prescaling and selection by rounding. IEEE Trans. Comput. **43**(8), 909–918 (1994)
3. Agarwal, R.C., Gustavson, F.G., Schmookler, M.S.: Series approximation methods for divide and square root in the power3/sup TM/processor. In: Proceedings 14th IEEE Symposium on Computer Arithmetic (Cat. No. 99CB36336), pp. 116–123. IEEE (1999)
4. Matula, D.W., Panu, M.T., Zhang, J.Y.: Multiplicative division employing independent factors. IEEE Trans. Comput. **64**(7), 2012–2019 (2014)
5. Antelo, E., Lang, T., Montuschi, P., Nannarelli, A.: Digit-recurrence dividers with reduced logical depth. IEEE Trans. Comput. **54**(7), 837–851 (2005)
6. Antelo, E., Lang, T., Montuschi, P., Nannarelli, A.: Low latency digit-recurrence reciprocal and square-root reciprocal algorithm and architecture. In: 17th IEEE Symposium on Computer Arithmetic (ARITH 2005), pp. 147–154. IEEE (2005)
7. Kikkeri, N., Seidel, P.M.: Formal verification of parametric multiplicative division implementations. In: 2005 International Conference on Computer Design, pp. 599–602. IEEE (2005)
8. Even, G., Seidel, P.M.: Pipelined multiplicative division with IEEE rounding. In: Proceedings 21st International Conference on Computer Design, pp. 240–245. IEEE (2003)
9. Ito, M., Takagi, N., Yajima, S.: Efficient initial approximation for multiplicative division and square root by a multiplication with operand modification. IEEE Trans. Comput. **46**(4), 495–498 (1997)
10. Kumar, D., Saha, P., Dandapat, A., et al.: Hardware implementation of methodologies of fixed point division algorithms. Int. J. Smart Sens. Intell. Syst. **10**(3), 630–645 (2017)

11. Morgenshtein, A., Fish, A., Wagner, I.A.: Gate-diffusion input (GDI)-a technique for low power design of digital circuits: analysis and characterization. In: 2002 IEEE International Symposium on Circuits and Systems. Proceedings (Cat. No.02CH37353), vol. 1, p. I. IEEE (2002)
12. Sucharitha, D., Raj, N.P., Sravya, R.B., Raja, V.S.: GDI logic based design of hamming-code encoder and decoder for error free data communication. In: 2019 3rd International Conference on Computing Methodologies and Communication (ICCMC), pp. 1–5. IEEE (2019)
13. Bellaouar, A., Elmasry, M.: Low-Power Digital VLSI Design: Circuits and Systems. Springer, Boston (2012). https://doi.org/10.1007/978-1-4615-2355-0
14. Rabaey, J.M., Chandrakasan, A., Nikolic, B.: Digital Integrated Circuits, vol. 996. Prentice-Hall (1996)
15. Rabaey, J.M., Chandrakasan, A.P., Nikolic, B.: Digital Integrated Circuits: A Design Perspective, vol. 7. Pearson Education, Upper Saddle River (2003)
16. Weste, N.H., Harris, D.: CMOS VLSI Design: A Circuits and Systems Perspective. Pearson Education India (2015)

Emerging Technologies and IoT

Automatic Toll Gates Using AI

Tatavarthi Dhiraj[1]([✉]), Melwin Mathew[1], and A. Rammohan[2]

[1] School of Electronics Engineering, Vellore Institute of Technology, Vellore 632014, India
[2] Automotive Research Center, Vellore Institute of Technology, Vellore 632014, India

Abstract. The infrastructure and mechanism of toll gates have been evolving over the years, ultimately to reduce queuing time and to make the method of payment as efficient as needed. Different kinds of infrastructure are being proposed and implemented in different parts of the world, which are working correctly but have some disadvantages of their own and some not compatible and suitable for other nations. This paper aims to provide an efficient solution for the Automatic Toll Collection System. An Artificial intelligence-based toll gate system is proposed, which has very high latency, no requirement for additional installation of any module into the vehicle, which reduces the cost for vehicle manufacturers, owners, and tollgate management. The system works by Capturing vehicle images at the highway toll gate and with the help of image processing and object recognition technique of machine learning, the corresponding vehicle type is identified automatically. The system is based on a variety of vehicle detection and number plate detection methods rather than the current working systems of toll collection like sensor-based RFID tags, smart cards, and manual observation. The system proposed in this paper mainly includes two modules: vehicle detection and its type and secondly number plate recognition from the image. The vehicle type detection module is implemented using the YOLO framework, which takes the vehicle features and segments the detected vehicle into three classes, namely car, van, and lorry. To tackle security concerns and unique identification for auxiliary requests, the system is developed with number plate recognition.

Keywords: Vehicle detection · Number plate recognition · YOLO · Convolution networks · KNN · GUI · CNN

1 Introduction

The contemporary world has seen a radical increase in the massive congestion of automobiles at toll-booths. In the preceding years, the manual collection was widely practiced across India. For this system to work uneventfully, a considerable workforce is required as the situation needs to be monitored perpetually. The toll collector decides the amount to be paid upon the type of the vehicle, its features, journey type, and pre-determined monetary values set by the government. To overthrow the hitches met in the manual system, Electronic Toll Collection (ETC) came into existence. The primary goal of such systems is to allow clearance for vehicles with minimal setback through the toll plaza. One such system available in India is FASTtag, based on Radio Frequency Identification Technology (RFID), which deducts the toll amount directly from the user's virtual

© Springer Nature Singapore Pte Ltd. 2021
V. Arunachalam and K. Sivasankaran (Eds.): ICMDCS 2021, CCIS 1392, pp. 103–121, 2021.
https://doi.org/10.1007/978-981-16-5048-2_9

wallet. The RFID based systems primarily require two components, tag, and reader. The RFID tag is fixed on the front screen of the vehicle, whereas the reader is fixed at the toll plaza. Although the system has been successful in reducing the delay at the toll gates, there have been certain issues that have caused further doubts in the usage of FASTtag. Doubts such as misplacing another tag worth a lower denomination to save money or even reading of tag might be difficult in foggy or rainy conditions, which further causes delay, and a manual override is needed for such situations.

To overcome these circumstances, the proposed system uses the principle of object recognition, a branch of computer vision where there has been a sudden surge in the development of recognition technology and high-performance computing in digital image processing over the years. A vehicle consists of many complicated features where each constraint can be used to differentiate and analyze them. In the proposed model, two cameras are used, one for number plate detection and the other for vehicle type detection. The system mainly consists of two modules for input: vehicle detection, vehicle type recognition, and second number plate recognition. Both of the modules take place parallel and separately. Vehicle recognition system has indeed become a vital part of any intelligent or smart transportation system. In this paper, YOLO algorithm that is built upon Convolutional Neural Network (CNN) and deep learning is used and also the second module is number plate recognition, Opencv, and a machine learning model KNN (K near neighbor). Finally, a user interface is built for viewing vehicle entry data by tollgate officials.

The system propose in the paper has the following steps:

Capturing Vehicle and Number Plate Image: Capture the images of the vehicle and its number plate by two separate cameras, a real-time camera is used for vehicle detection module, and a standby camera is used for number plate detection.

Vehicle Detection and Recognition: The video from real-time camera is continuously sent to the processor, when the vehicle is detected an image capture occurs and is sent to YOLO algorithm to identify the vehicle and sort it into any of the three primary classifications. Further sub-classifications of the vehicle can be created based on the length of the bounding box of the image.

Number Plate Detection and Recognition: An image captured by the standby camera is taken as input for this module k-NN and character segmentation are used.

Data Storage: After detecting and recognizing the vehicle and number-plate information such as Vehicle type, Number plate, Time of detection are sent to the data server for storage. These data can be retrieved but can never be edited.

Price Allocation: Based on the input, the price is allocated, and the amount is deducted from their wallets (Fig. 1).

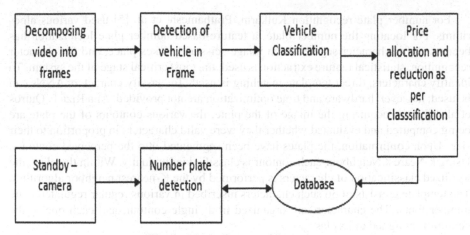

Fig. 1. Block diagram of the system

2 Related Work

For vehicle detection and recognition, many researchers have pressed on using sensor-based tags and off the shelf detectors. Tags stores the vehicle's unique registration number, vehicle type, and other details required.

The tags and readers are based on the principle of Radio Frequency Identification (RFID) technology. The tags stores the vehicle's unique registration number. The major components of the RFID based system comprise an RFID transmitter, receiver, and any microcontroller. If there is a sufficient balance in a registered account, then toll charges can be deducted automatically and with the help of a GSM module, transaction details are sent users via SMS [1]. There have also been other systems based on detectors and smart cards, which act as both storage for vehicle details and virtual wallet for money. Recently, the branch of computer vision has boomed with the rapid development of digital image processing. Watcharin et al. [2] use deep learning to classify the vehicles. CNN is the neural network used in image recognition. This paper mainly emphasizes on the performance and efficiency of vehicle type classification and vehicle color classification. Saripan et al. [3] have taken a tree-based approach for the vehicle classification system. Decision tree, a supervised machine learning model has been used, it has branches and nodes similar to that of the tree-based structure model. To categorize the input data divide and conquer algorithm has been used. It also uses color classifiers for the classification module. Complex algorithms have been used in the above papers, in the paper Zhan et al. [4], have taken a simpler and effective algorithm for extracting the vehicle type parameters, which is via counting the number of black pixels include in-vehicle body contour. Two different algorithms are used in detecting the vehicle, background subtraction, and threshold segmentation. Background subtraction and image segmentation are algorithms primarily for moving object detection in video surveillance systems. Moving objects are segmented by using the difference between the input images and background, and finally the color is inversed to find the number of pixels. Establishing a strong initial background is the key to background subtraction.

For number plate recognition Kulkarni, Prathamesh, et al. [5] used various algorithms. For locating the number plate, a feature-based number plate localization has been used, for character segmentation image scissoring takes place, and for character recognition, statistical feature extraction is used, the most critical stage of the system. To identify characters, direct template matching is used. To classify characters ANNs can be used; however, hardware and time optimization are not provided. Ana Riza F. Quiros et al. [6] upon acquiring the image of the plate, the various contours of the plate are being computed and evaluated whether they were valid characters in proportion to their size. Upon confirmation, the plates have been segmented into the perceived contours. Using k-Nearest Neighbour each contour is classified individually. Within the plate, the localized classification of characters is performed by the K-nearest neighbor algorithm. The template consists of 36 such characters inscribed in various regular regulated plate number fonts. The characters are organized in a single contour, and each one of the contour is assigned to its class.

3 Algorithm

The Automatic Tollgate requires three inputs: vehicle type, number plate, and time of entry at the toll gate. To acquire the inputs, the system uses two modules vehicle type recognition and number plate recognition. An image of the car is fed to the vehicle type recognition module and the vehicle type is returned to the user. When the type is returned, the timestamp is also returned as the time of entry. Secondly, a stand-by camera captures the number plate which is sent to the database for security concerns. Based on features such as Time of Entry and Vehicle type, the price is allocated as per the specified regulations of NHAI (Fig. 3).

3.1 Vehicle Type Recognition

It is a decisive and crucial model for the automated tollgate pricing system. NHAI divides all vehicles into 4 different pricing categories, car/jeep/van into one, LCV,3 or 4 axles, HCM/EME, and more than 7 axles. Vehicle detection is done using YOLOv3 (you only look once) which uses CNN (convolution neural network). The YOLOv3, an object detector that is pre-trained on a large scale dataset, the COCO dataset, and other model files. It is a 53 convolution layer that is followed by 2 connected layers, which are simply 1×1 reduction layer and followed by 3×3 convolution layers. The processed input image is divided into $S \times S$ grids, and if such an object has fallen into the grid then the grid will be responsible for detecting, each grid also forecasts the bounding boxes and confidence scores of objects, the bounding box is used to predict the 4 coordinates for a box, t_x, t_y, t_w, t_h. If the cell has been offset by the top left corner of the image by coordinates $(c_x; c_y)$ and the bounding box which has prior width and height p_w, p_h respectively; then the predictions has been correlated to:

$$b_x = (t_x) + c_x \tag{1}$$

$$b_y = (t_y) + c_y \tag{2}$$

$$b_w = p_w t_w \tag{3}$$

$$b_h = p_h t_h \tag{4}$$

In case the detected vehicle is a car then further classification is not required, else the detected vehicle is either a tuck or a car then there is need of further classification into LVC, ¾ axel or a large vehicle, the further classification is done through the length of the vehicle it is calculated using t_h component which is the height of detected object bounding box, a few test images are taken and ranges of length boundaries of each class is figured out, to classify vehicles further through the length. All the testing images are taken from the same distance because in tollgate all the vehicles will go in the same lane and the camera will be there at a fixed spot. Considering the length of the box in the image and original vehicle, a linear equation will be formed, from this equation, the original length of the vehicle can be estimated, Table 1 and Table 2 show the length range for different classes of vehicle classification and a corresponding class is given for billing system.

Table 1. Variable range for truck classification

Classification	Length minimum	Maximum length
LCV	75	110
2 axle	111	140
3 axle	141	200
4–6 axle	201	285
7 and more axle	286	315

Table 2. Range for bus classification

Classification	Length minimum	Maximum length
LCV	–	135
2 axle	136	230
3 axle	231	270
4–6 axle	271	–

3.2 Number Plate Recognition

Number plate detection can be performed either on the front-facing image or on back facing of a vehicle because number plate is present only on these positions, image is preprocessed and converted to grayscale and threshold image. Edge detection is the most accurate solution to address these requirements. The reason edge detection is that detection of edge with low error rate, i.e. the detection should accurately capture as many edges as present in the image. The edge point detected from the operator should accurately localize on the center of the edge. A detected edge in the image would be only marked once, where possible image noise should not create false edges.

Among edge detection techniques developed so far, Canny edge detection filter or algorithm is one of the most well-defined methods which provides good and reliable detection. To fulfill the above requirements Canny filter uses the calculus of variations, a technique which finds the function which optimizes a given functional. The optimal function in Canny's filter is defined by the sum of four exponential terms, and it can be approximated by the first derivative of a Gaussian. Canny edge detection algorithm consists of differnet steps. First Gaussian filter is applied to smooth the image to remove the noise, after which the intensity gradients of the image are found. Now non-maximum suppression is applied to remove the duplicate responses.Finally double threshold applied to determine potential edges and track the edge by hysteresis.

After applying the detector, we get a threshold image in which all possible contours are detected, the contour is a line connecting all the possible points along the boundary in an image with the same intensity. Contours come handy in for shape detection and shape analysis. For each counter a basic possible character check is performed to know is the counter is useful or not, if there are no characters in a counter, then the particular contour is removed. In possible character check, for a contour to be a possible character, it should have bounding area of more than 80 pixels, bonding height more than 8, bounding width more than two, and with an aspect ratio between 0.25 to 1. After getting all the possible characters in the image, the characters are segmented to form a group of size matching characters which are near by comparing with all the characters in the dataset image shown in Fig. 2, and this segmentation is to group possible, similar and near characters into the same category ideally these groups of characters are considered to be characters of a plate.

To categorize two given possible contour characters are in same group or not, five parameterized checks is performed; parameters are change in area, height and width between the possible characters, also distance and angle between the characters. To calculate the change of parameters the Eqs. (5), (6), (7), (8) and (9) are correspondingly used.

$$change_h = (char_2.h - char_1.h)/(char_1.h) \tag{5}$$

$$change_a = (char_2.a - char_1.a)/(char_1.a) \tag{6}$$

$$change_w = (char_2.w - char_1.w)/(char_1.w) \tag{7}$$

$$DistanceBetween_{char} = \left(\left((char_2.y + \frac{(char_2.h)}{2}) - (char_1.y + (\frac{char_1.h}{2})) \right)^2 + \left((char_2.x + \frac{(char_2.w)}{2}) - (char_1.x + \frac{char_1.w}{2}) \right)^2 \right)^{\frac{1}{2}} \tag{8}$$

$$AngleBetween_{char} = \tan\left(\frac{\left(char_2.y + \frac{(char_2.h)}{2}\right) - \left(char_1.y + \left(\frac{char_1.h}{2}\right)\right)}{\left(char_2.x + \frac{(char_2.w)}{2}\right) - \left(char_1.x + \frac{char_1.w}{2}\right)}\right) + \tag{9}$$

0 1 2 3 4 5 6 7 8 9

A B C D E F G H I J K L M N O P Q R S T U V W X Y Z

0 1 2 3 4 5 6 7 8 9

A B C D E F G H I J K L M N O P Q R S T U V W X Y Z

0 1 2 3 4 5 6 7 8 9

A B C D E F G H I J K L M N O P Q R S T U V W X Y Z

0 1 2 3 4 5 6 7 8 9

A B C D E F G H I J K L M N O P Q R S T U V W X Y Z

0 1 2 3 4 5 6 7 8 9

A B C D E F G H I J K L M N O P Q R S T U V W X Y Z

Fig. 2. Training dataset for character recognition

The change in the area should be less than 0.5, width change less than 0.8, and a height change of less than 0.2. The angle between them should be less than 12°, if 2 possible characters satisfy all these parameters then these are grouped. From the grouped characters the starting of the first character to end of the last character is considered as a single plate, this extracted number plate is further processed for text detection in the image, a machine learning-based KNN(k near neighbor) is used for extracting text, around 5 photos of each character is given for training, there are 10 numbers from 0 to 9 and 26 alphabets from A to Z, so around $36 \times 5 = 180$ samples are given while testing a single character is taken each time, that character is compared with all the images in train module, based on best match with the train images top 5 matches will be taken and the most relevant character will be given out.

3.3 Server and System Interface

From the central station, collected information of the vehicle, such as vehicle type, time of entry, and plate number, will be sent to the server. Based on the inputs received from the vehicle type recognition module, the price to be allocated for the respective vehicles is processed. On a particular day, if the vehicle passes through the toll booth once, the amount will be billed based on the vehicle type and is deducted from registered bank accounts. And if the same vehicle passes again through the same booth before midnight, an extra amount is deducted which is less than the time vehicle first passes through. In this system, the Microsoft SQL server is used. In Microsoft application (GUI), data from the server is pulled and displayed for user convenience. An interface is required for an easy visual of the information taken in by the system and for processed information, price allocated. The interface used for this system consists of two forms, a login form, and another form to display the necessary information as required. The above two kinds primarily consist of essential components such as text boxes and buttons.

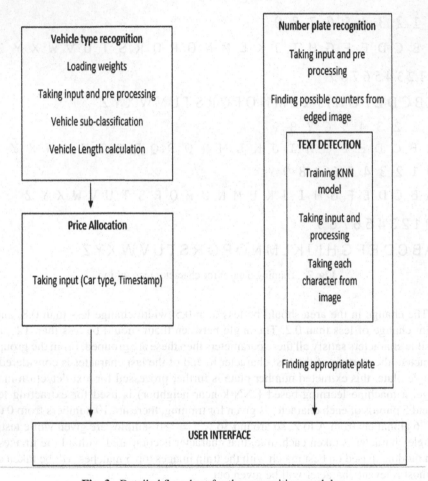

Fig. 3. Detailed flowchart for the recognition modules.

4   Results and Discussion

As there are two modules, vehicle type detection, and vehicle number plate detection, each module have a different input image followed by different outputs which are sent to the server and from server to toll application.

4.1   Vehicle Type Detection

A test image Fig. 4 a of an LCV a kind of minibus it was taken from a distance of 15 feet for vehicle type detection, the vehicle is detected as a bus but the length is calculated to 790 cm from "h" which indicates the length of the bounding box, for this image "h" is 127, basing on the length vehicle is categorized to LCV as shown in Fig. 4b vehicle in Fig. 4a is identified and highlighted by a rectangular box.

$$\text{Length} = 6.22 \times \text{th} \tag{10}$$

(a)

(b)

Fig. 4. a. Image of an LCV captured from 15 m away b. Output of Fig. 4a from vehicle type detection

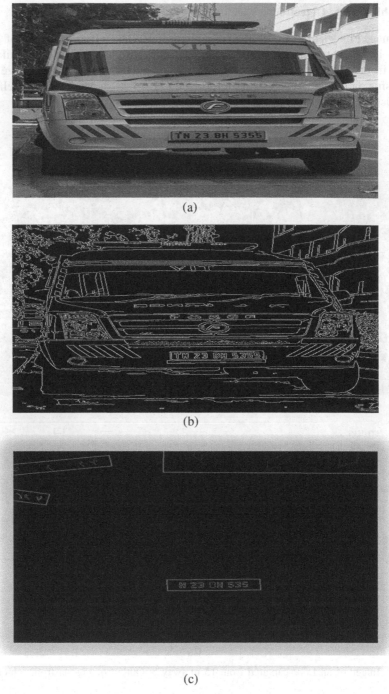

(a)

(b)

(c)

Fig. 5. a. An input image of an LCV taken from 16 m range b. Edge detected image of input c. Displays filtered and possible plates detected image d. Detected number plate

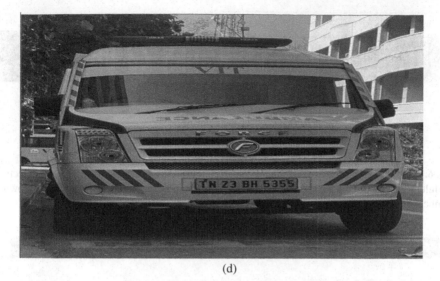

(d)

Fig. 5. (*continued*)

4.2 Number Plate Detection

For number plate detection, the front-facing image of the same LCV vehicle is taken, converted to grayscale, edge detection is performed with the canny filter in OpenCV. It is a technique used to extract very useful structural information from various vision objects and drastically reduce the amount of data to be processed, with a range from 30 to 200, from edged image all the counter are detected using find counter function, image is vectors of possible characters is taken, all the possible counters with a defined length which is rectangular in shape are taken, from the possible counters the one with appropriate length, width and with characters is chosen as number plate, outputs of all steps are shown in Fig. 5 the number plate part is cropped from the main car image, further on the cropped plate, each character is separated into individual components, this process is known component analysis. Then K-NN detection module is used to identify the corresponding character. Features from the image after component analysis will be classified by using K-Nearest Neighbor (KNN) algorithm. This process will classify the character by determining the the most similar object based on the training data. The KNN algorithm has two processes, namely training and testing. The training process is the data validation stage. The number of training data is 60% of the total dataset images. The testing process classifies the images based on the training data (Fig. 6).

4.3 Toll Application

The outputs of vehicle type and number plate detection are sent to the local server, the application will take the data from the server and display on its UI, a new entry is appended at the end, UI has four columns namely plate number, timestamp, vehicle type, and price, if the vehicle is charged an amount for its trip and again if the same vehicle is

imgPlate
TN 23 BH 5355
imgThresh
TN 23 BH 5355
plate number: TN23BH5355

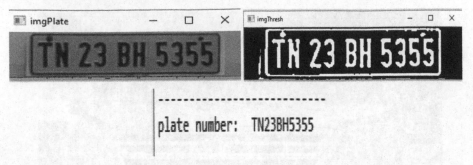

Fig. 6. Text detection from extracted number plate, left top: extracted plate from the plate detection module, right top: binary image of plate extracted, bottom: snapshot of python console showing number of detected plate

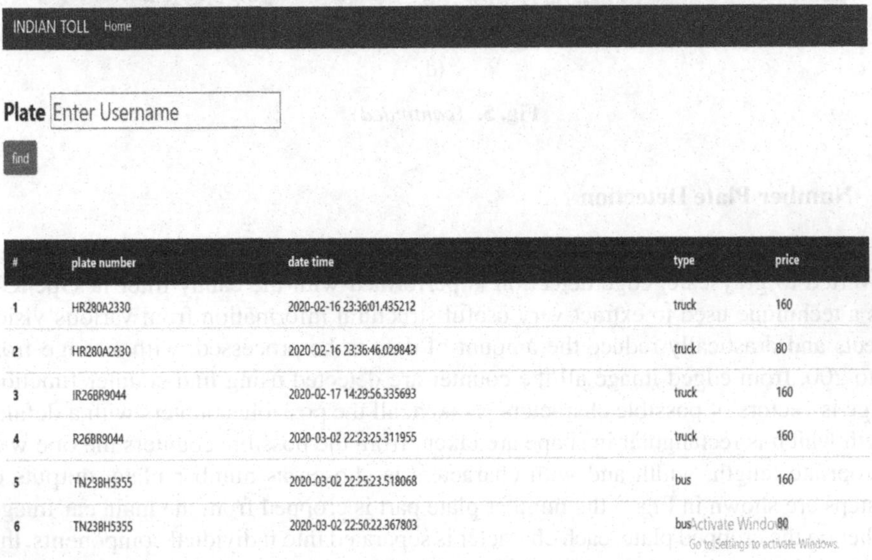

INDIAN TOLL Home
Plate Enter Username
find
plate number date time type price
1 HR280A2330 2020-02-16 23:36:01.435212 truck 160
2 HR280A2330 2020-02-16 23:36:46.029843 truck 80
3 IR26BR9044 2020-02-17 14:29:56.335693 truck 160
4 R26BR9044 2020-03-02 22:23:25.311955 truck 160
5 TN23BH5355 2020-03-02 22:25:23.518068 bus 160
6 TN23BH5355 2020-03-02 22:50:22.367803 bus 80
Activate Windows
Go to Settings to activate Windows.

Fig. 7. User interface with updated data

returning within 24 h of its last full payment, then the amount to be paid will be reduced by almost 50%. For example, let a vehicle is passing the toll and an amount of Rs.160, if the vehicle is returning from the toll back within 24 h then the amount detected is 80. In Fig. 7 5th entry shows detection of the vehicle for a single journey and the 6th entry shows the change in pricing if the vehicle is returning in 24 h. Figure 8 is showing the records of one particular vehicle, Application also has a feature to find all the records of one particular vehicle using its plate number.

To test the working of the prototype different axle vehicles images are used, the same axle vehicle could be of different lengths, the length range of different axle varies in bus and trucks. The results of each module are discussed individually.

Plate TN23BH5355

find

#	plate number	date time	type	price
1	TN23BH5355	2020-03-02 22:25:23.518068	bus	160
2	TN23BH5355	2020-03-02 22:50:22.367803	bus	80
3	null	null	null	null

Fig. 8. Vehicle history in the user interface

Fig. 9. Result of vehicle type detection on a van

Figure 9 shows the response of the prototype for a van, which is categorized to the car, actually this van in identified to be a truck by Yolo but after the length categorization, it is correctly identified to the category of car.

Fig. 10. Result of vehicle type detection on a 2 axle truck captured from 16 m away

In Fig. 10 a two axle truck is first identified as the truck in the Yolo module then in length calculation with a length of 120 it is identified as a 2 axle truck and the 3-axle vehicle in Fig. 11 is classified into a 3-axle class after length module with a length of 157.

Fig. 11. Result of vehicle type detection on a 3 axle truck captured from 16 m away

Fig. 12. Result of car image in number plate with a rectangular box around the detected plate and displayed in console

Fig. 13. Result of dull lighting car image in number plate with a rectangular box around the detected plate and displayed in console

Figures 12a, 13a, 14a are the results of the number plate identification module, as this is an most crutial module in this prototype various images of different vehicles like a car and truck are taken in different views for testing to check the working of number plate detection module in various conditions, Fig. 12 a and Fig. 13 a are the images of two different cars taken from two different camara views from front and back view. Figure 12 a and Fig. 13 b are the snapshots of python console shows the decoded plate numbers of the car, plate numbers are decoded correctly though images are in different views similarly Fig. 14 a is the image of an Indian truck taken from the front view and Fig. 14 b is the decoded plate number of the vehicle, for Indian trucks detecting plate number from back view if not possible because those backplates are not properly visible and at the time that number will be covered, and because of this always number plate should be captured from the front view.

```
10 possible plates found
-------------------------------------------------
plate number:  AP07TW0130
```

Fig. 14. Result of truck image in number plate with a rectangular box around the detected plate and displaed in console

Figure 15 and Fig. 16 shows how the response of the module for different number plates like in the numbers of the plate is split into two rows and detection is not accurate. The module is giving good accuracy for a single row vehicle number plate shown in Fig. 15, but in a multi-row number plate, only one row is detected rest other numbers are ignored by the module. This could be one of the drawbacks of the prototype, which needs to be rectified further.

Fig. 15. Result of truck with completely detected number plate in number plate detection module

Fig. 16. Result of truck with partially detected number plate in number plate detection module.

Figure 17 shows the web user interface of toll management application, the data are shown in the table are the different vehicles data that are passed through the toll, depending on the type of the vehicle price will be charged.

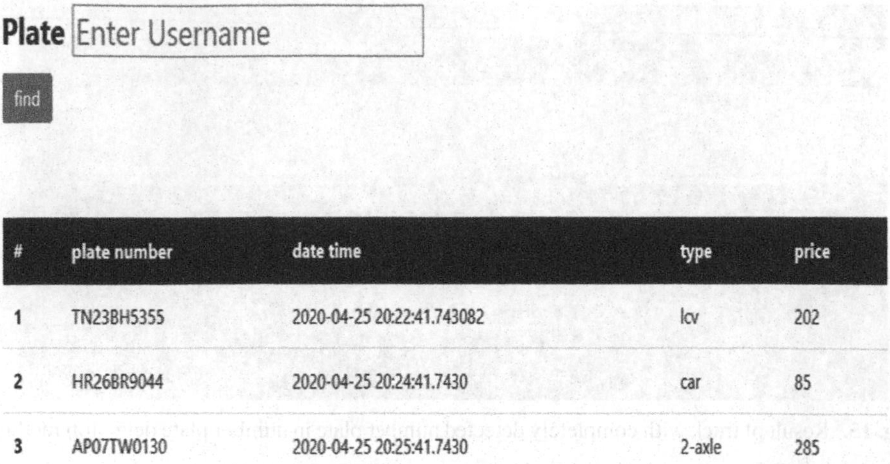

Plate Enter Username

find

#	plate number	date time	type	price
1	TN23BH5355	2020-04-25 20:22:41.743082	lcv	202
2	HR26BR9044	2020-04-25 20:24:41.7430	car	85
3	AP07TW0130	2020-04-25 20:25:41.7430	2-axle	285

Fig. 17. Screenshot of web interface for toll management

5 Conclusion and Future Work

In this research work, various systems involving toll gates and the respective constraints for them. By analyzing them the system is found to be more effective not only in reducing waiting time but also in reducing external factors such as cost and reduction in counterfeiting.

By Capturing moving vehicles of a highway toll station and with help of digital image processing and recognition, vehicles will be detected, and the vehicle type will be recognized automatically, using YOLOv3 for vehicle type detection is very accurate and it takes less memory compared to other object detection algorithms, but it takes a lot of time to process an image, so there is a need of some better model which is faster and accurate simultaneously to detect the vehicle type. In the number plate recognition model by using k-NN, this algorithm is fast in response but less accurate compared to other classifier models, this is improved using image segmentation and a pre-defined set of the font for the characters. An exception for some test images, extraction of text from an image is not accurate because of factors such as various and unidentified font and sizes, this could be further developed by methods of deep learning to find an improved model for text conversion to reduce such discrepancies. Also, this model can be further improved if an overall database of the vehicle number plates from the RTO's is linked to the toll collection database to increase the accuracy and security of the system.

Abbrevations

char	Character
CNN	Convolutional Neural Network
ETC	Electronic Toll Collection
HCM	Highway Capacity Manual vehicle
k-NN	k-Nearest Neighbors

LCV	Light Commercial Vehicle
NHAI	National Highway Authority of India
RFID	Radio Frequency Identification Technology
YOLO	You Only Look Once
$Char_1$	first character
$Char_2$	second character
Sqrt	square root
h	height
w	width
Tan	tangent
t_x	x coordinate of top left point in bounding box
t_y	y coordinate of top left point in bounding box
t_w	width of bounding box
t_h	height of bounding box
p_w	prior width
p_h	prior height

References

1. Pandith, H., Devaki, P.: Implementation of Automated Toll System for Highways And Bridges (2019)
2. Zhan, W., Wan, Q.: Real-time and automatic vehicle type recognition system design and its application. In: International Symposium on Intelligence Computation and Applications. Springer, Heidelberg (2012)
3. Maungmai, W., Nuthong, C.: Vehicle classification with deep learning. In: 2019 IEEE 4th International Conference on Computer and Communication Systems (ICCCS). IEEE (2019)
4. Saripan, K., Nuthong, C.: Tree-based vehicle classification system. In: 2017 14th International Conference on Electrical Engineering/Electronics, Computer, Telecommunications and Information Technology (ECTI-CON). IEEE (2017)
5. Chopra, K., Gupta, K.: Smart vehicle card using IoT. In: 2019 International Conference on Machine Learning, Big Data, Cloud and Parallel Computing (COMITCon). IEEE (2019)
6. Laghari, A.A., Sulleman Memon, M., Pathan, A.S.: RFID based toll deduction system. I.J. Information Technologyand Computer Sci. 4, 40–46 (2012)
7. Khan, M.A., Sharif, M., Javed, M.Y., Akram, T., Yasmin, M., Saba, T.: License number plate recognition system using entropy-based features selection approach with SVM. In: IET Image Processing, vol. 12, no. 2, pp. 200–209 (2018)
8. Kulkarni, P., et al.: Automatic number plate recognition (ANPR) system for indian conditions. In: 2009 19th International Conference Radioelektronika. IEEE (2009)
9. Quiros, A.R.F., et al.: A kNN-based approach for the machine vision of character recognition of license plate numbers. In: TENCON 2017–2017 IEEE Region 10 Conference. IEEE (2017)

A Prototypical Semantic Based Driver Deeds Prophecy to Prevent Accidents Using Intelligent Techniques

Abburi Venkata Jaswanth and P. Mohan Kumar$^{(\boxtimes)}$

School of Information Technology and Engineering, VIT University, Vellore, India

Abstract. At the present time vehicles are becoming more affordable, individual vehicle owner ship is increasing day by day. This leads to more vehicles on the road, and bad public transport is also becoming another reason to travel in individual vehicles. Also the poor knowledge of traffic rules and carelessness leads to more traffic blockage. In the recent years the number of accidents have been increased manifold due to stress/usage of social networks leads to lack of concentration of driver while driving. In this paper a solution to minimize the accident rate by analyzing the characteristics of the driver based on driver characteristics and route is assigned to him. Further a prototype uses intelligence semantic technique was designed based on the analyses which will be supportive for driver to drive vehicle in a safe mode was detailed with sample test in the real time mode as resultants.

Keywords: Driver · Semantic intelligence · Vehicles

1 Introduction

Accidents cannot be prevented when it occurs without human intervention. We can predict the accidents that might occur with human intervention. By observing certain entities like speed of the vehicle, the lane crossing, driving under influence of alcohol and violation of traffic rules. Our motive is to observe these kinds of driver behavior and provide some alert signals like speed of the vehicle is high and steering angle is continuously changing or hard left/right and redirect them to less traffic roads. So that we might reduce the probability of occurrence of accidents. Usage of Semantic web has increased significantly nowadays by popular companies, like Net Base Solutions and Cycorp Inc. Websites like tracking genie will provide user details like speed and the location where the vehicle was travelling. This data cannot be used in real time by the user. Our system too will get the data and process it. After processing, it will give the real time results to the user and it will give indication to avoiding accidents. Accidents are majorly caused due to over speed, illegal line changes etc. In olden day's vehicle's maximum speed was very less and more over there were very less number of vehicles on road. Nowadays vehicles are becoming more affordable. The vehicle count also increased. Due to this there will be very high number of accidents happen and governments has not considered on those. Accidents are mainly caused due to traffic.

© Springer Nature Singapore Pte Ltd. 2021
V. Arunachalam and K. Sivasankaran (Eds.): ICMDCS 2021, CCIS 1392, pp. 122–133, 2021.
https://doi.org/10.1007/978-981-16-5048-2_10

The traffic congestion will mainly occur due to situations like where there are more number of vehicles. To avoid this situation the major solutions are to expansion of roads. There are some advancement in now a days like to avoid accidents like automatic driving vehicles using artificial intelligence. For the above model there is no need of driver. For this we can reduce the accident count. But it is not affordable to so many people. So based on the above reasons we need a better solution that can be cost efficient with real time results.

1.1 Problem Specification

Accidents cannot be prevented when it occurs without human intervention. We can expect the accidents that might arise with human intervention. By observing certain entities like pace of the car, the lane crossing, driving below have an impact on of alcohol and violation of site visitors rules. Our reason is to observe these varieties of driver behavior and offer some alert indicators like pace of the vehicle is excessive and guidance perspective is continuously converting or hard left/right and redirect them to less traffic roads. So that we might reduce the possibility of prevalence of accidents. The reason of this undertaking is to offer accident prevention by way of analyzing the traits of the driving force based on driving force characteristic, direction is assigned to him. For Example, motive force who's driving abnormally is redirected to less visitor's direction there by system can lessen street accidents. For this we are coping with some demanding situations like Identifying rash driving, analyzing human behavior, pace and guidance angle. The following parameters are used to pick out the driver traits. The first one is speed which constitute speed of the vehicles in that area. Second one is to accumulate Steering perspective for each vehicle, vehicle identity and braking nature. For Identifying rash driving, we're producing the facts of equal automobiles for each one minute. Driver traits are categorized as follows, if the rate of the vehicle is very excessive and steerage attitude is tough left to hard right or tough right to difficult left then he's harsh motive force. If the velocity of the automobile is normal and steerage attitude is slight left to mild proper then he is ordinary driver. If the speed of the automobile is ordinary and guidance attitude is tough left to hard right then he is harsh driver. If the velocity of the automobile is very high and guidance perspective is slight left to slight right then he is harsh motive force.

2 Proposed Work

In this when the data has been generated the data will be processed in real time. To process it in real time through semantic web RDF is required and it's generated by the RDF4J package. After importing the package we need to define RDF schema. For this we have taken vehicle as a class. After generating the RDF data we are sending the data to rules of inferences. The list of rules of inferences that we generated are when the driver drives the vehicle with high speed, braking with harsh and the steering angle as hard right or right or straight or left or hard left we are classifying the driver as a harsh. If the vehicle speed is high, braking is normal and the steering angle is left to hard right or right to hard left we are classifying the driver as a harsh. If the vehicle speed is moderate and the braking as harsh and steering angle as left to hard right and right to hard left also we are classifying the driver as a harsh. If the vehicle speed is normal, braking as harsh and the steering angle data as right to hard left or left to hard right we are classifying the driver as harsh. Similarly we are classifying the driver to safe when the harsh condition doesn't happen. After the classification we are sending the data to the web page where the user can access.

2.1 System Architecture

The structure diagram Fig. 1 of the "Semantic version for Driver characteristics" is proven below. The main capabilities are Real time information generation, RDF Repository, Rules of Inference, Driver classification, net page. The functioning of each element is defined below. In this application we are taken into consideration the vehicle as a category and the attributes are Time stamp, Acceleration, Braking, Speed, Steering angle. Admin need to specify the no of automobiles in our system. Once we specified the number of automobiles right now the values for different vehicles might be generated randomly through our system. For each one minute, the software generates and facts the data values. As a feature of examining these potential information sources, we led probes e-schedules for countless, and have looked into various accessible geo referencing frameworks. Through the aftereffects of a factual investigation and by figuring area acknowledgment precision results, we investigated in detail the potential use of schedule area information to distinguish the driver's expectations. So as to abuse the various assorted information inputs accessible in current vehicles, we research the reasonableness of various Computational Intelligence (CI) strategies, and propose a novel fluffy computational displaying approach. At long last, we layout the effect of applying propelled CI and Big Data examination systems in current vehicles on the driver and society by and large, and talk about moral and lawful issues emerging from the organization of shrewd self-learning autos.

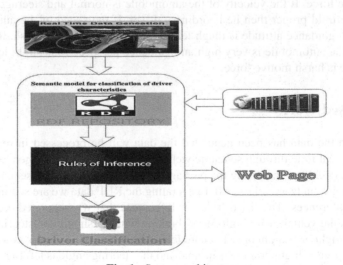

Fig. 1. System architecture

2.2   System Configuration

Whenever the facts values are generated it will send the ones values to the server. In the server we're producing the RDF (Resource Description Framework) dynamically for the input information. We are using RDF4j by maven dependencies. To generate RDF in actual time we want to outline the RDF schema in RDF4J. To employ it we need to setup path in eclipse as first we need to create a maven undertaking in that we want to specify the organization id, its miles like java package. We need to set up the pom record dependencies, it is the most important element on this and we want to add dependencies as a way to replicate in maven dependencies. Using these dependencies the RDF for the given facts were generated. To upload those dependencies we want to specify the corresponding organization Id and the model. For our venture we need rdf4j-runtime artifact Id with organization Id as org.Eclipse.Rdf4j with version as 2.0M2. And the other one has artifact Id as log back-conventional with group Id as ch.Qos. Logback with model as 1.0.13. After setting the dependencies we want to refresh the project to understand whether the dependencies are added or not. In maven dependencies package deal jar documents aren't brought then we need to update or utility and once more we want to restart the above process. After that we need to configure the java compiler by using including apache maven plug in and the maven compiler to the pom. Xml report. After putting it we want to configure the logger with the aid of going to logback. Xml file a good way to be available in sources folder. By putting it we had finished the RDF technology tool. After that we need to outline the RDF schema in java class. We have taken the automobile as a category and the items are Time stamp, Acceleration, Speed, Steering angle, Braking. After defining the schema we want to create a connection. Using this we're passing the statistics to the schema as input. To add the information

```
<?xml version="1.0" encoding="UTF-8"?>
<rdf:RDF
        xmlns:rdf="http://www.w3.org/1999/02/22-rdf-syntax-ns#"
        xmlns:rdfs="http://www.w3.org/2000/01/rdf-schema#"
        xmlns:owl="http://www.w3.org/2002/07/owl#"
        xmlns:xsd="http://www.w3.org/2001/XMLSchema#"
        xmlns:ex="http://www.semanticweb.org/arjun/ontologies/2018/11/untitled-ontology-17#">

<rdf:Description rdf:about="http://www.semanticweb.org/arjun/ontologies/2018/11/untitled-ontology-17#vehical">
        <rdf:type rdf:resource="http://www.w3.org/2002/07/owl#Class"/>
</rdf:Description>

<rdf:Description rdf:about="http://www.semanticweb.org/arjun/ontologies/2018/11/untitled-ontology-17#vehicle0">
        <ex:ACC rdf:datatype="http://www.w3.org/2001/XMLSchema#string">4</ex:ACC>
        <ex:BREAKING rdf:datatype="http://www.w3.org/2001/XMLSchema#string">normal</ex:BREAKING>
        <ex:DT rdf:datatype="http://www.w3.org/2001/XMLSchema#string">2019/04/02 11:26:02</ex:DT>
        <ex:S_A rdf:datatype="http://www.w3.org/2001/XMLSchema#string">right</ex:S_A>
        <ex:SPEED rdf:datatype="http://www.w3.org/2001/XMLSchema#string">16</ex:SPEED>
</rdf:Description>

<rdf:Description rdf:about="http://www.semanticweb.org/arjun/ontologies/2018/11/untitled-ontology-17#vehicle1">
        <ex:ACC rdf:datatype="http://www.w3.org/2001/XMLSchema#string">3</ex:ACC>
        <ex:BREAKING rdf:datatype="http://www.w3.org/2001/XMLSchema#string">normal</ex:BREAKING>
        <ex:DT rdf:datatype="http://www.w3.org/2001/XMLSchema#string">2019/04/02 11:26:02</ex:DT>
        <ex:S_A rdf:datatype="http://www.w3.org/2001/XMLSchema#string">hard left</ex:S_A>
        <ex:SPEED rdf:datatype="http://www.w3.org/2001/XMLSchema#string">46</ex:SPEED>
</rdf:Description>

<rdf:Description rdf:about="http://www.semanticweb.org/arjun/ontologies/2018/11/untitled-ontology-17#vehicle2">
        <ex:ACC rdf:datatype="http://www.w3.org/2001/XMLSchema#string">0</ex:ACC>
        <ex:BREAKING rdf:datatype="http://www.w3.org/2001/XMLSchema#string">harsh</ex:BREAKING>
        <ex:DT rdf:datatype="http://www.w3.org/2001/XMLSchema#string">2019/04/02 11:26:02</ex:DT>
        <ex:S_A rdf:datatype="http://www.w3.org/2001/XMLSchema#string">straight</ex:S_A>
        <ex:SPEED rdf:datatype="http://www.w3.org/2001/XMLSchema#string">76</ex:SPEED>
```

Fig. 2.   RDF generation

we need to corresponding object we want to present the command as Conrad (object name, f.createLiteral (value_to_assign)); by adding the commands for all the objects the corresponding RDF schema will be generated for the data. From this we can access the RDF data. After accessing the RDF data it was forwarded to the proposed algorithm as sample shown in Fig. 2.

3   Survey on Road Accidents

See Table 1.

Table 1. Road accidents survey.

Survey	Activities drivers involved while driving
96%	Talking to passengers
89%	Adjusting vehicle climate conditions
72%	Eating snacks
50%	Using mobile
42%	Tending to children
32%	Reading map publications
20%	Grooming
10%	Prepared for work

3.1   Activities During Driving

Automatic Vehicle Identification (AVI) which, other than their low disappointment rate, have the upside of giving disaggregated information per sort of vehicle. The procedure incorporates an arbitrary woods methodology to distinguish the most grounded fore-runners of mishaps, and the alignment/estimation of two characterization models, to be specific, Support Vector Machine and Logistic relapse. We find that, for this stretch of the roadway, vehicle organization does not assume a first-request job. Our best model precisely predicts 67.89% of the mishaps with a low false positive rate of 20.94%. These outcomes are among the best in the writing despite the fact that, and instead of past endeavors, (i) we don't utilize just a single parcel of the informational index for adjustment and approval yet lead 300 redundancies of haphazardly chosen segments; (ii) our models are approved on the first unequal informational index (where mishaps are very uncommon occasions), as opposed to on falsely adjusted information. Activities performed by the driver while driving shown in the given table (Table 2).

3.2   Human Factors with Accident Occurrence

Driver under the impact of liquor causes serious harm to life and property just as the loss of the economy. Liquor and medications is the main reason for street mishaps. Because

Table 2. Driver activities

Contributing human factors	Number of accidents	% influenced
Overtaking on undivided road (5 buses, 12 cars, 27 M2Ws)	55	22%
Improper lane change/usage	40	18%
Driving under the influence of alcohol	30	15%
Pedestrian dangerous behavior	12	6%
Driver in attention	8	55

of alcoholic driving, drivers lose their control and accident occurs. In recent years the quantity of accidents have been expanded complex because of use of cell phone while driving, forceful driving, driver yawning habitually, keeping an eye on children, rationally discouraged, eating, preparing and so forth prompts absence of focus of driver while driving. The project is developed based on the methods discussed in Context-Aware Driver Behavior Detection System in Intelligent Transportation Systems by Saif Al-Sultan proposing a solution where a five-layer context-conscious architecture is proposed, capable of collecting contextual information about the driving environment, which will give rise to thinking about certain unreliable context - based information. A probabilistic model based on Dynamic Bayesian Networks (DBNs), is used which combines contextual information on the driver, the vehicle, and the environment in four types of driving conduct (normal, drunk, rude, and fatigue). The dynamic behavior model captures the static and time aspects of the driver's behavior, resulting in a robust and accurate behavior. The evaluation of behavioral detection using summary data demonstrates how valid our pattern is and how important it is to include contextual data on drivers, vehicles and the environment. Division of the original path, rotation of the car's steering wheel, movement of pedals etc. is described by dvssce measure. These parameters are continually observed and, when changes in these occur that cross a specified threshold, the probability of the driver being drowsy is dramatically increased. The performance of the driver is constantly observed by a camera to detect the eyes of the driver like the eye closure, blinkage, head rotation, and Perclos, etc. It shows that a driver is drowsy if any performance is found. In physiological measures, drowsiness is detected, such as a continual review of the rates, brain and the pulses. In this assessment, ECG (Electrocardiogram) and EEG (Electroencephalogram) can be used to detect driver submissiveness while driving.

3.3 Detection of Drowsiness

Driving pattern abnormalities can be detected through such parameters as steering wheel movement, lane output, pedal speed movement, braking, etc. Systems based on these measures are the general process. Steering wheel movements are measured by angle sensors on the steering column (Fig. 3).

The standard steering wheel angle variation, steering wheel speed, steering wheel action rate, the high frequency part of the steering wheel angle, etc. are various metrics of

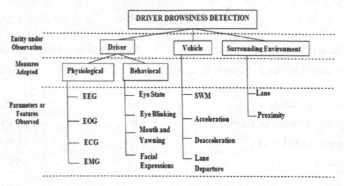

Fig. 3. Driver drowsiness approach

steering wheel movement. The vehicle position in respect of the center lane is monitored by an external camera. The departure from the lane depends upon the road marking, and is therefore not always effective. In addition, this measure depends heavily on the weather conditions and lighting.

3.4 Working Principle

The real time working of the system was elaborated in this session. Based on the system as detailed in the configuration and the survey made with relevant to the driver characters with respect to the vehicle and the road he is driving the system tends to gather the data and record initially. Based on the time variants and the driving status such has speed, steering moments and the climate conditions to the message display will be provided to the driver in front. This was done by the proposed system based on the semantic mapping of the collected data from the vehicle. This was monitored by the intelligent technique deployed in the system. It waits for a time variation of 0–30 s and alert signal will be given to the driver later based on the negative response 30–60 s wait time alert signal will be arise to driver, on negative response the intelligence system activates phase II section i.e., automation of minimizing the speed and bringing the vehicle to normal mode limit. The water stored in the front mirror edges will get activated default invoked by intelligence system and water will be sprayed over the mirror such that driver will get alertness by getting the vision of road blur due to water and he may reduce speed. In parallel the wiper too will be active. This also based on the response of driver. If delayed then the intelligent system will give the warning status in the display and monitors the speed limit. Thirdly the system default tends to block the fuel flow to engine and automates the speed reduction to normal mode to final off state. This is deployed in the automated smart vehicles. In case of battery mode vehicles the required power to activate the engine will get dissipated by giving alarm signal and thus bringing the speed limit to normal mode. Thus the observed resultant was detailed in the below session.

4   Results and Discussions

On opening the app, a map is displayed where one can search for different location in our website itself (Fig. 4).

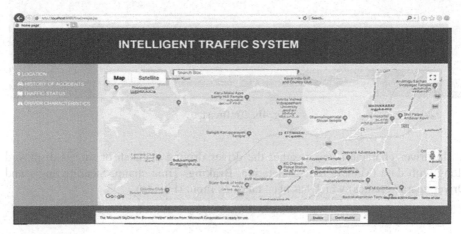

Fig. 4. Map search

Ongoing to history of accidents one can know about the different types of accidents like common forms of teenagers driving, types of distraction which causes accidents etc. (Fig. 4a).

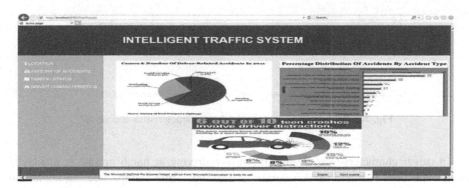

Fig. 4a. History of accidents

Ongoing to traffic status track the traffic from his location to his destination in our website itself (Fig. 4b).

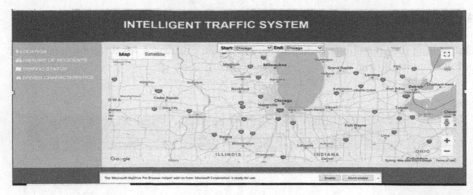

Fig. 4b. Traffic status

In driver characteristics, weather the driver driving at harsh or safe is displayed along with data (Vehicle Id, Acceleration, Braking, Time stamp, Steering angle and Driver characteristics) which has been taken as input (Fig. 4c).

```
</rdf:RDF>vehicle0
"4"
"normal"
"2019/04/02 11:26:02"
"right"
"16"
SAFE DRIVING
--------vehicle0, "4", "normal", "2019/04/02 11:26:02", "right", "16",SAFE DRIVING
vehicle1
"3"
"normal"
"2019/04/02 11:26:02"
"hard left"
"46"
SAFE DRIVING
--------vehicle1, "3", "normal", "2019/04/02 11:26:02", "hard left", "46",SAFE DRIVING
vehicle2
"0"
"harsh"
"2019/04/02 11:26:02"
"straight"
"76"
SAFE DRIVING
--------vehicle2, "0", "harsh", "2019/04/02 11:26:02", "straight", "76",SAFE DRIVING
vehicle3
"4"
"normal"
"2019/04/02 11:26:02"
"left"
"79"
SAFE DRIVING
--------vehicle3, "4", "normal", "2019/04/02 11:26:02", "left", "79",SAFE DRIVING
vehicle4
```

Fig. 4c. Sample of prediction of driver characteristics at time t0

In driver characteristics, weather the driver driving at harsh or safe is displayed along with data (Vehicle Id, Acceleration, Braking, Time stamp, Steering angle and Driver characteristics) which has been taken as input (Fig. 4d).

```
--------vehicle15, "1", "harsh", "2019/04/02 11:26:02", "hard left", "13",HARSH DRIVING
vehicle16
"4"
"harsh"
"2019/04/02 11:26:02"
"straight"
"56"
SAFE DRIVING
--------vehicle16, "4", "harsh", "2019/04/02 11:26:02", "straight", "56",SAFE DRIVING
vehicle17
"3"
"harsh"
"2019/04/02 11:26:02"
"straight"
"23"
SAFE DRIVING
--------vehicle17, "3", "harsh", "2019/04/02 11:26:02", "straight", "23",SAFE DRIVING
vehicle18
"3"
"harsh"
"2019/04/02 11:26:02"
"left"
"37"
SAFE DRIVING
--------vehicle18, "3", "harsh", "2019/04/02 11:26:02", "left", "37",SAFE DRIVING
vehicle19
"1"
"normal"
"2019/04/02 11:26:02"
"left"
"36"
SAFE DRIVING
--------vehicle19, "1", "normal", "2019/04/02 11:26:02", "left", "36",SAFE DRIVING
```

Fig. 4d. Sample of prediction of driver characteristics at time t1

5 Conclusion

A prototypical semantic based driver deeds prophecy to prevent accidents using intelligent techniques as designed in this work. The application can be used for any type of vehicles (cars, buses, motor cycles etc.). The track genie web was referred for simulating data sets and implementing the concepts The system perform in two ways one to give alertness to the driver and make him to be conscious by means of the semantic mapping results display based the data gathered relevant to the vehicle running mode, driver character and the relevant road he is driving and phase two as automation in avoidance of accidents using intelligent techniques based on the data gathered and in addition sensors were provided to monitor climate conditions to avoid traffic. The system will be much support for the real time road scenarios nowadays if implemented. But presently this approach was deployed in only high cost smart vehicles. The proposed prototype is suitable for non-fuel vehicles too i.e., battery mode vehicles utilized as intra travel with in the specified distance. Thus the work is concluded automation to be deployed at minimum cost for normal vehicles too by considering the fact life is more important than money. Whenever the users increase we can get the better results. The speed of vehicle is categorized as 1. *high speed (>80)*, 2. *moderate speed (>40 and <80) and* 3. *Lowspeed <40)*. Different types of steering angle data as hard right, right, straight, left, hard left and the braking of the vehicle is observed similarly in braking the data as harsh and the normal. Some of the conditions were classified the driver too harsh as follows i) when the driver drives vehicle with high speed, braking with harsh and the steering angle as left to hard right or hard left to right or straight or left to hard right or right to hard left then the driver as a harsh. ii) Similarly if the vehicle speed is high, braking is normal and the steering angle is left to hard right or right to hard left the driver as a harsh and if the vehicle speed is moderate and the braking as harsh and steering angle as left to hard right and right to hard left also we are classifying the driver as a harsh. iii) If the vehicle speed is normal, braking as harsh and the steering angle data as right to hard left or left to hard right we are classifying the driver as harsh. Similarly we are classifying the driver to safe when the harsh condition doesn't happen. After getting the result from the server it will show the result in the web page as vehicle data with the corresponding driver characteristic (Vehicle Id, Acceleration, Braking, Time stamp, Steering angle and Driver characteristics).

References

1. Ji, Q., Zhu, Z., Lan, P.: Real-time Nonintrusive monitoring and prediction of driver fatigue. IEEE Trans. Veh. Technol. **53**, 1052–1106 (2004)
2. Al-Sultan, S., Al-Bayatti, A.H., Zedan, H.: Context-aware driver behavior detection system in intelligent transportation systems. IEEE Trans. Veh. Technol. **62**(9), 4264–4275 (2013). https://doi.org/10.1109/TVT.2013.2263400
3. Kumar, P., Singh, M.P., Singh, J.P.: Driver alert system for accident avoidance by Nidhi Sinha. In: 2015 5th International Conference on Communication Systems and Network Technologies (2015)
4. Hankey, J.M., Dingus, T.: The Development of Design Evaluation Tool and Model of Attention Demand. Virginia Tech Transportation Institute Monk C.A (Science Applications International Corporation) (2000)
5. Chen, Z., Wu, C., Zhong, M., Lyu, N., Huang, Z.: Identification of common features of vehicle motion under drowsy/distracted driving: a case study in Wuhan China. Accid. Anal. Prev. **81**, 251–259 (2015)
6. Sahayadhas, A., Sundaraj, K., Murugappan, M.: Detecting driver drowsiness based on sensors: a review. Sensors **12**, 16937–16953 (2012)
7. Goswami, T.D., Zanwar, S.R., Hasan, Z.U.: Android based rush and drunk driver alerting system. Int. J. Eng. Res. Appl. **4**(2), 50–53 (2014). ISSN 2248-9622
8. Mandalia, H.M., Salvucci, D.D.: Using support vector machines for lane change detection. Proc. Hum. Factors Ergon. Soc. Annual Meet. **49**, 1965–1969 (2015). 49th Annual Meeting
9. Kumar, P., Perrollaz, M., Lefvre, S., Laugier, C.: Learning-based approach for online lane change intention prediction. In: 2013 IEEE Intelligent Vehicles Symposium (IV), June 2013, pp. 797–802 (2013)
10. Liebner, M., Baumann, M., Klanner, F., Stiller, C.: Driver intent inference at urban intersections using the intelligent driver model. In: 2012 IEEE Intelligent Vehicles Symposium (IV), June 2012, pp. 1162–1167 (2012)
11. Shalev-Shwartz, S., Shammah, S., Shashua, A.: On a formal model of safe and scalable self-driving cars. arXiv:1708.06374 (2017)
12. Hoermann, S., Stumper, D., Dietmayer, K.: Probabilistic long-term prediction for autonomous vehicles. In: 2017 IEEE Intelligent Vehicles Symposium (IV), June 2017 (2017)
13. Sun, J., Zhang, Y., He, K.: Providing context-awareness in the smart car environment. In: Proceedings of the IEEE CIT, July 2010, pp. 13–19 (2010)
14. Singh, H., Bhatia, J.S., Kaur, J.: Eye tracking based driver fatigue monitoring and warning system. In: Proceedings of the IEEE IICPE, January 2011, pp. 1–6 (2011)
15. Sakairi, M., Togami, M.: Use of water cluster detector for preventing drunk and drowsy driving. In: Proceedings of the IEEE Sensors, November 2010, pp. 141–144 (2010)
16. Dai, J., Teng, J., Bai, X., Shen, Z., Xuan, D.: Mobile phone based drunk driving detection. In: Proceedings of the Pervasive Health, March 2010, pp. 1–8 (2010)
17. Bar, T., Nienhuser, D., Kohlhaas, R., Zollner, J.M.: Probabilistic driving style determination by means of a situation based analysis of the vehicle data. In: Proceedings of the IEEE ITSC, October 2011, pp. 1698–1703 (2011)
18. Daza, I., et al.: Drowsiness monitoring based on driver and driving data fusion. In: Proceedings of the IEEE ITSC, October 2011, pp. 1199–1204 (2011)
19. Qing, W., WeiWei, Y.: A driver abnormality recondition model based on dynamic Bayesian network for ubiquitous computing. In: Proceeding of the ICACTE, August 2010, vol. 1, pp. 320–324 (2010)
20. Imamura, T., Yamashita, H., Zhang, Z., Bin Othman, M.R., Miyake, T.: A study of classification for driver conditions using driving behaviors. In: Proceedings of the IEEE SMC, October 2008, pp. 1506–1511 (2008)

21. Jiang, S., Hagelien, T.F., Natvig, M., Li, J.: Ontology-based semantic search for open government data. In: 2019 IEEE 13th International Conference on Semantic Computing (ICSC) (2019)
22. Park, S.H., Ha, Y.G.: Large imbalance data classification based on MapReduce for traffic accident prediction, 8 December 2014
23. Birek, L., Grzywaczewski, A., Iqbal, R., Doctor, F., Chang, V.: A novel Big Data analytics and intelligent technique to predict driver's intent. Comput. Ind. **99**, 226–240 (2018). https://doi.org/10.1016/j.compind.2018.03.025
24. Nagy, A., Tick, J.: Improving traffic management with big data analytics, 20 October 2016
25. Basso, F., Basso, L.J., Bravo, F., Pezoa, R.: Real-time crash prediction in an urban expressway using disaggregated data. Transp. Res. Part C Emerg. Technol. **86**, 202–219 (2018)

Driver Pattern Recognition System

Shreya Raut[✉], K. J. Vivek, Omkar Joshi, and M. Arun

Vellore Institute of Technology, Vellore, India

Abstract. The safety of vehicles is influenced by several parameters, particularly drivers, vehicles, and road conditions. The relationships between them are fairly complex. Consequently, existing methods that analyze driving safety and driving pattern uses image processing which might invade the privacy of the individual in vehicle.

This paper focuses on the detection of correctness of driving style of an individual using decision tree algorithm, where the decision is made based on the three sensor inputs monitoring different behavior of the driver. The model predicts human driving behaviors and distinguishes among various driving behavior i.e., to classify the steering behavior. In accordance with this, different types of steering behavior, variable steering angle ratio of steer-by-wire vehicle was designed to meet the requirements of different driving habits, also find out whether the driver is driving safely by placing his hands-on steering with proper posture on seat. The algorithms used were ID3 and C4.5 for determining driver state which gave an accuracy of 95 and 96% respectively.

Keywords: Decision tree · ID3 · C4.5 · Steer-by-wire · Hands-on-wheel · Pattern recognition

1 Introduction

The safety of people in vehicle is influenced by several parameters, particularly driver, vehicle, and road conditions. Most of the accidents happen due to driver; not having a steady hand, improper grip on the steering wheel, or by chance if he/she falls asleep. Also, with increasing popularity of ADAS systems on vehicles, the steering performance by driver of the vehicle put forward higher prerequisites. Thus, the steer-by-wire technology, Hands-on-wheel is becoming particularly important.

Among various parameters involved in protection of vehicle, our project focuses only on driver's pattern for recognition. Sensors involved in the same are used for (i) Capacitive sensor for detecting Hand on Wheel. (ii) Resistive pressure sensor for detecting any driver posture. (iii) Angle of steering is acquired using hall sensor for obtaining under-steer or over-steer.

The data received from the sensor is fed to decision tree for detecting driver's state or pattern. The decision tree is formed using C4.5 and ID3 algorithm which gave us an accuracy of more than 95.

Supported by Vellore Institute of Technology, Vellore.

V. Arunachalam and K. Sivasankaran (Eds.): ICMDCS 2021, CCIS 1392, pp. 134–148, 2021.
https://doi.org/10.1007/978-981-16-5048-2_11

2   Background

2.1   Hands-on-Wheel (HoW) Detection

Fujikura has been developing a system that recognizes the driver's grasp on the steering wheel. This product weighs the change in capacitance between the human body and the electrodes set on a steering wheel, and the circuit translates the capacitance value to a voltage value. Based on the analysis results of the voltage values by the micro-controller, the system determines the state of driver's grasp and transmits the results to a higher system (Fig. 1) [1].

IEE has developed a capacitive sensing device that integrates into the steering wheel to track if the driver's hand is actually on the steering wheel. For today's driver assistance systems, this is vital knowledge, since the driving remains with the driver and the hands have to stay on the steering wheel. With autonomous driving in mind, if the certain conditions are met, the vehicle can take over the driving control and the driver can take his hands off the steering wheel.

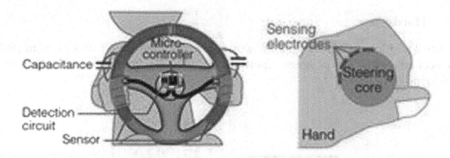

Fig. 1. Sensor model to detect grip and Hand gripping.   (Source: Sensor System to Detect Driver's Grip on Steering Wheel, Automotive Module Engineering Division)

2.2   Steer-by-Wire (SbW)

The steering sensor (Hall-sensor) is designed to interpret what the driver is choosing to do to the vehicle and pass the message down to the controller. Similarly, there is another sensor at rotor that reads feedback information that is sent back to controller. For instance, the controller will determine how much angle change is felt on the wheel or what kind of responses should be experienced to the driver. In short, the controller will sort out the information that as desired or not [2,3].

2.3   Pattern Recognition

The fundamental concept is to extract trends from the measurements of the actions of the driver and the vehicle response that represent the driving ability level of the driver. The experimental results indicate the feasibility of using a pattern-recognition technique to classify the handling capacity of a driver. This project ends with discussions of the problems and possible work to allow realistic use of the proposed technique [6].

3   Methodology

The proposed method involves hardware and software, the former is used for collecting data from the sensors and analyzes the information obtained from respective sensor and classifies them as "proper-data" or "improper-data" and further sends the classified data to Decision tree for collective analysis of all sensor input and deciding the driver condition.

3.1   Hardware

Figure 2 and Fig. 3, former shows how actual implementation takes place in real life scenario while latter shows experimental setup for interfacing of sensors for collecting data.

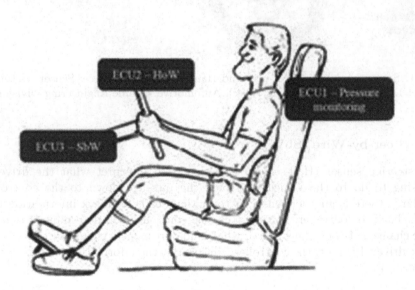

Fig. 2. Actual placement of ECU for monitoring

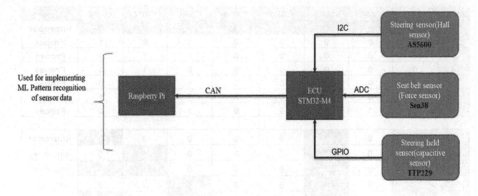

Fig. 3. Block diagram of experimental setup

The three sensors were used to collect data as follows:

1. **Capacitive sensor:** There are total of 8-capacitive sensor (Fig. 4) on the steering wheel which are used to determine the location of the hand. Since, there are 8 different sensors involved in determining, we created a truth-table which will enable us to understand how many input is "proper" and "improper", implying, no more than two input or no input should be received from the sensor, meaning, at any given time, only one or two hand can be placed on the steering wheel. Any input more than three will suggest us that, there might be a third person involved, who might've held the steering wheel by mistake or intentional and any input coming from such input should be discarded. If no input is received, naturally, there is no hand on the wheel, resulting in informing the system.

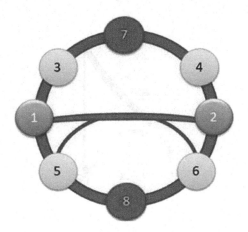

Fig. 4. Location of 8-capacitive sensor

Sl No	CAP1	CAP2	CAP3	CAP4	CAP5	CAP6	CAP7	CAP8	Output1
1	0	0	0	0	0	0	0	0	improper
2	0	0	0	0	0	0	0	1	Proper
3	0	0	0	0	0	0	1	0	Proper
4	0	0	0	0	0	0	1	1	Proper
5	0	0	0	0	0	1	0	0	Proper
6	0	0	0	0	0	1	0	1	Proper
7	0	0	0	0	0	1	1	0	Proper
162	1	0	1	0	0	0	0	1	improper
163	1	0	1	0	0	0	1	0	improper
164	1	0	1	0	0	0	1	1	improper
165	1	0	1	0	0	1	0	0	improper
166	1	0	1	0	0	1	0	1	improper
167	1	0	1	0	0	1	1	0	improper
168	1	0	1	0	0	1	1	1	improper
169	1	0	1	0	1	0	0	0	improper
254	1	1	1	1	1	1	0	1	improper
255	1	1	1	1	1	1	1	0	improper
256	1	1	1	1	1	1	1	1	improper

Fig. 5. Database of capacitive sensor

2. **Force sensor:** The Force sensor is used to measure the pressure applied on the seat belt. Figure 6 shows the arrangement of the seat belt in a vehicle. Figure 7 shows the placement of the sensor on the seat belt strap. The mentioned location is considered because when the driver inclines towards the wheel, there is an increase in the pressure on the strap near waist, as shown in Fig. 8.

Fig. 6. Seat belt design setup

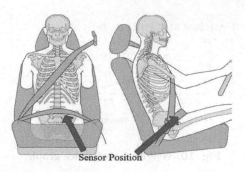

Fig. 7. Normal position of driver and sensor position indicated using arrow

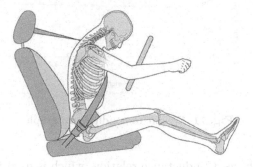

Fig. 8. Improper position of the driver due to inclination towards steering wheel

We created a database for determining standard force to weight on the seat belt. The sensor values collected are analog which are converted to digital with a resolution of 12-bit (Eq. 1)

$$Vout = \frac{3ADC}{2^n} \qquad (1)$$

Initial calibration needs to be done. The calibration is achieved by determining the resistance from change in the weight on the sensor, the resistance is measured using multi-meter. Figure 9 and Fig. 10 show the change in resistance with variation in weight.

Caliberation		
Weight(Kg)	Resistance(kOhm)	Conductance(mS)
0	100	0.01
0.01	40	0.025
0.1	16	0.0625
1	11	0.09091
10	10.25	0.09756

Fig. 9. Calibrations data

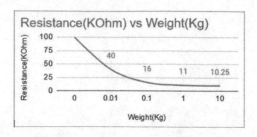

Fig. 10. Weight to resistance graph

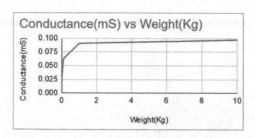

Fig. 11. Weight to conductance graph

Figure 11, Weight vs. Conductance relation, which is used to calculate slope. The Slope obtained from above calculation was 0.005733. Next, the conductance for different voltage output, needs to be found, which is calculated using formula (Eq. 2)

$$G = \frac{Vout}{10(6 - Vout)} \tag{2}$$

$$Flb = \frac{G}{S} \tag{3}$$

Using the output of conductance obtained from Eq. 2 and slope, Eq. 3 allows us to find the relationship between force to voltage value. The following table shows the dataset created for weight ranging from 0–10 Kg (assumed).

3. **Vehicle Dynamics:** In this work we study steady-state cornering conditions of vehicle, without imposing other restrictive conditions. The cornering behaviour is used as responsiveness of a vehicle to driver input, or ease of control. Current system is open-loop system, meaning, the driver observes the vehicle direction and corrects his/her input accordingly to achieve desired motion. In order to measure the response from the driver (in an open loop system), we use under-steer gradient as a measure of performance under steady state condition. [9] At certain speed a car can physically take through a corner – trying and taking more than this will break traction, resulting in under-steering. Similarly, in case of oversteering.

ADC Value	Analog Value(V)	Sensor Conductance(mS)	Weight(Kg)	Output2
0	0	0	0	Improper
1	0.001220703125	0.000004329615348	0	Improper
2	0.00244140625	0.000008660993139	0.001	Improper
3	0.003662109375	0.00001299413445	0.001	Improper
4	0.0048828125	0.00001732904035	0.001	Improper
5	0.006103515625	0.00002166571193	0.002	Improper
6	0.00732421875	0.00002600415026	0.002	Improper
7	0.008544921875	0.00003034435643	0.002	Improper
8	0.009765625	0.0000346863315	0.003	Improper
9	0.01098632813	0.00003903007658	0.003	Improper
10	0.01220703125	0.00004337559273	0.003	Improper
11	0.01342773438	0.00004772288104	0.004	Improper
3149	3.843994141	0.03793454875	3.001	Proper
3150	3.845214844	0.03796809234	3.004	Proper
3151	3.846435547	0.03800167396	3.007	Proper
3152	3.84765625	0.03803529366	3.009	Proper
3153	3.848876953	0.03806895153	3.012	Proper
3154	3.850097656	0.03810264761	3.015	Proper
3155	3.851318359	0.03813638199	3.017	Proper
3156	3.852539063	0.03817015471	3.02	Proper
3157	3.853759766	0.03820396585	3.023	Proper
3158	3.854980469	0.03823781548	3.025	Proper
3159	3.856201172	0.03827170365	3.028	Proper
3160	3.857421875	0.03830563044	3.031	Proper
4089	4.991455078	0.1053013798	8.331	Improper
4090	4.992675781	0.1054547705	8.343	Improper
4091	4.993896484	0.1056085334	8.355	Improper
4092	4.995117188	0.1057626698	8.367	Improper
4093	4.996337891	0.1059171812	8.38	Improper
4094	4.997558594	0.1060720689	8.392	Improper
4095	4.998779297	0.1062273343	8.404	Improper

Fig. 12. Database of force sensor

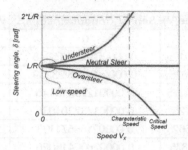

Fig. 13. Change of steer angle with speed (source: IIT Hyderabad)

Figure 13, shows with under-steer, angle increases as a square of speed, reaching twice the initial angle. In case of over steering, the steering angle decreases twice that of speed and reach zero. In simple words, there is an optimum angle range for a given speed, which is to be maintained, any deviation from range, might result in under steering or over steering. Since, the gradient value changes according to speed. In our study, we have assumed certain condition for ease of showing the process and calculation, Fig. 14 shows the values assumed.

Radius of curvature of curve(R)	40 m
Wheel base(L)	2.35 m
Lateral Acceleration(m/s^2)	3.09 m/s^2
Speed(mps)	11.2 mps
Radius of curvature of curve	40 m

Fig. 14. Assumption (towards left direction)

Considering above assumptions, we calculate steady state cornering (k) using Eq. 4, which implies

(a) Neutral Steering

$$k = 0 \tag{4}$$

(b) Under Steering

$$k < 0 \tag{5}$$

(c) Over Steering

$$k > 0 \tag{6}$$

Similar to force sensor calculation for ADC values, we use Eq. 8 to find respective digital value for given angle. The Fig. 15 shows the digital value and gradient for given angle at fixed speed (assumed vales)

$$k = \frac{Steering angle - \frac{57.3*L}{R}}{Lateral Acceleration} \quad (7)$$

$$Steering angle = \frac{N}{4096} * 360 \quad (8)$$

$$Torque = \frac{pi * (R^4) * G}{2L} * (Twisting angle) \quad (9)$$

ADC Value	Angle	Torque	Result(k)	Output3(K)
0	0	0	-1.10	Incorrect
1	0.087890625	1.363183594	-1.10	Incorrect
2	0.17578125	2.726367188	-1.00	Incorrect
3	0.263671875	4.089550781	-1.00	Incorrect
4	0.3515625	5.452734375	-1.00	Incorrect
5	0.439453125	6.815917969	-0.90	Incorrect

34	2.98828125	46.34824219	-0.10	Correct
35	3.076171875	47.71142578	-0.10	Correct
36	3.1640625	49.07460938	-0.10	Correct
37	3.251953125	50.43779297	0.00	Correct
38	3.33984375	51.80097656	0.00	Correct
39	3.427734375	53.16416016	0.00	Correct
40	3.515625	54.52734375	0.00	Correct

127	11.16210938	173.1243164	2.50	Incorrect
128	11.25	174.4875	2.60	Incorrect
129	11.33789063	175.8506836	2.60	Incorrect
130	11.42578125	177.2138672	2.60	Incorrect
131	11.51367188	178.5770508	2.60	Incorrect
132	11.6015625	179.9402344	2.70	Incorrect

Fig. 15. Database of hall sensor

Figure 16 shows the actual experimental setup used to obtain result.

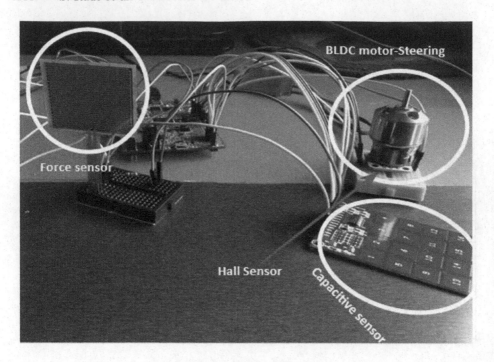

Fig. 16. Experimental setup

3.2   Software

The composition of the Decision Tree is as follows:

1. **Root Node:** The starting point of the tree is known as the Root Node. After root node, further nodes are split.
2. **Internal Nodes:** These node are decision taking nodes, with the help of which the nodes are split and also is predicting the outcome.
3. **Leaf/Terminal Nodes:** These nodes gives us the result of each classes.
4. **Branches:** It represents relations between the nodes. Every branch represents an answer like yes or no.

ID3 ALGORITHM: It's one of the algorithms used to construct a decision tree. The definition of Entropy and Information Gain is used to construct a decision tree. **Entropy:** This measures the impurity or uncertainty present in the data. Using the entropy value we divide the tree further into nodes.

$$ENTROPY = -\sum p(x) log p(x) \tag{10}$$

Information Gain: This feature helps us deciding the feature which most affects the Output the system.

$$Gain = entropy(parent) - [WeightedAverage] * entropy(children) \tag{11}$$

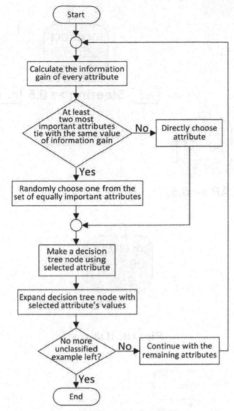

Flowchart of the traditional ID3 algorithm

Fig. 17. ID3 flowchart

Flowchart explanation:

1. Select most important attribute. (R)
2. For root node, assign the same as a decision variable.
3. For each value of R, build a descendant of the node.
4. Classification labels are assigned to leaf node.
5. For correctly classified data the iteration is stopped.
6. If the data is not classified correctly, it continues to iterate.

The accuracy of the ID3 ALGORITHM Tree is 95%.

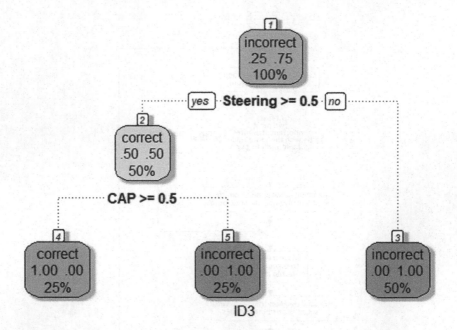

Fig. 18. ID3 tree

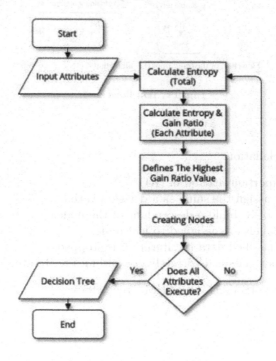

Fig. 19. C4.5 flowchart

C4.5 ALGORITHM: C4.5 is formed after pruning the formed tree by removing the branches of less importance and replacing them with leaf node. Pruning helps in faster decision making while considering all the important features.

As a rule of thumb, it is best to prune a decision tree using the smallest tree cp, which is within one standard deviation of the smallest xerror tree. The best xerror in this case is 0.6 with a standard deviation of 0.3561. So, we want the smallest tree with less than 0.3561 xerror. This is the tree with cp = 0.5, so we're going to prune our tree with a cp slightly larger than 0.5, i.e. cp = 0.52.

The accuracy of the C4.5 ALGORITHM Tree is 96%.

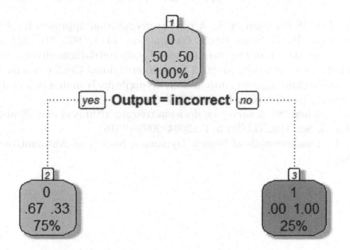

Fig. 20. C4.5 tree

4   Conclusion

In this paper we have proposed a system for predicting the condition of the driver by using data from three sensors: 1. Pressure Sensor: detects if there changes in movement of the driver, 2. Capacitive Sensor: detects the position of hands on steering wheel, 3. Hall sensor: implement steer by wire and detect whether it is under steer, over steer or neutral. The data collected from sensors was processed in STM32 and then sent to Raspberry Pi for prediction of the condition of the driver. The machine learning algorithm used was decision tree. Two algorithms were used for creation of decision: 1. ID3 and 2. C4.5 which uses Entropy and Information gain for classification. ID3 predicted the value after giving test set with 95 and C4.5 gave the result with 96% accuracy.

References

1. Fujikura Techincal Review No 47 November 2017: Sensor System to Detect Driver's Grip on Steering Wheel, Automotive Module Engineering Divison (2017)

2. Rodriguez, F., Uy, E.: Brushless DC motor drive for steer-by-wire and electric power steering applications. In: Proceedings: Electrical Insulation Conference and Electrical Manufacturing and Coil Winding Technology Conference (Cat. No.03CH37480). https://doi.org/10.1109/EICEMC.2003.1247944
3. Fleming, W.J.: Overview of automotive sensors. IEEE Sens. J. 1(4) (2001) https://doi.org/10.1109/7361.983469
4. Gowda, N., Darshan, M.S., Karthik, P.H.: Potentiometer Operated Steering. Imperial J. Interdiscip. Res. (IJIR) 3(4), 628 (2017), ISSN: 2454–1362
5. Mühlbacher-Karrer, S., Faller, L., Hamid, R., Zangl, H.: A wireless steering wheel gripping sensor for hands on, off detection. In: IEEE Sensors Applications Symposium (SAS), Catania, vol. 2016, pp. 1–5 (2016). https://doi.org/10.1109/SAS.2016.7479878
6. Zhang, Y., Lin, W.C., Chin, Y.S.: A pattern-recognition approach for driving skill characterization. IEEE Trans. Intell. Transp. Syst. 11(4), 905–916 (2010)
7. Liying, W.: The design of the steering wheel with antifatigue driving for vehicles based on pattern recognition. In: 2012 Fifth International Conference on Intelligent Computation Technology and Automation, Zhangjiajie, Hunan, pp. 340–343 (2012). https://doi.org/10.1109/ICICTA.2012.91
8. Sharma, H., Kumar, S.: A survey on decision tree algorithms of classification in data mining. Int. J. Sci. Res. (IJSR) 5(4), 2094–2097 (2016)
9. Gillespie, T.: Fundamentals of Vehicle Dynamics. Society of Automotive Engineers Inc. (1992)

Fingerprint Integrated E-Health Monitoring System Using IoT

N. Keerthana[✉], K. Lokeshwaran, P. S. Kavinkumar, T. Kaviyan, M. Manimaran, and S. Elango

Department of Electronics and Communication Engineering,
Bannari Amman Institute of Technology, Sathyamangalam, Erode 638 401, Tamil Nadu, India
keerthanan.ec18@bitsathy.ac.in

Abstract. Health has the foremost importance in our daily life. For the past few decades, people are getting infected with an increased number of diseases due to improper health care. Health care is prominent for every being to lead a successful life. Health monitoring concepts are acquainted with developed and developing countries. Health monitoring using IoT helps people by providing smart, reliable health care services. This framework monitors the patient's body temperature, heartbeat rate, and blood oxygen level with different sensors. Transmission of information from a body sensor is stored in the cloud using Node MCU and converts data into readable signals with proper security measures. This information's are sent as a message to the doctor and guardian of the patient. This system is beneficial for elderly and bedridden patients to monitor their health condition properly.

Keywords: Internet of Things (IoT) · Sensor system · Cloud · E-health monitoring

1 Introduction

Health is said to be the state of physical, mental and social well-being. But recently, we are facing many health issues due to improper health care, inadequate services. Nowadays, medical sensors play an essential role in an E-Health monitoring system and promote innovative research and invention. People use a thermometer to check the home temperature and take some precautions before consulting the doctor [1]. E-Health monitoring using IoT helps us find the patient's health condition in the house and informs the doctor through message for better medical care at the earliest. In the existing model, Arduino was used along with a Wi-Fi module to store the data in the cloud, and a GSM module is used to send message to the authorized person [8]. In the proposed model, the Infrared temperature sensor, MAX30102- Pulse oximeter and pulse rate sensor are used to measure the body temperature, blood oxygen level and heartbeat rate, respectively, with the help of LCD. The data are stored in the cloud via NodeMCU (ESP8266 Wi-Fi SOC), and the details are sent as a message to the doctor and guardian of the patient to ensure the earliest medical care [2].

© Springer Nature Singapore Pte Ltd. 2021
V. Arunachalam and K. Sivasankaran (Eds.): ICMDCS 2021, CCIS 1392, pp. 149–159, 2021.
https://doi.org/10.1007/978-981-16-5048-2_12

Internet of Things is a platform that connects everything embedded with sensors and software. The term 'things' in IoT represents everything we are accessing in our day to day life [3, 4]. It is working on many platforms. It is a technology which is increasing at present, and a lot of innovations are developed. In future, it will become a common platform where all things can connect. IoT has many features where the standard features are connectivity, analyzing, integrating, and artificial intelligence. In this work, the IoT concept is used to store the data in the cloud, examine with the base knowledge and send an alert message to the authorized persons. IoT applications include Machine to machine communication, Machine to infrastructure communication and Telehealth (i.e.) patient data monitoring, analyzing and predicting the disease at the earliest [5, 6].

In this work, the cheap and absolute system is proposed using ESP8266 and fingerprint sensor to ensure security. The objective of the work is to get real-time medical information of the patient via IoT. To ensure all sensors work concurrently and give the message to the authorized persons. As an outcome, Doctors can quickly diagnose and treat the disease or disorder in the preliminary stage by using advanced technologies. A physician can provide medical assistance for the minor illness based on the data received from the health monitoring system messages anywhere [7, 9].

The rest of the works as follows, related work in Sect. 2, tell the health monitoring system's recent development. Section 3 discusses the proposed methodology, followed by the hardware description. Working and Implementation of the proposed model is discussed in Sect. 4 and 5, respectively. The conclusion is given in Sect. 6.

2   Related Work

Many works have been done in the field of health monitoring with the help of the IoT system. Here some works in the field of E-health are discussed. The patient monitoring system monitors the basic health parameters like temperature, pulse rate, blood pressure, and ECG. For this temperature, heartbeat, ECG sensors are used withSST89E516RD2, which acts as a microcontroller, and a Wi-Fi module is used for data transmission. GSM is used to send the alert note [1]. In [2], implemented the health monitoring system that monitors the patient's temperature and pulse rate with an Arduino Microcontroller's help. These data are stored in the cloud for future purpose. These details are displayed on LCD.

The patient monitoring system using IoT with the help of temperature, BP, heartbeat and vibration sensors to monitor the temperature, blood pressure, pulse rate, and body movements of the patient, respectively, is designed [3]. In this, the health details are sent to the doctor with the help of the GSM module. In [6], the authors have developed a telehealth application that monitors the health condition and provides chronic diseases' workout recommendations. In [7] intended a smart healthcare monitoring system sed in the hospitals to monitor the patients' health parameters like heartbeat rate. This setup is done to monitor the patient's health condition and environmental conditions like room temperature, co and co2 level in the ambient.

3   Proposed Methodology

Designing of Health monitoring system is a challenging task for every researchers, engineers, and student. A Health monitoring system is Portable and widely used in areas like homes, hospitals, sports etc. They are designed based on the needs of the user. The model is created using Node MCU (ESP8266), which is used primarily for IoT based projects because it is open-source software that includes firmware that runs on ESP8266 Wi-Fi Soc. The biomedical sensors are integrated with the microcontroller to give accurate and reliable data for monitoring health care, as shown in Fig. 1. The health parameters like temperature, blood oxygen level and pulse rate are monitored by the Infrared Temperature sensor and Pulse oximeter sensor. The sensor data are transmitted to the cloud via NodeMCU, where they are processed, analyzed, and compared with the data provided earlier. Once the data is verified, the alert message will be sent to the doctor and the patient's guardian. Patient's data will be used by stored in the cloud, and doctors can provide medical assistance based on the previous reports. The data of the patients are protected with the help of the fingerprint-based security system. This helps to avoid mismatching and loss of data. It also allows doctors to observe the patient with well-maintained data and provide proper medication at any time.

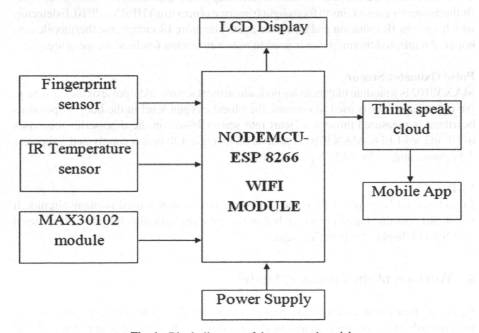

Fig. 1. Block diagram of the proposed model

Proposed Hardware Model Description

Node MCU:
In the proposed model, the biomedical sensors are connected to the NodeMCU ESP8266, a microcontroller that includes a Wi-Fi module. It makes it ease of transferring and storing the data to the cloud without external hardware assistances. Then the data are processed in the cloud, and the alert messages are sent to the mobile. NodeMCU is an open-source, bank card sized microcontroller (Ten silica 32-bit RISC CPU Xtensa LX106) mainly used for IoT based applications. It includes Lua based firmware, runs on ESP8266 Wi-Fi SOC and hardware is based on ESP -12 modules with an operating voltage of 3.3v.

Fingerprint Sensor
R305 is an optical biometric fingerprint sensor module that is small in size with low power consumption and excellent performance. The Features of the Fingerprint module are as follows, and it holds the capacity to store 980 fingerprints. It has a lifetime of 100 million times, and its matching method is based on the ratio of 1:1 and 1:N.

Infrared Temperature Sensor
The infrared temperature sensor senses electromagnetic waves from 700 nm to 14000 nm. IR thermometer uses a Lens to focus light from one object to a THERMOPHILE detector, which absorbs IR radiation and turns into heat. The more IR energy, the thermopile gets hotter. An infrared thermometer is used to measure human forehead temperature.

Pulse Oximeter Sensor
MAX30102 is a module that includes both a heartbeat sensor and a pulse oximeter sensor. An oximeter sensor is used to measure the blood oxygen level in the body. A person's heartbeat is measured through a Heart rate sensor based on the time-series responses of IR and red LEDs. MAX30102 operates on a single 1.8vpower supply and a separate 3.3v power supply for LED'S present inside.

LCD:
Liquid Crystal Display (LCD) is the displaying device that is used in many circuits. It is flat and contains liquid crystal cells that do not emit light directly; instead, it uses a backlight to display the panel's image.

4 Working of the Proposed Model

Figure 2 shows how to extort the patient's medical data from different sensors that continuously monitor the patient's health condition. Then the data are stored in the cloud and analyzed with the knowledge base. Later the message is sent to the authorized persons.

Working of the System
The proposed idea comprises the three stages shown in Fig. 3, which explains the model's complete working.

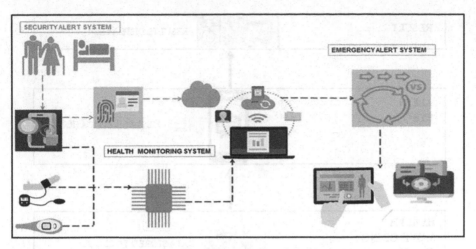

Fig. 2. Proposed model

- Security Alert System
- Health Monitoring System
- Emergency Alert System

4.1 Security Alert System

In this system, every patient is given a unique id and biometrics; medical details are added to the cloud at registration. Once the patient keeps his biometric, his /her details will be shown, and the cloud will allocate the space for data storage.

4.2 Health Monitoring System

In this system, various health parameters like temperature, blood oxygen level and heartbeat rate are monitored using biomedical sensors like Infrared temperature sensor, MAX30102 Pulse oximetry and pulse rate sensor. The data is sent to the cloud with the help of the microcontroller. These data are stored in the memory allocated.

4.3 Emergency Alert System

In this system, the patient's data is compared with the knowledge base, which is already provided, shown in Table 1. If the data are normal, it sends the message "NORMAL" to the authorized person. If the values are mismatched, it will send a notification "AB-NORMAL" to the authorized person and seek a medical emergency. This will also help the doctors predict the disorder in the preliminary stage and quickly diagnose them with advanced technologies like data mining.

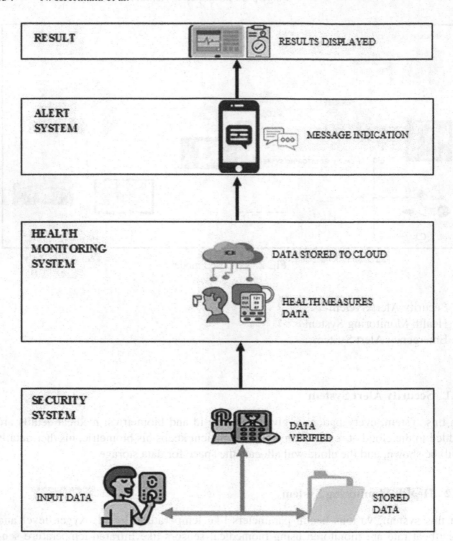

Fig. 3. System-level stages of the proposed model

Table 1. Threshold values

Components	Normal range
Infrared temperature sensor	36.5–37.5 °C/97.7–99.5 °F
Blood oxygen level	95–100%
Pulse rate sensor	60–100 beats/minute

5 Implementation

In this project, the fingerprint sensor is used to get the patient details with the unique id for maintenance and security. Once the fingerprint of a person is verified and matched with the cloud's data, the IR temperature sensor placed above the fingerprint module detects the person's temperature. The health monitoring system monitored the heartbeat rate, the patient's blood oxygen level with sensors' help and placed on the patient's body. This sensor sends the data to the cloud using NodeMCU which act as a controller cum Wi-Fi module. The data are stored and processed with the knowledge base and sends an intimation message to the authorized person, as shown in Fig. 3. As the name "E-Health Monitoring system using IoT" implies that health is monitored automatically with biomedical sensors, IoT and microcontroller. The result of the proposed system shown in Figs. 7 and 8 will significantly help the doctors and patients observe keenly. This will help the patients take care of their health correctly with less expense to hospitals. Doctors can quickly identify and maintain the patient's records to monitor their health condition and give them better medical assistance in all situations. The proposed system is modest, easy to understand, and constructs the doctors and patients' bond for a better life.

The system's working explained in Fig. 4, and the corresponding sample test case in Table 2 helps us understand the proposed model's functioning. After the verification of fingerprint for security, the cloud allocates the storage memory and monitors the patients' health parameters. These data are sent to the cloud and analyzed with the base data, and then an alert message is sent. If all the values, i.e. temperature, blood oxygen level and pulse rate, match the base data, then the message will be 'All the values are Normal'. If the values are mismatched, then the alert message will be 'All the values are Abnormal'. In some cases, if any one of the three values is mismatched, then the alert will be 'Abnormal value of the particular parameter'. This system provides the plot of the health parameters in a detailed manner shown in Fig. 5. Test sample of a single patient is given in Table 3 shows the detailed view on actual value and the observed value of the patient health parameter with a plot in Fig. 6.

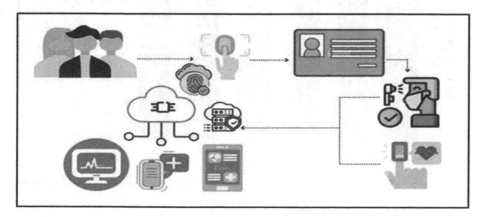

Fig. 4. Implementation of the system

Table 2. Test samples

Patent	Temperature (°F)	Blood oxygen level (%)	Pulse rate (Beats/Minute)	Message
1.	98	96	70	All values are Normal
2.	100	98	80	Abnormal value of Temperature
3.	99	90	70	Abnormal value of blood oxygen level
4.	99.9	80	50	All values are abnormal
5.	99.1	99	65	All values are normal
6.	101	96	85	Abnormal value of temperature

Table 3. A test sample of a single patient

Health parameters	Actual value	Obtained value
Temperature	97.7–99.5	101
Blood oxygen	90–100	85
Pulse rate	60–100	80

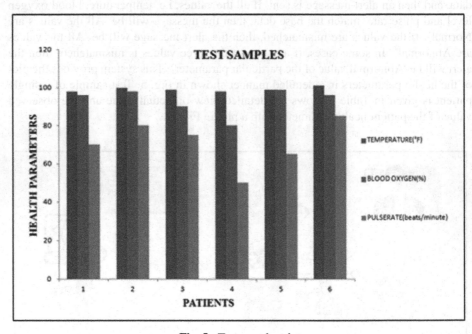

Fig. 5. Test samples plot

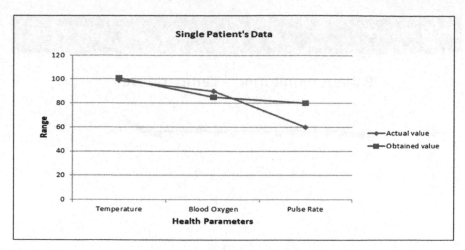

Fig. 6. Sample plot of single patient

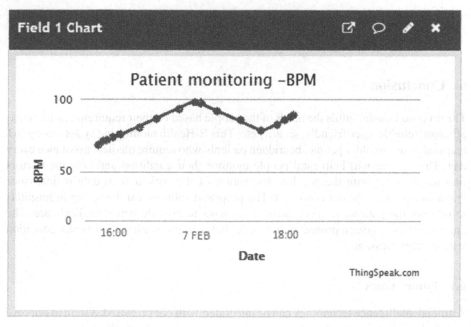

Fig. 7. Sample result of the proposed model (BPM)

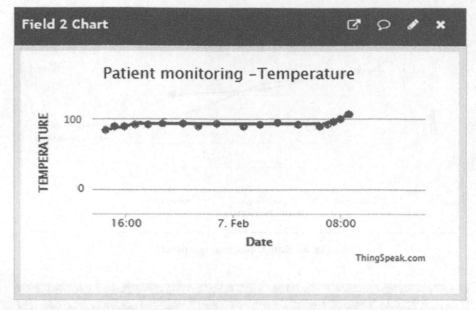

Fig. 8. Sample result of the proposed model (temperature)

6 Conclusion

The proposed model fulfils the needs of the people based on their requirements like cost-efficient, reliable, user-friendly, security etc. This E-Health monitoring system using IoT helps take care of older people, bedridden patients who require medical assistance every day. This system will help rural people monitor their condition and help the doctors find the disorder with the regular observation of the patient with data maintenance and analysis of the health condition. The proposed solution can be set up in hospitals to monitor the patients in more massive amounts to provide better medical care. The emergency alert system present in the model helps users monitor their health condition with an alert message.

6.1 Future Work

Artificial intelligence technology can be integrated with our proposed system to improve the work of the system. Data mining will help to explore the medical details of many patients. This will work on patterns and allows doctors to analyze the patient's reports and give them the proper medical assistance at an appropriate time.

References

1. Surekha, N., Yamuna, N., Kumar, J.A., Kumar, K.G.N., Kaushal, R.K.: Patient monitoring system using IOT. Int. J. Innov. Res. Adv. Eng. (IJIRAE) **5**, 176–182 (2018)

2. Patil, S., Pardeshi, S.: Health monitoring system using IOT. InT. Res. J. Eng. Technol. (IRJET) **5**(4), 1678–1682 (2018)
3. Banka, S., Madan, I., Saranya, S.S.: Smart health monitoring using IOT. Int. J. Appl. Eng. Res. **13**, 15, 11984–11989 (2018)
4. Neyja, M., Mumtaz, S., Huq, K.M.S., Busari, S.A., Rodriguez, J., Zhou, Z.: An IoT-based e-health monitoring system using ECG signal. In: GLOBECOM 2017 - IEEE Global Communications Conference, Singapore, pp. 1–6 (2017). https://doi.org/10.1109/GLOCOM.2017. 8255023
5. Godi, B., Viswanadham, S., Muttipati, A.S., Samantray, O.P., Gadiraju, S.R.: E-healthcare monitoring system using IoT with machine learning approaches. In: 2020 International Conference on Computer Science, Engineering and Applications (ICCSEA), India, pp. 1–5 (2020). DOI: https://doi.org/10.1109/ICCSEA49143.2020.9132937.
6. Gomez, O., Oviedo, B., Zhuma, E.: Patient monitoring system based on internet of things. Procedia Comput. Sci. **83**, 90–97 (2016). ISSN 1877–0509
7. Islam, M.M., Rahaman, A., Islam, M.R.: Development of smart healthcare monitoring system in IoT environment. Springer Nature Singapore Pte Ltd., 26 May 2020. https://doi.org/10.1007/ s42979-020-00195-y
8. Valsalan, P., Baomar, T.A.B., Baabood, A.H.O.: IoT based health monitoring system. J. Crit. Rev. **7**(4) (2020). ISSN-2394-5125
9. Sathya, M., Madhan, S., Jayanthi, K.: IoT based health monitoring system and challenges. Int. J. Eng. Technol. **7**(1.7), 175–178 (2018)

Intelligent Control of Aerator and Water Pump in Aquaculture Using Fuzzy Logic

Sudheer Kumar Nagothu(✉) 🄳

RVR & JC College of Engineering, Chowdavram, Guntur 522019, Andhra Pradesh, India
nsudheerkumar@rvrjc.ac.in

Abstract. Indian farmers are in search of various options to increase their income, Fish farming is one among them. In fish farming, water quality management is a very important criterion for the optimum growth and survival of the fish. The fitness and suitability parameters of water are used to define the quality of water for the optimal growth of fish. In the current paper, three parameters such as salinity, dissolved oxygen, and temperature of the water are considered and when these parameters value varies from their optimal range, corrective actions such as adding freshwater and rotation of aerator are discussed. A fuzzy logic technique is implemented to decide the status of fresh water pump and aerator by considering the input parameters salinity, temperature, and dissolved oxygen.

Keywords: Fuzzy logic · Smart aquaculture · Fish farming

1 Introduction

In the recent years production in aquaculture has increased tremendously. Species such as shrimp and fish are grown in the Ponds due to their good price and export income [1]. In fish farming various parameters are considered such as preparation of the pond, providing Bio security, maintaining the proper stocking density, feeding of fish, exchange of water, treatment for water and soil, harvesting and marketing, labor management etc. [2, 3]. Water quality management is a major issue in fish farming which creates a proper environment for the growth of fish. In this paper we are mainly concentrating on the water quality parameters such as salinity, Dissolved Oxygen and temperature [4]. They are measured daily with the help of various sensors. As the water quality parameters tend to change throughout the day, it will be better practice to measure them at fixed time on each day [5]. The measured parameters can be to the farmer app using Internet of Things, that can be monitored by the farmer [6–8]. By monitoring the real-time data of water in aquaculture, using IoT, it will be easy to maintain an optimum environment for the proper growth of the fish [9, 10]. The data can be collected using controllers such as Arduino or Raspberry Pi and corrective actions can be taken which can also be sent to the individual mobile app [11, 12, 14].

V. Arunachalam and K. Sivasankaran (Eds.): ICMDCS 2021, CCIS 1392, pp. 160–171, 2021.
https://doi.org/10.1007/978-981-16-5048-2_13

2   Materials and Methods

A fuzzy logic controller of MATLAB is used to evaluate the performance of the smart aquaculture fuzzy inference system. Stand-alone applications can be developed using the fuzzy inference engine toolbox. The initial step in a fuzzy inference system is input and output fuzzification using the membership function. In the current research paper, the trapezoidal membership function is used for the input parameters temperature, Dissolved Oxygen, and salinity. The output parameters motor pump and an Aerator has two conditions on and off. The fuzzy rule base is used in the fuzzy inference system to provide the state of output parameters. The Fuzzy inference system for smart aquaculture is shown in Fig. 1.

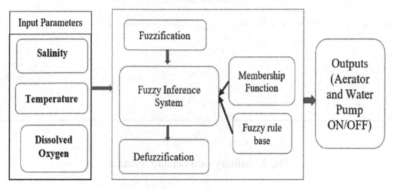

Fig. 1. Fuzzy inference system

2.1   Categorizations of Input and Output Parameters

To maintain water quality to an optimum level for the proper growth of fish, it is necessary to continuously monitor the parameters such as salinity, dissolved oxygen, and temperature. The input parameters are defined using Trapezoidal membership functions as they are easy to implement and computation also will be faster.

2.1.1   Salinity

Variation of salinity can be tolerated in younger fish but not in adults. The unit for salinity is ppt which stands for parts per thousand. Many species can tolerate the variations of salinity such that the normal range for salinity can vary from 7 to 31 ppt. Due to hot weather, the water in ponds evaporates, so there is a possibility for an increase of salt concentration in the pond water. The increase in salinity will affect the growth of the fish. An increase in salinity can be neutralized by adding freshwater. Ranges and categories of salinity are given in Table 1, and they have been defined using trapezoidal membership functions as shown in Eq. 1–3. The membership function can be visualised in Fig. 2.

$$\text{Salinity}_{\text{low}}(x) = \begin{cases} 1, & x < 5 \\ \frac{10-x}{5}, & 5 \le x < 10 \end{cases} \quad (1)$$

$$\text{Salinity}_{\text{normal}}(x) = \begin{cases} \frac{x-5}{5}, & 5 < x < 10 \\ 1, & 10 < x < 25 \\ \frac{30-x}{5}, & 25 < x < 30 \end{cases} \quad (2)$$

$$\text{Salinity}_{\text{high}}(x) = \begin{cases} \frac{x-25}{5}, & 25 \le x \le 30 \\ 1, & x > 30 \end{cases} \quad (3)$$

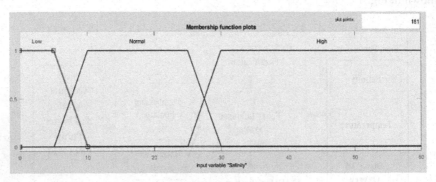

Fig. 2. Salinity membership function

2.1.2 Temperature

Growth and regular activities of fish or controlled by an important parameter known as temperature. The biological and chemical activities in fish will be increased by twice for every 10 °C addition in temperature. In other words, when the temperature is increasing from 30 °C to 40 °C the requirement of dissolved oxygen will be double at 40 °C compared to the 30 °C. Which gives a relationship between temperature and oxygen such that the requirement of DO is more in hot water compared to cool water. Ranges and categories of temperature are given in Table 2 and they have been defined using trapezoidal membership functions as shown in Eq. 4–6. The membership function can be visualised in Fig. 3. The normal range is around 26 °C to 31 °C. The temperature value can by varied using fresh water pump and aerator.

$$\text{Temp}_{\text{low}}(x) = \begin{cases} 1, & x < 20 \\ \frac{30-x}{10}, & 20 \le x < 30 \end{cases} \quad (4)$$

$$\text{Temp}_{\text{normal}}(x) = \begin{cases} \frac{x-20}{5}, & 20 < x < 25 \\ 1, & 25 < x < 30 \\ \frac{35-x}{5}, & 30 < x < 35 \end{cases} \quad (5)$$

$$\text{Temp}_{\text{high}}(x) = \begin{cases} \frac{x-30}{5}, & 30 \le x \le 35 \\ 1, & x > 35 \end{cases} \quad (6)$$

2.1.3 Dissolved Oxygen

Dissolved oxygen plays an active role in the optimal growth of fish. It has to be maintained at an adequate level. The optimal range of dissolved oxygen is between 4 and 7. Dissolved oxygen is measured in terms of parts per million (ppm). When dissolved oxygen is maintained at a low level the fish growth will be reduced and they will be exposed to two diseases. It even causes mortality issues in fish. The source for dissolved oxygen is photosynthesis and atmospheric air diffusion. The air from the atmosphere will be diffuse into the water using aerator. Various factors will affect the dissolved oxygen in water such as temperature, respiration, etc. Ranges and categories of Dissolved oxygen are given in Table 3 and they have been defined using trapezoidal membership functions as shown in Eq. 7–9. The membership function can be visualised in Fig. 4.

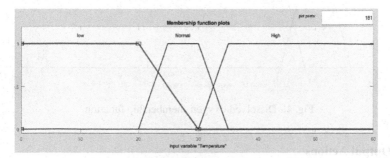

Fig. 3. Temperature membership function

$$DO_{low}(x) = \begin{cases} 1, & x < 2 \\ \frac{6-x}{4}, & 2 \leq x < 6 \end{cases} \tag{7}$$

$$DO_{normal}(x) = \begin{cases} \frac{x-2}{2}, & 2 < x < 4 \\ 1, & 4 < x < 6 \\ \frac{8-x}{2}, & 6 < x < 8 \end{cases} \tag{8}$$

$$DO_{high}(x) = \begin{cases} \frac{x-6}{2}, & 6 \leq x \leq 8 \\ 1, & x > 8 \end{cases} \tag{9}$$

Table 1. Ranges and categories of salinity (ppt)

Range	Category
(0–7)	Low
(7–31)	Medium
(>31)	High

Table 2. Ranges and categories of temperature (°C)

Range	category
(0–26)	Low
(26–31)	Normal
(31–50)	High

Table 3. Ranges and categories of DO (ppm)

Range	Category
(0–4)	Low
(4–7)	Medium
(7–20)	High

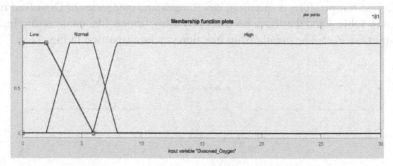

Fig. 4. Dissolved oxygen membership function

2.1.4 Output Actions

The corrective actions to maintain the water quality are to use a fresh water pump and the aerator pump. The freshwater can increase dissolved oxygen content and can be used to reduce the salinity and temperature of the water. As the temperature and dissolved oxygen are related to each other, changing one will affect the other. The aerator pump can be used to increase the dissolved oxygen content in the water and also to reduce the temperature of the water [13]. A sample aerator is shown in Fig. 5.

Table 4 gives samples of data which contains input parameters and output actions with respect to the input parameters. From Table 4 it can be observed that corrective output actions are needed to be taken to maintain the input parameters temperature, Dissolved Oxygen, and salinity in the normal range.

The fuzzy logic designer for smart aquaculture can be visualized in Fig. 6. The Mamdani fuzzy inference system is used in the current research paper. From the figure, it can be visualized that there are 3 input parameters (temperature, dissolved oxygen, and salinity) and 2 output parameters (Aerator and Fresh Water pump).

The fuzzy logic rules set for the input parameter and output action is given in Table 5. With respect to the various categories of input parameters, the corrective actions can be done through an aerator and freshwater pump as shown in Table 5.

The fuzzy rules are included in the fuzzy inference system using the rule editor of the MATLAB inference system. From Fig. 7, it can be visualized that input parameters used logic and operation to provide the outputs.

3   Simulation and Results

The simulation of smart aquaculture using a fuzzy inference system can be shown in Fig. 8. When the input parameters temperature, dissolved oxygen, and salinity are varying, what are all the corrective actions Aerator and freshwater pump can do to maintain the input parameters in the optimal range can be seen in Fig. 8. The system can be imported into MATLAB And with the test data available the model can be tested. We have given the input test data for the proposed smart aquaculture system which is collected at various instances of time. The outputs are observed and assessed whether they are matching with the intended criteria as per the rule base.

Fig. 5. Aerator in work

Table 4. A sample of input parameters and output actions

Input parameters			Output actions	
Temperature (°C)	DO (ppm)	Salinity (ppt)	Aerator	Water pump
20	15	40	Off	On
25	6	3	Off	Off
40	5	25	On	On
30	6	20	Off	Off
28	7	50	Off	On
45	15	35	Off	On
20	3	6	On	Off

The surface plot for the aerator and smart water pump with respect to various input parameters is shown in Figs. 9, 10, 11, 12 and 13. DO vs salinity surface plot of Fig. 9 shows that aerator is on when DO value is low. DO vs Salinity surface plot of Fig. 10 shows that water Pump will be on when Salinity is high. The temperature vs Salinity surface plot of Fig. 11 shows that the aerator is on when the Temperature value is high. The temperature vs Salinity surface plot of Fig. 12 shows that the water pump is on when Temperature or Salinity value is high. Figure 13 gives Temperature vs DO surface plot for fresh water pump.

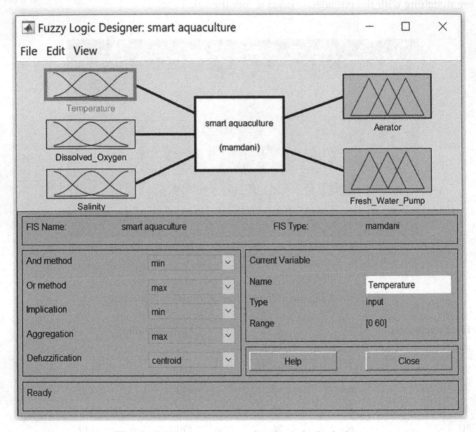

Fig. 6. Smart aquaculture using fuzzy logic designer

Table 5. Fuzzy logic rule set

Sl. no.	Temperature (°C)	DO (ppm)	Salinity (ppt)	Aerator	Fresh water pump
1	Low	Low	Low	On	Off
2	Low	Low	Normal	On	Off
3	Low	Low	High	On	On
4	Low	Normal	Low	Off	Off
5	Low	Normal	Normal	Off	Off
6	Low	Normal	High	Off	On
7	Low	High	Low	Off	Off
8	Low	High	Normal	Off	Off
9	Low	High	High	Off	On
10	Normal	Low	Low	On	Off
11	Normal	Low	Normal	On	OFF
12	Normal	Low	High	On	On
13	Normal	Normal	Low	Off	Off
14	Normal	Normal	Normal	Off	Off
15	Normal	Normal	High	Off	On
16	Normal	High	Low	Off	Off
17	Normal	High	Normal	Off	Off
18	Normal	High	High	Off	On
19	High	Low	Low	On	Off
20	High	Low	Normal	On	On
21	High	Low	High	On	On
22	High	Normal	Low	On	Off
23	High	Normal	Normal	On	On
24	High	Normal	High	On	On
25	High	High	Low	Off	Off
26	High	High	Normal	Off	On
27	High	High	High	Off	On

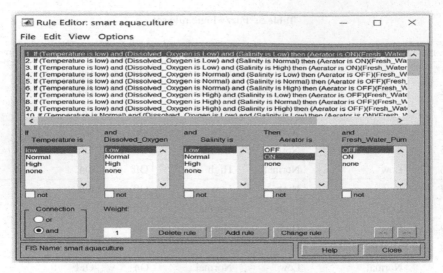

Fig. 7. Verbal fuzzy rules

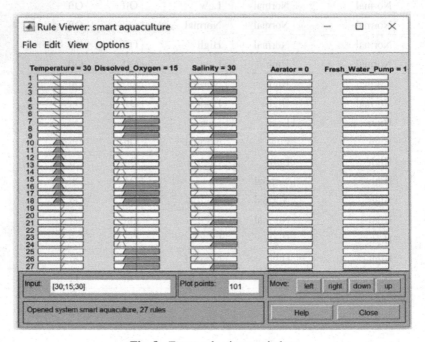

Fig. 8. Fuzzy rule viewer window

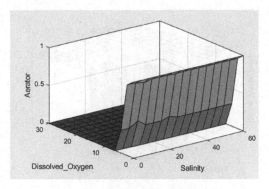

Fig. 9. DO vs salinity surface plot for aerator

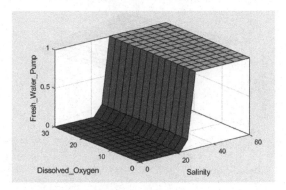

Fig. 10. DO vs salinity surface plot for pump

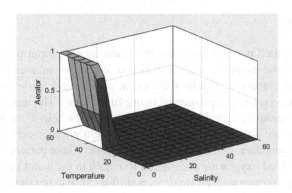

Fig. 11. Temperature vs salinity surface plot for aerator

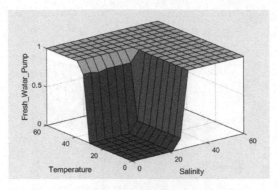

Fig. 12. Temperature vs salinity surface plot for pump

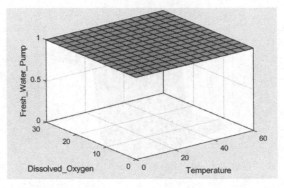

Fig. 13. Temperature vs DO surface plot for pump

4 Conclusion

In the current research paper to maintain the water quality, input parameters salinity, dissolved oxygen, and temperature are considered. When the parameters vary from their optimal range the corrective actions such as an aerator and freshwater pump on/off are proposed. The system is implemented using fuzzy logic. The input and outputs are fuzzified using trapezoidal membership functions. With the help of the Fuzzy rule base, the output actions are obtained. In the proposed system we have achieved an accuracy of 96% for the testing data. In the current research paper, three parameters temperature, salinity, and dissolved oxygen are considered to maintain the water quality. Parameters such as pH, nitrogen compound, and hydrogen sulfide can also be considered to maintain the water quality for the optimal growth of fish.

References

1. Rana, D., Rani, S.: Fuzzy logic based control system for fresh water aquaculture: a MATLAB based simulation approach. Serb. J. Electr. Eng. **12**(2), 171–182 (2015)

2. Nagothu, S.K., Kumar, O.P., Anitha, G.: Autonomous monitoring and attendance system using inertial navigation system and GPRS in predefined locations. In: 2014 3rd International Conference on Eco-friendly Computing and Communication Systems, Mangalore, pp. 261–265 (2014). https://doi.org/10.1109/Eco-friendly.2014.60
3. Nagothu, S.K., Anitha, G., Annapantula, S.: Navigation aid for people (joggers and runners) in the unfamiliar urban environment using inertial navigation. In: 2014 6th International Conference on Advanced Computing (ICoAC), Chennai, pp. 216–219 (2014). https://doi.org/10.1109/ICoAC.2014.7229713
4. Raju, K.R.S.R., Varma, G.H.K.: Knowledge based real time monitoring system for aquaculture using IoT. In: 2017 IEEE 7th International Advance Computing Conference (IACC), Hyderabad, pp. 318–321 (2017).https://doi.org/10.1109/IACC.2017.0075
5. https://thefishsite.com/articles/water-quality-parameter-analysis-for-the-feasibility-of-shr imp-culture
6. Nagothu, S.K., Kumar, O.P., Anitha, G.: GPS aided autonomous monitoring and attendance system. Procedia Comput. Sci. **87**, 99–104 (2016). https://doi.org/10.1016/j.procs.2016.05.133
7. Nagothu, S.K.: Weather based smart watering system using soil sensor and GSM. In: 2016 World Conference on Futuristic Trends in Research and Innovation for Social Welfare (Startup Conclave), Coimbatore, pp. 1–3 (2016). https://doi.org/10.1109/STARTUP.2016.7583991
8. Nagothu, S.K.: Automated toll collection system using GPS and GPRS. In: 2016 International Conference on Communication and Signal Processing (ICCSP), Melmaruvathur, Tamilnadu, India, pp. 0651–0653 (2016). https://doi.org/10.1109/ICCSP.2016.7754222
9. Nagothu, S.K., Anitha, G.: INS - GPS integrated aid to partially vision impaired people using Doppler sensor. In: 2016 3rd International Conference on Advanced Computing and Communication Systems (ICACCS), Coimbatore, pp. 1–4 (2016). https://doi.org/10.1109/ICACCS.2016.7586386
10. Nagothu, S.K., Anitha, G.: Low-cost smart watering system in multi-soil and multi-crop environment using GPS and GPRS. In: Satapathy, S.C., Kamakshi Prasad, V., Padmaja Rani, B., Udgata, S.K., Srujan Raju, K. (eds.) Proceedings of the 1st International Conference on Computational Intelligence and Informatics: ICCII 2016, pp. 637–643. Springer Singapore, Singapore (2017). https://doi.org/10.1007/978-981-10-2471-9_61
11. Nagothu, S.K., Anitha, G.: INS-GPS enabled driving aid using Doppler sensor. In: 2015 International Conference on Smart Sensors and Systems (IC-SSS), Bangalore, pp. 1–4 (2015). https://doi.org/10.1109/SMARTSENS.2015.7873619
12. http://www.fao.org/3/ac210e/AC210E09.htm. Accessed 15 Nov 2020
13. https://www.alibaba.com/product-detail/2HP-fish-farming-aerator-paddlewheel-aerator_6 0140721127.html. Accessed 15 Nov 2020
14. Nagothu, S.K., Anitha, G.: Automatic landing site detection for UAV using supervised classification. In: Rao, P.J., Rao, K.N., Kubo, S. (eds.) Proceedings of International Conference on Remote Sensing for Disaster Management. SSGG, pp. 309–316. Springer, Cham (2019). https://doi.org/10.1007/978-3-319-77276-9_27

A Review on Cybersecurity of Internet of Things

S. Balaji, Abhinav Jaishanker[✉], Sarthak Gokhale, Sakshi Sinhal,
and M. Rajeshkumar

School of Electrical Engineering, VIT University, Vellore 632014, Tamil Nadu, India
sbalaji@vit.ac.in

Abstract. Internet of things (IOT) is the fastest growing technology in today's world and has changed the world completely. It has become an integral part of our lives and from smart home to smart cities everything is connected to the internet which has reduced the human effort and made our lives easier. As it is all about the internet, so with it comes some repercussion which are the cyber threats. These threats need to be dealt with in a proper and a phased manner so that it won't lead to any device failure or data breaches. As there have been a lot of attacks in the past so the issue of cybersecurity in IOT is of huge importance and needs to get much more attention. This paper discusses about the ways in which the important sectors like smart cities, healthcare and industries, apply IOT on day-to-day basis and the different ways in which these sectors deal with the cybersecurity issues. This paper deeply analyses the various kinds of cyber threats as well as the consequences the system has to face because of these attacks and what preventive measures can be taken to avoid the attacks.

Keywords: Confidentiality · Authentication · Cyber-physical systems · Big data · Personal medical device · Advanced metering infrastructure · Smart meter · External communication infrastructure

1 Introduction

Today millions of devices are connected with internet and power in order to interact with other devices of similar kind. This technology has improved our live to such an extent that it has made it efficient, easier, saves time and money. With advanced sensors and added connectivity, business revenue flows in an unprecedented manner, people have started believing in this technology more. The challenge that we forget to deal is, today the entire world is becoming smart and has enabled technology in their infrastructure, with this, the technology which we deem smart is acting as a toy for malicious hackers to take control of our personal space. Usage of any Internet enabled device must not pose a constant fear in the user's mind that their personal information is getting controlled by the system. When a fridge becomes internet enabled it becomes a device cybercriminal can now exploit, same as our phone or laptop. The more the number of devices gets connected to the internet, the more they get prone to the attack. This market is on a rise and with it the cyber threats and potential risk is simultaneously increasing. Security of IOT has become a Herculean task. When constant pressure is put on designers and manufacturers to create new products and with enhanced quality, they often forget to prioritize security. Many manufacturers are themselves not aware of the threats their devices can cause as they only focus on revenue and savings. Securing these connected devices completely is a challenge and although it threats can't be eliminated completely; they can be mitigated up to a certain level. Precautions should also be taken by the user while using the device to have a check whether they don't show any undesired behavior. Networks should be properly encrypted to deny any unauthorized entry. Passwords to these devices should be often changed to avoid hacking and also the default passwords must not be forgotten to update. These are a few measures that can be implemented at a personal level.

As we see in today's world, everything in our life has become online, from buying vegetables to grocery, clothes to work from home, paying digitally to getting income online, ordering food to online classes, according to the latest research, the total number of connected IOT device will reach 75 billion by 2025, with almost 30% of them installed in industrial environments. Cyberattacks has increased during the pandemic by a large number, this gave us a thought to do wide research in this topic and come up with some brilliant solutions which we will try to discuss in the research paper. This was the motivation behind choosing this topic. There are a few listed reasons of why Internet of Things is an attractive target for hackers: They function in a very large network and scale. A million devices can be hacked or taken control over to fuel Distributed Denial of Service (DDoS) attacks, compromising a single device or a network can open door to a million other devices. These devices are always functioning; hence their attack layer can be properly studied, and information can be processed and hacking them gets easier. They have passwords that can be easily decrypted, first because they are default admin or system password and second because the local technicians are not that capable to manage the device with very strong passwords in such installations.

The entire paper will deal with many different areas of IOT which are more prone to cyber threats and a deep analysis has been done on the way the system is attacked and a solution approach has also been outlined to benefit the readers. Table 1 summarizes the topics discussed in the paper.

Table 1. Cybersecurity topics dealt in this paper

Cyber security subtopics	Preliminary
Wearables and smart homes	A comprehensive study on the various wearable and smart-home devices and the associated security risks
Industrial IOT	An overview on industry 4.0 and the threats and vulnerabilities faced by it
Health care	Overview about the various cyber threats faced by the healthcare industry and its effect
Smart grid	A detailed study and analyzation of the cyber security threats faced by the smart grid system
Smart city	A generic study on the main smart city components and how are they attacked
Connected and autonomous vehicles	Proper study of the system with analyzation of the sensors and external infrastructure involved in threat

2 Cyber Security in Smart Homes and Everyday IOT Devices

2.1 Cybersecurity in Wearable Devices

Wearable technology or wearable electronics are smart devices that have various uses right from health monitoring of patients to gaming and fashion accessories. These devices generally have minimal processing capabilities and perform a simple operation. Some wearable devices include smart watches, VR headsets, fitness trackers, smart clothing and jewelry etc. These devices are worn by a user to provide information and ease of access to the main devices like mobile phone or laptop it is pairing with. Wearable devices are defined by six main characteristics which are un-monopolizing, unrestrictive, observable, controllable, attentive and communicative [3]. Intruders and hackers may have various objectives for attacking, for example, financial gain, influencing public opinion, blackmailing someone etc. The goals of intruders vary from individual attackers to sophisticated organized-crime organizations [2]. Some of the key risks and some motives of attackers are mentioned below.

The primary security threat associated with the wearable smart devices is the third-party usage of all our personal data like location, sleep schedule, mental and physical wellness, and in some cases even our history of calls, messages, mails, card payments etc. which is being constantly recorded by the device. These devices are typically low cost hence they don't have advanced security features to protect the device as well as the user. They collect a variety of sensitive personal information which could be misused if in wrong hands.

Data Confidentiality. It is the control and authorization mechanism of an IOT device by which it verifies if the user (or the external device) accessing the data have the necessary permissions. This mechanism may grant or deny permission to access the data that is recorded by the IOT device. However, the issue that arises here is that the device is small and low cost, hence a complicated control mechanism is not possible. This is a critical issue as an IOT device may be connected to several other external devices through Wi-Fi, Bluetooth etc.

Privacy. Each device collects a lot of data through various sensors attached to it. The large amount of data needs to be handled carefully as the system can be easily manipulated to access the data. There are several "Terms and conditions" and "Privacy policy" that each device has and often these are very large documents with hundreds of pages of conditions. The users don't read these and generally give all the permissions that the device asks for.

Trust. It is the factor in IOT which assures the user that their data is in safe hands. There may be instances when the company is not being transparent about their policies. They may try to confuse the users with complicated and lengthy documents about how their data is handled, how safe is the data, what they intend to do with the data etc. In such cases a doubt arises, and it makes the company less trustworthy.

Wearable devices pose several new safety challenges to developers and manufacturers because of its unique characteristics like small size and curved shapes, limited display area, low processing power, a lot of sensors-all these features crammed into one device. In such a scenario designing a completely secure system becomes a challenge [1]. All the IOT devices are connected to the internet constantly thereby exposing them to the risk of some malware or virus penetrating the system. Any attack on the wearable devices can cause physical harm to the user. For example, if a fitness tracker is hacked it can show wrong readings of vital parameters of the user, or if a health monitoring system is infiltrated, it can pose a threat to the life of the patient. Another risk is the loss of the device itself. The stolen device exposes the user to the risk of getting all their data into wrong hands. Even the expensive wearable devices don't have and mechanism to protect them from risks if they are stolen [3]. Table 2 mentions some security vulnerabilities and the attack type in some popular wearable devices that have been discovered in the past.

Some key security and safety aspects to keep in mind while purchasing a wearable IOT device are illustrated in the Fig. 1 below:

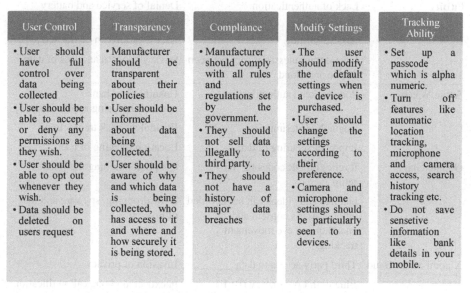

User Control	Transparency	Compliance	Modify Settings	Tracking Ability
• User should have full control over data being collected • User should be able to accept or deny any permissions as they wish. • User should be able to opt out whenever they wish. • Data should be deleted on users request	• Manufacturer should be transparent about their policies • User should be informed about data being collected. • User should be aware of why and which data is being collected, who has access to it and where and how securely it is being stored.	• Manufacturer should comply with all rules and regulations set by the government. • They should not sell data illegally to third party. • They should not have a history of major data breaches	• The user should modify the default settings when a device is purchased. • User should change the settings according to their preference. • Camera and microphone settings should be particularly seen to in devices.	• Set up a passcode which is alpha numeric. • Turn off features like automatic location tracking, microphone and camera access, search history tracking etc. • Do not save sensetive information like bank details in your mobile.

Fig. 1. Some safety and security aspects

2.2 Cybersecurity in Smart Homes

With the advent of IOT systems, everything around us are connected to each other and to the internet. This kind of hyper connectivity has led to several innovations aimed at easing our day-to-day work and one such innovation is smart homes. Smart homes are nothing, but houses equipped with devices connected to the cloud which can be controlled remotely using a mobile application or even using our voice. They have several features like temperature and humidity control, home automation to control the lights, fans, curtains and almost every other home appliance.

A smart home provides the promise of enhanced security, comfort, efficiency, power saving and even ecological sustainability. For example, smart homes can help the elderly live independently and comfortably-they can automate almost all devices, set reminders, smart robot vacuum can clean the house and they can even send an alarm to relatives and neighbors in case of any emergency.

All these features sound very alluring, however there are several security and privacy risks attached with them. The primary issue with a smart home environment is that it is a relatively ad-hoc system without dedicated system management resources, and the user generally has less technical knowledge [7].

Table 2. Use case of some security vulnerabilities and security attacks found in various wearable devices

Device	Vulnerability	Attack type
FitBit	Lack of authentication	Denial of service and battery drainage
	Passive sniffing	User location can be tracked [3]
	Intercepting messages sent between device and cloud	Privacy concern and loss of data
Apple Watch	Poor backend authentication	Unauthorized bank transactions using apple watch [4]
	Rogue NFC terminals	Fraudulent bank transactions
	Improper securing of data	Location tracking of user
Google Glass	It relies on QR codes for Wi-Fi setup	QR photobombing malware
	pictures and videos can be recorded without user's consent and unauthorized eye movement tracking	Eavesdropping, spyware and loss of privacy
Xiaomi Smart Band	Third party access to data	Invasion of privacy
	Bluetooth Low Energy (BLE) security flaw	unexpected phone call notification, SMS notification and changing the date and time [5]

2.3 Threats

A threat in IOT means the various risks or dangers it may be exposed to. These threats pose a great challenge to the developer and a considerable security concern to the user. Some of the security threats in wearable devices are mentioned below in Fig. 2:

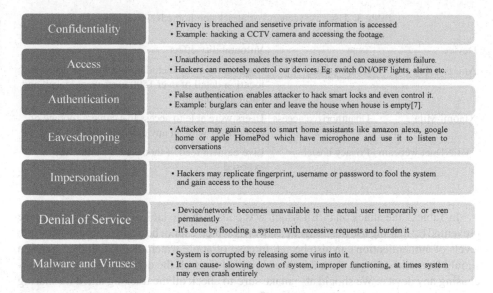

Confidentiality	• Privacy is breached and sensetive private information is accessed • Example: hacking a CCTV camera and accessing the footage.
Access	• Unauthorized access makes the system insecure and can cause system failure. • Hackers can remotely control our devices. Eg: switch ON/OFF lights, alarm etc.
Authentication	• False authentication enables attacker to hack smart locks and even control it. • Example: burglars can enter and leave the house when house is empty[7].
Eavesdropping	• Attacker may gain access to smart home assistants like amazon alexa, google home or apple HomePod which have microphone and use it to listen to conversations
Impersonation	• Hackers may replicate fingerprint, username or passsword to fool the system and gain access to the house
Denial of Service	• Device/network becomes unavailable to the actual user temporarily or even permanently • It's done by flooding a system with excessive requests and burden it
Malware and Viruses	• System is corrupted by releasing some virus into it. • It can cause- slowing down of system, improper functioning, at times system may even crash entirely

Fig. 2. Security threats in wearable devices

2.4 Vulnerabilities

Vulnerability means the susceptibility of the device to be attacked, i.e., the various weakness the device has which can make it an easy target for attackers. Some common vulnerabilities are mentioned below and Table 3 lists out some smart home devices and their vulnerabilities in the past.

Weak Encryption and Outdated Protocols. Encryption is the process of protecting the system and its architecture from any kind of unauthorized activity. However, many a times the ciphering techniques used may be weak and may have loopholes, thus exposing the device to attacks. Most smart home environments existing today are just devices connected to an already existing house. The house was originally not designed to accommodate the smart devices. This results in a variety of different devices from different manufacturers being used together to create a smart home, but in this process the security protocols are often outdated.

Firmware Failure and Insecure Application. Old IOT devices are easy target for attackers. The hardware devices are almost never updated, and they run on older software which are more vulnerable to attack most smart home devices are controlled by some kind of mobile apps. However, it is easy to replicate these apps and gain control over the device.

Heterogeneous Architecture and Insecure Wi-Fi Network. In an environment where different kinds of devices from different brands and manufacturers are being integrated to form one system, the architecture is very important.

Wi-Fi attacks are on the rise as people often leave their networks open and unprotected thereby giving hackers easy access to their data and activity [6].

Table 3. Use case scenario of attacks on home IOT systems

Device	Type	Vulnerability effect
Amazon ring	Data breach	Login credentials including user ID, password and location detail of over 1500 users were leaked and published online
Xiaomi Mija	Unauthorized access	Users were able to access live camera footage of other users without any authentication
TRENDnet webcam	Privacy breach	Live camera feed of thousands of users was exposed

In Table 2, the attack on FitBit which was caused due to lack of authentication can be prevented by making use of stronger passwords which cannot be easily guessed. Multiple levels of authentication can also be set. In case of apple watch, the backend encryption should be made stronger. As a user, we should change all the default passwords on purchasing any device. We should also make sure to check all the tracking and data sharing permission we have given to the device. There are several new malwares that can access user's camera without our knowledge, one solution for this is to use a camera shutter in case of devices like mobiles and laptops. One must not keep a device's connections like Bluetooth, Wi-Fi and hotspot ON at all times unnecessarily as these are easy terminals for hackers to access our device. In Table 3, attacks like data breach and privacy breach have more to do with the security measures and encryption that are implemented by the manufacturer. As a user we should buy devices from trusted manufacturers who follow latest and advanced security protocols.

3   Cybersecurity in Industry 4.0

The first industrial revolution started in the late 18th century with the introduction of mechanization, water and steam power. The second was a century later and primarily saw the wide-spread use of electricity as a source of energy and mass production of goods. The third industrial revolution saw the advent of microprocessors and chips, computers and system automation. Finally, the industry 4.0 saw the merging of the physical and virtual world-It has cyber-physical systems [12] which leverage off of what was done in the computer and automation world, but it's highly instrumented with cloud technology, wireless sensors, data collection, data analytics, machine learning, artificial intelligence and other smart technologies and this is what is transforming the manufacturing world.

Industry 4.0 is driven by factors such as the global socio-economic changes, understanding the importance of using resources more efficiently, and introduction of cloud technologies, the use of IOT and IIOT, the availability of big data and above all, the evolving needs of the customers. Industry 4.0 has enabled the transformation of factories into smart factories and has improved the overall performance [11].

3.1 Need for Cybersecurity

In today's era of hyper connectivity there are billions of devices connected to each other. They have access to data stored in the other devices. In such a scenario, threat to the security and protection of data and the connected devices is inevitable. If this issue is not resolved it will pose a major threat [13]. It is of utmost importance to improve cybersecurity in Industries since the impact of the threats can compromise physical security, because production downtimes, spoil the products and even damage equipment which will ultimately result in financial and reputational losses. The motivation behind a cyberattack or a hack may be varying-bringing down a competitor, monetary benefit, gaining access to sensitive private data of a company and in some cases even political agenda.

Cyber criminals are coming up with various methods to harm industries and this calls for an improved security system. The already existing systems are mostly outdated and are not sufficient to protect the evolving industry needs. The fact that industry 4.0 uses a complex system of physical devices and software services makes it even more difficult to protect as each of them follow their own protocols which is different from the other.

[15] correctly states that industrial control systems (ICS) are extensively used across a spectre of sectors, such as electricity, waste, water, oil and natural gas, and so far, multiple security incidents have been reported across these sectors. Although these incidents are considered to be isolated, yet they are quite alarming. With the interconnection of critical infrastructures, new cyber-security risks arise that need to be identified, studied and addressed, before it is too late. Similarly, [14] states that organizations generally do not officially report the cyber-attacks they may be subjected to and I agree with this. Reporting such incidents would expose their vulnerability to such attacks and they will have to face public scrutiny. Several million dollars are paid to hackers and cyber-criminals every year as ransom by corporates. This has also led to companies investing large amounts in developing new technologies and strategies to protect them from future attacks.

3.2 IOT Architecture and the Security Threats

The IOT architecture in general consists of four layers as mentioned below. Table 4 summarizes the various layers and security threats associated with each layer are analyzed in the Fig. 3 below.

Perception layer is characterized with a number of sensing devices like RFID, sensors, actuators etc. which collect information. It is also known as the sensing layer [11]. Network layer is the layer that collects the data from the sensing layer and transfers it to the processing system. In this layer, the cloud services, internet gateways, switching and routing devices are operated using latest technologies like ZigBee, WIFI, LTE, Bluetooth etc. [14]. Service layer and Support layer are for managing all the services and it is also responsible for secure computing, i.e., it makes sure that the data is being accessed only by authorized personnel. Application layer is the layer that is responsible for interfacing with the user directly in the form of applications and services.

Table 4. Various layers and their associated threats

Parameters	Perception layer	Network layer	Service layer	Application layer
Components	Barcodes RFID tags RFID reader-writers BLE devices Intelligent sensors, GPS	WLAN Cloud network Social networks Wireless sensor networks	Database Service API's Service management	Smart applications and management Interfaces
Security threats and vulnerabilities	Unauthorized access Malicious code attacks Noisy data Availability	Denial of service Network congestion Routing attack Data breach	Malicious information Spoofing Manipulation	Phishing attacks Malicious code attacks Configuration threats

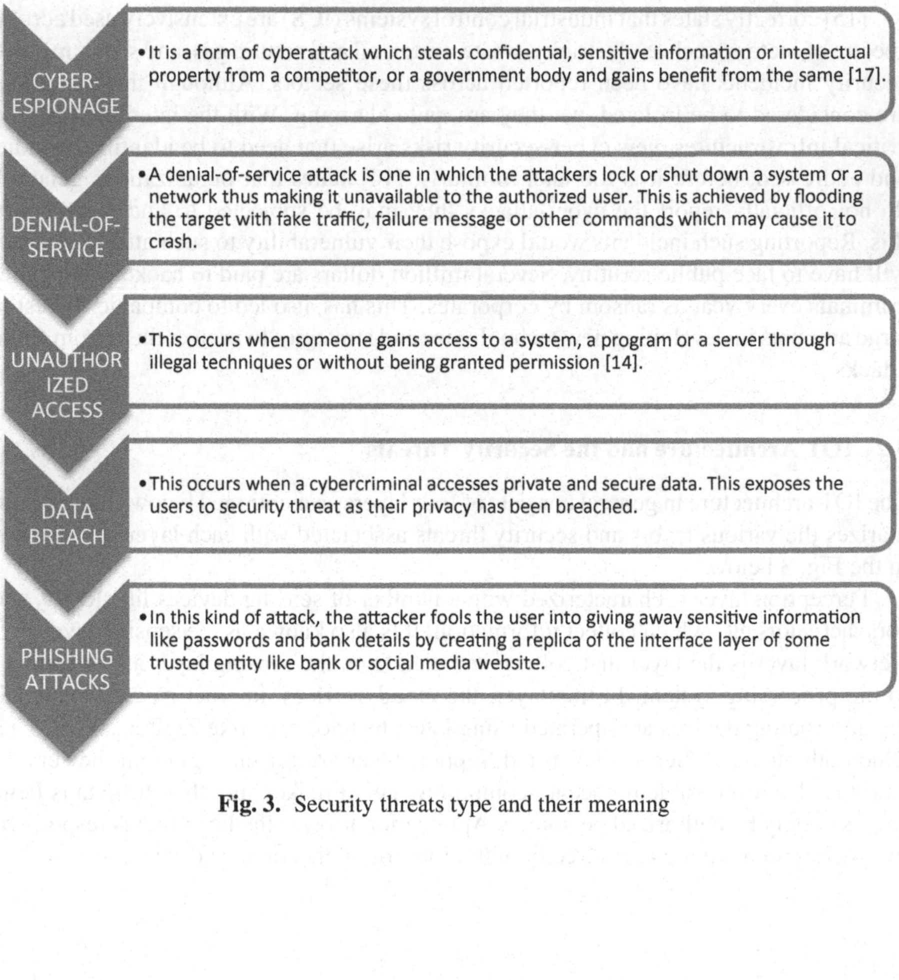

CYBER-ESPIONAGE
- It is a form of cyberattack which steals confidential, sensitive information or intellectual property from a competitor, or a government body and gains benefit from the same [17].

DENIAL-OF-SERVICE
- A denial-of-service attack is one in which the attackers lock or shut down a system or a network thus making it unavailable to the authorized user. This is achieved by flooding the target with fake traffic, failure message or other commands which may cause it to crash.

UNAUTHORIZED ACCESS
- This occurs when someone gains access to a system, a program or a server through illegal techniques or without being granted permission [14].

DATA BREACH
- This occurs when a cybercriminal accesses private and secure data. This exposes the users to security threat as their privacy has been breached.

PHISHING ATTACKS
- In this kind of attack, the attacker fools the user into giving away sensitive information like passwords and bank details by creating a replica of the interface layer of some trusted entity like bank or social media website.

Fig. 3. Security threats type and their meaning

3.3 Use Case Scenario

No system in the world is absolutely perfect and safe. Every system has its flaws which exposes it to a number of risks and these risks may be varying like mechanical breakdown, low efficiency or easily prone to cyberattacks. For several years, harmful cybercriminals have been targeting the industrial control systems (ICSs) that manage our crucial infrastructures. Industrial control systems (ICSs) are embedded cyber-devices that operate crucial infrastructures like energy, transportation, water supply systems etc. [10]. There have been multiple instances in the past where there have been major security breaches, intentional cyber-attacks, virus attacks and even unintentional malware attacks on Industrial control systems.

One of the most popular attack in history is STUXNET, a worm that attacks SCADA systems, which attacked Iran's nuclear program and caused substantial damage. Table 5 gives some examples of major cyber-attacks in history.

Table 5. Examples of cyber attacks

Industry affected	Name *(year)*	Description
Davis-Besse Nuclear Power Station (USA)	Slammer (2002)	Slowsdownthe network and denial of service [15]
British Coastguard, Delta Airline (USA), French Stock Exchange [15] (FRA)	Sasser (2004)	Systems Brought down, Flight delays & cancellations, High profile Infections etc.
French Navy (FRA)	Conficker (2009)	Gains administrator access, propagates to other vulnerable machines, self-updates, downloads & installs further malware
Oil industry (Exxon, Shell, BP and others)	Night Dragon (2009)	RATsdistributed using spear-phishing
Iran'sNatanz nuclear facility (IRN)	Stuxnet (2010)	Destroyed a fifth of Iran's Nuclear centrifuges [16]
Multinational companies in Middle east	Shamoon (2012)	Malware used to target large energy companies in the Middle East, including Saudi Aramco and RasGas
Energy and aerospace	APT33 (2017)	A cyber-espionage group targeting the aviation and energy sectors

4 Health Care and IOT

4.1 Introduction

Healthcare one of the most important industry. As technology has improved healthcare facilities have also improved drastically. In today's world healthcare is a sector which needs the most attention and advancement in techniques of treatment. IOT has reached every sector of society and have as well reached the healthcare sector where it is being used in several positive ways. The combination of IOT and healthcare have helped the patients as well as the healthcare workers in a lot of ways and has eased the process of providing the correct treatment.

Table 6. Industries experiencing the highest incident rates

2014	2015	Most frequently occurring incident categories
Financial services	Healthcare	Unauthorized access
Information and communication	Manufacturing	Malicious code
Manufacturing	Financial services	Sustained probe/scan
Retail and wholesale	Government	Suspicious activity
Energy and utilities	Transportation	Access or credentials abuse

As shown in Table 6, healthcare industry is the industry which is hit the most as of 2015 because of various reasons which makes the healthcare system very much vulnerable. The combination of IOT and healthcare has led to various equipment like heart monitoring implants, insulin pumps, pacemakers and many equipment of these kind which has helped in keeping the health track of patients very easy and has made that process very smooth. A lot of wearables are there in the market like the smart watch through which a person can keep track of his heart rate, blood pressure and overall body condition. This is the most prime of example of IOT and healthcare. The data is getting stored safely and the user can monitor all the time. IOT and healthcare combination in basically used to keep the health track of the patients who need care 24 × 7. The data is stored and as soon as there is some discrepancy in the health data the doctors as well as the patient can take some action and react to that. This can prevent a lot of causalities and can save a lot of lives. Several applications are already there which sell medicines and can be used for booking appointment with the doctors which has changed the scenario completely and the process has never been smoother. In today's world the data which is managed by the healthcare industry is one of the most sensitive data. It actually has everything related to a person's health and all his detail which makes it much more vulnerable [20]. There have been already a lot of attacks on the healthcare data. The biggest of them was the Anthem Blue Cross data breach in 2015 which affected around 78.8 million people in which a lot of personal information of the patients was stolen. As technology is advancing so rapidly and the number of IOT devices are increasing data breaches would be increasing as well.

4.2 Ways in Which Healthcare is Hit and Methods to Prevent It

With the growing technology and health scare there has been a huge rise in Personal medical devices (PMD) to manage health data and keep a check about the body condition

[21]. In this the devices discussed are the ones which are fitted inside the body and do coordinate with the organ and assist the process. These devises handle important functions inside the body, so the battery life of these devices becomes a very important aspect which needs to be considered at every stage.

PMD's basically include devices like pacemaker, implantable cardiac defibrillator, insulin pumps etc. The structure of these kind of devices is kind of delicate and they have non-rechargeable batteries, so we need to change the device after a certain period of time. This make the device to be used with more caution. As the structure of these devices is very basic so adding cryptographic protection becomes very difficult as well as impractical [21].

These devices need to be secured of malicious activities. Some methods like encryption key can be made and provided to the proper users or providing credential certificates to access data [19]. The size of the devices can be increased a bit so that proper and more advanced encryption technique can be applied to the device. If advanced techniques are used it would affect the battery life of the device. As these devices are implanted in the body so making rechargeable batteries or changing them again and again is not possible. This is the part where these devices can further be improved. As there are a lot of devices in the hospitals and most of them are connected to the internet so it gives the hackers a lot of ways to enter the hospital network. The purpose of the hackers is to enter the hospital network using any of the device and generally steal huge patient data. They just use these small devices as the gateway to enter the network [19]. Various other threats like session med jacking, network failure also affect the system in many ways and can be harmful. IOT has become a major part of every industry and a very integral part of healthcare sector. So, there need to be ways to tackle these cybersecurity issues. Some of the ways in which these issues can be tackled are [19]: -

Monitoring the device-to-device network and several layers of security should be used so that the process of getting inside the network becomes tougher and complex. Permission for accessing the information should only be given to limited users and so that and only related to people can view the data. The software as well the hardware used in the medical devices should be latest otherwise getting into the network would be easy for the hackers and can lead to loss of huge data.

Some common type of attacks which happens regularly and affect most of the system, specific action should be taken based on the attack so that these can be handled with more care and the risk of data loss or any other technical mishap can be reduced. DDoS is a very brutal threat to the system so a response plan should be ready as well as a strong network system should be maintained against those attacks at all time so that these can't much affect the system.

In [22] case-oriented assessment methodology has been highlighted and the ways in which that situation could be dealt by providing security to each layer. In [20] some ways have been identified for the movement of healthcare sector in the forward direction which include regular testing of the environment, having strict laws against cybercrimes and by inheriting cybersecurity in the patient care culture as an important thing and the most important thing is that confidentiality should be maintained by any means necessary through anonymization of data.

5 Smart Grid

5.1 Introduction

Smart grid is a system which eases the process of generation, transmission and distribution of electricity to the consumers. It includes a lot of operations and processes such as smart meters, smart appliances, renewable energy resources etc. It's a two-way channel where the both the consumers as well as the suppliers are in benefit. Basically, it's a bulk generation of electricity, then transmitting it through transmission lines and continuously regulating its usage. It has several advantages like sustainability, increased efficiency reliability, flexibility.

This system allows the consumers to keep check on their electricity usage from time to time so that they can manage their electricity bills. This will result in a more reliable and efficient management of the usage which would increase the transparency of the entire system.

As it is a two-way system which means the flow of information is bi-directional which helps the suppliers as well. The system consists of various intelligent electronic devices (IED) such as sensors, meters, smart devices which help the suppliers in managing the power generation and its consumption by creating a demand response report according to the usage of the producers.

5.2 Study on Security

So, as all the devices and its subparts are connected to the internet so that brings into picture how much secure is the system from hackers and what risk our data is facing. There are majorly 3 stages which can be hit and can result in major security concerns are the Generation systems, Transmission system and the Distribution system. If the hacker gets into one of these any systems, it could create the downfall of the entire process [23]. The generation system uses IP-Based protocol IEC 61850 so this makes the system at risk of DoS/DDoS attack which can damage and obstruct or delay information to the smart grid. These attacks severely hamper the availability of the smart grid system.

One of the major software systems that are being used in smart grids and the main part of the transmission system is SCADA (Supervisory control and Data Acquisition). It is an automotive centralized control system which monitors and controls the entire process. It's basically the most important part of the software in smart grid at the load end so a hack into this can create a complete ruination of the entire system. The major features of SCADA are Alarm handling, Trend Curve Patterns, Data Access and Retrieval and Computer Networking and Processing. Improper working of any of these features or malware injection in the software system can cause the downfall of the entire system [23, 24]. If the adversary gets inside the software and make any changes in the frequency measurements of any other variable and then sends it to the control system, it can directly affect the stability and performance of the system. The RTU's and the PLC's can also be hit by Cross-Site Request Forgery attacks.

The distribution system consists of Advanced Metering Infrastructure (AMI) is known as the backbone of the smart grid system. It's basically includes the system through which the communication from the consumer side happens to the suppliers. It includes smart meters, communication channels and data acquisition systems [24]. This system depends upon wi-fi, LAN, HAN, WLAN which threatens the reliability of the system as it is all over the internet so if any adversary gets into the network the communication channels and the data management system, false information could be sent to the supplier and the system can get completely disrupt the system. There are a lot of attacks through which the smart grid system can be affected as shown in Fig. 4 [24–26].

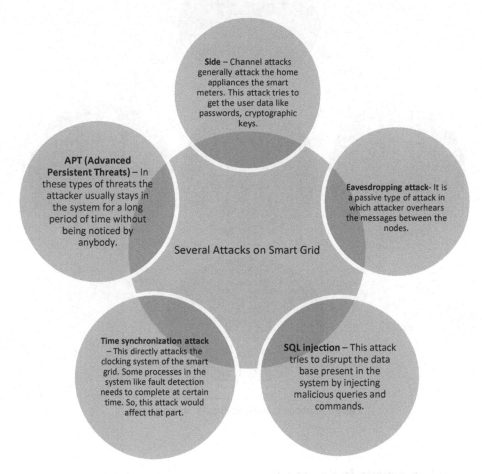

Fig. 4. Several ways in which smart Grid can be attacked

5.3   Methods to Prevent Attacks

With the increasing number of IOT devices day by day, the cyber threats to the smart grid system increase with them. These attacks need to be mitigated in some so that it can follow the requirements of CIA Triad which are Confidentiality, Integrity and Availability. The requirements to fulfil the objectives of the CIA Triad are Authenticity, Authorization,

Accountability, Privacy, Dependability, Survivability, and Safety Criticality [24]. The most important methods used to fulfil the requirements are highlighted in Fig. 5 [25, 26]:-

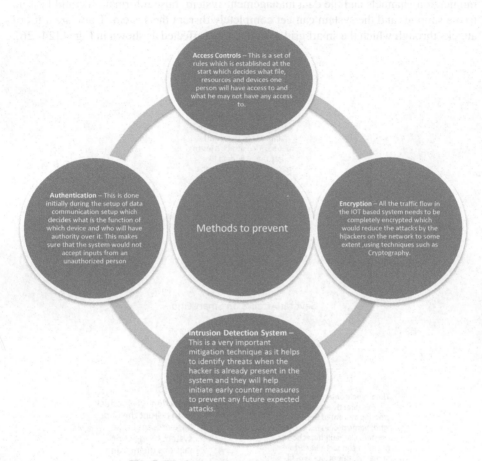

Fig. 5. Methods to prevent attacks on smart grid

6   Cybersecurity in Smart City

A Smart City is a framework that predominantly uses Internet of Things and devices such as connected sensors, lights and meters, machine learning, cloud computing to collect and analyze data, that are transmitted using wireless technology, then this data is used to improve infrastructure, utility and services. These kind of Information and Communication Technology (ICT) is necessary to address the growing urban challenges and help government, citizens and enterprises to lead a better quality of life. The connected devices like smartphones, connected cars, connected homes, allow us to remotely manage, monitor and control them. Such a technology is definitely needed to improve the physical challenges in life that includes, decreasing air pollution, streamlining trash collection and dissipation, decreasing traffic congestion, improved disaster recovery, better sanitization and sustainable energy distribution. A Smart City associates with decreased emission of greenhouse gases, cuts cost, increased safety and increased efficiency.

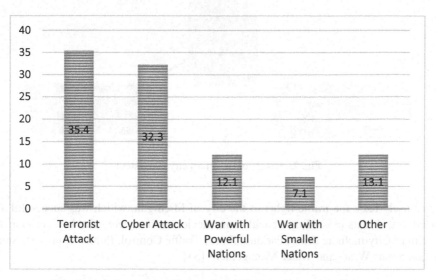

Fig. 6. Attack types and their ratio in US *(source:securityaffairs.co)*

6.1 Cyber Threats

Our location, our personal data, our cellular network that we use in these connected devices always pose a threat to our security. Though these technologies are needed for our economy development but however attractive it may seem, we can't neglect its backdrops. We need to accept that we can be tracked, our data can be hacked and a lot more can happen than what we imagine. Threats to Smart City components is more dangerous as an attack on a small system of this wide infrastructure can open the entire system and compromise them. Some of the possible weak points of the system includes: Traffic Control System, Smart Street Lighting [30]. Today the number of IOT connected devices has reached to almost 20 billion and Fig. 6 shows that recently there has been an explosion in the cyberattacks that target both data and physical assets. The smart city ecosystem comprises of three layers [33] as shown in Fig. 7.

Hacking wireless sensors is very easy to launch a cyberattack, for example, Rubbish level sensors can be used to generate a false alarm of foul smell from the garbage, which in turn will waste the time of the Municipality authorities to find and clean the non-existent garbage. Similarly, a small glitch took place in 2012, where the computer itself summoned 1200 jury on duty which resulted in heavy traffic jam all over California. During 2017, hackers turned on 156 severe weather sirens in Dallas in the middle of the night, causing a surge of 911 calls and distress. In 2014, a research was conducted

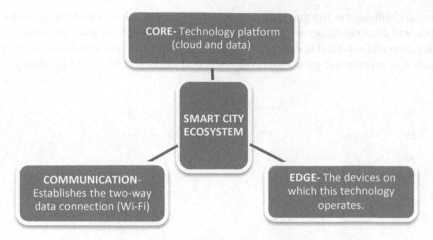

Fig. 7. Layers of the smart city ecosystem

to purposely hack the traffic lights of the city of Michigan, which was successful and proved that threats existed that could cause accidents if severe. The key components of a Smart City include: Smart Parking, Smart Traffic Control, Public Transport, Smart Energy, Smart Waste and Water Management [31].

6.2 Smart Meters

Smart meters via Advanced Metering Infrastructure (AMI) enables two-way communication between utilities and customers. They allow remote management of in-field devices that may allow malicious hackers to make unwanted changes in the configuration and settings of these devices. One way would be to change the transformation ratio of the device and the other would be to modify the memory that stores these measurements. With regard to the remote management, the hacker could be the energy meter user who would inject frames locally from their residence that would supplant the identity of the network and then carry out desired operations. They could send frames to the meters of the same phase and carry out operations like completely cutting off the supply of the other users.

6.3 Smart Transportation and Traffic

It allows smooth flow of cargo and passengers, which includes all modes of transportation from air, rail, and water to roadways. Intelligent Transportation Systems (ITS) is the application of advanced and emerging technologies to save time, lives, money and the environment. Researchers from Kaspersky Labs purposely attempted to hack Moscow's transportation system, data was easily accessed, and they were able to easily control the traffic speed and the traffic light [32]. Such an attempt from a hacker could lead to traffic congestion and road accidents. The data leaked can be sold to the third parties, modified, falsified or even deleted.

Transport infrastructure is subject to cyber dependency. Information infrastructure is responsible to track the goods, a breach in any part of this infrastructure can lead to theft of company or user data, and also their communication and connectivity systems can be compromised. These can lead to derailment of the trains from their path due to diverted signal by the hackers, can case loss of life, financial loss to enterprises.

Connected and Autonomous vehicles can be further attacked in the transportation infrastructure as discussed later in this paper. To organize traffic movement spontaneity, various intelligent modes of payment are inculcated in the ITS [35]. ITS facilities are open to threat on the highways, exposed gauges, ports and network antennas might be tampered by the hackers causing failure in uploading data and reporting. Public vehicles such as e-bikes may be stolen due to connectivity hazard caused by an outsider and the user may not be able to return it to the dock station, they could be damaged to run out of battery and other vandalism issues. Table 7 below gives a glimpse of attacks in the smart city component that caused severe damages. Ransomware attack on the public Muni Transport system could have been prevented if the system was updated and the latest antivirus software was installed. Another possibility was by formatting the system and disconnecting it from the internet. DDoS attacks like the one that happened in Finland could have been prevented by having proper VPN, firewalls installed in the system. Content filtering, load balancing, anti-spam could have been able to provide consistent network protection.

Table 7. Use case scenario of attacks in smart city

Event	Year	Country	Effect
Public Muni Transit System Ransomware attack	2016	San Francisco	Bitcoins were demanded to unlock computer and data
Airbnb hotel cameras were hacked	2019	China	Guests were spied and were demanded money
DDoS at heating device	2016	Finland	Temperature went down below freezing point but heat didn't kick in

6.4   Smart Water Management

Owing to Smart City planning, there has been a recent advancement in Water Distribution and Management using IoT. Smart Water System refers to a technology that uses wide range of hardware and software instruments, including sensors, meters and data processing and visualization tools, actuators and web applications which can connect people with water systems.

Water plays a crucial role in our environment and as a fact none of the internet connected devices come without a hazard. A proper secure system cannot be compromised here as water deals with billions of health and social well-being of citizens. A number of sensors are employed in this technology to measure the chemical composition, pressure in the pipes and the pumps, changing water quantity in the reservoir and the distribution system leading drinking water to households and wastewater form industries to the rivers by itself processing them clean. Sensors are further employed to direct water to the fields as a means of smart irrigation system to itself sprinkle water to the crops by measuring the soil moisture, humidity and temperature. Sensors are easily accessible by the malicious hackers and they can launch an attack. The attack would first involve taking control of a botnet of computers with an eye to detecting smart irrigation systems on local networks [36].

6.5 Key Mitigations to Follow

Most of the companies in the world provide their employees with gadgets to work with, which needs replacement every 4–5 years. Gadgets such as phones, tablets, drives, fax machines, copiers and old computers contains confidential information that could put the business at risk. Deleting files from the recycle bin, need not necessarily wipe off the data. Thus, proper disposal of these cyber waste is very necessary for an enterprise. A team should be made to teach all the company staff, employees, and interns to properly burn the data from the hard disk. Yibin et al. [34] presented a mobile-cloud-based smart city framework, which is an active approach to avoid data over-collection. By putting all of the user's data into the cloud, the security of user's data can be greatly improved. As suggested in the paper [30], a proposed three plan approach should be followed to avoid being susceptible to the above-mentioned hacks. Mutual Authentication is another measure to be mitigated. Every time a Smart City is connected to a network, it should be authenticated prior to receiving or transmitting data, where two parties will have to prove their identity to one another only the can the transfer happen.

7 Connected and Autonomous Vehicle

A Connected and Autonomous Vehicle (CAV) consists of numerous sensors, on board computers, controllers and software which are capable of replacing human driver and have full access to control the vehicle by itself monitoring the surrounding. Recent developments have been successful in developing quite enhanced version of these cars that have increased safety, efficiency, comfort and convenience but every good thing comes at a price and here it's the digital security.

7.1 Study of a CAV

The Society of Automotive Engineers (SAE) has defined six levels of driving automation which ranges from fully manual-level 0, driver assistance-level 1, partial automation-level 2, conditional automation-level 3, high automation-level 4 to fully automation-level 5. We have become closer to level 5 automation, in which vehicles can fully operate autonomously, from steering, accelerating, and braking to responding to other obstacles or road or weather conditions. This can all be credited to Artificial Intelligence and data generated from sensors in roads, speed bumps or traffic lights.

We do realize that when we connect cars with local cellular network or Wi-Fi, we give access to the hackers to steal our personal data and our destination so that they can track us at every point. IoT enabled technology allows people to turn on their home appliances from their car. They may unknowingly give access to the hackers to these devices by connecting over these networks so they might get the control. Imagine a lock system of your door being hacked and the robber getting entry to your house. These threats make us ponder upon how we can get a full proof solution. Nowadays, everything can be equipped from our very own mobile phone. Manufacturers of CAV's are not backdated in this area as well. They have ensured to make a configuration so as to allow users to equip each and every component of their car ranging from seat orientation, operating windows, headlights and other operands. With smart technology we need smart security. Below we have given a few insights on how these devices get third party control and a few solutions to fill the knowledge gap within.

Connected and Autonomous Vehicles needs to go in depth of the supply chain starting from the hardware, software and the infrastructure to know the risk in each component. More importantly these risks should be in knowledge of each and every member who is responsible to design the car. In most of the cases we see that the manufacturing of the vehicle is outsourced in the sense the work is divided at every stage, for example control unit system of the car made by a company will be send to a different company that will be manufacturing the hardware. Here they have a deal so as to focus only in the hardware and further send the car for other additions by some other company. Hence such intermediate manufacturers are not interested in knowing the connected safety hazards of the vehicle as they have a contract and they have done their part effectively. Also, they do not have access to the source code of the control unit to make improvements.

The present autonomous cars incorporate many types of factors in order to sense the surrounding environment and the security is much dependent on the type of the sensors, the vehicle infrastructure, and the communication infrastructure. There is a three-layer framework (sensing, communication and control) through which automotive security threats can be understood [37, 38]: Sensing layer incorporates the vehicle dynamics and the environmental sensors, they are vulnerable to threats like eavesdropping, jamming and spoofing. Communication layer comprises of in-vehicle and V2X communications, threat to them is eavesdropping, spoofing, human and Sybil attacks. Control layer responsible for all the autonomous behavior of the vehicle including speed, braking and steering. They can be compromised when both Sensing, and Communication layer are attacked.

7.2 Multiple Sensors in a CAV

Sensor technology in a CAV works in manner that is makes the car get connected to a lot many networks that may be public. These networks are open source and can easily get hacked losing the identity of the user and his personal data. Below we have listed the most important sensors that are used in a CAV and how they get attacked. A few leads on how to reduce these malware attacks and their mitigation are also discussed.

Global Positioning Systems. GPS is an open-source technology and freely accessible by anyone. It can be jammed in a complex procedure to develop counterfeit GPS signals that can be broadcasted with the realistic signals and show a position much different from the actual target. This can mislead and lead to crimes like it can divert the path of vehicles transporting goods and initiate a big theft [38].

Inertial Measurement Units. They consist of accelerometers, inclination sensors and gyroscopes that are required to provide velocity, acceleration and orientation data. They continuously monitor the dynamics of the environment and provide the necessary information to the autonomous vehicle such as when to speed up and when to slow down depending upon the steepness and the gradient of the road. They provide low level feedback inputs to the control system of the vehicle so that it can make the necessary change in the operation of the vehicle to safely travel. They can again be spoofed, in a way to give misleading data about the topography. But here the attacker will need to have physical access to the sensor to interfere with its readings. He will have to know the range of tolerance and thorough understanding of how the sensors communicate [38].

LiDAR, Radar, Camera. Light Detection and Ranging, Radar and Cameras are presently included in the automated vehicles. They allow the vehicle to sense each and every object, buildings, cars, animals and pedestrians. Radar works to detect objects made of metal. cameras provide 360-degree vision of the surrounding. These sensors can be spoofed in a manner such that when a real light signal from a distant object is sensed by the vehicle, the attacker can inject the same signal but at a very high intensity so that it interferes with the realistic signal and shows a false object nearby. This can cause the vehicles to stop or can allow it to collide with other vehicles [38].

7.3 Keys to Prevent Spoofing of Sensors

Efforts have been put to secure our vehicle networks and signals from jamming and spoofing. We must ensure to use encrypted communication on the vehicle's communication network. This will be helpful in preventing counterfeit signals to inject into our network. Further, continuous monitoring of the signal must be done to ensure that its behavior is within the range of its functioning and doesn't change drastically. Additional sensors can be used in the vehicle so that even if the main signal is attacked, we may get information from the second to tally the data points. The variation in their values can be valuable to provide us enough understanding about the spoofing. Data identification of the sender, data authentication are additional measures to be mitigated.

7.4 External CAV Communication Infrastructure

Autonomous driving is related to connected vehicles. Vehicles have achieved level-5 self-driving, although this is mainly achieved through sensors attached to the vehicle itself. However, V2X communication which consist of three infrastructure-vehicle to vehicle (V2V), vehicle to infrastructure (V2I) and vehicle to cloud communications for connected vehicles is also used for autonomous driving. V2V is the data exchange between the vehicles wirelessly and V2I is the data exchange between the vehicle and the infrastructure such as traffic lights as examples. V2X communication are facilitated when autonomous vehicles can operate as nodes within vehicular and hoc networks (VANETs). VANETs compose two type of wireless nodes [37, 41] as shown in Fig. 7 (Fig. 8):

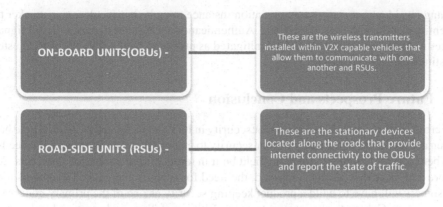

Fig. 8. Nodes of the VANETs

It is considered that these types of communications avoid traffic congestion by exchanging various types of information regarding road conditions with other vehicles through the Internet. They use both sensor technology and radio-based communication. The principle behind the working of this communication infrastructure is when two vehicles or ITS (Intelligent Transportation Station) are in radio communication range, they can connect automatically. This allows all the connected vehicles and traffic infrastructure such as lights, signs and tolls to share information like position, speed, direction. These surroundings actively communicate their state and changing conditions around them to the vehicle. A vehicle beforehand communicates that it is going to take a turn. A traffic control beforehand communicates that the light signal is going to turn red in about two minutes and a sign communicates that the next turn-off is five miles ahead. This kind of information is necessary to optimize the traffic control infrastructure to maximize the traffic flow, minimize the fuel usage and pollution. Again, they are not away from cyber-attacks. The security aspect of this infrastructure must be completely secure as there are cases in which the vehicles are in complete control by the sensors that are dependent directly on the messages received from connected vehicles [39].

7.5 V2X Attacks and Security

The major concern that lies in this part of the CAV is that the message that is delivered to the intruder node of the receiver in the vehicle should not be altered by an intruder. The receiver node must be able to identify whether the received message is legitimate or corrupted [39]. Data verification and data authentication are key to prevent these attacks. VANETs exists for a very short duration of time and the alien attackers in the vicinity of the vehicle is continuous along the vehicle, thus a more flexible means of communication is needed to be deployed in this area. These types of attacks can cause Denial of Service (DoS) where normal functioning of the system is disrupted. V2V Infrastructure will open threats to them being accessible through the publicly connected open networks like internet, which are again dangerous as already discussed above [37, 42].

Public-key infrastructure methods uses Public-Key cryptography which can be considered to ensure trustworthiness of the messages received. The vehicle can continuously change its identifier every communication instance to make it difficult for an attacker to identify or follow the specific vehicle. Authentication techniques that uses digital signatures to verify messages can also be mitigated as proposed by the students of Rochester Institute of Technology [40].

8   Future Prospects and Conclusion

There is an ever-increasing demand for security in IOT and its related systems. There has been a lot research in the field of cyber security to cater to the constantly evolving needs. Cyber security is an up-and-coming field be it in terms of research or job prospects. As more and more devices get connected, the need for security increases. Developers and designers will have to build a product keeping security as one of the primary concerns. Loss due to Cyber-attacks amount to several billion dollars each year and unless the security aspects are improved, this amount will keep going up.

IOT based technologies face countless security threats and with the evolution of technology the threats and vulnerabilities keep increasing. In our paper we discussed and documented the security concerns faced by 6 different domains in IOT, namely-smart cities, connected and autonomous vehicles, industry 4.0, smart grids, healthcare and wearable technology and smart homes. An overview of the major challenges faced like-confidentiality, authentication etc. was briefly discussed. It is concluded that most of the development of cybersecurity in IOT space is in the nascent stage and there is a lot left to be done. No IOT system is entirely safe and they may be easily prone to some type of cyberattack. In order to overcome this, the manufacturer and the end user need to take preventive measures. Future IOT systems should be designed and built while keeping security as one of the primary parameters. Users should be aware of the IOT system and use it responsibly. We hope that this survey proves to be useful to fellow IOT enthusiasts and researchers in the field of IOT and cybersecurity.

References

1. Kraus, A.: Watch out for wearables: new security risks posed by wearables & IoT (2019). https://www.zeguro.com/blog/new-security-risks-posed-by-wearables-iot
2. Mohamed, A., Geir, M.K.: Cyber security and the internet of things: vulnerabilities, threats, intruders and attacks. J. Cyber Secur. Mob. 4(4), 65–88 (2015)
3. Ching, K.W., Singh, M.M.: Wearable technology devices security and privacy vulnerability analysis. Int. J. Netw. Secur. Appl. 8(3), 19–30 (2016)
4. Tracy, K., Mathew, J.: Apple watch: 8 security issues (2015). https://www.bankinfosecurity.com/apple-watch
5. Ojha, Y.: I hacked Mi Band 3, and here is how I did it. Part I(2018). https://medium.com/@yogeshojha/i-hacked-xiaomi-miband-3-and-here-is-how-i-did-it-43d68c272391
6. Abdullahi, A.: Cyber security challenges within the connected home ecosystem futures. Procedia Comput. Sci. 61, 227–232 (2015)
7. Lin, H., Bergmann, N.: IoT privacy and security challenges for smart home environments. Information 7(3), 44 (2016). https://doi.org/10.3390/info7030044
8. Anil, L., Satinderjeet, S., Natasha, D., Rela, S.S.M.: Uses of different cyber security service to prevent attack on smart home infrastructure. Int. J. Technol. Res. Eng. 1(11), 5809–5813, 2347–4718 (2014)

9. Abdullah, T., Waleed, A., Sharaf, M., Adel, A.: a review of cyber security challenges, attacks and solutions for internet of things based smart home. IJCSNS Int. J. Comput. Sci. Netw. Secur. **19**(9), 139–146 (2019)
10. Hemsley, K.E., Fisher, E., Mon, R.: History of Industrial Control System Cyber Incidents. United States. https://doi.org/10.2172/1505628, https://www.osti.gov/servlets/purl/1505628
11. Lu, Y., Xu, L.D.: Internet of Things (IoT) cybersecurity research: a review of current research topics. IEEE Internet Things J. **6**(2), 2103–2115 (2019)
12. Vaidya, S., Ambad, P., Bhosle, S.: Industry 4.0 – a glimpse. Procedia Manuf. **20**, 233–238 (2018)
13. Thames, L., Schaefer, D.: Industry 4.0: an overview of key benefits, technologies, and challenges. In: Thames, L., Schaefer, D. (eds.) Cybersecurity for Industry 4.0. SSAM, pp. 1–33. Springer, Cham (2017). https://doi.org/10.1007/978-3-319-50660-9_1
14. Ervural, B., Ervural, B.: Overview of cyber security in the industry 4.0 era. In: Industry 4.0: Managing The Digital Transformation. SSAM, pp. 267–284. Springer, Cham (2018). https://doi.org/10.1007/978-3-319-57870-5_16
15. Benias, N., Markopoulos, A.P.: A review on the readiness level and cyber-security challenges in Industry 4.0. In: 2017 South Eastern European Design Automation, Computer Engineering, Computer Networks and Social Media Conference (SEEDA-CECNSM), Kastoria, pp. 1–5 (2017)
16. Dawson, M.: cyber security in industry 4.0: the pitfalls of having hyperconnected systems. J. Strat. Manag. Stud. **10**(1), 19–28 (2018)
17. Pereira, T., Baretto, L., Amaral, A.: Network and information security challenges within industry 4.0 paradigm. Procedia Manuf. **13**, 1253–1260 (2017)
18. Djenna, A., Eddine Saïdouni, D.: Cyber attacks classification in IoT-based-healthcare infrastructure. In: 2018 2nd Cyber Security in Networking Conference (CSNet), Paris, pp. 1–4 (2018)
19. Anil, C., Thaier, H.: Security and privacy issues with IoT in healthcare. EAI Endorsed Trans. Perv. Health Technol. Ghent **4**(14) (2018)
20. Coventry, L., Branley, D.: Cybersecurity in healthcare: a narrative review of trends, threats and ways forward. Maturitas **113**, 48–52 (2018). https://doi.org/10.1016/j.maturitas.2018.04.008
21. Mohan, A.: Cyber security for personal medical devices Internet of Things. In: 2014 IEEE International Conference on Distributed Computing in Sensor Systems, Marina Del Rey, CA, pp. 372–374 (2014)
22. Strielkina, A., Illiashenko, O., Zhydenko, M., Uzun, D.: Cybersecurity of healthcare IoT-based systems: regulation and case-oriented assessment. In: The 9th IEEE International Conference on Dependable Systems, Services and Technologies, DESSERT, 1–7 (2018)
23. Pandey, R.K., Mishra, M.: Cyber security threats-Smart grid infrastructure. In: National Power Systems Conference, pp. 1–6 (2016)
24. Gunduz, M.Z., Das, R.: Cyber-security on smart grid: threats and potential solutions. Comput. Netw. **169**(107094), 1–14 (2020)
25. Kimani, K., Oduol, V., Langat, K.: Cyber security challenges for IoT-based smart grid networks. Int. J. Crit. Infrastruct. Prot. **25**, 36–49 (2019)
26. Danda, B.R., Bajracharya, C.: Cyber security for smart grid systems: status, challenges and perspectives. In: Proceedings of the IEEE SoutheastCon 2015, Fort Lauderdale, Florida, pp. 1–6 (2015). https://doi.org/10.1109/SECON.2015.7132891
27. Yang, Y., Littler, T., Sezer, S., McLaughlin, K., Wang, H.F.: Impact of cyber-security issues on Smart Grid. In: 2011 2nd IEEE PES International Conference and Exhibition on Innovative Smart Grid Technologies, pp. 1–7 (2011). https://doi.org/10.1109/isgteurope.2011.6162722
28. Khclifa, B., Abla, S.: Security concerns in smart grids: threats, vulnerabilities and countermeasures. In: 2015 3rd International Renewable and Sustainable Energy Conference (IRSEC), pp. 1–6 (2015). https://doi.org/10.1109/irsec.2015.7454963

29. SLPowers. Healthcare Industry Most Targeted For Cyber Attacks. https://www.slpowers.com/Healthcare-Industry-Most-Targeted-For-Cyber-Attacks

30. Alibasic, A., Al Junaibi, R., Woon, J.A.W.L., Omar, M.A.: Cybersecurity for smart cities: a brief review. In: International Workshop on Data Analytics for Renewable Energy Integration, DARE 2016: Data Analytics for Renewable Energy Integration, pp 22–30 (2016)

31. Lin, P., Swimmer, M., Urano, A., Hilt, S., Vosseler, R.: Article on The Global Technical Support and R&D Center of TREND MICRO. https://documents.trendmicro.com/assets/

32. Fadilpasic, S.: Smart traffic sensors are vulnerable to cyberattacks (2016). https://www.itproportal.com/2016/04/19/

33. Pandey, P., Golden, D., Peasley, S., Kelkar, M.: Making Smart Cities Cyber Secure. https://www2.deloitte.com/content/dam/Deloitte/de/Documents/risk/Report_making_smart_cities_cyber_secure.pdf

34. Li, Y., Dai, W., Ming, Z., Qiu, M.: Privacy protection for preventing data over-collection in smart city. IEEE Trans. Comput. **65**(5), 1339–1350 (2016). https://doi.org/10.1109/tc.2015.2470247

35. Huq, N., Vosseler, R., Swimmer, M.: Cyberattacks Against Intelligent Transportation Systems Assessing Future Threats to ITS Trend Micro Forward-Looking Threat Research (FTR)Team. https://documents.trendmicro.com/assets/white_papers/wp-cyberattacks-against-intelligent-transportation-systems.pdf

36. Foltyn, T.: Article on "Smart irrigation system vulnerable to attacks" (2018). https://www.welivesecurity.com/2018/08/21/smart-irrigation-systems-vulnerable-warn-researchers/

37. Mahdi, D., et al.: Survey on "Attacks and defences on intelligent connected vehicles", Digital Communications and Networks, pp. 1–27 (2020). https://researchers.mq.edu.au/en/publications/attacks-and-defences-on-intelligent-connected-vehicles-a-survey

38. Parkinson, S., Ward, P., Wilson, K., Miller, J.: Cyber threats facing autonomous and connected vehicles: future challenges. IEEE Trans. Intell. Transp. Syst. **18**(11), 2898–2915 (2017). https://doi.org/10.1109/tits.2017.2665968

39. Junko, T.: An overview of cyber security for connected vehicles. IEICE Trans. Inf. Syst. **E101.D**(11), 2561–2575 (2018). https://doi.org/10.1587/transinf.2017ICI0001

40. Bureau, S.: Student researchers seek to improve cybersecurity of vehicle-to-vehicle communications. Rochester Institute of Technology News (2020). https://www.rit.edu/news/student-researchers-seek-improve-cybersecurity-vehicle-vehicle-communications

41. El-Rewini, Z., Sadatsharan, K., Selvaraj, D.F., Plathottam, S.J., Ranganathan, P.: Cybersecurity challenges in vehicular communications. Veh. Commun. 100214 (2019). https://doi.org/10.1016/j.vehcom.2019.100214

42. Stepehen, M.W.: Article on techgenix.com "cybersecurity risks for autonomous IOT-ready cars" (2016). http://techgenix.com/cybersecurity-risks-autonomous-cars/

43. Samydurai, R.V.: Security on Internet of Things (IOT) with challenges and countermeasures. IJEDR **5**(1) (2017), ISSN: 2321–9939

44. Iqbal, M.A., Olaleye, O.G., Bayoumi, M.A.: A review on Internet of Things (Iot): security and privacy requirements and the solution approaches global journal of computer science and technology: e network. Web Secur. **16**(7) (2016)

45. Broomead, B.: Article on "IOT device cyber vulnerabilities" (2020). www.securitymagazine.com/articles

ANFIS Based Smart Wound Monitoring System

Sudheer Kumar Nagothu[(✉)] [iD]

RVR & JC College of Engineering, Chowdavaram, Guntur 522019, Andhra Pradesh, India
nsudheerkumar@rvrjc.ac.in

Abstract. Every part of the human body is very important. When a wound occurs on the human body part, a proper environment needs to be provided in order to heal it. If the wound is not Adequately healed it may lead to other complications such as the removal of a body part. Various internal and external factors come into play when the healing of wounds occurs. In the current research, a smart wound monitoring system is proposed using artificial neural and fuzzy inference systems which will give the current status of the wound in terms of Alerting, normal, and better. Internet of things, which is being used in various research areas such as agriculture, smart homes, industrial applications, etc., is used here to alert the doctor or the corresponding person when the wound status is critical. The efficient ANFIS algorithm has provided good training accuracy for the wound monitoring system.

Keywords: IoT · ANFIS · Smart wound monitoring

1 Introduction

Wound monitoring is an essential phenomenon in the healing process. If the external and internal conditions are not in favor of wound healing, it will take more time to get the wound healed, in extreme conditions, the body part may need to be removed [1]. Certain research investigations are conducted to assess the healing of wounds by measuring the physical characteristics such as body temperature, Size, and color of the wound, etc. [2]. The patient would need to be continuously monitored in order to heal it properly [3]. Various wearable sensors are available in the market which will help to measure the human body parameters such as temperature, heartbeat, blood pressure, etc. When there is an abnormality in the reading of sensors, medical help should be immediately arranged [2, 4]. The Internet of things technology has been used in various applications such as agriculture, industrial, Medical, etc. [5]. When there is an abnormality in the body parameters, a nearby medical person can be alerted using IOT [6, 7]. The abnormality in sensor readings can be measured using various machine learning technologies such as decision trees, fuzzy logic, and CNN models [8, 9]. These machine learning models were used in various applications such as fire alerting systems using it, student attendance system, smart watering system, etc. [10–14].

© Springer Nature Singapore Pte Ltd. 2021
V. Arunachalam and K. Sivasankaran (Eds.): ICMDCS 2021, CCIS 1392, pp. 197–208, 2021.
https://doi.org/10.1007/978-981-16-5048-2_15

Table 1. Body temperature

Standard	Range
Very high	>41.5 °C
High	(38–41.5) °C
Normal	(35.1–37.9) °C
Low	<35 °C

Table 2. Air temperature

Standard	Range
High	(29–50) °C
Normal	(17–28) °C
Low	<16 °C

Table 3. Air humidity

Standard	Range
High	(60–100)%
Normal	(20–59)%
Low	(0–19)%

Table 4. Oxygenation

Standard	Range
High	>100%
Normal	(95–100)%
Low	<94.5%

2   Materials and Methods

An adaptive neuro-fuzzy inference system has been used to measure the status of wound. With respect to the training data used for the current research the ANFIS model has generated fuzzy rules, Which is preferred for the current research problem because of its uniqueness in matching the input with the desired output and it also has good optimization. There will be five layers in the ANFIS model which includes input layer and membership function layer, normalisation layer, output membership function layer and output layer. ANFIS model for the smart wound monitoring system can be visualized in Fig. 1. A MATLAB simulation approach was used for the current research problem to implement the ANFIS model. Various parameters such as body temperature, and atmospheric temperature and humidity, the oxygen level in the body are used to evaluate the wound status. The wound status is categorised into three levels such as alerting, normal and better. When the women's status is alerting, the nearby health professional will be alerted for a precautionary measure. The input parameters body temperature, air temperature and humidity, Oxygenation level, ranges are given in Tables 1, 2, 3 and 4 respectively. When the body temperature, air temperature, and humidity, oxygen levels are at a normal level, a supportive environment will be provided for the wound to get healed.

2.1 Smart Wound Monitoring Implementation Through ANFIS

In the current research triangle membership functions are considered for the four input parameters as it is simple to implement and they work in a more efficient manner. The fuzzy inference model can be visualized in Fig. 2 to which Sugeno engine model is used for implementation. Triangular membership function plot for internal and external parameters of the wound can be visualised in Figs. 3, 4, 5, 6 and 7. Figure 3 gives the triangular membership function for body temperature and Fig. 4 gives the triangle membership function for air temperature Fig. 5 gives triangular membership function for air humidity, Fig. 6 gives triangular membership function for Oxygenation.

Data for analysing the wound has been collected at various time and day intervals and it was tabulated as shown in Table 5. Based on wound status 3 values 1, 0, −1 are assigned when wound status is Alerting, Normal and Better respectively.

Wound status with respect to the internal and external parameters is also given. A sample set of 2800 is used for training and 400 is used for testing. The input data has been converted to the desired output by using the ANFIS model. When membership functions are defined for both input and output parameters the ANFIS will generate the rules to evaluate the output.

For the current research problem, the ANFIS model has generated 108 rules for the given training data. The rules can use a combination of various logical operations such as AND, OR gates, and it can be visualised in Fig. 7. For the input parameters considered such as body and atmospheric temperature, oxygen level the rules proposed will estimate the status of the wound. As fuzzy Sugeno Model has parameters which can be adjusted compared to Mamdani model, in the current research paper Sugeno Model is used.

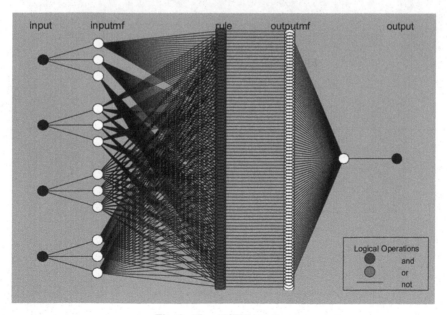

Fig. 1. The ANFIS structure

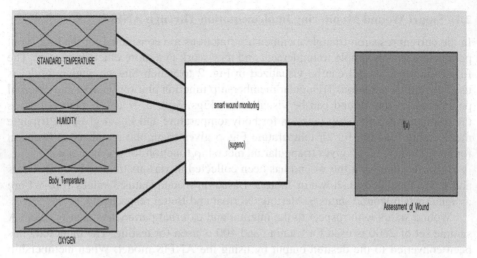

Fig. 2. ANFIS Sugeno engine

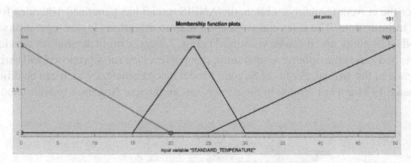

Fig. 3. Standard temperature MF plot

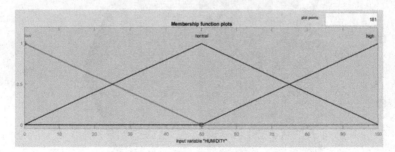

Fig. 4. Humidity MF plot

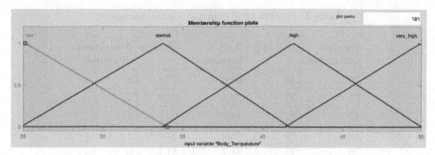

Fig. 5. Body temperature MF plot

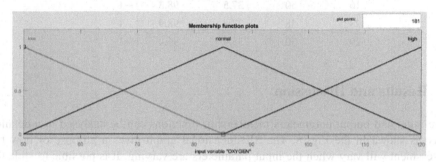

Fig. 6. Oxygenation MF plot

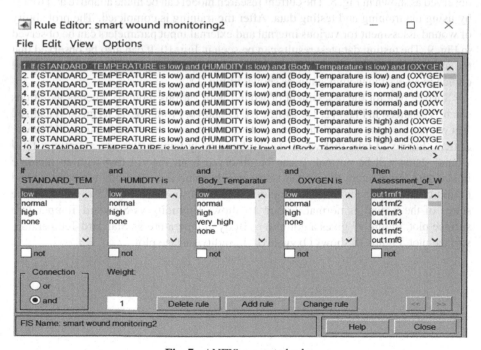

Fig. 7. ANFIS generated rules.

Table 5. Sample input data and wound assessment

Standard temperature	Humidity	Body temperature	Oxygen	Assessment of wound
20	28	46.6	97.1	1
21	97	39.5	83.5	1
40	87	39.7	60.6	1
19	84	48.8	82.6	1
26	73	31.7	51.1	0
34	82	35	90.1	0
16	50	37.5	98.3	−1
23	58	37.8	98.9	−1
29	30	35.9	96.4	−1

3 Results and Discussion

The input and output parameters membership functions can be analysed in a detailed way as shown in the Fig. 8. The 3-Dimensional graph gives a glimpse of how the assessment will vary when the input parameters are varying. It is possible to slide the input parameters from one side to the other and the variation in wound assessment can be observed as shown in Fig. 8. The current research model can be made adaptive and robust by using the training and testing data. After the training is completed. The probability of wound assessment for various internal and external input parameters can be observed in Fig. 9. The testing data test results can be seen in Fig. 10. It can also be observed that the average testing error is minimum, which assures that the ANFIS model is a good choice to assess the wound status as shown in Fig. 11.

Surface plot for the assessment of wound with various input parameters variations can be visualized in Figs. 12, 13, 14, 15, 16, 17 and 18. From Fig. 12 it can be visualized that with an increase in humidity and standard temperature the wound status will become critical. Figure 13 tells that when standard and body temperature are at optimal level wound status will be normal. It can be observed from Fig. 14 that with an increase in standard temperature the wound status will become critical. Body temperature and humidity have to be maintained at optimum level as shown in Fig. 15 to maintain the status of the wound as normal. Figure 16 shows Humidity vs Standard Temperature surface plot. Figure 17 gives a glimpse of Body Temperature vs Standard Temperature surface plot. Figure 18 shows Oxygen vs Humidity surface plot.

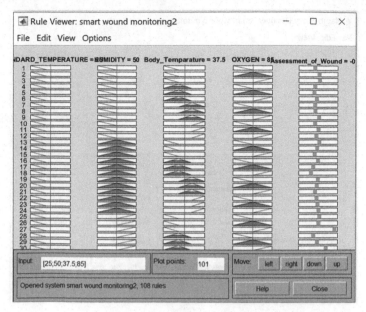

Fig. 8. ANFIS rules viewer

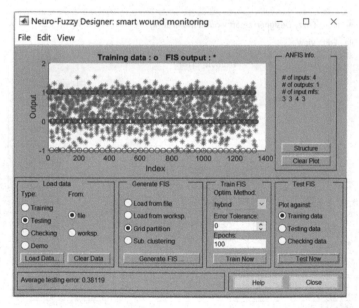

Fig. 9. ANFIS training data Test results

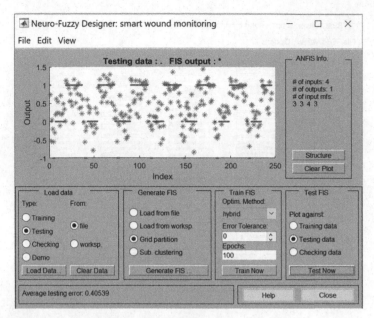

Fig. 10. ANFIS testing data test results

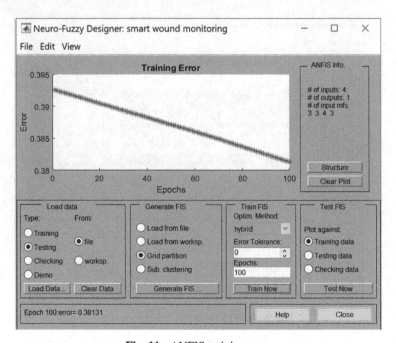

Fig. 11. ANFIS training error

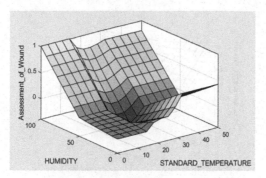

Fig. 12. Standard temperature vs Humidity surface plot

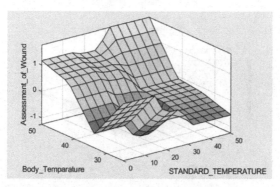

Fig. 13. Standard temperature vs Body temperature surface plot

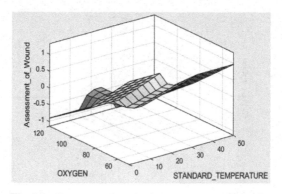

Fig. 14. Oxygen vs Standard temperature surface plot

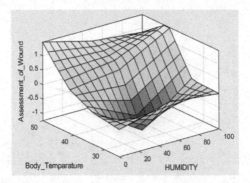

Fig. 15. Body temperature vs Humidity surface plot

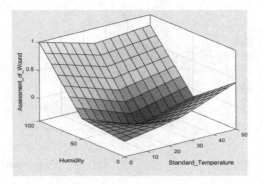

Fig. 16. Humidity vs Standard temperature surface plot

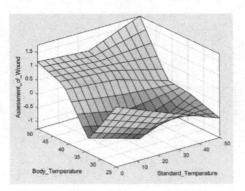

Fig. 17. Body temperature vs Standard temperature surface plot

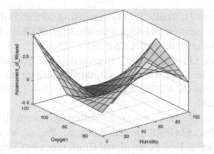

Fig. 18. Oxygen vs Humidity surface plot

4 Conclusions

In this paper, a smart Wound monitoring system has been proposed using an adaptive neuro-fuzzy inference system. The proposed model has taken various internal and external parameters of the Wound such as body and atmospheric temperature, humidity, and oxygenation level to assess the status of Wound. When the Wound status is alerting, the person who is monitoring the patient will be intimated for further actions. ANFIS model is used in the current research to implement the smart Wound monitoring system for its reliability and robustness. The proposed model will aid in timely healing of the wound.

References

1. Sattar, H., et al.: An IoT-based intelligent wound monitoring system. IEEE Access **7**, 144500–144515 (2019). https://doi.org/10.1109/ACCESS.2019.2940622
2. Farahani, B., Firouzi, F., Chang, V., Badaroglu, M., Constant, N., Mankodiya, K.: Towards fog-driven IoT eHealth: promises and challenges of IoT in medicine and healthcare. Futur. Gener. Comput. Syst. **78**, 659–676 (2018)
3. Brown, M.S., Ashley, B., Koh, A.: Wearable technology for chronic wound monitoring: current dressings, advancements, and future prospects. Front. Bioeng. Biotechnol. **6**, 47 (2018)
4. Sarwar, B., Bajwa, I.S., Jamil, N., Ramzan, S., Sarwar, N.: An intelligent fire warning application using IoT and an adaptive neuro-fuzzy inference system. Sensors **19**(14), 3150 (2019)
5. Nagothu, S.K., Kumar, O.P., Anitha, G.: Autonomous monitoring and attendance system using inertial navigation system and GPRS in predefined locations. In: 3rd International Conference on Eco-friendly Computing and Communication Systems, Mangalore, pp. 261–265 (2014). https://doi.org/10.1109/Eco-friendly.2014.60
6. Nagothu, S.K., Anitha, G., Annapantula, S.: Navigation aid for people (joggers and runners) in the unfamiliar urban environment using inertial navigation. In: Sixth International Conference on Advanced Computing (ICoAC), Chennai, pp. 216–219 (2014). https://doi.org/10.1109/ICoAC.2014.7229713
7. Nagothu, S.K., Kumar, O.P., Anitha, G.: GPS aided autonomous monitoring and attendance system. Procedia Comput. Sci. **87**, 99–104 (2016). ISSN 1877–0509, https://doi.org/10.1016/j.procs.2016.05.133
8. Nagothu, S.K.: Weather based smart watering system using soil sensor and GSM. In: 2016 World Conference on Futuristic Trends in Research and Innovation for Social Welfare (Startup Conclave), Coimbatore, pp. 1–3 (2016). https://doi.org/10.1109/STARTUP.2016.7583991

9. Nagothu, S.K.: Automated toll collection system using GPS and GPRS. In: 2016 International Conference on Communication and Signal Processing (ICCSP), Melmaruvathur, pp. 0651–0653 (2016). https://doi.org/10.1109/ICCSP.2016.7754222

10. Nagothu, S.K., Anitha, G.: INS - GPS integrated aid to partially vision impaired people using Doppler sensor. In: 2016 3rd International Conference on Advanced Computing and Communication Systems (ICACCS), Coimbatore, pp. 1–4 (2016). https://doi.org/10.1109/ICACCS.2016.7586386

11. Nagothu, S.K., Anitha, G.: Low-cost smart watering system in multi-soil and multi-crop environment using GPS and GPRS. In: Satapathy, S., Prasad, V., Rani, B., Udgata, S., Raju, K. (eds.) Proceedings of the First International Conference on Computational Intelligence and Informatics. Advances in Intelligent Systems and Computing (AISC), vol. 507, pp. 637–643. Springer, Singapore (2017). https://doi.org/10.1007/978-981-10-2471-9_61

12. Nagothu, S.K., Anitha, G.: INS-GPS enabled driving aid using Doppler sensor. In: 2015 International Conference on Smart Sensors and Systems (IC-SSS), Bangalore, pp. 1–4 (2015). https://doi.org/10.1109/SMARTSENS.2015.7873619

13. Nagothu, S.K.: Anti-theft alerting and monitoring of animals using integrated GPS and GPRS in Indian scenario. Pak. J. Biotechnol. 15(Special Issue I), 56–58 (2018)

14. Nagothu, S.K., Anitha, G.: Automatic landing site detection for UAV using supervised classification. In: Rao, P.J., Rao, K.N., Kubo, S. (eds.) Proceedings of International Conference on Remote Sensing for Disaster Management. SSGG, pp. 309–316. Springer, Cham (2019). https://doi.org/10.1007/978-3-319-77276-9_27

Nano-scale Modelling and Process Technology Device

Design and Optimization of a 50 nm Dual Material Dual Gate (DMDG), High-κ Spacer, FiNFET Having Variable Gate Metal Workfunction

Abhishek Bhattacharjee[✉], Tanmoy Majumder, Rajib Laskar, Shradhya Kar, Tamanna Laskar, Nabadipa Dey, and Amanisha Chakraborty

Department of Electronics and Communication Engineering, Tripura Institute of Technology, Narsingarh, Agartala, Tripura (West), India

Abstract. This paper proposes a dual-material dual gate (DMDG) FiNFET architecture that shows superior electrostatic control over the conventional FiNFET and planar MOS devices. The difference in the work function of the used gate metals and improved electrostatic integrity provided by the high-κ spacers mainly led to the performance improvements. Moreover, the proposed DMDG structure explores the possibility of a symmetric FiNFET architecture which will be highly beneficial from circuit application point of view.

Keywords: FiNFET · DMDG · Planar · Device physics

1 Introduction

Gradually, as the semiconductor industry is progressing to commercially use the 3-D gate all around (GAA) devices [1–5] in lower technology nodes, the dimensions of the channel are shortened to take the maximum advantage of utilizing the area by accommodating as many components as possible [6, 7]. This has led to various short channel effects (SCEs) such as increase in leakage current, increase in tunneling current through the gate, random dopant fluctuations (RDF), drain-induced-barrier–lowering (DIBL), Channel length Modulation (CLM), Punch- through etc. [8–10]. To combat these detrimental effects modifications in device architectures has been made and modern transistors like FiNFETs, silicon nanowire FETs are gradually replacing bulk MOSFETs [1–10]. FiNFET devices are gaining strong interest among the device researchers because of their power/performance advantages, better control over channel and scalability and hence they are being widely accepted as a strong contender for modern IC's. But the complexity of structures largely affects the performance of the device [1–3]. To improve the electrostatic integrity, as the FiNFET devices are scaled down continuously, the short channel effects are also increasing. The reduction of thickness of gate oxide, close to physical limit increases the gate leakage current. Most of the challenges which the modern day FiNFETs are facing are mainly due to fabrication technology restrictions. One important design parameter of FinFET is the fin thickness [5–8], which is generally

© Springer Nature Singapore Pte Ltd. 2021
V. Arunachalam and K. Sivasankaran (Eds.): ICMDCS 2021, CCIS 1392, pp. 211–216, 2021.
https://doi.org/10.1007/978-981-16-5048-2_16

kept equal to or smaller than gate length. But a major advantage is FiNFET scaling does not depend on oxide thickness (t_{ox}). Since the Fin devices can also operate at a lower operating voltage, the overall power consumption is also lesser which provides a strong ground for choosing it in modern day circuits [9, 10].

1.1 Device Structure

Keeping the above mentioned points in mind, we investigate in this paper using Cogenda 3D TCAD numerical simulator tool, the scaling behavior of a 50 nm channel length DMDG FiNFET as shown in Fig. 1 using the following parameters: length of channel L = 50 nm; thickness of gate oxide t_{ox} = 5 nm; doping concentration of the channel regions $N_A = 10^{16} cm^{-3}$; doping concentration of the source/drain contact regions $N_D = 10^{20} cm^{-3}$; fin height H_{fin} = 12 nm and fin width W_{fin} = 50 nm. The device parameters are enlisted in Table 1.

Table 1. Device parameters of the proposed FiNFET

Device parameters	Value
Physical gate length	50 nm
Oxide thickness	5 nm
Fin thickness	0.9 nm
Supply voltage	0.5 V
Channel doping	$1 * 10^{16} cm^{-3}$
Source/drain doping	$1 * 10^{20} cm^{-3}$
Threshold voltage	0.2 V

For more clarity of the readers the extracted .sim file and .drw files of the proposed device are shown in Fig. 2 and 3 respectively.

2 Result and Discussion

The performance parameters have been extracted for the proposed DMDG FinFET device using the following as standards:-

On Current (I_{ON}): The on-current (I_{ON}) have been calculated at V_{gs} = 1.5 V and drain voltage of V_{ds} = 0.5 V.

Off Current (I_{OFF}): It is the leakage current of the FiNFET in off state. It have been measured at V_{gs} = 0 V and a drain voltage V_{ds} = 0.5 V.

I_{ON}/I_{OFF} **Current ratio:** The I_{ON}/I_{OFF} ratio is measured as I_{ON} at V_{gs} = 1.5 V and I_{OFF} at V_{gs} = 0 V with V_{ds} = 0.5 V. For improved switching, higher value of I_{ON}/I_{OFF} is expected.

Subthreshold Swing (SS): Subthreshold Swing is calculated as the change in Vgs per decade change in Vds.

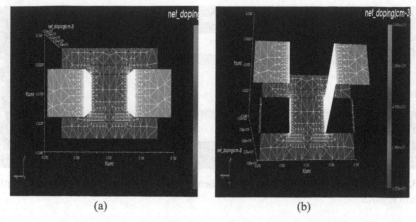

(a)   (b)

Fig. 1. (a) 3-D top view (b) side view of the proposed DMDG FiNFET.

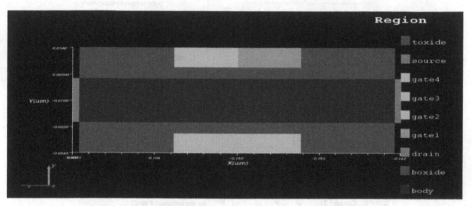

Fig. 2. .sim file of the proposed FiNFET extracted from Cogenda TCAD showing different regions

The simulated V-I characteristics of Dual material Dual gate (DMDG) FinFET is shown in Fig. 4(a). It is clear from the figure that the drive current of the proposed device is improved as compared to conventional FiNFET and planar MOSFET devices because of the improvement in electrostatic integrity over the channel because of front and back gates and difference in work function of the gate material used. The improved electrostatic coupling results in better concentration of fringe electric field lines in case of the proposed device.

From Fig. 4(b) it can be seen that gate length scaling does not have a considerable impact on the on current of the device as the improvement is only slight for $L_G = 40$ nm as compared to $L_G = 60$ nm. This further solidifies the fact that scaling has negligible effect on channel formation in case of a FiNFET. Since the difference in work function is maximum for Cu-Ti gate combination, best result in terms of I_{on} and I_{on}/I_{off} is obtained for this combination as shown in Fig. 4(c). This is mainly because of increase in concentration of vertical fringe electric field due to enhanced coupling. Lastly, since high-k gate oxide HfO_2, can help the internal fringe field lines of force to terminate on

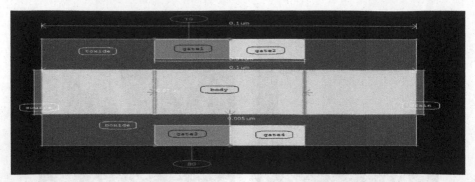

Fig. 3. .drw file of the proposed FiNFET extracted from Cogenda TCAD showing lengths of different regions

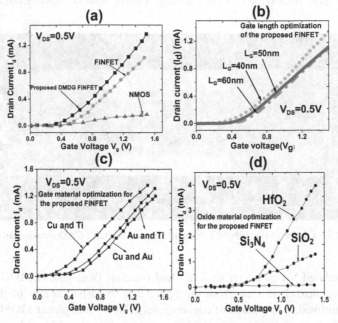

Fig. 4. (a) Comparison of I_d-V_{gs} characteristics of the proposed FiNFET, normal FiNFET and MOSFET. (b) Gate length optimization of the proposed FiNFET (c) Gate material optimization of the proposed FiNFET (d) Oxide material optimization of the proposed FiNFET.

the channel region of the FiNFET better as compared to Si_3N_4 and SiO_2, best results can be seen in this case from Fig. 4(d).

The better drain current performance due to difference in workfunction of front and back gates is also reflected in subthreshold swing and DIBL performance of the device as shown in Fig. 5(a) and (b) respectively. The device having Cu and Ti as gates shows the steepest S/S and lowest DIBL mainly because of a higher vertical electric fringe field concentration near the channel region owing to a superior coupling between back and

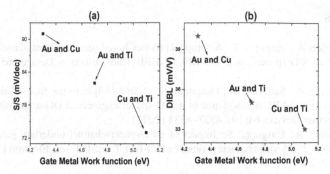

Fig. 5. (a) Variation of Subthreshold Swing (S/S) and (b) Drain induced barrier lowering (DIBL) with gate mateiral work function difference for the proposed FiNFET.

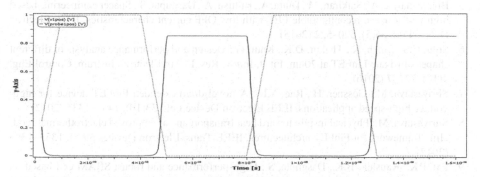

Fig. 6. Transient characteristics of the proposed DMDG FiNFET.

front gates. We have also simulated a CMOS Inverter with proposed DMDG FiNFET, the transient characteristics of which is shown in Fig. 6. The obtained propagation delay is 50 ns which is 30% and 26% less than normal FiNFET and MOSFET respectively.

3 Conclusions

A symmetric Dual Material Dual Gate (DMDG) FiNFET is designed, analyzed and optimized in this paper. It is found that the influence of two gates wrapping the channel with different work functions improves the electrostatic integrity and the influence of vertical electric field thus helping in channel formation. This is reflected in the improved current drive and reduced inverter delay as compared to single gate planar FiNFET, and bulk MOSFET devices. Moreover, it is also demonstrated that more the difference in work function between the front and the back gates, higher the current drive and on-off current ratio. Finally, shorter gate lengths and high-k gate dielectric is found to be beneficial for better performance.

Acknowledgements. Authors are grateful to Tripura Institute Of Technology (TIT), Agartala for providing financial and lab assistance to carry out this research work.

References

1. Bhattacharjee, A., Dasgupta, S.: A compact physics-based surface potential and drain current model for an S/D spacer-based DG-RFET. IEEE Trans. Electron Devices **65**(2), 448–455 (2018)
2. Bhattacharjee, A., Saikiran, M., Dasgupta, S.: A first insight to the thermal dependence of the DC, analog and RF performance of a S/D spacer engineered DG-ambipolar FET. IEEE Trans. Electron Devices **64**(10), 4327–4334 (2017)
3. Bhattacharjee, A., Dasgupta, S.: Impact of gate/spacer-channel underlap, gate oxide EOT, and scaling on the device characteristics of a DG-RFET. IEEE Trans. Electron Devices **64**(8), 3063–3070 (2017)
4. Bhattacharjee, A., Dasgupta, S.: Optimization of design parameters in dual-κ spacer-based nanoscale reconfigurable FET for improved performance. IEEE Trans. Electron Devices **63**(3), 1375–1382 (2016)
5. Bhattacharjee, A., Saikiran, M., Dutta, A., Bulusu, A., Dasgupta, S.: Spacer engineering-based high-performance reconfigurable FET with low OFF current characteristics. IEEE Electron Device Lett. **36**(5), 520–522 (2015)
6. Sohi, C.S., Singh, K., Thakur, D.K., Kaur, G.: Design and performance analysis of different shapes of trigate FinFET at 20nm. Int. J. Innov. Res. Electr. Electron. Instrum. Control Eng. **4**(10), 72–77 (2016)
7. Shrivastava, M., Gossner, H., Rao, V.R.: A novel drain-extended FinFET device for high-voltage high-speed applications. IEEE Electron Device Lett. **33**(10), 1432–1434 (2012)
8. Shrivastava, M.: Physical insight toward heat transport and an improved electrothermal modeling framework for FinFET architectures. IEEE Trans. Electron Devices **59**(5), 1353–1363 (2012)
9. Pal, P.K., Kaushik, B.K., Dasgupta, S.: High-performance and robust SRAM cell based on asymmetric dual-k spacer FinFETs. IEEE Trans. Electron Devices **60**(10), 3371–3377 (2013)
10. Pal, P.K., Kaushik, B.K., Dasgupta, S.: Low-power and robust 6T SRAM cell using symmetric dual-k spacer FinFETs. In: 29th International Conference on Microelectronics Proceedings - MIEL at Belgrade, Serbia (2014)

Tunnel FET Based SRAM Cells
– A Comparative Review

Rasheed Gadarapulla and Sridevi Sriadibhatla

Vellore Institute of Technology, Vellore, India
{gadarapulla.rasheed,sridevi}@vit.ac.in

Abstract. This paper reviews some of the recent developments in Tunnel FET based SRAM cells. Tunnel Field Effect Transistor (TFET) is a potential contender to outperform CMOS at low voltages. Unique characteristics of TFET such as band-to-band tunneling, subthreshold swing (SS) < 60 mV/dec, and very low leakage current are suitable for designing ultra-low-power circuits. Novel techniques are proposed in recent years to address the issue of low ON-current (I_{ON}) and ambipolarity in TFET. We will review the performance of various TFET based SRAM cells in terms of stability, access times, and power consumption during the read and write operation. Parameters such as read static noise margin (RSNM), write SNM (WSNM), read delay, and write delay, read power, write power, and leakage power are considered for comparing various TFET based SRAM cells. The study shows that the heterojunction TFET based SRAM is superior to homojunction TFET based SRAM in terms of lower power consumption and faster access times.

Keywords: Tunnel FET · Subthreshold swing · SRAM · Stability · Heterojunction

1 Introduction

Continuous scaling of MOSFET for the past few decades has led to various short channel effects in the recent nanometer-scale devices. The effects of scaling give rise to increased leakage power consumption, especially at low voltages. Hence, designing low power circuits with these devices has become a challenge. Due to the thermal diffusion-based current flow mechanism in MOSFET, the SS is also limited to 60 mV/dec [1]. The scaling of MOS devices in the order of few nanometers has almost reached its physical limits. To overcome the short channel effects at low voltages, there is a need for an alternate device. In this quest, both industry and academia have examined many innovative devices. One such energy-efficient device is the Tunnel Field Effect Transistor. The current conduction mechanism in TFET is based on the principle of band-to-band tunneling of carriers. This mechanism helps in favorable properties of TFET such as steep SS (less than 60 mV/dec) and very low leakage current. Because of these unique characteristics, TFET is an excellent choice for designing ultra-low-power circuits with low leakage current. However, some limitations of TFET such as low I_{ON} and ambipolar

© Springer Nature Singapore Pte Ltd. 2021
V. Arunachalam and K. Sivasankaran (Eds.): ICMDCS 2021, CCIS 1392, pp. 217–228, 2021.
https://doi.org/10.1007/978-981-16-5048-2_17

nature of the current act as impediments in designing efficient ultra-low-power circuits. Various techniques are proposed in the literature to improve the I_{ON} of the TFET. Gate engineering techniques of the TFET include increasing the dielectric constant of the gate oxide or decreasing the thickness of the gate oxide [22], use of high-κ gate material [18], wrap-around gate structure [23], introducing a spacer dielectric on both sides of the gate [24], asymmetrical gate structure [11, 12]. Asymmetrical gate structure, as the name suggests is an approach of having different properties of the gate on the source and drain sides. This approach helps in suppressing ambipolar conduction as well as reducing the I_{OFF} for a given I_{ON} [11]. Using this approach in [11], gate nearer to the source with low work function and gate nearer to the drain with high work function has shown improved I_{ON}/I_{OFF} ratio. In [12], a hetero-gate structure TFET is proposed with high-κ material gate oxide on the source side and low-κ material on the drain side to improve I_{ON}. I_{ON} can also be improved by tunnel junction engineering methods such as increasing the source doping concentration [26], introducing a strongly doped source pocket leading to PNPN TFET [27], using a heterojunction tunneling transistor (HETT) as in [13] constituting of SiGe/Si materials. Different materials such as III-V semiconductors, Germanium, nanowires, carbon-based nanomaterials are being investigated by the researchers to address the low I_{ON} limitation of the TFET. III-V compound semiconductors when used as heterojunction in TFET can aid in attaining high I_{ON} and low I_{OFF} simultaneously [2]. III-V semiconductors are particularly favorable due to their smaller bandgap, direct bandgap nature, and higher tunneling rates [28]. The capability of TFETs in improving the power savings of low-voltage adiabatic circuits especially for low operating frequencies is shown in [39].

Ambipolarity refers to the same TFET displaying both n-type and p-type behavior with the electrons and holes making the major contribution in the current transport, at the same drain voltage VDS [2]. Ambipolar current in a TFET is not desirable and has to be suppressed as it leads to high I_{OFF} [2]. Several techniques such as decreasing the drain doping concentration [10], making a drain-gate underlap [14], using a heterojunction [13], or asymmetric TFET structures [11, 12] have been proposed to suppress the ambipolar current.

Since TFETs have distinct electrical properties compared to conventional MOSFET, there is a need to find the significance of these properties on TFET based circuits. For this purpose, a single device characterization alone is not enough. Till now, the assessment of the performance of TFET based circuits has been majorly done using mixed-mode i.e., device/circuit analysis based TCAD simulations [3–7] and look-up table (LUT) based Verilog-A models for TFETs [8, 9].

The Static Random Access Memory (SRAM) cell is one of the most important digital circuits, mainly used in the higher levels of memory hierarchy as registers and data cache in processors. SRAM is a volatile memory with faster access times used to store data that is most frequently accessed by the processor. The design of the SRAM cell using TFETs provides a good opportunity to determine the merits of TFETs over the traditional MOSFETs. The article begins with an introduction in Sect. 1, the basic structure of TFET in Sect. 2, SRAM cells based on recent TFETs in Sect. 3, comparative study of various TFET based SRAMs in Sect. 4, and conclusion in Sect. 5.

2   Basic Structure of TFET

The TFET is a reverse-biased p-i-n structure with a gate on top of a dielectric layer. The structure of TFET resembles a conventional MOSFET except that the source and drain regions are oppositely doped whereas it is similarly doped in MOSFET. Figure 1(a) and 1(b) represent the schematic of n-type and p-type TFET respectively along with biasing arrangement. The drain is N+ doped and the source is P+ doped in an n-type TFET. Whereas in a p-type TFET, the drain is P+ doped and the source is N+ doped. In other words, the type of TFET is determined by the type of dominant carrier in the channel when the TFET is in on-state. The channel is an intrinsic or lightly doped n-type or p-type semiconductor. The source-channel junction is the region where tunneling happens. TFET is a unidirectional device which means the charge carriers travel in only one direction i.e., from source to drain, and hence the current flows in opposite direction i.e., from drain to source [21]. The dielectric layer isolates the channel from the gate electrode.

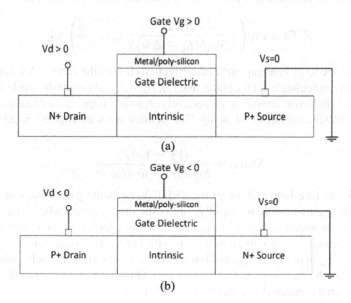

Fig. 1. (a). n-type TFET [2] (b). p-type TFET [2]

The working principle of TFET is band-to-band tunneling (BTBT) of charge carriers. BTBT can be controlled by applying gate bias in the channel region [15, 16]. The energy band diagram of TFET in OFF-state and ON-state is shown in Fig. 2(a) and 2(b) respectively. When a positive gate voltage is applied to the n-type TFET, the bands in the channel region are pushed down due to which the conduction band of the channel goes below the valence band of the source. This creates a tunneling window through which the carriers tunnel at the source-channel junction giving rise to the band-to-band tunneling current.

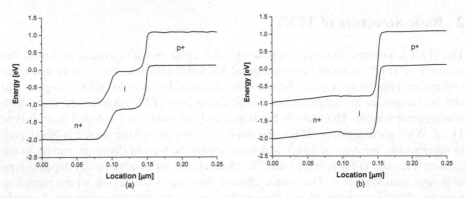

Fig. 2. (a). Energy band diagram of n-type TFET in OFF-state and (b) Energy band diagram of n-type TFET in ON-state [18]

The tunneling probability T (E) based on the study in [17] is given as

$$T(E) \propto \exp\left(-\frac{4\sqrt{2m^*}E_g^{\frac{3}{2}}}{3|e|\hbar(E_g + \Delta\Phi)}\sqrt{t_{ox}t_{Si}\frac{\varepsilon_{Si}}{\varepsilon_{ox}}}\right)\Delta\Phi \tag{1}$$

where Eg is the energy bandgap, m* is the effective mass of the carrier, $\Delta\Phi$ is the energy window where tunneling can take place, and t_{ox}, t_{Si}, ε_{ox}, and ε_{Si} are the oxide and silicon thickness and dielectric constants, respectively. Another important advantage of TFET is its < 60 mV/dec subthreshold swing. The definition for average SS is given in [18] as:

$$SS_{AVG} = \frac{(V_T - V_{OFF})}{log(I_{VT}) - log(I_{OFF})} \tag{2}$$

where V_T is the threshold voltage of the TFET, V_{OFF} is the gate voltage at which the drain current begins to increase rapidly, I_{VT} is the drain current when $V_{GS} = V_T$ and I_{OFF} is the drain current at $V_{GS} = V_{OFF}$. The low I_{ON} problem in a conventional TFET has been addressed in [18] with a double-gate TFET (DGTFET) structure using a high-K dielectric leading to improved I_{ON} and lower subthreshold swing. The schematic diagram of DGTFET is shown in Fig. 3. The double-gate TFET provides better control over the channel potential compared to a single-gate TFET [2].

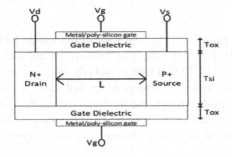

Fig. 3. Schematic diagram of DGTFET [2]

3 SRAM Cells Based on Recent TFET Structures

3.1 Double Pocket Double Gate Tunnel Field Effect Transistor (DP-DGTFET) Based 7T SRAM Cell

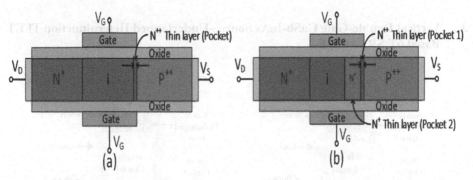

Fig. 4. Schematic of (a) SP-DGTFET and (b) DP-DGTFET [19]

In [19], a silicon-based DP-DGTFET is proposed, it is a homojunction TFET because the source, channel, and drain are all made of the same material. A pocket 2 of thickness 10 nm with a doping concentration of $N_D = 2.8 \times 10^{18}$ cm^{-3} is introduced besides the existing pocket 1 in the proposed structure. The introduction of the pocket at the source-channel junction of the TFET results in an increase in lateral electric field in the tunneling junction, which in turn results in increased band bending and ultimately leads to reduced tunnel barrier at the source-channel junction [27]. The performance of DP-DGTFET is shown to be better than Single Pocket Double Gate Tunnel Field Effect Transistor (SP-DGTFET) in terms of I_{ON}, the threshold voltage (Vt), SS$_{avg}$, I_{ON}/I_{OFF} ratio, and I_{ON}/C_{gg}. The proposed device has an I_{ON} of 120.58 μA/μm, I_{ON}/I_{OFF} ratio of 2.54×10^{10}, Vt of 0.336 V, and SS$_{avg}$ of 45.86 mV/dec at Vds = 1 V. The proposed structures in [19] are illustrated in Fig. 4.

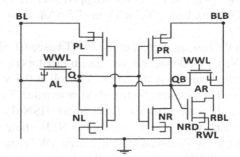

Fig. 5. 7T SRAM cell based on DP-DGTFET [19]

DP-DGTFET based SRAM cell is depicted in Fig. 5. In this SRAM cell, the pull up devices draw power from the bitlines BL, BLB. A separate read buffer and column voltage collapse write assist are employed in the proposed cell to improve the read and write stabilities [19]. The DP-DGTFET based 7T SRAM cell offers an 8X higher write margin, 1.3X modest write delay, comparative RSNM, and read delay while consuming 2.2X modest write power, and comparable read power contrasted to the current 7T SRAM cell in [34] (at Vdd = 0.5 V).

3.2   Vertical Double-Gate GaSb-InAs Source-Underlapped Heterojunction TFET Based 6T SRAM Cell

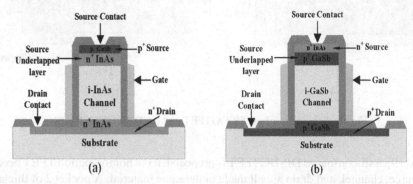

Fig. 6. (a) n-TFET device having n$^+$- doped underlap layer of InAs between source and channel and (b) p-TFET device having p$^+$- doped underlap layer of GaSb between source and channel [20].

In [20], the authors utilized the vertical double-gate GaSb-InAs source-underlapped heterojunction TFET proposed in [32] to design a 6T SRAM cell. The GaSb-InAs heterojunction TFET is an excellent choice because of its broken-gap band alignment which results in a large drive current [33]. Figure 6(a) shows an n-type TFET device having n$^+$- doped underlap layer of InAs between source and channel whereas a p-type TFET device having p$^+$- doped underlap layer of GaSb between source and the channel is shown in Fig. 6(b). The 10 nm underlapped n-TFET (p-TFET) draw an I$_{ON}$ of 235 µA/µm (210 µA/µm), I$_{OFF}$ of 0.3 nA/µm (1.5 nA/µm) at 0.5 V supply voltage [32].

This work assesses the leakage current of the TFET based 6T SRAM cell in standby mode for different pull-up, pull-down, and pass-gate transistors ratios (PU: PD: PG) and also performs the stability analysis of the 6T SRAM cell at 0.5 V supply voltage. The stability of an SRAM cell is measured by the SNM parameter. To analyze the stability of 6T SRAM cell, the authors have evaluated hold SNM (HSNM), read SNM (RSNM), write SNM (WSNM), static voltage noise margin (SVNM), static current noise margin (SINM), write-trip voltage (WTV) and write-trip current (WTI) parameters for different PU: PD: PG (1:1:1, 1:5:2, 2:5:2) configurations. The results thus obtained are compared with FinFET based 6T SRAM cell. The authors conclude from the comprehensive stability analysis, that the TFET based SRAMs have superior HSNM and RSNM compared to the FinFET based SRAMs however the latter has higher WSNM. Figure 7 illustrates a basic 6T SRAM cell.

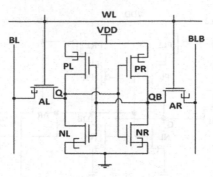

Fig. 7. Basic 6T SRAM cell

3.3 InAs Double-Gate Homojunction TFET Based 9T SRAM Cell

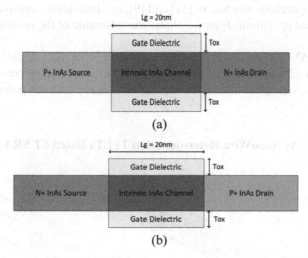

Fig. 8. Schematic of InAs Double-gate homojunction TFET (a) n-type (b) p-type [25]

In this work [25], the authors used a double gate p-i-n InAs TFET based Universal TFET model developed by Notre Dame University [29]. The schematic of InAs Double-gate homojunction TFET is shown in Fig. 8. InAs is an interesting choice for TFET fabrication, due to its direct band-gap and wide range of compositionally tunable band-alignment for tunnel barrier reduction [30]. The channel length of the device is 20 nm.

In [25], the proposed 9T SRAM cell consists of cross-coupled inverters, power cut-off transistors PL1, PR1, access transistors AL, AR for a write operation, and read buffer with a separate transistor ND. The bitlines BL, BLB drives the power cut-off transistors, PL1 and PR1. These transistors are used to cut the pull-up path during the write operation to provide the dispute free discharge of the '0' going node. For a read operation, an independent bitline RBL is used. A single wordline WL is used for both the

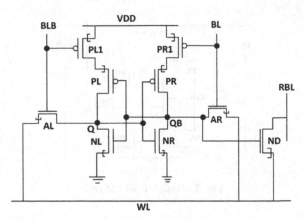

Fig. 9. 9T SRAM cell based on InAs double gate TFET [25]

read and write operations whereas in [31] and [9], two individual wordlines are used for reading and write operations. Figure 9 shows the schematic of the proposed 9T SRAM cell.

The 9T SRAM cell in [25], achieved 1.15X better write margin, 25% modest write delay, 73% and 13% reduction in write energy and average energy per operation, and 7% saving in leakage power (at VDD = 0.3 V) compared with the previous 9T TFET cell in [31].

3.4   AlGaSb/InAs NanoWire Heterojunction TFETs Based 6T SRAM Cell

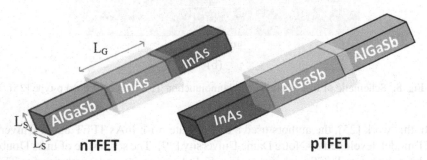

Fig. 10. Sketch of n- and p-type TFET device architectures. The red and blue colors indicate the n- and p-doping types, respectively (green: intrinsic semiconductor, transparent-grey: oxide). TFET dimensions are: LG = 20 nm, nanowire cross-section (LS) = 7 nm, EOT = 1 nm [35]. (Color figure online)

The authors in this work [35], have examined the performance of basic digital, analog, and mixed-signal circuits using TFETs and compared the same with the predictive technology model (PTM) platform of 10 nm node FinFET [36]. The TFET employed for this purpose is an AlGaSb/InAs NanoWire Heterojunction TFET proposed in [37], the schematic of which is shown in Fig. 10. The nanowire is square-shaped with a side of $L_S = 7$ nm, a gate length of $L_G = 20$ nm, and an equivalent oxide thickness EOT = 1 nm. Circuit simulations are done using look-up-tables (LUTs) obtained from TCAD simulations and calibrated against full-quantum results.

The authors in [38] have proved that the basic 6T SRAM cell can function without serious performance degradation compared to more complex cells such as 8T cell, provided that (1) outward-ATs are used and (2) the bit-lines (BLs) are precharged to VDD/2 for the read operation. The SNM for the read and write operation is calculated for the 6T SRAM cell to determine the stability of the cell. The analysis is done on a conventional 6T SRAM cell with outward-faced ATs (access transistors), the sketch of which is shown in Fig. 7. The authors conclude based on the outcomes that TFET technology has clear advantages over FinFET for VDD lower than 0.4 V.

4 Comparative Summary of TFET Based SRAM Cells

In this section, a performance comparison of various TFET based SRAM cells discussed above is presented. In this survey, both homojunction and heterojunction TFET based SRAM cells are considered. Various parameters of different TFET based SRAM cells such as RSNM, WSNM, read delay, write delay, leakage power, read and write power are compared to identify the better one in terms of better stability, fast access times, and low power requirements. The parameters are tabulated below in Table 1.

Table 1. Comparison of performance of TFET based SRAM cells.

Parameter	Homojunction TFET		Heterojunction TFET	
	Si DP-DGTFET 7T [19]	InAs DGTFET 9T [25]	GaSb-InAs TFET 6T [20] (PU:PD:PG = 1:5:2)	AlGaSb/InAs NW 6T [35]
Supply voltage (V)	0.5	0.4	0.5	0.5
RSNM (mV)	168.88	114	48.3	115 (@ V_{DD} = 0.3 V)
WSNM (mV)	236.38	133	82.46	126 (@ V_{DD} = 0.3 V)
Leakage power	0.412 pW	30.9 pW	3.74 nW	
Write delay	3.554 nS	10.4 pS	0.346 nS	43.81 nS
Read delay	2.292 nS	5 nS	5.502 nS	2.754 nS
Read power	7.33 nW	–	12.728 nW	–
Write power	0.16 μW	–	3.62 nW	–

In general, the heterojunction TFETs are better than homojunction TFETs because the heterojunction TFET decreases the effective bandgap which leads to increased I_{ON}.

Another advantage is it inhibits the ambipolar behavior of TFET due to which lower I_{OFF} and lower SS can be obtained. From Table 1, it is evident that the vertical double-gate GaSb-InAs source-underlapped heterojunction TFET based 6T SRAM cell has a very low write delay but slightly higher read delay than the AlGaSb/InAs NanoWire Heterojunction TFETs based 6T SRAM cell at 0.5V V_{DD}. The Si – homojunction double pocket DGTFET based 7T SRAM accomplishes very low leakage power (less than half pW), lower write delay, and read power except higher write power at 0.5 V_{DD}. The Si-DPDGTFET based 7T SRAM performs the read operation faster than other cells in consideration due to its very low read delay.

5   Conclusion

A detailed survey of recent TFET based SRAM cells was discussed in this paper. A comparative study of both homojunction and heterojunction TFET based SRAMs is performed for a supply voltage of 0.5 V. The vertical double-gate GaSb-InAs source-underlapped heterojunction TFET based 6T SRAM cell offers better power savings. The Si DP-DGTFET based 7T SRAM cell has the least leakage power, better read and write stability compared to other cells. It also has the best read access time and least power consumption for read operation in comparison with other cells. The stability and speed of SRAM cells can be further improved by employing TFETs with a higher I_{ON}/I_{OFF} ratio and lower subthreshold swing.

References

1. Sze, S.M., Ng, K.K.: Physics of Semiconductor Devices, vol. 10. Wiley, Hoboken (1995)
2. Saurabh, S., Kumar, M.J.: Fundamentals of Tunnel Field-Effect Transistors. CRC Press, Boca Raton (2016)
3. Singh, J., et al.: A novel Si-Tunnel FET based SRAM design for ultra low-power 0.3V VDD applications. In: Proceedings of the 15th Asia and South Pacific Design Automation Conference (ASP-DAC), Taipei, pp. 181–186. IEEE (2010)
4. Singh, J., et al.: TFET based 6T SRAM cell. U.S. Patent 20 120 106 236 A1, 27 October (2010)
5. Mookerjea, S., et al.: Experimental demonstration of 100nm channel length In0.53Ga0.47As-based vertical inter-band tunnel field effect transistors (TFETs) for ultra low-power logic and SRAM applications. In: IEEE International Electron Devices Meeting (IEDM), Baltimore, MD, USA, pp. 1–3. IEEE (2009)
6. Strangio, S., et al.: Impact of TFET unidirectionality and ambipolarity on the performance of 6T SRAM cells. IEEE J. Electron Devices Soc. 3(3), 223–232 (2015)
7. Chen, Y.-N., Fan, M.-L., Hu, V.P.-H., Su, P., Chuang, C.-T.: Design and analysis of robust tunneling FET SRAM. IEEE Trans. Electron Devices 60(3), 1092–1098 (2013)
8. Lee, Y., et al.: Low-power circuit analysis and design based on heterojunction tunneling transistors (HETTs). IEEE Trans. Very Large Scale Integr. VLSI Syst. 21(9), 1632–1643 (2013)
9. Morris, D.H., Avci, U.E., Young, I.A.: Variation-tolerant dense TFET memory with low VMIN matching low-voltage TFET logic. In: 2015 Symposium on VLSI Technology (VLSI Technology), Kyoto, pp. T24–T25. IEEE (2015)

10. Koswatta, S.O., Nikonov, D., Lundstrom, M.S.: Computational study of carbon nanotube p-i-n tunnel FETs. In: IEEE International Electron Devices Meeting. IEDM Technical Digest, Washington, DC, pp. 518–521. IEEE (2005)
11. Saurabh, S., Kumar, M.J.: Novel attributes of a nanoscale dual material gate tunnel field effect transistor. IEEE Trans. Electron Devices **58**, 404–410 (2011)
12. Choi, W.Y., Lee, W.: Hetero-gate-dielectric tunneling field-effect transistors. IEEE Trans. Electron Devices **57**, 2317–2319 (2010)
13. Koester, S.J., et al.: Are Si/SiGe tunneling field-effect transistors a good idea? ECS Trans. **33**(6), 357–361 (2010)
14. Abdi, D.B., Kumar, M.J.: Controlling ambipolar current in tunneling FETs using overlapping gate-on-drain. IEEE J. Electron Devices Soc. **2**, 87–190 (2014)
15. Seabaugh, A.C., Zhang, Q.: Low-voltage tunnel transistors for beyond CMOS logic. Proc. IEEE **98**(12), 2095–2110 (2010)
16. Ionescu, A.M., Riel, H.: Tunnel field-effect transistors as energy efficient electronic switches. Nature **479**(7373), 329–337 (2011)
17. Knoch, J., Appenzeller, J.: A novel concept for field-effect transistors - the tunneling carbon nanotube FET. In: 63rd Device Research Conference Digest, DRC 2005, Santa Barbara, vol. 1, pp. 153–156. IEEE (2005)
18. Boucart, K., Ionescu, A.M.: Double-gate tunnel FET with high-κ gate dielectric. IEEE Trans. Electron Devices **54**, 1725–1733 (2007)
19. Ahmad, S., Ahmad, S.A., Muqeem, M., Alam, N., Hasan, M.: TFET-based robust 7T SRAM cell for low power application. IEEE Trans. Electron Devices **66**(9), 3834–3840 (2019)
20. Mohammed, M.U., Chowdhury, M.H.: Reliability and energy efficiency of the tunneling transistor-based 6T SRAM cell in sub-10 nm domain. IEEE Trans. Circuits Syst. II Express Briefs **65**(12), 1829–1833 (2018)
21. Avici, U.E., Morris, D., Young, I.A.: Tunnel field-effect transistors: prospects and challenges. IEEE J. Electron Devices Soc. **3**(3), 88–95 (2015)
22. Verhulst, A., et al.: Si-based tunnel field-effect transistors for low-power nano-electronics. In: 69th Device Research Conference, Santa Barbara, CA, pp. 193–196. IEEE (2011)
23. Morita, Y., et al.: Performance enhancement of tunnel field-effect transistors by synthetic electric field effect. IEEE Electron Device Lett. **35**, 792–794 (2014)
24. Chattopadhyay, A., Mallik, A.: Impact of a spacer dielectric and a gate overlap/underlap on the device performance of a tunnel field-effect transistor. IEEE Trans. Electron Devices **58**, 677–683 (2011)
25. Ahmad, S., Alam, N., Hasan, M.: Robust TFET SRAM cell for ultra-low power IoT applications. AEU – Int. J. Electron. Commun. **89**, 70–76 (2018)
26. Sandow, C., Knoch, J., Urban, C., Zhao, Q.-T., Mantl, S.: Impact of electrostatics and doping concentration on the performance of silicon tunnel field-effect transistors. Solid-State Electron. **53**, 1126–1129 (2009)
27. Nagavarapu, V., Jhaveri, R., Woo, J.: The tunnel source (PNPN) n- MOSFET: a novel high performance transistor. IEEE Trans. Electron Devices **55**, 1013–1019 (2008)
28. Woodall, J.M.: Fundamentals of III-V Semiconductor MOSFETs. Springer, Boston (2010). https://doi.org/10.1007/978-1-4419-1547-4
29. Lu, H., Ytterdal, T., Seabaugh, A.: Universal TFET Model. (Version 1.6.8). nanoHUB (2015). https://doi.org/10.4231/D3901ZG9H
30. Liu, H., Narayanan, V., Datta, S.: Penn State III-V Tunnel FET Verilog-A Model Manual (Version 1.0.1). nanoHUB. https://doi.org/10.4231/D30Z70X8D
31. Amir, M.F., Trivedi, A.R., Mukhopadhyay, S.: Exploration of Si/Ge tunnel FET bit cells for ultra-low power embedded memory. IEEE J. Emerg. Sel. Top. Circuits Syst. **6**(2), 185–197 (2016)

32. Sharma, A., Akkala, A.G., Kulkarni, J.P., Roy, K.: Source underlapped GaSb-InAs TFETs with applications to gain cell embedded DRAMs. IEEE Trans. Electron Devices **63**(6), 2563–2569 (2016)

33. Mohata, D., et al.: Barrier-engineered arsenide–antimonide heterojunction tunnel FETs with enhanced drive current. IEEE Electron Device Lett. **33**(11), 1568–1570 (2012)

34. Liu, J.S., Clavel, M.B., Hudait, M.K.: An energy-efficient tensile-strained Ge/InGaAs TFET 7T SRAM cell architecture for ultralow-voltage applications. IEEE Trans. Electron Devices **64**(5), 2193–2200 (2017)

35. Strangio, S., et al.: Digital and analog TFET circuits: design and benchmark. Solid-State Electron. **146**, 50–65 (2018)

36. Predictive Technology Model Website. http://ptm.asu.edu

37. Baravelli, E., Gnani, E., Gnudi, A., Reggiani, S., Baccarani, G.: TFET inverters with n-/p-devices on the same technology platform for low-voltage/low-power applications. IEEE Trans. Electron Devices **61**(2), 473–478 (2014)

38. Strangio, S., et al.: Impact of TFET unidirectionality and ambipolarity on the performance of 6T SRAM cells. IEEE J. Electron Devices Soc. **3**(3), 223–232 (2015)

39. Núñez, J., Avedillo, M.J.: Approaching the design of energy recovery logic circuits using TFETs. IEEE Trans. Nanotechnol. **19**, 500–507 (2020)

Analog and Mixed Signal Design

Performance Analysis of LNA for IoT Application Using Noise Cancellation Technique

Reeya Agrawal$^{(\boxtimes)}$

GLA University, Mathura, India
reeya.agrawal@gla.ac.in

Abstract. A quantitative and yield analysis of low noise amplifier has been done using a noise amplifier cancellation technique for high sensitivity receiver. Wide bandwidth, low noise figures (N_F), and high power gain are achieved by using a common source path and common gate path with a single inductor at a common source path. Proposed LNA is designed using UMC 90 ηm complementary metal-oxide-semiconductor technology, proposed low noise amplifier packaged, achieves a maximum power gain of 20.5 dB, the noise figure of 2–2.5 dB at 1.2 V supply.

Keywords: Complementary metal oxide semiconductor (C_{MOS}) · Low noise amplifier (LN_A) · Common source (C_S) · Common gate (C_G)

1 Introduction

Wireless Sensor Networks (WSNs) have been attracting a lot of interest in the research community lately. These devices are implemented in numerous areas such as safety of the environment, industrial process control, and field monitoring, to provide short-range contact with significant fault tolerance. The key problems in developing WSNs are low voltage, low cost, system measurements, and high integration. However, these networks rely on the battery. For a longer service life, it is important, therefore, to minimize the power consumption of its recipients and to preserve the sensitivity of the recipient [1–4]. Fundamental topologies of the WSN's are seen in Fig. 1. According to low capacity, low cost, and high integration, C_{MOS} technologies are used in practice to improve both power consumption and lifetime of WSN [5–10]. Analog and radio frequency architecture are built into structures of these technologies.

An electronic amplifier that amplifies a very low-power signal without greatly degrading the signal-to-noise ratio is a low-noise amplifier (LNA). An amplifier will increase both the signal's power and the noise present at its input, but any extra noise will also be introduced by the amplifier [11–15]. To mitigate the additional noise, LNAs are planned. By using low-noise materials, operating points, and circuit topologies, designers will eliminate additional noise. Such architecture objectives, such as power gain and impedance synchronization, must be balanced by eliminating additional noise.

To this end, LN_A is the first part of WSN's R_F receiver. Its main goal is to increase the lowest noise level possible on weak R_F signals produced by the antenna. The combination

© Springer Nature Singapore Pte Ltd. 2021
V. Arunachalam and K. Sivasankaran (Eds.): ICMDCS 2021, CCIS 1392, pp. 231–241, 2021.
https://doi.org/10.1007/978-981-16-5048-2_18

of benefit, noise statistic, input impedance combination, efficiency, straight-linearity, and energy consumption also exists. Both C_S and C_G topologies have become the most frequently used topologies in LN_A design architecture [16–21].

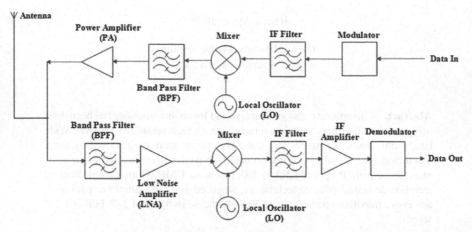

Fig. 1. Basic diagram of the low noise amplifier

A variety of researchers studied LN_A techniques at high frequencies ranging from MHz up to several GHz (front end of the receiver). In [22], an N_F of around 1.5 dB with 650 MHz is offered with 0.5 µm Bi C_{MOS} LN_A under a supply of 2.9 V and uses 15.4 mW of power. Belostotski and Haslett developed LN_A in C_{MOS} 90 nm bulk method to achieve a sub-0.2 dB noise level between 800 and 1400 MHz, thus consuming a current of 43 mA from a supply of 1V.

A 3 dB 1.2–11.9 GHz bandwidth with 0.18 µm C_{MOS} method has been developed for an IC device which is 9.7 dB [23]. They also found that a 4.5–5.1 dB N_F existed for the whole UWB band. It consumes 20 mW even and occupies an area of a 1.8V supply of just 0.59 mm². Jussila and Sivonen [24] developed an LN_A using a 0.13 µm C_{MOS} technique, which provided a 3.0dB noise level with a 2.1 GHz intercept point (IIP_3) third-order input of +10.5 dBm. The current usage of a circuit, as mentioned, is approximately 10.5 mA from a 1.2 V supply. C_S LN_A inductively degenerated 2.2 GHz was developed by Fan et al. [25] using TSMC technology 0.35 µm C_{MOS}. LN_A was estimated to be 1.92 dB N_F and 8.4 dB power gain and 9 mA absorbed 1.8 V power supply. Reiha and Long recently made a 15.1 dB LN_A, 2.1 dB (min.) noise numbers with 0.13 µm technologies, operating over a maximum of 3.1–10.6 GHz. They reported that LN_A was created by LN_A [26]. Power consumption of 0.87 mm² IC from a 1.2 V power to 9 mW was constrained by the reactive feedback-based current-reuse approach [27]. With a forward gain of 8 dB, an efficiency-optimized three-stage wideband DLNA with a Smooth Noise of 2.9 dB was observed over the UWB band of 7.5 GHz. The device will absorb 12 mA of current from a 1.8 V_{DC} voltage. Noise efficiency for LN_A developed by Deal et al. is excellent. It functions at 4–9 GHz, with 9–20 GHz LN_A and noise of 1.75 dB, which gives an N_F 2.75 dB [28]. In comparison to [29], all LN_A with a shunt peak load resistive configuration has a satisfactory S_{11} over 10 dB extreme width band.

LN_A reported a gain of 14.6 dB at 60 GHz while drawing 16 mA out of a 1.5 V supply, an IIP_3 at 6.8 dBm with a range of noise below 5.5 dB at [30]. The goal is to present a C_{MOS} sensor node technology performance review for the front end of ultra-low-power and mixed-signal receiver.

In different applications including hospitals, pollution control, processing environments, and agriculture Wireless Sensor Networks are commonly used. These programmers' designs impose major restrictions on the WSN node's energy use. To optimize battery life and make the energy from the atmosphere in service, ultra-low-power (ULP) radiofrequency (RF) front-end circuits are essential. The maximum voltage is also reduced, as the feature size is reduced in standard complementary semiconductor metal oxide (CMOS) technology. The overall power voltage of this function is also limited. Although low voltage supply operations help mitigate the loss of transfer to energy collected devices, they also lead to constraints on existing topologies of the circuit and their running speed. This makes circuits very important and extensively studied at very low input voltages [31]. During the operations, high transit frequency F_T of short cell CMOS technology, such as superior efficiency, speed saturation, and agility loss, can be substituted for energy usage by low power RF circuitry with high bandwidth. This compromise was initially seen in low-performance RF architecture metrics. While this bias metric can be useful, it does not affect the intrinsic gain in the output conduction, gds, and Drain-source VDS voltage. These are all very important for ULV and ULP designs. The paper offers an expanded bias metric to fix these noise-efficient ULV and ULP architecture problems and to illustrate their applicability by generating an ultra-wideband LNA ULP amplifier [32].

The first element of the front-end layout of the receiver is a low-noise amplifier (LNA). This is the front end of the first amplification block. As the antenna signal is very weak, ~ 1μVp is available. The first step is the LNA that increases the weak input signal of the antenna. When the wireless network market is large, the optimum design of their modules becomes an essential function. The noise generation and amplification of receiver circuits have major repercussions. As a consequence, without noise, we obtain a meaningful signal. The LNA is very simple from a topological viewpoint. In architecture, a single chip part is combined for industrial purposes with the NMOS transistor. This reduces the cost and reliability of the machine. The length of the scaling canal was reduced by nanometres in the MOS VLSI method and the frequency of transit was improved by gigahertz [33].

The LNA is intended to provide adequate proximity and power consumption to enable a long battery life, especially in portable handheld applications. In the optimization of architecture, there are also certain compromises between benefit, NF, linearity, and stability. The LNA is the first active substance on the receiver's front and is generally referred to as one of the blocks of hunger. It is due to the very high energy consumption that an LNA must be equated with a wide-scale, high gain, low noise, and high linearity, with high power and high voltages. These mixed requirements have been a complicated subject in the production of low-power and low-voltage UWB LNAs. This article includes some well-known strategies for the construction of broadband LNAs [34].

A common approach is the use of distributed amplifiers, as shown in Fig. 2(a) provides a high bandwidth range of the multi-gigahertz spectrum. The distributed amplifier suffers from high power consumption, however, and because of the need for different steps and different inducers, they occupy a huge chip area. Also used is the common gate (CG) transistor. The impedance at the input of a CG transistor is 1/gm where gm is the transduction of the transistor. Configuring gm to 20 ms is a 50-input wideband match, which is facing two major difficulties as far as wideband matching is concerned. The first is that, if μ is the coefficient of thermally acoustic noise and $\alpha = g_m/g_{d0}$ in an appropriate condition, the minimum noise (NF), and the other is that the gm is binding on the input criterion and cannot be raised or lowered to boost NF and increase or decrease the power consumption. Noise and feedback are two methods used to optimize the performance of the CG stage circuit. A conventional noise cancellation technique in LNAs is shown in Fig. 2(c).

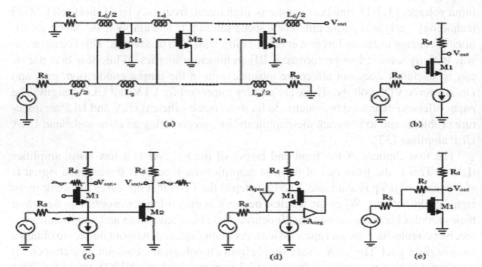

Fig. 2. Wideband LNA architectures (a) Distributed LNA (b) CG LNA (c) Noise Cancellation (d) Feedback LNA (e) Resistive shunt feedback LNA

Noise cancelation techniques have been shown to optimize the NF, but due to intermediate steps and high voltage supply, this costs higher power usage. A fusion of input and feedback, as seen in Fig. 2(d) was used for splitting NF, obtaining and matching the entry into parasites, adding additional parasite power, and limiting operating bandwidths. These scenarios prove to be a challenging task to provide a low energy and broadband approach with a CG input. Another feasible alternative for broadband LNA design is the resistive shunt feedback architecture. This involves the use of a feedback resistor, as seen in Fig. 2(e), to render a 50-input fit for wideband. It utilizes less power, lower noise, and greater benefits in comparative frequency ranges relative to other circuits. Objects are grouped accordingly. Section 2 explains the recipient's front end and architectural LNA analysis. Section 3 shows typical techniques for decreasing control. Section 4 contains a performance table with other work and findings for inductive degenerated LNA.

2 Design Analysis

Basic Idea

C_G amplifier is impaired by greater intense voltage and has headroom problems in inductor-free LN_A than in C_S topology because a current or other source is needed for C_G amplifier to separate R_F signal flow in the field. In this configuration, a C_S amplifier is then adopted to design the key direction of gain. As Fig. 2(a) showed. C_S amplifier requires additional components to achieve input impedance matching, but N_F will suffer greatly from passive resistors or active devices. Thereby, a 50-input matching network without noise or with a low noise contribution is needed [35] to achieve reasonable noise efficiency for inductor-free LN_A based on C_S topology. C_G Topology is used for input matching because of its inherent advantage in changing input impedance. To minimize noise contribution, noise cancellation technology for C_G amplifiers was used. A low-noise inductive network matching with a C_S amplifier can also be accomplished [36–39].

Systemic Analysis

For structural experiments, two behavioral amplifiers representing two paths are known for a proposed system [Fig. 3]. With an adder, it is possible to add output signals of two paths [40–44]. Total voltage gain (A_V^T) is equal to $A_V^T = A_{V,Cs} + A_{V,CG}$.

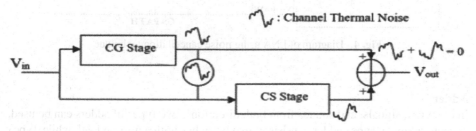

Fig. 3. Block diagram of LNA

3 Design of Proposed LNA

CS Path

A C_s amplifier is one of three topologies commonly used as a voltage or transconductance amplifier, main field-effect transistor (FET). In this case, the signal reaches the port and leaves the drain. Another terminal is the "normal" terminal. The source is only connected terminal [45–49].

CG Path

As seen in Fig. 4 C_G amplifiers are followed to create a C_G path to achieve input impedance equilibrium, consisting of M_4, R_2, and DC source I_1. The circuit's input impedance is mainly regulated by M_1 (g_{m1}) [50–54] transduction. Consequently, g_{m1} was picked to fit an R_G of approximately 20 mS as shown in Fig. 4.

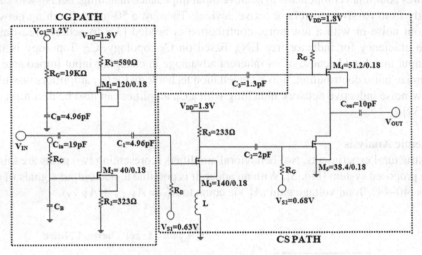

Fig. 4. Diagram of LNA using noise cancellation technique

Adder

In overview, signals, and sounds from both directions, two types of adders can be used, as seen in Fig. 5. Type$_1$ adder consists of two branches with a normal load, while Type$_2$ adder has one shunt current branch [55–57].

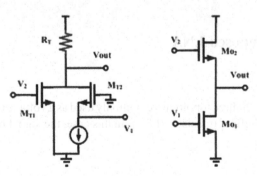

Fig. 5. Types of adder

Type$_1$ extension has greater flexibility to adjust voltage gain ratio between two active paths while changing M_{T1} and M_{T2} Trans conductors separately. This means the use of energy, however. As Type$_2$ adder machines are less, their noise quality in ordinary cases is higher than that of Type$_1$. The M_{O2} noise of Type$_2$ can therefore be degraded [58–60] by M_{O1}. For consideration of adder in this design, Type$_2$ was then selected. As seen in Fig. 6. Type$_2$ adder is reused as the second stage of the C_S amplifier.

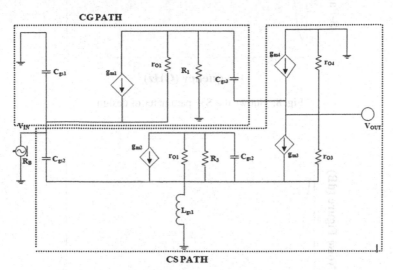

Fig. 6. Small-signal of LNA

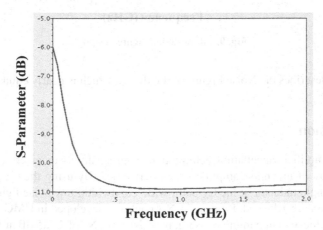

Fig. 7. Shows S_{11} parameter of design

Figure 7 describes the S_{11} parameter of the system which shows that the reflection coefficient should be less than zero whereas Fig. 8 shows the S_{21} parameter of the proposed LNA.

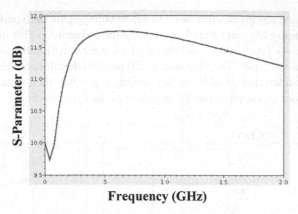

Fig. 8. Shows the S_{21} parameter of design

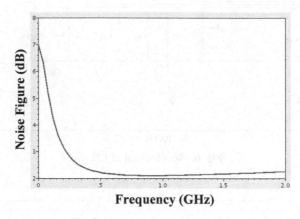

Fig. 9. Shows noise figure design

Figure 9 describes the Noise Figure of the design which is nearly equal to as shown in the figure.

4   Conclusion

Using noise amplifier cancellation technique for high sensitivity receivers, a quantitative and yield study of low noise amplifiers was performed. By using the C_S path and C_G path with a single inductor at the C_S path, wide bandwidth, low noise figure (N_F), and high power gain are achieved. Proposed LNA packing, developed in UMC 90 um C_{MOS} technology, achieves a maximum power gain of 20.5 dB, N_F of 2–2.5 dB at 1.2 V supply.

References

1. Shams, N., Abbasi, A., Nabki, F.: A 3.5 to 7 GHz wideband differential LNA with gm enhancement for 5G applications. In: 2020 18th IEEE International New Circuits and Systems Conference (NEWCAS), Montréal, QC, Canada, pp. 230–233 (2020)

2. Yadav, N., Pandey, A., Nath, V.: Design of CMOS low noise amplifier for 1.57GHz. In: 2016 International Conference on Microelectronics, Computing and Communications (MicroCom), Durgapur, pp. 1–5 (2016)
3. Kim, J., Silva-Martinez, J.: Low-power, low-cost CMOS direct-conversion receiver front-end for multistandard applications. IEEE J. Solid-State Circuits 48(9), 2090–2103 (2013)
4. Lai, M.-T., Tsao, H.-W.: Ultra-low-power cascaded CMOS LNA with positive feedback and bias optimization. IEEE Trans. Microw. Theory Techn. 61(5), 1934–1945 (2013)
5. Belmas, F., Hameau, F., Fournier, J.-M.: A low power inductors LNA with double Gm enhancement in 130 nm CMOS. IEEE J. SolidState Circuits 47(5), 1094–1103 (2012)
6. Sobhy, E.A., Helmy, A.A., Hoyos, S., Entesari, K., Sanchez-Silencio, E.: A 2.8-mW sub-2-dB noise-figure inductor less wideband CMOS LNA employing multiple feedback. IEEE Trans. Microw. Theory Tech. 59(12), 3154–3161 (2011)
7. Parvizi, M., Allidina, K., El-Gamal, M.N.: An ultra-low-power wideband inductor less CMOS LNA with tunable active shunt-feedback. IEEE Trans. Microw. Theory Tech. 64(6), 1843–1853 (2016)
8. Bruccoleri, F., Klumperink, E.A.M., Nauta, B.: Wide-band CMOS low-noise amplifier exploiting thermal noise canceling. IEEE J. SolidState Circuits 39(2), 275–282 (2004)
9. Chen, W.-H., Liu, G., Zdravko, B., Niknejad, M.A.: A highly linear broadband CMOS LNA employing noise and distortion cancellation. IEEE J. Solid-State Circuits 43(5), 1164–1176 (2008)
10. Blaakmeer, S.C., Klumperink, E.A.M., Leenaerts, D.M.W., Nauta, B.: Wideband balun-LNA with simultaneous output balancing, noise-canceling, and distortion-canceling. IEEE J. Solid-State Circuits 43(6), 1341–1350 (2008)
11. Shim, J., Yang, T., Jeong, J.: Design of low power CMOS ultra-wideband low noise amplifier using noise-canceling technique. Microelectron. J. 44(9), 821–826 (2013)
12. Chen, K.-H., Liu, S.-I.: Inductorless wideband CMOS low-noise amplifiers using noise-canceling technique. IEEE Trans. Circuits Syst. I Reg. Pap. 59(2), 305–314 (2012)
13. Wang, H., Zhang, L., Yu, Z.: A wideband inductor less LNA with local feedback and noise-canceling for low-power low-voltage applications. IEEE Trans. Circuits Syst. I Reg. Pap. 57(8), 1993–2005 (2010)
14. Razavi, B.: Low-noise amplifier. In: RF Microelectronics, 2nd edn., pp. 263–266. Publishing House of Electronics Industry, Beijing (2012)
15. Lee, T.H.: "Noise". In: The Design of CMOS Radio-Frequency Integrated Circuits, 2nd edn., pp. 259–262. Publishing House of Electronics Industry, Beijing (2012)
16. Razavi, B.: "Noise". In: Design of Analog CMOS Integrated Circuits, pp. 212–213. China Machine Press, Beijing (2013)
17. Kim, J., Hoyos, S., Silva-Martinez, J.: Wideband common-gate CMOS LNA employing dual negative feedback with simultaneous noise, gain, and bandwidth optimization. IEEE Trans. Microw. Theory Tech. 58(9), 2340–2351 (2010)
18. Kim, J., Silva-Martinez, J.: Wideband inductor less balun-LNA employing feedback for low-power low-voltage applications. IEEE Trans. Microw. Theory Techn. 60(9), 2833–2842 (2012)
19. Liao, C., Liu, S.: A broadband noise-canceling CMOS LNA for 3.1–10.6-GHz UWB receivers. IEEE J. Solid-State Circuits 42(2), 329–339 (2007)
20. Liu, J.Y.-C., Chen, J.-S., Hsia, C., Yin, P.-Y., Lu, C.-W.: A wideband inductor less single-to-differential LNA in 0.18µm CMOS technology for digital TV receivers. IEEE Microw. Wireless Compon. Lett. 24(7), 472–474 (2014)
21. Costa, A.L.T., Klimach, H., Bampi, S.: A 2-decades wideband low-noise amplifier with high gain and ESD protection. In: Proceedings of the 28th Symposium on Integrated Circuits and System Design (SBCCI), September 2015, pp. 1–6 (2015)

22. Arshad, S., Ramzan, R., Muhammad, K., Wahab, Q.: A sub-10 mW, noise-canceling, wideband LNA for UWB applications. Int. J. Electron. Commun. **69**, 109–118 (2015)
23. Chou, H.-T., Chen, S.-W., Chiou, H.-K.: A low-power wideband dual feedback LNA exploiting the gate-inductive bandwidth/gain-enhancement technique (2013)
24. Nguyen, T.-K., Kim, C.-H., Ihm, G.-J., Yang, M.-S., Lee, S.-G.: CMOS low-noise amplifier design optimization techniques. IEEE Trans. Microw. Theory Tech. **52**(5), 1433–1442 (2004)
25. Srigayathri, V., Vasanthi, M.S.: Design of low noise amplifier for multiband receiver. In: 2016 International Conference on Wireless Communications, Signal Processing and Networking (WiSPNET), Chennai, pp. 1603–1605 (2016)
26. Dakua, P.K., Varma, A.S.N., Kabisatpathy, P., Mishra, S.: Study on design and performance analysis of low noise high-speed amplifier. In: 2016 International Conference on Signal Processing, Communication, Power and Embedded System (SCOPES), Paralakhemundi, pp. 1105–1108 (2016)
27. Farhat, E.O., Adami, K.Z., Casha, O., Grech, I., Bij de Vacate, J.G.: Design of a wideband CMOS LNA for low-frequency band SKA application. In: 2015 IEEE International Conference on Electronics, Circuits, and Systems (ICECS), Cairo, pp. 567–571 (2015)
28. Verma, P.K., Jain, P.: A low power high gain low noise amplifier for wireless applications. In: 2015 Communication, Control and Intelligent Systems (CCIS), Mathura, pp. 363–367 (2015)
29. Kaamouchi, M.E., et al.: A 2.4 GHz fully integrated ESD-protected low noise amplifier in 130-nm PD SOI CMOS technology. IEEE Trans. Microw. Theory Tech. **55**, 2822–2831 (2007)
30. Fatin, G.Z., Fatin, H.Z.: A wideband balun LNA. Int. J. Electron. Commun. (AEU) **68**, 653–657 (2014)
31. Hsu, M.T., Chang, Y.C., Huang, Y.Z.: Design of low power UWB LNA based on common source topology with current-reused technique. Microelectron. J. **44**, 1223–1230 (2013)
32. Ku, K.W., Huang, C.C.: A low power CMOS low noise amplifier for wireless communication. In: 19th International Conference on Microwaves, Radar and Wireless Communications, Warsaw, Poland, 21–23 May 2012 (2012)
33. Lin, T.H., Kaiser, W.J., Pottie, G.J.: Integrated low-power communication system design for wireless sensor networks. IEEE Commun. Mag. **42**, 142–150 (2004)
34. Nguyen, T.K., Kim, C.H., Ihm, G.J., Yang, M.S., Lee, S.G.: CMOS Low-noise amplifier design optimization techniques. IEEE Trans. Microw. Theory Tech. **52**, 1433–1442 (2004)
35. Rajput, S.S., Jamuar, S.S.: Low voltage analog circuit design techniques. IEEE Circuits Syst. Mag. **2**, 24–42 (2002)
36. Tsang, T.K., El-Gamal, M.N.: Gain and a frequency controllable sub-IV 5.8 GHz CMOS LNA. ISCAS **4**, 795–798 (2002)
37. Zhuo, W., et al.: A capacitor cross-coupled common-gate low-noise amplifier. IEEE Trans. Circuits Syst. II **52**, 875–879 (2005)
38. Ziabakhsh, S., Alavi-Rad, H., Yagoub, M.C.E.: A high- gain low-power 2–14 GHz ultra-wideband CMOS LNA for wireless receivers. Int. J. Electron. Commun. (AEU) **66**, 727–731 (2012)
39. Zokaei, A., Amirabadi, A.: A 0.13 μm dual-band common-gate LNA using active post distortion for mobile WiMAX. Microelectron. J. **45**, 921–929 (2014)
40. Azizan, A., Murad, S.A.Z., Ismail, R.C., Yasin, M.N.M.: A review of LNA topologies for wireless applications. In: 2014 2nd International Conference on Electronic Design (ICED), Penang, pp. 320–324 (2014)
41. Zhuo, W., Li, X., Shekhar, S., Embabi, S.H.K., et al.: A capacitor cross-coupled common-gate low-noise amplifier. IEEE Trans. Circuits Syst. II Express Briefs **52**, 875–879 (2005)
42. Li, X., Shekhar, S., Allstot, D.J., et al.: Gm-boosted common-gate LNA and differential Colpitts VCO/QVCO in 0.18-μμm CMOS. IEEE J. Solid-State Circuits **40**, 2609–2619 (2005)

43. Samavati, H., Rategh, H.R., Lee, T.H.: A 5-GHz CMOS wireless LAN receiver front end. IEEE J. Solid-State Circuits **35**, 765–772 (2000)
44. Linten, D., Aspemyr, L., et al.: Low-power 5 GHz LNA and VCO in 90 nm RF CMOS. In: IEEE Symposium on VLSI circuits, pp. 372–375 (2004)
45. Karimi, G.R., Nazari, E.: An ultra-low-voltage amplifier design using forward body bias folded cascade topology for 5 GHz application. In: IEEE Conference on Industrial Electronics and Applications, pp. 1838–1842 (2010)
46. Chang, C.-P., Chen, J.-H., Wang, Y.-H.: A fully integrated 5 GHz low-voltage LNA using forward body bias technology. IEEE Microw. Wirel. Compon. Lett. **19**, 176–178 (2009)
47. Kargaran, E., Kazemi, M.M.: Design of 0.5V, 450μW CMOS LNA using current reuse and forward body bias technique. In: IEEE European Conference on Circuits and Systems for Communications, pp. 93–96 (2010)
48. Wu, D., Ru, H., et al.: A 0.4-V low noise amplifier using forward body bias technology for 5 GHz application. IEEE Microw. Wirel. Compon. Lett. **43**, 543–545 (2007)
49. Lorenzo, M.A.G., de Leon, M.T.G.: Comparison of LNA topologies for WiMAX applications in a standard 90-nm CMOS process. In: IEEE Conference on Computer Modelling and Simulation, pp. 642–647 (2010)
50. Hsieh, H.-H., Wang, J.-H., et al.: Gain-enhancement techniques for CMOS folded cascode LNAs at low-voltage operations. IEEE Trans. Microw. Theory Tech. **56**, 1807–1816 (2008)
51. Dehqan, A., Kargaran, E., et al.: Design of 0.45V,1.3mW ultra high gain CMOS LNA using gm-boosting and forward body biasing technique. In: IEEE International Midwest Symposium on Circuits and Systems, pp. 722–725 (2012)
52. Wang, R.-L., Chen, S.-C., Huang, C.-L., Gao, C.-X., Lin, Y.-S.: A 0.8V folded-cascade low noise amplifier for multi-band applications. In: IEEE Asia Pacific on Circuits and Systems, pp. 1387–1389 (2008)
53. Nguyen, T.-K., Kim, C.-H., et al.: CMOS low-noise amplifier design optimization techniques. IEEE Trans. Microw. Theory Tech. **52**, 1433–1442 (2004)
54. Li, C.-H., Liu, Y.-L., Kuo, C.-N.: A 0.6-V 0.33-mW 5.5-GHz receiver front-end using resonator coupling technique. IEEE Trans. Microw. Theory Tech. **59**, 1629–1638 (2011)
55. Hong, E.-P., Hwang, Y.-S., Yoo, H.-J.: A low-power folded RF front-end with low flicker noise for direct conversion receiver. In: IEEE Conference on Electron Devices and Solid-State Circuits, pp. 453–456 (2007)
56. Tang T., Mo, T., Chen, D.: A low-noise amplifier using subthreshold operation for GPS-L1 RF receiver. In: IEEE Conference on Electrical and Control Engineering, pp. 4257–4260 (2011)
57. Perumana, B.G., Chakraborty, S., et al.: A fully monolithic 260-W, 1-GHz subthreshold low noise amplifier. IEEE Microw. Wirel. Compon. Lett. **15**, 428–430 (2005)
58. Do, A.V., Boon, C.C.: A subthreshold low-noise amplifier optimized for ultra-low-power applications in the ISM band. IEEE Trans. Microwave Theory Tech. **56**, 286–292 (2008)
59. Wei, M.-D., Chang, S.-F., et al.: A CMOS fully-differential current-reuse LNA with gm-boosting technique. In: European Microwave Integrated Circuits Conference, pp. 378–381 (2011)
60. Walling, J.S., Shekhar, S., Allstot, D.J.: A gm-boosted current-reuse LNA in 0.18um CMOS. In: IEEE Radio Frequency Integrated Circuits (RFIC) Symposium, pp. 613–616 (2007)

Design of Low Voltage LDO Voltage Regulator for Battery Operated Wireless Sensor Nodes

Piyushkumar M. Chaniyara (✉) (iD)

VLSI Divison, School of Electronics, VIT University, Vellore, India

Abstract. This paper presents the low voltage low dropout voltage regulator for battery operated wireless sensor nodes. The gain boosted folded cascode operational amplifier presented here is use as an error amplifier with improved gain (80.16 dB). For low power operation and low quiescent current (1.2 uA) error amplifier is operated in sub threshold region. The voltage regulator presented here is inherently stable without any external RC compensation network with 30 nF as load capacitor. The proposed voltage regulator has line regulation of 0.031% with good power supply rejection ratio (PSRR) −60 dB at 1.5 kHz and −40 dB at 1 GHz. All the simulation results are carried out in CMOS 90 nm technology using cadence virtuoso tool.

Keywords: Low power · Low dropout regulator · Subthreshold · Battery operated wireless sensor nodes · LDO · PSRR

1 Introduction

In past few years due to advancement in technology scaling, it becomes possible to accommodate more number of transistors on a single chip. Hence, integration of various circuits like ADC, memory, RF circuits becomes possible to accommodate on single chip. Therefore, power supply management of all these circuits becomes an important design consideration.

In case of wireless sensor distributed nodes network, it is highly desirable such network has to work actively for a month or years from battery supply voltage. For such an application power supply block is required to have very low quiescent current for long battery life. Sensor nodes are sensitive to noise. Therefore, it is desirable for voltage regulator have good PSRR and line regulation for stable operation. To fulfill such requirement many topologies of LDO regulator circuits were proposed.

In [1] quiescent current is lowered but with high supply voltages (1.2 to 3.6 V). In [2] proposed architecture with low on chip capacitance requirement but has large quiescent current (14–53.5 uA) with moderate line regulation (0.2). In [3] has used extra circuits to achieved good PSRR (~70 dB) and line regulation (~0.02%) but has high quiescent current (28u). In [4] has proposed bulk driven technique to increase the PSRR (−42 dB) but layout design for such a system implementation become difficult. In [5] has achieved high PSRR (−51 dB) but has high voltage drop (400 mv) across the pass transistor. In

© Springer Nature Singapore Pte Ltd. 2021
V. Arunachalam and K. Sivasankaran (Eds.): ICMDCS 2021, CCIS 1392, pp. 242–254, 2021.
https://doi.org/10.1007/978-981-16-5048-2_19

[6] has very low quiescent current (26 nA) but has high voltage drop (500 mv) across the pass transistor.

In this paper, we have proposed low power LDO regulator circuit design with low quiescent current, good line regulation performance and high PSRR. For low power operation most of the transistors in circuits used in LDO regulator circuit design are operated in subthreshold region except the power transistor, feedback transistors and BGR MR transistor.

The rest of the paper is organized as follows. In Sect. 2 Basics of subthreshold operation is provided. In Sect. 3, basic parameters of voltage regulator is explained. In Sect. 4 Error Amplifier Architecture is explained. In Sect. 5 Low power BGR implementation is explained. In Sect. 6, complete system architecture is given. In Sect. 7, Simulation results and previous literature results are discussed in tabular form. In Sect. 8, conclusion is provided.

2 Basics of Subthreshold Operation

In subthreshold region operation of CMOS transistor very week inversion layer of channel is formed between drain and source [7]. In subthreshold region, current flow through the transistor is less (1 nA–1000 nA Approx.). The controlling Voltage condition for N-MOS transistor to operate in subthreshold region is VGS < VTH. Here VGS and VTH is gate to source voltage and threshold voltage of transistor respectively.

Drain current flowing through transistor in subthreshold region is

$$I_D = \frac{W}{L} I_0 e^{\frac{V_{GS} - V_{TH}}{nV_T}} (1 - e^{-\frac{V_{DS}}{V_T}})$$

Where $\frac{W}{L}$ is the aspect ratio of MOSFET, n slope factor of subthreshold region, I_0 is current $(=\mu COX(n\text{-}1)VT2)$, VGS is gate-source voltage, VDS is drain-source voltage, VT is the thermal voltage(kBT/q) [7, 8].

The formulas of various parameters associated with of MOSFET in sub-threshold region are described below:

Transconductance formula:

$$gm = \frac{I_D}{nV_T} \tag{1}$$

Drain Resistance formula:

$$r_d = \frac{nV_T}{\lambda_D I_D} \tag{2}$$

Transconductance Formula due to body bias effect:

$$g_{mb} = \frac{\lambda_B I_D}{nV_T} \tag{3}$$

Gain formula:

$$A_{V0} = \frac{1}{\lambda_D} \tag{4}$$

where g_m is the transconductance, g_{mb} is transconductance with body bias effect, ID is the drain current, λ_D is the channel length modulation taken into account, g_{mb} is the transconductance due to body bias, A_{V0} is the gain of the MOSFET.

It is been observed that gain is a variable of channel length modulation parameter for subthreshold region operation of N-MOS transistor. Therefore, in order to increase the gain, it is desirable to increase length of MOS transistors [9].

3 Parameters of Voltage Regulator

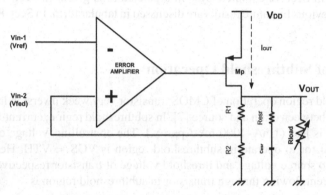

Fig. 1. LDO regulator circuit architecture

As shown in Fig. 1 basic LDO regulator circuit architecture with P-MOS as a pass element.

$$\text{Line regulation} = \frac{\Delta V_{OUT}}{\Delta V_{DD}}$$

At low frequency line regulation for LDO regulator circuit is as follows.

$$\Delta V_{OUT} = \frac{R_L}{R_L + R_{PASS}} * \Delta V_{DD} - \Delta V_{FB} * A_{ERROR\_AMP} * g_{PASS} * R_L \qquad (5)$$

Here R_L is load resistance and R_{PASS} effective resistance of Pass transistor, ΔV_{FB} is change in feedback voltage, A_{ERROR_AMP} is voltage gain of error amplifier, g_{PASS} is trans conductance of pass transistor.

$$\Delta V_{FB} = \Delta V_{OUT} * \frac{R_2}{R_1 + R_2} \text{ and } R_L << R_1 + R_2 \qquad (6)$$

Now re writing Eq. (5).

$$\left[1 + \frac{R_2}{R_1 + R_2} * A_{ERROR\_AMP} * g_{PASS} * R_L\right] * \Delta V_{OUT} = \frac{R_L}{R_L + R_{PASS}} * \Delta V_{DD}$$

$$\frac{\Delta V_{OUT}}{\Delta V_{DD}} =\sim \frac{R_1 + R_2}{R_2} * \frac{1}{(R_L + R_{PASS}) * A_{ERROR\_AMP} * g_{PASS}} \tag{7}$$

From above Eq. (7) we can infer that by increasing error amplifier gain A_{ERROR_AMP} we can minimize line variation at LDO regulator circuit output [10].

$$\text{Load regulation} = \frac{\Delta V_{OUT}}{\Delta I_{OUT}}$$

From above Fig. 1 we can analyze.

$$\Delta V_{OUT} = \Delta I_{OUT} * \{(R_1 + R_2)\|R_L\}$$

$$\Delta I_{OUT} = A_{ERROR\_AMP} * g_{PASS} * \Delta V_{FB} \tag{8}$$

From Eq. (6) we can re write Eq. (8) as follow.

$$\frac{\Delta V_{OUT}}{\Delta I_{OUT}} =\sim \frac{1}{A_{ERROR\_AMP} * g_{PASS}} * \frac{R_1 + R_2}{R_2} \tag{9}$$

From above Eq. (9) we can infer that by increasing gain of error amplifier we can improve load regulation [11].

4 Error Amplifier Architecture

In existing topologies of low power gain boosted op-amps all the transistors are operated in strong inversion region with different topologies of auxiliary amplifier to increase gain, slew rate and stability. However, the minimum power achieved is in terms of mW operation.

Here proposed op-amp topology of error amplifier all the transistors in the design are operated in subthreshold region with minimum power consumption approximately 0.6 uW.

Here proposed error amplifier topology is shown in Fig. 2(a). It is fully differential output of Op-Amp is converted to single sided by current mirror technique at transistors M10 and M11.

In Fig. 2(b) and (c) shows two auxiliary amplifiers N_AMP and P_AMP used in Fig. 2(a). Auxiliary amplifier are designed in fully differential topology which is advantageous in terms of avoiding noise signal from power supply. In fully differential amplifier both output terminal should have proper common mode voltage level to avoid clipping or reduction of output swing. So here common mode feedback circuit (CMFB) circuit is used to sense common mode voltage level of both terminal and average voltage is compared with reference voltage and feed back to amplifier.

Use of N_AMP and P_AMP is advantageous in terms of increase overall Op-Amp gain by factor by $(1 + A_{AUX})$ times, due to increase in output impedance by A_{AUX}. Here A_{AUX} is the gain of N_AMP and P_AMP. In overall Op-Amp design we achieve gain of 80.16 dB with phase margin is 66° and unity gain frequency is around 28.79 MHz. The simulation results are shown in Fig. 3. Theroritical derivation of gain A_V is.

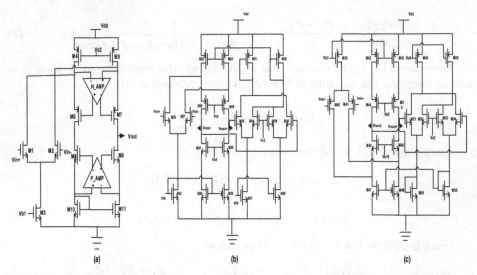

Fig. 2. (a) Circuit level architecture error amplifier (Op-Amp). (b) Circuit level architecture of N_AMP. (c) Circuit level architecture of P_AMP.

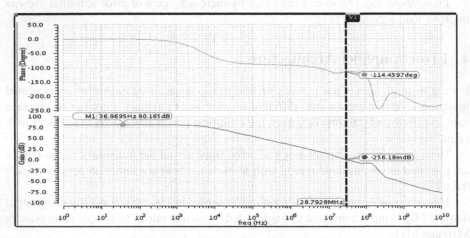

Fig. 3. Gain and phase plot of Op-Amp design

$$A_V = - g_{m1}[g_{m6}r_{ds6}r_{ds4}A_{N\_AMP}|| g_{m8}r_{ds8}r_{ds10}A_{P\_AMP}] \tag{10}$$

Where A_{N_AMP} and A_{P_AMP} given by

$$A_{N\_AMP} = - g_{m20}[r_{ds27}r_{ds29}g_{m27}||r_{ds23}r_{ds25}g_{m25}] \tag{11}$$

$$A_{P\_AMP} = - g_{m40}[r_{ds47}r_{ds45}g_{m45}||r_{ds42}g_{m44}r_{ds44}] \tag{12}$$

Figure 4 is the plot of PSRR (Power Supply Rejection Ratio) versus frequency of Op-amp design. The PSRR of op-Amp is −63 dB up to 160 kHz frequency. In this Op-Amp circuit the CMRR (Common Mode Rejection Ratio) achieved is 74.2 dB.

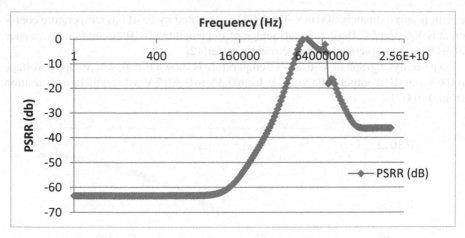

Fig. 4. PSRR of Op-Amp design

5 BGR Architecture

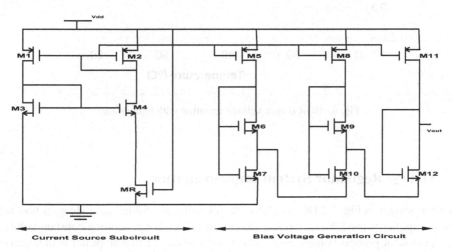

Fig. 5. Band gap reference circuit used in LDO regulator circuit design

In Fig. 5 BGR (Band Gap Reference) circuit all the transistors are operated in sub-threshold region except transistor MR is operated in linear region. Here transistors M1-M4 act as a current source sub circuit. Transistors M5, M8, M11 are used to mirror the current generated from current source sub circuit.

Transistors pair M6-M10 and M9-M12 are two source coupled pairs used to generate reference voltages from the mirrored current provided by M5 and M8 respectively [12]. All the transistors aspect ratio are tuned in such a way that VOUT generated by BGR circuit is approximately 300 mV. The VOUT generated by BGR has temperature coefficient is 300 ppm/°C. Here main advantage of implemented BGR circuit is with absence of BJT layout implementation of circuit is easier[12].

The analysis graph of VOUT Vs Temperature is shown Fig. 6, where supply voltage is 0.6 V and BGR output voltage varies from 0.3 V to 0.3012 V with temperature variation from 0–100 °C.

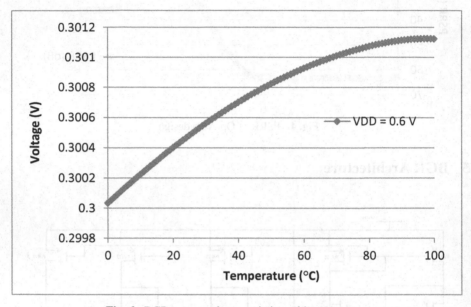

Fig. 6. BGR output voltage variation with temperature

6 Voltage Regulator System Implementation

Here as shown in Fig. 7 LDO regulator circuit with gain folded cascode gain boosted error amplifier is used. Voltage reference circuit is used for generating constant voltage irrespective of process voltage and temperature variation. Error amplifier is in negative feedback loop with output voltage of power transistor through feedback network. So, if output voltage is higher than required voltage then feedback voltage VFB will increases, error amplifier will subtract it from reference voltage and difference voltage will be given to the PMOS pass transistor, due to large difference voltage PMOS transistor effective gate to source voltage |VGS| decreases and output voltage level decreases. Hence output will be in continuous monitoring negative feedback loop and very less voltage variation at output node is observed due to voltage variation in supply voltage.

In LDO system implementation feedback network is designed with PMOS transistors instead of using resistor as in conventional LDO system. The transistor feedback network is advantageous in terms of layout area decrease and complexity in layout also decreases. Here cascode structure of transistor is advantageous in terms of improving PSRR.

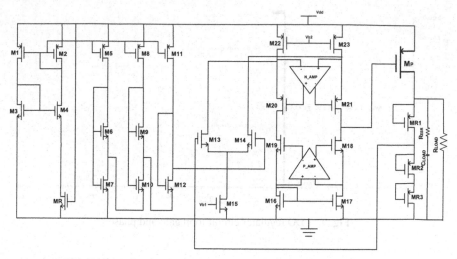

Fig. 7. Circuit level architecture of complete LDO regulator circuit

At low frequencies LDO regulator circuit output is given by

$$VOUT = VREF(1 + R2/R1) \tag{13}$$

Here R1 and R2 are feedback resistors (MR1, MR2, MR3 in Fig. 7) and VREF is output of BGR circuit.

7 Simulation Results and Comparison Table

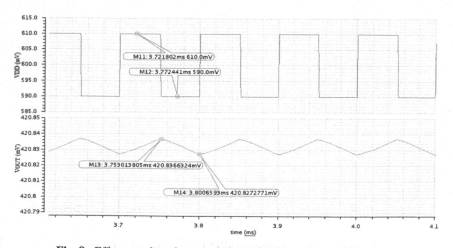

Fig. 8. Effect supply voltage variation at LDO regulator circuit output

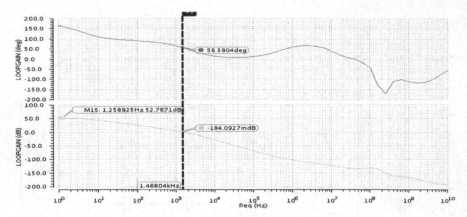

Fig. 9. LDO regulator circuit loop gain and phase

In Fig. 8 shows supply variations in square wave and corresponding voltage variation at LDO circuit output which is used to measure the line regulation of LDO regulator circuit. We have considered here 20 mV supply voltage variation and LDO output we are able to observe minimum variation of 9.3 uV variation. We are able to achieve line regulation of 0.0318%.

In Fig. 9 shows loop gain (52.7 dB) and Loop phase of LDO regulator circuit with Loop phase margin approximately 56.58°.

As shown in Fig. 10 for LDO regulator circuit we are able to achieve PSRR approximately −52.73 dB at 1.5 kHz and −40 dB at 1 GHz.

LDO regulator circuit output voltage variation with temperature variation is very less approximately 0.0019 V with variation in temperature from 0 to 70°. Corresponding graph is shown in shown in Fig. 11.

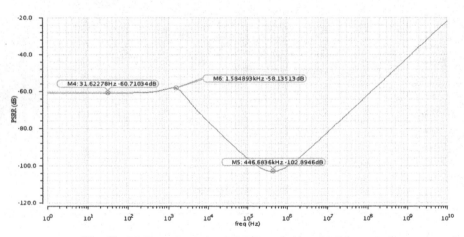

Fig. 10. LDO regulator circuit PSRR variation with frequency

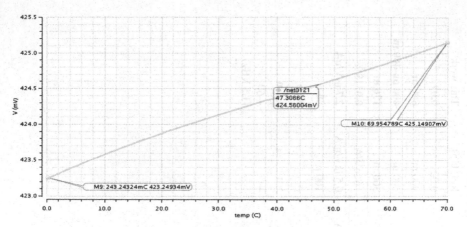

Fig. 11. LDO regulator circuit output voltage variation with temperature

Literature Table

	Ref. [13]	Ref. [3]	Ref [14]	Ref. [1]	Ref. [16]	Ref. [15]	This work
Technology (μm)	0.18	0.18	0.35	0.13	0.09	0.021	0.09
V_{SUPPLY} (V)	1.2	1.8	1.2–3.3	900 m	1	900 m	600 m
V_{OUT}(V)	1	1.5	1.0–3.1	462 m	500 m	600 m	400 m–460 m
V_{DO}(V)	200 m	300 m	200 m	438 m	500 m	300 m	170 m
Line regulation	–	0.024%	1.5%	0.31%	27 mV/V	16 mV/A	0.0318%
Load regulation	–	0.7 mV/4 mA	1.7%	1.16 mV/4 mA	1.06 mV/uA	0.5 mV/mA	2.7 mV/uA
C_L(F)	1 u	–	None	50 p	–	100 p	30 n
$I_{LOAD(MAX)}$ (A)	150 m	4 m	100 m	–	15 u	–	15 u
$I_{Q(MAX)}$ (A)	8.5 u	28 u	42 u	11.6 u	26 n	5 u	1.1 u
PSRR (dB)	–	–70 dB (1 kHz)	–	–51 dB (1 kHz)	–63 dB (1 Hz)	–	–60 (1.5 kHz)

8   Conclusion

In this paper for proposed LDO regulator circuit it is possible to operate LDO regulator circuit at low voltages by designing low voltage (600 mV) subthreshold gain boosted folded cascoded error amplifier.

The line regulation (~0.031%) and load regulation (2.7 mV/uA) parameters of an LDO regulator circuit is improved by improving gain (80dB) of an error amplifier using gain boosting technique.

PSRR (−60.07 dB @ 1.5 kHz, −40 dB @ 1 GHz) of LDO regulator circuit is improved by using folded cascode topology in an error amplifier design.

CMRR of LDO regulator circuits improved by using high impedance differential input configuration of an error amplifier.

BGR circuit of LDO circuits also have good PSRR and temperature coefficient (300 ppm/°C) in required output voltage range and power consumption of BGR circuit is reduced by operating the transistors in subthreshold region.

Voltage dropout across power transistor is also improved (170 mV) by proper tuning of transistors of LDO regulator circuit.

Though proposed LDO regulator circuit design require an external 30 nF capacitor but wireless sensor nodes are very sensitive to PSRR and line regulation it become worthy to use external capacitance for such good line regulation.

References

1. Gruber, S., et al.: An ultra-low power voltage regulator for wireless sensor nodes. In: 22nd International Conference on Microelectronics (ICM 2010) (2010)
2. Chong, S.S., Chan, P.K.: A quiescent power-aware low-voltage output capacitorless low dropout regulator for SoC applications. IEEE (2011). 978-1-4244-9474-3
3. Majidzadeh, V., Schmid, A., Leblebici, Y.: A fully on-chip LDO voltage regulator for remotely powered cortical implants. IEEE (2009). 978-1-4244-4353-6
4. Izadpanahi, N., Maymandi-Nejad, M.: Enhancing power supply rejection of low-voltage low-dropout voltage regulators using bulk driven PMOS. IEEE (2012). 978-1-4673-1148-9/12
5. Luo, L., De Gannes, K., Fricke, K., Senjuti, S., Sobot, R.: Low-power CMOS voltage regulator architecture for implantable RF circuits. IEEE (2012). 978-0-7695-4813-5/12
6. Wen, F.-C., Hsu, H.-S., Hong, Z.-H., Liao, Y.-T.: A low-power 0.5V regulator with settling enhancement for wireless sensor nodes. IEEE (2013). 978-1-4673-5762-3/13
7. Chaniyara, P.M., Srivastava, P.K., Suresha, B., Reddy, A.S.: Design of sampled analog wavelet processor architecture for cochlear implant application. Analog Integr. Circ. Sig. Process. 86(2), 171–180 (2015). https://doi.org/10.1007/s10470-015-0642-8
8. Leung, K.N., Mok, P.K.T.: A CMOS voltage reference based on weighted (delta) VGS for CMOS low-dropout linear regulator. IEEE J. Solid-State Circuits 38(1), 146–150 (2003)
9. Magnelli, L., Amoroso, F., Crupi, F., Cappuccino, G., Iannaccone, G.: Design of a 75-nW, 0.5-V subthreshold complementary metal-oxide-semiconductor operational amplifier. Int. J. Circuit Theory Appl. 42, 967–977 (2014)
10. Wu, C.S.: Low cost dual output voltage level low dropout linear regulator using a novel MUX based adjustable reference voltage generator. MS thesis, National Cheng Kung University, January 2008
11. Shyu, Y.S.: Low operating current analog integrated circuits. Ph.D. thesis, National Chaio-Tung University, Taiwan, June 2002

12. Uno, K., Hirose, T., Asai, T., Amemiya, Y.: A 300 nW, 15 ppm/°C, 20 ppm/V CMOS voltage reference circuit consisting of subthreshold MOSFETs. IEEE J. Solid-State Circuits **44**(7), 2047–2054 (2009)

13. Heidrich, J., Brenk, D., Essel, J., Heinrich, M., Jung, M.: Design of a low-power voltage regulator for RFID applications. In: IEEE Region 8 SIBIRCON, Russia (2010)

14. Zheng, C., Ma, D.: Design of monolithic CMOS LDO regulator with D2 coupling and adaptive transmission control for adaptive wireless powered bio-implants. IEEE Trans. Circuits Syst.— I Regul. Pap. **58**(10), 1225–1228 (2011)

15. Chen, W.-C., Su, Y.-P., Lee, Y.-H., Wey, C.-L., Chen, K.-H.: 0.65V-input-voltage 0.6V-output-voltage 30ppm/°C low-dropout regulator with embedded voltage reference for low-power biomedical systems. In: IEEE International Solid-State Circuits Conference (2014)

A Source Degenerated Cascode LNA with High Gain and Low Noise Figure Using Layout Optimized High Q Inductors

Sobhana Tayenjam[1]() ⓘ, Venkata Vanukuru[2] ⓘ, and S. Kumaravel[2] ⓘ

[1] Vellore Institute of Technology, Vellore 632014, India
sobhana.tayenjam@vit.ac.in
[2] GLOBALFOUNDRIES, Bangalore 560045, India

Abstract. The abstract should summarize the contents of the paper in short terms, i.e. 150–250 words. In low noise amplifier (LNA) design, a prominent trade-off usually exist between noise-figure (NF) and gain. In this paper, impact of quality-factor (Q) of the inductors used in LNA design on the overall noise-figure and gain parameters are discussed. To understand the efficacy of the dependency of Q of inductors on NF, LNA with inductor available in UMC 0.18 μm Process Design Kit and LNA with parameterized-cell (pcell) based layout optimized high Q tapered inductors are realized, simulated and compared. Simulations study are carried out on a cascode source degenerated LNA. First, the LNA design is studied for different values of finite Q using library inductors. It is observed that the noise figure is reduced by about 65% (2.66 dB–1.61 dB) and gain is improved by about 30.2% (7.63–9.94) for the same design when Q of the inductors are increased from 10 to 30. Finally, the design is implemented using layout optimized high Q tapered inductors achieving lower noise figure of 1.2 dB with a better gain value of 16.45 and input return loss of −29.31 dB.

Keywords: Gain · Inductance · LNA · Noise-figure · Quality-factor

1 Introduction

With the growing importance of wireless communication systems, the demands for fully integrated radio- frequency (RF) front-end designs are huge. Low noise amplifiers (LNA) being the backbone of a receiver system plays a critical role in successfully delivering the received RF signals. LNA basically amplifies unwanted noise from the weak RF signals received through antenna and further enhances the received RF signal while maintaining an optimum signal-to-noise ratio (SNR) without any distortion. Some important characteristics of an LNA design includes: low noise figure, high gain, low power, high linearity, high stability with good impedance matching over the required range of frequency. To achieve the desired features from an LNA design, it is indeed crucial to choose the right topology. Several variants of LNAs are present in literature so far. However, source degenerated inductor topology are known to reduce noise figure and provide high gain. So, in this paper, cascode source degenerated inductor topology is

© Springer Nature Singapore Pte Ltd. 2021
V. Arunachalam and K. Sivasankaran (Eds.): ICMDCS 2021, CCIS 1392, pp. 255–268, 2021.
https://doi.org/10.1007/978-981-16-5048-2_20

considered for the study. Generally, LNA designs consist of inductors which are crucial in providing better noise performance. Optimizing noise figure is an important aspect of LNA design. In LNA designs, better noise performance are usually achieved at the cost of higher power transfer. So, to improve noise performance several optimization techniques are adopted [1]. Using high Q on-chips inductors for the design is one of the potential technique to improve NF. In [4], cascode LNA are thoroughly studied to discuss the impact of large gate inductor on NF variations. In this paper, the impact of quality-factor (Q) of the inductors used in the design on the gain and noise figure of the LNA are analyzed. The NF and gain analysis is done through simulation study for different values of Q using UMC 0.18 μm CMOS technology. Once the importance of inductors' Q is figured out, layout optimized inductors with high Q are incorporated for designing the three inductors and is observed to give a better a noise performance than the LNA design with same structure and standard library inductors.

2   Performance Parameters

In LNA design several parameters are considered to judge the performance of the circuit. The major performance metrics of LNA are as follows:

Noise-Figure (NF): NF is the measure of SNR degradation introduced by the LNA block to the signal in receiver system. The overall noise performance of the receiver front-end is dominated by the noise performance of the LNA which is determined in terms of *NF*. *NF* relation of the RF front-end block is given as:

$$NF_{frontend} = NF_{LNA} \frac{NF_{subsequent} - 1}{G_{LNA}} \tag{1}$$

Where $NF_{frontend}$, NF_{LNA}, $NF_{subsequent}$ are the NF of the entire front-end blocks, NF of the LNA and NF of the subsequent blocks respectively and G_{LNA} is the power gain of the LNA. Noise-figure (*NF*) of an LNA is given by:

$$NF_{LNA} = \frac{N_{device} + G_m N_{in}}{G_m N_{in}} \tag{2}$$

where N_{device} and N_{in} denotes the device noise and input noise.

Noise-Factor (F): For LNA design, F is the amount of unwanted noise added to the incoming RF signal and is derived as:

$$F = \frac{SNR_{in}}{SNR_{out}} \tag{3}$$

Where, SNR_{in} and SNR_{out} are the signal to noise ratio at the input and output of the device respectively.

Power-Gain (G): G of an LNA is the parameter with which the power signal amplification ability of the LNA is determined and is measured as:

$$G = \frac{P_{out}}{P_{in}} \tag{4}$$

Where, P_{out} is the output signal power and P_{in} is input signal power. The measurement unit of G is decibel (dB) on a logarithmic scale.

Linearity: Linearity is defined as the ability of an LNA to increase the input signal power level without hampering the original signal content. Linearity measurement are done on the basis of 1-dB compression point (P1dB) and Input-Referred Third-Order Intercept Point (IIP3). P1dB refers to the input power which instigate the linear gain to be reduced by 1 dB because of device saturation. On the other hand, IIP3 is a terminology developed by assuming the possibility of modeling the non-linearity of LNA with the use of a low order polynomial. Mathematically, IIP3 refers to the power of the input signals at the point where amplitudes of the third-order inter-modulation term and the linear fundamental term are equal.

Stability: Stability is an LNA is the parameter that helps in assuring that the LNA free from unwanted oscillations. For an LNA, the design is ensured to be free from any sort of oscillation with any source or load impedances at any range of frequency if it is unconditionally stable. An LNA is considered unconditionally stable if its input and output impedances have positive real part.

Impedance Matching: Impedance matching is a concept which implies that a certain amount of impedance is required at the input source and also at output load for LNA design. In RF circuit, impedance matching is required for maximum power transfer between the input source and output. Maximum power transfers occurs in impedance matching when the source impedance complex conjugate and the load impedance are equal. It should also be noted that perfect impedance matching could be achieved for a specific frequency alone and for the rest of the frequency the matching get degraded gradually and becomes non-existent at the end. For LNA design, impedance matching not only performs the task of maximizing the power transfer but also in minimizing the noise-factor. In LNA, input impedance matching is much needed because in a receiver chain, a passive BPF usually comes before the LNA block and transfer characteristics of filters are generally sensitive to termination quality [2]. The impedance at the input and output are known as input impedance and output impedance respectively. The input and output impedance matching for an LNA are measured by the S11 and S22 parameters respectively through two-port analysis. The standard value of input and output impedance is 50 Ω for most of the RF circuits.

Power-Dissipation: It refers to the amount of power consumed by the LNA from the DC power supply and is measured in terms dBm. Power-dissipation is a major concern in most of the devices specially in cases of portable or wireless devices and it is always desirable to have minimum power-dissipation for longer device operation time.

3 Common LNA Topologies

For LNA design, several circuit topology are available. Performance of an LNA is highly dependent upon its topology. So, the topology for the design of LNA is generally decided according to the performance requirement of the circuit. Some of the common CMOS LNA topologies are: common-source (CS), common-gate (CG), Cascode.

Common-Source LNA with Shunt Resistor: In LNA design, impedance matching for 50 Ω at the input is a critical task. One of the simple topology to achieve this is the CS LNA with a shunt resistor at the input port as shown in Fig. 1, where R1 represent the shunt resistor. Drawback of this topology is that the use of shunt resistor degrades the input signal when it attenuates past the gate-transistor (M) due to the added thermal noise of R1 in the signal path. This leads to a very poor NF of the design, due to which this topology is often avoided.

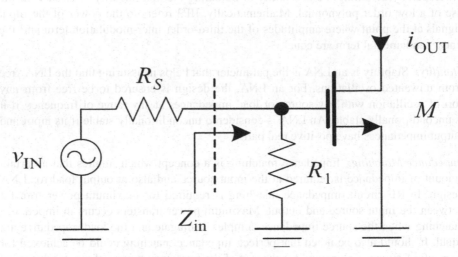

Fig. 1. CS-LNA with shunt input resistor.

Common-Gate LNA: This LNA topology is mainly used when excellent input match is required. Figure 2 shows an LNA with CG topology. The input impedance of CG LNA is given by:

$$Z_{in} = \frac{1}{sC_{gs} + g_m} \approx \frac{1}{g_m} \tag{5}$$

Where, g_m, C_{gs} represents the transconductance and the parasitic gate-source capacitance of the transistor respectively. So, with proper biasing and transistor sizing, input impedance matching can be achieved in CG LNA as the channel resistance causes the input resistance at the source terminal to be resistive in nature [3].

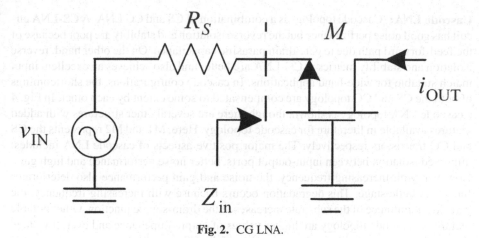

Fig. 2. CG LNA.

Common-Source LNA with Inductive Degeneration: The LNA topologies discussed so far suffers from poor NF performance due to added noises from the input resistances in the signal path. In inductive degenerated CS LNA topology, an inductor is inserted at the source of the transistor which dominates the real part of the input impedance with its inductive characteristic. Figure 3 shows the structure of a inductive degenerated CS-LNA with Ls as the source degenerated inductor. A negative feedback is provided by Ls to the amplifier that stabilizes gain of the LNA. Ideally, the inductive degeneration caused by Ls is free from noise with a strong input signal. Here, the series resonant input matching network pre-amplify the input signal. The main drawback of this topology is the large area due to the presence of passive inductors. So, overall the CS-LNA with inductive degeneration topology results in a good narrow-band match with low NF and thus makes it a suitable choice for various narrow-band LNA designs.

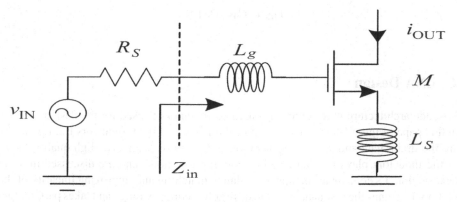

Fig. 3. CS-LNA with inductive degeneration.

Cascode LNA: Cascode topology is a combination of CS and CG LNA. A CS-LNA circuit has good noise performance but the reverse isolation and stability are poor because of the feed-forward path due to gate-drain parasitic capacitance. On the other hand, reverse isolation and stability metrics in CG-LNA are better and also achieves an excellent input match suitable for wide-band applications. In cascode configurations, the shortcomings of both the CS and CG topology are compensated to some extent by each other. In Fig. 4 a cascode LNA topology is shown, though there are several other structures with added features available in literature for cascode topology. Here, M1 and M2 represents the CS and CG transistors respectively. The major positive aspects of cascode LNA includes: improved isolation between input-output ports, better noise performance and high gain. However, with increasing frequency, the noise and gain performance also deteriorates for the cascode stage. This degradation occurs because with increasing frequency, the parasitic admittance of the substrate increases at the drain-source junction. Other notable features of cascode topology are higher values of output impedance and overall voltage gain of the structure being equivalent to that of the CS-stage gain.

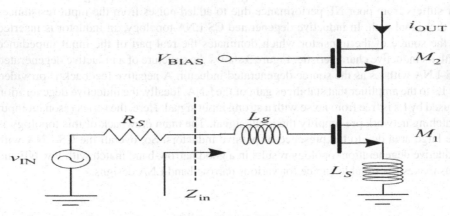

Fig. 4. Cascode LNA.

4   LNA Design

Cascode architecture with source degenerated inductors is used for the design of LNA in this paper. Figure 5 shows the circuit of the LNA designed. Inductors Ld, Lg and Ls are the drain, gate and source degeneration inductors respectively. High quality-factor of the inductors plays a major role in achieving low noise and are discussed more in next section. Ls contributes in input impedance matching and improving linearity of the system. Lg, tunes the resonant circuit to desirable frequency range and takes part in input matching too. C1 is the coupling capacitance to block DC. Ld and C2 together forms the output matching network and tunes output load at resonant frequency for high gain and output power transfer [5, 6]. M2 is the cascode device that minimizes unwanted interaction between tuned input and output. M3 and Rref forms a current mirror with M1 and are used for proper biasing of the circuit along with Rbias.

Input matching network of a source degenerated LNA is shown in Fig. 6. Input impedance (Zin) of cascode LNA with source degeneration can be given as:

$$Z_{in} = s(L_g + L_s) + \frac{1}{sC_{gs}} + \frac{g_m L_s}{C_{gs}} \tag{6}$$

At resonance, real part of input impedance is matched to 50 Ω to avoid unwanted signal sensitivity and $\omega^2 = C_{gs}(L_g + L_s) = 1$, so Zin becomes:

$$Z_{in} = \frac{g_m L_s}{C_{gs}} \tag{7}$$

Cascode LNA suffers a low gain, however, high Q_{in} at the input matching stage gives improvement to the overall transconductance (G_m) and is given by:

$$G_m = \frac{I_{out}}{V_s} = \frac{\frac{g_m}{sC_{gs}}}{R_s + Z_{in}} = \frac{g_m}{1 + s(R_s C_{gs} + g_m L_s) + s^2(R_s C_{gs} + g_m L_s)} \tag{8}$$

Quality-factor of the input matching stage (Q_{in}) is the ratio of total power stored to the dissipated power and is given as:

$$Q_{in} = \frac{1}{2\omega R_s C_{gs}} \tag{9}$$

For source degenerated LNA, the NF at resonance is given by:

$$NF = 1 + \frac{\gamma}{R_s g_m}\omega^2(R_s C_{gs} + g_m L_s)^2 \tag{10}$$

In [7], it is given that when the correlations between noise currents are not considered, the noise factor (F) can be written as:

$$F = 1 + \frac{\overline{i^2}_{Rgg,o} + \overline{i^2}_{Rss,o} + \overline{i^2}_{Rtail,o} + \overline{i^2}_{ng,o} + \overline{i^2}_{nd,o}}{\overline{i^2}_{Rs,o}} \tag{11}$$

where, $\overline{i^2}_{Rgg,o}$, $\overline{i^2}_{Rss,o}$ and $\overline{i^2}_{Rtail,o}$ are mean square noise currents generated at the output by the mean square noise voltages $\overline{v^2}_{Rgg,o}$, $\overline{v^2}_{Rss,o}$ and $\overline{v^2}_{Rtail,o}$ and $\overline{i^2}_{Rs,o}$, $\overline{i^2}_{ng,o}$ and $\overline{i^2}_{nd,o}$ are the mean square noise current at output due to R_s, mean square gate noise current $\overline{i^2}_{ng}$ and mean square channel noise current $\overline{i^2}_{nd}$ respectively. The above equation shows the relation between the inductor performance and the F of the LNA. With high quality inductor the noise current that adds to the F could be reduced and hence a better F could be achieved.

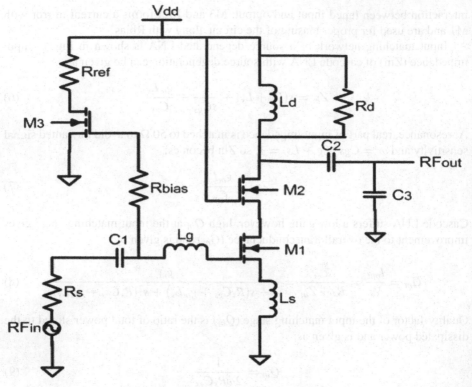

Fig. 5. Cascode LNA with source degeneration.

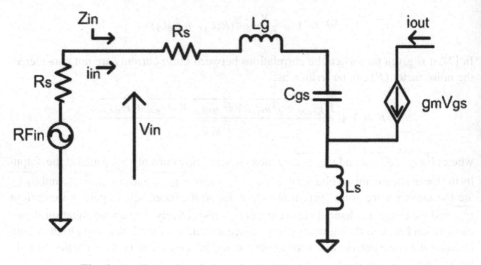

Fig. 6. Small signal equivalent circuit of the input match network.

5 Simulations Study

5.1 Impact of Inductors' Q on Noise Figure and Gain

NF and gain are two such parameters known for depicting the most prominent trade-off in an LNA design [8]. Here, to study the impact of inductors' Q on noise figure and gain, the LNA design is implemented using library inductors with added resistance to give a finite value of Q. These added resistance (R) is calculated as:

$$R = \frac{\omega L}{Q}$$

where, ω, L and Q denotes the resonant frequency, inductance and quality-factor of the inductor respectively. The LNA is simulated for different values of inductors' Q (10, 20, 30). The S11, S22, S21 and NF simulation curves for Q values of 10, 20 and 30 are shown in Fig. 7, 8, and 9 respectively. The NF values noted for Q values of 10, 20 and 30 are 2.66 dB, 1.89 dB and 1.61 dB respectively. Thus, achieving a reduction of about 65%. Gain (S21) values are also observed to improve by about 30.2%. For Q values of 10, 20 and 30, gain values observed are 7.63 dB, 9.25 dB and 9.94 dB respectively. Figure 10 shows the NF and gain analysis curves for the different Q. With increasing Q both NF and gain showed improvements in its own terms. These result shows that increasing Q of inductors in LNA is a beneficial method for providing a balanced improvement in both NF and gain.

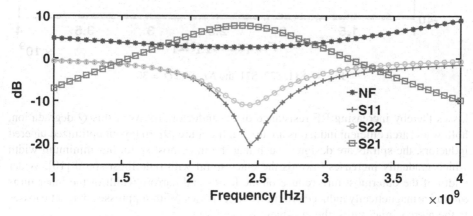

Fig. 7. S11, S22, S21 and *NF* with $Q = 10$.

5.2 LNA with High-Q Layout Optimized Inductors

Layout optimization is one of the promising techniques that improves Q in inductor modeling. Tapered inductors wherein the width varies from inner to outer turns are used to design Lg, Ls and Ld. In spiral inductors, magnetic field strength is stronger inside core region of the inductor than at the edges, inner turns suffer from increased magnetic

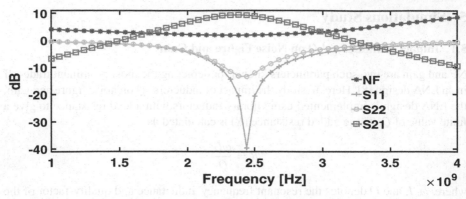

Fig. 8. S11, S22, S21 and *NF* with $Q = 20$.

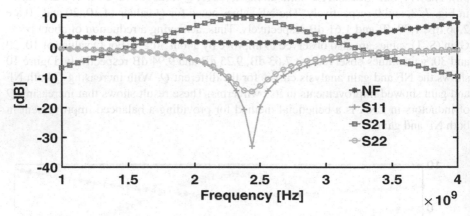

Fig. 9. S11, S22, S21 and *NF* with $Q = 30$.

losses thereby increasing RF resistance of the inductor. To avoid this Q degradation, hollow and area efficient inductors are used in literature [9]. In layout optimized tapered inductors, the spirals are designed such that the innermost spiral has minimum width which gradually increases towards the outer spiral with outermost spiral [10]. Wider width of the outermost turn reduce ohmic losses and narrow width of the inner turns minimize magnetically induced proximity effect losses. With suppressed magnetic losses in the narrow inner turns, the Q values are increased.

Here, the same LNA design discussed in previous section is implemented using layout optimized inductors. Figure 11 shows the layout view of tapered inductors used to model Lg, Ls and Ld respectively. Table 1 shows the specifications and performance parameters used to model these inductors. Parameters used to design the LNA are listed in Table 2. Figure 12 shows the input output match, *NF* and gain of the designed LNA with tapered inductors. At 2.44 GHz, input reflection coefficient (S11) and output reflection coefficient (S22) shows a peak value of -29.31 dB and -16.37 dB respectively with

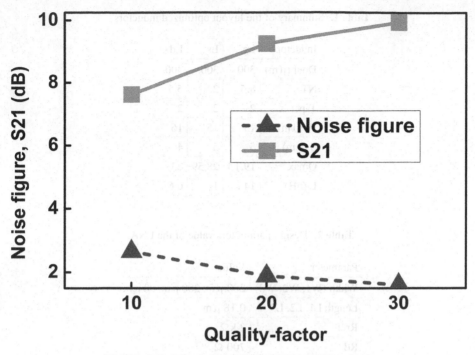

Fig. 10. *NF* and gain for different values of inductor *Q*.

a gain value noted of 16.45. The noise figure value observed is 1.2 dB. Table 3 shows the performance comparison of the designed LNA with some of the previous work. It is observed that the designed LNA shows best *NF* with an optimum gain among the compared works.

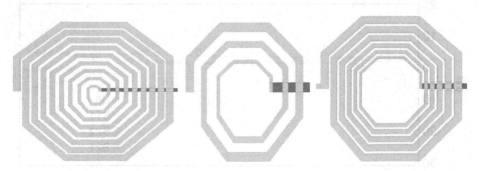

Fig. 11. Layout view of the tapered inductor Lg, Ls and Ld.

Table 1. Summary of the layout optimized inductors.

Inductor	Lg	Ls	Ld
Dout (μm)	300	300	300
NT	8.5	2.5	5.5
Taper	2	2	2
W (μm)	15	15	16
S (μm)	5	5	4
Qmax	19.13	28.59	23
L (nH)	14	1	6.6

Table 2. Design parameters value of the LNA.

Parameter	Value
Width (W1, W2, W3)	200 μm, 200 μm, 90 μm
Length L1, L2, L3	0.18 μm
Rref	2 kΩ
Rd	700 Ω
Rbias	3 kΩ
C1, C1	10 nF
C3	750 fF
Vdd	1.8 V

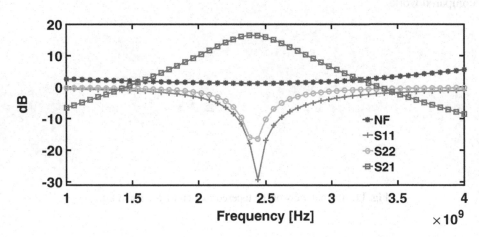

Fig. 12. S11, S22, S21 and NF with layout optimized inductors.

Table 3. Performance comparison of the designed LNA with previous works.

	[11]	[12]	[13]	[14]	This work
Process	0.18 μm	0.18 μm	0.18 μm	0.18 μm	0.18 μm
Frequency (GHz)	5	2.4	5	2.44	2.44
Vdd (V)	0.6	1.8	0.6	0.6	1.8
Power (mW)	1.68	2.7	0.8	3.8	3.56
Gain (dB)	14.1	11.2	10.2	14.6	16.45
Input return loss S11 (dB)	−12.7	−11	−17.9	−15	−29.31
Noise figure (dB)	3.65	2.15	4.1	2.9	1.2
IIP3 (dBm)	−8.6	−6.5	−15	4.19	−4.35

6 Conclusion

High Q inductors are shown to benefit LNA design in achieving low noise and higher gain. LNA designed with different values of inductor Q are analyzed showing an improvement by about 30% in gain and a reduction of about 65% in NF with high Q values. Finally, the LNA is designed using layout optimized high Q inductors achieving a much lower NF of 1.2 dB and a high gain of 16.45 dB at 2.44 GHz.

References

1. Hasaneen, E.-S.: On-chip inductor technique for improving LNA performance operating at 15 GHz. Circuits Syst. **03**, 334–341 (2012)
2. Lee, T.H.: The Design of CMOS Radio-Frequency Integrated Circuits, 2nd edn. Cambridge University Press, Cambridge (2003)
3. Li, X.J., Zhang, Y.P.: CMOS low noise amplifier design for microwave and mmWave applications. Prog. Electromagn. Res. **161**, 57–85 (2018)
4. Belostotski, L., Haslett, J.W.: Noise figure optimization of inductively degenerated CMOS LNAs with integrated gate inductors. IEEE Trans. Circuits Syst. I Regul. Pap. **53**(7), 1409–1422 (2006)
5. Tiwari, S., Vanukuru, V.N.R., Mukherjee, J.: Noise figure analysis of 2.5 GHz folded cascode LNA using high-Q layout optimized inductors. In: 2015 IEEE Asia Pacific Conference on Postgraduate Research in Microelectronics and Electronics (PrimeAsia), Hyderabad, pp. 94–97 (2015)
6. Kumar, S., Kumari, S.: Design of low power, high gain lna for wcdma range and parameters extraction using artificial neural network (ANN). In: 2015 IEEE Power, Communication and Information Technology Conference (PCITC), Bhubaneswar, pp. 436–441 (2015)
7. Jin, X., Hoe, D.H.K.: Optimization of short channel cmos lnas by geometric programming. In: 2012 IEEE 55th International Midwest Symposium on Circuits and Systems (MWSCAS), p. 912 (2012)
8. Molavi, R., Mirabbasi, S., Hashemi, M.: A wideband cmos lna design approach. In: IEEE International Symposium on Circuits and Systems, Kobe, vol. 5, pp. 5107–5110 (2005)
9. Burghartz, J.N., Rejaei, B.: On the design of RF spiral inductors on silicon. IEEE Trans. Electron Devices **50**(3), 718729 (2003)

10. Tayenjam, S., Vanukuru, V., Sundaram, K.: High- Q variable pitch spiral inductors for increased inductance density and figure-of-merit. IEEE Trans. Electron Devices **66**(10), 4481–4485 (2019)
11. Hsieh, H., Wang, J., Lu, L.: Gain-enhancement techniques for CMOS Folded Cascode LNAs at low-voltage operations. IEEE Trans. Microwave Theory Tech. **56**, 1807–1816 (2008)
12. Toofan, S., Rahmati, A., Abrishamifar, A., Lahiji, G.: A low-power and high-gain fully integrated CMOS LNA. Microelectron. J. **38**, 1150–1155 (2007)
13. Chang, C., Chen, J., Wang, Y.: A fully integrated 5 GHz low voltage LNA using forward body bias technology. IEEE Microwave Wireless Compon. Lett. **19**(3), 176–178 (2009)
14. Kumaravel, S., Kukde, A., Venkataramani, B., Raja, R.: A high linearity and high gain Folded Cascode LNA for narrowband receiver applications. Microelectron. J. **54**, 101–108 (2016)

Comparative Study of Latch Type and Differential Type Sense Amplifier Circuits Using Power Reduction Techniques

Reeya Agrawal[✉]

Department of Electronics and Communication Engineering, GLA University, Mathura, India
reeya.agrawal@gla.ac.in

Abstract. A quantitative and yield analysis of different types of sense amplifiers has been done. Furthermore, power reduction techniques such as sleep transistor technique, footer stack technique, sleep stack technique, and sleepy keeper technique also have been done over sense amplifiers. Observations specifically concentrate on the dissipation of power of various combinations of sense amplifiers. The findings of the simulation reveal that the suggested implementation of the sleep transistor technique system in the current mode differential sense amplifier often leads to a drastic decrease, in power dissipation considering 1.2 V power supply voltage.

Keywords: VMDSA (voltage mode differential sense amplifier) · CMDSA (current mode differential sense amplifier) · VLSA (voltage latch sense amplifier) · CLSA (current latch sense amplifier) · SRAMC (Static Random Access Memory Cell) · Sense Amplifier (SA)

1 Introduction

Improved density and efficiency of very large scale integrated circuit (VLSI) circuits have been obtained by scale down transistors. Local connections are called wires and are used to connect transistors within integrated circuits. Clock and power routing wires within a chip are known as global links on a chip. The latency of global communication becomes essential for many applications, such as buses between cache memories and processors [1], as VLSI technology scales down to the sub-micron level. With length [2] delay in this global interconnection on the chip raises four-way. Different signaling methods were suggested to transmit signals by interconnection and to reduce delay; different kinds of transceivers were employed. In recent years, the design of low power storage has been powered by the exponential output of battery-operated computers. Leakage current has made the SRAMC system a power-hungry block from both static and dynamic perspectives as the transistor count increases. SRAM block is now also an important part of system-on-chip (SOC) architecture.

Sense amplifiers are used primarily to read SRAMC content and dynamic random access memory (DRAM). Their conception means an acceptable spectrum of noise and

V. Arunachalam and K. Sivasankaran (Eds.): ICMDCS 2021, CCIS 1392, pp. 269–280, 2021.
https://doi.org/10.1007/978-981-16-5048-2_21

high-quality information that reflects the material of a specific memory cell. They are very sensitive to noise. Fast sense amplifiers are critical for many circuits to achieve low latency, with bit-line reading in memories being the most common domain. Interconnection is becoming a major source of on-chip delay with the emergence of sub-micrometer complementary metal-oxide-semiconductor (CMOS) chips, rapid sense amplifiers are also likely to be needed e.g. as high-speed signal repeaters that must cross large chips [3–5].

The demand for mobile devices and a battery-operated embedded system is growing with greater breadth as the very large scale integrated circuit (VLSI) industries grow. Cache memory is the central part of the memory that plays a key role in the data execution, cache occupying 60% to 70% of the chip region [6–8]. As chip consumption increases rapidly, microprocessor velocity is then decreased. One million transistors also increase and degrade the efficiency of single-chip failure rates, so the industry is working to build a low-speed and low-power memory circuit, which keeps the development of the VLSI system informed. The emphasis is on the sense amplifier (SA) in this article. In current high-performance microprocessors, more than half of the transistors are for cache memories and in the future, this proportion is projected to increase [9–12]. SRAMC is usually the option for built-in stock because it is robust in such chips in a noisy environment. The design of low-power, high-performance processors, therefore, received considerable attention. The device can use the necessary memory cells by integrating them in SRAMCs that are the right size for the system requirement. In an area, speed and power lead to improvements. In all SRAMC memory blocks, SA is an important element that responds to high frequency. Memories time for access and power consumption is calculated primarily by the configuration of the sense amplifier. One of the main peripheral circuits in memory devices is SA [13–15]. SA is a power-operated circuit that reduces the time of signal propagation from the cell to the logic circuit on the memory cell periphery and converts the arbitrary logical levels of the peripheral Boolean circuits from a bit to the digital logic levels [16]. Their output significantly influences both memory access time and the total dissipation of memory capacity. CMOS memories, as with other integrated circuits (ICs), are needed to increase speed, increase power, and keep dissipation at low energy. When it comes to SA memory design these goals are quite contradictory. Usually, with increased memory space the parasite space of the bit line is increased. This bit line has increased steadily with more energy-hungry memories [17–20].

2 Power Reduction Techniques

This section contains techniques of low power reduction that have been introduced in various types of amplifiers, such as VMDSA, CMDSA, VLSA, and CLSA.

2.1 Sleep Transistor Technique

Sleep Transistor Technique [21] is the most well-known method. A P_{MOS} transistor "Sleep" is situated between V_{DD} and network pull-up and an N_{MOS} transistor is positioned between the pull-down network and G_{ND} as shown in Fig. 1.

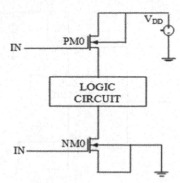

Fig. 1. Circuit diagram of sleep transistor technique

2.2 Sleepy-Keeper Technique

In this P$_{MOS}$ and N$_{MOS}$ transistor approach structure, pull-up sleep transistor N$_{MOS}$ transistor linked to pull-down sleep transistor P$_{MOS}$ applied parallel between pull-up network and V$_{DD}$ and pull-down network and GND. This method reduces the control of outflow wells and preserves the exact logic of a small field circuit. The N$_{MOS}$ transistor linked between the V$_{DD}$ and pull-up network is turned ON in sleep mode to retain the data value '1'. Similarly, the P$_{MOS}$ transistor joint between the pull-down network and GND is switched ON to maintain the data value '0'. Similarly, the P$_{MOS}$ transistor joint between the pull-down network and GND is switched ON to maintain the data value '0' as shown in Fig. 2 [1].

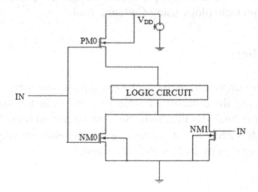

Fig. 2. Circuit diagram of sleepy keeper technique

2.3 Forced-Stack Technique

Another power reduction technique is the stacking strategy, which pushes an individual transistor into two half-size transistors [22]. The result of transistor stacking contributes

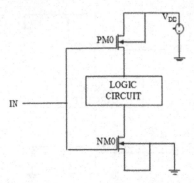

Fig. 3. Circuit diagram of forced stack technique

to a reduction in the decrease in sub-threshold current. This strategy saves the actual state while the transistor is in an off state as shown in Fig. 3.

These circuits became known as high-density circuits because of their numerous transistors used and also because of the high leakage rate concerning technological developments. The input power supply was then reduced by attempting to reduce the energy consumption rate. However, due to the reduction, data stability will be decreased. In both static and dynamic memories the access time is approximately the same [23, 24]. Section 1 provides a brief presentation on the semiconductor industry and a brief introduction to power reduction techniques have been discussed in Sect. 2. Each sense amplifier with its circuit diagram has been described in Sect. 3. Section 4 describe the comparison table of power consumption of different sense amplifiers. The conclusions are present in Sect. 5. The goal of this paper is to design low power sense amplifiers in customary gpdk 90ηm technology using Cadence Tool.

3 Sense Amplifiers

Sense Amplifier is an important memory design aspect. The sense amplifiers become separate circuit class to the diversity of SA's in semiconductor memories and to the effect they have on the final specifications. Sensing operation must be non-destructive, provided that SRAMCs need no data to refresh circuits after sensing [25]. The criteria for a sensory amplifier usually include the following:

- Gain (A) = V_{out}/V_{in}.
- Sensitivity (S) = V_{IN} min – minimum detectable signal.
- Rise time (t_{rise}), fall time (t_{fall}) – 10% to 90% of the signal transient.

Generally, sense amplifier classified into two types (Table 1):

1. Differential Type Sense Amplifier:
2. Latch Type Sense Amplifier

Table 1. Difference between differential type and latch type sense amplifier

Differential type sense amplifier	Latch type sense amplifier
Less access time or high delay	Fast access time or less delay
Due to more delay than latch type it consumes less power than latch type	Power consumption is high
As it has Pre-Charge circuitry in its circuit it gives high voltage swing	It gives poor voltage swing
The area is large, due to this complicated in designing	Whereas its area is small, so easy to design

3.1 Differential Type Sense Amplifier

All the elements necessary for differential sensing are included in the basic metal oxide semiconductor (MOS) sense amplifier circuit. An amplifier is capable of rejecting popular noise and of amplifying the real difference between the indicators. Since the operating rate is very sluggish; the main difference amplifier is not in memories due to significant power dispersion and an inherently high offset [26].

3.1.1 Voltage Mode Differential Sense Amplifier

All elements needed for differential sensing are found in a simple MOS differential voltage sense amplifier circuit as seen in Fig. 4.

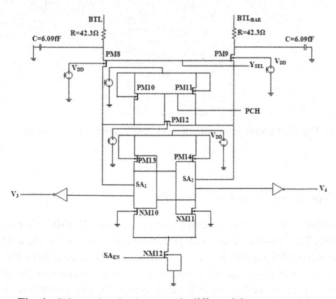

Fig. 4. Schematic of voltage mode differential sense amplifier

A differential amplifier requires a single-ended, small-signal output. The useful-ness of a differential amplifier is characterized by its ability to amplify true contrast between signals by ignoring common noise. Simple differential voltage amplification is not implemented in memories [27, 28] because of the very slow operating speed provided at substantial power dissipation and inherently high offset.

3.1.2 Current Mode Differential Sense Amplifier

The current sense amplifier consists of two parts: a) current transporting circuit with characteristics of unity-gain current transfer, b) current sense amplifier that senses dif-ferential current. Figure 5 shows a schematic of CMDSA. It is made up of four P_{mos} transistors (PM_8, PM_9, PM_{10}, and PM_{11}) with positive feedback [29, 30]. For all read cycles, internal nodes SA_1 and SA_2 are pre-equalized to have the same delay and latching using a P_{mos}.

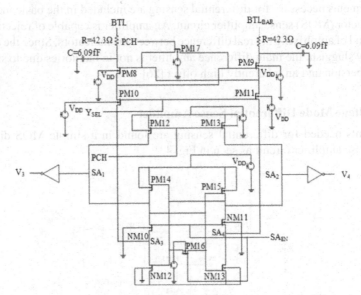

Fig. 5. Schematic of current mode differential sense amplifier

3.2 Latch Type Sense Amplifier

The sense amplifier type consists, similar to a six transistor SRAMC of a pair of intercon-nected inverters. The sensing begins with preloading and equalizing the latch-type SA in the high-gain metastable region. Since the input is not segregated from the outputs in a latch-type SA, the insulation transistors are necessary for isolation of the latch-type SA, the insulation transistors are necessary for isolation of the latch-type SA of the bit-lines and preventing the complete unloading of a "0" bit-line that costs additional power and time [31].

3.2.1 Voltage Latch Sense Amplifier

Voltage latch sense amplifier schematics developed in this work are shown in Fig. 6. In this design, internal nodes are pre-charged via bit-lines. Circuit architecture works directly via input bit-lines, centered on its internal nodes. When WL is pulled high and priors to sense amplifier trigger, NM_{12} is OFF, and PM_8 and PM_9 pass transistors are ON. As differential increases on bit-lines, a random bit on sense amplifier's internal nodes has an appropriate difference in voltage. The cross-linked inverters consist of PM_{10}, NM_{10}, PM_{11}, and NM_{11} amplify the differential voltage to its maximum swing output when sensor signal SA_{en} is asserted [32].

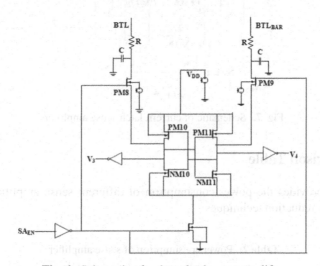

Fig. 6. Schematic of voltage latch sense amplifier

3.2.2 Current Latch Sense Amplifier

In cache memory architecture SA is a circuit of great importance. One of the bit-lines discharges during reading operation while the other bit-line stays at supply voltage. Figure 7 indicates a schematic of a current latch sense amplifier.

The slow discharge is due to the capacitance of large bit-line and bit cells access transistor is small. For this purpose, SA is used to amplify to digital levels a small difference between the values of bit-line voltages. The operation of the circuit is as follows. The differential voltage on bit-lines is transmitted to CLSA inputs SA_3 and SA_4. When SA_{EN} is pulled high both outputs SA_1 and SA_2 start discharging. Suppose, $SA_3 = V_{DD}$ and $SA_4 = V_{DD} - \Delta V$. Owing to its higher V_{gs}, this results in higher current through NM_{12} than NM_{13}. This triggers the discharge of output V_3 faster than V_4 [33].

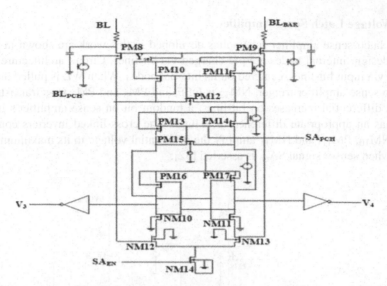

Fig. 7. Schematic of current latch sense amplifier

4 Comparison Table

This section provides the power consumption of different sense amplifiers with and without power reduction techniques.

Table 2. Power consumption of sense amplifier

S. no.	Sense amplifiers	Power consumption
1	VMDSA	86.66 μW
2	CMDSA	54.245 μW
3	VLSA	419.502 μW
4	CLSA	152.899 μW

Table 2 reveal that the overall dissipation of power in VMDSA is 86.66 μW, which is the lowest relative to other SA, and Fig. 8 describe the comparison of power consumption of different sense amplifiers of Table 2 in chart form.

Also, it was evaluated from Table 3 that the application of techniques of low power reduction such as the sleep transistor technique absorbs the lowest power in CMDSA whereas Fig. 9 describes the comparison of power consumption of different sense amplifier using the power reduction technique of Table 3 in chart form.

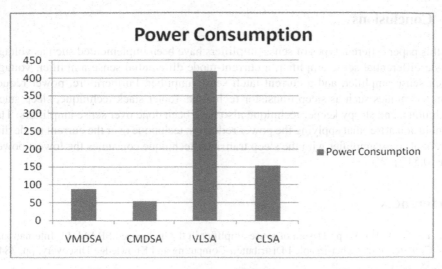

Fig. 8. Power consumption of different sense amplifier

Table 3. Power reduction techniques over sense amplifiers

Techniques used	Power consumption			
	VMDSA	CMDSA	VLSA	CLSA
Footer stack	52.94 μW	0.5545 μW	257.102 μW	109.838 μW
Sleep transistor	53.21 μW	0.5482 μW	255.344 μW	64.79 μW
Sleepy-keeper	53.18 μW	0.5436 μW	261.103 μW	108.154 μW

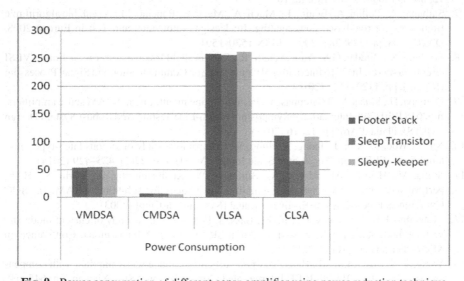

Fig. 9. Power consumption of different sense amplifier using power reduction technique

5 Conclusions

In this paper different types of sense amplifiers have been implemented such as voltage mode differential sense amplifier, a current-mode differential sense amplifier, voltage latch sense amplifier, and a current latch sense amplifier. Furthermore, power reduction techniques such as sleep transistor technique, footer stack technique, sleep stack technique, and sleepy keeper technique also have been done over sense amplifiers. The conclusion arises that applying the power reduction technique over the current mode differential sense amplifier with the sleep transistor technique consumes the lowest power (i.e. 0.548 μW).

References

1. Tao, Y.-p., Hu, W.-p.: Design of sense amplifier in the high-speed SRAM. In: International Conference on Cyber-Enabled Distributed Computing and Knowledge Discovery, pp. 384–387 (2015)
2. Garg, M.R., Tonk, A.: A study of different types of voltage & current sense amplifier used in SRAM. Int. J. Adv. Res. Comput. Commun. Eng. 4, 30–35 (2015)
3. Natarajan, A., Shanker, V., Maheshwari, A.: Sensing design issue in deep submicron CMOS SRAM. In: IEEE Computer Society Annual Symposium on VLSI, pp. 42–45 (2005)
4. Pandey, K., Yadav, V.: Design and analysis of low power latch sense amplifier. IOSR J. Electron. Commun. Eng. 9, 69–73 (2014)
5. Priya, G., Baskaran, K., Krishnaveni, D.: Leakage power reduction techniques in deep submicron technologies for VLSI applications. In: International Conference on Communication Technology and System Design. ELSEVIER (2011)
6. Abdollahi, A., Fallah, F., Pedram, M.: A robust power gating structure and power mode transition strategy for MTCMOS design. IEEE Trans. Very Large Scale Integr. (VLSI) Syst. 15, 80–89 (2007). ISSN 1063-8210
7. Sathanur, A., Pullini, A., Benini, L., Macii, A., Macii, E., Poncino, M.: A scalable algorithmic framework for row-based power-gating. In: Design Automation and Test in Europe 2008. DATE 2008, pp. 379–384 (2008). ISSN 1530-1591
8. Sridhara, K., Biradar, G.S., Yanamshetti, R.: Subthreshold leakage power reduction in VLSI circuits: a survey. In: 2016 International Conference on Communication and Signal Processing (ICCSP), pp. 1120–1124 (2016)
9. Dounavi, H., Sfikas, Y., Tsiatouhas, Y.: Periodic aging monitoring in SRAM sense amplifiers. In: 2018 IEEE 24th International Symposium on On-Line Testing And Robust System Design (IOLTS), Platja d'Aro, pp. 12–16 (2018)
10. Na, T., Woo, S., Kim, J., Jeong, H., Jung, S.: Comparative study of various latch-type sense amplifiers. IEEE Trans. Very Large Scale Integr. (VLSI) Syst. 22(2), 425–429 (2014)
11. Sinha, M., Hsu, S., Alvandpour, A., Burleson, W., Krishnamurthy, R., Borhr, S.: High-performance and low-voltage sense-amplifier techniques for sub-90nm SRAM. In: SOC Conference, Proceedings. IEEE International [Systems-on-Chip] (2003)
12. Mohammad, B., Dadabhoy, P., Lin, K., Bassett, P.: Comparative study of current mode and voltage mode sense amplifier used for 28nm SRAM. In: 24th International Conference on Microelectronic, 07 March 2013
13. Wang, Y., Zhao, F., Liu, M., Han, Z.: A new full current-mode sense amplifier with compensation circuit. In: 2011 9th IEEE International Conference on ASIC, Xiamen, pp. 645–648 (2011)

14. Dutt, R., Abhijeet: High-speed current mode sense amplifier for SRAM applications. IOSR J. Eng. **2**, 1124–1127 (2012)
15. Wei, Z., Peng, X., Wang, J., Yin, H., Gong, N.: Novel CMOS SRAM voltage latched sense amplifiers design based on 65nm technology, pp. 3281–3282 (2014)
16. Arora, D., Gundu, A.K., Hashmi, M.S.: A high-speed low voltage latch type sense amplifier for non-volatile memory. In: 2016 20th International Symposium on VLSI Design and Test (VDAT), Guwahati, pp. 1–5 (2016)
17. Agrawal, R., Tomar, V.K.: Analysis of cache (SRAM) memory for core I ™ 7 processor. In: 9th International Conference on Computing, Communication and Networking Technologies (ICCCNT), 402 (2018)
18. Schinkel, D., Mensink, E., Klumperink, E., van Tuijl, E., Nauta, B.: A double-tail latch-type voltage sense amplifier with 18ps setup+hold time. In: 2007 IEEE International Solid-State Circuits Conference. Digest of Technical Papers, San Francisco, CA, pp. 314–605 (2007)
19. Tripathi, V.M., Mishra, S., Saikia, J., Dandapat, A.: A low-voltage 13T latch-type sense amplifier with regenerative feedback for ultra speed memory access. In: 2017 30th International Conference on VLSI Design and 2017 16th International Conference on Embedded Systems (VLSID), Hyderabad, pp. 341–346 (2017)
20. Hemaprabha, A., Vivek, K.: Comparative analysis of sense amplifiers for memories. In: 2015 International Conference on Innovations in Information, Embedded and Communication Systems (ICIIECS), Coimbatore, pp. 1–6 (2015)
21. Jefremow, M., et al.: Time-differential sense amplifier for sub-80mV bit line voltage embedded STT-MRAM in 40nm CMOS. In: 2013 IEEE International Solid-State Circuits Conference Digest of Technical Papers, San Francisco, CA, pp. 216–217 (2013)
22. Rajendra Prasad, S., Madhavi, B.K., Lal Kishore, K.: Design of 32nm forced stack CNTFET SRAM cell for leakage power reduction. In: IEEE Conference on Computing, Electronics and Electrical Technologies, pp. 629–633 (2012)
23. Mishra, J.K., Srivastava, H., Misra, P.K., Goswami, M.: A 40nm low power high stable SRAM cell using separate read port and sleep transistor methodology. In: 2018 IEEE International Symposium on Smart Electronic Systems (iSES) (Formerly iNiS), Hyderabad, India, pp. 1–5 (2018)
24. Sultana, T., Jagadesh, S., Naveen Kumar, M.: A novel dual-stack sleep technique for reactivation noise suppression in MTCMOS circuits. IOSR J. VLSI Signal Process. **3**, 32–37 (2013)
25. Deepika, K.G., Priyadarshini, K.M., Raj, K.D.S.: Sleepy keeper approach for power performance tuning in VLSI design. Int. J. Electron. Commun. Eng. **6**(1), 17–28 (2013)
26. Kaushik, C.S.H., Vanjarlapati, R.R., Krishna, V.M., Gautam, T., Elamaran, V.: VLSI design of low power SRAM architectures for FPGAs. In: 2014 International Conference on Green Computing Communication and Electrical Engineering (ICGCCEE), pp. 1–4 (2014)
27. Choudhary, R., Padhy, S., Rout, N.: Enhanced robust architecture of single Bit SRAM cell using drowsy cache and super cut-off CMOS concept. Int. J. Ind. Electron. Electr. Eng. **3**, 63–68 (2011)
28. Gajjar, J.P., Zala, A.S., Aggarwal, S.K.: Design and analysis of 32 bit SRAM architecture in 90nm CMOS technology. Int. Res. J. Eng. Technol. (IRJET) **03**(04), 2729–2733 (2016)
29. Agrawal, R., Tomar, V.K.: Analysis of cache (SRAM) memory for core I ™ 7 processor. In: 9th International Conference on Computing, Communication and Networking Technologies (ICCCNT), 40225 (2018)
30. Vanama, K., Gunnuthula, R., Prasad, G.: Design of low power stable SRAM cell. In: 2014 International Conference on Circuit Power and Computing Technologies (ICCPCT), pp. 1263–1267 (2014)

31. Saun, S., Kumar, H.: Design and performance analysis of 6T SRAM cell on different CMOS technologies with stability characterization. IOP Conf. Ser. Mater. Sci. Eng. **561**, 012093 (2019)

32. Bhaskar, A.: Design and analysis of low power SRAM cells. In: 2017 Innovations in Power and Advanced Computing Technologies (i-PACT), Vellore, pp. 1–5 (2017)

33. Zhang, Y., Wang, Z., Zhu, C., Zhang, L., Ji, A., Mao, L.: 28nm latch type sense amplifier coupling effect analysis. In: 2016 International Symposium on Integrated Circuits (ISIC), Singapore, pp. 1–4 (2016)

Design and Implementation of ASIC for Time Recorder in TSMC 180 nm CMOS Technology

Saroja V. Siddamal(✉) ⓘ, Suhas B. Shirol, Shraddha B. Hiremath, Jayashree Mallidu, and Nalini C. Iyer

KLE Technological University, Hubballi, India
{sarojavs,suhasshirol,shraddha_h,jayashree.mallidu,
nalinic}@kletech.ac.in

Abstract. The authors present ASIC design of time recorder which finds application in monitoring the total amount of time that a device is in operation or the number of times the device is in uses since last repair, or last calibration. ASIC is implemented in TSMC 0.18 with power supply of 3.3 V/1.8 V. Frequency of 1.024 MHz is produced by the oscillator. The oscillator is designed to for maximum current of 100 μA. For all PVT corners the frequency variation is less 10%. The back end implementation is done using industry standard Cadance tool. The die size of the core is 1.500 mm * 1.500 mm. At 1.8 v supply the power consumed is 1.47 mW. The ASIC is fabricated from at mini@sic runway shuttle.

Keywords: Mixed signal ASIC · Placement and route · Low power · Power analysis

1 Introduction

The experience of complete chip design is presented in this paper. The authors has considered event recorder as usecase. In paper [1] which is a datasheet of an elapsed-time recorder. The devive tracks time when the event signal is high Its also calculates the accumulated on-time.

In paper considered for reference is a datasheet of maxium IC [2]. This IC records the number of events occured. The authors in [3] have proposed the ASIC design elapsed time counter in UMC 180 nm technology. The design and implementation is done using industry standard cadance tool. In paper [4] a datasheet for event logger is a 8 pin DIL battery powered. The counters are designed to count the real time clock and the eplased time. The paper [5] the authors have discussed oscillator. The authors in [6] discuss the power lost due to switching activity when the device under test is in funtinal mode due to scan chain. A novel gating technique is proposed to reduce the switching activity. The work is carried out using UMC 180 nm CMOS technology. The authors in paper [7] have presented the design of mixed signal ASIC.

© Springer Nature Singapore Pte Ltd. 2021
V. Arunachalam and K. Sivasankaran (Eds.): ICMDCS 2021, CCIS 1392, pp. 281–287, 2021.
https://doi.org/10.1007/978-981-16-5048-2_22

2 Architecture of Time Recorder

The architecture of the time recorder is as shown in Fig. 1. It communicates through I^2C interface.

Once EVENT pin goes HIGH, glitch filter validates the toggling. The filtered EVENT edge increments EC register by one. Simultaneously EDC and ETC counters start counting with 8 kHz clock. The rest of the section discussed main sub-modules of the architecture.

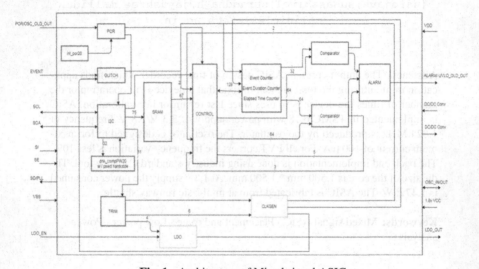

Fig. 1. Architecture of Mixed signal ASIC

Glitch Filter: An event greater the 70 ms is considered as true event. This event is used to increment the Event Counter. The event occurred is passed through the glitch filter shown in Fig. 2.

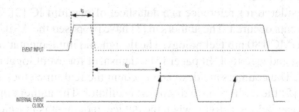

Fig. 2. Timing diagram of glitch filter

This filter outputs a signal '1' when the event is held high for 70 ms. Any event less than 70 ms, glitch filter outputs '0' which is considered as false event. The timing characteristic of glitch filter is shown in Table 1.

Table 1. Timing characteristics of glitch filter

Parameter	Symbol ms	Min ms	Typ ms	Max ms
Glitch duration	t_G		70	
CLK period to event counters	t_{EI}	95	100	105

I^2C Communication: The ASIC communicates to the external devices through I^2C which operates at 400 kHz. The two SDA and SCL pins are used for the task. The data is sent on SDA and clock pulse on SCL. The communication is of master-slave type. The operation of I^2C communication is as shown in Fig. 3 and Fig. 4.

The data from the **SDA** pin is sampled at falling edge of SCL and is written at SCL's rising edge.

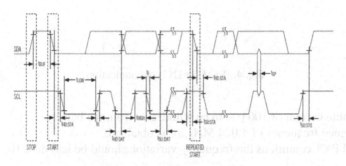

Fig. 3. I2C Timing diagram

When power is supplied, the POR signal is generated from the POR block. This signal is an active low, which triggers the reset conditions in the I^2C slave module. After the reset signal the slave starts the set-up sequence, in which it waits for the master to fill all the initial counter, comparator limit, configuration and command register values in the memory. After the setup sequence is completed slave passes a ready signal to the SRAM controller for its further operation.

START Condition: The master generates the start condition to begin a new data transfer. A start condition is generated when SDA transits from high to low and SCL remains high.

STOP Condition: The master generates stop condition to initiate the end of data transfer with the slave. This condition is generated when SDA transits from low to high and SCL remains high.

On Chip Oscillator: A CMOS RC ring oscillator is used to in the design. The oscillator operates at 1.8 V supply. It is an on-chip oscillator designed to meet the following objectives.

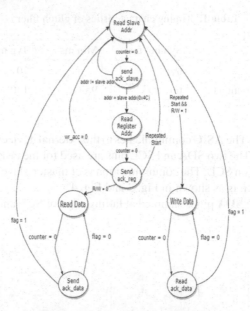

Fig. 4. FSM for I2C communication

- A maximum current of 100 μA to be withdrawn from the battery.
- The designed frequency of 1.024 MHz to be obtained.
- Under all PVT conditions the frequency variation should be less than 10%.

To achieve the above said objectives the design specifications in Table 2 are considered.

Table 2. Oscillator design and achieved specifications

Parameter	Min	Typ	Max	Min		Typ	Max	Units
	Designed specification			Achieved specification				
Frequency (F)	0.95	1	1.05	0.84		1.006	1.07	MHz
Duty cycle (DS)	–	50	–	20		45	65	%
Supply current (I)	–	–	<100	5.46		7.01	22.36	μA
Power supply (V_{DD})	1.71	1.8	1.9	1.71		1.8	1.9	V
Leakage current (I_{leak})	–	0	<5	–		1.5	2.5	nA
Temperature Range	−40	27	125	−40		27	125	°C

The design of an oscillator block consists of an RC Ring based oscillator, a multi-plexer and a seven-stage frequency divider circuit. The oscillator block is an RC Ring based oscillator which has a temperature CTAT current source, voltage regulator, main RC ring block and Output Buffer.

Oscillator Resuts: The design is simulated using spectra simulator in cadence virtuoso platform. The achieved specifications are as shown in Table 2. The design is implemented using TSMC 180 ηm CMOS Logic as shown in Fig. 5. The area consumed is 138 μm * 68 μm.

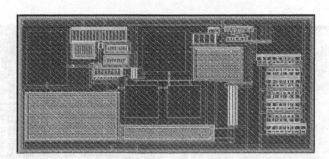

Fig. 5. Layout of oscillator

3 Back End Implementation of Time Recorder

Time Recorder is a test chip with16 pin DIL Fig. 6. The physical implementation is done using Cadance tool.

Sl.no	Pin Name	Description
1.	POR	Bidirectional pin Power on reset signal
2.	EVENT	Event Trigger Signal
3.	SDA	I²C serial data Input/Output.
4.	SCL	I2C serial clock.
5.	TESTMODE	When '1' ,ASIC is in test mode and '0', ASIC is in Function mode
6.	SI	Test mode input
7.	SO	Scan Out in Test Mode
8.	GND	Ground
9.	ALARM/SE	Function mode Alarm output, Test mode acts as scan enable
10.	OSC_IN/OUT	This is bidirectional pin; Oscillator output and Input Clock signal .
11.	1.8 VDD	1.8V Supply for core
12.	DC-DC IN	DC/DC converter Input
13.	DC-DC_OUT	DC/DC converter Output
14.	LDO OUT	LDO output: This pin gives output 1.8V from LDO
15.	LDO_EN	LDO Enable: This pin is used to Enable or Disable the LDO block
16.	VCC	3.3V DC input voltage

Fig. 6. a) ASIC pin details b) Description of pinouts

Physical implementation is done using industry standard CAD Tool Cadance innovous. It consists of 6 metal routing layers. P&R is carried out to get the final GDS II format.

Timing Analysis: Timing performance of a design is verified using industry standard tempus tool. Care is taken to meet timing closure.

Power Planning: Power measurement is done using Voltas IC Total of 1.497 mW of power requirement is seen for typical voltage of 1.8 V.

Physical Verification: Mentor graphics tool is used for performing DRC. The design area is 2,449,225 μm^2.

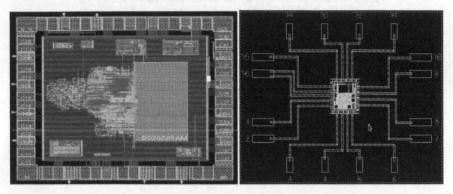

Fig. 7. a) Time recorder GDS II format b) Bounding diagram for DIL 16

The Fig. 7 shows the GSD II file taped out to TSMC foundry fabrication.

4 Conclusion

The work authors have presented a chip tape out. Mixed Signal ASIC is designed using industry standard Cadance tool. The time recorder is implemented in TSMC 180 ηm technology. 100 μA of current is drawn from the battery. For typical case at 1.8 v supply the power consumed is 1.47 mW. The core area is 1500 μm *1500 μm.

References

1. https://datasheets.maximintegrated.com/en/ds/DS1683.pdf
2. https://datasheets.maximintegrated.com/en/ds/DS1682.pdf
3. Rajaram, S., Balamurugan, N.B., Gracia Nirmala Rani, D., Singh, V. (eds.) VDAT 2018. CCIS, vol. 892. Springer, Singapore (2019). https://doi.org/10.1007/978-981-13-5950-7
4. https://datasheets.maximintegrated.com/en/ds/DS1602.pdf
5. Kalburgi, S., et al.: Ultra low power low frequency on-chip oscillator for elapsed time counter. In: 32nd International Conference on VLSI Design and 18th International Conference on Embedded Systems (VLSID-2019), pp. 251–256, IEEE (2019). https://doi.org/10.1109/VLSID.2019.00062

6. Nekar, H., Siddamal, S.V.: Design and implementation of novel scan architecture for test power reduction. Procedia Comput. Sci. **171**, 2556–2562 (2020). ISSN 1877-0509. https://doi.org/10.1016/j.procs.2020.04.277
7. Siddamal, S.V., Shirol, S.B., Kotabagi, S.S., Hiremath, S.B., Iyer, N.C.: Design and implementation of mixed signal ASIC-event logger in TSMC 0.18 μm CMOS technology. In: Sabut, S.K., Ray, A.K., Pati, B., Acharya, U.R. (eds.) Proceedings of International Conference on Communication, Circuits, and Systems. LNEE, vol. 728, pp. 451–457. Springer, Singapore (2021). https://doi.org/10.1007/978-981-33-4866-0_55

A Design of Low Power Resistorless Sub-threshold CMOS Bandgap Voltage Reference

Priya Vinayak Kulkarni[1](✉) and Rajashekhar B. Shettar[2]

[1] Department of Electronics and Communication Engineering, B.V. Bhoomaraddi College of Engineering and Technology, Vidyanagar, Hubballi 580031, Karnataka, India
[2] School of Electronics and Communication Engineering, KLE Technological University, Vidyanagar, Hubballi 580031, Karnataka, India

Abstract. The present work focuses on the analysis and design of a resistorless sub-threshold voltage reference. A low power CMOS voltage reference is developed using 180 nm process technology. In conventional band gap reference bipolar transistors (BJT's) and resistors are used, where BJT's are parasitic in nature and resistors consume larger area on the silicon chip and therefore the cost of the chip will be increased. From conventional band gap reference, BJT's and resistors are replaced with MOS transistors which operate in linear region and sub-threshold region respectively to generate the required proportional to absolute temperature (PTAT) and complementary to absolute temperature (CTAT) voltages. The proposed voltage reference circuit generates a stable voltage of 414.96 mV at 270C under 1.8 V of power supply. This circuit operates stable in the temperature range of −200C to 1200 C. Silicon chip area is 0.000916 mm^2 and power consumption is 0.0016 μW. When the proposed work is compared with similar architectures 88% of reduction in chip area and 79% of reduction in power consumption is observed. These are the two important observed outcomes from this proposed work.

Keywords: Temperature coefficient · Band gap · Sub-threshold · Triode · CTAT · PTAT

1 Introduction

The band gap voltage reference source is used in most of the integrated circuits. The traditional voltage reference makes use of Zener diodes as the forward biased diodes, which are reliant on temperature to a great extent. Temperature independency is the main characteristic of band gap reference. Regardless of disparity in power supply and changes in temperature the band gap reference gives constant voltage [1]. In the year 1964, it was documented that the disparity between two bipolar transistors base emitter voltage is straightforwardly proportional to the absolute temperature (PTAT) if they operate at uneven current densities. When compared to metal oxide semiconductor transistors, the bipolar transistors use large power [2–5]. For handy devices, the stumpy voltage and stumpy power operations are in demand. Because these are battery operated, stabilized

© Springer Nature Singapore Pte Ltd. 2021
V. Arunachalam and K. Sivasankaran (Eds.): ICMDCS 2021, CCIS 1392, pp. 288–300, 2021.
https://doi.org/10.1007/978-981-16-5048-2_23

over supply voltage, process and temperature variations also required. These requirements can be achieved by using bandgap voltage references but output voltage generated by conventional BGR (band gap reference) is equal to the silicon energy gap that is around 1.25 V but it is not suitable for low supply voltage operation [6, 7]. Figure 1 shows the conventional band gap reference, has two nodes that generate controlled voltages and currents by two same resistors for generating CTAT and PTAT currents. In the deep sub-micron technologies, it cannot be used. Therefore, in this project by replacing the BJTs and resistors by means of MOSFETs recital of BGR is improved. Silicon (Si) chip area is also saved and thus power consumption of the circuit is also reduced. Temperature dependencies can be suppressed by the combination of MOS transistors which operates in different regions like sub-threshold, saturation and linear regions [6]. To reduce the power expenditure of the devices the BGR generators operated below 1-V power supply are in demand and they are widely used in flash memories, DRAMs, ADCs and various analog devices [4].

Curvature compensation is enhanced further to achieve a superior temperature dependence (TD) performance over a wide range of temperature. In addition to this, it has also improved lower noise and line regulation. Sizes of the circuit and power efficiency are two critical issues in the design of band gap references. It is expensive for IC design when band gap references are based on BJTs and resistors. Total size of the circuit is large and it consumes more power and it is difficult to reach the desired noise and precision specifications.

Applications of band gap reference

- Used in voltage regulators (78xx, 79xx devices etc.)
- Used in low power applications
- Used in DRAM's, ADC's and various analog circuits.

Advantage of conventional band gap reference

- Conventional band gap references will provide stabilized output over power supply and temperature variations.

Disadvantages of conventional band gap reference

- Conventional BGR needs at least two resistors, area is increased and power consumption is also increased.
- Not suitable for low power applications.

This work is done to improve the performance of voltage reference by replacing bipolar and also resistors with MOSFETs which works in linear and sub threshold region.

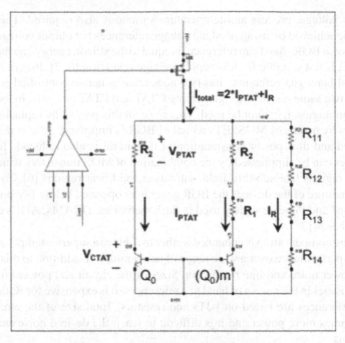

Fig. 1. Conventional band gap reference

2 MOSFET Operations in Different Regions

In sub-threshold region, when Vgs < Vth there is no channel formation between drain and source and there is no conduction of current, hence the transistor is considered as switched off. Here, the ideal current should be zero but there is a weak inversion current called as sub-threshold leakage current. The exponential relationship between the current and Vgs as given by [6, 10].

$$I_D \cong I_{D0} e^{\frac{Vgs-Vth}{nVt}} \tag{1}$$

where I_{D0} = current when Vgs will be equal to Vth
Vt = thermal voltage which is equal to kT/q
n = incline factor which is equal to $1 + CD/Cox$
CD – depletion layer capacitance
Cox – oxide layer capacitance

$$I_D \cong I_{DO} e^{(k(Vgs-Vth)-Vs)/Vt} \tag{2}$$

where k is channel divider

$$k = Cox/(Cox + C_D) \tag{3}$$

Highest possible transconductance to current ratio is delivered by these MOSFET's is,

$$\frac{g_m}{I_D} = \frac{1}{nV_T} \tag{4}$$

In this region MOSFETs behavior is similar to bipolar transistor.

In linear region, when Vgs > Vth and Vds < Vgs – Vth the drain current is given by,

$$I_D = \frac{\mu_n C_{ox} W}{L} V_{ds} \left((V_{gs} - V_{th}) - \frac{V_{ds}}{2} \right) \tag{5}$$

In the above equation when Vds << 2Vgs – 2Vth,

$$I_D \approx \frac{\mu_n C_{ox} W}{L} V_{ds} (V_{gs} - V_{th}) \tag{6}$$

Where I_D shows a linear variation vs. V_{ds}. The path between source to drain can be indicated as linear resistor, which is given by,

$$R_{on} = 1 \left/ \left(\frac{\mu_n C_{ox} W}{L} (V_{gs} - V_{th}) \right) \right. \tag{7}$$

When Vds << 2Vgs – 2Vth, the device operates in triode region.

Where (Vgs – Vth) is 'overdrive voltage' W/L is 'aspect ratio'. The MOS transistor performs similar to a resistor, where this value is controlled by overdrive voltage and aspect ratio [8, 9].

3 Proposed CMOS Voltage Reference

3.1 Schematic

The planned circuit schematic diagram has been depicted in Fig. 2. V_{dd} of 1.8 V has been selected for the proposed design and it is designed under 180 nm technology. Biasing in this circuit is not dependent on the power supply. It is supply independent and biasing can be obtained by the 4 transistors M0, M1, M3 and M4. These four transistors always work in saturation region and these will govern the current flowing through the circuit. The two transistors which operate in triode region and acts as voltage-controlled resistors are M5 and M6. The required voltage to remain M5 and M6 in triode region is provided by the gate node of M3 and M4. The next two transistors M7 and M8 operate in sub-threshold region acts as bipolar transistors of conventional voltage reference. Width of M7 and M8 transistors are kept high to keep them always in sub-threshold region. When the power supply is switched on the loop is formed by the four MOSFETs M0, M1, M3 and M4, there is a situation in which all MOSFETs transmit a zero current through both the branches. To eradicate this problem M2 transistor is used which acts as a 'start-up' circuit.

The final sizes of transistors are represented in Table 1, after some adjustments made from the simulations. All the transistors that govern the current which operates in saturation have the same width and length. Aspect ratio of these four transistors (M0, M1, M3 and M4) kept same. The transistors M5, M6 which operates in triode region have the same aspect ratio. The transistors M7, M8 which operates in sub-threshold region have the same aspect ratio.

Table 1. Sizes of MOSFETs of proposed band gap reference

Parameter	M0	M 1	M2	M 3	M4	M5	M6	M7	M8
Width (μm)	1	1	240	1	1	240	240	15	15
Length (μm)	2	2	2	2	2	2	2	2	2

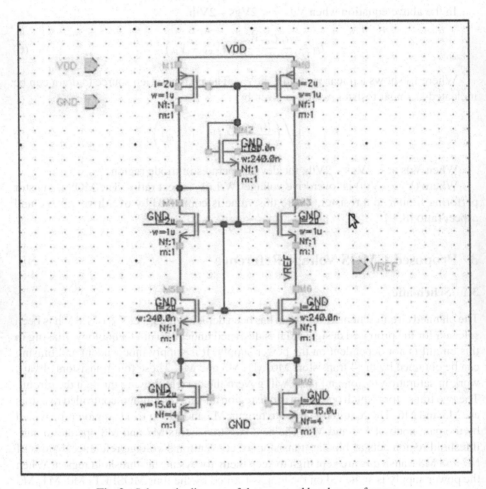

Fig. 2. Schematic diagram of the proposed band gap reference

The Fig. 3 shows the test schematic of the circuit. The input and output parameters are also shown. Vdc and Gnd are the two input parameters, Vref is the output parameter. The input parameter Vdc = 1.8 V is connected to the two PMOS transistors. The output voltage or the voltage reference generated from the circuit is measured across the M6 transistor. After setting this test, schematic simulations are done. Variations in Vref is studied for different parameters like temperature variations. Design is tested at 5 different corners such as TT, FF, FNSP, SNFP and SS.

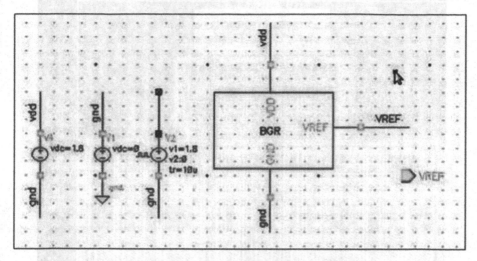

Fig. 3. Test schematic of proposed bandgap reference

M1 and M2 are connected to ground and M3 and M4 are connected to Vdd and hence there is no current between these two branches. To charge the M1 and M2 equal to gate voltage of M3 and M4, the transistor M9 is turned on. Once it is done the M9 works in cutoff region and hence the startup device is switched off. M7 and M8 which are operated in sub-threshold region, produces CTAT voltage. Variations in reference voltage are dependent on PTAT and CTAT voltages of the circuit. The required PTAT voltage is generated by the transistors which operate in triode region (M5 and M6). With the addition of these two voltages (PTAT and CTAT) the required voltage reference is obtained. Variance of V_{ref} is not dependent on the transistors M0, M1, M3 and M4.

3.2 Layout

The proposed circuit has to be laid on the silicon wafer. Errors like DRC (design rule check) and LVS (layout vs schematic) are eradicated to keep the layout of proposed schematic error free. The Fig. 4 shows the layout of planned schematic. This layout occupies a chip area of 0.00096 mm^2.

In electrical networks, an undesired electrical behavior is represented by a parasitic element. It could be an extra resistor, capacitor, inductor or a combination of these elements. These are associated with devices and interconnect. The effects of parasitic are electrical failures; impacts circuit performance, slower signal transitions or increased delays. Parasitic extractions are also done. Post layout simulations are done and verified. The Fig. 5 and Fig. 6 show AV extractions at 120 $^\circ$C and –20 $^\circ$C respectively.

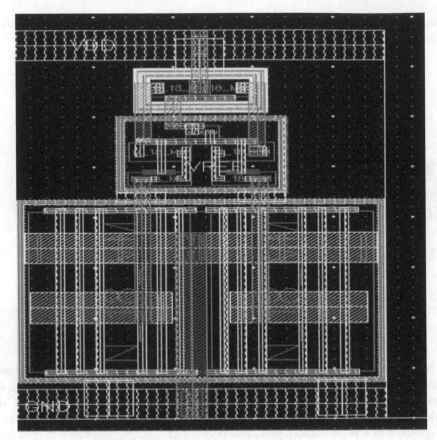

Fig. 4. Layout of planned band gap reference

4 Results and Analysis

This circuit is simulated in 180 nm CMOS technology. From the BSIM3 model of technology device and process parameters are obtained.

4.1 Temperature Variations from –20° to 120 °C

For the determined W/L ratios of the transistors the temperature variations are parabolic in nature as shown in Fig. 7. Which varies between a minimum of Vref = 425.65 mV at 850C and maximum of Vref = 433.96 mV at 1200C. A small fluctuation in Vref of order 8.31 mV is observed in excess of the mentioned temperature range. Temperature coefficient of this is equal to 143.3 ppm/°C.

$$TC_{eff} = \frac{V_{REFmax} - V_{REFmin}}{(T_{max} - T_{min})V_{ref\ (27\,°C)}} \tag{8}$$

$$TC_{eff} = \frac{433.9 - 425.65}{(120 - (-20)\ 414.7} \tag{9}$$

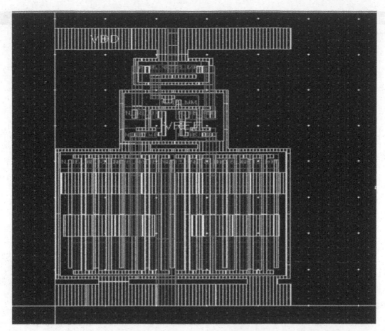

Fig. 5. AV extractions at 120 $^\circ$C

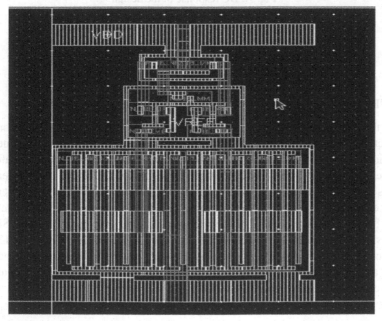

Fig. 6. AV extractions at –20 $^\circ$C

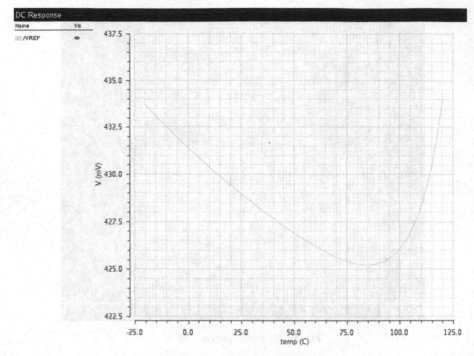

Fig. 7. DC response of the design

$$TC_{eff} = 143.3ppm/^{\circ}C \tag{10}$$

4.2 Impact of Process Variations

One of the examples for design of experiments kind of technique in semiconductor manufacturing is process corner, which indicates a disparity in various parameters of fabrication. Helpful in IC (integrated circuit) design on a semiconductor wafer. The boundries of variations in different parameters are represented by the five corners. This design is identified as inadequate design margin when there is a problem in circuit at these process extremes. In this scrutiny, the whole design is simulated for output reference voltage for all 5 process corners of the simulator (TT, FF, SS, SNFP and FNSP). The Table 2 shows the voltage variations across the temperature range of –200C to 1200C at five process corners. Temperature coefficient is calculated for each process corners. It is worst at FNSP process corner which is high. Temperature coefficient is low at SNFP process corner is good compared to the others.

4.3 Transient Analysis

The transient analysis is also carried out and verified at few distinctive conditions. In this analysis circuit is simulated in time domain. Power supply has been inclined down

Table 2. Comparison of voltage reference across five process corners

Corner	Variation	TC (ppm/$^\circ$C)
FF	12.48	215.3
FNSP	13.15	226.8
TT	8.31	143.3
SNFP	3.124	53.89
SS	9.956	171.2

first and then inclined up after 50 µs to settle the final value as shown in Fig. 8. No oscillations are observed in output reference voltage.

4.4 Comparison Between Proposed Architecture with Other Architectures

The Table 3 shows the comparison between proposed architecture and others. The proposed architecture is done with 180 nm CMOS technology. Observations from the table show that the proposed work is better than all other similar works. The huge reduction in power consumption and area is observed.

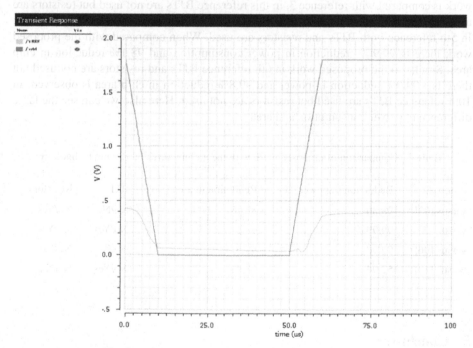

Fig. 8. Transient response of proposed voltage reference

Table 3. Comparison of proposed work with different architectures.

Ref. No	Temp coefficient (ppm/°C)	Power (μW)	Vin (Volts)	Tech. (μm)	Vref (mV)	BJT used	Resistor used	Area (mm²)
1	5	16.3	0.75	0.18	469	Yes	No	0.0053
2	43	0.33	1.2	0.13	240	No	No	0.0016
3	14.4	0.134	1	0.18	546.3	No	Yes	0.0094
4	8.79	0.048	1	0.18	479	Yes	No	0.0012
5	0.55	54	1.8	0.18	1100	Yes	Yes	0.048
6	28.4	3.9	1.8	0.18	466.5	No	No	0.22
7	15.7	0.3	1.4–3	0.35	745	Yes	No	0.05
9	-----	1.4	3.7	0.5	1121	No	No	0.4
10	-----	0.0034	0.8	0.18	550	Yes	No	0.00135
proposed	53.89	0.0016	1.8	0.18	414.7	No	No	0.000916

Improvements in the project such as power reduction and chip area reduction compared with the other references in 180 nm technology are listed in Table 4. When proposed work is compared with reference 3, in this reference BJTs are not used but resistors are used. Power consumption is decreased by 98.8% and area is also decreased by 89.78%. In 5th reference both BJTs and resistors are used. When compared with the proposed work there is 99.90% reduction in power consumption and 98.1% reduction in chip area. Similar to the proposed work in 6th reference BJTs and resistors are not used but there is a 99.9% reduction in power and 99.8% reduction in chip area is observed. In 10th reference BJTs are used but resistors are not used. Here also we can see the large difference in power consumption and area.

Table 4. Comparison of proposed work with the architectures of 180 nm technology

Proposed	Reduction in power (%)	Reduction in area (%)	BJT	Resistors
versus [03]	98.80	89.78	No/No	No/Yes
versus [05]	99.99	98.1	No/Yes	No/Yes
versus [06]	99.90	99.5	No/No	No/No
versus [10]	52.94	28.83	No/Yes	No/No

5 Conclusion

Because of very good and precise characteristics of diode connected BJTs, band gap references are most prevalently used references in many analog and digital applications.

The traditional band gap references chomp through huge quantity of area and power because of BJTs, op-amps and resistors which are connected in the circuit. Therefore, the newly designed schematic does not make use of BJTs, operational amplifiers and resistors. Hence consumes a smaller amount area and power when compared to the existing designs. The proposed circuit totally consists of 9 MOSFETs. The circuit is implemented in 180nm CMOS technology. The MOSFETs M7 and M8 are operated at sub-threshold region which substitutes the bipolar transistors. Similarly, the MOSFETs M5 and M6 which are operated in the triode region substitutes the resistors. By escalating transconductance value in the sub threshold region resistance is also found to be reduced. The voltage reference design with Vref of 414.7 mV at 270C with Vdd = 1.8 V. For the proposed schematic, the layout is prepared in Cadence environment. The errors such as DRC and LVS are cleared and verified. The chip area consumed in the planned layout is 0.000916 mm^2 and the power consumption is found to be around 0.0016 μW. The anticipated architecture is very much competent in terms of area reduction and power consumption. The planned work has been simulated for all five process corners (TT, FF, SS, SNFP and FNSP) under the temperature range of $-200C$ to 1200C and supply variations. From the simulations carried out, it can also be also concluded that there is no start up circuit requirement in the planned architecture. Present study optimized process parameters considering less chip area and low power consumption whereas temperature coefficient has increased. Work can be carried out to reduce the temperature coefficient. Curvature compensations can be carried out.

References

1. Gomez Caicedo, J.A., Mattia, O.E., Klimach, H., Bampi, S.: 0.75 V supply nanowatt resistorless sub-bandgap curvature-compensated CMOS voltage reference. Analog Integr. Circ. Sig. Process **88**(2), 333–345 (2016). https://doi.org/10.1007/s10470-016-0722-4
2. Campana, R.V., Klimach, H., Bampi, S.: 0.5 V supply resistorless voltage reference for low voltage applications. Salvador, Brazil (Sept 2015)
3. Khot, P., Shettar, R.B.: Design of area efficient and low power bandgap voltage reference using sub-threshold MOS transistors. In: VLSI Design and Test (VDAT), 19th International Symposium on, pp. 1–5 (2015)
4. Mattia, O.E., Klimach, H., Bampi, S.: 0.9 V, 5 nW, 9 ppm/0C resistorless sub-bandgap voltage reference in 0.18 μm CMOS. In: Circuits and Systems (LASCAS), IEEE 5th Latin American Symposium on, pp. 1–4 (2014)
5. Hongal, R., Shettar, R.B.: Design and implementation of curvature corrected bandgap voltage reference – 1.1 using 180 nm technology. In: 5th Nirma University International Conference on Engineering (NUiCONE) (2015)
6. Somvanshi, S., Kasavajjala, S.: A low power sub-1V CMOS voltage reference. In: Anti-counterfeiting, Security, and Identification in Communication, ASID. 3rd International Conference on, pp. 20–22 (Aug 2009)
7. Uneno, K., Hirose, T., Asai, T., Amemiya, Y.: A 300 nW, 15 ppm/0C, 20 ppm/V CMOS voltage reference circuit consisting of subthreshold MOSFETs. IEEE J. Solid-State Circuits **44**(7), 2047–2054 (2009)
8. Mok, P.K.T., Leung, K.N.: Design considerations of recent advanced low-voltage low-temperature-coefficient CMOS bandgap voltage reference. In: IEEE Custom Integrated Circuits Conference (2004)

9. Buck, A.E., McDonald, C.L., Lewis, S.H., Viswanathan, T.R.: A CMOS bandgap reference without resistors. IEEE J. Solid-State Circuits **37**(1), 81–83 (2002)

10. Mattia, O.E., Klimach, H., Bampi, S.: Resistorless BJT and curvatures compensation circuit at 3.4 nW for CMOS bandgap voltage references. Electron. Lett. **50**(12), 863–864 (2014)

Comparative Performance Analysis of P-I-N Detector with Different Amplifiers and Pulse Generators for Quality Improvement of Distorted Signal

Manoj Kumar Dutta[✉] and Mohineet Kaur

BIT Mesra, Deoghar Campus, Jharkhand 814142, India

Abstract. Optical detector is a very important part of an optical network. The efficiency of an optical transmission system is greatly affected by the sensitivity of photoetector. The working capability of an optical receiver depends on amplifiers and the modulation technique used for the same. In this paper the sensitivity of a p-i-n photodetector has been compared for different commonly used amplifiers viz, EDFA, Optical amplifier and SOA using different modulation schemes. The comparison is done in terms of BER, Q- factor and power analysis of the received signal. The result suggests that the P-I-N along with EDFA and NRZ modulation scheme gives the best result. Optisystem professional software is used for the simulation purpose.

1 Introduction

The ever increasing demand of on-line applications like e-commerce, online education system, different multimedia based application, online medical advice etc., require enormous bandwidth. Optical fiber can provides huge usable bandwidth. Optical fiber along with WDM/DWDM is used for this purpose [1–4]. The invention of the optical fiber amplifier is the innovation making it possible to realize the WDM system efficiently. Whenever signal in optical domain travels through fiber, it becomes impaired and distorted by different effects such as, self-phase modulation (SPM), four-wave mixing (FWM) and cross-phase modulation (XPM). Apart from these nonlinear effects the travelling signal also degrades due to different unavoidable losses, like losses due to fiber attenuation, tap loss, splices loss etc. Because of these nonlinear effects and the inbuilt noises of the fiber, the quality of the transmitting signal degrades significantly. As a result the OSNR at the receiver goes below the recoverable value. For reliable transmission of the optical signal over distance, it is very much essential to compensate the losses as much as possible. Transmission distance in optical communication can be increased by using either regenerators or optical amplifiers. Advantage of optical amplifiers over regenerators is that it can boost the power without any optoelectronic conversation and hence reduce the system manufacturing cost.

© Springer Nature Singapore Pte Ltd. 2021
V. Arunachalam and K. Sivasankaran (Eds.): ICMDCS 2021, CCIS 1392, pp. 301–310, 2021.
https://doi.org/10.1007/978-981-16-5048-2_24

2 Relevant Theory and Mathematical Calculation

2.1 P-I-N Photodetector

In the p-n junction photo-detector the frequency response is limited due to junction capacitance and this junction capacitance can be reduced by the use of an intrinsic semiconductor layer between p & n layers. When light falls on this portion electron hole pairs are generated and drift randomly into the depletion region and a delayed displacement current is produced. The type of semiconductor material and the energy of the incident photon determine penetration of the incident light.

The gain of the p-i-n photodetector can be written as,

$$G = \frac{1}{1 - (v_d/V_B)^n} \tag{1}$$

Where, v_d = carrier drift velocity and V_B = Breakdown voltage of the diode.

The 3 dB bandwidth can be estimated as

$$f_{3dB} = \frac{0.35}{t_r} \tag{2}$$

t_r is the rise time.

2.2 SOA

Ssemiconductor optical amplifiers has gain equal to,

$$G = 1 + \frac{P_{amp,sat}}{P_{s,in}} \ln(\frac{G_0}{G}) = G_0 \exp(-\frac{G-1}{G} \frac{P_{s,out}}{P_{amp,sat}}) \tag{3}$$

Where, G_0 is small signal gain, $P_{s,in}$ is power input and $P_{s,out}$ is power output.

The 3-dB BW is equal to

$$
\begin{aligned}
B_{SOA} = 2(f - f_0) &= \frac{2\Delta f_{FSR}}{\pi} \sin^{-1}[\frac{1 - \sqrt{R_1 R_2 G}}{2(\sqrt{R_1 R_2 G})^{1/2}}] \\
&= \frac{c}{\pi n L} \sin^{-1}[\frac{1 - \sqrt{R_1 R_2 G}}{2(\sqrt{R_1 R_2 G})^{1/2}}]
\end{aligned} \tag{4}
$$

2.3 EDFA

Gain of EDFA

$$G_{max} = \min\{\exp(\rho\sigma_e L), 1 + \frac{\lambda_p}{\lambda_s}\} \tag{5}$$

EDFA output power is given by,

$$P_{s,out} = \min\left\{P_{s,in} \exp(\rho\sigma_e L), P_{s,in} + \frac{\lambda_p}{\lambda_s} P_{p,in}\right\} \tag{6}$$

2.4 Optical Amplifier

Gain of optical amplifier is

$$G = G_0 \exp[-\frac{G-1}{G}\frac{P_{out}}{P_{intsat}}]\tag{7}$$

$P_{int\,sat} = Ah\upsilon / \sigma_a \tau$.

A = mode-field area, h = Planck's constant, υ = frequency at the propagating signal, σ_a = absorption cross-section, and $\tau = E_r$ metastable lifetime in silica.

2.5 Noise Figure (NF)

Noise figure is defined as,

$$NF = \frac{SNR_{in}}{SNR_{out}} = \frac{1 + 2n_{sp}(G-1)}{G}\tag{8}$$

Quality factor can be written as,

$$Q = \frac{(R_b.P_s)^2}{\sigma_{ase}}\tag{9}$$

Where, R_b = bit rate, P_s = signal power in dBm, σ_{ase} = noise induced by parametric gain.

BER in WDM system is [5–7],

$$BER = \frac{1}{2}erfc(\frac{Q}{\sqrt{2}}) = \frac{\exp(-Q^2/2)}{Q.\sqrt{2\pi}}\tag{10}$$

3 Result and Discussion

Figure 1 represents the layout diagram for the calculating the different comparative performance analysis. Table 1 represents the parametric values of PIN photodiode. Figure 2, 3 and 4 depicts eye diagram representation of EDFA, Optical amplifier and SOA for NRZ pulse respectively and Table 2, 3 and 4 represents the different eye diagram parameters respectively. Figures show that the highest Q factor is achieved when EDFA is used as the amplifier followed by SOA and optical amplifier. This result suggests that p-i-n photodetector sensitivity is maximum when EDFA is used and lowest when optical amplifier is used. This inference is valid only when NRZ pulse is used for modulation. The result changes if Gaussian pulse is used instead of NRZ pulse. In that case the maximum Q factor is obtained by EDFA followed by optical amplifier and SOA, as shown by the Fig. 5, 6 and 7 respectively. Table 5, 6 and 7 represents the different eye diagram parameters of EDFA, Optical amplifier and SOA respectively. Figure 8, 9 and 10 represents the power vs frequency output of EDFA, Optical amplifier and SOA respectively for NRZ pulse. Figure 11, 12 and 13 represents the power vs frequency output of EDFA, Optical amplifier and SOA respectively for Gaussian pulse. This figure supports the same results obtained by the eye diagram analysis. The results obtained in this paper may be useful by the optical design engineers for choosing suitable amplifiers and modulation technique to get the optimum photodetector efficiency.

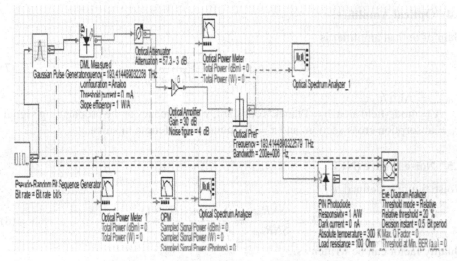

Fig. 1. Layout diagram for the simulation study

Table 1. Parametric values of PIN photodetector

Responsivity	Dark current	Absolute temp	Load resistance	Thermal noise current	Shot noise current
1 A/W	0 nA	300 K	100 Ω	0 nA	0 nA

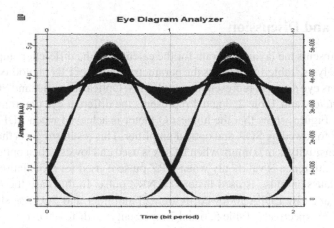

Fig. 2. Eye diagram of EDFA for NRZ pulse

Table 2. Eye diagram parametric values of EDFA for NRZ pulse

Max. Q factor	Min. BER	Eye height	Threshold	Decision inst.
38.1736	2.11302e−319	3.58489e−006	6.93073e−008	0.3125

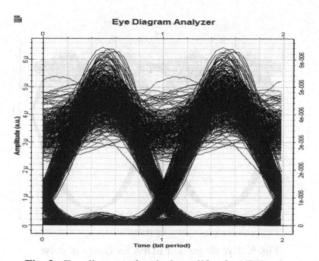

Fig. 3. Eye diagram of optical amplifier for NRZ pulse

Table 3. Eye diagram parametric values of optical amplifier for NRZ pulse

Max. Q factor	Min. BER	Eye height	Threshold	Decision inst.
7.18086	2.33222e−013	2.40232e−006	4.35354e−007	0.328125

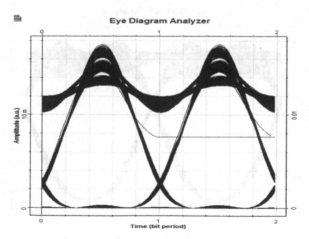

Fig. 4. Eye diagram of SOA for NRZ pulse

Table 4. Eye diagram parametric values of SOA for NRZ pulse

Max. Q factor	Min. BER	Eye height	Threshold	Decision inst.
25.8711	3.8836e-148	0.0119846	0.000276311	0.328125

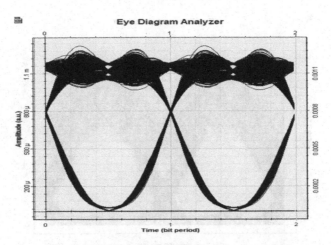

Fig. 5. Eye diagram of EDFA for Gaussian pulse

Table 5. Eye diagram parametric values of EDFA for Gaussian pulse

Max. Q factor	Min. BER	Eye height	Threshold	Decision inst.
21.7779	1.57535e−105	0.000954199	0.00024793	0.5

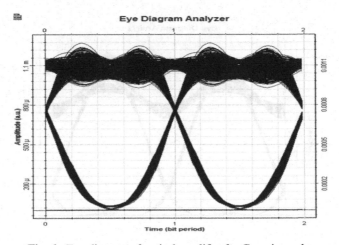

Fig. 6. Eye diagram of optical amplifier for Gaussian pulse

Table 6. Eye diagram parametric values of optical amplifier for Gaussian pulse

Max. Q factor	Min. BER	Eye height	Threshold	Decision inst.
21.5016	6.30318e−103	0.000913576	0.000236239	0.5

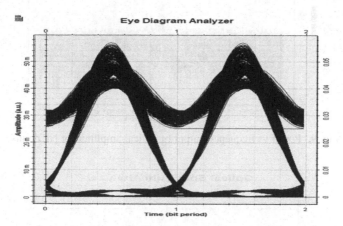

Fig. 7. Eye diagram of SOA for Gaussian pulse

Table 7. Eye diagram parametric values of SOA for Gaussian pulse

Max. Q factor	Min. BER	Eye height	Threshold	Decision inst.
10.5327	2.58313e−026	0.0315758	0.00981251	0.640625

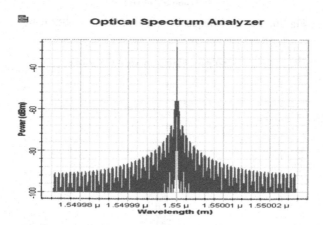

Fig. 8. Power vs frequency output of EDFA for NRZ pulse

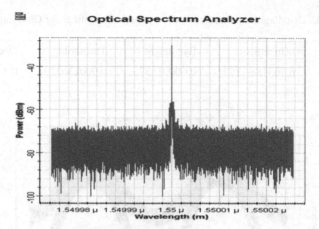

Fig. 9. Power vs frequency output of optical amplifier for NRZ pulse

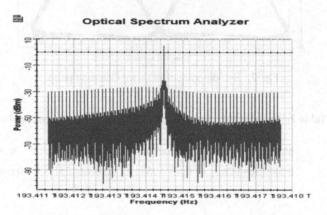

Fig. 10. Power vs frequency output of SOA for NRZ pulse

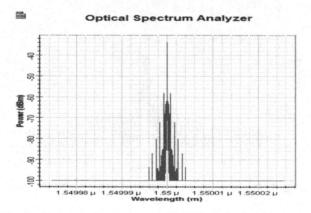

Fig. 11. Power vs frequency output of EDFA for Gaussian pulse

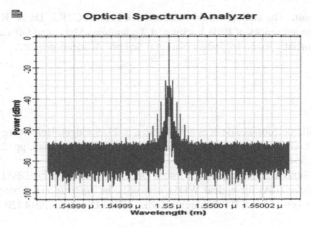

Fig. 12. Power vs frequency output of optical amplifier for Gaussian pulse

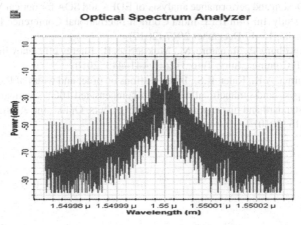

Fig. 13. Power vs frequency output of SOA for Gaussian pulse

4 Conclusion

Photodetector is a very important part of optical communication system. The performance of the network heavily depends on the efficiency of photodetector. The sensitivity of the detector changes with the associated amplifier, the modulation scheme used and fiber nonlinearites present. In this paper a comparative study of p-i-n diode for various types of amplifiers and modulation scheme is reported. The performance analysis is done in presence of nonlinear effects. Analysis of the results and the corresponding graphs suggests that the p-i-n photodetector sensitivity becomes maximum when it is attached with the EDFA and the NRZ pulse. The results discussed here is very important for a network and optical system designer for efficiently designing of an optical transmission system.

Acknowledgement. The authors would like to thank Prof. R.C. Jha, Dr. R. K. Sarkar, Dr. S. Karmakar and the authorities of Birla Institute of Technology, Mesra and Off-campus Deoghar. This work is financially supported Indian National Science Academy project.

References

1. Alamo, A.: Microelectronics devices and circuits, p. 23. Springer, Heidelberg (2005)
2. Agarwal, G.P.: Optical communication: its history and recent progress, pp. 23–28. Springer, Heidelberg (2004)
3. Dutta, M.K.: Study and comparison of Erbium Doped Fiber Amplifier (EDFA) and Distributed Raman Amplifier (RA) for optical WDM networks. In: International Conference on Fibre Optics and Photonics 2014, IIT Kharagpur India, 13–16 December 2014 (2014). ISBN: 978-1-55752-882-7
4. Singh, S.: Boost up of four wave mixing signal in semiconductor optical amplifier for 40 Gb/s optical frequency conversion. Opt. Commun. **281**(9), 2618–2626 (2008)
5. Dutta, M.K.: Design and performance analysis of EDFA and SOA for optical WDM networks: a comparative study. In: 14th IEEE India Council International Conference INDICON 2017, IIT Roorkee, India, 15–17 December 2017 (2017)
6. Zhang, Y., Chowdhury, P., Tornatore, M., Mukherjee, B.: Energy efficiency in telecom optical networks. IEEE Commun. Surv. Tutor. **12**(4), 441–445 (2010)
7. Singh, M., Sharma, A.K., Kaler, R.S.: Investigations on order and width of RZ super Gaussian pulse in pre-, post- and symmetrical dispersion compensated 10Gb/s optical communication system using standard and dispersion compensating fibers. Optik –Int. J. Light Electron Opt. **121**(7), 609–616 (2010)

Design and Implementation of Bi-directional IO for Elapsed Time Counter Application

Shraddha B. Hiremath$^{(\boxtimes)}$, Saroja V. Siddamal, Nalini C. Iyer, and Sujata Kotabagi

KLE Technological University, Hubballi, India
shraddha_h@bvb.edu

Abstract. IO plays an important role in communicating the core circuitry with external world. This paper discusses the design and implementation of bi-directional IO for elapsed time counter. It is used as both input and output port having following blocks level shifter, pre-driver, driver and Schmitt trigger. The design operates at two different voltage levels. The core operates at 1.8 V which is named as VDDC and the IO voltage level is at 3.3 V named as VDDIO. The range of frequency at which the IO should function properly is up to 10 MHz. Different levels of voltage at input and output side with its lowest and highest values are set as one of the specification. The designed IO functions with the capacitive load of 150 fF and 5 pF is present at input core and output pad respectively. The resulting rise time and fall time are to be a maximum of 10% of signal time period. Similarly the rise to rise delay and fall to fall delay must be less than 25% of the signal time period. The duty cycle should not exceed the 40–60 barriers. IO design should satisfy the design constraints and specification under all process corners, operating temperatures and voltage conditions (PVT).

Keywords: IO · Core · Rise time · Fall time · Rise to rise delay · Fall to fall delay · Duty cycle

1 Introduction

An elapsed time counter is used to count seconds when power supply is applied [8]. The IO cells are situated at the periphery of the chip and provide immunity to the chip from noise and other untimely threats [1]. Input/output (IO) circuits enable a chip to communicate with the external world. The electrical signal outside the chip is unknown and possibly unsafe for the internal circuitry. If any of incoming signals is having voltage level more than the core level, then it may lead to failure of the core. IO helps to isolate the chip from such an environment and helps to convert the external signal to a form where the internal circuit can process it [2, 9].

IO consists of two main blocks transmitter and receiver. The signal from the core circuit enters transmitter which consist of level up shifter, pre-deriver and driver. Level up shifter converts the core level voltage (VDDC) to IO level voltage (VDDIO). Pre-deriver consist NAND and NOR logic which help to decide whether the IO should act as transmitter or receiver. P and N driver are controlled by the signals produced by pre-driver. The block diagram of transmitter is shown in Fig. 1.

© Springer Nature Singapore Pte Ltd. 2021
V. Arunachalam and K. Sivasankaran (Eds.): ICMDCS 2021, CCIS 1392, pp. 311–321, 2021.
https://doi.org/10.1007/978-981-16-5048-2_25

Receiver block consist of Schmitt trigger, Level down shifter and core buffer. Schmitt trigger acts as a noise rejecter. It helps to reshape sloppy, or distorted rectangular pulses. Level down shifter converts the IO level voltage (VDDIO) to core level voltage (VDDC). The signal enters the core through core buffer [3].

The block diagram of receiver is shown in Fig. 2.

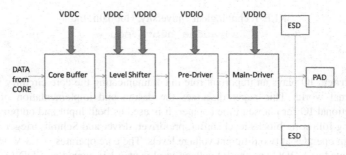

Fig. 1. Transmitter

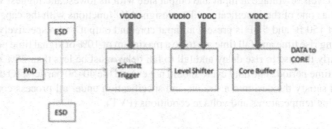

Fig. 2. Receiver

2   Design Specifications

The design specifications of the proposed bidirectional IO is as shown in Table 1.

Table 1. Design specifications

Parameter	Symbol	Min	Typ	Max
IO-level supply voltage	VDDIO	3.0 V	3.3 V	3.6 V
Core-level supply voltage	VDDC	1.65 V	1.8 V	1.9 V
Low-level input voltage	VIL			0.2VDDIO
High-level input voltage	VIH	0.8VDDIO		
Low level output voltage	VOL		0.8 V	

(*continued*)

Table 1. (*continued*)

Parameter	Symbol	Min	Typ	Max
High-level output voltage	VOH		2.4 V	
Operating temperature	T	−40 °C	27 °C	125 °C
Output duty cycle	DCD	40%	50%	60%
Maximum Frequency	Fmax			10 MHz

3 Proposed Design of Bidirectional IO

3.1 Transmitter Design

Transmitter design consists of a combination of design of level up shifter, pre-driver logic and driver.

3.1.1 Level up Shifter

The conventional level up shifter as shown in Fig. 3 consists of two cross coupled PMOS(P_1 and P_2) and two NMOS (N_1 and N_2) driven by complimentary input signal A and B. When the two inputs A and B are low and high, N_1 and N_2 are OFF and ON respectively. N_2 pulls down V_{OUT} and P_1 becomes ON and P_2 turns off since it is cross coupled and V_{OUT} decreases to ground level. Note that the node voltage of V_{OUT} is determined by the driver currents of pull-up transistor P_2 and pull-down transistor N_2. Therefore, if the driver current P_2 larger than that of N_2, the V_{OUT} cannot be discharged [4].

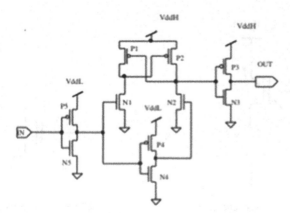

Fig. 3. Conventional level up shifter

3.1.2 Pre-driver

In order to drive the strong geometrically wide driver, a pre-driver is necessary. The pre-driver interfaces the small core logic circuit to the large capacitances include the gate capacitance and the parasitic capacitance of the metal route of the driver. It consists of NAND and NOR logic as shown in Fig. 4. Pre-driver must be able to drive the large capacitance in the driver transistors. Sizing of pre-driver transistors is adjusted such that their rise time matches with the fall time for typical PVT conditions [5].

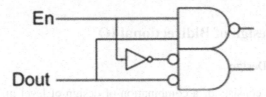

Fig. 4. Pre-driver for transmitter

3.1.3 P-driver and N-driver

To design the P-driver, V_{OH} is connected in place of the load capacitance as shown in Fig. 5. Then vary the width of the PMOS until the current is greater than 2 mA at all process corners. During this cycle the NMOS or the N-driver is turned OFF. Similarly, V_{OL} is connected in place of the load as shown in Fig. 6 and vary the width of the NMOS until the given requirements are fulfilled. Further, verification of the same is done by inducing a 2 mA current and checking the V_{OUT}. Here the V_{OUT} should be less than V_{OL} and should be more than V_{OH}.

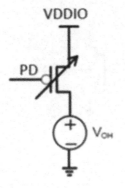

Fig. 5. P-driver schematic

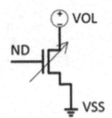

Fig. 6. N-driver schematic

3.2 Receiver Design

Receiver design consists of a combination of design of Schmitt trigger, Level down shifter.

3.2.1 Schmitt Trigger

The Schmitt trigger circuit as shown in Fig. 7 is an inverter circuit with two extra transistors for providing the hysteresis. Now after addition of 2 extra transistors M_6 and M_3 the circuit is capable to provide hysteresis. When input is LOW the M_1 and M_2 are off and M_4 and M_5 are ON and output is logic level high. When input is equal to threshold point of M_1 then M_1 will be ON but M_2 remains in OFF condition only, so output will be HIGH and M_3 will be ON, so M_1 makes to pull the voltage between M_1 and M_2 while M_3 try to pulls up voltage to V_{DD}-V_T. So M_2 will be in ON condition, whenever input crosses the threshold voltage of M_2 then output switches to LOW logic level. Hence switching point shifted to higher voltage referred as V_{IH}. Similarly vice versa when input is falling from higher logic level the PMOS comes into the picture. The difference between V_{IH} and V_{IL} referred as a Hysteresis voltage [6].

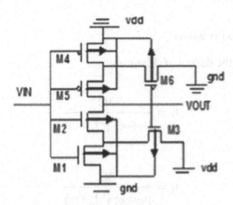

Fig. 7. Schmitt trigger

3.3 Level Down Shifter

Level down shifter is used for converting the voltage level from 3.3 V to 1.8 V. Since the pad operates at 3.3 V and core operates at 1.8 V. There is requirement of level down shifter to convert the signals coming from Schmitt trigger to core voltage signals. Figure 8 shows the circuit of level down shifter. It consists of a simple inverter chain of thick gate and the thin gate. The 3.3 V thick-oxide transistors have to be used here as the drive transistors, because the 3.3 V signal swings at the gates. Because of this, the channel length chosen to handle 3.3 V is excessive, and unnecessarily limits the drain current [9]. The driver is used to invert the signal i.e., the input signal is inverted with respect to input. To control the rise and fall time progressive sizing is used [7].

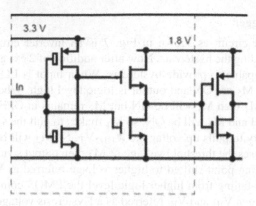

Fig. 8. Level down shifter

3.4 Mathematical Expressions

Equations involved in the design of driver are

Rise time

$$t_r = \frac{3C}{\mu_p c_{ox} \left(\frac{W}{L}\right)_p V_{DD}}$$

(1)

Fall time

$$t_f = \frac{3C}{\mu_p c_{ox} \left(\frac{W}{L}\right)_p V_{DD}}$$

(2)

Equation 1 and 2 are used to obtain (W/L) ratio of PMOS and NMOS driver circuits.

3.5 Mathematical Expressions

Figure 9 shows complete transmitter schematic consisting of level up shifter, pre-driver and driver.

Figure 10 shows complete receiver schematics consisting of Schmitt trigger and level down shifter.

4 Performance Analysis and Simulation

Simulation results for the transmitter and the receiver at different process corner, different operating temperature and voltages are detailed using UMC180 technology. The given results are the maximum, typical and minimum values for different delays.

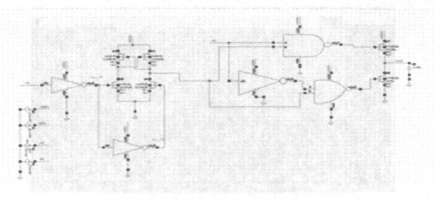

Fig. 9. Transmitter schematic

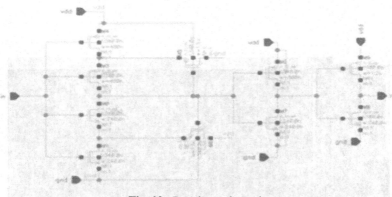

Fig. 10. Receiver schematic

4.1 Transmitter Result Analysis and Simulation

Table 2 and Fig. 11 shows the rise time, fall time, rise to rise delay, fall to fall delay and duty cycle of the transmitter at 10% variation of VDDIO = 3.3 V and VDDC = 1.8 V. The minimum values are obtained for the process corner fast (ff) and at operating temperature of −40 °C. The maximum values are obtained for the process corner slow (ss) and at operating temperature of 125 °C. The typical condition is taken to be process corner typical (tt) and the operating temperature as 27 °C.

Table 2. Transmitter analysis across PVT (1.8 V, 3.3 V) with 10% variation

	Rise time	Fall time	Rise-rise delay	Fall-fall delay	Duty cycle
Max	7.44 ns	3.593 ns	3.480 ns	3.508 ns	50.76
Typ	5.341 ns	2.592 ns	2.432 ns	2.569 ns	50.66
Min	1.209 ns	1.233 ns	1.676 ns	1.852 ns	50.56

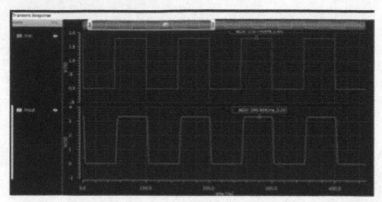

Fig. 11. Transmitter simulation showing level shifted wave-forms from core level voltage of 1.8 V to IO level voltage of 3.3 V at PVT (1.8 V, 3.3 V)

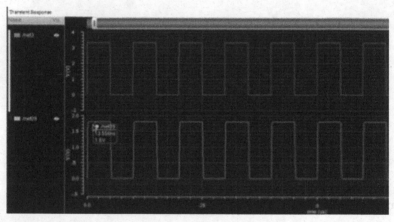

Fig. 12. N-driver simulation PVT (1.8 V, 3.3 V) with marker indicating the voltage value at 2 mA which is less than V_{OL} (0.8 V)

4.1.1 Driver Design Validation

Table 3, Figs. 12 and 13 gives the justification for the proposed design by verifying the values of V_{OH} and V_{OL} at 10% variation of $V_{DDIO} = 3.3$ V and $V_{DDC} = 1.8$ V. These values must not be lesser than 2.4 V and greater than 0.8 V respectively.

4.2 Receiver Result Analysis and Simulation

Table 4 and Fig. 14 and shows the rise time, fall time, rise to rise delay, fall to fall delay and duty cycle of the receiver at 10% variation of $V_{DDIO} = 3.3$ V and $V_{DDC} = 1.8$ V. The minimum values are obtained for the process corner fast fast (ff) and at operating

Table 3. Driver design validation across PVT (1.8 V, 3.3 V) with 10% variation

	P-driver	N-driver
Minimum	3.036 V	0.120 V
Typical	3.137 V	0.126 V
Maximum	3.151 V	0.212 V

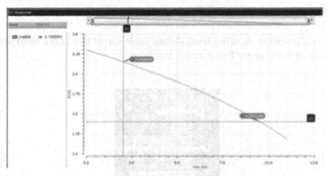

Fig. 13. P-driver simulation PVT (1.8 V, 3.3 V) with marker indicating the voltage value at 2 mA which is more than Voh (2.4 V)

temperature of −40 °C. The maximum values are obtained for the process corner slow slow (ss) and at operating temperature of 125 °C. The typical condition is taken to be process corner typical typical (tt) and the operating temperature as 27 °C.

Table 4. Receiver analysis across PVT (1.8 V, 3.3 V) with 10% variation

	Rise time	Fall time	Rise-rise delay	Fall-fall delay	Duty cycle
Max	8.39 ns	3.593 ns	3.480 ns	3.226 ns	51.36
Typ	4.702 ns	1.666 ns	2.432 ns	2.396 ns	50.95
Min	1.039 ns	1.11 ns	1.175 ns	1.929 ns	50.76

4.3 Floor Plan for Layout

Figure 15 shows the floor plan of transmitter which consist of level up shifter, pre-drive and driver. The estimated area of the IO cell width is 62.62 μm and height is 140.12 μm.

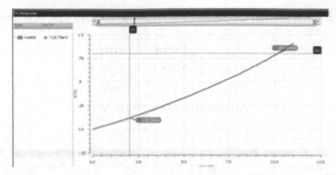

Fig. 14. Receiver simulation showing level shifted wave-forms from core level voltage of 1.8 V to IO level voltage of 3.3 V at PVT (1.8 V, 3.3 V)

Fig. 15. Floor plan of transmitter

5 Conclusion and Future Scope

5.1 Conclusion

The designed IO cell satisfies the given design constraints and specifications. The individual blocks of the IO cell are specifically designed and fine-tuned such that the signal integrity is maintained.

5.2 Future Scope

The IO cell is designed to fit into the elapsed time counter mixed signal IC. The addition of ESD circuit, slew rate optimization circuit and impedance control circuit will further increase its application in bigger and complex IC.

References

1. Maxims DS1602 device datasheet. https://datasheets.maximintegrated.com/en/ds/DS1602.pdf
2. Hall, S.H., Hall, G.W., McCall, J.A.: High-Speed Digital System Design: A Handbook of Interconnect Theory and Design Practices. Citeseer (2000)
3. Abraham, S.: GPIO design, layout, simulation and ESD clamp placement calculator. The University of Texas at Arlington (2014)
4. Kumar, M., Arya, S.K., Pandey, S.: Level shifter design for low power applications. arXiv preprint arXiv:1011.0507 (2010)
5. Weste, N.H.E., Harris, D.: CMOS VLSI design: a circuits and systems perspective. Pearson Education India (2015)
6. Kumar, M., Kaur, P., Thapar, S.: Design of CMOS Schmitt trigger. Int. J. Eng. Innov. Technol. (IJEIT) **2**, 252–255 (2012)
7. Ali, N.B.Z., Zwolinski, M., Al-Hashimi, B.M.: Testing of level shifters in multiple voltage designs. In: 14th IEEE International Conference on Electronics, Circuits and Systems 2007, ICECS 2007, pp. 435–438. IEEE (2007)
8. Kalburgi, S., et al.: Ultra low power low frequency on-chip oscillator for elapsed time counter. In: 2019 32nd International Conference on VLSI Design and 2019 18th International Conference on Embedded Systems (VLSID), pp. 251–256, Delhi, NCR, India (2019). http://ieeexplore.ieee.org/stamp/stamp.jsp?tp=&arnumber=8711177&isnumber=8710751
9. Pattanashetty, V.B., Iyer, N.C., Viswanath, H.L., Kore, S.: Inclusive device to connect people with the surrounding world. In: Fong, S., Akashe, S., Mahalle, P.N. (eds.) Information and Communication Technology for Competitive Strategies. LNNS, vol. 40, pp. 485–493. Springer, Singapore (2019). https://doi.org/10.1007/978-981-13-0586-3_49

Communication Technologies
and Circuits

FPGA Based High Speed 8-Tap FIR Filter

Bogi Kartheek$^{(\boxtimes)}$ and N. Purnachand

School of Electronics Engineering, VIT-AP University, Inavolu 522237, A.P., India

Abstract. FIR (Finite Impulse Response) filters play a predominant role in digital signal processing due to their phase linearity. It can be easily implemented in the hardware and is very stable compared to IIR due to its non-feedback nature. The main drawback of FIR filter is that it takes more time to compute since there are more coefficients. Hence it is very essential to speed up the multiplication process of the FIR filter system. One of the best techniques to improve the speed is to use memory-based computation using Anti-Symmetric product coding (APC) and Odd multiple storage (OMS) techniques. This paper uses the APC-OMS based multiplier in the design of 8-TAP FIR filter. The APC-OMS multiplier used in the 8-TAP FIR filter reduces the LUT size. The design is implemented and verified using Verilog HDL on a Xilinx Zynq-7000 series FPGA. The proposed design reduces the FPGA area utilization and improves the performance compared to the some of the state-of-the-art works. The proposed design can be operated at a maximum clock frequency of 464.04 MHz.

Keywords: FIR filters · Odd multiple storage · Anti-symmetric product coding · FPGA · Look-up-table

1 Introduction

The finite impulse response (FIR) filter is the significant filter to be used in digital signal processing Applications. "FIR digital filters find extensive applications in mobile communication systems such as channel equalization, matched filtering, and pulse shaping, due to their absolute stability and linear phase properties" [2]. FIR filters are used for certain applications where phase sensitivity is essential. Some of the applications are data communication, seismology, and mastering. FIR filters are designed on FPGA mainly because of its dedicated Hardware. The multiplier in FIR filter is designed using APC-OMS technique. FIR filter structure consists of Multipliers, Adders and Delay elements are shown in Fig. 1.

"Memory-based computing is a class of dedicated systems, where the computational functions are carried out by look-up tables (LUT)" [3, 5]. "Memory-based computing is well suited for many digital signal processing (DSP) algorithms, which involve multiplication with a fixed set of coefficients" [7]. "Optimization of LUT for Memory based computing can be performed using the APC-OMS technique and the odd multiples of the fixed coefficients are required to store in LUT which is termed as the odd multiple storage (OMS)" [4]. "While in the antisymmetric product coding (APC) approach, the product words are stored as antisymmetric pairs" [6].

© Springer Nature Singapore Pte Ltd. 2021
V. Arunachalam and K. Sivasankaran (Eds.): ICMDCS 2021, CCIS 1392, pp. 325–334, 2021.
https://doi.org/10.1007/978-981-16-5048-2_26

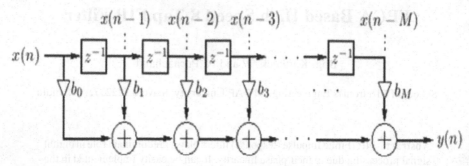

Fig. 1. Structure of FIR filter.

The equation of nth order digital filter (FIR) can be written as:

$$y(n) = \sum_{i=0}^{N} b_i * (x[n-i]) \tag{1}$$

- x[n] represents the I/p of the signal
- y[n] represents the o/p of the signal
- N represents order of an FIR filter (Delay points)
- N+1 represents no. of Taps.

2 Related Works

In [9], the authors proposed a high-speed FIR filter using adders and shifters and implemented the design on a Xilinx FPGA and achieved a maximum clock frequency of 235.026 MHz. The author has used add and shift method instead of multiplier to reduce chip size.

In [8], the authors proposed the design of FIR by means of vedic multiplier and implemented on Xilinx FPGA and achieved maximum clock frequency of 109 MHz.

In [7], the authors proposed LUT based multiplier design using APC-OMS based technique and implemented using TSMC 90nm technology. The author also synthesized CSD- based multiplier using the same technology library and compared it with LUT design and described the area utilization of LUT design is efficient over CSD- based multiplier.

In [11], the authors proposed an efficient FIR filter EMS multiplier and implemented using virtex-7, and achieved a maximum clock frequency of 433.46 MHz for the 16-TAP filter of input word size 4. Operating frequency can be higher by using APC-OMS based multiplier.

In [12], the authors proposed a FIR filter using birecorder multiplier and implemented. In a Xilinx FPGA and achieved maximum frequency of 157.227 MHz.

3 Techniques for Optimization of Memory

3.1 APC for the Optimization of Look up Table

The word length L = 5 of an input X and its values can be seen in the first and the third column of Table 1. Product values are defined by the multiplication of corresponding

X input with the fixed coefficient A. The sum of the product values, which are situated at the 2nd and 4th column equals 32A.The values situated at third column are two's compliment to the values which are situated at the first column of the Table 1. The final APC words are to be seen corresponding to different Addresses, which were written for different input values. These address inputs are located in the 5th column of Table 1. The terms u and v are defined as product values and are situated at second and fourth column. The subsequent equation determines the values of both u and v.

$$v = \frac{(u+v)}{2} - \frac{(v-u)}{2} \quad and \quad u = \frac{(u+v)}{2} + \frac{(v-u)}{2} \tag{2}$$

We know (u + v) = 32A, substituting this equation in Eq. (2)

$$v = 16A - \left[\frac{(v-u)}{2}\right] \quad and \quad u = 16A + \left[\frac{(v-u)}{2}\right] \tag{3}$$

In Eq. 3, we can see the negative symmetry on u and v. since considering the nature we can reduce the LUT size to half by storing the [v−u]/2 for the inputs situated at the same row of the table. The values in 2nd and 4th are known as product values. Those values are asymmetric to each other. The product can be found by using the next equation.

$$Product\ word = (APC\ word) * (sign\ value) + 16A \tag{4}$$

The product word can be found by the addition of 16A to the multiplication equation of sign value of MSB of input X with APC word. If the MSB (most significant bit) of input X is 0 then the sign value is −1. Likewise, if the MSB of the input is 1, then the sign value is −1.

3.2 OMS for Optimization of Look up Table

Address inputs from APC are taken as inputs in OMS (odd multiple storage) method. Those address inputs are situated in the 1st column of Table 2. And the corresponding product values of the address inputs are located in the 2nd column. The Required input values of shifted input are accessed by doing a left shift operation. Shifted APC can be found in the 5th column.

An active high signal (RESET signal) is given to reset the LUT output to derive the APC word 0. For 00000(X), the encoded word "16A" can be derived by left shifting the "2A" 3 times. It is stored at the address 1000.

Product value of input(X) 00000 is 0. For the input 00000(X), the APC word to be stored is 16A. APC words are said to be dissimilar to each other due to its procedure.

The inputs and product values are said to be unsigned values. It reduces half of the LUT size. Initially it requires 32 address locations, now it is reduced to half. It will be further reduced when these values are given to OMS technique.

Addresses from APC design are given as an input to OMS (odd multiple storage) in order to further reduce the size of LUT. The LUT size can be reduced by only storing the odd address and its corresponding product values.

Table 1. APC words of dissimilar various I/p values (L = 5)

Input (X)	Product values	Input (X)	Product values	Address (x3'x2'x1'x0)	APC words
00001	A	11111	31A	1111	15A
00010	2A	11110	30A	1110	14A
00011	3A	11101	29A	1101	13A
00100	4A	11100	28A	1100	12A
00101	5A	11011	27A	1011	11A
00110	6A	11010	26A	1010	10A
00111	7A	11001	25A	1001	9A
01000	8A	11000	24A	1000	8A
01001	9A	10111	23A	0111	7A
01010	10A	10110	22A	0110	6A
01011	11A	10101	21A	0101	5A
01100	12A	10100	20A	0100	4A
01101	13A	10011	19A	0011	3A
01110	14A	10010	18A	0010	2A
01111	15A	10001	17A	0001	A
10000	16A	10000	16A	0000	0

Odd multiple storage design reduces the LUT size further lower than the APC (Anti-symmetric product coding). A maximum of three left shifts are produced by using Barrel shifter. It may possibly be further used to derive rest of all the even multiples of coefficient A.

In the Table 2, it has been seen that all the stored APC words are the odd multiples of coefficient A. Address d3, d2, d1, d0 derives the storage address of the APC words which defines the 5-bit input values.

Odd multiple storage technique can be the efficient way to reduce the size of the LUT. This can further reduce the design and resource utilization of any FPGA. Here it leads to reduce power dissipation as the resources are low.

4 Implementation of the Look up Table Multiplier

4.1 Design on Look up Table Multiplier Using APC-OMS Based Technique

The subsequent block diagram in Fig. 2 is the multiplier, which uses the APC-OMS technique. It is a Look up Table (LUT) multiplier. Address Generator and the control circuit block takes 5bit input X of L = 5 and generates output of 4bit address. Control circuit is used to control Barrel shifter by using S0 and S1. Address decoder takes d0, d1, d2 and d3 as inputs and decodes nine outputs. The nine outputs are given as I/p's for LUT block, there it generates 9 words with the width of 4bit.

Table 2. OMS Words of dissimilar various I/p values (L = 5)

Input (X') x3'x2'x1'x0'	Product values	No. of shifts	Shifted input (X")	Stored APC word	Address d3d2d1d0
0001	A	0	0001	A	0000
0010	2*A	1			
0100	4*A	2			
1000	8*A	3			
0011	3A	0	0011	3A	0001
0110	2*3A	1			
1100	4*3A	2			
0101	5A	0	0101	5A	0010
1010	2*5S	1			
0111	7A	0	0111	7A	0011
1110	2*7A	1			
1001	9A	0	1001	9A	0100
1011	11A	0	1011	11A	0101
1101	13A	0	1101	13A	0110
1111	15A	0	1111	15A	0111

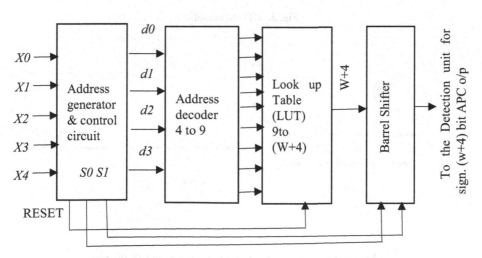

Fig. 2. Look up table multiplier using APC-OMS technique

The shifted product value from Barrel shifted goes to sign determination of input (X). The sign can be determined by the MSB (most significant bit) of the input X. If the input has the MSB as 0. Then the sign value should be taken as −1 and if the MSB of the input is 1, then the sign value is taken as −1.

5 Simulation Results

The 8-TAP FIR filter using APC-OMS based lookup table (LUT) multiplier is coded in Verilog HDL and simulated and synthesized in Xilinx vivado 2018.3. Figure 3, 4, 5, 6, 7, 8 and 9 and Table 3 shows the o/p waveforms of the FIR filter and its RTL schematic, synthesis, and summary report. Summary reports show the LUT utilization percentage amongst the Overall LUT's and also flip-flops utilization. This shows the consumption of Area and resources are very low. So, gradually the power consumption also reduces. Since, it is an 8-tap FIR filter, it requires 8 clock cycles to produce the output.

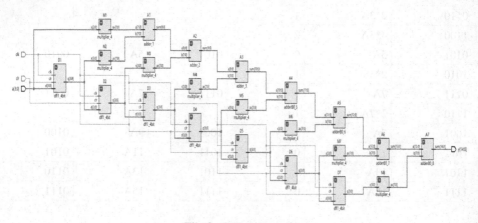

Fig. 3. RTL Schematic

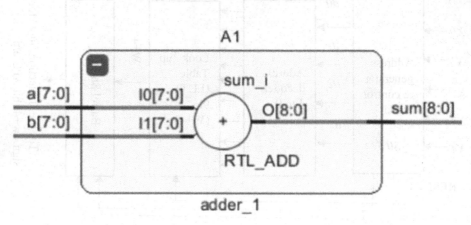

Fig. 4. Schematic diagram of adder module in FIR filter

Schematic diagram of Adder module of FIR filter is shown in the Fig. 4. Schematic block generates RTL_ADD (register transfer level) to describe an adder. Input A[7:0] and b[7:0] is given to the RTL input I0[7:0] and I1[7:0] and generates the output of O[8:0]. The output can be taken as sum [8:0]. Likewise, the synthesis diagram of D-Flip-Flop

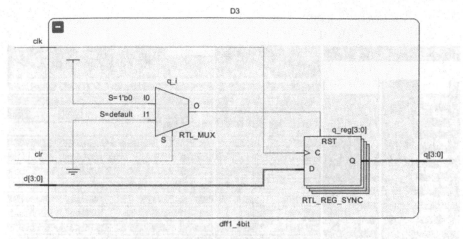

Fig. 5. Schematic diagram of D-Flip flop module in FIR filter

uses RTL_MUX and RTL_REG_SYNC. There are 7 such adders used to design the FIR filter. Since, 8-TAP filter requires 7 adders to design it.

From Fig. 5, the D-flip flop delays one clock period for the input signal to give the output. The delayed input can be convoluted with the multiplier and to be added with the next delayed input.

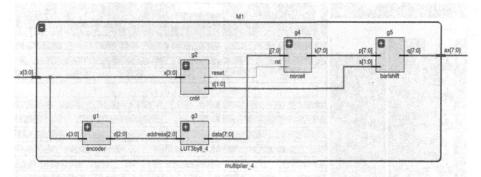

Fig. 6. Schematic diagram of Multiplier module in FIR filter

RTL Schematic is done using Xilinx vivado tool. The schematic diagram shows the multipliers, adders and the D-Flip flops. D Flip flops are used to delay the inputs. Here there are 8 multipliers, since it is an 8tap FIR filter and 7 D-Flip flops. The 7 Flip-flops represents the order of FIR filter. The multiplier has encoder, control, LUT3X8, nor cell and Barrel shifter. Control block is used to manage the complete signal. Nor cell is used for RESET operation. Figure 6 shows the schematic representation of the multiplier module. The barrel shifter shifts the products words based on the select lines S0 and S1.

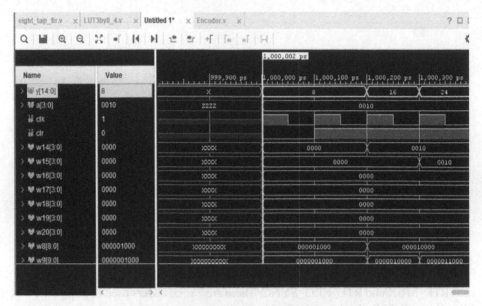

Fig. 7. Simulation result of 8-TAP FIR filter

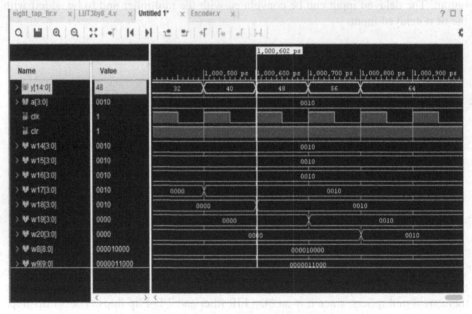

Fig. 8. Simulation result of 8-TAP FIR filter

From Fig. 7 and 8, the given input can be convoluted with the multiplier with symmetrical coefficients of 4. It gives linear phase response due to its stability. The simulation runs in ps(picoseconds) scale.

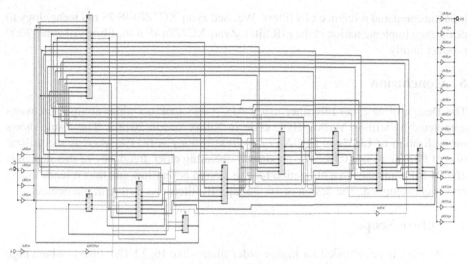

Fig. 9. Synthesis (schematic) on Zynq-7000 board library

Synthesis represents the design of FIR filter on zynq-7000 board and the usage of I/O ports, net lists, buffers and flip-flops of the board library.

In Fig. 7, we have given 0010 as an input (a [3:0]) and y [14:0] as an output. It took 8 cycles to produce output. The output y [14:0] is an amplified output. The usage of multipliers, symmetric coefficients upsurges the amplitude and response of the input signal. The maximum frequency response can be determined by creating the timing constraints in Xilinx. XDC file can be created at Top module of the design hierarchy. The input clock waveform of 10 ns is given to the implemented design to get the analysis of design regarding setup and hold time violations. The implemented design is free of setup and holds time violations and attained the max frequency of 464.04 MHz.

Table 3. Summary of synthesis report

Synthesis results			
	[8]	[9]	Proposed work
FPGA & technology	virtex-5 (65 nm)	Spartan-3 (45 nm)	zynq-XC7Z014S (28 nm)
# slices	-	144	26
FPGA slice LUTs	204	92	29
FPGA slice flip-flops	-	-	28
Max. clock frequency	109 MHz	235.02 MHz	464.04 MHz

The proposed work is compared with two other technologies. The usage of FPGA and Technology, no. of slice LUT's, no. of FPGA slice Flip-Flops and Maximum clock frequency is written in 1st column of Table 3. The utilisation of slice LUT's are lesser than the compared reference FIR filters. We used zynq-XC7Z014S 28 nm technology to design and implementation of the FIR filter. Zynq-XC7Z014S is the library of zynq-7000 product family.

6 Conclusion

The Design of an 8-tap FIR filter using APC-OMS look up table multiplier remains completed by writing Verilog HDL code in Xilinx vivado 2018.3. The result shows the utilization of LUT's in FPGA (zynq-7000) library is 0.11% whereas the utilization of Flip-Flops is 0.03%. The maximum operating clock frequency of this design is 464.04 MHz and the Area utilization for this design is very low and thus it leads to less power consumption. The design of 16, 32 tap FIR filters can further implemented.

7 Future Scope

The design can be extended for higher order filters (like 16, 32 TAP filters) where high performance is required. It can be used in different FIR applications like mastering, study of seismology etc.

References

1. Proakis, J.G., Manolakis, D.G.: Digital Signal Processing: Principles, Algorithms and Applications. Prentice-Hall, Upper Saddle River, NJ (1996)
2. Vinod, A.P., Lai, E.: Low power and high speed implementation of FIR filters for software define radio receivers. IEEE Trans. Wirel. Commun. 5(7), 1669–1675 (2006)
3. Schaller, R.R.: Technological innovation in the semiconductor industry: a case study of the international technology roadmap for semiconductors (itrs), Ph.D. dissertation, George Mason University (2004)
4. Meher, P.K.: New approach to LUT implementation and accumulation for memory-based multiplication. In: Proceedings of the IEEE ISCAS, pp. 453–456 (May 2009)
5. Meher, P.K.: Memory-based hardware for resource-constraint digital signal processing systems. In: 2007 6th International Conference on Information, Communications and Signal Processing. IEEE (2007)
6. Meher, P.K.: New look-up-table optimizations for memory-based multiplication. In: Proceedings of the 2009 12th International Symposium on Integrated Circuits. IEEE (2009)
7. Meher, P.K.: LUT optimization for memory-based computation. IEEE Trans. Circ. Syst. II Express Briefs 57(4), 285–289 (2010)
8. AlJuffri, A.A., et al.: FPGA implementation of scalable microprogrammed FIR filter architectures using Wallace tree and Vedic multipliers. In: 2015 3rd International Conference on Technological Advances in Electrical, Electronics and Computer Engineering (TAEECE). IEEE (2015)
9. Thakur, R., Khare, K.: High speed FPGA implementation of FIR filter for DSP applications. Int. J. Model. Optim. 3(1), 92–94 (2013)
10. Paul, L., Paul, R.: Modified APC-OMS technique for memory based computing. Procedia Technol. 25, 606–612 (2016)
11. Vinitha, C.S., Sharma, R.K.: An efficient LUT design on FPGA for memory-based multiplication. Iran. J. Electr. Electron. Eng. 15(4), 462–476 (2019)
12. Jayashree, M.: Design of high speed and area efficient FIR filter architecture using modified adder and multiplier. Int. J. Eng. Tech. 4, 537–543 (2018)

Design of Reconfigurable Multiply-Accumulate Unit with Computational Optimization

J. Christopher Vishal[1], S. Sai Sri Charan[1], Arpit Kumar[1], and K. Sivasankaran[2(✉)] (iD)

[1] VLSI Design Students, Vellore Institute of Technology, Vellore 632014, Tamil Nadu, India
{christophervishal.j2020,saisri.charans2020,
arpit.kumar2020}@vitstudent.ac.in
[2] Department of Micro and Nano Electronics, SENSE, Vellore Institute of Technology, Vellore 632014, Tamil Nadu, India
ksivasankaran@vit.ac.in

Abstract. The Multiply and Accumulate Unit is a significant module in graphic hardware accelerators which is widely used in Signal processing and Neural Network applications where high computational over-head is involved. In general, reconfigurability in hardware will provide an additional advantage for optimization when process intensive or computationally expensive operations are considered. In this paper, a reconfigurable architecture is designed for performing multiply - accumulate, multiplication and addition operations with improved efficiency by incorporating a multiplier algorithm. After analyzing the available literature, it is observed that the speed of existing conventional multipliers used in the Multiply - Accumulate unit is limited by the processing delays in the adders used for partial products addition. Hence, a ripple carry adder is included in Multiply - Accumulate unit to perform partial product addition which will show significant improvement in area and power consumption. This also includes a Sign Identification Unit for handling the signed and unsigned data before and after processing the operands. The reconfiguration logic is designed with the help of a set of multiplexers and de-multiplexers to improve data throughput rate and to optimize power consumption. The Power and Timing analysis is done for the reconfigurable MAC unit using the Synthesis tools.

Keywords: Ripple carry adder · Sign Identification Unit · Reconfigurable

1 Introduction

The Multiply-Accumulate Unit is used to perform convolution operations, Fast Fourier Transform (FFT), Discrete Cosine Transform (DCT) and Discrete Fourier Transform (DFT) in signal and image processing applications. It is also predominantly used in the computation of the activation function in neural networks for AI based applications and accelerators.

Many researchers have been constructing different designs of advanced MAC unit architecture to improve the overall efficiency of the system in terms of area, throughput, power etc. Initially, the proposed MAC unit Architecture in [1] will take inputs from

© Springer Nature Singapore Pte Ltd. 2021
V. Arunachalam and K. Sivasankaran (Eds.): ICMDCS 2021, CCIS 1392, pp. 335–349, 2021.
https://doi.org/10.1007/978-981-16-5048-2_27

a memory location and feed the inputs to the multiplier block, which will perform multiplication and give the result to the adder where the previously stored result will be added to the existing result and the new result will be stored in corresponding memory location. This whole process is done in a single clock cycle.

The re-configurability in MAC units [2] provides additional hardware flexibility by introducing pipelining and multi word length support. But it restricts the reconfigurable feature only in-terms of hardware which is a major drawback when present-day computational requirements are considered.

In the proposed work of the high speed ALU design [3] carry save addition [4] has been incorporated to reduce the total number of half adders and full adders used in the design, which will improve the overall throughput of the MAC unit by introducing parallelism among the full-adder and half-adder operations. It will also support in reducing the overall area of the unit which will eventually decrease the power consumption. In general, the MAC units suffer heavy computational overheads in the multiplication operations due to the less efficient hardware used to perform multiplication, C.S Wallace proposed a design [5] which accelerates the processing of partial products in the multiplication operation by reducing the area and forcing more parallelism.

It is also found that Wallace Tree Multiplier offers improved throughput from a comparative study [6, 7] on different other conventional multipliers in terms of area, delay and power. So, in this paper we will incorporate a Wallace Tree based multiplier for improving the overall efficiency in terms of area and power. Also, the drawback in the proposed design where the re-configurability was enabled only in terms of hardware will be extended in this work by enabling reconfigurable architecture the module will enable peripherals to select any one of the desired operations such as addition, multiplication and multiply – accumulate. The design is checked for its efficiency by analyzing the Timing and Power components of the overall RTL using the synthesis tool which provides a detailed analysis and report on these components considering the critical paths.

2   Reconfigurable MAC

The Reconfigurable MAC unit's architecture is illustrated in Fig. 1. It is constructed with the following modules 1) Sign Identification Unit, 2) Addition Unit, 3) Multiplication Unit [8] and 4) Reconfiguration Control Unit. The SIU (Sign Identification Unit) is used to process the signed operands by doing sign computation separately and passes the input operands accordingly to the necessary modules based upon the configured operation. The addition unit is used to perform the addition operation on operands of variable word length such as 4 bits, 8 bits and 16 bits. The Multiplication Unit performs the multiplication operation on variable word length same as Addition Unit. The Multiplication Unit has four 4 × 4 multiplier leaf blocks constructed with Wallace Tree Algorithm to enforce minimum propagation delay. In the Multiplication Unit different pipeline stages of registers are induced to match different output throughput requirements.

The Addition Unit also has various levels of pipeline stages to match the same requirement as the Multiplication Unit. The Accumulation Unit has a register that stores the previous multiplication data and performs an accumulative addition on the present incoming data with the previously stored product data. The carry look ahead adder is used

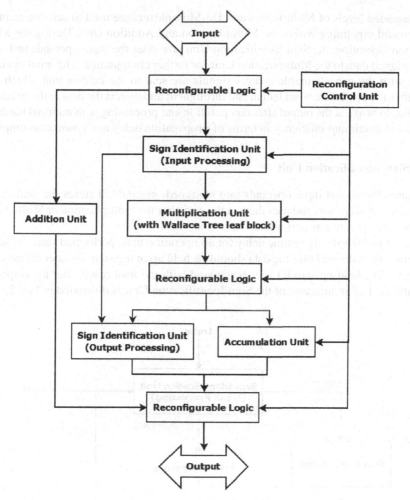

Fig. 1. Reconfigurable MAC

to perform the accumulation on the data inputs. All the units above are reconfigurable through the signals generated from the Reconfiguration Control Unit, it works based on a Finite State Machine controlled by reconfigurable logic signals given as input to the entire module. Minimum power consumption can be derived with efficient usage of the reconfigurable logic on different word length of operands and different throughput controls [9].

2.1 Working of the Reconfigurable MAC Unit

The designed architecture will support selection of variable word length, operation selection and throughput control selection to choose the pipeline stages in the Addition and Multiplication Unit.

Cascaded levels of Multiplexers and De-Multiplexers are used to achieve reconfiguration and pipelining within the Multiplication and Addition Unit. During the Multiplication Operation, the Sign Identification Unit processes the input operands and sends the unsigned data to the Multiplication Unit for further computation. The input operands along with the reconfigurable control signals are sent to the control unit which then identifies the operation, word length and throughput and directs the data to the necessary modules to arrive at the output after computation and processing with minimal hardware usage and maximum efficiency in terms of propagation delay and power consumption.

2.2 Sign Identification Unit

SIU turns the signed input operands into unsigned operands. It stores the signs of the input data into registers and uses them at the end after the multiplication or Multiply and accumulate operation is performed.

The time complexity or time delay for an operation to be performed varies based on operands bit width and thus the data should be held up in registers for later access using registers. The held-up sign bit is concatenated with the final result after the respective operations. The architecture of the Sign Identification Unit is illustrated in Fig. 2.

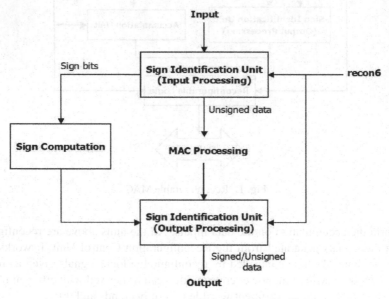

Fig. 2. Architecture of Sign Identification Unit

2.3 Multiplication Unit

In order to enforce concurrent operation, the 16×16 multiplication is fragmented into four 8×8 individual multiplication process as shown in Fig. 3. These fragmented computations could be performed in parallel with individual reconfigurable hardware blocks which will eventually reduce the overall computational delay and also reduces the hardware overhead by splitting the hardware resources. This decomposition also provides an ability to the reconfigurable logic to disable certain 8 × 8 blocks when computations are performed on minimum word length operations. The four 16 bit product values obtained are then processed with the three operand 16-bit adder and an 8-bit adder as shown.

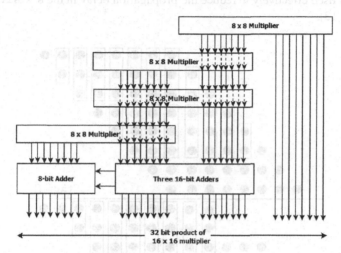

Fig. 3. Fragmentation of 16 × 16 multiplication into four 8 × 8 multiplication

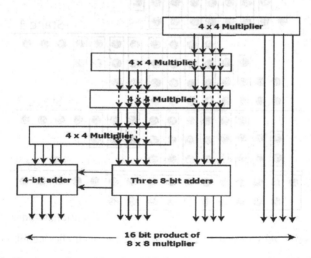

Fig. 4. Fragmentation of 8 × 8 multiplication into four 4 × 4 multiplication

Wallace Tree Multiplier (8 × 8 Leaf Block)

The pipelined architecture is designed by using four 8 × 8 Wallace Tree Multiplier leaf blocks to arrive at four 16-bit products which will be used for further computations. The process involved in Wallace Tree Multiplier is represented in Fig. 5. In Wallace Tree Multiplier the partial products of the 8 × 8 multiplication are processed in parallel thus reducing the delay and dependency in computation of the previous stage's addition and carry which is observed in conventional array multipliers [10]. Thus, the Wallace Tree Multiplier is used effectively to reduce the propagation delay in the 8 × 8 computation process [11, 12].

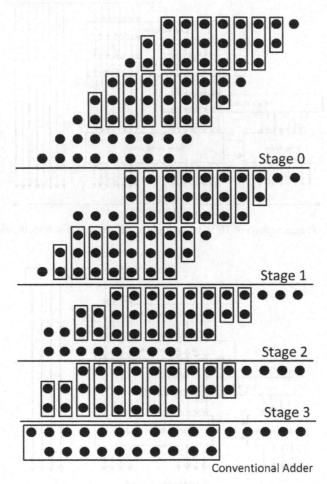

Fig. 5. Representation of 8 × 8 Wallace tree multiplier algorithm

The designed 16 × 16 pipelined multiplication structure is shown in Fig. 6. The multiplier is constructed with different pipeline stages in order to meet different throughput requirements. This enables the module to compute the output in different clock cycle periods which could be controlled using the recon 8 signal. Two pipeline stages are

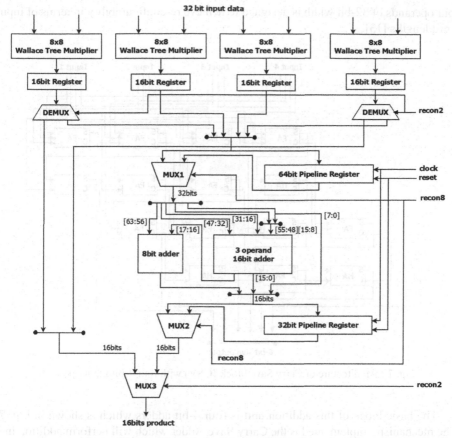

Fig. 6. 16×16 pipelined multiplication unit

incorporated with multiplexers and registers. The multiplier unit is reconfigurable to operate on different word length such as 4-bits, 8-bits and 16-bits by using the recon 1 and recon 2 control signals. The 8×8 pipelined architecture is similarly designed with four 4×4 Wallace Tree Leaf blocks as shown in Fig. 4.

2.4 Addition Unit

The basic operation of the addition unit is to add the input operands and feed the result to the output. But the conventional adder is inefficient in terms of Area, power and propagation delay. Every stage will be dependent on the previous stage which will negatively affect the throughput of the overall unit. Hence it is necessary to select an efficient addition architecture to improve the efficiency of the overall system. There are multiple types of adders to provide the efficiency in terms of different metrics out of which the Carry Save Adder is proved to be best if the input word length is high and will provide efficiency in terms of delay between the stages. In this paper, an adder which will add either sixteen operands of 8-bit width (or) eight operands of 16-bit width (or) four operands of 32-bit width is designed to achieve re-configurability in terms of input word lengths [13].

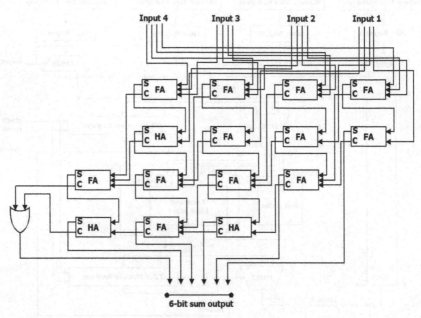

Fig. 7. Architecture of Carry Save block (CSV) with four 4-bit input operands

The basic block of this addition unit is four 4-bit adders which is shown in Fig. 7. The mechanism implemented is the Carry Save Adder which will perform addition in 3 stages. In the first stage, it will add all the operands by ignoring the carry propagation. In 2nd stage, it will propagate all the carry bits that were generated. Finally, in the 3rd stage it will combine the results with the carry bits and feed the result to the output. In this way, the propagation delay between the stages will be reduced to a great extent. Using the above-mentioned basic block, the process of addition of four operands each of 8-bits is illustrated in Fig. 8. The addition block will be fetched with a 128-bit input in which sixteen operands of 8-bit width (or) eight operands of 16-bit width (or) four operands of 32-bit width can be accommodated as illustrated in Fig. 9. For sixteen 8-bit operations, sixteen 8-bit inputs can be given directly to the four 8-bit CSV blocks. For eight 16-bit operations, CSV blocks 1 and 2 will be fed with upper nibbles of eight 16-bit inputs, i.e., [15:8]. Similarly, CSV blocks 3 and 4 will be fed with lower nibbles of eight 16-bit inputs i.e., [7:0]. For four 32-bit operation, bit positions of all the four inputs from [31:24], [23:16], [15:8], [7:0] are given to CSV blocks 1, 2, 3, 4 respectively.

For eight 16-bit operations, CSV blocks 1 and 2 will be fed with upper nibbles of eight 16-bit inputs, i.e., [15:8]. Similarly, CSV blocks 3 and 4 will be fed with lower nibbles of eight 16-bit inputs i.e., [7:0]. For four 32-bit operation, bit positions of all the four inputs from [31:24], [23:16], [15:8], [7:0] are given to CSV blocks 1, 2, 3, 4 respectively.

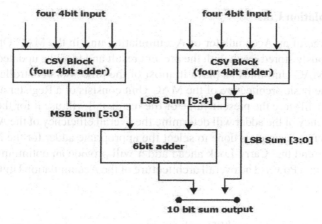

Fig. 8. Demonstration of addition of four 8-bit input operands

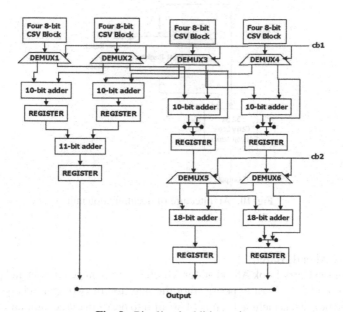

Fig. 9. Pipelined addition unit

Here the de-multiplexers are controlled by two signals, cb1 and cb2. When cb1 = 0 and cb2 = 0, sixteen 8-bit addition operation will be performed and the output can be fetched from Register-1. When cb1 = 1 and cb2 = 0, eight 16-bit addition operation will be performed and the output can be fetched from Register-2. When cb1 = 1 and cb2 = 1, four 32-bit addition will be performed and the output can be fetched from Register-3. In this way, the addition operation can be done. Similarly, the higher order addition operation will need more CSV blocks and outputs must be driven accordingly.

2.5   Accumulation Unit

The basic usage of an Accumulator or Accumulation unit in the MAC Operation is to add the previously stored result with the present result and feed the updated value to the output. This MAC Unit finds its place in most of the processors/controllers which has ALU in it. The basic architecture of the MAC Unit consists of a Register and an Adder. The Register will store the present value of the result and will use it for the next cycle.

The efficiency of the adder will determine the overall efficiency of the Accumulation Operation. Hence a survey is done to select the appropriate adder for the MAC Unit as in [14]. It is found that Carry-Look ahead adder will provide an optimum efficiency in terms of Area and Power. The overall architecture of the Accumulation Unit is illustrated in Fig. 10.

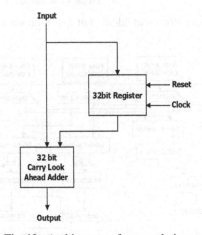

Fig. 10. Architecture of accumulation unit

Carry Look Ahead Adder

The delay of the Carry Look Ahead adder which is based on generation and propagation of carry is found to be least in performing the addition of two operands based on their data size and hence it is included in this MAC unit to perform the accumulation (unsigned addition operation).

The generation and propagation mechanism of the Carry Look Ahead adder provides better results in-terms of delay, since the carry is calculated even before the sum bits of the successive stages are computed using carry generate operation where the carry will be propagated to the after stages following the carry propagate operation.

2.6   Reconfiguration Control Unit

The Reconfigurable Control Unit is used to identify and distinguish the operations, word length, data type identification if it is signed or unsigned and finally it also provides the pipeline stage selection with which the required throughput requirements are

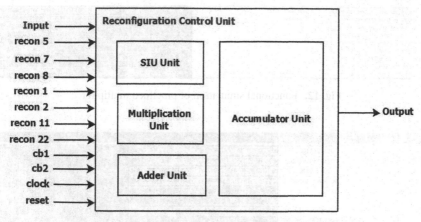

Fig. 11. Architectural representation of reconfiguration control unit.

achieved thus making it operationally efficient [15]. The overall architectural design of the Reconfiguration Control Unit is illustrated in Fig. 11.

The recon 5 signal is used by the SIU to identify the signed and unsigned operation. An unsigned operation will be performed if the signal is low and when it is high the signed operation will be performed. The SIU will do the sign storage and computation accordingly based on this input signal. The recon 1 and recon 2 signals are used to select the word length. It processes a 4-bit data if recon 1 = 0 and recon 2 = 0, 8-bit data will be computed if recon 1 = 1 and 16-bit operation will be performed on the operands if recon 2 = 1. The Reconfiguration Control Unit also enables individual operation selection by using recon 11 and recon22 signals. The unit performs addition operation on the input operands if recon 22 = 1. The multiplication operation shall be selected by using the turning the recon 11 and recon 22 low that is recon 11 = 0 and recon22 = 0. The multiply and accumulate operation is selected if recon 11 = 1 and recon 22 = 0. The throughput of the multiplication unit can also be altered as different pipelining stages can be selected or bypassed based on the input signal recon 7 and recon 8 for 8-bit and 16-bit pipelined multiplications respectively.

3   Results and Discussion

The RTL design is done using Verilog HDL and functionally simulated and verified in ModelSim, A Mentor software. The functional simulation results are shown in Figs. 12, 13, and 14.

The simulation waveform obtained for the pipelined multiplier is illustrated where the input operands of 4-bit, 8-bit and 16-bits are given and the respective reconfiguration is done using the recon 1 and recon 2 control signals as shown in Fig. 12.

The simulation waveform for the pipelined adder is illustrated where the addition for sixteen operands of 8-bit width (or) eight operands of 16-bit width (or) four operands of 32-bit width will be done based on cb1 and cb2 control signals as shown in Fig. 13.

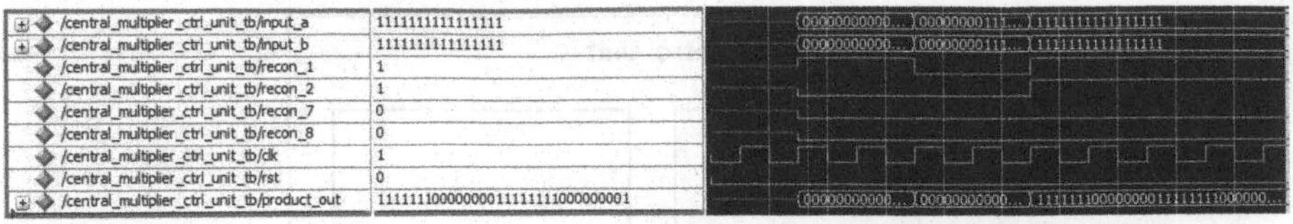

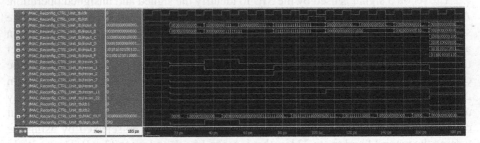

/central_multiplier_ctrl_unit_tb/input_a	1111111111111111
/central_multiplier_ctrl_unit_tb/input_b	1111111111111111
/central_multiplier_ctrl_unit_tb/recon_1	1
/central_multiplier_ctrl_unit_tb/recon_2	1
/central_multiplier_ctrl_unit_tb/recon_7	0
/central_multiplier_ctrl_unit_tb/recon_8	0
/central_multiplier_ctrl_unit_tb/clk	1
/central_multiplier_ctrl_unit_tb/rst	0
/central_multiplier_ctrl_unit_tb/product_out	1111111000000001111111110000000001

Fig. 12. Functional simulation of pipelined multiplier

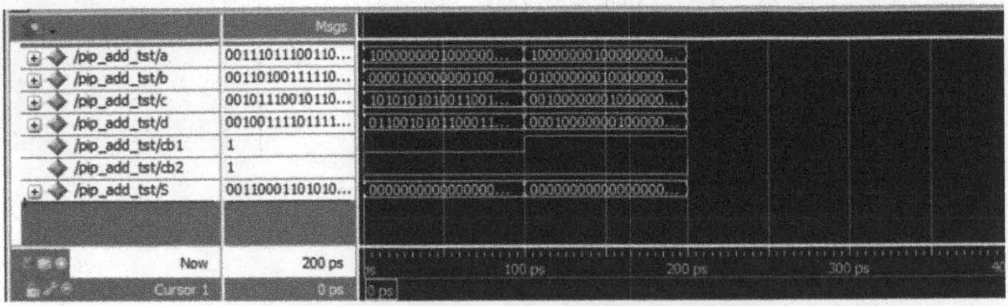

Fig. 13. Functional simulation of addition unit

Fig. 14. Simulation results of reconfigurable MAC unit

One of the operations from multiplication, addition or Multiply-Accumulate can be selected using the recon 11 and recon 22 control signals. The bit width for these operations can be configured as 4-bit, 8-bit or 16-bit using recon 1 and recon 2 control signals. If the recon 5 signal is asserted low, then the entire unit performs the unsigned operation. If the recon 5 is asserted high, then the signed operation is performed on the input operands as shown in Fig. 14.

The proposed design is synthesized on Intel Quartus Prime Lite Edition 18.0.0 with Cyclone IV E FPGA as the target device. After the synthesis, it is observed that the proposed architecture consumes 1,166 logic elements (CLBs), 243 registers and 208 pins to map the design onto the target device. The CLB (Configurable Logic Block) is the basic recurring logic resource on the FPGA. The register on the FPGA consists of a clock, an input port, an output port and an enable. The pins on FPGA include the user IOs, power pins etc.

The timing analysis of the proposed design is done using the Time Quest Timing Analyzer on Intel Quartus Prime Lite. The timing analysis results of the proposed architecture is shown below in Table 1.

Table 1. Timing analysis of the reconfigurable MAC

Parameters	Model 85 °C	Model - 0 °C
Maximum clock frequency	50.08 MHz	53.66 MHz
Setup slack	2.033 ns	3.365 ns
Hold slack	0.428 ns	0.395 ns

The maximum clock frequency achieved will depict the execution speed of the circuit. The setup slack is given as the delta difference in time between the data required time and data arrival time whereas the hold slack is the delta difference in time between the data arrival time and the data required time. The timing requirements of a design are met only if the Slack is positive. The maximum frequency of operation obtained is 50.08 MHz for 85 °C model by using Wallace tree multiplier as a leaf block in the Pipelined multiplier architecture of the reconfigurable MAC unit. The power dissipated by the reconfigurable MAC unit is calculated by using PowerPlay Power Analyzer in Intel Quartus Prime for 8-bit and 16-bit input operands as shown in Tables 2 and 3.

Table 2. Frequency and power comparison of different bit widths

Parameters	Reconfigurable MAC (with Wallace tree multiplier as leaf block)	
Operand bit width	8	16
Clock frequency (MHz)	53.13	50.34
Power dissipated (mW)	220.86	221.38

Table 3. Power analysis for the reconfigurable MAC unit

Power dissipated (mW)	8-bit	16-bit
Static power	98.82	98.83
Dynamic power	58.20	58.30
I/O thermal power	63.73	64.26
Total power	220.86	221.38

The comparison of proposed MAC Unit, MAC Unit with array multiplier [9] and MAC unit with Wallace multiplier [9] in terms of power dissipation is illustrated in Table 4.

Table 4. Comparison of power dissipation of MAC unit models [9]

Power dissipated	Proposed MAC unit	MAC with array multiplier [9]	MAC with wallace multiplier [9]
Total power (mW)	221.38	1067	1061

4 Conclusion

The reconfigurable MAC architecture will provide the flexibility to the user in terms of word length of input operands, data type and the operation to be carried out. The reconfiguration control unit is the key block to decide the different operations to be done on different input operands. The inclusion of Wallace tree multiplier as a leaf block in pipelined multiplier replacing conventional array multiplier to reduce the propagation delay and improve the throughput. The carry save addition mechanism is incorporated in the Addition Block which will work efficiently if the input operand word length is high. Also, the carry save addition will reduce the propagation delay of the outputs. By considering all the above-mentioned results, it's evident that the reconfigurable MAC unit designed is efficient in terms of throughput, delay and power.

References

1. Dakua, P.K., Sinha, A., Shivdhari & Gourab: Hardware implementation of MAC unit. Int. J. Electron. Commun. Comput. Eng. **3**(1), 79–82 (2012)
2. Li, Y., Chen, J.: A reconfigurable architecture of a high performance 32-bit MAC unit for embedded DSP. In: Proceedings of 5th International Conference on Semiconductor Manufacturing, ASIC 2003, vol. 2, pp. 1285–1288 (2003)
3. Gurjar, P., Solanki, R., Kansilwal, P., Vucha, M.: VLSI implementation of adders for high speed ALU. In: 2011 Annual IEEE India Conference India Conference (INDICON), 1–6 December 2011. IEEE (2011)
4. Kamboh, H.M., Khan, S.A.: FPGA implementation of fast adder. In: 7th International Conference on Computing and Convergence Technology (ICCCT), pp. 1324–1327 (2012)
5. Wallace, C.S.: A suggestion for a fast multiplier. IEEE Trans. Electron. Comput. **EC-13**(1), 14–17 (1964). https://doi.org/10.1109/PGEC.1964.263830
6. Kim, S., Papaefthymiou, M.C.: Reconfigurable low energy multiplier for multimedia system design. In: IEEE Computer Society Workshop on VLSI 2000: System Design for a System-on-Chip Era (2000)
7. Janveja, M., Niranjan, V.: High performance wallace tree multiplier using improved adder. ICTACT J. Microelectron. **3**(1), 370–374 (2017). https://doi.org/10.21917/ijme.2017.0065

8. Challa Ram, G., Sudha Rani, D., Balasaikesava, R., Bala Sindhuri, K.: Design of delay efficient modified 6 bit wallace multiplier. In: IEEE International Conference on Recent Trends in Electronics Information Communication Technology, 20–21 May 2016, India (2016)
9. Kumar, M.S., Ashok Kumar, D., Samundiswary, P.: Design and performance analysis of multiply-accumulate (MAC) unit. In: International Conference on Circuit, Power and Computing Technologies (ICCPCT) (2014)
10. Wey, C.-L., Li, J.-F.: Design of reconfigurable array multipliers and multiplier-accumulators. In: The IEEE Asia-Pacific Conference on Circuits and Systems, 6–9 December 2004 (2004)
11. Prakash, E., Raju, R., Varatharajan, R.: Effective method for implementation of wallace tree multiplier using fast adders. J. Innov. Res. Solutions (JIRAS) 1(1) (2013)
12. Jaiswal, K.B., Kumar, N., Seshadri, P., Laxminarayan, G.: Low power Wallace tree multiplier using modified full adder. In: Proceedings of 3rd International Conference on Signal Processing, Communication and Networking, pp. 1–4 (2015)
13. Koyada, B., Meghana, N., Omair Jaleel, M., Jeripotula, P.R.: A comparative study on adders. In: 2017 International Conference on Wireless Communications, Signal Processing and Networking (WiSPNET), 22–24 March 2017 (2017)
14. Patil, P.A., Kulkarni, C.: A survey on multiply accumulate unit. In: 4th International Conference on Computing, Communication Control and Automation, ICCUBEA 2018, 23 April 2019 (2019)
15. Tatas, K., Koutroumpezis, G., Soudris, D., Thanailakis, A.: Architecture design of a coarse-grain reconfigurable multiply-accumulate unit for data-intensive applications. Integration 40(2), 74–93 (2007). https://doi.org/10.1016/j.vlsi.2006.02.011

Development of an Automated System
for Tomato Harvesting and Pest Detection

S. Elango$^{(\boxtimes)}$, A. Srinigha, G. P. Vigashini, J. Vishnupriya, and V. Yashwanthi

Department of Electronics and Communication Engineering, Bannari Amman Institute of
Technology, Sathyamangalam, Erode 638 401, Tamil Nadu, India
{elangos,srinigha.ec19,vigashini.ec19,vishnupriya.ec19,
yashwanthi.ec19}@bitsathy.ac.in

Abstract. Digital farming is a viable solution for the current challenges faced in
the agricultural industry. Tomato is one of the most important crops in agriculture.
The production of this crop is high as well as the infection of the plant is enormous.
The monitoring of the pest infection and harvesting of the tomato plant in the
farm is a challenging issue by the labour, which leads to time delay, charges for
labour and might be damage. In this paper, an automated system is developed for
harvesting and pest monitoring in the tomato plant. The computerized systems
enabled with a camera fixed in the system that captures images for pest detection
and a robotic arm for plucking the fruit from the plant and making the operation
faster. This automated system makes the process quicker and reduces the effort of
farmers. This system provides more significant support during harvesting since it
continuously observes the field and picks the fruit at the correct time. In the area
of 1 hectare, the bot can harvest tomatoes at the fastest speed of 90–120 min.

Keywords: Digital farming · Agricultural industry · Pest detection · Tomato
harvesting · Smart agriculture · Convolutional neural network

1 Introduction

Tomato Lycopersicon esculentum is a vital vegetable grown in India. India is considered
the second-largest country in the volume of tomato production. Indian economy is mainly
dependent on the agriculture sector and contributes about 17% of the total GDP. Tomato is
considered one of the three most important crops. Gujarat, Bihar, Maharashtra contribute
the maximum tomato production in the country. Pests are a significant threat in the field
of agriculture. These pests damage the plants in two primary kinds. One is about direct
damage, where the insects eat the leaves and burrowing holes in stems and fruits. The
second is indirect harming, where the insect transmits the bacterial, fungal or viral
infection to the crop. Tomato plants are affected by diseases and decrease crop yield [1].
Progressing digital farming would be the best reaction for current troubles in the farming
industry by using a machine to give steady information on passed on an area and provide
the proper assessment in various farming pieces [2]. Automation is an essential criterion
in food production [3]. The project aims to help the farming field by introducing tomato

© Springer Nature Singapore Pte Ltd. 2021
V. Arunachalam and K. Sivasankaran (Eds.): ICMDCS 2021, CCIS 1392, pp. 350–359, 2021.
https://doi.org/10.1007/978-981-16-5048-2_28

harvesting and pest detector at low cost. The bot help farmers to harvest tomatoes and monitor the plant's health. This bot is mainly to detect ripened fruit and harvest the fruit at the right period. CNN technology is used for harvesting and pest detection.

The bot helps the farmer to detect pests in the leaf and spray pesticide to the infected leaf. The automated machine helps to reduce human resources in the agricultural field and to replace active robots. This undertaking aims to set the fundamental idea of moving the device to comprehend the chance of modernized developing. This examination's interest is that this procedure is essential, and image processing is might be unique to oblige processors confined estimation properties [4].

Farmers suffer many problems while cultivating a tomato plant, starting from seedling it, ending with tomato cultivation. Since there are different tomatoes, everyone has the other method of cultivating them. Primary-season tomatoes need 50 to 60 days to reach harvest from transplanting; middle -season tomatoes need an average of about 60 to 80 days; final-season tomatoes need 80 or more days [5].

A major common problem in farming is a pest, which eradicates the cultivation. They are accountable for two significant kinds of damage to growing crops. The first is an immediate injury to plants brought about by bugs eating leaves and tunnelling gaps in stems, foods grown from the ground/roots. The second is aberrant harm, where the bugs themselves do practically no damage yet send bacterial, viral or parasitic disease to a harvest [6]. To prevent pest, the bot will spray organic pesticides in the field. The plant and fruit are toxic-free and eco-friendly.

Section 1 discusses the introduction, and the survey is given in Sect. 2. Section 3 presents the proposed work, and analysis is provided in Sect. 4. The conclusion is given in Sect. 5.

2 Literature Review

According to the research 2020, India is the world's second-largest tomato crop producer next to china and accounts for around 11% of the total global food growth. In 2020 statistics analysis, the volume of this crop production amounted to roughly 21 million metric tons in area. The development of automation is divided into many categories like IoT, remote sensing, and so more. A 400 kg weight robot called the robot of the ministry of agriculture was developed. This robot was functioned to detect the branch and collect tomatoes and was more efficient and carried out the work in 20 s [7]. Panasonic presented their project about harvesting robot in the year 2015. Their bot's primary function was to pick tomatoes with sensors and locomote [8]. In a few countries, automation is being carried out in food industries. So researches are going on regarding the process of using the same in agricultural sides [9]. A robot was designed in a way to pick tomatoes with scissors using a 3D movement system. The CCD camera is also used in this project for colour detection purpose [10]. Few existing projects related to this harvesting and pest monitoring have some drawbacks, and those projects cost so high, extensive in size.

A robot was designed to develop a vision algorithm, and this robot collected one tomato at a time. Moreover, this robot showed 70% of success rate [11]. By involving colour property, segmentation property and morphological property estimation ANN, Espinoza et al. proposed work for identifying Frankliniella occidentalis and Bemisia tabaci with the help of shape and colour identification process. This work attained 85% efficiency [12].

Indonesia is considered one of the biggest agricultural countries. Few studies state that robotic technology implementation and efficiency enhancement have not yet taken up extensive agricultural process. In [1], low-cost agricultural robot architecture is proposed. This robot surveys the farm area, treats and harvests the ripened tomatoes. Wireless technology is involved here so that the farmer communicates with the robot through a wireless line using a radio wave. This radio wave is also combined with Bluetooth to simplify communication. Moreover, the farmer can check the farm with the help of a camera equipped with the robot. Farmers can also control robot movement using the user interface, which contains control icons.

Several studies are going on to identify plant disease by processing the leaves' images and classifying the leaves. In [13] the study refers to the comparison of extensive datasheets to the art method. Moreover, 14828 tomato leaves images are infected by nine diseases. The CNN - Convolutional Neural Network learning algorithm is also involved. To get clear idea about symptoms and disease region in leaves, visualization methods are used.

In [13], a robot was developed for tomato harvesting, and the study consists of a four-wheel independent steering system. This robot was functioned to provide a low-speed steering control which is based on Ackerman steering geometry. PDI Algorithm - Proportional-Integral-Derivative was used in the laser navigation control system. The time taken by this robot for detecting and pitching the ripened tomato was 15 s per tomato. This study gives a piece of clear information about the usage of tomato harvesting robot in the greenhouse.

In recent developments in the sector of Deep Neural Networks have improved object detection accuracy. In paper [13], the approach to detect pests and diseases based on deep learning using camera devices for image capturing with various resolutions. The main goal is to find a suitable deep learning architecture for the task. It is well known that pests and plant diseases are a significant threat in agriculture. So a faster detection of pest and diseases in plants will be of great use in agricultural sectors. The approach is presented in detecting pests and diseases in tomato plants using images captured by different camera devices with variation in resolutions based on deep learning. Faster R-CNN, Single Shot Multi-box Detector (SSD), Region-based Fully Convolutional Network (R-FCN) so these three detectors are considered in this process. The research involves a deep learning-based classification process that improves accuracy. Lycopersicon esculentum improves health by safeguarding chronic diseases, in particular cancer, osteoporosis and contaracts. Image processing is adopted to monitor the diseases from plantation to harvesting. Artificial neural network hypothesis being utilized.

3 Proposed Work

The main principle of the project is to harvest tomato and monitor pest in the infected leaf. The Raspberry pi based automated device is mainly used to reduce the farmer's effort and make the operation faster. Image acquisition and classification are made by using an image processing technique. Here, used CCN (Convolutional Neutral Network) for classification of tomato image. The growth of the plant should be 3 to 5 ft tall. The robotic arm with the gripper will identify its ripens period by the colour specificity of the fruit.

The components used here are Raspberry pi, Ultrasonic sensor, Relay module, Pi camera, Robotic arm, Temperature & humidity sensor, Servomotor, Load cell sensor, Power supply, Air pump, Sprayer and Wi-Fi module.This robotic system's central controller is raspberry pi 3B, which consists of a quad-core 1.2G Hz Broadcom BCM2837 64 bit CPU. The controller controls the four primary elements such as servomotor for camera rotation, robotic arm, pi camera and sensor materials.

3.1 Flowchart of the Proposed Method

The flowchart for the project is depicted in Fig. 1. It consists of majorly four process, Bot movement, Image acquisition, image analysis, spraying pesticide based on the conditions.

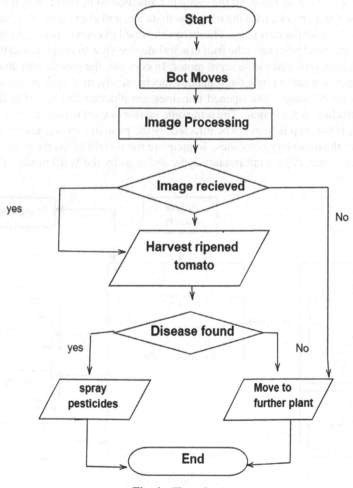

Fig. 1. Flow chart

Initially, the bot starts moving using its gear motors, and it moves to its respective field. Using the ultrasonic sensor, it will detect the plant. The pi camera attached to the bot is used for the image processing of the plant. Once it captured the image, it will send data to the raspberry pi and starts its image processing technique. By differentiating the background in the captured image, Image processing is accompanied to found tomato.

The captured raw image is converted into a grayscale image. The modified mage converted into a binary image in the form of "0" and "1".

First, it will pluck the ripened tomato from the plant by using a robotic arm; it is designed to pluck the fruit and not the plant branches. Next step it will check whether the plant leaf is healthy or unhealthy. If the plant leaf is healthy, the bot moves to the other plant. Suppose the bot detect the pest infection in the leaf. In that case, it will find the disease symptoms and spray the pesticide by seeing the texture and colour of that leaf according to the various type of the disease given in the input algorithm.

The Raspberry pi controls all the elements attached to it. In this bot, the DC servo motor is used, which calculates the inter-row distance, and after harvesting and monitoring, the bot turns to the next plant. The stereo-visioned pi camera is used to monitor the colour, distance and position of the fruit in a 360-degree view of the plant and the rotation of the camera is achieved by the servo motor. In contrast, the robotic arm attached with a soft gripper is used to pluck the tomatoes mechanically, and there would not be any damage to the tomatoes. The ripened tomatoes are plucked and stored in the bucket, which is attached to the system. The ultrasonic sensor is used to detect obstacles during movement. If the crop is found to be infected by the pest, the sprayer attached to the air PMP sprays the necessary pesticides. To measure the weight of the harvested tomatoes, load cells are used. All the information is passed to us by the WIFI module (Fig. 2).

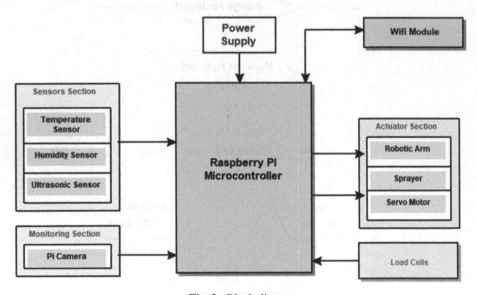

Fig. 2. Block diagram

The figure for the arm and gripper is given in Fig. 3.

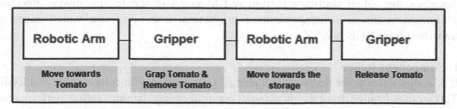

Fig. 3. Block diagram of arm and gripper

The pi camera fixed in that raspberry pi will be focusing the fruit at 360° The gripper fixed with a robotic arm is used to remove the tomato from the plant's stem. In this bot, the farmer can spray organic pesticides as well as inorganic pesticides (Table 1).

3.2 Pest Detection Parameters

Table 1. Types of diseases and its pesticide to spray

Raw image	Disease	Pesticide to spray
	Healthy leaf	No pesticide to spray
	Bacterial spot	Spray copper fungicide
	Late blight	Spray fungicides
	Yellow leaf curl virus	Spray carbonates

a*-Component Image

It is three-dimensional colour models of chrominance and brightness. a* component describes the colour distribution from red to green in the feature image. Because a*component image is independent of brightness, it is non-linear which needs to transform from RGB to XYZ.

I–Component Image

It is a source image for fusion. It is linear as a connection with colour space and RGB. This section detailed data collection and its pre-processing, data annotation, performance verification, and robotic vision.

Dataset

Images of tomatoes are taken from the field and examined carefully to decide the correctness of images and diseases type. It will start differentiating by the colour of the fruit and various diseases like moulded, rotten etc. In the way to brief the pre-processing, it has four processes. The dataset will be subdivided by digital fill light, digital subtraction light, high ISO noise reduction, and automatic white balancing mainly applied for image processing in Fig. 4.

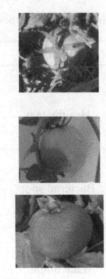

Fig. 4. Dataset images

Data Annotation

There are two objections mainly used for training to be annotated in many ways. R-CNN used to find the variety and location of tomato infection in the captured image. Faster R-CNN used for labelling. The primary function is to mark the location of pest infection in the images. The segmentation is to obtain a more accurate condition of a crop by mask R-CNN. This process is used to keep the shape and spot of disease with improper polygons.

During data processing, the image is carried out under flipping, cropping, zooming and shearing. It will divide into testing and training. In training, it will do the process from dataset1 to dataset n and undergo classification. In testing, it verifies the performance of the task. From the two categories, it undergoes fruit maturity and detection of pest using convolutional neural network technique. From the CNN, robot vision undergoes navigate, find objects, inspect, and handle parts orbits before an application is made. It finally classifies tomatoes and detects pest by features in the below Fig. 5.

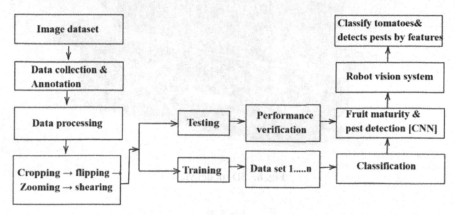

Fig. 5. Block diagram of image processing technique

4   Analysis and Implementation

This study involves different dataset augmentation methods of the final classification task. Here the classification is based on Convolutional Neural Network (CNN) method. The central theme is harvesting tomato and also monitoring pest using Raspberry pi. This project can be made at an affordable price, assuring the tomato's high safety during the robot's harvesting process. The project budget is around Rs. 5,250. The bucket attached with the bot can carry a maximum of 15 to 18kg of vegetables. This paper's deep learning will be useful for the agricultural field as the technique has clear identification, high accuracy, and efficiency. The bot's dimension is 70×55 cm. The three-dimensional view of the automated system shown in the Fig. 6.

The automated system is shown in Fig. 7. The central controller used is raspberry pi which controls the sensors and robotic arm effectively. With the gripper's help, the fruit is picked and delivered to the basket using the tube attached to the system. The PMP sprayer fixed in front of the robot sprays the pesticides on the pest by visualizing using a stereo camera. The bot will pluck only the ripened tomato from the plant by utilizing a robotic arm. The primary intention is to pluck only the fruit and not the branches nor leaves of the plant. In the next subsequent stage, it will check whether the plant leaf is desirably healthy or undesirable. If the plant is in a good state, then the machine proceeds towards the next plant if it is not in a desirable condition. The bot identifies the kind of disease that is being infected to the plant. It sprays the necessary pesticides by noticing

Fig. 6. 3D model view

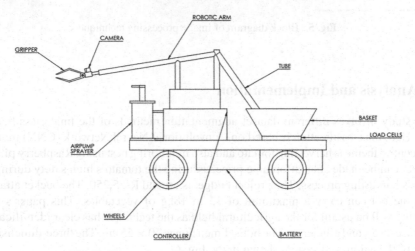

Fig. 7. Tomato harvesting and pest detection robot model

its texture and colour according to the various types of diseases stated in the inbuilt algorithm.

When harvesting, it will compute the tomatoes weight and tally the number of tomatoes that the system has stored in it. The pi camera attached to the raspberry pi provides clear cut images and can focus the plant in a 360-degree view. The robotic arm is attached to a gripper used to pluck the tomatoes from the plant's stem. The machine designed to spray both organic as well as inorganic pesticides as per their needs.

5 Conclusion

In this paper, a tomato harvesting and pest detection automation system is presented. This paper focuses on a technical method to enhance farming and agriculture through new technology. It is observed that the proposed plan will be an excellent benefit for the farmers to improve agricultural productions and reduce loss, and it is the best way to replace workers at this time. The machine gives an option for setting pesticides in the form of both organic and artificial ones. Moreover, this would be one of the effective technology in the field of the agricultural industry. The agro robot could help the farmer evaluate their residence domain, treat the tomato plants and harvest the prepared tomatoes.

References

1. Fuentes, A., Yoon, S., Kim, S.C., Park, D.S.: A robust deep-learning based detector for real-time tomato plant diseases and pests recognition. Sensors 17(9), 2022 (2017)
2. Dewi, T., Risma, P., Oktarina, Y., Muslimin, S.: Visual servoing design and control for agriculture robot; a review. In: 2018 International Conference on Electrical Engineering and Computer Science (ICECOS), pp. 57–62 (2018). https://doi.org/10.1109/ICECOS.2018.860 5209
3. Zhang, L., Jia, J., Gui, G., Hao, X., Gao, W., Wang, M.: Deep learning based improved classification system for designing tomato harvesting robot. IEEE Access 6, 67940–67950 (2018). https://doi.org/10.1109/ACCESS.2018.2879324
4. Bhargava, A., Bansal, A.: Fruits and vegetables quality evaluation using computer vision: a review. J. King Saud Univ. Comput. Inf. Sci. 33(3), 243–257 (2018)
5. Takahahi, Y., Ogawa, J., Saeki, K.: Automatic tomato picking robot system with human interface using image processing. In: The 27th Annual Conference of the IEEE Industrial Electronics Society, vol. 1, pp. 433–438 (2001)
6. Barbedo, J.G.A.: A review on the main challenges in automatic plant disease identification based on visible range images. Biosyst. Eng. 144, 52–60 (2016). https://doi.org/10.1016/j.bio systemseng.2016.01.017
7. Li, J., Tang, W., Wang, J., Wang, X., Zhang, X.: Multilevel thresholding selection based on variational mode decomposition for image segmentation. Signal Process. 147, 80–91 (2019)
8. Barbedo, J.G.A.: Factors influencing the use of deep learning for plant disease recognition. Biosyst. Eng. 172, 84–91 (2018). https://doi.org/10.1016/j.biosystemseng.2018.05.013
9. Kondo, N., Nishitsuji, Y., Ling, P., Ting, K.: Visual feed-back guided robotic cherry tomato harvesting. Trans. Am. Soc. Agric. Eng. 39(6), 2331–2338 (1996)
10. Espinoza, K., Valera, D.L., Torres, J.A., López, A., Molina-Aiz, F.D.: Combination of image processing and artificial neural networks as a novel approach for the identification of Bemisia tabaci and Frankliniella occidentalis on sticky traps in greenhouse agriculture. Comput. Electron. Agric. 127, 495–505 (2016)
11. Sembiring, A., Budiman, A., Lestari, Y.D.: Design and control of agricultural robot for tomato plants treatment and harvesting. J. Phys. Conf. Ser. 930(1), 012019 (2017)
12. Brahimi, M., Boukhalfa, K., Moussaoui, A.: Deep learning for tomato diseases: classification and symptoms visualization. Appl. Artif. Intell. 31(4), 299–315 (2017)
13. Syahrir, W.M., Suryanti, A., Connsynn, C.: Color grading in tomato maturity estimator using image processing technique. In: Proceedings of IEEE International Conference Computer Science Information Technology (ICCSIT), pp. 276–280 (2009)

LUT and LUT-Less Multiplier Architecture for Low Power Adaptive Filter

Ankita Gupta, Vijetha Kanchan, Shyam Kumar Choudhary, and R. Sakthivel$^{(\boxtimes)}$

School of Electronics Engineering, VIT Vellore, Vellore 632014, Tamil Nadu, India
{ankita.gupta2020,vijetha.kanchan2020,
shyamkumar.choudhary2020}@vitstudent.ac.in, rsakthivel@vit.ac.in

Abstract. This paper presents a multiplier less architecture for delayed LMS adaptive filter in its direct form and transposed form. Multipliers are required to compute the FIR filter partial product and coefficient updation. With increase in filter order, the complexity involved with conventional multipliers also increases and its implementation becomes uneconomical. Moreover, presence of multipliers in the critical path of the filter increases its computational time and power consumption. Many multiplier-less approaches such as Distributed Arithmetic (DA) have been adapted to design FIR filters with constant coefficients. The main advantage of DA-based designs is that it utilizes a lookup table (LUT) that stores the filter partial product. With some modifications, the LUT based multipliers can be optimized and can also be implemented in adaptive filters in its transposed form. Another approach is to eliminate the LUT required for the multiplier block by utilizing symmetries in odd multiples of filter partial product. From the implementation of a multiplier less adaptive filter on FPGA, reduction of power consumption was achieved for transposed form of DLMS ADF with the proposed LUT-based multiplier as compared to direct form of DLMS ADF with lutless multiplier.

Keywords: Delayed LMS · FIR filter · Adaptive filter · LUT multiplier · LUT-less multiplier · Transposed ADF

1 Introduction

An adaptive filter is a digital filter which causes any contaminated input of a system to converge to the response desired from the system. Unlike standard filters which are highly application specific and pass only a certain frequency of signals, Adaptive filters are more versatile; in the sense that they can be applied to any system to extract the desired response from a corrupted input signal (Fig. 1). Because of its versatility, ADFs' are now popularly used for noise cancellation, channel equalization in digital signal processing, in bio-medical applications like enhancing ECG signals, geological applications like in detecting seismic activities, in telecommunication, etc. The main component of ADF is the FIR filter which can be realized in its direct form or transposed form [1]. The coefficients of the FIR filter are updated regularly using adaptive algorithms like

© Springer Nature Singapore Pte Ltd. 2021
V. Arunachalam and K. Sivasankaran (Eds.): ICMDCS 2021, CCIS 1392, pp. 360–372, 2021.
https://doi.org/10.1007/978-981-16-5048-2_29

Least Mean Square (LMS), Recursive Least Square (RLS), Forward Linear Prediction, Steepest Descent etc. Of these, the LMS algorithm is most popularly used, owing to its simple structure and ease of implementation [2].

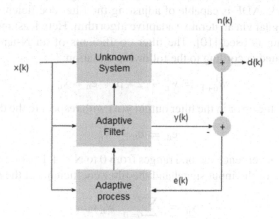

Fig. 1. Adaptation process of ADF

Optimizing the ADF architecture involves reducing the critical path, which is dominated mainly by the multipliers used to generate filter partial products and also the partial product in weight/coefficient updating to some extent. There are several algorithms for high speed multipliers using booth encoding and modified booth encoding [3]. Several implementations with filters were proposed: [4, 5] To generate a regular partial product array with fewer partial product rows and negligible overhead, thereby lowering the complexity of partial product reduction and reducing the area, delay, and power of Modified Booth Encoding (MBE) multipliers. At $(n - 1)^{th}$ bit '1' is added to the partial product array and then truncating the nth. It reduces the partial product rows from n/2 + 1 to n/2 by incorporating the last neg bit into the sign extension bits of the first partial product row, and almost no overhead is introduced to the partial product generator. [6] an optimization for binary radix-16 (modified) Booth recoded multipliers to reduce the maximum height of the partial product columns to n/4 for n = 64-bit unsigned operands. However, the circuitry involved with these encoding techniques is complex and difficult to implement.

Another possible scope of optimization is pipelining the filter structure but due to its recursive nature, conventional ADF cannot be pipelined. Hence certain modifications were suggested in [7, 8] to enable pipelining and meet the timing requirements. In this article, we intend to compare the performance of DLMS ADF with LUT-less multiplier and Transposed form DLMS ADF with LUT based multiplier in terms of power, timing and area utilized.

The rest of this article is organized as follows. In Sect. 2 a brief background of ADF is discussed along with the necessary modifications. In Sect. 3 transposed form ADF with delayed LMS algorithm is reviewed and in Sect. 4.1 and 4.2 the proposed LUT based and LUT less architectures are elaborated.

2 Review of Adaptive Filters

[2, 9] a basic Adaptive filter (ADF) block diagram is shown in the Fig. 2. It consists of a linear Finite Impulse Response (FIR) Filter, a weight updating block and an error computation block. ADF is capable of adjusting the filter coefficients automatically to adapt the input signal via an iterative adaptive algorithm. Here least mean square (LMS) adaptive algorithm is used [10]. The filter coefficients of an N-tap filter for the nth iteration are updated according to the following equation:

$$w_{n+1}^i = w_n^i + 2 * \mu * e_n * x_{n-i} \tag{1}$$

Where e(n) is the error in the filter output y(n) with respect to the desired signal d(n).

$$e_n = d_n - y_n \tag{2}$$

and μ is the convergence factor. i ranges from 0 to N − 1 The output of the filter y(n) is the convolution of the input signal and the filter coefficients at the nth time instant.

$$y_n = \sum_{i=0}^{N-1} w_n^i x_{n-i} \tag{3}$$

Thus the ADF computes the error between the desired signal and the output signal and based on the error, it generates filter coefficients to try and adapt the input signal to the desired response. It can be noted that ADFs require a finite amount of adaptation time initially to identify the response that is desired from the system and then it eventually converges.

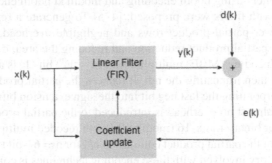

Fig. 2. Block diagram of ADF

In real time application, the conventional LMS ADF is inefficient in terms of longer critical path and more no. of multipliers. Also, from Eq. 2 it can be observed that ADF is recursive in nature i.e. the coefficients for the future instance depends on the present output. Hence conventional ADF blocks cannot be pipelined. To overcome this drawback, a delayed LMS algorithm is used [7, 11–16]. This modification involves introducing a delay in the error and input signal that is fed to the coefficient update block as shown in the Fig. 3. The coefficients are therefore updated as follows:

$$w_{n+1}^i = w_n^i + 2 * \mu * e_{n-m} * x_{n-i-m} \tag{4}$$

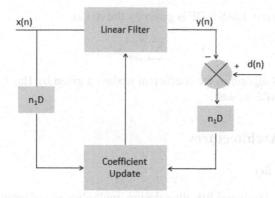

Fig. 3. Block diagram of DLMS ADF

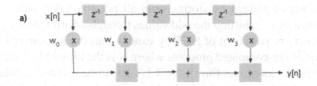

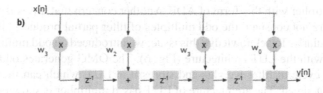

Fig. 4. a. Direct form of FIR filter b. Transposed form of FIR filter

3 Transpose Form LMS Adaptive Filter

In conventional ADF or DLMS ADF the FIR filter is generally implemented in the direct form as shown in the Fig. 4a. Another form of implementing FIR filters is the transposed form [17] as shown in the Fig. 4b. In contrast to the direct form, here the input signal is not time shifted; instead the sum of partial products of two consecutive stages is time shifted. The transposed form has therefore benefits over the direct form, owing to its inherent pipelined structure. Since the input signals are not time shifted, the partial products are generated independently in the same clock period. For fixed coefficients, the FIR filter realized in direct form and transposed form are mathematically identical but it is not so in case of ADF where the coefficients are updated regularly. However, the performance of the transpose-form LMS adaptive filter falls between that of the direct-form LMS algorithm and a delayed LMS algorithm with the worst-case delay [1]. The output y(n) of the transposed form LMS ADF is given by the eq (5).

$$y_n = \sum_{i=0}^{N-1} w_{n-i}^i x_{n-i} \tag{5}$$

The delayed LMS algorithm for coefficient updation given by Eq. 4 can be applied in transposed form ADF as well.

4 Proposed Architectures

4.1 LUT Multiplier

In an LUT - multiplier based FIR filter design, multiplication of input values with fixed coefficients are performed by a look up table consisting of all possible precomputed product values ($x_n * w_i^n$) corresponding to all possible values of input multiplicand (x_n). The LUT is further optimized by storing only all possible odd values and the even values are obtained by left shifting the odd values through a barrel shifter [18, 19]. This reduces the memory requirement of LUT by exactly half the amount required to store 2^N combinations of pre-computed products where N is the bit width of the input signal. In case of adaptive filters (direct form), this LUT has to be updated regularly since the coefficients are updated in regular intervals. Also, since the input signal is time shifted it takes more no. of clock cycles to evaluate filter partial products. However, in transposed ADF, since the partial product evaluations are done independently, it is more effective to use LUT multiplier with this form of ADF. Another concern that arises is that since the coefficients are not constant, the odd multiples of filter partial products also have to be evaluated regularly. To acknowledge this issue, we introduced an odd multiple generator (OMG) [20] with the LUT architecture (Fig. 6). The OMG generates odd multiples in every update cycle of filter weights and stores it in LUT, which can then be selected based on input signal. The architecture of LUT based multiplier is shown in Fig. 5 with following major blocks- 4 to 3 bit encoder, 3 to 8 line decoder, Memory array with OMG, Control unit, NOR cell and Barrel Shifter.

For an n-bit input, there can be 2^n possible bit combinations and hence 2^n different input values. Here, a 4-bit input value $X = x_3x_2x_1x_0$ is considered with a possibility of $2^4 = 16$ variant values. This is given as an input to the 4-to-3 bit encoder. The output of this encoder can be expressed as

$$d_0 = \overline{(\overline{x_0 x_1})(\overline{x_1 x_2}).(x_0 + (\overline{x_2 x_3}))} \tag{6}$$

$$d_1 = \overline{(\overline{x_0 x_2})(x_0 + (\overline{x_1 x_3}))} \tag{7}$$

$$d_2 = x_0 x_3 \tag{8}$$

Depending on the values of d_0, d_1 and d_2, the decoder activates one of the eight outputs which are then passed through a memory unit. This memory unit is embedded with an Odd Multiple Generator (OMG) and a memory array of size W x A where W is the bit width of the product and A is the no. of odd values possible. Here, we consider

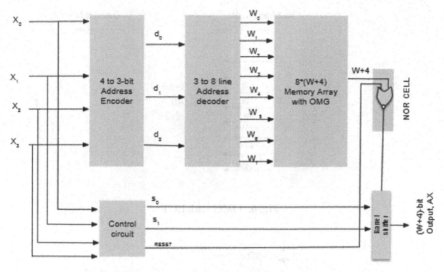

Fig. 5. LUT multiplier with OMG

the coefficients to be 4 bit wide. Therefore, the size of the memory array is 8 x 8. The function of OMG is to generate all possible odd values of the product $w_i * X$ for every update in w_i. The design of OMG [20] is such that it exploits the symmetries between odd multiples. For instance, here since the weight w_i and input X are 4 bit wide, there are 8 possible odd multiples of w_i*X - w_i, $3w_i$, $5w_i$, $7w_i$, $9w_i$, $11w_i$, $13w_i$, $15w_i$ of which only w_i, $3w_i$, $5w_i$, $7w_i$ needs to be generated. The other set of odd multiples can be generated by adding an offset of $2^3 w_i$ to this set. All the 8 odd multiples are then stored in the memory array. The output of the decoder is given as input to the memory array. This acts like a select line to pop out the required product value stored in the memory array. The popped value is then given to NOR cell [18] which is nothing but an array of NOR gates and the no. of gates required depends upon the no. of bits of the output from the memory unit. Each bit of the output is taken as one of the input to NOR gate present in the NOR cell and the other input of the NOR gate is the RESET signal coming from the control unit [18] whose expression can be written as

$$\text{RESET} = \overline{(x_0 + x_1)} . \overline{(x_2 + x_3)} \tag{9}$$

The RESET signal is common to all the NOR gates in the cell. If the RESET is high then all the outputs coming from the NOR cell is 0, while for RESET = 0, it then depends on the values from the memory unit. A barrel shifter [18] is then appended to the NOR cell. The block of this is made in two stages by using AOI (And Or Inverter) which is two AND gates preceding an OR gate. The structure of the AOI is shown in Fig. 7. The number of left shifts done by barrel shifter on the input value X depends on the output s_0 and s_1 signals from the control unit whose input is directly connected to the X values. The expression of s can be shown as.

$$s_0 = \overline{(x_0 + \overline{(x_1 + \bar{x}_2)})} \tag{10}$$

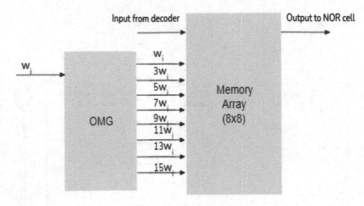

Fig. 6. OMG with LUT

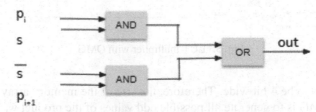

Fig. 7. AOI circuit

$$s_1 = \overline{x_0 + x_1} \tag{11}$$

The input value of X = 0100 gives the RESET = 0 thus making the input of the barrel shifter to depend on the values coming as complemented form of the output of memory unit through the NOR cell. This input value of x sets s_1 to 1 and s_0 to 0 which results shifting the input to the barrel shifter by two units. Since a NOR cell is used for RESET operation, the weights are stored in their complemented form in the memory unit.

4.2 LUT-Less Multiplier

The concept of LUT-less multiplier emerged from the shortcomings of LUT multiplier with direct form ADF [20]. The basic concept remains the same; segregating odd values of all possible filter partial product values and generating even values using barrel shifter. Only modification is that the odd multiples are no longer stored; instead they are generated in situ in hardware and an appropriate value is selected through a 4:1 mux demarcated as Odd Multiple Selector (OMS) in the block dig of Fig. 8.

The architecture of the LUT-less multiplier is shown in the Fig. 8. It consists of an encoder whose internal schematic is referred from [18] with W-bit input coefficient expressed as:

$$w(i) = \sum_{j=0}^{W-1} w(i, j)2^j = 2\sum_{j=0}^{W-2} w(i, j)2^j + w(i, 0) \tag{12}$$

Here $w(i,j)$ would be the jth-bit of $w(i)$ in a W-bit representation where i ranges from 0 to N-1, N being the no. of taps of the linear filter. The output of the encoder is d_2, d_1 and d_0, similar to the LUT multiplier. An Odd Multiple Generator (OMG) is also used with x_i as 4-bit input. It is embedded with a shifter and adder whose function is to shift the input sample and generate odd multiples - x_i, $3x_i$, $5x_i$, $7x_i$. These shifted inputs are then given to the Odd Multiple Selector (OMS) and subsequently to a 2-to-1 mux. This OMS selects one of the 4 input values generated by OMG using the select lines named as d_0 and d_1. The value of these select lines d_0 and d_1 are indirectly decided by the coefficient $w(i)$.

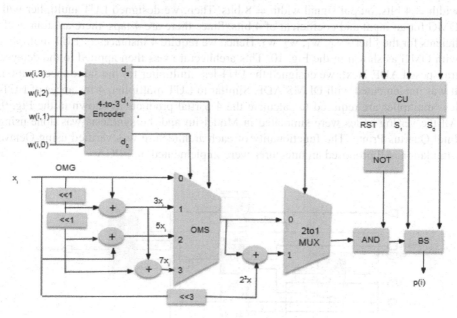

Fig. 8. LUT-less multiplier

For the 2-to-1 mux, one of the inputs is taken directly from the OMS and the other input is OMS with an offset of 2^3x_i added to it. This offset is added to generate the other set of odd multiples $9x_i$, $11x_i$, $13x_i$ and $15x_i$. The selection of these two inputs depends on the select line d_2 which is the output of the encoder. The output of this 2-to-1 mux is then given to the AND cell with another input being the active low RESET signal obtained from the control unit. The internal schematic of this control unit is same as given in [18] for equations refer Sect. 4.1 (LUT multiplier) Eq. 10, Eq. 11 and Eq. 9. The barrel shifter is identical to the schematic elaborated in LUT multiplier in Sect. 4.1, the working functions being the same: to left shift the values given as input from the AND cell by an amount decided by the select lines s_0 and s_1 coming from the control unit. The final output of this LUT-less multiplier structure can be obtained from the barrel shifter and is represented as

$$p(i) = [2\sum_{j=0}^{W-2} w(i, j)2^j + w(i, 0)]x_i \qquad (13)$$

The objective of this LUT-less multiplier is to give the output value p(i) which is the product of the input value x_i and w(i). For instance, if the coefficient value of w(i) is 1 (0001), and the input sample at that instant is $x_i = 9$ (1001), then output comes as $(x_i)*(w(i))$ i.e. p(i) = 00001001.

5   Implementation

For implementing, first we design delayed LMS adaptive filter and delayed transposed adaptive filter using verilog. No. of taps = 4, input signal width = 4 bits, coefficient width = 4 bits, output signal width = 8 bits. Then, we designed LUT multiplier with OMG for an input and coefficient of 4 bits. Since there are 4 taps, there are four coefficients for the filter - w_0, w_1, w_2, w_3. Hence we require 4 instances of LUT multiplier with OMG as shown in the Fig. 10. This architecture was then applied to the delayed transposed ADF. Next, we designed the LUT-less multiplier for the same specification. It was implemented with DLMS ADF. Similar to LUT multiplier, 4 instances of LUT-less multiplier are required to calculate the 4 partial products as shown in the Fig. 9. All the verilog codes were simulated in Modelsim and the synthesis was done using Intel Quartus Prime. The functionality of each architecture was verified using Octave Simulation. All proposed architectures were implemented on FPGA.

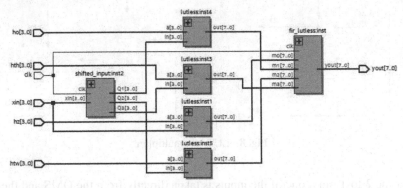

Fig. 9. RTL view of standard DLMS ADF with LUT-less multiplier

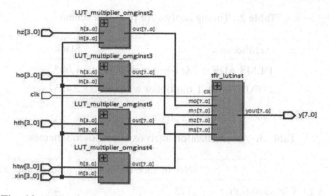

Fig. 10. RTL view of transposed DLMS ADF with LUT multiplier

6 Results

6.1 Performance Comparison - Power

From the FPGA implementation of the said architectures, it was found that transposed form of DLMS ADF with proposed LUT multiplier consumed lesser power as compared to direct form of DLMS ADF with LUT-less multiplier. Reduction of power by 1.5% was achieved. A summary of the total power consumption is given in Table 1. For evaluating total power consumption, the Power Analyzer tool in Intel Quartus Prime was used.

Table 1. Power analysis of proposed schemes

Architecture	Power (mW)
DLMS ADF + LUT-less multiplier	135.16
DTADF + LUT multiplier with OMG	133.14

6.2 Performance Comparison - Timing

From the Timing Analyzer in Intel Quartus Prime, the slack for each architecture is summarized in Table 2. The slack for transposed form of DLMS ADF with proposed LUT multiplier is more positive as compared to DLMS ADF with LUT-less multiplier. Greater positive slack provide our tool room for optimization on other design criteria, such as area and power.

6.3 Performance Comparison – Area

To estimate the approximate area utilization of the proposed schemes, we used Xilinx ISE. Table 3 summarizes the total slice LUTs and registers required for both schemes. The LUT-less architecture consumes lesser area as compared to LUT based scheme.

Table 2. Timing analysis of proposed schemes

Architecture	Slack
DLMS ADF + LUT-less multiplier	1.605
DTADF + LUT multiplier with OMG	2.425

Table 3. Area utilization analysis of proposed schemes

Architecture	No. of slice LUTs used	No. of slice registers used
DLMS ADF + LUT-less multiplier	175	48
DTADF + LUT multiplier with OMG	288	102

7 Future Scope

There is a lot of scope for optimization in both the architectures. Foremost, in both the architectures only unsigned input values and coefficients are considered. For processing signed integers, certain modifications are required. With sign-magnitude representation and using EX-OR gates, signed integers can also be processed. Further, the architecture can be pipelined [20] to meet the timing requirements. The same architecture can be modified for processing signals with more bit width. The LUT-less multiplier can also be implemented with transposed form of DLMS ADF for similar performance.

8 Conclusion

In this article, a new approach of LUT based multiplier is presented with a transposed form of DLMS ADF. To reduce the LUT size over the conventional design, Odd Multiple Generator (OMG) is used to update the coefficients in LUT. The article also presents a novel LUT-less multiplier architecture with direct form of DLMS ADF. Both the architectures are found to have similar performance with slight reduction of power in transposed architecture. However with more taps on the linear filter and a wider bit width, since LUT-multiplier is memory based it may consume even lesser power as compared to LUT-less multiplier. Also memories are much denser as compared to combinational logics. LUT-based architecture consumes more area as compared to LUT-less design. Hence, it is a tradeoff between the performance and area consumed for the two specified architectures.

It can also be concluded that a multiplier less approach in designing Adaptive filters is far more efficient in terms of power consumed and timing. The analysis of the presented architectures is performed through FPGA implementation in Intel Quartus prime.

References

1. Jones, D.L.: Learning characteristics of transpose-form LMS adaptive filters. IEEE Trans. Circuits Syst.-11: Analog Digit. Signal Process. **39**(io), (1992)
2. Tan, L., Jiang, J.: Digital Signal Processing Fundamentals and Applications, 3rd edn. Elsevier Inc., The Boulevard, Langford Lane, Kidlington, Oxford, UK (2019)
3. Kang, J.-Y., Gaudiot, J.L.: A simple high-speed multiplier design. IEEE Trans. Comput. **55**(10), 1253–1258 (2006)
4. Kuang, S.R., Wang, J.P., Guo, C.Y.: Modified booth multipliers with a regular partial product array. IEEE Trans. Circuits Syst. II Express Briefs **56**(5), 404–408 (2009)
5. He, Y., Chang, C.-H.: A new redundant binary booth encoding for fast 2n-bit multiplier design. IEEE Trans. Circuits Syst. I Regul. Papers. **56**(6), 1192–1201 (2008)
6. Antelo, F., Montuschi, P., Nannarelli, A.: Improved 64-bit radix- 16 booth multiplier based on partial product array height reduction. IEEE Trans. Circuits Syst. I Regul. Papers. **64**(2), 409–418 (2017)
7. Long, G.-H., Ling, F., Proakis, J.G.: The LMS algorithm with delayed coefficient adaptation. IEEE Trans. Acoust. Speech Signal Process. **37**(9), 1397–1405 (1989)
8. Meher, P.K., Park, S.Y.: Area-delay-power efficient fixed-point LMS adaptive filter with low adaptation-delay. IEEE Trans. Very Large Scale Integr. (VLSI) Syst. **22**(2), 362–371 (2014)
9. Haykin, S.: Adaptive Filter Theory, 5th edn. Prentice-Hall, Upper Saddle River, NJ, USA (1996)
10. Safarian, C., Ogunfunmi, T., Kozacky, W.J., Mohanty, B.K.: FPGA implementation of LMS-based FIR adaptive filter for real time digital signal processing applications. IEEE (2015)
11. Van, L.-D., Feng, W.-S.: An efficient systolic architecture for the DLMS adaptive filter and its applications. IEEE Trans. Circuits Syst. II Analog Digit. Signal Process. **48**(4), 359–366 (2001)
12. Meher, P.K., Maheshwari, M.: A high-speed FIR adaptive filter architecture using a modified delayed LMS algorithm. In: Proceedings of IEEE International Symposium Circuits System (ISCAS), pp. 121–124
13. Mankara, P.J., Pundb, A.M., Ambhorec, K.P., Anjankard, S.C.: Design and verification of low power DA-adaptive digital FIR filter. In: 7th International Conference on Communication, Computing and Virtualization (2016)
14. Meher,P.K., Park, S.Y.: Critical-path analysis and low-complexity implementation of the LMS adaptive algorithm. IEEE Trans. Circuits Syst. I Regul. Papers. **61**(3), 778–788 (2014)
15. Meyer, M.D., Agrawal, D.P.: A modular pipelined implementation of a delayed LMS transversal adaptive filter. In: Proceedings of IEEE International Symposium Circuits System, pp. 1943–1946 (May, 1990)
16. Yi, Y., Woods, R., Ting, L.-K., Cowan, C.F.N.: High speed FPGA based implementations of delayed LMS filters. J. VLSI Signal Process. Syst. Signal Image Video Technol. **39**(1–2), 113–131 (2005)
17. Datix, F.F., Rosa, V.S., Costa, E., Flores, P., Bampi, S.: VHDL generation of optimized FIR filters. In: International Conference on Signals, Circuits and Systems (2008)
18. Meher, P.K.: New approach to look-up-table design and memory based realization of FIR digital filter. IEEE Trans. Circuits Syst. I Regul. Papers. **57**(3), 592–603 (2010)
19. Park, S.Y., Meher, P.K.: Low-power, high throughput, and low-area adaptive FIR filter based on distributed arithmetic. IEEE Trans. Circuits Syst. II Exp. Briefs **60**(6), 346–350 (2013)
20. Sarma, R.K., Khan,M.T.: Student Member, IEEE, Shaik, R.A.: A novel time-shared and LUT-less pipelined architecture for LMS adaptive filter. IEEE Trans. Very Large Scale Integr. (VLSI) Syst. **28**(1) (2020)

21. Xu, D.., Chiu, J.: Design of a high-order FIR digital filtering and variable gain ranging seismic data acquisition system. In: Proceedings of Southeastcon, p. 6 (April 1993)
22. Cui, X., Liu, W., Chen, X., Swartzlander, E.E., Lombardi, F.: A modified partial product generator for redundant binary multipliers. IEEE Trans. Comput. **65**(4), 1165–1171 (2016)
23. Khan, M.T., Shaik, R.A.: Optimal complexity architectures for pipelined distributed arithmetic based LMS adaptive filter. IEEE Trans. Circuits Syst. I Regul. Papers. **66**(2), 630–642 (2019)
24. Meher, P.K.: LUT optimization for memory based computation. IEEE Trans. Circuits Syst. II Express Briefs **57**(4), 285–289 (2010)

Technology and Modelling for Micro Electronic Devices

FPGA Based Efficient IEEE 754 Floating Point Multiplier for Filter Operations

C. Thirumarai Selvi[1]($\boxtimes$), J. Amudha[2], and R. S. Sankarasubramanian[3]

[1] Sri Krishna College of Engineering and Technology, Coimbatore, Tamilnadu, India
thirumaraiselvi@skcet.ac.in
[2] Dr Mahalingam College of Engineering and Technology, Coimbatore, Tamilnadu, India
[3] PSG Institute of Technology and Applied Research, Coimbatore, Tamil Nadu, India

Abstract. The Existing and emerging information and communication technology (ICT) applications, such as smart cities, internet of things (IOT), autonomous vehicles, among other things, need more effective electronic and control systems and smaller sizes. This is a challenging problem for electronic designers to design such a system with low power consumption short development times and miniature in size for a world market. The development of chip-based systems (SOC) is an attractive and viable solution because SOC technologies allow customized designs for nanometric and low power consumption architectures and technologies. A SOC is developed by combining several previously designed and tested tiny modules. These modules are called as intellectual properties or IP cores for semiconductors. This work describes single, double and multiple precision multipliers for better timing and area performance. To achieve higher accuracy normalization is applied to the multiplier algorithm. The architecture design is implemented by Verilog HDL. Simulation is done by Modelsim 6 and synthesis done by Xilinx tool.

Keywords: IEEE 754 · Floating point multiplier · FPGA · VHDL · Xilinx

1 Introduction

Please Increasing the usage of mobile computing platforms in commercial and regular activities, requires greater efficiency, tiny size and sophisticated functionality in the equivalent electronic system. Multimedia and communication technologies are important for constructing digital signal processing systems. Thus, there is a need for implemented in VLSI hardware, DSP modules allow output, silicon area and power consumption circuits suitable for the particular application. There are comprehensive and frequent DSP algorithms that involve intensive computation, which is typically done by a general-purpose microprocessor making the system bottleneck. In customized VLSI hardware, this sort of algorithm could be performed. In order to improve overall device performance in terms of silicon region, speed and power consumption. After implementing the algorithms for digital signal processing in VLSI, these circuits could be incorporated into a system on chip (SOP) device through an instantiation of intellectual property (IP).

© Springer Nature Singapore Pte Ltd. 2021
V. Arunachalam and K. Sivasankaran (Eds.): ICMDCS 2021, CCIS 1392, pp. 375–386, 2021.
https://doi.org/10.1007/978-981-16-5048-2_30

The intellectual of properties of semiconductors, also known as IP cores are proved and reusable units that can be applied at various levels of abstraction: generic logic and chip layout. They are categorized into soft, firm and hard IP cores and are part of a growing phase. Electronic design industry trend because it decreases design time and may increase the overall performance of the system.

Low power consumption and system design based on modular applications are two of the key electronic design challenges imposed by current and future applications, such as IoT and deep learning. An evolving approach to energy saving in the design of electronic system is approximately computing, which is advantageous for many low precision tolerant applications.

Arithmetic logic units (ALUs) are very significant processor components that perform different arithmetic and logical operations, such as multiplication, division, addition, subtraction, cubing, squaring, etc. Of all these operations, the greatest multiplication is elementary and most widely used activity in the ALUs.

Binary multiplication is somewhat similar to the technique used in the decimal number system, involving multiplication of multiplicands by multipliers, one bit at a time, and a partial product is created in each case. Then the multiplicand is multiplied each bit of the multiplier, the partial products has been generated. Finally, all the partial products are summed together to create the final product result. An approach to fractional multiplier numbers is to first count the number of decimal places for both multiplicand and multiplier after the binary stage, then the count the number of decimal places after the binary point. The sum of these two numbers is calculated to give a total that can be denoted by the number P. In short, the binary point in the product is place before total number of places P count from the right-side direction. A partial product value zero is generated by zero multiplication. A multiplication by 1 produced the multiplicand bits to move to the left by one-bit location. Multiplication is performed using adders hardware and results are obtained using standard methods adopted for the binary number system.

Deep neural networks are usually trained on graphical processing units (GPUs). Several deep learning structures such as Caffe and tensor flow, use 32- bit single precision floating point numbers by default to perform deep neural network computations. Furthermore, the single-precision floating point unit data path is complicated and the hardware cost of implementing single-precision units is costly. These contribute to high energy consumption and high latency when deep neural networks are implemented in specialized hardware. In order to minimize hardware costs, some research work has been focused on reducing the cost of hardware in recent years. The numerical precision needed by deep computation of the neural network.

Half precision numbers are also used in deep learning training and inference operations in some other occupations. Single precision and higher precision formats are well supported in the floating-point unit (FPU) of general-purpose processors in order to provide better accuracy for scientific computations. On the one hand, however, the use of low precision formats (half precision) is able to preserve high accuracy for deep learning computation. Deep learning, on the other hand, is computationally intensive and thus low precision computation is needed to enhance the overall speed efficiency. Given these considerations, to accelerate deep learning computation in general purpose processors, support for half-precision operations in FPU.

The reduced precision computation is usually used along with the mixed precision computation in deep learning computation to control the accuracy of the computation. The reduced precision approach is commonly used to multiply since the multiplication mechanism is slow and the multiplier requires a significant amount of energy. The region of the multiplier can be reduced with reduced precision multiplication, and the speed of multiplication operations can be increased.

1.1 Floating Point Arithmetic

IEEE 754-2008 defines standard format for binary floating point include three components: single sign bit (s), w-bit biased component and p-bit mantissa. Figure 1 represents the structure of floating point arithmetic. Table 1 describes the various precision formats for IEEE 754-2008. Table 2 describes the sign, exponent and mantissa format for the different precisions.

S	E(w-bit)	M(p-bit)

Fig. 1. Binary floating-point format defined in IEEE 754-2008

Table 1. Basic precision formats specified in IEEE 754-2008

Data width	Precision
16 bit	Half Precision (HP)
32 bit	Single Precision (SP)
64 bit	Double Precision (DP)
128 bit	Quadruple Precision (QP)

Table 2. Floating-Point format defined in IEEE 754-2008

Format	Sign	Exponent	Mantissa	Bias	e_{max}	e_{min}
16-bit HP	1	5	10	15	15	-14
32-bit SP	1	8	23	127	127	-126
64-bit DP	1	11	52	1023	1023	-1022
128-bit QP	1	15	112	16383	16383	-16382

The primary benefit of the format of floating points is that they compared to fixed, there is a much wider variety of values point format. An extra benefit of the floating-point number they are more versatile than fixed point numbers, since they are having little to no versality. Other important benefits are the greatly expanded dynamic range available for many applications. In dealing with larger values, this wide dynamic range is very useful. Internal representation of floating point, details the format is more accurate than the fixed-point format. The characteristics of floating-point operation compared to the fixed-point arithmetic are listed in Table 3. Floating-point arithmetic operation has wide dynamic range, easier programming, higher efficiency, low design cost and faster time to market. Floating point arithmetic found crucial for the following applications. In military and radar applications floating point operations are very essential because of its high precision. For computing large FFT in floating point operations are very good in FIR filter operation. This is more suitable in the systems where gain coefficients are varied with respect to time for higher dynamic range.

Table 3. Characteristics of floating point and fixed-point arithmetic

Characteristics	Floating point	Fixed point
Dynamic range	Much larger	Smaller
Resolution	Comparable	Comparable
Speed	Comparable	Comparable
Ease of programming	Much easier	More difficult
Compiler efficiency	More efficient	Less efficient
Power consumption	Comparable	Comparable
Chip cost	Comparable	Comparable
System cost	Comparable	Comparable
Design cost	Less	More
Time to market	Faster	Lesser

This work presents the novel implementation of binary multiplier architecture for multi-precision which results in reduced area, lower latency and lesser hardware area compared to the existing methodologies.

2   Literature Survey

Sohn et al. [1] proposed an improved architecture for a fused floating-point add–subtract unit. The fused floating-point add–subtract unit is useful for digital signal processing (DSP) applications such as fast Fourier transform (FFT) and discrete cosine transform (DCT) butterfly operations. For both single and double precision, the suggested designs are implemented. Compared to a separate floating point add-subtract unit saves area and power consumption. Swartzlander et al. [2] suggested an improved architecture for a two-term dot product unit with a floating point. For a broad range of digital signal processing applications, including complex multiplication and fast Fourier transform and discrete cosine transform butterfly operations, the floating point used dot product unit is useful.

For a fused floating point three term adder, Shon et al. [1] suggested an enhanced architecture. Compared to a network of convolutional floating point two term adders, which is referred to as a separate architecture, the fused floating point three term adder conducts two additions in a single device to achieve better efficiency and better precision. The proposed design is implemented and synthesized with a 45 nm CMOS standard cell library for single and double accuracy. The improved three term adder fused floating point decreases the area and power consumption compared to a separate three term adder floating point.

Naresh et al. [3], spoke about the fact that the for computing, floating point operations are useful. They have a wide dynamic range, but they require considerably more resources than the integer operations. A 32 bit IEEE 754 standard floating point arithmetic unit has been developed using VHDL code and all addition, subtraction, multiplication and division operations are checked on Xilinx. Once the model of Simulink has been generated using MAT-VHDL code laboratory. It is possible to regenerate the lab and the VHDL code with the optimized and checked outcomes on Xilinx to see the improvement of parameters. Rami reddy et al. [4] proposed a high speed ASIC implementation suggested a floating point arithmetic unit that can, deduct, multiply, split functions to 32-bit operations using the IEEE 754-2008 standard. The algorithm is implemented using VHDL and synthesized using Cadence RTL compiler for 180 nm TSMCC. Bhaskar Chittaluri [5] developed an area efficient IEEE-754 double precision floating point arithmetic unit. The proposed design achieves the lesser partial products which increases the speed of computation.

Marcus [6] introduces a new 24-bit binary multiplier architecture. For use in data intensive applications, a single precision floating point multiplier that needs low delay benefits. The framework was synthesized using Xilinx ISE architecture suite 14.7. ISM was simulated with the performance. The implemented framework was contrasted implementations of 8-bit, 16 bit and 24-bit binary multipliers in terms of path delay.

Ramalakshmana et al. [7] have proposed a Vedic multiplier using CSLA adder gives better output in terms of delay. In the design of high-speed arithmetic logic units, the internet of things and digital signal processing applications, multipliers play a key role. Two Vedic sutras intended for multiplication are intended to increase the multiplier efficiency with the use of different adders. The output parameters are obtained in Vedic multipliers by using various adders such as carry select adder, ripple carry adder and BEC adders, very few gates and least delay. The Vedic multiplier using the CSLA adder offers better delay output compared to the Vedic multiplier using other adders. The multiplier is implemented on Spartan 3E FPGA and simulation is done using VHDL.

Liu et al. [8] implemented an approximate computing, as used in error tolerant applications. It is a promising technique for high performance and low power circuits. The design of approximate redundant binary (RB) multipliers is discussed in this work. For the RB multipliers, two approximate Booth encoders and two RB 4:2 compressors based on RB (full and half) adders are suggested. In the RB multiplier, the approximate architecture of the RB normal binary (NB) converter is also studied by taking into account the error features of both the approximate Booth encoders and the RB compressors. In the approximate RB multipliers, both approximate and exact normal partial product arrays are used to satisfy different precision requirements. To illustrate the validity of the proposed designs, case studies of error-resilient applications are also presented.

3   Proposed Method

In the proposed modified floating-point multiplication as in the FIR filter operation, the filters coefficient is multiplied with input image sequences. During the multiplication the floating-point numbers are multiplied, then adding the exponent. Here the sign of the multiplicands is Exor-ed. Then to increase the accuracy normalization is applied. Figure 2 brings the flowchart of the proposed method.

The following list the different steps for floating point multiplication

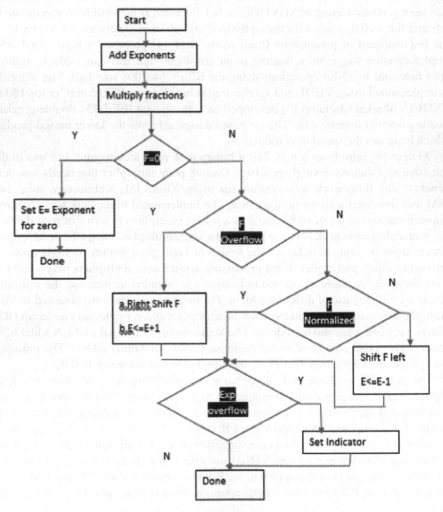

Fig. 2. Flowchart for the proposed floating-point multiplier

1. For the given data, separate the sign, exponent and mantissa.
2. Now check whether inputs are zero, infinity or an invalid representation in IEEE-754 standard.
3. Multiply mantissas and incorporate exponents, as well as determine a sign of the product.
4. Therefore, no normalization is necessary if the MSB is 1 in the outcome of multiplication of mantissas. Until a '1' is obtained, the mantissa is pushed to the left. The current exponent is lowered by 1, for each shift operation. Finally, concatenate the last results with the symbol, exponent and mantissa. The floating-point cores have been written in language for VHDL hardware description using Xilinx tools for ISE.

The designed floating-point can be used for implementing the FIR filter operation to compute one dimensional discrete wavelet transform (1D-DWT) and two-dimensional discrete wavelet transform (2D-DWT) [9]. The computation results of 1D-DWT generate high pass and low pass filter coefficients. When this calculation extended to 2D-DWT produces high-high (HH), low-low (LL), high-low (HL) and low-high (LH) filter coefficients. This low-low frequency components are used for image reconstruction. The RTL schematic of 2D-DWT and its synthesis results are displayed in Fig. 8 and Fig. 9.

4 Results

Single precision and multi precision multiplication results for binary and hexadecimal values are depicted from Figs. 3, 4, 5, 6. The overview results of the floating-point multiplication for single precision and double precision floating point values are synthesized using the Xilinx Virtex 5 FPGA family are provided in Tables 4, 5, 6. The improved performance of reduced area and increased speed of operation of the proposed technique with the conventional method [7] is represented in Fig. 7.

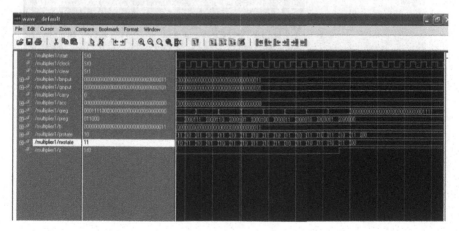

Fig. 3. Synthesis results of single precision floating point multiplier

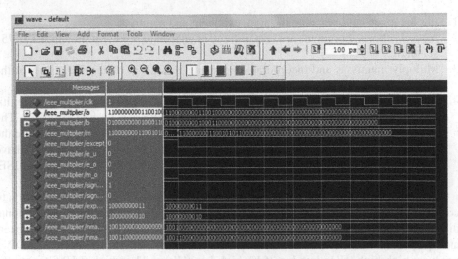

Fig. 4. Simulation results of double precision floating point multiplier

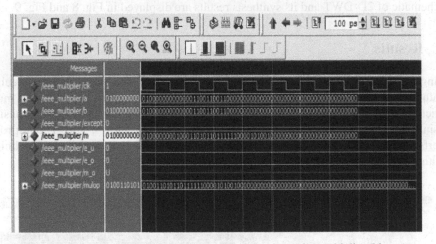

Fig. 5. Simulation results of double precision floating point multiplier (binary)

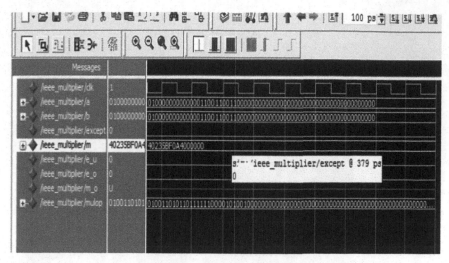

Fig. 6. Simulation results of double precision floating point multiplier (hexadecimal)

Table 4. Synthesis results for multipliers

Bit-width (Exponent, Mantissa)	FF	LUTs (area)	DSP48Es	Freq (Mhz)(timing)
24 (6, 17)	27	59	5	587.98
32 (8, 23)	35	74	5	576.45
43 (11, 31)	46	95	7	569.17
64 (11, 52)	67	250	15	568.10

Table 5. Power consumption in watts

	Bit width (Exponent, Mantissa)			
Power		24 (6, 17)	32 (8, 23)	43 (11, 31)	64 (11, 52)
	Quiescent	1.095	1.095	1.095	1.095
	Dynamic	0.006	0.006	0.006	0.006
	Total	1.101	1.101	1.101	1.101

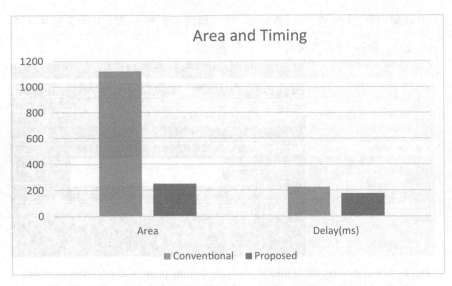

Fig. 7. Area and timing comparison of conventional and proposed methods

Table 6. Basic precision formats specified in IEEE 754-2008

Logic resources	Used	Available	Utilization
No. of slices	877	192,00	1%
No. of LUTs	765	192,00	1%
Total power	0.72210 W		
FPGA device	Virtex-5		

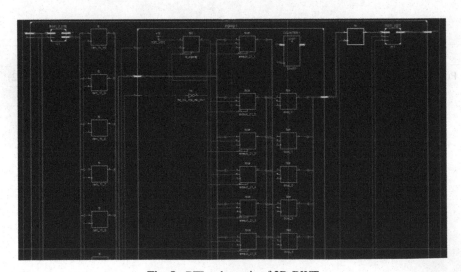

Fig. 8. RTL schematic of 2D-DWT

Device Utilization Summary				[-]
Slice Logic Utilization	Used	Available	Utilization	Note(s)
Number of Slice Registers	1,784	12,480	14%	
Number used as Flip Flops	1,775			
Number used as Latches	7			
Number used as Latch-thrus	2			
Number of Slice LUTs	11,079	12,480	88%	
Number used as logic	10,952	12,480	87%	
Number using O6 output only	9,386			
Number using O5 output only	40			
Number using O5 and O6	1,526			
Number used as Memory	106	3,360	3%	
Number used as Shift Register	106			
Number using O6 output only	106			
Number used as exclusive route-thru	21			
Number of route-thrus	147			
Number using O6 output only	51			
Number using O5 output only	92			
Number using O5 and O6	4			
Number of occupied Slices	3,026	3,120	96%	

Fig. 9. Synthesis results of 2D-DWT

5 Conclusion

The designed binary multipliers are simulated using Xilinx and synthesized by mod-elsim. The proposed new multi-precision binary multiplier architecture results reduced delay and hardware. The modified system had latency much shorter than all the current implementations compared in all modes i.e., 8-bit, 16-bit and 24-bit modes. The sys-tem design produced results as per the exceptions and will have high performance with drastic reduction in hardware. Also, the multiplier was used to implement basic FIR filter response. This FIR filter was useful to compute one dimensional discrete wavelet transform and two-dimensional discrete wavelet transform.

References

1. Sohn, J., Swartzlander, E.E., Jr.: A fused floating-point three-term adder. IEEE Trans. Circuits Syst. I Regul. Pap. **61**, 2842–2850 (2014)
2. Swartzlander, E.E., Jr., Saleh, H.H.: FFT implementation with fused floating-point operations. IEEE Trans. Comput. **61**, 284–288 (2013)
3. Grover, N., Soni, M.K.: Design of FPGA based 32-bit floating point arithmetic unit and verification of its VHDL code using MATLAB. I. J. Inf. Eng. Electron. Bus. **6**, 1–14 (2014)
4. Rami Reddy, C., HomaKesav, O., Maheswara Reddy, A.: High speed single precision floating point unit implementation using Verilog. Int. J. Adv. Electron. Comput. Sci. **2**(8), 803–808 (2015) ISSN: 2393–2835
5. Chittaluri, B.: Implementation of area efficient IEEE-754 double precision floating point arithmetic unit using Verilog. Int. J. Res. Stud. Sci. Eng. Technol. **2**(12), 15–21 (2015)
6. George, M.L.: Improved 24-bit binary multiplier architecture for use in single precision floating point multiplication. Int. J. Commun. Syst. Netw. Technol. **7**(2), 34–40 (2018). https://doi.org/10.18486/ijcsnt.2018.7.2.03
7. Ramalakshmanna, Y., Yaswanth Varma, V., Sai Kumar, P., Nalini Prasad, T.: Modified Vedic Multiplier Using CSLA Adders. J. Comput. Theor. Nanosci. **16**(4), 1255–1269(15) (2019)

8. Liu, W., et al.: Design and analysis of approximate redundant binary multipliers. IEEE Trans. Comput. **68**(6), 804–819 (2019). https://doi.org/10.1109/TC.2018.2890222
9. Tausif, M., Khan, E., Hasan, M., Reisslein, M.: Lifting-based fractional wavelet filter: energy-efficient DWT architecture for low-cost wearable sensors. Adv. Multimedia **2020**, 13 (2020), Article ID 8823689. https://doi.org/10.1155/2020/8823689

Design Framework of 4-Bit Radix-4 Booth Multiplier Using Perpendicular Nanomagnetic Logic in MagCAD

Anshul Dalal, Manoj Choudhary, and S. Balamurugan($\boxtimes$)

Department of Electrical and Electronics Engg,
Vellore Institute of Technology, Vellore 632014, Tamil Nadu, India
sbalamurugan@vit.ac.in

Abstract. Currently, researchers have been relentlessly working towards developing technologies that can potentially replace Complementary Metal Oxide Semiconductor (CMOS) technology as the scaling of CMOS technology has nearly reached its physical size limitations at the nanoscale. Nanomagnetic Logic (NML), one such promising advancement in the field of post-CMOS technology uses nanomagnets to transmit and compute data. It is a non-volatile, power-efficient technology that provides the potential to exploit the third dimension. In this paper, we have designed and implemented a 4-bit Radix-4 Booth Multiplier using And-Or-Inverter Graph (AOIG) representation in MagCAD tool using perpendicular Nano magnetic logic (pNML) technology. Subsequently, we have optimized the design using Majority Invertor Graph (MIG) manipulation techniques, a new method for efficient logic representation of boolean expressions using majority and inverter gates. MagCAD tool incorporates all the necessary design rules, physical models, libraries and technological parameters. After the design phase, a register-transfer-level (RTL) model is extracted in VHDL and it is simulated in Xilinx ISE to analyze and compare the performances of both the circuits. We evince a reduction in critical path delay, latency and area by, nearly 10%, 29% and 40% respectively after optimizing the layout of the Booth multiplier design using Majority-Inverter-Graph manipulation rules.

Keywords: Post-CMOS · MagCAD · Majority inverter graph (MIG) · Majority logic · And-or-inverter graph (AOIG) · Modified booth multiplier · Perpendicular nano-magnetic logic (pNML)

1 Introduction

We have witnessed an exponential growth in the speed and power efficiency of the electronic chips and a commensurate decrease in their physical dimensions in the past few decades. We are very close to reaching the physical limitations of silicon based CMOS technology, beyond which it cannot be further scaled down [1]. Due to the technological and economical limitations, increased associated power leakages and the limitations on the various trade-off factors, scaling the current technology further down has become

© Springer Nature Singapore Pte Ltd. 2021
V. Arunachalam and K. Sivasankaran (Eds.): ICMDCS 2021, CCIS 1392, pp. 387–403, 2021.
https://doi.org/10.1007/978-981-16-5048-2_31

exceedingly difficult. The post-CMOS scenario raises many challenges for researchers who have been working on developing new technologies that could potentially replace CMOS technology and continue to power the growth of electronics industry. Quantum-Dot cellular automata (QCA), Nano magnetic technology (NML), single electron tunneling technology (SET), spin electronics are some examples of such technologies. In all these technologies, the basic logic elements are majority, minority gates and inverters. Nanomagnetic technology is a promising advancement in the beyond CMOS technology research [2, 3]. When compared to the CMOS technology, Nanomagnetic technology offers potential advantages. It can store binary information, it is intrinsically non-volatile, consumes low power and is remarkably compact [4, 5]. Majority and Minority gates are used for logic implementation in NML, analogous to NAND and NOR gates used in CMOS technology.

Digital signal processing, communication systems, digital filters and arithmetic logic unit are some of the most computationally demanding fields and high performance multipliers are ubiquitously used in these applications [6]. The capacity of these applications are heavily dependent on the performance of these multipliers. Since efficiency, speed and compactness of multipliers has become so critical, researchers have been extensively working on designing optimized digital multiplier topologies. The research hitherto culminated in Modified Booth multiplier algorithm; a fast signed binary multiplication algorithm which is widely used in highly multiplication-intensive applications [6]. In this paper, we have designed and implemented the 4-Bit Radix-4 Booth multiplier based on And-Or-Inverter Graph (AOIG) logic representation in MagCAD tool using pNML technology [5]. Subsequently, we have optimized the design using Majority-Inverter Graph [7] manipulation technique, a novel method for efficient logic representation of Boolean expressions using majority and inverter gates. Both the designs were implemented in MagCAD tool using 9 layers of perpendicularly stacked magnetic circuits in MagCAD. Once the circuit is implemented, a VHDL file and various other necessary files were generated in MagCAD [8], which were used to test the functionality and performance of the circuits in Xilinx ISE.

2   Background

Nanomagnetic technology uses magnetic field for processing, transmission and storage of data [8]. Arrays of single-domain dipole field-coupled nanoscale magnets are used for transmission of data. Their magnetization of these dipole is manipulated for computation and transmission of data. Two stable magnetization states are used to represent binary information. When compared to the CMOS technology nanomagnetic technology offers potential advantages. It can store binary information, it is intrinsically non-volatile, consumes low power and is remarkably compact [9]. Different implementations of Nanomagnetic logic are currently under research amongst which the most propitious implementations are the perpendicular nanomagnetic logic (pNML) [10] and in-plane nanomagnetic Logic (iNML) [10, 11] technology. pNML offers advantages over iNML technology. pNML employs a global, perpendicular clock field, reducing the power consumption. It also allows 3D stacking of layers of magnetic circuit, significantly reducing the area occupied [12]. Exploiting the potential offered by the third dimension is clearly one of the best options available for us. Throughout this paper we have used pNML technology for design implementation.

MagCAD is a part of the ToPoliNano design suite [13], an open source software EDA tool to simulate and implement circuits based on emerging nanotechnologies [5]. MagCAD can be used to design, simulate and compare 3D multilayered NML circuits, exploring the advantages provided by the third dimension. Each layer is represented with different color provided in Layer Toolbar (see Fig. 7). The validity of MagCAD was experimentally verified by Riente Fabrizio [5, 13]. MagCAD supports two implementations, in-plane NML (iNML) and perpendicular NML (pNML). We have used pNML technology to design our circuit. After the circuit has been designed, an RTL file is generated in VHDL by MagCAD. It is used to simulate the circuit in Xilinx ISE to verify the behavior of the design [5]. This paper is divided into 7 sections. Section 1 gives a brief introduction about the beyond-CMOS technology. Section 2 gives background of Nanomagnetic (NML) technology and MagCAD, a tool for 3D implementation of nano-magnetic circuits. Section 3 explains modified booth multiplier: encoder and decoder. Section 4–5 deal with implementation of multiplier using AOIG in MagCAD and its optimization using MIG manipulation techniques. Finally, in Sect. 6–7, simulation results are presented followed by conclusion.

3 Modified Booth Multiplier

Booth multiplier algorithm is a multiplication algorithm used for multiplying two signed binary numbers. Booth Algorithm is ideally used where the multiplier circuits are expected to perform multiplications as fast as possible. An extensive amount of research is being performed on developing multipliers that produce minimal number of partial products rows and accumulate them as fast as possible [4]. In order to do that, Modified Booth Algorithm was developed, a crucial improvement in the design of binary multipliers. Modified Booth Algorithm, faster than the Booth Algorithm, addresses the limitations of Booth Algorithm.

The Modified Booth Algorithm consist of following three stages which must be optimized in order to optimize the multiplier (see Fig. 1),

1. Generation of the partial products (pp) using encoder and decoder.
2. Accumulate the generated partial products until the last two rows remain.
3. Compute the final multiplication results by adding the last two partial product rows.

For two 'n' bit integers, it involves 'bit pairing' of the booth encoded bits and reduces the number of partial products (see Fig. 2) rows to be accumulated from 'n' to 'n/2'. Given 2 n-bit two's complement integers with multiplier and multiplicand as MR and MD respectively [6], their product P is defined as,

$$P = MR*MD = \sum_{i=0}^{i=2n-1} P_i * 2^i \tag{1}$$

Here Pi, are the bits of the output product P, where multiplier MR and multiplicand MD in two's complement are expressed as,

$$MR = -mr_{n-1} * 2^{n-1} + \sum_{i=0}^{i=n-2} mr_i * 2^i \tag{2}$$

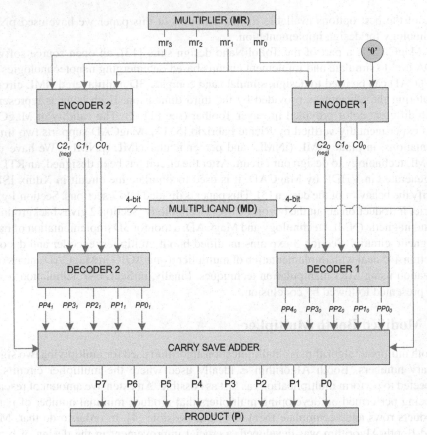

Fig. 1. Block representation of modified booth multiplier for 4 × 4 multiplication

$$MD = -md_{n-1}*2^{n-1} + \sum_{i=0}^{i=n-2} md_i*2^i \qquad (3)$$

where mr_i and md_i are the bits of multiplier and multiplicand respectively.

Generation of partial product arrays for 4 × 4 multiplication using Booth's algorithm is shown below (see Fig. 2).

3.1 Booth Encoder

The modified booth recoding involves grouping 3 bits at a time. This technique is advantageous as it reduces the number of partial products by half. Due to this the critical path delay and the area of the circuit is reduced [13] (see Fig. 3). The inputs to the encoder circuit are the multiplier bits and the outputs of encoder are C2, C1, C0. The C2 bit decides whether the multiplicand should be added to or subtracted from multiplier and the C1 or C0 bits indicate that the multiplicand should be multiply by 1 or 2 respectively (see Table 1).

$$C0_i = \overline{mr}_{2i+1} \,\&\, mr_{2i} \,\&\, mr_{2i-1} + mr_{2i+1} \,\&\, \overline{mr}_{2i} \,\&\, \overline{mr}_{2i-1} \qquad (4)$$

				md_3	md_2		md_1	md_0
			$\times$	mr_3	mr_2		mr_1	mr_0
			1					
$PP_0 \rightarrow$			1	$PP4_0$	$PP3_0$	$PP2_0$	$PP1_0$	$PP0_0$
$PP_1 \rightarrow$	1	$PP4_1$	$PP3_1$	$PP2_1$	$PP1_1$	$PP0_1$		$C2_0(neg)$
						$C2_1(neg)$		
P7	P6	P5	P4	P3	P2		P1	P0

Fig. 2. Partial product (PP) arrays for 4×4 signed multiplication with modified booth multiplier

Table 1. Truth table of encoder

mr_{2i+1}	mr_{2i}	mr_{2i-1}	Operation performed on multiplicand $(mr_{2i-1} + mr_{2i} - 2mr_{2i+1})$ *MD	C2	C1	C0
0	0	0	0*MD	0	0	0
0	0	1	1* MD	0	1	0
0	1	0	1* MD	0	1	0
0	1	1	2* MD	0	0	1
1	0	0	−2* MD	1	0	1
1	0	1	−1* MD	1	1	0
1	1	0	−1* MD	1	1	0
1	1	1	0* MD	0	0	0

$$C1_i = mr_{2i} \oplus mr_{2i-1} \tag{5}$$

$$C2_i = mr_{2i+1} \,\&\, \overline{mr}_{2i} + mr_{2i+1} \,\&\, \overline{mr}_{2i-1} \tag{6}$$

In terms of majority logic gate, above expressions are represented as follows:

$$C0_i = \bar{M}\left(\bar{M}\left(M\left(mr_{2i}, \overline{mr}_{2i+1}, 0\right), mr_{2i-1}, 0\right), \bar{M}\left(\bar{M}\left(\overline{mr}_{2i}, mr_{2i+1}, 0\right), \overline{mr}_{2i-1}, 0\right), 0\right) \tag{7}$$

$$C1_i = \bar{M}\left(\bar{M}\left(\overline{mr}_{2i}, mr_{2i-1}, 0\right), \bar{M}\left(\overline{mr}_{2i-1}, mr_{2i}, 0\right), 0\right) \tag{8}$$

$$C2_i = \bar{M}\left(\bar{M}\left(\overline{mr}_{2i}, \overline{mr}_{2i-1}, 1\right), \overline{mr}_{2i+1}, 1\right) \tag{9}$$

where M is majority function, $\bar{M}$ is minority function, $i=\{0,1\}$ and $mr_{-1} =$ '0'. In MagCAD each magnetic layer is represented with different color provided in Layer Toolbar (see Fig. 7).

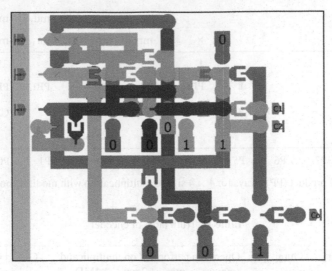

Fig. 3. pNML layout of AOIG based encoder circuit in MagCAD

3.2 Booth Decoder

The decoder stage follows immediately after encoding stage. The output bits C2, C1, C0 from the decoding unit along with two multiplicand bits are input to the decoder [14]. As already mentioned the former decide whether multiplicand should be added or subtracted from multiplier and also whether multiplicand should be multiplied with 1 or 2 before performing the operation (see Fig. 4). The decoder generates the partial product bits [15]. These partial products are accumulated in the succeeding stage.

$$PPj_i = C2_i \oplus (md_{j-1} \& C0_i + md_j \& C1_i) \tag{10}$$

where $j = \{0, 1, 2, 3, 4\}$ and $md_{-1} = \text{`0'}$. In terms of majority logic gate, above expression is represented as follows:

$$PPj_i = M\left(M\left(\overline{C2_i}, 0, w\right), M\left(\bar{w}, 0, C2_i\right), 1\right) \tag{11}$$

$$w = M\left(M\left(C1_i, 0, md_j\right), M\left(C0_i, 0, md_{j-1}\right), 1\right) \tag{12}$$

3.3 Full Adder

Full adder is a crucial component of the multiplier circuits. It takes three single-bit inputs and produce two outputs, namely *Sum* and C_{out} [16]. The circuit diagram for the full adder and its implementation in pNML layout in MagCAD is given below (see Fig. 5).

$$Sum = C_{in} \oplus A \oplus B \tag{13}$$

$$C_{out} = A\&B + B\&C_{in} + C_{in}\&A \tag{14}$$

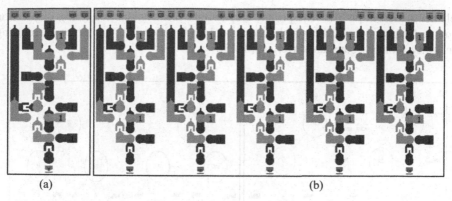

(a)   (b)

Fig. 4. pNML layout of AOIG based (a) Selector and (b) Decoder circuit in MagCAD.

In terms of majority logic gate, above expressions can be represented as follows:

$$Sum = M(M(\overline{C}_{in}, M(\overline{A}, B, 0)M(A, \overline{B}, 0), 1), 0),$$
$$M(C_{in}, \overline{M}(M(\overline{A}, B, 0), M(A, \overline{B}, 0), 1), 0), 1) \tag{15}$$

$$C_{out} = M(A, B, C_{in}) \tag{16}$$

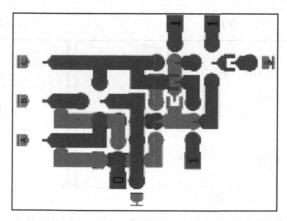

Fig. 5. pNML layout of AOIG based full adder

4 Implementation of Modified Booth Multiplier in MagCAD Using AOIG

MagCAD incorporates design rules, physical models, design parameters and technological libraries that contain all the functions and basic blocks needed to design circuits using pNML technology [5]. Majority, minority gates and inverter are the basic logic elements used in pNML. The primitive operations like conjunction (and), disjunction (or) and negation (not) along with several boolean functions can be implemented using majority, minority gates and inverters [8, 15].

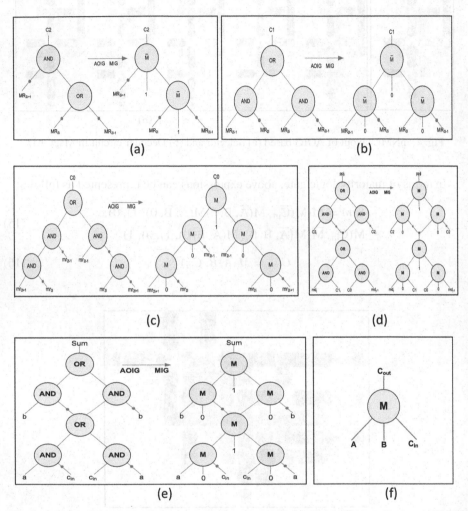

Fig. 6. AOIG to MIG conversion of encoder outputs (a) C1 (b) C2 (c) C0, decoder output (d) PPij and Full adder outputs (e) Sum (f) C_{out}

The equivalent MIG of the And-Or-Inverter-Graph (AOIG) of booth encoder, decoder and full adder are implemented in pNML (see Fig. 6). In the pNML implementation of AOIG representation of booth multiplier, we have used 9 different layers, layer-0 through layer-8. The encoder has been implemented using 5 layers (see Fig. 3). Encoder-1 is present in layer-0 through layer 4, while encoder-2 is present in layer-4 through layer-9. The output of the encoder is fed to the decoder, also implemented using 2 layers. Decoder-1 is implemented using layer-0 and layer-1, while decoder-2 uses layer- and

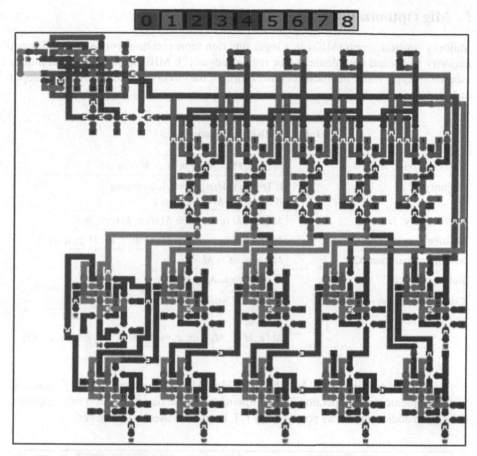

Fig. 7. AOIG based 4 × 4 modified booth multiplier in MagCAD and layer toolbar

layer-6 and layer-7 (see Fig. 4). The output of decoder-1 and decoder-2 are available in layer-1 and layer-6 (see Fig. 7).

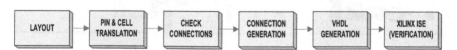

Fig. 8. Flow chart for design and verification

The output of the decoder is fed to the full adder array placed in the layer 4–6. The final product is present in layer-4. RTL files written in VHDL are generated [15] and these files are used to simulate the design in Xilinx ISE to verify its behavior/functionality (see Fig. 8).

5 Mig Optimization

Majority inverter graph (MIG) is a logic function representation consisting of 3-input majority nodes and complemented or regular edges [7]. MIG manipulation techniques (see Table 2) [7] result in efficient optimization of the circuit by reduction of size, depth and switching activity.

Table 2. MIG manipulation rules

Commutativity: $\Omega.C$	$M(p, q, r) = M(q, p, r) = M(r, q, p)$
Majority: $\Omega.M$	If $(p==q)$, $M(p,p,r)=M(q,q,r)=p=q$ If $(p = \bar{q})$, $M(p, \bar{p}, z) = z$
Associativity: $\Omega.A$	$M(p, u, M(q, u, r)) = M(r, u, M(q, u, p))$
Distributivity: $\Omega.D$	$M(p, q, M(u, v, r)) = M(M(p, q, u), M(p, q, v), r)$
Inverter propagation: $\Omega.I$	$\bar{M}(p, q, r) = M(\bar{p}, \bar{q}, \bar{r})$
Relevance: $\psi.R$	$M(p, q, r) = M\left(p, q, r_{p/\bar{q}}\right)$
Complementary associativity: $\psi.C$	$M(p, u, M(q, \bar{u}, r)) = M(p, u, M(q, p, r))$
Substitution: $\psi.S$	$M(p, q, r) =$ $M\left(v, M\left(\bar{v}, M_{v/u}(p, q, r), u\right), M\left(\bar{v}, M_{v/\bar{u}}(p, q, r), \bar{u}\right)\right)$

It is defined over the set $(B, M, ^{-}, 0, 1)$ [7]. Here M is a 3-input majority logic gate and $^{-}$ is a complementation operator. The following primitive transformation rules, referred to as Ω, in addition to Ψ, as proposed by [7], have been used in this paper.

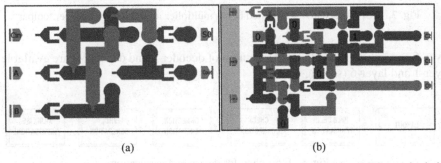

(a)   (b)

Fig. 9. (a) Optimized full adder and (b) Optimized booth encoder using MIG manipulation techniques

Encoder produces three output, namely C2, C1 and C0, of which MIGs of C2 and C1 cannot be optimized any further. So to optimize our circuit, we have manipulated the MIGs of full adder Sum, as shown in [16] and encoder output C0 to reduce the number of levels/depth in the respective graphs (see Fig. 9). First the AOIG was converted into corresponding MIG. Subsequently, using above given rules each MIG is manipulated in such a way that the resultant MIG have either fewer levels or fewer majority gates or both, compared to the original MIG (see Fig. 10). Using this technique, number of levels in majority logic network of encoder output C0 and full adder Sum were reduced from 3, 4 levels to 2, 2 levels respectively (see Table 3). Transformation rules such as $\psi.S$, $\psi.C$, $\Omega.D, \Omega.M$ are used to optimize full adder Sum and encoder output C0 (see Fig. 11).

Table 3. Flow of MIG manipulation of sum and encoder (C0)

Function	Expressions	Rule	Depth
$Sum = c_{in} \oplus a \oplus b$	$O\begin{pmatrix} A(\bar{b}, O(A(\overline{c_{in}}, a), A(c_{in}, \bar{a}))), \\ A(b, \overline{O}(A(\overline{c_{in}}, a), A(c_{in}, \bar{a}))) \end{pmatrix}$ $\downarrow$ $M\begin{pmatrix} M(\bar{b}, M(M(\overline{c_{in}}, a, 0), M(c_{in}, \bar{a}, 0), 1), 0), \\ M(b, \bar{M}(M(\overline{c_{in}}, a, 0), M(c_{in}, \bar{a}, 0), 1), 0), 1 \end{pmatrix}$ $\downarrow$ $M(c_{in}, \bar{M}(a, b, c_{in}), M(a, b, \overline{c_{in}}))$	AOIG→MIG $\Psi.S(c_{in}=a)$ $\Omega.M$	4 4 2
$CO_i =$ $(\overline{mr}_{2i+1} \& mr_{2i}$ $\& mr_{2i-1}) +$ $(mr_{2i+1} \& \overline{mr}_{2i} \&$ $\overline{mr}_{2i-1})$	$O\begin{pmatrix} A(A(\overline{mr}_{2i+1}, mr_{2i}), \ mr_{2i-1}), \\ A(A(mr_{2i+1}, \overline{mr}_{2i}), \ \overline{mr}_{2i-1}) \end{pmatrix}$ $\downarrow$ $\bar{M}\begin{pmatrix} \bar{M}(M(mr_{2i}, \overline{mr}_{2i+1}, 0), mr_{2i-1}, 0), \\ \bar{M}(\bar{M}(\overline{mr}_{2i}, mr_{2i+1}, 0), \overline{mr}_{2i-1}, 0), 0 \end{pmatrix}$ $\downarrow$ $\bar{M}(C1_i, \bar{M}(mr_{2i}, \overline{mr}_{2i+1}, 0), \bar{M}(\overline{mr}_{2i}, mr_{2i+1}, 0))$	AOIG→MIG $\Psi.S(mr_{2i+1}=mr_{2i})$ $\psi.C, \Omega.D, \Omega.M$	3 3 2

6 Simulation Results

The behavior and functionality of the designs have been verified. VHDL generated in MagCAD were used to simulate the designs in Xilinx ISE. Table 4 shows that the encoder optimized (see Fig. 9b) using MIG manipulation rules is faster and has lesser bounding box area than the AOIG based encoder. All the simulation results are obtained using the default parameters (see Fig. 14). Changing these parameters will also influence the performance of the circuits designed. Table 5 and Table 6 show that the design optimized using MIG manipulation rules is approximately 29% faster than AOIG based design and has 10% lesser critical path delay and 40% lesser bounding box area. It has been experimentally shown by Riente [17] that pNML circuits have lesser static and dynamic power consumption than CMOS based circuits.

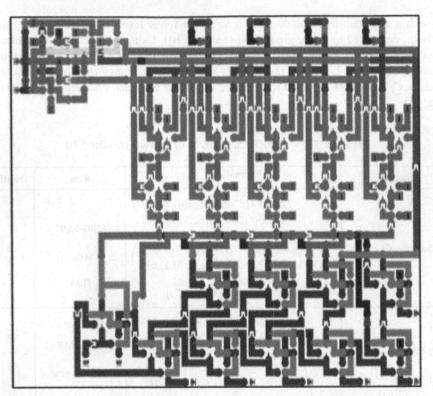

Fig. 10. 4 × 4 Modified booth multiplier optimized by MIG manipulation techniques

The simulation results of the design based on AOIG and the design optimized using MIG manipulation techniques, as obtained in Xilinx ISE are shown below (see Fig. 12–13).

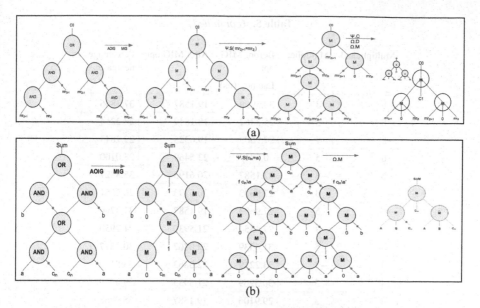

Fig. 11. MIG optimization of (a) Encoder output (C0) and (b) Full adder sum

Table 4. Latency of booth encoder before and after MIG optimization for each combination

Multiplier bits			Before MIG opt	After MIG opt	Percentage decrease
B2	B1	B0	Latency (us)		
0	0	0	3.4333	1.3721	60.0355
0	0	1	3.7305	1.6059	56.9521
0	1	0	3.7305	2.3078	38.1369
0	1	1	4.0341	2.5481	36.8359
1	0	0	3.4333	2.5481	25.782
1	0	1	3.7305	2.3078	38.1369
1	1	0	3.7305	2.3078	38.1369
1	1	1	4.0341	2.7821	31.0354

Table 5. Latency of modified booth multiplier for arbitrary multiplicand and multiplier inputs before and after MIG optimization

Multiplicand	Multiplier	Before MIG opt	After MIG opt	Percentage decrease
		Latency (us)		
−8	−5	30.0721	21.1062	29.8148
−8	−3	30.0721	20.1261	33.0738

(*continued*)

Table 5. (*continued*)

Multiplicand	Multiplier	Before MIG opt	After MIG opt	Percentage decrease
		Latency (us)		
−8	3	30.5969	19.1587	37.3836
−8	5	25.3362	18.1849	28.2254
−8	7	27.9603	19.6325	29.7843
−6	−5	30.5843	23.5469	23.0100
−6	−3	32.1587	20.6193	35.8827
−6	3	27.9603	20.6193	26.2551
−6	5	27.9603	19.1587	31.4790
−6	7	27.4354	21.5930	21.2950
−4	−5	31.6339	22.0862	30.1817
−4	−3	33.2219	22.0862	33.5190
−4	3	30.5969	21.5935	29.4259
−4	5	29.9106	19.1587	35.9468
−4	7	30.5969	21.5867	29.4480
2	−5	32.1587	22.5731	29.8071
2	−3	32.6962	24.5206	25.0048
2	3	29.0225	20.6193	28.9541
2	5	26.3858	21.1061	20.0095
2	7	28.4851	20.6193	27.6137
4	−5	31.1091	20.6193	33.7194
4	−3	33.7458	23.5469	30.2229
4	3	28.4851	20.6193	27.6137
4	5	28.4851	20.6193	27.6137
4	7	29.0225	21.5930	25.5989
0	0	21.6562	18.1849	16.0289
1	1	26.9106	20.1324	25.1877
−1	−1	29.0099	21.1062	27.2449

Table 6. Critical path delay and bounding box area before and after MIG optimization

Design	Before MIG optimization		After MIG optimization	
	Critical path delay (us)	Bounding box area (um^2)	Critical path delay (us)	Bounding box area (um^2)
Booth encoder	0.2365	18.9	0.1859	13.5
Booth multiplier	0.4199	277.2	0.3782	167.58

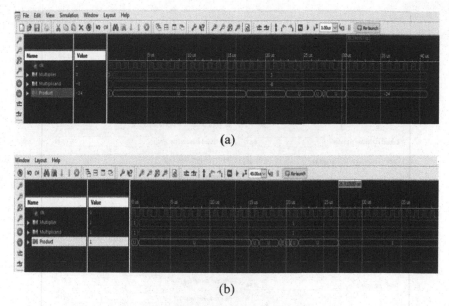

Fig. 12. Simulated waveforms of AOIG based design for the inputs (a) 3×-8 and (b) 1×1.

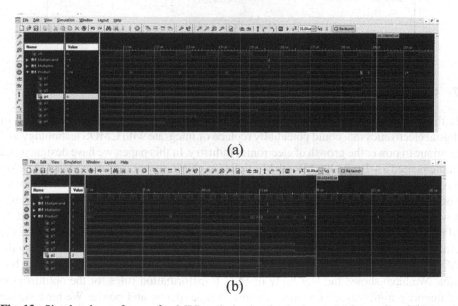

Fig. 13. Simulated waveforms after MIG optimization for the inputs (a) 3×-8 and (b) 1×1.

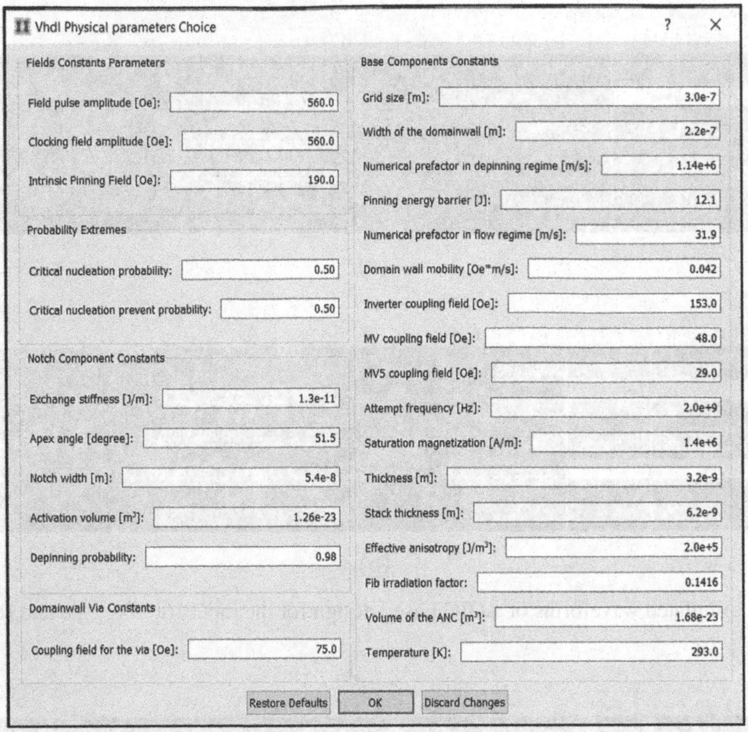

Fig. 14. Geometrical and physical parameters used in MagCAD

7 Conclusion

In this paper, we have presented the implication of pNML technology on the field of digital electronics that could potentially replace or integrate with CMOS technology and continue to power the growth of electronics industry. In this paper, we have designed and implemented a 4-Bit Radix-4 Booth Multiplier in pNML technology using MagCAD. We have designed two separate circuits; one based on AOIG representation and the other optimized using MIG manipulation techniques. The functionality of both the circuits have been verified in Xilinx ISE using the RTL files written in VHDL generated by MagCAD. The latency, critical path delay and bounding box areas are obtained for the circuits (see Tables 4, 5 and 6). The MIG optimized circuit is nearly 29% faster than the AOIG based circuit and has 10% lesser critical path delay and 40% lesser bounding box area. We have shown the feasibility of MIG transformation rules for the optimization of majority logic-based networks in terms of area, delay, and power. We have shown the feasibility of multi-layer layout for modified Booth Multiplier in pNML technology. Further research must be carried out to explore advantages offered by pNML technology.

References

1. Roadmap, I.T.R.S. International Technology Roadmap for Semiconductors 2.0 (ITRS2. 0). Semiconductor Industry Association. http://www.itrs2.net/2013-itrs.html (2015)

2. Riente, F., Turvani, G., Vacca, M., Roch, M.R., Zamboni, M., Graziano, M.: Topolinano: a CAD tool for nano magnetic logic. IEEE Trans. Comput. Aided Des. Integr. Circuits Syst. **36**(7), 1061–1074 (2017)

3. Agarwal, S., Harish, G., Balamurugan, S., Marimuthu, R.: Design of high speed 5: 2 and 7: 2 compressor using nanomagnetic logic. In: International Symposium on VLSI Design and Test, pp. 49–60. Springer, Singapore (2018). https://doi.org/10.1007/978-981-13-5950-7_5

4. Kumar, S., Marimuthu, R., Balamurugan, S.: Design and analysis of 4-bit squarer circuit using minority and majority logic in MagCAD. In: Das, K.N., Bansal, J.C., Deep, K., Nagar, A.K., Pathipooranam, P., Naidu, R.C. (eds.) Soft Computing for Problem Solving. AISC, vol. 1057, pp. 409–417. Springer, Singapore (2020). https://doi.org/10.1007/978-981-15-0184-5_36

5. Riente, F., Garlando, U., Turvani, G., Vacca, M., Roch, M.R., Graziano, M.: MagCAD: tool for the design of 3-D magnetic circuits. IEEE J. Exploratory Solid-State Comput. Devices Circuits **3**, 65–73 (2017)

6. Kang, J.Y., Gaudiot, J.L.: A simple high-speed multiplier design. IEEE Trans. Comput. **55**(10), 1253–1258 (2006)

7. Liu, W., Qian, L., Wang, C., Jiang, H., Han, J., Lombardi, F.: Design of approximate radix-4 booth multipliers for error-tolerant computing. IEEE Trans. Comput. **66**(8), 1435–1441 (2017)

8. Amaru, L., Gaillardon, P.E., De Micheli, G.: Majority-inverter graph: a new paradigm for logic optimization. IEEE Trans. Comput. Aided Des. Integr. Circuits Syst. **35**(5), 806–819 (2015)

9. Almatrood, A., Singh, H.: A comparative study of majority/minority logic circuit synthesis methods for post-CMOS nanotechnologies. Engineering **9**(10), 890 (2017)

10. Turvani, G., Riente, F., Plozner, E., Vacca, M., Graziano, M., Gamm, S.B.V.: A PNML compact model enabling the exploration of 3D architectures. IEEE Trans. Nanotechnol. **99**, 1 (2017)

11. Becherer, M., Csaba, G., Porod, W., Emling, R., Lugli, P., Schmitt-Landsiedel, D.: Magnetic ordering of focused-ion-beam structured cobalt-platinum dots for field-coupled computing. IEEE Trans. Nanotechnol. **7**(3), 316–320 (2008)

12. Niemier, M.T., et al.: Nanomagnet logic: progress toward system-level integration. J. Phys. Condens. Matter **23**(49), 493202 (2011)

13. Turvani, G., et al.: Efficient and reliable fault analysis methodology for nanomagnetic circuits. Int. J. Circuit Theory Appl. **45**(5), 660–680 (2017)

14. Kuang, S.R., Wang, J.P., Guo, C.Y.: Modified booth multipliers with a regular partial product array. IEEE Trans. Circuits Syst. II Express Briefs **56**(5), 404–408 (2009)

15. Chaitanya, C.V. and Kumar, P. Design and Analysis of Booth Multiplier with Optimised Power Delay Product. In: International Conference on Computer Communication and Informatics (ICCCI), pp. 1–6. IEEE (2018)

16. Amaru, L.G.: New Data Structures and Algorithms for Logic Synthesis and Verification. Springer, Cham (2017). https://doi.org/10.1007/978-3-319-43174-1

17. Riente, F., Melis, D., Vacca, M.: Exploring the 3-D integrability of perpendicular nanomagnet logic technology. IEEE Trans. Very Large Scale Integr. Syst. **27**, 1711–1719 (2019)

Transmission Gate Based PFD Free of Glitches for Fast Locking PLL with Reduced Reference Spur

Radhika Singh[1]($\boxtimes$), K. K. Abdul Majeed[1] (iD), and Umakanta Nanda[2]

[1] Department of Micro and Nanotechnology, School of SENSE, VIT Vellore, Vellore 632014, India
[2] School of Electronics Engineering, VIT-AP University Amaravati, Amaravati 52223, India

Abstract. This work has been paying attention to design and implement a Transmission gate phase frequency detector (TG-PFD) for Fast locking and low Reference Spur PLL working in Giga-Hertz choice. It has been experiential that the projected TG-PFD could completely erase delay for reset thereby eliminating dead region and blind region as well. By inclusion of the transmission gate into the PFD, could enhance the magnitude of the output signal and hence could improve the loop band and obtained a PLL with reduced locking time. Leakage current minimized as a result of adding CMOS inverters at the output of the TG-PFD and thereby obtained better reference spur for the Phase Locked Loop implemented using TG-PFD. Reference Spur of -77.2 dBc, locking time of 2.83 μs have been obtained for the designed PLL using projected TG-PFD in 180 nm CMOS technology which is exactly matching with the mathematical analysis done by this paper.

Keywords: Transmission Gate Phase Frequency Detector (TG-PFD) · Dead zone · Blind zone · Loop bandwidth

1 Introduction

PLL is a closed-loop feedback system that is an essential and effective tool used for detection and tracking of desired frequency signal vital for large scope vehicles its area ranges from satellites to interstellar ships [1–4]. Figure 1 represents the basic building block of PLL and it consists of five different blocks. For better performance of PLL like low power, low phase noise, fast lock-in, and low reference spur it's important to develop and optimize each block individually [5, 6]. For designing Charge pump circuit less phase offset is adaptable and with less leakage current [7]. VCO has one of the other significant factors in optimizing the phase noise of the Phase Locked Loop structure as it has been found to be one of central sources for out of band phase noise [8]. The PLL working is to lock the reference signal through clock VCO output signal.

Phase Frequency Detector is vital essential block of PLL, which acting a key role in determining its acquisition time and reference spur [9, 10]. It detect phase error between CLK_{ref} signal and CLK_{vco} signals which gives output in the form of a voltage that

© Springer Nature Singapore Pte Ltd. 2021
V. Arunachalam and K. Sivasankaran (Eds.): ICMDCS 2021, CCIS 1392, pp. 404–414, 2021.
https://doi.org/10.1007/978-981-16-5048-2_32

depends on the signal's phase difference. UP signal and DN signal are the output of Phase Frequency Detector at growing edge of reference signal "UP" goes to logic high and it stills continues being high logic till the growing edge of the VCO output signal. "DN" goes logic high at the growing edge of the VCO output signal and stays logic high till the reference signal goes high. When both the signals are at a rising edge "UP" and "DN" both go to zero. There are techniques to reach up to zero value of UP and DN earlier there was a separately reset circuit to reset the PFD. Conventional linear PFDs with reset circuit [11–16] has proposed earlier for function; though, as they may source very less gain, glitches at the output, very precise loop bandwidth, bigger acquisition time and very huge reference spur, linear PFD without separate reset circuit would be a possible alternative.

In these work the reset is done without any separate circuit and also able to reduce the glitches at output by the use of transmission gate and CMOS inverter.

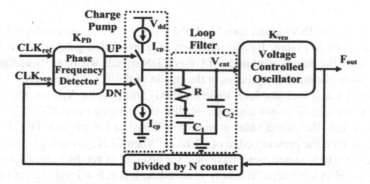

Fig. 1. Simple block diagram of phase locked loop

1.1 Traditional Phase Frequency Detector

Conventional functional diagram of a PFD and its transfer characteristics is shown in Fig. 2. Delay for the reset circuitry in a PFD may cause dead zone and blind zone [10–16] in its transfer characteristics it generate larger lock-in time for the PLL. In transfer characteristic of conventional PFD there is flat line near to 0° and near 360° phase difference that represents Dead zone and Blind zone respectively. There are many PFD circuits has been proposed [10] where Dead zone region & Blind zone region has been minimized [9]. Spikes are there at the output of the phase frequency detector can mislead the value of UP signal and DN signal[10] and that UP voltage value and DN voltage value may not be proportional to the phase difference of the reference input signal and VCO output signal. This would lock the PLL into undesirable phase and frequency and it may also cause to raise leakage current.

2 Proposed Transmission Gate Based PFD (TG-PFD) Design

Transistor level implementation of Transmission gate based PFD (TG-PFD) design is depicted in Fig. 3. It consists of four transmission gate (TG$_1$ to TG$_4$), eight CMOS

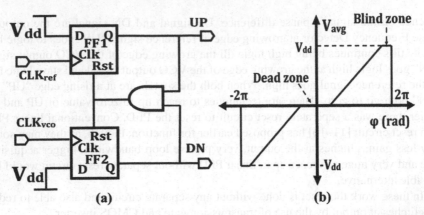

Fig. 2. (a) Traditional PFD architecture (b) Transfer characteristics of traditional PFD

inverters (INV1 to INV8), and four N-MOSFETs (N_1 to N_4) are connected in such a fashion as given in Figure. By the inclusion of transmission gate in to the TG-PFD, could increase the output magnitude of UP and DN signals where as by adding CMOS inverters could eliminate the glitches at the output of the TG-PFD as well.

Initially CLK_{ref} is at low level logic then TG_1 will pass the V_{dd} and that will store at node 'a' because N_1 nmos transistor is OFF and at rising edge of CLK_{ref} TG_1 will not be activated. The stored value at node a will pass at UP through TG_2. UP will be at high state until the growing edge of CLK_{vco}. When CLK_{vco} is at high level logic N_2 nmos transistor turn on and these make path for node 'b' to get discharged the value and make UP equal to logic zero. Similarly when CLK_{vco} is at low level logic it turn on the TG_3 and V_{dd} stored at node 'd' and N_2 nmos turn off and there is no path to ground so UP remain at its previous value. When CLK_{vco} is at high level logic transmission gate TG_4 will be on and TG_3 get off but the value stored at node 'd' will pass through node 'e' and DN equals to high logic state and now N_2 nmos turn on and make UP equal to zero. If at the same time CLK_{ref} is at high level logic these make DN immediately logic zero by making N_4 nmos transistor turn on. So in this way these proposed PFD reset when both UP signal and DN signal are high level logic simultaneously. There is no need of reset circuitry to reset PFD as logic gate is used to reset the Conventional PFD. By inclusion of transmission gate could increase the b, e node voltages in to maximum and hence could enhance the TG-PFD gain. By adding CMOS inverters, "INV1 to INV4" and by the inclusion of a direct reset processing technique with a minimum delay could eliminate the glitches at the output of UP signal and DN signal and hence could minimize the leakage current.

When both CLK_{ref} and CLK_{vco} are at high level logic, reset process is initiated through N1, N2, N3 and N4 NMOS transistors due to its unique reset technique it reduces the reset delay as a result dead zone & blind zone & glitches are eliminated which results in reducing leakage current and improved PFD gain.

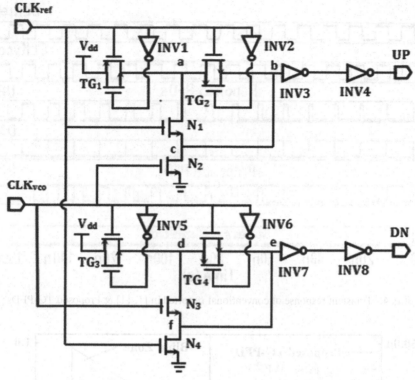

Fig. 3. Proposed transmission gate based PFD (TG-PFD)

2.1 Analysis of Proposed TG-PFD

Transient analysis of proposed TG-PFD has been done using "CADENCE" 180 nm technology with input voltage (V_{dd}) of 1.8 V and it show in Fig. 4. It has been noted from Fig. 4 that whenever CLK_{ref} is leading than CLK_{vco}, UP and DN signal voltage value is directly proportional to phase difference of these two signals. When CLK_{ref} signal leads CLK_{vco} signal pulse width of UP signal will be increasing simultaneously pulse width of DN signal will decrease and the vice versa happens when CLK_{vco} signal leads the CLK_{ref} signal. The transient analysis of traditional PFD reported in [10, 16] are also depicted in Fig. 4 there spikes are present in UP signal and DN signal where as it can be seen the spikes are totally removed from the proposed TG-PFD. Transfer characteristics plot also tells the presence of dead zone and blind zone, it can be seen that the proposed TG-PFD eliminated that zones and gives linear characteristic for the entire range of phase difference from 0° to 360°. When the input CLK_{ref} signal and CLK_{vco} signal are at high level logic, directly used to initiate the reset process of proposed TG-PFD through NMOS transistors from N1 to N4 which reaches to zero to UP and DN voltages value (Fig. 5).

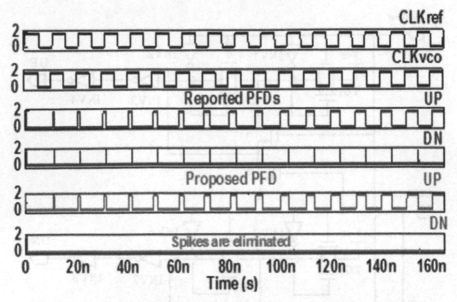

Fig. 4. Transient response of conventional reported in [1, 11] & Proposed TG-PFDs

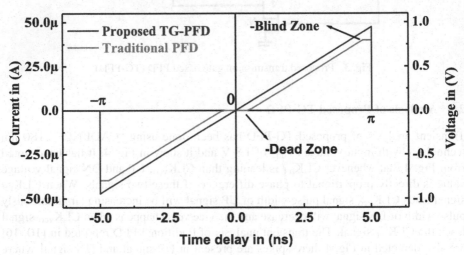

Fig. 5. Transfer characteristic of traditional PFD and planned TG-PFD simulated by cadence.

2.2 PLL Leakage Current

Reference spur is one of the important parameter of PLL which will be mainly determined by the leakage current generated from the PFD + Charge Pump block during the lock-in condition of PLL. When the PLL is in a Lock-in position, there should not be any UP and DN signal but practically on conventional PFD, there is a little amount of UP and DN signal spikes are generating as depicted in Fig. 6. These spikes deviates the performance of PLL because the Charge pump would generate a minute leakage current due to the glitches at the output of the PFD. That may cause spurious tones at the output of the spectrum of the PLL. The implemented TG-PFD is able to abolish spikes at UP and DN on the Lock-in position so there will not be any leakage current in the case of the proposed TG-PFD.

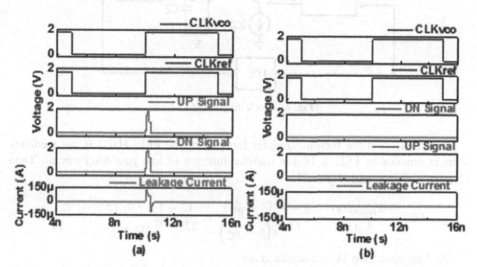

Fig. 6. PFD + CP block leakage current analysis of (a) traditional PFD + charge pump block and (b) Proposed TG-PFD + charge pump

3   Performance Analysis of PLL Implemented using TG-PFD

Fundamental working diagram of the PLL architecture is depicted in Fig. 8 and the closed loop transfer function of PLL using proposed Transmission gate based PFD has been found out in order to compare the step response obtained from transfer function with that from CADENCE circuit simulation result (Fig. 7).

3.1   Loop Gain $L_0(s)$

Open loop gain $L_0(s)$ can be determined by equation of open loop transfer function [8]. In this design, divider ratio N is equal to 128, to get stable PLL, high loop bandwidth (BW). The values of the resistor (R), capacitor (C) and b of lowpass filter components is 1 kΩ, 277 pF and 12 respectively the values of $K_{vco} = 20$ GradV^{-1}, and $K_{pc} = 23.87e^{-6}$.

The loop gain, $L_0(s)$ for the configuration of the PLL using TG-PFD is given in Fig. 1 could be determined from the standard equation as

$$L_o(s) = G1(s)H1(s) \tag{1}$$

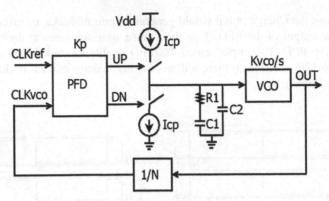

Fig. 7. Block diagram of PLL

Where $G_1(s)$ is the forward transfer function of the PLL, $H1(s)$ is the feedback transfer function of PLL & $F(s)$ is transfer function of low pass filter circuit. Then $G(s) = \frac{kpckvcoF(s)}{s}$ and $H(s) = \frac{1}{N}$

$$F(s) = \frac{V_{control}(s)}{I_{cp}(s)} = \frac{b-1}{C} \frac{\left(s + \frac{1}{RC}\right)}{s\left(s + \frac{b}{RC}\right)} = \frac{12-1}{277e^{-12}} \frac{s + \frac{1}{1e^3 \times 277e^{-12}}}{s(s + \frac{12}{1e^3 \times 277e^{-12}})} \qquad (2)$$

And the open loop TF as calculated as:

$$L_o(s) = \frac{K_{pc}K_{vco}(b-1)}{Nc} \frac{s + \frac{1}{RC}}{s^2(s + \frac{b}{RC})} = \frac{23.87e^{-6} \times 20e^9(12-1)}{128 \times 277e^{-12}} \frac{s + \frac{1}{1e^3 \times 277e^{-12}}}{s^2(s + \frac{12}{1e^3 \times 277e^{-12}})}$$

$$(3)$$

Loop band width of the designed Phase Locked Loop architecture is normally determined as the unity gain frequency (ω_c) [9, 10] which could be defined from open loop transfer function $L_o(s)$. The constant values are substituted as from the reference [17]. The reference frequency CLK$_{ref}$ = 20 MHz and N = 128 to get stable PLL and high loop bandwidth.

By applying the values of I_{CP} = 150 μA, C = 227p Farad, R = 1k Ω, b = 12, N = 128, K_{vco} = 20 GradV^{-1}, & K_{pc} = 23.87 ΩA/rad Eq. (3) could be expressed as:

$$L_o(s) = \frac{1.48e^{14}s + 5.3469e^{20}}{s^3 + 43.32e^6 s^2} \qquad (4)$$

Plot the bode plot of the Eq. (4) and obtained the Unity gain frequency or loop band width is found to be 700 kHz, is given in Fig. 8.

From (3), as $L_o(s)$ consists of 2 pole at origin, and phase margin could be asserted as transfer function zero and pole ($\tau_p = b \ \tau_z = b/(RC)$) as

$$\phi_m(\omega) = tan^l(\omega_c \tau_z) - tan^l(\omega_c \tau_p) = 44.89° \qquad (5)$$

The proposed phase margin of open loop transfer function of designed Phase Looked Loop is equal to 44.89°, it is constant throughout the entire PLL operation and hence we can say that PLL is stable.

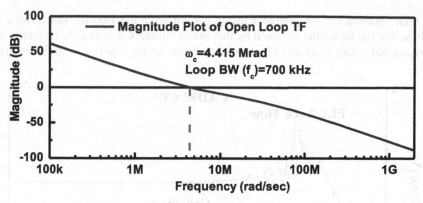

Fig. 8. Open loop TF of phase locked loop using TG-PFD

3.2 Closed Loop TF

The acquisition time could be calculated from the bode plot of Closed loop transfer function and it could be expressed as

$$TF = \frac{NK_{pc}K_{vco}F(s)}{Ns + K_{pc}K_{vco}F(s)}$$

Substitute the values of Eq. (2) in the above equation then

$$TF = T_c(s) = \frac{437e^6s + 1.579e^{15}}{2.305e^{-8}s^3 + s^2 + 3.414e^6s + 1.23e^{13}} \tag{6}$$

Step response for the Eq. (6) has plotted in MATLAB and it is depicted in Fig. 9. The acquisition time or locking time has calculated as 2.85 μs. Node voltage from PLL block diagram V_{cnt} has plotted in Fig. 10 and acquisition time or locking time of 2.83 μs

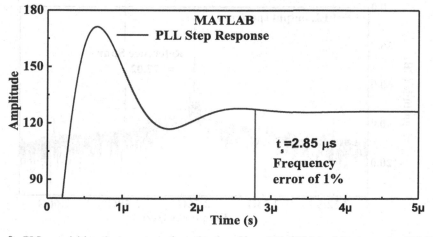

Fig. 9. PLL acquisition time response from the closed loop TF of PLL architecture using TG-PFD

has been obtained for 1% tolerance and it is clear from the Fig. 10. Hence we could analyze that the lock time obtained by the circuit simulation is exactly matching with the mathematical analysis and which is much better results reported in the literature.

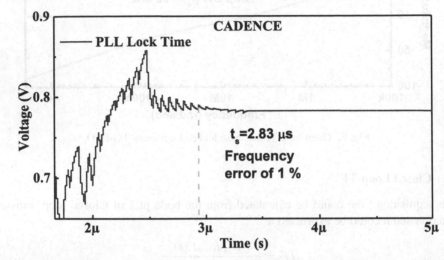

Fig. 10. Transient response of control voltage in CADENCE for the PLL using TG-PFD

3.3 Output Spectrum of PLL Using TG-PFD

The PLL architecture using TG-PFD has modeled by "CADENCE Virtuoso" using 180 nm technology. It's output spectrum is to be analyzed in order to calculate its reference spur. PLL spectrum given in Fig. 11 and the reference spur could be about − 77.02 dBc at 20 MHz offset.

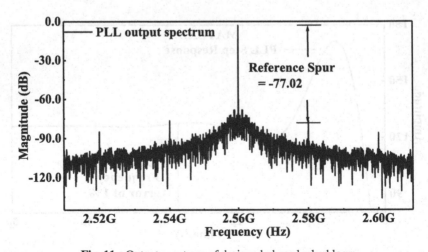

Fig. 11. Output spectrum of designed phase locked loop

Table 1. Comparison table of PLL parameters of proposed and reported work

Parameter	[5]	[6]	[1]	[13]	[14]	[15]	[16]	[17]	This work
Technology	180	180	180	350	65	180	600	180	180
N	128	128	128	32	44	48	300	64	8
Loop BW (MHz)	–	0.9	0.7	0.12	5	0.5	2	0.4	0.7
Lock time (μs)	1.548	1.753	2.95	18	4	21 m	–	20	2.77
Reference spur	−72.2	−56.7	−75.92	–	−41	−55	–	−54	−77.2

4 Conclusion

A simple transmission gate based phase frequency detector (TG-PFD) has been proposed here. It has been noted that the designed TG-PFD could completely eliminate the reset delay by adopting direct resetting circuitry that could eliminate dead zone and blind zone from its transfer characteristics. By the inclusion of the transmission gate into the PFD, could observe that there is an enhancement in its output magnitude and the output glitches have been eliminated by the cascaded CMOS inverter. And hence the proposed TG-PFD is one of the best choices for the PLL to have fast lock-in as well for better reference spur and it is very clear from the Table 1. Reference Spur of −77.2 dBc and lock-in time of 2.83 μs are obtained for the PLL architecture using designed TG-PFD has been designed using 180 nm CMOS technology which is exactly matching with the mathematical analysis done by this paper.

References

1. Abdul Majeed, K.K., Kailath, B.J.: Low power PLL with reduced reference spur realized with glitch-free linear PFD and current splitting CP. Analog Integr. Circ. Sig. Process. **93**(1), 29–39 (2017). https://doi.org/10.1007/s10470-017-1013-4
2. Nanda, U., Acharya, D.P.: Adaptive PFD selection technique for low noise and fast PLL in multi- standard radios. Microelectron. J. **64**, 92–98. Elsevier (2017)
3. Nanda, U., Acharya, D.P., Nayak, D., Rout, P.K.: High performance PLL for multiband GSM applications. Int. J. Nanoparticles Inderscience **10**(3), 244–258 (2018)
4. Nanda, U., Acharya, D.P., Nayak, D.: Process variation tolerant wide-band fast PLL with reduced phase noise using ADCC strategy. Int. J. Electron. **108**(5), 705–717. Taylor and Francis (2020)
5. Kuppalath, A.M.K., Kailath, B.J.: Nonlinear PFD free of glitches and blind zone for a fast locking PLL with reduced reference spur. IEICE Electron. Express **13**(2016), 20160328 (2016)
6. Abdul Majeed, K.K., Kailath, B.J.: Analysis and design of low power nonlinear PFD architectures for a fast locking PLL. In: 2016 IEEE Students' Technology Symposium (TechSym), Kharagpur, 2016, pp. 136–140 (2016)
7. Nanda, U., Acharya, D.P., Patra, S.K.: A new transmission gate cascode current mirror charge pump for fast locking low noise PLL. Circ. Syst. Sig. Process. **33**(9), 2709–2718 (2014). https://doi.org/10.1007/s00034-014-9785-6

8. Abdul Majeed, K.K., Kailath, B.J.: CMOS current starved voltage controlled oscillator circuit for a fast locking PLL. In: 2015 Annual IEEE India Conference (INDICON), New Delhi, 2015, pp. 1–5(2015)

9. Abdul Majeed, K.K., Kailath, B.J.: PLL architecture with a composite PFD and variable loop filter. IET Circ. Devices Syst. 12(3), 256–262 (2018)

10. Kailath, B.J., Majeed, K.K.: Composite PFD based low-power, low noise, fast lock-in PLL. Materials Circuits and Devices. VLSI Post-CMOS Electron. Volume 1: Des. Model. Simul. Chap. 6, pp. 135–157 (2019)

11. Abdul Majeed, K.K., Kailath, B.J.: A novel phase frequency detector for a high frequency PLL design. Procedia Eng. 64, 377–384 (2013)

12. Majeed, K.K.A., Kailath, B.J.: Low power, high frequency, free dead zone PFD for a PLL design. In: 2013 IEEE Faible Tension Faible Consommation, Paris, pp. 1–4 (2013)

13. Nanda, U., Acharya, D.P.: An efficient technique for low power fast locking PLL operating in minimized dead zone condition. In: IEEE International Conference on Devices for Integrated Circuits, 23–24 March, pp. 396–400 (2017)

14. Nanda, U., Acharya, D.P., Patra, S.K.: Design of an efficient phase frequency detector to reduce blind zone in a PLL. Microsyst. Technol. 23(3), 533–539 (2016). https://doi.org/10. 1007/s00542-016-2970-8

15. Nanda, U., Acharya, D.P., Patra, S.K.: Low noise and fast locking PLL using a variable delay element in the phase frequency detector. J. Low Power Electron. Am. Sci. Publishers 10, 53–57 (2014)

16. Taheri, S., Ghaderi, N., Amani, A.: A new high speed phase detection circuit with π phase difference detection. In: ICEE (2017)

17. Gardner, F.M.: Charge-pump phase-lock loops. IEEE Trans. Commun. 28(11), 1849–1858 (1980)

18. Yang, C.-Y., Liu, S.-I.: Fast-switching frequency synthesizer with a discriminator-aided phase detector. IEEE J. Solid-State Circ. 35(10), 1445–1452 (2000)

19. Hsu, C.-W., Tripurari, K., Yu, S.-A., Kinget, P.R.: A sub-sampling-assisted phase-frequency detector for low-noise PLLs with robust operation under supply interference. IEEE Trans. Circ. Syst. I Regul. Pap. 62(1), 90–99 (2015)

20. Huang, P.-C., Chang, W.-S., Lee, T.-C.: 21.2 A2.3 GHz fractional-N divider less phase-locked loop with-112dBc/Hz in-band phase noise. In: IEEE International Solid State Circuits Conference Digest of Technical Papers, 9–13 February, vol. 9, no. 13, pp. 362–363 (2014)

21. Lim, K., Park, C.-H., Kim, D.-S., Kim, B: A low-noise PLL design by loop BW optimization. IEEE J. Solid State Circ. 35(6), 807–815 (2000)

22. Woo, K., Liu, Y., Nam, E., Ham, D.: Fast-lock hybrid PLL combining fractional-N and Integer-N modes of differing bandwidths. IEEE J. Solid-State Circ. 43(2), 379–389 (2008)

Electronics for Green Technology

A Highly Sensitive Gold-TiO2 Coated Dual-Core PCF-SPR Sensor with a Large Detection Range

Sanjida Sultana[1], Md. Faiyaz Bin Haassan[1], Shovasis Kumar Biswas[2], and Hriteshwar Talukder[1]([⊠])

[1] Department of Electrical and Electronic Engineering, Shahjalal University of Science and Technology, Sylhet, Bangladesh
hriteshwar-eee@sust.edu

[2] Department of Electrical and Electronic Engineering, Independent University, Dhaka, Bangladesh

Abstract. This study is based on the design and numerical investigation of a high-accuracy plasmonic biosensor. A dual-core Photonic Crystal Fiber (PCF) has been designed to obtain superior characteristics to its kindred. As for the plasmonic layer, a thin layer of titanium dioxide over a layer of gold has been used both of which contribute to the occurrence of Surface Plasmon Resonance (SPR). Circular airholes positioned in a rectangular manner pave the way to light entrapment. A Perfectly Matched layer (PML) is placed to help absorb the reflected light. The analysis of this structure's performance was carried out considering the wavelength and amplitude sensitivity, the figure of merit (FOM), and the sensor resolution. The values go as fine as 22,000 nm/RIU for wavelength sensitivity, 3446 RIU^{-1} for amplitude sensitivity, and 4.54×10^{-6} for the sensor's resolution. Also, the maximum FOM found is 241.76 RIU^{-1}. The proposed structure, where the external sensing technique is used, shows excellent micro-scale sensing properties. To achieve such attributes, different structural parameters like pitch, gold and TiO_2 thickness, and air-hole diameters were altered. Keeping in mind the feasibility of fabrication, the design was kept simple while balancing the optimum properties.

Keywords: Surface plasmon resonance · Polariton · Sensitivity · Confinement loss · Fabrication · Sensor resolution

1 Introduction

The quantum of the continuous oscillation of plasma is known as plasmon. These plasmons generate surface plasmonic waves (SPW) along the surface. The coupling of this plasmon with a photon i.e., an optical oscillation creates another particle named polariton. The polariton that travels along a metal-dielectric surface is known as surface plasmon polariton (SPP). SPPs are excited by both photons and electrons. A photon excites an SPP when both the frequency and the momentum of the photon and SPP match identically. The phenomenon of surface plasmon resonance (SPR) abides by this theory. SPR was first numerically demonstrated by Ritchie et al. in 1957 [1]. Later on, Kretschmann

© Springer Nature Singapore Pte Ltd. 2021
V. Arunachalam and K. Sivasankaran (Eds.): ICMDCS 2021, CCIS 1392, pp. 417–429, 2021.
https://doi.org/10.1007/978-981-16-5048-2_33

built an SPR sensor based on prism coupling [2]. He used a light beam on one surface of the prism to pole-polarize and to reflect on the metal surface. This method is known as prism coupling and has been used worldwide. Leidberg et al. theoretically found the SPRs [3]. For this, he conducted the same prism-coupling technique in 1983 [2].

When resonance occurs, a sharp Gaussian peak for the confinement loss of the core-guided light is observed for a specific analyte refractive index (RI). Generally, Gold (Au), Silver (Ag), TiO_2, Copper (Cu) etc. are used as metal conductor layer. A dielectric material is introduced along with the surface of the metal layer to create an environment for SPR phenomenon. A liquid or gaseous material is inserted as the analyte and it generally has RIs ranging from 1 to 2.5.

Although prism coupling method to induce SPR is robust, it's hard to implement this process for its bulkiness, complexity, and heavy weight. To overcome these issues, R.C. Jorgenson first introduced SPR-based photonic crystal fiber (PCF) sensors in 1993 [4]. Photonic crystal fibers are a type of optical fiber with airholes introduced in the cladding instead of a solid silica glass. The air holes are arranged in such a manner that the guided light gets trapped inside the intended core using the air hole-silica boundary. When light falls on the air hole-silica boundary in a specific angle, the total internal reflection phenomenon occurs and light gets reflected back to core instead of refracting through air medium. The reflected light then falls on another hole-silica interface and reflects back into the core using the same principles. A well-organized arrangement can trap this guided light inside the core. This simple phenomenon is the main principle while designing and fabricating a PCF. The popular hole arrangements of PCFs are circular, hexagonal, rectangular, pentagonal, and hybrid. A specific area of the PCF gets filled with analyte and a thin metal layer is introduced between the silica glass and the analyte so that the SPR occurs. Silver (Ag) is extensively used as the plasmonic metal for creating sharp loss peak though it gets oxidized easily and isn't chemically stable [5]. The chemical instability increases the chances of chemical reaction between the analyte and silver layer. Therefore, the use of gold is much appreciated since gold provides higher stability.

There are two ways of coating a PCF with a plasmonic layer. The internal coating generally uses one or two air holes as analyte channels, and the metal layer surrounds these air holes to create plasmonic modes. In external coating, the gold layer surrounds the whole PCF, and the analyte cavity surrounds the whole structure. Rifat et al. designed an internally coated PCF sensor with maximum wavelength sensitivity (WS) of 3000 nm/RIU and a maximum amplitude sensitivity (AS) of 418 RIU^{-1} in 2015 [6]. Z. Fan et al. designed a internally coated PCF-SPR sensor which had WS of 7040 nm/RIU [7]. Rifat et al. designed another PCF sensor with internal coating with much better sensing capability in 2018 [8]. This sensor's max WS was 11000 nm/RIU and AS was 1420 RIU^{-1}. The number of externally coated PCFs is much higher because this approach is easier to fabricate than the internal-sensing technique. Sanjida et al. designed an open-channel structure which has 5000 nm/RIU WS [9]. Md. Nazmus Sakib et al. designed a circularly-slotted PCF which had WS of 16000 nm/RIU and AS of 780 RIU^{-1} [10]. A lot of research has been done on externally-coated photonic crystal fibers [11–13, 15]. The objective of this study is the further improvement and development in the structure and sensing capability of the PCFs. A new structure with higher sensing capability and relatively lower confinement loss has been proposed in this work.

In this proposed structure, two micro-channel based dual core structure has been specified by removing two air holes from the rectangular lattice. The air hole lattice is arranged in a rectangular fashion. An external coating of the gold layer with TiO$_2$ as an adhesive agent used to induce plasmonic resonance. The TiO$_2$ layer has significant effect on the sensing ability of the proposed structure. The Gold–TiO$_2$ layer is introduced in one side of the crystal. There are four leaky channels to transfer the light energy from core to plasmonic mode. The structure operates in a large RI range of 1.22–1.38 with the maximum WS of 22,000 nm/RIU in the RI range of 1.37–1.38. The maximum AS found is 3446 RIU^{-1} for the same range of analyte RI. This modified structure shows much better overall sensitivity profile compared to the other available structures.

2 Geometric Structure and Modeling

The design of our photonic crystal fiber is given in Fig. (1). This structure has a 4×5 rectangular lattice. The distance between two air holes i.e., pitch is $\Lambda = 3.2$ µm. Two air holes were removed to create core guided mode. Two more air holes of the last row were removed, and the diameters of two air holes near the metal layer were decreased to ensure energy transfer from core-guided mode to spp mode. The diameter of these two airholes is $d_2 = 0.36\Lambda$. The large air holes have a diameter of $d_1 = 0.5\Lambda$. The air hole between the two smaller air holes is made slightly bigger to create channels for the energy transfer. The diameter of that hole is $d_3 = 0.85\Lambda$. The circular core 6 µm from the center of the PCF has been cut for smooth transfer of energy. This side of the PCF is selectively coated with gold and TiO$_2$. The TiO$_2$ is used as an adhesive agent for the gold layer. The gold layer thickness is 50 nm. We have kept the TiO$_2$ layer to 13 nm which is significantly lower than the gold thickness.

The study of this structure was completely done by simulation and numerical evaluation. We used COMSOL Multiphysics 5.5 to simulate the structure and do the mathematical evaluations, and the graphs were created using MATLAB. A virtual perfectly matched layer (PML) was added around the structure to apply the scattering boundary conditions in the simulation. The simulation was done for 204325 number of degrees. The mesh analysis had 29164 domains and 2304 boundary elements to achieve high accuracy.

3 Theoretical Understanding of the Structure

Silica is the main material of the fiber core. The RI of silica depends on the wavelength of intended light. The effective RI of Silica can be calculated using the Sellmeier equation [16],

$$n_{eff}(\lambda) = \sqrt{1 + \frac{B_1\lambda^2}{\lambda^2 - C_1} + \frac{B_2\lambda^2}{\lambda^2 - C_2} + \frac{B_3\lambda^2}{\lambda^2 - C_3}} \tag{1}$$

The values of the constants are B1 = 0.69616300, B2 = 0.407942600, B3 = 0.897479400, C1 = 0.00467914826, C2 = 0.0135120631 and C3 = 97.9340025 for

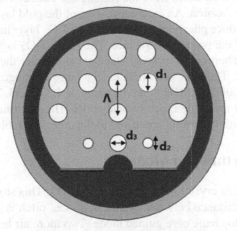

Fig. 1. Geometry of the proposed structure

silica and found experimentally. Here, n_{eff} = effective RI and λ = wavelength of the light.

From Drude-Lorentz model, the relative permittivity of the Au layer is calculated [17]. Supposing Au is the permittivity of Au and the angular frequency is ω,

$$\epsilon_{Au} = \epsilon_\infty - \frac{\omega_D^2}{\omega(\omega + j\gamma_D)} + \frac{\Delta\epsilon\Omega_L^2}{(\omega^2 - \Omega_L^2) + j\Gamma_L\omega} \tag{2}$$

The values of these parameters in the above equation are, $\epsilon_\infty = 5.9673$, $\Delta\epsilon = 1.09$, $\Gamma_L = 16.69$, $\gamma_D = 2.534$, $\Omega_L = 103.46$. Note that, $\omega = \frac{2\pi c}{\lambda}$.

The RI of TiO2 is determined using the equation below [19],

$$n_{ti} = \sqrt{5.913 + \frac{2.441 \times 10^7}{\lambda^2 - 0.803 \times 10^7}} \tag{3}$$

To analyze the performance of a PCF, the confinement loss of the core mode is a significant parameter. If L_c is the confinement loss and K_0 is the wave number, the following equation calculates the confinement loss of a structure [18],

$$L_c(dB/cm) = 8.686K_0 Im(n_{eff}) \times 10^4 \tag{4}$$

Wavelength sensitivity is the difference between the two resonant wavelengths in per unit RI difference. It can be calculated by the following equation [21],

$$S_\lambda = \frac{\Delta\lambda_{peak}}{\Delta n_a} \ (nm/RIU) \tag{5}$$

Here, Δn_a is the difference of RI of the two resonant wavelengths and $\Delta \lambda_{peak}$ is the difference of the resonant wavelengths.

Another important parameter, amplitude sensitivity is obtained from the following equation [15],

$$S_a\left(RIU^{-1}\right) = -\frac{1}{\alpha(\lambda, n_a)} \frac{\delta\alpha(\lambda, n_a)}{\delta n_a} \qquad (6)$$

The sensor resolution is the parameter that states the sensing capability of the change in the analyte RI. This is measured by the following equation [21],

$$R(RIU) = \Delta n_a \times \frac{\Delta\lambda_{min}}{\Delta\lambda_{peak}} \qquad (7)$$

where Δn_a is the change in analyte RI. Another key parameter to calculate the detection capability is the figure of merit (FOM) of the PCF. It is calculated by [10],

$$FOM = \frac{m(nm/RIU)}{FWHM\,(nm)} \qquad (8)$$

Higher FOM means higher spectral width, which means the structure has a higher detection limit.

4 Result Analysis

The simulation was run for the parameters $d_1 = 0.5\Lambda$, $d_2 = 0.33\Lambda$, $d_3 = 0.55\Lambda$ and $\Lambda = 3.2\,\mu m$. The gold and TiO_2 layers have thicknesses of 50 nm and 13 nm respectively. The mesh analysis is done within 29164 domains and 2304 boundary elements.

Figure (2) shows different guided mode where Fig. (2a) demonstrates core-guided mode, Fig. (2b) shows spp modes, and Fig. (2c) shows the resonance condition. Under resonance condition, the real part of both the core guided and plasmonic mode effective RI are equal.

We took the step size of 0.01 RIU while sweeping through the total analyte RI range which means $\Delta n_a = 0.01$. The $\Delta \lambda_{peak}$ means the difference of the gaussian peak's wavelength of two consecutive analyte RIs. Figure (3a) demonstrates the resonant situation with confinement loss curve. At resonance condition, the spp modes and the core mode intersect. The resonant wavelengths or peak locations are shown in Fig. (3b). The curve joining the resonant wavelengths is non-linear and rather exponential which demonstrates a steady increase of WS with the increment of analyte RI.

Moreover, the sharp peak of confinement loss curve occurs at the wavelength where the spp and core mode intersect. This satisfies the condition of Gaussian peak occurring under the resonant condition.

The structure functions within a long range analyte RI- from 1.22 to 1.38. The confinement loss (CL) is very minimal at the lower RIs and increases gradually as the RI increases. The loss curve reaches its highest at $n_a = 1.37$ and then decreases at $n_a = 1.38$. The highest loss recorded for this structure is 87.83 db/cm at 1.37 analyte RI. Figure (4) shows all the CL curves for analyte RI in the range of 1.22–1.38. The structure

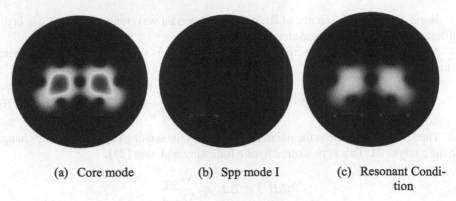

(a) Core mode   (b) Spp mode I   (c) Resonant Condi-
                                                      tion

Fig. 2. Different modes of the guided light

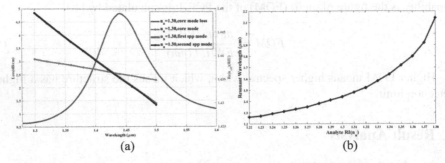

(a)   (b)

Fig. 3. (a) Core and spp mode intersection at resonance, (b) Resonant wavelength curve

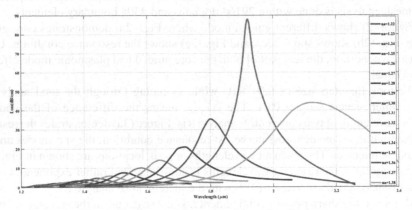

Fig. 4. Confinement loss curve for analyte RI sweep

breaks down before $n_a = 1.22$ and after $n_a = 1.38$. A key sensitivity factor- the AS of this structure is shown in Fig. (5).

The AS curves show a gradual increase of AS as the analyte RI increases. The AS is maxed out in the range of 1.37–1.38 and the maximum value of this AS is 3446 RIU^{-1}.

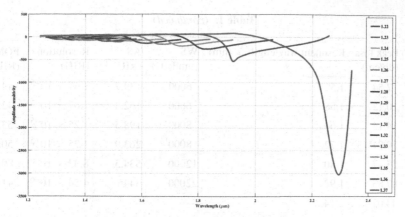

Fig. 5. Amplitude sensitivity curve for analyte RI

Using the Eq. (5), the wavelength sensitivity has been calculated for the total RI range. The lowest WS is 1000 nm/RIU for 1.22–1.23. It starts increasing with the increase in RI and the maximum WS found is 22000 nm/RIU for RI shift of 1.37–1.38. All the AS and WS data are summarized in Table (1). The sensor resolution is a key factor to detect the minimum sensing range for the slightest change of analyte RI. Using the Eq. (7), sensor resolutions have been calculated. The value gets as low as 4.54×10^{-6} for 1.37 to 1.38. That means the sensor can sense and detect the change of 10^{-6} order in the analyte RI.

Figure (8) demonstrate the change of FOM with the change of RI. The highest FOM recorded here is 241.76 RIU^{-1} for 1.37–1.38 shift. All the data found are summarized in Table 1, which gives a brief detail on the performance of the sensor.

Table 1. Results of RI sweep for x-polarized light

RI	Peak loss (db/cm)	Resonant wavlength, λ (nm)	WS (nm/RIU)	AS (RIU^{-1})	Resolution (RIU)	FOM (RIU^{-1})
1.22	1.403	1.26	1000	53.76	1×10^{-4}	13.33
1.23	1.59	1.27	2000	57.58	5×10^{-5}	21.51
1.24	1.8531	1.29	2000	62.27	5×10^{-5}	23.26
1.25	2.129	1.31	2000	67.97	5×10^{-5}	22.22
1.26	2.458	1.33	2000	74.6	5×10^{-5}	21.28
1.27	2.854	1.35	3000	82.03	3.33×10^{-5}	30.61
1.28	3.334	1.38	3000	84.89	3.33×10^{-5}	28.85
1.29	3.948	1.41	3000	98.85	3.33×10^{-5}	27.03
1.30	4.813	1.44	4000	110.4	2.5×10^{-5}	34.19
1.31	5.937	1.48	4000	119.35	2.5×10^{-5}	32.00

(continued)

Table 1. (*continued*)

RI	Peak loss (db/cm)	Resonant wavlength, λ (nm)	WS (nm/RIU)	AS (RIU⁻¹)	Resolution (RIU)	FOM (RIU⁻¹)
1.32	7.54	1.52	6000	139.7	1.67×10^{-5}	44.44
1.33	10.12	1.58	6000	162.3	1.67×10^{-5}	42.55
1.34	14.14	1.64	8000	198.5	1.25×10^{-5}	53.69
1.35	20.94	1.72	8000	263.9	1.25×10^{-5}	50.96
1.36	35.47	1.80	12000	534.5	8.33×10^{-6}	80.00
1.37	87.83	1.92	22000	3446	4.54×10^{-6}	241.76
1.38	44.02	2.14	–	–	–	–

5   Performance Analysis by Varying Geometric Parameters

5.1   Effects of Varying Air Hole Diameters

Variation of d_1

The simulation was run for $d_1 = 0.4\Lambda$ and $d_1 = 0.5\Lambda$ and the results are displayed in Fig. (6). Figure (6a) shows the confinement loss, and Fig. (6b) shows the AS of the structure. For $n_a = 1.37$, The loss is 19.4 db/cm for $d_1 = 0.4\Lambda$. Confinement loss increased to 47.61 db/cm for $d_1 = 0.5\Lambda$.

On the other hand, the amplitude sensitivity rises from 684.2 RIU⁻¹ to 1276 RIU⁻¹ for $d_1 = 0.4\Lambda$ and $d_1 = 0.5\Lambda$ respectively. The loss and amplitude sensitivity both increased with the increase in diameter of the air hole.

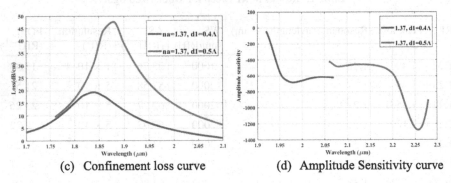

(c) Confinement loss curve   (d) Amplitude Sensitivity curve

Fig. 6. Change in confinement loss and amplitude sensitivity due to varying d_1

Variation of d2

The diameter d_2 is varied in the range of $0.30\Lambda - 0.36\Lambda$ with a step size of 0.03. The confinement losses for $n_a = 1.37$ are 54.58 db/cm, 47.61 db/cm, and 43.43 db/cm for

0.30Λ, 0.33Λ, and 0.36Λ, respectively. For RI 1.38, confinement losses are 45.39 db/cm, 45.83 db/cm and 47.28 db/cm. Figure (7) shows all the plots of these trials. The loss decreases with the increase of the diameter for 1.37. For 1.38, the increment of loss is comparatively very low. Hence, the optimum diameter of d_2 in our structure is 0.36Λ.

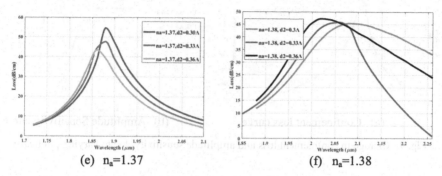

(e) n_a=1.37   (f) n_a=1.38

Fig. 7. Change in confinement loss due to varying d_2

Variation of d3

The diameter of d_3 for analyte RI 1.37 and 1.38 was varied. The trials were done for 0.25Λ, 0.55Λ and 0.85Λ. For RI 1.37, the found losses are 87.9 db/cm, 87.83 db/cm, 58.21 db/cm and for 1.38, 33.84 db/cm, 44.02 db/cm, 25.83 db/cm respectively. The peak location shifted with the variation of the diameter. The lowest confinement loss found is in 0.85Λ for both the RI. Figure (8) demonstrates the graphs of data found in these trials.

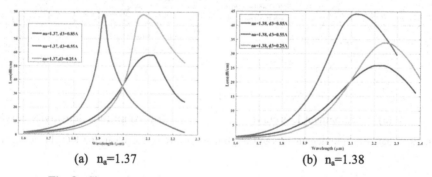

(a) n_a=1.37   (b) n_a=1.38

Fig. 8. Change in confinement loss for different RI due to varying d_3

5.2 Pitch Variation

The pitch is defined as the distance between the two adjacent air holes of a structure. The simulation was run for pitch sizes 3.2 μm and 3.3 μm. As seen from Fig. (9), the CL decreases with the increment of pitch size. But the amplitude sensitivity is the highest when the pitch size is 3.2 μm, which is 3024 RIU^{-1}. As the AS increment with the pitch size reduction is significantly high compared to the loss increment, the optimum performance of this structure will be found when $\Lambda = 3.2\ \mu m$.

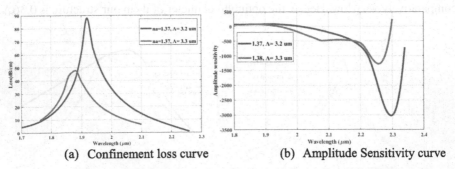

(a) Confinement loss curve   (b) Amplitude Sensitivity curve

Fig. 9. Change in confinement loss and amplitude sensitivity due to varying pitch size

5.3 Metal Layer Thickness Variation

TiO$_2$ Layer Thickness
Though TiO$_2$ layer is used as an adhesive agent between the gold and silica layer, its thickness significantly affects the SPR phenomenon, which ultimately leads to the change in the sensitivity of the structure.

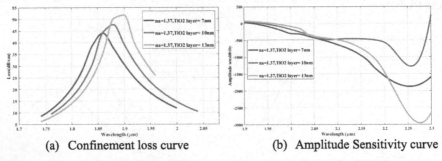

(a) Confinement loss curve   (b) Amplitude Sensitivity curve

Fig. 10. Change in confinement loss and amplitude sensitivity due to varying TiO$_2$ layer thickness

Figure (10) shows that the loss increases with the increment of the TiO$_2$ layer's thickness. Also the amplitude sensitivity increases. The maximum AS is 2954 RIU^{-1} for TiO$_2$ thickness of 13 nm and $n_a = 1.37$.

Gold Layer Thickness
For $n_a = 1.37$, three iterations were done for gold layer thickness of 50 nm, 65 nm, and 80 nm. The steady increment of the confinement loss is observed with the reduction of thickness of the gold layer, whereas the maximum AS is found for the thinnest gold

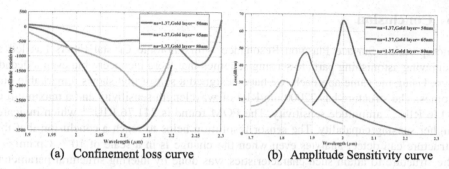

(a) Confinement loss curve   (b) Amplitude Sensitivity curve

Fig. 11. Change in confinement loss and amplitude sensitivity due to varying gold layer thickness

layer. The highest AS is 3446 RIU^{-1}, found for 50 nm of gold layer. Also, this is the highest recorded amplitude sensitivity in our structure (Fig. 11).

The performance analysis was done to determine the optimum structural parameters which provide the maximum utilization of the proposed sensor. From this section, the optimum parameters found are $\Lambda = 3.2$ μm, $d_1 = 0.5\Lambda$, $d_2 = 0.36\Lambda$, and $d_3 = 0.85\Lambda$. The TiO$_2$ and gold layer thicknesses are 13 nm and 50 nm respectively.

Table 2 shows the comparative analysis of our work with similar studies done by other researchers. Our structure is functional within a large analyte RI range which is not very common in PCF sensor studies. This large RI range enables the possibility of sensing higher number of liquids than other structures. Our sensor also has both improved WS and AS compared to the other structures mentioned in the table. High FOM and sensor resolution also indicates higher detection ability with very little change in the analyte RI.

Table 2. Comparison table with other structures

Ref. no	RI range	AS (RIU^{-1})	WS (nm/RIU)	FOM (RIU^{-1})	Resolution (RIU)
[1]	1.42–1.46	230	15000	45	6.66×10^{-6}
[8]	1.33–1.42	1420	11000	407	7.00×10^{-6}
[9]	1.33–1.39	396	5000	47	2.00×10^{-5}
[10]	1.40–1.46	780	16000	400	6.25×10^{-6}
[11]	1.350–1.395	641	11000	–	–
[12]	1.49–1.54	–	4782	–	2.09×10^{-5}
[13]	1.33–1.39	1250	10000	260.86	1.00×10^{-5}
[14]	1.333–1.404	–	4903	46.1	2.04×10^{-5}
[15]	1.33–1.41	2770	12600	–	7.94×10^{-6}
[18]	1.45–1.49	439.9	9000	–	3.33×10^{-5}
Our structure	1.22–1.38	3446	22000	241.76	4.54×10–6

6 Conclusion

Incorporating Surface Plasmon Resonance with Photonic Crystal Fibers has led to achieving astonishing particle-sensing schemes that were inconceivable even a decade ago. Using the same approach, we have designed a sensor that shows remarkable outcomes. The structure has 22000 nm/RIU of wavelength sensitivity and a maximum of 3446 RIU^{-1} amplitude sensitivity. The FOM found is 241.76 RIU^{-1} which indicates higher sensing capability. The sensor resolution helps to reach a conclusion that this structure can detect analytes even when the change is in a scale of 10^{-6}. Optimizing the structure to attain such characteristics was done by altering structural parameters from 10% to 30% of the original ones. Our structure, with its excellent real-time analyte detection properties, has important application in the fields of biology, biochemistry, and biosensing. Multifarious application of these sensing devices opens doors to tremendous progress in the biosensing field in near future.

Acknowledgement. This research is funded and fully supported by department of Electrical and Electronic Engineering of Shahjalal University of Science and Technology, Sylhet. The authors don't have any conflict of interest in this paper.

References

1. Hossain, M.B., et al.: Numerical development of high performance quasi Dshape PCF-SPR biosensor: an external sensing approach employing gold. Results Phys. **18**, 103281 (2020). (ISSN 2211–3797)
2. Luan, N., Yao, J.: Refractive index and temperature sensing based on surface plasmon resonance and directional resonance coupling in a PCF. IEEE Photon J. **9**(2), 1–7 (2017)
3. Liedberg, B., Nylander, C., Lunström, I.: Surface plasmon resonance for gas detection and biosensing. Sens. Actuators **4**, 299–304 (1983). (ISSN 0250–6874)
4. Monfared, Y.E., Ponomarenko, S.A.: Extremely nonlinear carbon-disulfide-filled photonic crystal fiber with controllable dispersion. Opt. Mater. **88**, 406–411 (2019)
5. Rifat Ahmmed, A., et al.: Photonic crystal fiber based plasmonic sensors. Sens. Actuators B **243**, 311–325 (2017)
6. Rifat, A.A., Mahdiraji, G.A., Chow, D.M., Shee, Y.G., Ahmed, R., Adikan, F.R.: Photonic crystal fiber-based surface plasmon resonance sensor with selective analyte channels and graphene-silver deposited core. Sens. Basel **15**(5), 11499–11510 (2015). https://doi.org/10.3390/s150511499.PMID:25996510;PMCID:PMC4481892
7. Fan, Z., et al.: High sensitivity of refractive index sensor based on AnalyteFilled photonic crystal fiber with surface plasmon resonance. IEEE Photonics J. **7**(3), 1–9 (2015). https://doi.org/10.1109/JPHOT.2015.2432079
8. Rifat, A.A., Haider, F., Ahmed, R., Mahdiraji, G.A., Adikan, F.M., Miroshnichenko, A.E.: Highly sensitive selectively coated photonic crystal fiber-based plasmonic sensor. Opt. Lett. **43**(4), 891–894 (2018). https://doi.org/10.1364/OL.43.000891
9. Akter, S., Rahman, M.Z., Mahmud, S.: Highly sensitive openchannels based plasmonic biosensor in visible to near-infrared wavelength. Results Phys. **13**, 102328 (2019). (ISSN 2211–3797)
10. Sakib, M.N., et al.: Numerical study of circularly slotted highly sensitive plasmonic biosensor: a novel approach. Results Phys. **17**, 103130 (2020). (ISSN 2211–3797)

11. Li, X., Li, S., Yan, X., Sun, D., Liu, Z., Cheng, T.: High sensitivity photonic crystal fiber refractive index sensor with gold coated externally based on surface plasmon resonance. Micromachines **9**, 640 (2018)
12. De, M., Markides, C., Singh, V.K., Themistos, C., Rahman, B.M.A.: Analysis of a single solid core flat fiber plasmonic refractive index sensor. Plasmonics **15**(5), 1429–1437 (2020). https://doi.org/10.1007/s11468-020-01154-2
13. Rahman, M.M., Rana, M.M., Anower, M.S., Rahman, M.S., Paul, A.K.: Design and analysis of photonic crystal fiber-based plasmonic microbiosensor: an external sensing scheme. SN Appl. Sci. **2**(7), 1–11 (2020). https://doi.org/10.1007/s42452-020-2998-3
14. Dong, J., Zhang, Y., Wang, Y., Yang, F., Hu, S., Chen, Y., et al.: Sidepolished fewmode fiber based surface plasmon resonance biosensor. Opt. Express **27**, 11348–11360 (2019)
15. Li, T., Zhu, L., Yang, X., Lou, X., Yu, L.: A Refractive index sensor based on H-shaped photonic crystal fibers coated with Ag-Graphene layers. Sens. Basel **20**(3), 741 (2020). https://doi.org/10.3390/s20030741.PMID:32013213;PMCID:PMC7038478
16. Talukder, H., Isti, M.I.A., Nuzhat, S., Biswas, S.K.: Ultra-high negative dispersion based single mode highly nonlinear bored core photonic crystal fiber (HNL-BCPCF): design and numerical analysis. Braz. J. Phys. **50**(3), 263–271 (2020). https://doi.org/10.1007/s13538-020-00742-1
17. Vial, A., Grimault, A.-S., Mac´ıas, D.,et al.: Improved analytical fit of gold dispersion: application to the modeling of extinction spectra with a finite-difference time-domain method. Phys. Rev. B **71**(8), 085416 (2005)
18. Hassan, M.F.B., Sultana, S., Isti, M.I.A., Nuzhat, S., Biswas, S.K., Talukder, H.: Liquid benzene analyte based dual core surface Plasmon resonance sensor for chemical sensing. In: 2020 11th International Conference on Computing, Communication and Networking Technologies (ICCCNT), Kharagpur, India, pp. 1–6 (2020). https://doi.org/10.1109/ICCCNT49239.2020.9225505
19. DeVore, J.R.: Refractive indices of rutile and sphalerite. J. Opt. Soc. Amer. **41**(6), 416–419 (1951)
20. de Mol, N.J., Fischer, M.J.E.: Surface plasmon resonance: a general introduction. In: Mol, N.J., Fischer, M.J.E. (eds.) Surface plasmon resonance, pp. 1–14. Humana Press, Totowa, NJ (2010). https://doi.org/10.1007/978-1-60761-670-2_1
21. Isti, M.I.A., et al.: Asymmetrical D-channel photonic crystal fiber-based plasmonic sensor using the wavelength interrogation and lower birefringence peak method. Results Phys. **19**, 103372 (2020)

FPGA Implementation of ECC Enabled Multi-factor Authentication (E-MFA) Protocol for IoT Based Applications

S. Raja Sekar, S. Elango$^{(\boxtimes)}$, Sajan P. Philip, and A. Daniel Raj

Department of Electronics and Communication Engineering, Bannari Amman Institute of Technology, Sathyamangalam, Erode 638 401, Tamil Nadu, India
{rajasekar,elangos}@bitsathy.ac.in

Abstract. IoT platform creates attractive opportunities for our daily lives which make us smarter and more comfortable. IoT offers an incredible guarantee in the e-healthcare field by enhancing the quality of service with limited time-bound. The connectivity provided for e-healthcare devices poses overwhelming security and privacy concerns in this area. In this work, the Elliptic Curve Cryptography (ECC) based Multi-Factor Authentication (MFA) is employed between two entities to enhance security. The authentication is achieved using the Point multiplication operation, which provides more randomness. The three-factor authentication protocol for IoT based E-health devices is presented in this work. The architecture is coded using Verilog HDL, synthesized using Xilinx Synthesis Technology (XST) and ported in Zynq FPGA device (XC7Z020CLG484–1). The results show that the proposed three-factor mutual authentication protocol provides better security.

Keywords: Multifactor authentication · Point multiplication · FPGA · E-Health · IoT · ECC applications

1 Introduction

Internet of things is the internet in everything. Even the small gadgets around us are smart by analyzing the things and environment in our daily lives. Nowadays, billions of physical devices are connected to the internet and sharing the information independently of human actions. IoT helps people to live smart. These devices act autonomously in communicating the gathered data to the central coordinator automatically. IoT technology impacts every ground, including body applications, smart homes, smart cities, automated environment, weather detections, intelligent transportations etc. Due to IoT usage in every single field of life, IoT in health application is expected. IoT in healthcare cut down an unnecessary visit to doctors, hospital stays and re-admission. To provide smart devices in e-health systems, IoT is essential. The biosensors continuously monitor the vital signs, behavioural, other health-related information, and the data are transferred to the concern medical server at anywhere anytime. Medical devices with integrated IoT help in many tasks including remote patient monitoring, treatment progress observation,

© Springer Nature Singapore Pte Ltd. 2021
V. Arunachalam and K. Sivasankaran (Eds.): ICMDCS 2021, CCIS 1392, pp. 430–442, 2021.
https://doi.org/10.1007/978-981-16-5048-2_34

health issue indications etc. The benefits of IoT in healthcare include monitor the overall treatment processes, save time and money, integrates and adapt the hospitality model, make better health decisions for patients.

Authentication has a significant role in IoT to ensure the connected device can be trusted. It is the process of identifying the individual with what they have (possession factor), what they know (Knowledge factor) and what they are (inherence factor). Whenever the user makes a request, authentication occurs from starting to login into the account. When the device attempts to connect to the cloud, authentication is needed for each IoT device's unique identities. The unique ID's can be tracked and analyzed throughout its lifecycle, as shown in Fig. 1. To access the protected resource, which includes network database and other service applications, the particular organization only provides permission for the authenticated users. Authentication is of single, double and multiple ways. The efficient, secure purpose in e-health Multi-Factor Authentication (MFA) is introduced to protect the data transmission between the patient and the healthcare centres and members. It is a security system that uses more than one authentication method for the user's identity and in the transaction process. One of the considered problems with the traditional way is to maintain the password database. If it is captured by the attackers, the probability of guesses with the speed limit of the hardware used nowadays, obviously it will be cracked. MFA is more efficient than the traditional way of using only username and password. The Elliptic Curve Cryptography (ECC) based authentication is proposed to provide better authentication and security. This paper's framework includes the proposed protocol design, analysis of the algorithm with the brief explanation of the sample problem, Finite State Machine (FSM), simulation result of the proposed protocol.

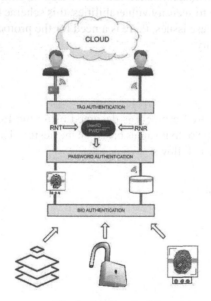

Fig. 1. IoT in e-health

2 Background

In this section, various security issues and solutions in the medical field are discussed. In recent years, various security schemes were proposed to solve the issue of sharing the keys between different users. Only a very few protocols have been implemented as hardware using FPGAs and embedded microcontrollers. Some work is proved using a simulator like AVISPA. Most of the mutual authentication protocols are theoretical, and their analysis is qualitative. Hardware implemented protocol is given in [1–7], a protocol for e-health application is presented in [7, 8], IoT Cloud-based environment is discussed in [4, 9, 10]. In [11], Zhang et al. propose a three-factor authenticated scheme for e-health systems to protect users' privacy. Their proposed method is secure in real-time applications. This protocol is prone to many attacks like de-synchronization, DoS, and insider attacks. In [8], A lightweight authentication bio hash function consisting of five-phases (setup, registration, login, authentication, and key agreement and ownership transfer) and three factors (password, smart card, biometric) for e-health IoMT application is presented. This authentication prevents insider attack, DoS attack, de-synchronization attack, offline password guessing attack. In [12], the remote authentication scheme's robustness using passwords and smart cards is not explained in detail. So biometric data (e.g. fingerprint, iris) with traditional authentication schemes are used. In general, three-factor-based authentication schemes are introduced to improve the security of the patient's information [13, 14]. A study [15] discussed the recent topics and issues related to the e-health applications and provided proper solutions to minimize them. Later, they will discuss what may occur in future regarding security and privacy issues and how to handle them. In [16], the authentication schemes based on Elliptic-curve cryptography (ECC) is discussed. Due to security vulnerabilities, this scheme is not suitable for IoMT systems. To overcome these issues, there is a need for the protocol which balances both area overhead and security.

3 Proposed Work

In this section, the proposed protocol is designed using the ECC point multiplication architecture to produce the output values based on the design. The step by step procedure for the protocol is given as follows:

3.1 Proposed Protocol

(See Fig. 2).

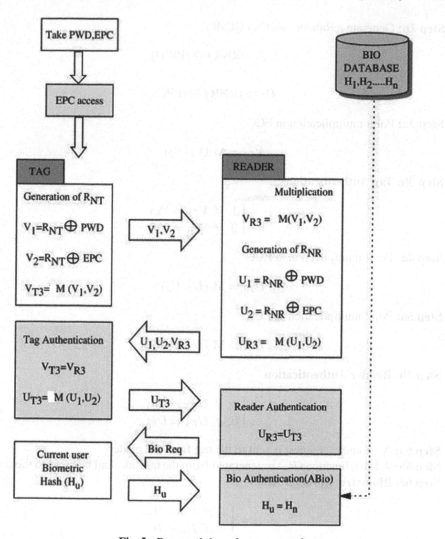

Fig. 2. Proposed three-factor protocol

3.2 Algorithm

Step 1a: Generate a Random number (RNT)
Step 1b: XOR RNT with PWD and EPC

$$V_1 = (RNT) \oplus (PWD) \tag{1}$$

$$V_2 = (RNT) \oplus (EPC) \tag{2}$$

Step 2a: Point multiplication in ECC

$$V_{R3} = M(V_1, V_2) \tag{3}$$

Step 2b: Generate a Random number (RNR)

$$U_1 = (RNR) \oplus (PWD) \tag{4}$$

$$U_2 = (RNR) \oplus (EPC) \tag{5}$$

Step 3a: Point multiplication in ECC

$$V_{T3} = M(V_1, V_2) \tag{6}$$

Step 3b: Tag Authentication

$$A_T = \begin{cases} 1, & \text{if } V_{T3} = V_{R3} \\ 0, & \text{if } V_{T3} \neq V_{R3} \end{cases} \tag{7}$$

Step 4a: Point multiplication in ECC

$$U_{T3} = M(U_1, U_2) \tag{8}$$

Step 5a: Point multiplication in ECC

$$U_{R3} = M(U_1, U_2) \tag{9}$$

Step 5b: Reader Authentication

$$A_R = \begin{cases} 1, & \text{if } U_{T3} = U_{R3} \\ 0, & \text{if } U_{T3} \neq U_{R3} \end{cases} \tag{10}$$

Step 6a: A Biometric request is sent to the tag from the reader
Step 6b: A Hash function (H_u) is generated from the tag side, and it is sent to the reader
Step 6c: Biometric Authentication

$$A_{Bio} = \begin{cases} 1, & \text{if } H_u = H_n \\ 0, & \text{if } H_u \neq H_n \end{cases} \tag{11}$$

Where H_n is the number of users in the database.

3.3 Point Multiplication

Point multiplication [17] is the process in which a point is successively added along the elliptic curve with itself repeatedly. In general, point multiplication is the multiplication of the point P with a scalar d using algebraic equations to find new point Q, i.e. $dP = Q$. In cryptosystems, the private key which is an integer is the scalar d and the public key is $T(xT, yT)$. This operation is known as the point multiplication, and it can be represented as $T = dP$. The point multiplication can be computed in several methods such as Double and Add algorithm, Windowed method, Sliding-window method, etc.

The Double and algorithm involves the following steps, which includes the Point addition and point doubling operations

(i) Initially, the Point P is doubled to obtain 2P, 4P…

(ii) The scalar value d is then converted into its binary form. (iii) For example,

$$26P = (11010_2) = (d_4 d_3 d_2 d_1 d_0)P \tag{12}$$

(iv) Then the bits are processed from left to right, i.e. $d0$ to $d4$ as the select line to a multiplexer.

(v) If the select line is 1 then the point is added, and the result is fetched to next mux.

(vi) If the select line is 0 then the point is directly carried to the next mux.

(vii) The Output of the final mux gives the point dP.

Thus, the algorithm is used to obtain point multiplication (dP). The number of Multiplexers used is based on the input number of bits of the point P. Based on the bit size required, the multiplexers are used to obtain the output.

3.4 Point Addition

In the case of Point Addition [18, 19], we find $R = P + Q$ where $P \neq Q$. The construction is stated as a line is drawn through the points P and Q to obtain the new point $-R$. Mirror this point $-R$ along the x-axis.

Theoretically, the Point addition is calculated as, given two points $P(a1,b1)$ and $Q(a2,b2)$ on the elliptic curve then the point $R(a3,b3) = P + Q$ is given by,

$$a3 = \left(s^2 - a1 - a2 \right) \bmod p \tag{13}$$

$$b3 = (s(a1 - a3) - b1) \bmod p \tag{14}$$

Where S is the slope between the points P and Q given by,

$$s = \left(((b_2 - b_1) mod\ p) * \left((a_2 - a_1)^{-1} mod\ p \right) \right) \bmod p \tag{15}$$

3.5 Point Doubling

In Point doubling [18, 19], we find $P + Q$ where $P = Q$ and therefore $R = P + P = 2$. The construction is stated as follows. First, draw a tangent line to point P and find the point of intersection of the line and curve. Now, reflect this point along x-axis. Thus, the reflected point is the result R of point doubling (Table 1).

Theoretically, the point doubling can be calculated as f, given the point $P(a1,b1)$ on an elliptic curve then the point $R(a3,b3) = P + P = 2P$ is given by,

$$a3 = \left(s^2 - 2a1 \right) \bmod p \tag{16}$$

$$b3 = (s(a1 - a3) - b1) \bmod p \tag{17}$$

Where S is the slope given by, (11)

$$s = \left(\left(\left(3a_1^2 - c_1 \right) \bmod p \right) * \left((2b_1)^{-1} mod\ p \right) \right) \bmod p \tag{18}$$

3.6   Example Calculation or Illustration

Table 1. Example calculation

1. Point Addition $(a_3, b_3) = (a_1, b_1) + (a_2, b_2)$

$P(a_1, b_1) = P(-48610, -58932) Q(a_2, b_2) = Q(-41200, -53980) p = 65537$

$S = \left| \left((-53980 - 58932) \times (-41200 + 48610)^{-1} \right) \right|_{65537} = 30903$

$a_3 = \left| \left(\left| (30903)^2 \right|_{65537} - |(48610 + 41200)|_{65537} \right) \right|_{65537} = 14518$

$b_3 = |(|30903 \times (-63128)|_{65537} - |58932|_{65537})|_{23} = 54227$

$(a_3, b_3) = P + Q = (14518, 54227)$

2. Point Doubling $(a_3, b_3) = P + P$

$P(a_1, b_1) = P(45731, -52832) c_1 = 1 p = 65537$

$S = \left| \left(\left| 3 \times (45731)^2 + 1 \right|_{65537} \times \left| (2 \times (-52832))^{-1} \right|_{65537} \right) \right|_{65537} = 15784$

$a_3 = \left| \left(\left| (15784)^2 \right|_{65537} - |91462|_{65537} \right) \right|_{65537} = 2594$

$b_3 = |(|15784 \times (43137)|_{65537} - |-52832|_{65537})|_{65537} = 63347$

$(a_3, b_3) = P + P = (57855, 62446)$

3. Point Multiplication $(x, y) = d \times P(a_1, b_1)$

$P(a_1, b_1) = P(-49321, -51020) d = 17 (x, y) = 17P$

3a. Point Doubling:	*3b. Point Addition:*
$1P = (-49321, -51020)$ $2P = (58359, 39527)$ $4P = (46186, 42864)$ $8P = (41006, 36181)$ $16P = (27279, 11362)$	$17P = (010001)_2$ $P = 16P + 1P$ $(x, y) = (4574, 38417)$

3.7   Finite State Machine (FSM)

FSM of the proposed protocol is given in Fig. 3. In Fig. 3, bit explanation and different states of the protocol based on the inputs are represented in Table 2 and 3.

4   Result and Analysis

The Verilog HDL code is developed, optimized, and synthesized using Vivado Design suite Xilinx 14.6 and analyzed the area and delay parameters.

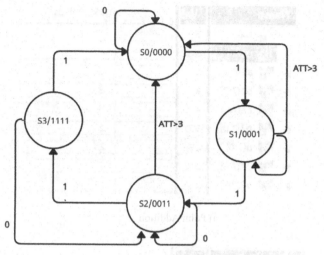

Fig. 3. State diagram

Table 2. Bit explanation

Output	Authentication	Biometric	Password	EPC
Bits	X	X	X	X

Table 3. FSM states

State	Input	Next state	Output
S0	0	S0	0000
	1	S1	0001
S1	0	S1	0001
	1	S2	0011
S2	0	S2	0011
	1	S3	1111
S3	0	S2	0011
	1	S0	0000

4.1 Simulation Result

The simulation results represent the Point Addition, Point Doubling, and Point Multiplication process is shown in Fig. 4. In the point addition, two points (2, 8) & (4, 5) are added, and the result is a point (2, 15). In the point doubling process, a point (9, 5) is

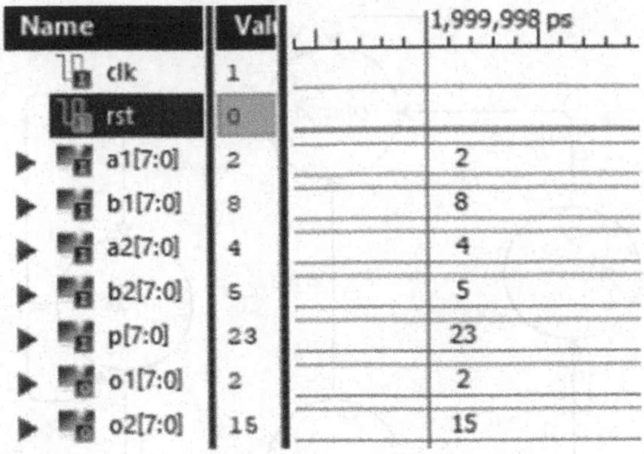

a) Point Addition

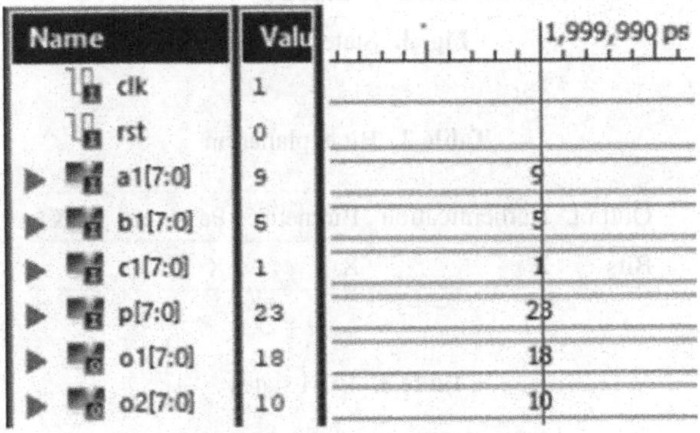

b) Point Doubling

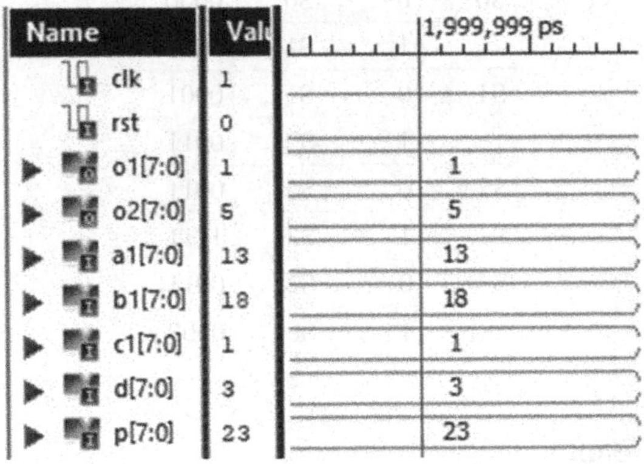

c) Point Multiplication

Fig. 4. Simulation output of point operations

doubled, and the result of doubling is (18, 10). In the Point Multiplication, a point (13, 18) is multiplied by 3 using the Double and Add method, and the result is (1, 5).

4.2 Synthesized Result and Analysis

The synthesizable Verilog HDL code is developed for each block of ECC algorithm and proposed protocol with 32-bit point multiplication using Vivado 14.6 and analysis of the performance parameters such as area and delay by synthesis the design with reference to the FPGA device XC7Z020CLG484-1 is given in Table 4 and 5.

Table 4. ECC operations

Logic utilization and delay	Point addition			Point doubling			Point multiplication		
	8-bit	16-bit	32-bit	8-bit	16-bit	32-bit	8-bit	16-bit	32-bit
Number of slice registers	20	36	84	20	36	84	190	385	784
Number of slice LUTs	3886	18360	88452	5402	17440	122297	80184	273824	1589237
Number of bonded IOBs	58	114	226	50	98	194	58	114	226
Logic delay (ns)	220	611	1400	344	691	2458	17940	47714	61813
Routing delay (ns)	191	301	615	240	252	917	4784	20459	29084
Total delay (ns)	411	912	2015	584	943	3374	22724	68172	90896

Table 5. Proposed authentication protocol synthesis results

Logic utilization and delay	Existing MFA [20] (32-bit)	Proposed MFA (32-bit)
Number of slice registers	3157	3200
Number of slice LUTs	3815896	3973185
Number of bonded IOBs	70	70
Logic delay (μs)	298	309
Routing delay (μs)	139	145
Total delay (μs)	437	454

Table 5 shows that the proposed mutual authentication protocol performance parameters are almost similar to the existing protocol, but it provides twice the amount of security than the existing protocol. Hence, the proposed protocol is highly suited for high secured applications.

5 Security Attacks

The informal analysis is discussed for the proposed protocol with various attacks scenarios is given in Table 6.

5.1 Replay Attack

A new session key will be generated, and once the identity of the tag and reader is successfully verified, the replay attack is prevented.

5.2 Man in the Middle Attack

Here the point multiplication algorithm is used. In the channel, only residue values are available for the attacker or Man in the Middle. With that residue values, the attacker in the unsecured channel cannot retrieve the key/password.

5.3 De-synchronization Attack

The protocol structure is designed so that the tag and reader's element does not depend on each other. A separate feature is created for tag and reader; no time synchronization is required between tag and reader in this protocol. Hence de-synchronization attack is not possible.

5.4 Stolen Smart Card Attack

If a smart card is stolen, the attacker may try to find the smart card's information. Here we use biometric as one of the factors of authentication. So the attacker cannot be able to track any information from the hash values.

5.5 Credential Stuffing

Credential stuffing is a kind of cyber-attack. The attacker can guess the password with the help of username and email address stored in the database since biometric authentication is used to avoid this type of attack.

Table 6. Attacks

Attacks	Existing MFA [20] (32-Bit)	Proposed MFA (32-Bit)
Man in the Middle attack	✓	Δ
De-synchronization attack	✗	✓
Replay attack	✗	✓
Stolen smart card attack	Δ	✓
Credential stuffing	Δ	✓

✓ - Prevented, Δ – Not Applicable ✗- Not Prevented

6 Conclusion

In this paper, the three-factor authentication protocol for IoT based E-health devices is proposed. To enhance the security between two entities in the healthcare environment multi-factor authentication is employed. The password authentication is achieved using the Point multiplication operation in ECC, which has better security and randomness. The smart card and biometric authentication are added with password authentication, which improves security. The password authentication architecture is coded using Verilog HDL and synthesized to Zynq FPGA device (XC7Z020CLG484-1) using Xilinx Synthesis Technology (XST). This three-factor authentication protocol implemented in FPGA preserves the user's security level. It offers an excellent service to patients with better security without compromising the hardware cost compared with existing MFA.

References

1. Liu, D., Liu, Z., Yong, Z., Zou, X., Cheng, J.: Design and implementation of an ECC-based digital baseband controller for RFID tag chip. IEEE Trans. Ind. Electron. **62**, 4365–4373 (2015). https://doi.org/10.1109/TIE.2014.2387333

2. Liu, Z., Liu, D., Li, L., Lin, H., Yong, Z.: Implementation of a new RFID authentication protocol for EPC Gen2 standard. IEEE Sens. J. **15**, 1003–1011 (2015). https://doi.org/10.1109/JSEN.2014.2359796

3. Hatzivasilis, G., Floros, G., Papaefstathiou, I., Manifavas, C.: Lightweight authenticated encryption for embedded on-chip systems. Inf. Secur. J. **25**, 151–161 (2016). https://doi.org/10.1080/19393555.2016.1209259

4. Li, N., Liu, D., Nepal, S.: Lightweight mutual authentication for IoT and its applications. IEEE Trans. Sustain. Comput. **2**, 359–370 (2017). https://doi.org/10.1109/tsusc.2017.2716953

5. Mujahid, U., Najam-Ul-Islam, M., Khalid, M.: Efficient hardware implementation of KMAP+: an ultralightweight mutual authentication protocol. J. Circuits, Syst. Comput. **27**, 1850033 (2018). https://doi.org/10.1142/S0218126618500330

6. Vijaykumar, V.R., Sekar, S.R., Elango, S., Ramakrishnan, S.: Implementation of 2n–2k-1 modulo adder based RFID mutual authentication protocol. IEEE Trans. Ind. Electron. **65**, 626–635 (2018). https://doi.org/10.1109/TIE.2017.2711864

7. Sureshkumar, V., Amin, R., Vijaykumar, V.R., Sekar, S.R.: Robust secure communication protocol for smart healthcare system with FPGA implementation. Futur. Gener. Comput. Syst. **100**, 938–951 (2019). https://doi.org/10.1016/j.future.2019.05.058

8. Aghili, S.F., Mala, H., Shojafar, M., Peris-Lopez, P.: LACO: lightweight three-factor authentication, access control and ownership transfer scheme for e-health systems in IoT. Futur. Gener. Comput. Syst. **96**, 410–424 (2019). https://doi.org/10.1016/j.future.2019.02.020

9. Dong, Q., Chen, M., Li, L., Fan, K.: Cloud-based radio frequency identification authentication protocol with location privacy protection. Int. J. Distrib. Sens. Netw. **14** (2018). https://doi.org/10.1177/1550147718754969

10. Gope, P., Amin, R., Hafizul Islam, S.K., Kumar, N., Bhalla, V.K.: Lightweight and privacy-preserving RFID authentication scheme for distributed IoT infrastructure with secure localization services for smart city environment. Futur. Gener. Comput. Syst. **83**, 629–637 (2018). https://doi.org/10.1016/j.future.2017.06.023

11. Zhang, L., Zhang, Y., Tang, S., Luo, H.: Privacy protection for e-health systems by means of dynamic authentication and three-factor key agreement. IEEE Trans. Ind. Electron. **65**, 2795–2805 (2018). https://doi.org/10.1109/TIE.2017.2739683

12. Arshad, H., Nikooghadam, M.: An efficient and secure authentication and key agreement scheme for session initiation protocol using ECC. Multimedia Tools Appl. **75**(1), 181–197 (2014). https://doi.org/10.1007/s11042-014-2282-x

13. Guo, D., Wen, Q., Li, W., Zhang, H., Jin, Z.: An improved biometrics-based authentication scheme for telecare medical information systems. J. Med. Syst. **39**(3), 1 (2015). https://doi.org/10.1007/s10916-015-0194-6

14. Srivastava, K., Awasthi, A.K., Kaul, S.D., Mittal, R.C.: A hash based mutual RFID tag authentication protocol in telecare medicine information system. J. Med. Syst. **39**(1), 1–5 (2014). https://doi.org/10.1007/s10916-014-0153-7

15. Suhardi, Ramadhan, A.: A survey of security aspects for internet of things in healthcare. In: Lecture Notes in Electrical Engineering. pp. 1237–1247. Springer (2016). https://doi.org/10.1007/978-981-10-0557-2_117

16. He, D., Zeadally, S.: An analysis of RFID authentication schemes for internet of things in healthcare environment using elliptic curve cryptography. IEEE Internet Things J. **2**, 72–83 (2015). https://doi.org/10.1109/JIOT.2014.2360121

17. Schinianakis, D.M., Fournaris, A.P., Michail, H.E., Kakarountas, A.P., Stouraitis, T.: An RNS implementation of an Fp elliptic curve point multiplier. IEEE Trans. Circuits Syst. I Regul. Pap. **56**, 1202–1213 (2009). https://doi.org/10.1109/TCSI.2008.2008507

18. Hankerson, D., Menezes, A., Vanstone, S.: Guide to Elliptic Curve Cryptography. (2004). https://doi.org/10.1007/b97644

19. . Washington, L.: Elliptic Curves: Number Theory and Cryptography (2004).https://doi.org/10.5860/choice.41-4097

20. Vijaykumar, V.R., Reghunath, R., Rajasekar, S., Elango, S.: A novel lightweight and low power tag-reader mutual authentication protocol for portable RFID based security systems. In: IEACon 2016 - 2016 IEEE Industrial Electronics and Applications Conference (2017). https://doi.org/10.1109/IEACON.2016.8067405

GPS Aided Hassle-Free Cycling Using Sensors

Sudheer Kumar Nagothu[✉] [iD]

RVR&JC College of Engineering, Chowdavaram, Guntur, Andhra Pradesh 522019, India
nsudheerkumar@rvrjc.ac.in

Abstract. Cycling has become part and parcel of the urban world. It is mainly used because it is one of the cheapest modes of transport and also used exercise equipment to burn calories. Here we are proposing an idea to make cycling a joyride using GPS and a heartbeat sensor. The person will plan the route using google maps, based upon which the motors attached to the cyclist arms will vibrate and guide the person. It's a common habit for cyclists to listen to music while cycling which will enable them to overcome tiredness. The speed of the cycle measured by an accelerometer and the heartbeat rate which is measured by a heartbeat sensor will control the music play rate.

Keywords: Heartbeat sensor · Cycling · Global Positioning System (GPS)

1 Introduction

Cycling has become part and parcel of human life. It not only helps to reduce the pollution in atmosphere but also provides good exercise for the humans. So, providing comfort to humans during cycling will help the humans to forget their tiredness and to do more cycling.

Normally the cyclist will plan their route before the begin cycling using google maps. This pre planned route will be used to guide the cyclist along the path. Because of the cycling the cyclist will get strained, to provide solace to cyclist while cycling music is played. The information of the speed of the cycle and the human's heartbeat rate are used to control the music rate.

The cyclist has to plan the route before he starts his journey using waypoints in google maps. These paths will guide him along the route using vibration motors. Motors will be attached to cyclist the shoulders and they will be vibrated to guide him according to the route he has planned. The motors are tied to the arms of cyclist, if he has to take right turn vibration motor will be operated on right arm, if he has to move or turn left vibration motor will be vibrated on left arm, if he has to go on straight path (when there is a turn ahead of him) both the vibration motors on left and right arm will be on [1–3].

While cycling sometimes he need to climb and sometimes he needs to descend from high elevation areas. In order to enjoy his cycling a music system is implemented by using the heartbeat sensor, and accelerometer data. Normally when the cyclist struggles to move the cycle his heartbeat will increase, at this time normally he prefers to listen slow music [4–7]. When the cycle moves at fast rate, he may prefer to listen fast music, the

V. Arunachalam and K. Sivasankaran (Eds.): ICMDCS 2021, CCIS 1392, pp. 443–450, 2021.
https://doi.org/10.1007/978-981-16-5048-2_35

music files are categorized based up on the bit rate and store in different files based up on the cyclist preference. With respect to the speed of the cycle and heart beat rate, respective music will be played. GPRS GPS integrated system finds application in various fields such as agriculture, people monitoring, smart attendance system, monitoring animals etc. [8–11] (Figs. 1, 2, 3).

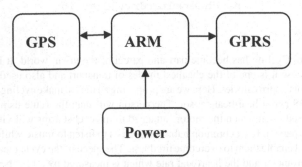

Fig. 1. Block diagarm

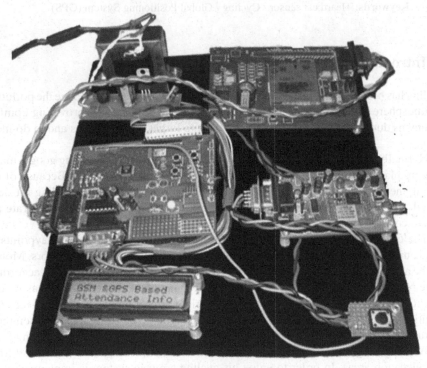

Fig. 2. Ciruit diagarm

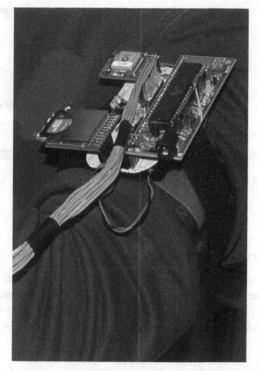

Fig. 3. Circuit diagarm attached to shoulder

2 System Working

The system mainly consists of heart beat sensor, accelerometer and INS. An ARM microcontroller is used to connect all the sensor. The latitude and longitude obtained from the INS are used know the person location, and if he deviates from the planned path, an alert in terms vibration will be given. The working of Heart beats sensor, and Accelerometer are given below.

2.1 Heart Beat Sensor Working

The Heartbeat sensor is used to measure the heart rate of the cyclist. This sensor consists of a photodiode and an infrared LED. The Bright LED and light detector are kept adjacent as shown in Fig. 4 and a finger is kept above these sensors, and infrared light is made to fall on the fingertip using an infrared light-emitting diode and a marginal amount of this signal is reflected from the finger inside the blood, whose intensity depends upon the volume of blood. The reflected signal is detected by the photodiode. With this arrangement, it is possible to measure the heartbeat rate. The small alteration in the reflected light amplitude can be converted in to a form of pulse using high gain amplifier.

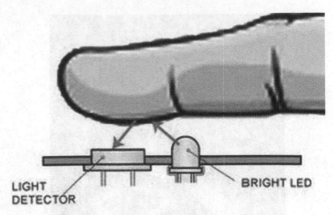

Fig. 4. Heart beat sensor working

2.2 Speed Measurement Using Accelerometer

The accelerometer sensor gives acceleration by integrating it we can get velocity or speed of the vehicle. This information is used here to play the music. By Comparing the Present location data with pre planned position data guidance will be given to the cyclist. Here Haver-Sine formula is used to find the deviation in distance and angle.

$$a = \sin^2(\frac{\phi_2 - \phi_1}{2}) + \cos(\phi_2) * \cos(\phi_1) \sin^2(\frac{\lambda_2 - \lambda_1}{2})$$

$$d = 2 * R_E * a \tan 2(\frac{\sqrt{a}}{\sqrt{(1-a)}})$$

Where λ_1, ϕ_1 is longitude & latitude of cyclist, λ_2, ϕ_2 is longitude latitude & of stored path position and R_E is radius of earth.

Fig. 5. Path using Google earth.

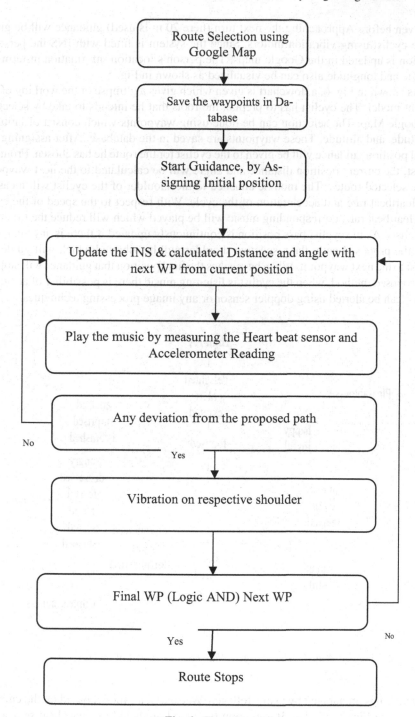

Fig. 6. Flow chart

Even before Approaching the next turn (here 20 m is used) guidance will be given to the cyclist using vibration motors. Since the system is fitted with INS the person's position is updated in the Google maps. The person's location information in-terms of latitude and longitude also can be visualized as shown in Fig. 5.

As shown in Fig. 6, a flowchart is given which gives a glimpse of the working of the current model. The cyclist has to preplan the roots that he intends to take by selecting in Google Map. The selection can be done using waypoints which consist of latitude, longitude, and altitude. These waypoints are saved in the database. After assigning the initial position guidance will be given to the cyclist for the route he has chosen. From the cyclist, the current position distance and angle will be calculated to the next waypoint in the selected routes. The module attached to the shoulder of the cyclist will measure the Heartbeat rate and acceleration of the cycle. With respect to the speed of the cycle and Heartbeat rate, corresponding music will be played which will reduce the tiredness of cyclists. As the cyclist pass position is continuously updated if there is any deviation from the proposed path, the respective shoulder will be vibrated which will guide the cyclist to the next waypoint. When he reaches the final position that guidance will stop. In the proposed method, when the cyclist is listening music there is possibility of accident, Which can be alerted using doppler sensor or any image processing techniques.

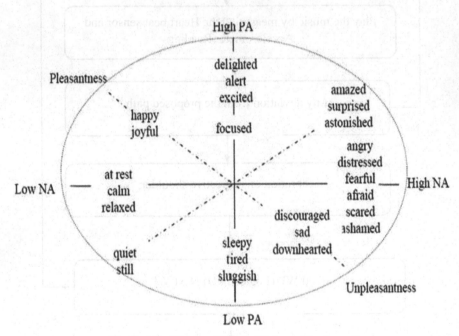

Fig. 7. The Tellegen-Watson-Clark model of mood

The songs are labeled by using Tellegen-Watson-Clark model based on the emotion as shown in Fig. 7 [12, 13]. Based upon the mood predicted by heart beat sensor and accelerometer corresponding song can be played.

The reaction in emotion among the listeners for a song will vary and classifying the music will be a different task. The Thayer's mood model classifies the songs into various levels such as happy, energetic, anxious, and calm. By measuring the parameters of a song such as rhythm, pitch, and intensity the song can be categorized into various modes such as contentment, depression, energetic, sad, exuberant, happy, etc. As shown in Table 1 the songs were categorized based upon the components of music such as pitch, intensity rhythm, and Timbre [14, 15]. From the table, it can be observed that when the intensity and timbre are normal and Pitch, Rhythm are extremely high the strong mood is categorized as happy.

Table 1. List of song moods using components of music

Songs mood	Timbre	Rhythm	Pitch	Intensity
Calm	Extremely low	Extremely low	Normal	Extremely low
Contentment	Low	Low	High	Low
Exuberant	Normal	High	High	High
Energetic	Normal	High	Normal	Extremely high
Frantic	Extremely high	Extremely high	Low	High
Happy	Normal	Extremely high	Extremely high	Normal
Sad	Extremely low	Low	Extremely low	Normal
Depression	Low	Low	Low	Low

3 Conclusions

A low-cost system has been proposed to provide some entertainment to cyclist while he is in riding. The tiredness faced by the cyclist can be reduced by providing some entertainment for the person. His cycling is also made easy by guiding the person along the route he has planned. Since frequent breaks (to check the route in map) are avoided, he can burn more calories by having uninterrupted journey. Songs were categorized as per Tellegen-Watson-Clark model and Bhat model. The songs were categorized into Contentment, Exuberant, Frantic, Sad, Depression, Energetic, Calm, Happy etc. based on songs pitch, intensity, rhythm and timbre. As music is played by analyzing the heartbeat of person and speed of the cycle, he can easily overcome the tiredness and will enjoy his ride.

References

1. Nagothu, S.K., Kumar, O.P., Anitha, G.: Autonomous monitoring and attendance system using inertial navigation system and GPRS in predefined locations. In: 2014 3rd International Conference on Eco-friendly Computing and Communication Systems, Mangalore, pp. 261–265 (2014). https://doi.org/10.1109/Eco-friendly.2014.60

2. Nagothu, S.K., Anitha, G., Annapantula, S.: Navigation aid for people (joggers and runners) in the unfamiliar urban environment using inertial navigation. In: 2014 Sixth International Conference on Advanced Computing (ICoAC), Chennai, pp. 216–219 (2014). https://doi.org/10.1109/ICoAC.2014.7229713
3. Nagothu, S.K., Kumar, O.P., Anitha, G.: GPS aided autonomous monitoring and attendance system. Procedia Comput. Sci. **87**, 99–104 (2016), ISSN 1877–0509. https://doi.org/10.1016/j.procs.2016.05.133
4. Nagothu, S.K.: Weather based smart watering system using soil sensor and GSM. In: 2016 World Conference on Futuristic Trends in Research and Innovation for Social Welfare (Startup Conclave), Coimbatore, pp. 1–3 (2016). https://doi.org/10.1109/STARTUP.2016.7583991
5. Rengarajan, M., Anitha, G.: Algorithm development and testing of low cost way point navigation system. Eng. Sci. Technol. Int. J. **3**(2), 411–414 (2013)
6. Nagothu, S.K.: Automated toll collection system using GPS and GPRS. In: 2016 International Conference on Communication and Signal Processing (ICCSP), Melmaruvathur, Tamilnadu, India, pp. 0651–0653 (2016). https://doi.org/10.1109/ICCSP.2016.7754222
7. Nagothu, S.K., Anitha, G.: Automatic landing site detection for UAV using supervised classification. In: Rao, P.J., Rao, K.N., Kubo, S. (eds.) Proceedings of International Conference on Remote Sensing for Disaster Management. SSGG, pp. 309–316. Springer, Cham (2019). https://doi.org/10.1007/978-3-319-77276-9_27
8. Ramalingam, R., Anitha, G., Shanmugam, J.: Microelectromechnical systems inertial measurement unit error modelling and error analysis for low-cost strapdown inertial navigation system. Def. Sci. J. **59**(6), 650–658 (2009)
9. Nagothu, S.K., Anitha, G.: INS - GPS integrated aid to partially vision impaired people using Doppler sensor. In: 2016 3rd International Conference on Advanced Computing and Communication Systems (ICACCS), Coimbatore, pp. 1–4 (2016). https://doi.org/10.1109/ICACCS.2016.7586386
10. Nagothu, S.K., Anitha, G.: Low-cost smart watering system in multi-soil and multi-crop environment using GPS and GPRS. In: Proceedings of the First International Conference on Computational Intelligence and Informatics Volume 507 of the Series Advances in Intelligent Systems and Computing, pp. 637–643. https://doi.org/10.1007/978-981-10-2471-9_61
11. Nagothu, S.K., Anitha, G.: INS-GPS enabled driving aid using Doppler sensor. In: 2015 International Conference on Smart Sensors and Systems (IC-SSS), Bangalore, pp. 1–4 (2015). https://doi.org/10.1109/SMARTSENS.2015.7873619
12. Trohidis, K., Tsoumakas, G., Kalliris, G., Vlahavas, I.: Multilabel classification of music by emotion, EURASIP. J. Audio Speech Music Process. **4**, 1–9 (2011)
13. Yang, D., Lee, W.: Disambiguating music emotion using software agents. In: Proceedings of the 5th International Conference on Music Information Retrieval (ISMIR 2004), Barcelona, Spain (2004)
14. Bhat, A.S., Amith, V.S., Prasad, N.S., Mohan, D.M.: An efficient classification algorithm for music mood detection in western and hindi music using audio feature extraction. In: 2014 Fifth International Conference on Signal and Image Processing, pp. 359–364 (2014). https://doi.org/10.1109/ICSIP.2014.63
15. Thanh, D.T., Shirai, K.: Machine learning approaches for mood classification of songs toward music search engine. In: 2009 International Conference on Knowledge and Systems Engineering. KSE 2009, pp. 144–149 (2009), 13–17 October 2009. https://doi.org/10.1109/KSE.2009.10

High-Performance Residue Arithmetic Based Elliptic Curve Cryptosystem Over GF(p) for Hardware Security

S. Elango[✉], P. Sampath, S. Raja Sekar, and Sajan P. Philip

Department of Electronics and Communication Engineering,
Bannari Amman Institute of Technology, Sathyamangalam, Erode, Tamil Nadu 638 401, India
elangos@bitsathy.ac.in

Abstract. Hardware security is an inevitable one in embedded portable devices. Hardware uniqueness is the key advantage of hardware-based security and a viable alternative to software security. In this paper, residue arithmetic circuits are used to design the point operations in Elliptic Curve Cryptography (ECC) over Galois Field GF (p). Point Multiplication operations in ECC over GF(p) using signed residue arithmetic architectures are developed. A Verilog HDL code is used to model the entire ECC architecture and implemented in Zynq FPGA (XC7Z020CLG484-1) for Proof of Concept (PoC) using TSMC 180 nm, 90 nm and 45 nm standard cell libraries. The ASIC synthesis results, Proposed ECC Point multiplication architectures save the chip area by 7%, improve the operation speed by 17% and PDP savings of 15% compared with direct implementation of point multiplication. Key generation, Encryption, and Decryption operations are done using ECC over GF(p), which shows evidence that this system can secure embedded portable devices.

Keywords: Elliptic Curve Cryptography (ECC) · GF(p) · Hardware security · Residue arithmetic · FPGA · ASIC

1 Introduction

Public Key Cryptography (PKC) is an asymmetric system that consists of two separate keys, namely public key and private key [1, 2]. The widely used PKC algorithms are Rivest–Shamir–Adleman (RSA) Algorithm, Elliptic Curve Cryptography (ECC), Diffie-Hellman Key Exchange, and Digital Signature Standard (DSS). Among the above algorithms, RSA and ECC are preferred for all the applications mentioned above.

ECC has received much attention and scientific interest since it ensures more security with limited key size through challenging underlying mathematical problems. The ECC places a footprint in various applications like Data Security, Key exchange, Digital signature, Authentication, E-Health applications, Internet of Things (IoT), and Vehicular communication. In ECC, the point addition, point doubling, and point multiplication are the key elements. ECC is resisting attacks attempted based on factorization and discrete logarithm.

© Springer Nature Singapore Pte Ltd. 2021
V. Arunachalam and K. Sivasankaran (Eds.): ICMDCS 2021, CCIS 1392, pp. 451–466, 2021.
https://doi.org/10.1007/978-981-16-5048-2_36

ECC algorithm includes a large number of arithmetic operations such as multiplication, addition, and subtraction. Hence the RNS is a suitable candidate to perform such massive arithmetic operations in large integers [3–5]. The point multiplication is performed by successive point doublings and point addition operations. The point operation in ECC relies on modular arithmetic. Thus, the modular arithmetic performance determines the overall performance of the public-key coprocessor in hardware security implementations [6]. Due to the development of low-cost embedded system applications, Lightweight hardware implementation of the crypto algorithms using FPGAs and ASIC design has been a popular research topic [7].

The paper is structured as follows: In Sect. 2, the related works connected to ECC. In Sect. 3, ECC over GF(p) is discussed and proposed VLSI architecture is given in Sect. 4. The Simulation results and analysis are presented in Sect. 5. Application of ECC for data encryption and decryption is presented in Sect. 6. The conclusion is drawn in Sect. 7.

2 Background

The equation for the elliptic curve is derived from the Weierstrass equation. The general form of the equation is

$$b^2 + c_1 ab + c_3 b = a^3 + c_2 a^2 + c_4 a + c_6 \tag{1}$$

The plane form of the Weierstrass equation is considered as the elliptic curve equation as given in (2)

$$b^2 = a^3 + c_1 a + c_2 \tag{2}$$

In general, as a part of providing better security, the key's length is also increased, and performing faster arithmetic operations on larger integers becomes a bottleneck problem in such situations. The computational delay is also increased.

The inception of Elliptic curve cryptosystems is proposed in [8, 9] over finite fields. In the late 1990s, elliptic curve systems started receiving commercial acceptance when accredited standards organizations specified elliptic curve protocols. This made private companies include these protocols in their security products. Since then, an abundance of research has been published on the security and efficient implementation of Elliptic Curve Cryptography (ECC).

Later the development of Elliptic Curve Cryptosystems was surveyed in the dimensions of speed, security, block size, field representation, and implementation issues. Selecting an appropriate field, Efficient implementation of arithmetic in the fields, and Elliptic curve selection are identified metrics that decide the cryptosystems' overall performance [10]. The applications of ECC is extended to e-passport and mobile e-commerce as an authentication protocol [11]. In [12], concentrated on improving the performance of point multiplication operation, which is a crucial element in ECC. RNS Montgomery multiplication with pipelining technique achieves area efficient and high speed of implementation. But the process is a serial approach since it uses a Montgomery multiplication scheme.

In [13], the author proposes a novel ECC processor over a restricted set of prime fields GF(p) by accelerating computationally expensive blocks of modular operations.

This processor supports all five National Institute of Standards and Technology (NIST) recommended primes *(p)* and combines programmability, parallelism, and security features within a system. In [7], presents the implementation of ECC in both the FPGA and ASIC. The concept of the Elliptic curve over the prime field and the binary field are discussed. The mathematical operations like addition, squaring, multiplication, and inversion for both the prime and binary fields are addressed. The design and implementation of the hardware structures for the point multiplication on elliptic curves with minimum overall delay are essential research topics.

The paper [14] deal with implementing ECC architecture represented in jacobian coordinates using various FPGA devices. The Point multiplication algorithms like Double and Add algorithm and Non-Adjacent Form (NAF) Recordings are discussed. The multiplier architecture is developed using the Radix-4 Booth encoded interleaved multiplication. However, it requires 191,815 clock cycles are needed for computation with a key size of 256.

In [6] the author surveyed Lightweight Cryptography using ECC. The fundamentals of ECC and different security schemes of ECC are presented. Moreover, the ECC applications like Digital Signature, Key generation, and Security establishment are discussed. As an outcome of the conducted survey, the general problem in ECC hardware is identified. Long latencies and hardware processing overhead when ECC is used for key establishment and digital signature applications. Thus new hardware architecture can reduce the complexity and latencies of a specific instance of ECC. The paper [15] deal with developing a high-speed Edward25519 based ECC processor for 256-bit point multiplication over the prime field. The latency of the point addition operation is higher than the point doubling operation. The Montgomery ladder algorithm is used for the point multiplication, which is a serial type that required more clock cycles to complete the process.

3   Elliptic Curve Cryptosystem Over GF(p)

In the Elliptic curve cryptosystem, point addition, doubling, and multiplication operations are classified into two types of Galois Field (GF), namely prime field GF(p) and binary field $GF(2^n)$ [16]. The field is the group of numbers that satisfies all addition and multiplication properties, including multiplicative inverse in [6, 7]. The binary field $GF(2^n)$ is denoted using n-bit word polynomial basis expression with a degree of $n-1$. Prime field GF(p) is the signed integer representation in a binary form where elements range from 0 to $p-1$. Each integer in the range has an additive inverse and multiplicative inverse except 0. Galois Field GF(p) number theory plays a significant role in public-key cryptography, and the GF has p integers. This finite number of elements within the field makes it more accessible to algorithmic computation [16]. In ECC, the affine and projective coordinates are the two coordinate systems that offer flexibility to calculate the point addition, point doubling, and point multiplication. Two coordinates P = (a,b) represent affine that consists of more multiplicative inverse operations.

In contrast, the projective is a three-coordinate system consisting of multiplication and temporary registers that eliminate the inverse operation requirement. Prime numbers are essential in crypto processing because the securities of many encryption algorithms are based on the chosen prime number. Factorizing the prime number is a complicated problem and has added advantage in the area of cryptography. Thus, the reverse process to find the prime numbers by factorizing is computer science's unsolved problem [14].

3.1 Point Addition

Let us consider the two different points $P\ (a_1,b_1)$, $Q(a_2,b_2)$ on the considered elliptic curve. The addition of two-point P, Q gives the third Point on the curve called R [19]. Point Addition operation is used to perform the addition of two points on the elliptic curves $R = P + Q$ where $P \neq Q$. The construction is as follows, draw a line that passes through the points P and Q on the curve to obtain the third Point R. Mirror this intersection point $-R$ along the a-axis gives R as given in Fig. 1.

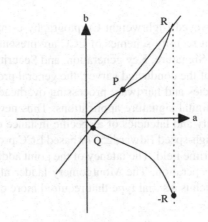

Fig. 1. Point addition

In GF(p) prime field, the curve equation is $b^2 = (a^3 + c_1a + c_2) \mod p$ with $c_1 = 1 \,\& \, c_2 = 0$, then the point addition operation for a given two points $P(a_1, b_1)$ and $Q(a_2, b_2)$ on the elliptic curve is $R(a_3, b_3) = P + Q$. Mathematically, the point a_3, b_3 and slope (S) over GF(p) are expressed as

$$a_3 = \left(S^2 - a_1 - a_2\right) \mod p \tag{3}$$

$$b_3 = (S(a_1 - a_3) - b_1) \mod p \tag{4}$$

$$S = \left(\frac{b_2 - b_1}{a_2 - a_1}\right) \mod p \tag{5}$$

The Eq. (5) is expressed as,

$$S = \left((b_2 - b_1) \times (a_2 - a_1)^{-1}\right) \mod p \tag{6}$$

3.2 Point Doubling

If two points are the same in the elliptic curve, then the point doubling operation is essential to find the third Point. Point doubling is adding two similar points on the elliptic curves $P + Q$ where $P = Q$ and hence, $R = P + P = 2P$ [19]. The construction of point doubling operation is slightly different from point addition. First, draw the line tangent to P and obtain another intersection point (R) between the line and elliptic curve. Now, mirror this Point of intersection along the a-axis. Thus, the mirrored Point is the result $-R$ of Point doubling as given in Fig. 2.

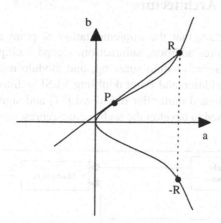

Fig. 2. Point doubling

In GF (p) prime field, the curve equation is $b^2 = \left(a^3 + c_1 a + c_2\right) \bmod p$ with $c_1 = 1$ & $c_2 = 0$, then the Point doubling operation for a given point $P(a_1, b_1)$ on the elliptic curve is $R(a_3, b_3) = P + P = 2P$. Mathematically, the point a_3, b_3 and slope (S) over GF(p) are expressed as

$$a_3 = \left(S^2 - 2a_1\right) \bmod p \tag{7}$$

$$b_3 = (S(a_1 - a_3) - b_1) \bmod p \tag{8}$$

$$S = \left(\frac{3a_1^2 + c_1}{2b_1}\right) \bmod p \tag{9}$$

The Eq. (9) is expressed as,

$$S = \left(\left(3a_1^2 + c_1\right) \times (2b_1)^{-1}\right) \bmod p \tag{10}$$

3.3 Point Multiplication

In general, point multiplication is the Multiplication of the point P with a scalar d to find new point Q, i.e., $dP = Q.\underbrace{P + P + P........P}_{d \text{ times}} = dP = O$. In point multiplication operation, the Point on the elliptic curve is successively added to itself for d scalar times. In ECC, the point multiplication operation is used for key generation application. The point multiplication can be using the Double and Add algorithm [14].

4 Proposed ECC Architecture

The Eqs. (3)–(9) indicates that the implementation of point addition and doubling operation in ECC requires addition, subtraction, signed multiplication, signed modulo (residue) multiplication, modulo squaring, and modulo multiplicative inverse. In this section, the point addition and Point doubling VLSI architecture are derived from the Eqs. (3)–(9). The signed multiplier discussed [17] and signed residue multipliers addressed in [18] are used to develop the architecture represented in Figs. 3 and 4.

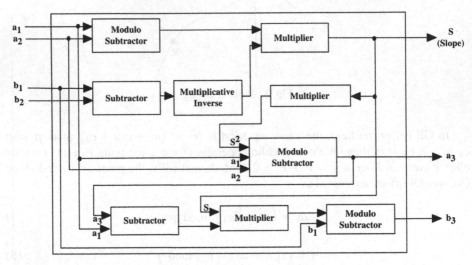

Fig. 3. Point addition architecture

The parallel point multiplication architecture proposed based on the double and add method is shown in Fig. 3. In the proposed point multiplication, the architecture consists of repeated point addition, doubling, Multiplexer, and Tri-state buffers. Architectures in Figs. 3 and 4 are used to develop the point multiplication structure. This architecture precomputes all the possible point doubling operation at the first instance when the MUX selection signal is 1. Then the computed value is immediately added with point addition. This precomputed Point doubling increases the operation speed. Tristate Buffers (B) is used to physically disconnect the previous output path when the MUX selection signal is 0. The proposed point multiplication architecture is represented in Fig. 5.

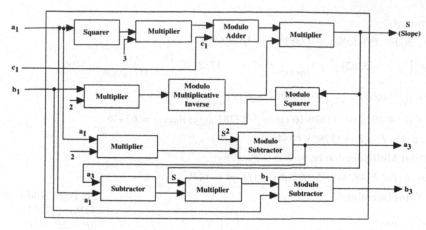

Fig. 4. Point doubling architecture

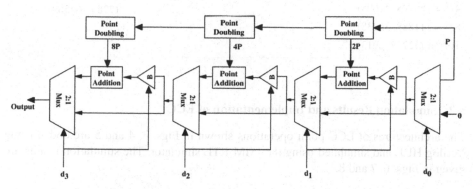

Fig. 5. Proposed point multiplication architecture

5 Results and Analysis

5.1 Numerical Calculation of ECC Operations

1. Point Addition $(a_3, b_3) = (a_1, b_1) + (a_2, b_2)$
$P(a_1, b_1) = P(34625, -42193)\, Q(a_2, b_2) = Q(42931, -53791)$ $p = 65537$
$S = \left\| \left((-11450) \times (42931 - 34625)^{-1} \right) \right\|_{65537} = 56083$
$a_3 = \left\| \left(\left\|(56083)^2\right\|_{65537} - \|(34625 + 42931)\|_{65537} \right) \right\|_{65537} = 39166\, b_3 = \|(\|56083 \times (-4541)\|_{65537} - \|-49123\|_{65537})\|_{65537} = 46072$
$(a_3, b_3) = P + Q = (39166, 46072)$
2. Point Doubling $(a_3, b_3) = P + P$

(continued)

(*continued*)

$P(a_1, b_1) = P(-53821, -47381) c_1 = 1 p = 65537$
$S = \left\| \left(\left\| 3 \times (-53821)^2 + 1 \right\|_{65537} \times \left\| (2 \times (-47381))^{-1} \right\|_{65537} \right) \right\|_{65537} = 54669$
$a_3 = \left\| \left(\left\| (54669)^2 \right\|_{65537} - \|-107642\|_{65537} \right) \right\|_{65537} = 57855$
$b_3 = \|(\|54669 \times (-111676)\|_{65537} - \|-47381\|_{65537})\|_{65537} = 62446$
$(a_3, b_3) = P + P = (57855, 62446)$
3. Point Multiplication $(x, y) = d \times P(a_1, b_1)$
$P(a_1, b_1) = P(48241, -51092) d = 11 (x, y) = 11P$

3a. Point Doubling:	**3b. Point Addition:** $11P = (01011)_2 P = 8P + 2P + 1P$
$1P = (48241, -51092)$	
$2P = (13606, 45101)$	$(x, y) = (7289, 64569)$
$4P = (58798, 41698)$	
$8P = (11888, 36238)$	
$16P = (12227, 8913)$	

5.2 Simulation Results and Implementation of ECC

The architectures of ECC point operations shown in Figs. 3, 4 and 5 are coded using Verilog HDL and simulated using the ISIM RTL simulator. The simulation results are given in Figs. 6, 7 and 8.

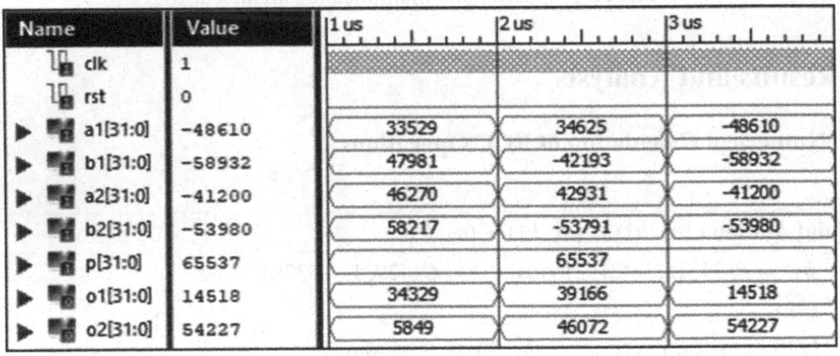

Name	Value	1 us	2 us	3 us
clk	1			
rst	0			
a1[31:0]	−48610	33529	34625	−48610
b1[31:0]	−58932	47981	−42193	−58932
a2[31:0]	−41200	46270	42931	−41200
b2[31:0]	−53980	58217	−53791	−53980
p[31:0]	65537		65537	
o1[31:0]	14518	34329	39166	14518
o2[31:0]	54227	5849	46072	54227

Fig. 6. Simulation result of a 32-bit point addition operation

In Public Key Cryptography (PKC), the point multiplication is used to generate the public key. The scalar d is granted as a private key, and the public key is the point multiplication output of d and random/base points on the curve $P_k(o_1, o_2) = d \bullet P(a_1, b_1)$. Figure 9 shows the simulation output of the key generation using point multiplication.

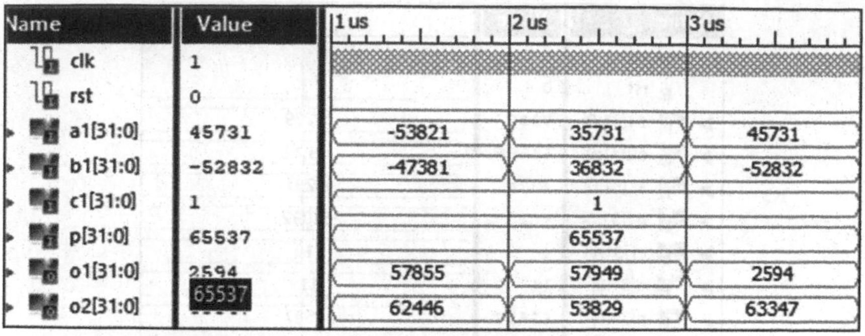

Name	Value	1 us	2 us	3 us
clk	1			
rst	0			
a1[31:0]	45731	-53821	35731	45731
b1[31:0]	-52832	-47381	36832	-52832
c1[31:0]	1		1	
p[31:0]	65537		65537	
o1[31:0]	2594	57855	57949	2594
o2[31:0]	65537	62446	53829	63347

Fig. 7. Simulation result of a 32-bit Point doubling operation

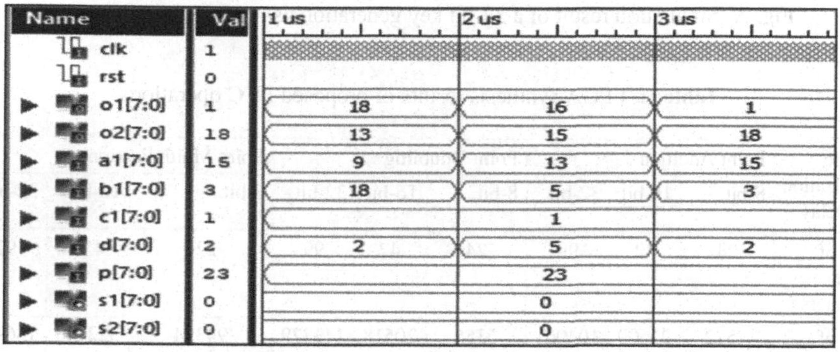

Name	Val	1 us	2 us	3 us
clk	1			
rst	0			
o1[7:0]	1	18	16	1
o2[7:0]	18	13	15	18
a1[7:0]	15	9	13	15
b1[7:0]	3	18	5	3
c1[7:0]	1		1	
d[7:0]	2	2	5	2
p[7:0]	23		23	
s1[7:0]	0		0	
s2[7:0]	0		0	

Fig. 8. Simulation result of an 8-bit Point multiplication operation

In Fig. 9, $d = 11$ is considered as the private key, and the random/base point is (a_1,b_1) $= (48241, -51092)$. Then the public key is computed from the point multiplication between d and (a_1,b_1), then the public key is $(o_1,o_2) = (7239,64569)$. It is impossible to find the d value (i.e., private key) from the public key.

5.3 FPGA Synthesis Results of Proposed ECC Operations

The FPGA synthesis results of proposed and existing ECC architectures are presented in Table 1. It shows the time delay and LUT's required to execute the algorithm concerning the Xilinx XC7Z020CLG484-1 FPGA device. Further, the proposed concept is verified by deploying 8-bit point multiplication using the Xilinx ZED Board. HDL supported debug Intellectual Property (IP) core is used along with the proposed design to implement the point multiplication operation successfully.

5.4 ASIC Synthesis Results of ECC Operations

The architectures of the proposed ECC point operations and existing ECC operation structures are synthesized in the ASIC platform by considering the CMOS technology

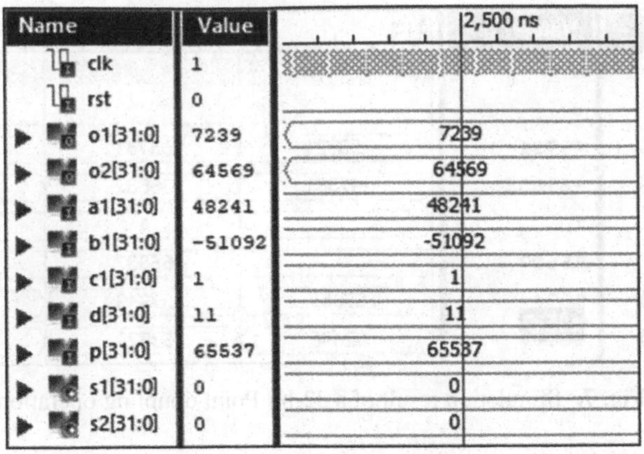

Name	Value	2,500 ns
clk	1	
rst	0	
o1[31:0]	7239	7239
o2[31:0]	64569	64569
a1[31:0]	48241	48241
b1[31:0]	-51092	-51092
c1[31:0]	1	1
d[31:0]	11	11
p[31:0]	65537	65537
s1[31:0]	0	0
s2[31:0]	0	0

Fig. 9. Simulation result of a 32-bit key generation using point multiplication

Table 1. FPGA synthesis results of proposed ECC operations

Logic Utilization & Delay	Point Addition			Point Doubling			Point Multiplication		
	8-bit	16-bit	32-bit	8-bit	16-bit	32-bit	8-bit	16-bit	32-bit
No. of slice registers	24	42	99	24	42	99	224	453	922
No. of slice LUTs	4572	21600	104061	6355	20518	143879	94334	322146	1869690
No. of bonded IOBs	58	114	226	50	98	194	58	114	226
Logic Delay (ns)	191	531	1217	299	601	2137	15600	41490	53750
Routing Delay (ns)	166	262	535	209	219	797	4160	17790	25290
Total Delay (ns)	357	793	1752	508	820	2934	19760	59280	79040

nodes of 180 nm, 90 nm, and 45 nm. The area, power, delay, and PDP synthesis results are given for 180 nm, 90 nm, and 45 nm from Tables 2, 3 and 4.

5.5 Performance Analysis of ECC Operations

In ASIC synthesis Tables 2, 3 and 4, the results indicate that the proposed Point doubling VLSI architecture shows a maximum area reduction of 6%, a maximum of 9% delay, and 17% PDP reduction compared with the existing implementation. Power consumption decrease to a maximum of 8% in the proposed Point doubling architecture. The area of the proposed point addition architecture is increased by 4%. Due to a 5% increase

Table 2. ASIC synthesis results of ECC operations (180 nm)

Multiplier	N	Area (μm^2)	Power (μW)	Delay (ns)	PDP (nJ)
180 nm					
ECC direct implementation					
Point addition	8	90854	33619	193	6.5
	16	494541	365424	918	336
	32	2438660	3044755	4114	12526
Point doubling	8	99326	28643	215	6.2
	16	463166	275964	996	275
	32	2619793	2483872	4238	10527
Point multiplication	8	1347546	418795	8330	3489
	16	15977957	1053757	78440	82657
	32	191735484	21055111	862841	18167213
ECC using residue arithmetic					
Point addition	8	94221	35425	201.6	7.1
	16	512866	385054	959	369
	32	2529022	3208314	4298	13789
Point doubling	8	95085	27133	197	5.3
	16	443388	261416	928	242
	32	2507921	2352930	3856	9072
Point multiplication	8	1329557	421049	7690	3238
	16	15764654	1059425	70740	74944
	32	180231348	21845213	709021	15488715

in power dissipation and delay, there is an increase in PDP of point addition by 10% compared with existing ECC.

In point multiplication, the proposed architecture achieves maximum area reduction of 6.5%. The precomputation of all the possible point doubling operation is done at the very first instance. The MUX selects the point doubling operation immediately when it is necessary, and the precomputed point doubling increases the operation speed. Hence there is a delay reduction of 17% and PDP reduction of 15% in the proposed VLSI point multiplication architecture. However, there is an increase in power consumption of proposed point multiplication by 4% due to more switching in multiplexer implementation. The graphical representation of the results is given in Fig. 10.

Table 3. ASIC synthesis results of ECC operations (90 nm)

Multiplier	N	Area (μm^2)	Power (μW)	Delay (ns)	PDP (nJ)
90 nm					
ECC direct implementation					
Point addition	8	40884	5670	103	0.6
	16	222543	59372	488	29
	32	1097397	472468	2506	1184
Point doubling	8	44697	5171	116	0.6
	16	208425	44999	532	24
	32	1178907	382709	2577	986
Point multiplication	8	606396	83822	4561	382
	16	7190081	169811	43451	7378
	32	86280968	3056598	477952	1460907
ECC using residue arithmetic					
Point addition	8	42399	5931	108	0.64
	16	230789	62293	512	31.8
	32	1138060	498544	2629	1310
Point doubling	8	42788	4894	107	0.5
	16	199525	42589	493	21
	32	1128564	362212	2370	858
Point multiplication	8	598301	84728	4241	359
	16	7094094	170698	38401	6555
	32	81104107	3180135	404202	1285417

Table 4. ASIC synthesis results of ECC operations (45 nm)

Multiplier	N	Area (μm^2)	Power (μW)	Delay (ns)	PDP (nJ)
45 nm					
ECC direct implementation					
Point addition	8	19216	7246	49	0.35
	16	104595	47397	199	9.4
	32	515777	359827	1053	379

(*continued*)

Table 4. (*continued*)

Multiplier	N	Area (μm^2)	Power (μW)	Delay (ns)	PDP (nJ)
Point doubling	8	21008	6128	54	0.33
	16	97960	37285	218	8.1
	32	554086	290006	1051	305
Point multiplication	8	285006	88775	2620	233
	16	3379338	136597	24120	3295
	32	40552055	1707463	217081	370658
ECC using residue arithmetic					
Point addition	8	19928	7493	51	0.38
	16	108471	49013	207	10
	32	534888	372095	1095	407
Point doubling	8	20110	5619	49	0.27
	16	93777	34188	198	6.7
	32	530425	265917	953	253
Point multiplication	8	281201	89029	2440	217
	16	3334224	136910	20840	2853
	32	38118930	1757358	182641	320966

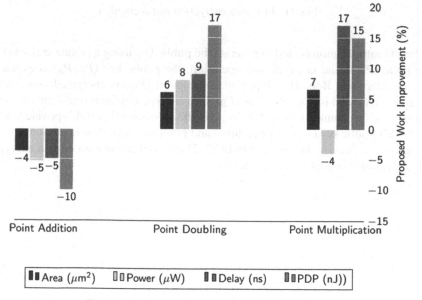

Fig. 10. Performance analyses of ECC operations

6 Application of ECC Point Operations in Hardware ECC Encryption and Decryption

The ECC point operations are used for data encryption and decryption. The complete ECC data encryption and decryption between Alice (sender) and Bob (receiver) require four processes: key generation, key exchange, encryption, and decryption, as shown in Fig. 11.

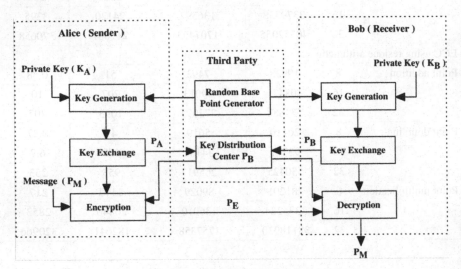

Fig. 11. ECC data encryption and decryption

Point multiplication is used to generate the public key using a private scalar key and base point (P). In the key exchange operation, the public key (P_A, P_B) is exchanged between Alice and Bob. The elliptic message point (P_m) is encrypted using Alice's private key (K_a) and Bob's public key (P_B). The encrypted point is transferred through a communication channel to Bob. Bob decrypts the message using Bob's private key (K_b) and Alice's public key (P_A). Point addition and point multiplication operations are used to encrypt and decrypt the message in ECC. The model calculation of data encryption and decryption using ECC is given below.

Elliptic Curve Equation: $b^2 = a^3 + c_1 a + c_2 \mod p$

Base Point: $P = (1, 18)$ $c_1 = 1$ $c_2 = 0$ $p = 23$

Alice	Bob
Private Key (Alice) $K_a = 3$	Private Key (Bob) $K_b = 5$
Public Key Generation using Private key and Base Point	
$P_A = (K_a \bullet P) \mod p$	$P_B = (K_b \bullet P) \mod p$
$P_A = 3 \bullet (1, 18) \mod 23$	$P_B = 5 \bullet (1, 18) \mod 23$
By Point Multiplication	By Point Multiplication
$P_A = (1, 5)$	$P_B = (1, 18)$

Key Exchange $P_A \leftrightarrow P_B$

Encryption (Alice)

Consider the message (in Elliptic Points): $P_m \leftarrow m$. Let's assume elliptic message points $P_m = (11, 13)$ then the Encrypted message point is
$P_E = (P_m + (K_a \bullet P_B)) \mod p$
$(K_a \bullet P_B) = (3 \bullet (1, 18)) \mod 23 = (1, 5)$
$P_E = ((11, 13) + (1, 5)) \mod 23$
Encrypted message point $P_E = (19, 22)$

P_E Transmitted through Channel

Decryption (Bob)

Consider the encrypted message point $P_E = (19, 22)$
The decrypted message point is $P_m = (P_E - P_k) \mod p$
$P_k = (K_b \bullet P_A) \mod p = 5 \bullet (1, 5) \mod 23 = (1, 5)$

$P_m = ((19, 22) - (1, 5)) \mod 23$

$P_m = ((19, 22) + (1, -5)) \mod 23$

Decrypted message point $P_m = (11, 13)$

---

7 Conclusion

Point doubling ECC operation using signed residue multiplier architectures have shown the appreciable amount of performance improvement when compared with existing work. Proposed ECC point multiplication architectures save the chip area by 7%, improves the operation speed by 17% and PDP savings by 15% compared with direct implementation of point multiplication. Hence this high-performance residue arithmetic based Elliptic Curve Cryptosystem over GF(p) architecture can be efficiently used to secure embedded hardware systems.

References

1. Adleman, L.M., Rivest, R.L.: The use of public key cryptography in communication system design: a public key cryptosystem can be synergistically combined with a traditional system to obtain the best features of both approaches. IEEE Commun. Soc. Mag. **16**, 20–23 (1978). https://doi.org/10.1109/MCOM.1978.1089778

2. Dolev, D., Yao, A.C.: On the security of public key protocols. IEEE Trans. Inf. Theory. **29**, 198–208 (1983). https://doi.org/10.1109/TIT.1983.1056650

3. Sung-Ming, Y., Kim, S., Lim, S., Moon, S.: RSA speedup with residue number system immune against hardware fault cryptanalysis. In: Kim, K. (ed.) ICISC 2001. LNCS, vol. 2288, pp. 397–413. Springer, Heidelberg (2002). https://doi.org/10.1007/3-540-45861-1_30

4. Kenny, J.R., Robinson, C.: Embedded software assurance for configuring secure hardware. IEEE Secur. Priv. **8**, 20–26 (2010). https://doi.org/10.1109/MSP.2010.150

5. Antão, S., Sousa, L.: The CRNS framework and its application to programmable and reconfigurable cryptography. Trans. Archit. Code Optim. **9**, 1–25 (2013). https://doi.org/10.1145/2400682.2400692

6. Lara-Nino, C.A., Diaz-Perez, A., Morales-Sandoval, M.: Elliptic Curve Lightweight Cryptography: A Survey. IEEE Access. **6**, 72514–72550 (2018). https://doi.org/10.1109/ACCESS.2018.2881444

7. Rashidi, B.: A survey on hardware implementations of elliptic curve cryptosystems. arXiv Prepr. arXiv:1710.08336 (2017)

8. Miller, V.S.: Use of elliptic curves in cryptography. In: Lecture Notes in Computer Science (including subseries Lecture Notes in Artificial Intelligence and Lecture Notes in Bioinformatics). pp. 417–426. Springer (1986). https://doi.org/10.1007/3-540-39799-X_31.

9. Koblitz, B.N.: Elliptic Curve Cryptosystems. Math. Comput. **4**, 203–209 (1987)

10. Koblitz, N., Menezes, A., Vanstone, S.: The state of elliptic curve cryptography. Towar. Quarter-Century Public Key Cryptogr. **19**, 103–123 (2000). https://doi.org/10.1007/978-1-4757-6856-5_5

11. Chabanne, H., Tibouchi, M.: Securing E-passports with elliptic curves. IEEE Secur. Priv. **9**, 75–78 (2011). https://doi.org/10.1109/MSP.2011.37

12. Esmaeildoust, M., Schinianakis, D., Javashi, H., Stouraitis, T., Navi, K.: Efficient RNS implementation of elliptic curve point multiplication over GF(p). IEEE Trans. Very Large Scale Integr. Syst. **21**, 1545–1549 (2013). https://doi.org/10.1109/TVLSI.2012.2210916.

13. Alrimeih, H., Rakhmatov, D.: Fast and flexible hardware support for ECC over multiple standard prime fields. IEEE Trans. Very Large Scale Integr. Syst. **22**, 2661–2674 (2014). https://doi.org/10.1109/TVLSI.2013.2294649.

14. Javeed, K., Wang, X., Scott, M.: High performance hardware support for elliptic curve cryptography over general prime field. Microprocess. Microsyst. **51**, 331–342 (2017). https://doi.org/10.1016/j.micpro.2016.12.005

15. Islam, M.M., Hossain, M.S., Hasan, M.K., Shahjalal, M., Jang, Y.M.: FPGA implementation of high-speed area-efficient processor for elliptic curve point multiplication over prime field. IEEE Access. **7**, 178811–178826 (2019). https://doi.org/10.1109/ACCESS.2019.2958491

16. Savas, E., Koc, C.K.: Finite field arithmetic for cryptography. IEEE Circuits Syst. Mag. **10**, 40–56 (2010). https://doi.org/10.1109/MCAS.2010.936785

17. Elango, S., Sampath, P.: Implementation of high performance hierarchy-based parallel signed multiplier for cryptosystems. J. Circuits, Syst. Comput. **29** (2020). https://doi.org/10.1142/S021812662050214X.

18. Sekar, E., Palaniswami, S.: Hardware implementation of residue multipliers based signed RNS processor for cryptosystems. Inf. MIDEM. **50**, 71–86 (2020). https://doi.org/10.33180/InfMIDEM2020.201.

19. Leonel, S., Samuel, A., Paulo, M.: Combining residue arithmetic to design efficient cryptographic circuits and systems. IEEE Circuits Syst. Mag. **16**(4), 1–2 (2016)

Performance Improvement of Inorganic Lead-Free Perovskite Solar Cell

Neelima Singh, Alpana Agarwal[✉], and Mohit Agarwal

Department of Electronics and Communication Engineering,
Thapar Institute of Engineering and Technology, Patiala 147001, India
alpana@thapar.edu

Abstract. This paper simulates the lead-free or non-toxic PSC (perovskite solar cell) based on cesium tin germanium halide ($CsSnGeI_3$). The effect of different electron transport layers is understood by mutually related the built-in potential (V_{bi}) with the open circuit voltage (V_{OC}). The simulation study reveals that electron transport layer (ETL) shows a crucial effect on the photovoltaic performance (PV performance) of solar cell. It is obtained from simulation, that ZnOS (Zincoxysulfide) as an ETL shows better device efficiency. Further, the PV performance is optimized based on the defect density (DD) of perovskite absorber layer. The proposed work depicts that at the optimum defect density of 1×10^{14} cm^{-3} a remarkable device efficiency is achieved *i.e.,* ~ 25.43%.

Keywords: Lead-free · All-inorganic · ETL · Defect density

1 Introduction

The increasing utilization of non-renewable source of energy enhances a global demand of renewable energy sources which makes solar energy as one of the most prominent candidates among various alternatives. The organic-inorganic lead halide based perovskite gains a huge attention due to its low cost, solution processing methodology, low charge carriers binding energy, excellent charge carrier mobility [1, 2]. Due to these outstanding properties, the solar cell device efficiency (η) surpasses to 23.7% [3–7]. However, despite of these gradual development the existence of noxious lead (Pb) will hamper its potential towards commercialization. This raises a considerable interest towards the development of non-toxic PSC. Several tin based alternatives are explored including $(MA/FA)SnI_3$, still limited device efficiency of ~ 9% is achieved with low device stability [8]. The limited stability is ascribed to the presence of organic group which is volatile in nature. In this context, $CsSnI_3$ is considered a feasible approach for the application of non-toxic PSC application. However, $CsSnI_3$ based perovskite exhibits phase instability ascribed to the rapid oxidation of Sn cation from (Sn (II) oxidation state to Sn (IV) oxidation state) [9]. To mitigate this instability issue Min Chen *et al.,* fabricates the Sn-Ge composite ($CsSnGeI_3$) which exhibits a PCE of ~ 7% with is considered as a potential alternative for the application of stable PSC [10]. Apart from synthesis, computational analysis is

© Springer Nature Singapore Pte Ltd. 2021
V. Arunachalam and K. Sivasankaran (Eds.): ICMDCS 2021, CCIS 1392, pp. 467–472, 2021.
https://doi.org/10.1007/978-981-16-5048-2_37

also explored by Raghvendra *et al.*, with the device efficiency of 13.29% [11]. Singh *et al.*, demonstrates that CsSnGeI3 is also taken as a feasible substitute for bottom cell for the application of all-perovskite tandem solar cell [12]. Despite of having significant advancement, effect of various charge transport layer (CTL) on the PV performance of all-inorganic non-toxic CsSnGeI3 based PSC is at nascent stage. Hence, the proposed simulation study shows the outcome of various ETL on the PV performance of solar cell. Furthermore, the device performance is realized based on the absorber defect density.

1.1 Device Parameters and Structure

The numerical simulation is performed using SCAPS 1D. SCAPS is a tool capable to solve continuity and Poisson's equations. This tool is widely utilized for the simulation of solar cell owing to its ability to simulate various defect configuration such as bulk, uniform, Gaussian. In our simulation the effect of various ETLs and perovskite absorber defect density is investigated on device performance. Table 1 shows the numerical parameters considered for simulation. Figure 1 shows the schematic of the simulated PSC.

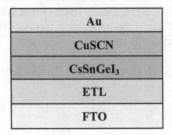

Fig. 1. Device schematic of non-toxic PSC.

Table 1. Material parameters for perovskite absorber layer, TCO layer, electron and hole transport layer [11–15]

Parameters	CuSCN	CsSnGeI3	TiO2	SnO2	STO	ZnOS
Thickness (μm)	0.350	0.400	0.070	0.070	0.070	0.070
Eg(eV)	1.8	1.5	3.26	3.6	3.2	2.83
qχ(eV)	3.4	3.9	4.2	4.5	4	3.6
ε_r	10	9	10	9	8.7	9
μe (cm²/Vs)	2×10^{-4}	9.74×10^2	100	100	5300	1×10^2
μh (cm²/Vs)	1×10^{-2}	2.13×10^2	25	25	660	25
N_D	0	0	10^{19}	10^{20}	10^{16}	2×10^{18}
N_A	10^{18}	10^{14}	0	0	0	0
N_t	10^{14}	10^{16}	10^{15}	10^{15}	10^{15}	10^{15}

2 Results and Discussion

This section includes the investigation of impact of various ETLs on the PV performance of non-toxic PSC. Further study includes the outcome of absorber DD on the non-toxic PSC.

2.1 Outcome of ETL on the Photovoltaic Performance of Non-toxic PSC

In this study the effect of different electron transport layers is analyzed to enhance the PV performance of non-toxic PSC. The optimization of ETLs is performed by finding the relation between built in potential (V_{bi}) with the open circuit voltage V_{OC}. The energy band alignment diagram and energy band diagram of simulated various ETLs are given in Fig. 2 and Fig. 3(a–d) respectively. It is obtained that SnO_2 as an ETL shows lowest device performance whereas ZnOS and TiO_2 shows high device performance as given in Table 2 and Fig. 4. It is also found from the Table 2 that V_{bi} is greatly depend on E_{CBETL}-E_{VBHTL} and φ_{FC}-E_{VBHTL}. Whenever, E_{CBETL}-E_{VBHTL} is smaller than φ_{FC}-E_{VBHTL} then the built-in potential nearer or equal to E_{CBETL}-E_{VBHTL}. However, when E_{CBETL}-E_{VBHTL} is greater than φ_{FC}-E_{VBHTL} then the built-in potential mainly influenced by φ_{FC}-E_{VBHTL}. Also, higher V_{bi} leads to highest V_{OC} and thus the power conversion efficiency. The lowest V_{OC} of SnO_2 is mainly due to its lower E_{CBETL}-E_{VBHTL} value of 0.70 eV hence its V_{OC} is limited to 0.74 eV. Due to higher V_{bi} of ZnOS and its higher efficiency, ZnOS (Zinc oxysulfide) is recommended as a potential ETL for $CsSnGeI_3$ based PSC.

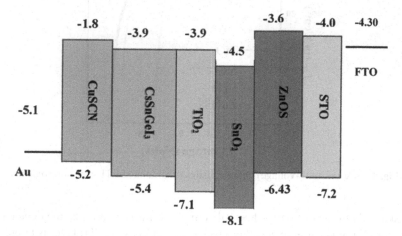

Fig. 2. Energy level alignment for various material used in simulation.

2.2 Outcome of DD of Absorber Layer on the PV Performance of Non-toxic PSC

The defect density within a perovskite absorber layer shows a crucial role on the PV performance. Despite of the ETL optimization the PCE is limited to ~ 20% with the

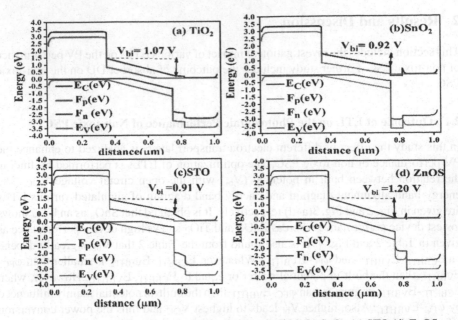

Fig. 3. Energy band diagram of simulated ETLs (a) TiO$_2$ (b) SnO$_2$ (c) STO (d) ZnOS.

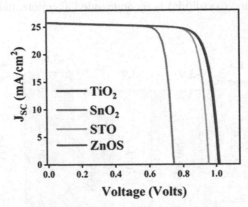

Fig. 4. J–V (current -voltage) characteristics of simulated ETLs for non-toxic PSC.

perovskite DD of the order of ~ 1×10^{16} cm^{-3}. To further optimize the device performance the DD of perovskite absorber layer with ZnOS as an ETL layer is altered from
1×10^{14} cm^{-3} to 1×10^{18} cm^{-3} as depicted in Fig. 5(a–b).

Figure 5a and b demonstrates the outcome of variation of DD on the photovoltaic
performance. It is illustrated from Fig. 5(a–b) that as the DD changes from 1×10^{16}
cm^{-3} to 1×10^{14} cm^{-3}, the V$_{OC}$, FF and η elevates s up to 1.19V, 82.52% and 25.43%.
However, small variation in J$_{SC}$ is observed. From the simulation, it can be summarized
that as DD of perovskite absorber layer reduces, it decreases the recombination due to
reduction of recombination centers. Moreover, the lifetime of the charge carrier enhances

Table 2. Impact of φ_{FC}-E_{VBHTL}, E_{CBETL}-E_{VBHTL}, V_{bi} on the PV performance of PSC.

Different ETL combination	φ_{FC}-E_{VBHTL}	E CB_ETL -E_{VB_HTL} (eV)	Vbi (V)	J_{SC} (mA/cm^2)	VOC (Volts)	η (%)	FF (%)
TiO$_2$	0.9	1.30	1.07	25.76	1.01	20.61	78.98
SnO$_2$	0.9	0.70	0.92	25.70	0.74	15.71	82.37
STO	0.9	1.20	0.91	25.80	0.95	20.00	81.30
ZnOS	0.9	1.60	1.20	25.76	1.01	20.77	79.10

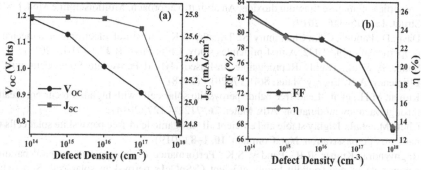

Fig. 5. Effect of variation of perovskite (CsSnGeI$_3$) defect density (a) V_{OC} and J_{SC} (b) FF and η.

with the decrement of the absorber layer defect density which further improves the device shunt resistance. Hence, the device performance of PSC is mainly determined by the DD of the perovskite layer. In addition, by optimizing the ETL layer and defect density of CsSnGeI$_3$ perovskite layer, PCE reaches upto ~ 25.43% which is the highest efficiency reported so far with this absorber layer.

3 Conclusion

This manuscript presents the numerical simulation of non-toxic CsSnGeI$_3$ based PSC. The simulation study reveals that the higher built- in potential leads to the higher device performance. Our proposed simulation suggests that different ETLs and defect density impact the PV performance significantly. It is also found that ZnOS as an ETL layer is considered as a promising candidate to attain device efficiency of ~ 20%. Further, with the optimization of DD of CsSnGeI$_3$ based perovskite layer the overall device performance reaches upto 25.43%.

Acknowledgement. We express our gratitude to Dr. Marc Burgelman (University of Gent, Belgium) for providing the access to SCAPS 1D software.

References

1. Kim, Y.H., et al.: Multicolored organic/inorganic hybrid perovskite light-emitting diodes. Adv. Mater. **27**, 1248–1254 (2015)
2. Dou, L., et al.: Solution-processed hybrid perovskite photodetectors with high detectivity. Nat. Commun. **5**, 1–6 (2014)
3. Kim, H.S., Hagfeldt, A., Park, N.G.: Morphological and compositional progress in halide perovskite solar cells. Chem. Commun. **55**, 1192–1200 (2019)
4. Higuchi, H., Negami, T.: Largest highly efficient 203 × 203 mm 2 CH 3 NH 3 PbI 3 perovskite solar modules. Jpn. J. Appl. Phys. **57**, 08RE11 (2018)
5. Zhou, D., Zhou, T., Tian, Y., Zhu, X., Tu, Y.: Perovskite-based solar cells: materials, methods, and future perspectives. J. Nanomaterials **2018**, Article id. 8148072 (2018)
6. Dash, D., Pandey, C.K., Chaudhary, S., Tripathy, S.K.: Structural, electronic, and mechanical properties of anatase titanium dioxide: An ab-initio approach. Multidiscipline Model. Mater. Struct. **15**, 306–316 (2019)
7. Dash, D., Pandey, C.K., Chaudhury, S., Tripathy, S.K.: Structural, electronic, and mechanical properties of cubic TiO2: A first-principles study. Chin. Phys. B **27**, 017102 (2018)
8. Shao, S., et al.: Highly Reproducible Sn-Based Hybrid Perovskite Solar Cells with 9% Efficiency. Adv. Energy Mater. **8**(4), 1702019 (2018)
9. Kumar, M.H., et al.: Lead-free halide perovskite solar cells with high photocurrents realized through vacancy modulation. Adv. Mater. **26**, 7122–7127 (2014)
10. Chen, M., et al.: Highly stable and efficient all-inorganic lead-free perovskite solar cells with native-oxide passivation. Nat. Commun. **10**, 1–8 (2019)
11. Raghvendra, Kumar, R.R., Pandey, S.K.: Performance evaluation and material parameter perspective of eco-friendly highly efficient CsSnGeI3 perovskite solar cell. Superlattices Microstructures **135**, 106273 (2019)
12. Singh, N., Agarwal, A., Agarwal, M.: Numerical Simulation of highly efficient lead-free perovskite layers for the application of all-perovskite multi-junction solar cell. Superlattices and Microstructures **149**, 106750 (2020)
13. Bishnoi, S., Pandey, S.K.: Device performance analysis for lead-free perovskite solar cell optimisation. IET Optoelectron. **12**, 185–190 (2018)
14. Rahman, S.I., Faisal, S., Ahmed, S., Dhrubo, T.I.: A comparative study on different HTMs in perovskite solar cell with ZnOS electron transport layer. In: 5th IEEE Region 10 Humanitarian Technology Conference 2017, R10-HTC 2017, pp. 546–550, Dhaka (2018)
15. Hossain, M.I., Alharbi, F.H., Tabet, N.: Copper oxide as inorganic hole transport material for lead halide perovskite based solar cells. Sol. Energy **120**, 370–380 (2015)

Photonic Processing Core for Reconfigurable Electronic-Photonic Integrated Circuit

M. Mubarak Ali[✉], G. Madhupriya, R. Indhumathi,
and Pandiyan Krishnamoorthy

Integrated Optics Lab, Centre for Nonlinear Science and Engineering (CeNSE),
SASTRA Deemed University, Thanjavur 613401, Tamil Nadu, India
mubarakali@sastra.ac.in, krishpandiyan@ece.sastra.edu

Abstract. This article proposes a reconfigurable silicon photonic processing core (PPC), an array of reversible photonic gates and reconfigurable switch matrix (RSM) arranged in a systematic way. The RSM includes tunable directional couplers (TDC), provides the features namely broadband operation, low insertion loss and compact layout. The reconfiguration of photonic processing core is accomplished using the silicon based electro-optic P-i-N carrier injection mechanism. The photonic processing core is modeled using the 2D finite difference beam propagation method (FD-BPM). Finally, a compact numerical model (CNM) is developed utilizing the transmission and loss characteristics. The all-pass ring-resonator (RR) is configured in the proposed photonic processing core and the performance metrics are measured with the values of free-spectral range (FSR) of 8 nm, full-width half-maximum (FWHM) of 0.63 nm, finesse value of 12.6984, and quality factor (Q-factor) of 2460. The developed CNM is coded using MATLAB to verify its suitability for reconfigurable electronic-photonic integrated circuit (RePIC) that supports high-performance computing applications.

Keywords: Photonic core · Tunable directional coupler · Reversible photonic gate · Reconfigurable electronic-photonic IC

1 Introduction

The application specific photonic integrated circuit perform dedicated functions, where the intended function is permanent after manufacturing. Reconfigurable photonic ICs are capable of performing multiple functionality in the same photonic IC after manufacturing, which reduces the development time, and cost leads to hardware flexibility. The reconfigurable photonic IC is implemented with different structures such as square, rectangular, triangular and hexagonal with array of either 2 × 2 MZI or 2 × 2 directional couplers. With the suitable configuration of each element, the required photonic applications can be mapped. The MZI based photonic array resulted more insertion loss and larger layout

© Springer Nature Singapore Pte Ltd. 2021
V. Arunachalam and K. Sivasankaran (Eds.): ICMDCS 2021, CCIS 1392, pp. 473–484, 2021.
https://doi.org/10.1007/978-981-16-5048-2_38

dimensions, which limits the dense integration of configurable Mach-Zhender interferometer (MZI) or directional coupler (DC) as the photonic elements [1].

In 2 × 2 MZI based crossbar switches the light either propagated to through/bar port or to the cross port. The MZI has the following problems such as the phase-error, larger-foot print and power imbalance in the upper and lower arms. The phase-errors in MZI switch leads to an undesirable interference effects other than required constructive and destructive interferences. However, with the inclusion of two phase-shifters at the upper and lower arm the unwanted interference effect will be compensated. Among two phase-shifters, one phase-shifter is used for controlling the phase-error and other is used to provide required phase shift.

For silicon based MZI switches, modulation and phase-shifting are realized using free carrier plasma dispersion effect by one of the following mechanism namely, carrier injection (forward biased P-i-N junction), carrier depletion (reverse biased P-N junction), and carrier accumulation (MOS capacitor structure). The carrier-injection produces insertion loss due to the free-carrier absorption [2]. At the same time, additional phase-shifter increases the insertion loss, the larger-foot print of the MZI structure is not suitable for large-scale integration of photonic components. A recent review of different types of photonic switches has been given in [3].

The intrinsic problems with directional coupler such as cross talk due to the undesirable coupling and the attenuation makes approximately 100% power transfer. Hence, with the selection of proper manufacturing process, the above mentioned problems can be tolerated. Reconfigurable photonic ICs are emerging due to its proven ability to solve complex real-world problems, features namely faster and power efficient operation makes it the best candidate for high-performance computing applications. The inherent wavelength multiplexing capability makes the photonic circuit to handle multiple light signals in parallel, which ensures faster operation. The photonic component which uses mode coupling mechanism [4–7] occupies less foot print compared to the photonic component which uses the interferometric principles. Due to this reduced footprint, it consumes lesser power compared to digital electronic realization counterpart.

The proposed photonic processing core include an array of reversible photonic gate [8–11] and tunable directional coupler based reconfigurable switch matrix, serves as the generic building block, that can be used to perform any photonic functionality with the required configuration. The circuit simulation approach is followed by deigning compact numerical model of the reconfigurable components simulated using finite-difference beam propagation method [12]. The proposed core find applications in the field of reconfigurable photonic ICs, programmable photonic arrays, deep learning networks, microwave photonics, waveguide meshes, digital photonics, optical switching and high speed data centers [13–18].

2   Photonic Processing Core

A photonic processing core comprises of twelve reversible photonic gate (RPG) as the basic processing element as depicted in Fig. 1, in which, six RPGs are responsible for horizontal (left to right and vice-versa) flow of light and another six RPGs are responsible for vertical (top to bottom and vice-versa) flow of light. The routing path of light is controlled through four reconfigurable switching matrix units. The designed reconfigurable directional coupler and the photonic switch matrices are controlled via forward biased P-i-N carrier injection plasma dispersion effect.

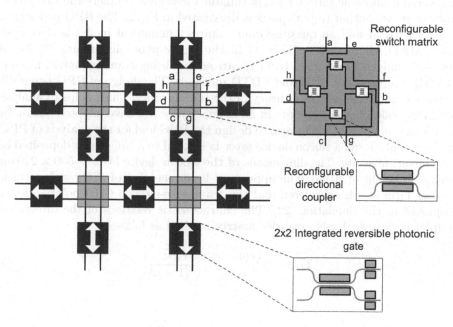

Fig. 1. The schematic representation of the proposed photonic processing core (Not to scale).

2.1   Reconfiguration Mechanism in Silicon Photonics

The silicon photonics plays a vital role in microwave photonics, optical sensing and data center applications. The electro-optic modulation in silicon photonics can be achieved by two means with the help of plasma dispersion effect. One is using creating a P-i-N junction, where a carrier injection mechanism is involved and the second one is using PN junction, where carrier depletion principle is used. The refractive index of the silicon is controlled by means of varying the density of charge carriers present in the silicon waveguide. The change in refractive index (Δn) by means of change in carrier density at 1550 nm is described by well known Soref equations as follows [19]. However, the change in carrier density also leads to the change in absorption ($\Delta\alpha$) of the waveguide, which can be described as follows:

$$\Delta n = -5.4 \times 10^{-22} \Delta N^{1.011} - 1.53 \times 10^{-18} \Delta P^{0.838} \tag{1}$$

$$\Delta\alpha = 8.88 \times 10^{-21} \Delta N^{1.167} + 5.84 \times 10^{-20} \Delta P^{1.109} \tag{2}$$

where ΔN and ΔP are the carrier densities of electrons and holes $[cm^{-3}]$ respectively.

2.2 Reversible Photonic Gate

A reversible photonic gate consists of tunable directional couplers and two phase-shifters at two output (input) ports is illustrated in Fig. 2. The RPG is designed using FD-BPM and an quasi-rigorous compact numerical model is developed using MATLAB to utilize the RPG in the larger photonic circuits [20, 21]. A detailed analysis of designed RPG is carried out using transfer matrix method (TMM), full vectorial BPM and FDTD methods. The design of RPG using different methods ensures the accuracy of the functionality, which helps to analysis the large scale photonic circuits in an efficient way. We have adopted silicon on insulator (SoI) photonic platform to design the RPG and for the analysis of PPC. In the SoI platform, a silicon device layer is bonded to a SiO_2 layer deposited on the silicon substrate. The dimensions of the silicon device layer is $500 \times 220\,\text{nm}$ with slab height of 90 nm. The upper and lower cladding of SiO_2 with a thickness of $1\,\mu\text{m}$ size is considered and the transverse-electric (TE) polarization is employed in the simulation [22]. The characteristic relations of the directional coupler is expressed using transfer matrix method as follows.

$$T_{DC} = \begin{bmatrix} \sqrt{(1-\kappa)} & i\sqrt{\kappa} \\ i\sqrt{\kappa} & \sqrt{(1-\kappa)} \end{bmatrix} \tag{3}$$

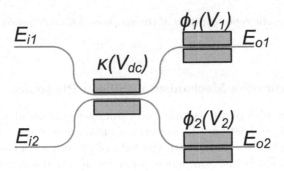

Fig. 2. The schematic representation of the designed reversible photonic gate (Not to scale).

where, κ represents the field-coupling factor of the directional coupler. The phase-shifter (PS) in the top and bottom ports of the output arm is given using the following relation.

$$T_{PS} = \begin{bmatrix} e^{j\phi_1} & 1 \\ 1 & e^{j\phi_2} \end{bmatrix} \tag{4}$$

where, the ϕ_1 and ϕ_2 are the phase-shifts introduced by the phase-shifters in the top and bottom phase-shifters respectively. The final linear transformation matrix of the proposed reconfigurable directional coupler is obtained using Eqs. (3) and (4).

$$T_{RPG} = \begin{bmatrix} e^{j\phi_1} & 1 \\ 1 & e^{j\phi_2} \end{bmatrix} \begin{bmatrix} \sqrt{(1-\kappa)} & i\sqrt{\kappa} \\ i\sqrt{\kappa} & \sqrt{(1-\kappa)} \end{bmatrix} \tag{5}$$

Finally, the input and output electric fields of the light with the transfer matrix T_{RPG} are described as follows.

$$\begin{bmatrix} E_{o1} \\ E_{o2} \end{bmatrix} = \begin{bmatrix} \sqrt{(1-\kappa)} & j\sqrt{\kappa} \\ j\sqrt{\kappa} & \sqrt{(1-\kappa)} \end{bmatrix} \begin{bmatrix} e^{j\phi_1} & 1 \\ 1 & e^{j\phi_2} \end{bmatrix} \begin{bmatrix} E_{i1} \\ E_{i2} \end{bmatrix} \tag{6}$$

where, the E_{i1}, and E_{i2} are the electric fields of the input lights. The parameters E_{o1}, and E_{o2} represents the output electric fields of the light. The voltage controlled field-coupling factor $\kappa(V_{dc})$ is described by means of plasma dispersion effect as follows.

$$\kappa(V_{dc}) = sin\left[\frac{\pi \Delta n_{eff}(V_{dc})L_c}{\lambda}\right] \tag{7}$$

where, L_c is the length of the coupling region. The driving scheme for the designed RPG is shown in Fig. 3. The reconfiguration is achieved using a dedicated driver circuit, the respective control signal is delivered by the FPGA. Here, in the proposed RPG, three control signals are required to control the central tunable directional coupler, and two phase-shifters in the top and bottom waveguides. The voltage controlled phase-shift in the top arm is given by the following relation.

$$\phi_1(V_1) = \left[\frac{2\pi L \Delta n_{eff}(V_1)}{\lambda}\right] \tag{8}$$

Similarly, the voltage controlled phase-shift at the bottom arm is given by,

$$\phi_2(V_2) = \left[\frac{2\pi L \Delta n_{eff}(V_2)}{\lambda}\right] \tag{9}$$

where, the Δn_{eff} is the change in effective refractive index, λ is the free-space wavelength, and L is the length of the phase-shifter. Hence, the voltage controlled input-output relationship of the reconfigurable directional coupler is given by,

$$\begin{bmatrix} E_{o1} \\ E_{o2} \end{bmatrix} = \begin{bmatrix} \sqrt{(1-\kappa(V_{dc}))} & j\sqrt{\kappa(V_{dc})} \\ j\sqrt{\kappa(V_{dc})} & \sqrt{(1-\kappa(V_{dc}))} \end{bmatrix} \begin{bmatrix} e^{j\phi_1(V_1)} & 1 \\ 1 & e^{j\phi_2(V_2)} \end{bmatrix} \begin{bmatrix} E_{i1} \\ E_{i2} \end{bmatrix} \tag{10}$$

where, the parameters $\kappa(V_{dc})$, $\phi_1(V_1)$, and $\phi_2(V_2)$ are the voltage controlled field-coupling coefficient, top and bottom phase-shift values respectively.

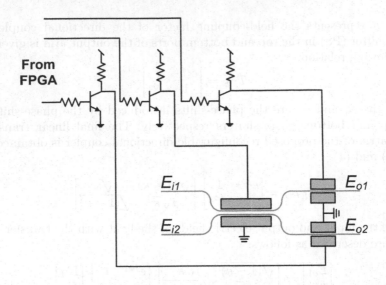

From FPGA

E_{i1} E_{o1}

E_{i2} E_{o2}

Fig. 3. The schematic representation of the designed reversible photonic gate.

2.3   Reconfigurable Switch Matrix

The reconfigurable switch matrix (RSM) shown in Fig. 4, comprises of four tunable directional couplers which allows an arbitrary routing mechanism broadly classified into two categories. One scheme is to allow the routing of signals from top to right, and top to bottom. The second one is to allow the signals from left to right, and left to bottom. The basic routing mechanism depends on the state of the individual tunable directional coupler (TDC) [4]. For example, the path $a{\rightarrow}f$, follows bar-state in TDC_4, and cross-state in TDC_1. At the same time, the path $h{\rightarrow}b$ demands TDC_4 to be in cross-state, TDC_1 to be in bar-state, and TDC_2 to be in bar-state. This is not allowed in the designed RSM. Instead the path $h{\rightarrow}b$ can utilize the bar-state of TDC_4, bar-state of TDC_3, and cross-state of TDC_2, provided the signal routed through TDC_3 and TDC_2 do not demand other than bar-state of TDC_3, and cross-state of TDC_2. The required routing path and the status of individual TDCs is controlled and monitored by the field-programmable gate array (FPGA), since the FPGA acts as the master electronic controller for the driver circuits associated with each RPGs, and RSMs [23]. The only limitation with the designed RSM is not suitable for routing the signals of same wavelength, since the TDC results in undesired interference effect while two signals of same wavelength traverses through the TDC. Hence, the designed TDC demands different wavelength of operation which are in the bandwidth of the TDC to ensure the same state of operation of the two different wavelength. For a single wavelength of operation, the directional coupler is restricted to handle one of the light signal at a time. The wavelength dependent operation of the directional coupler can be handled by the utilization of wavelength independent directional coupler designed by Gupta *et al.* [24].

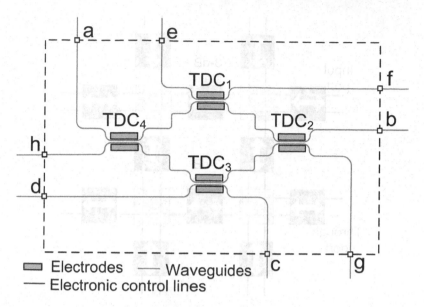

Fig. 4. The designed reconfigurable switch matrix (Not to scale).

3   Results and Discussion

3.1   Configuration of Photonic Processing Core (PPC) as Ring-Resonator

The proposed photonic processing core is configured to perform multiple functions using the same resources. Here in this section we configured the ring-resonator (RR) photonic functionality using the designed PPC is depicted in Fig. 5. In this configuration, the input and output couplers are considered as the access waveguide. The vertical couplers are configured to be in bar-state, the two couplers in the horizontal orientation is configured to be in 3-dB state and provides 90°, as a total phase-shift of 180° is accumulated due to two couplers in 3-dB state, this leads to destructive interference at the through output port under resonance wavelength. Similarly, the constructive interference state is achieved by configuring four RPGs into 90° to create a net phase-shift of 360°, which results in constructive interference effect. Using this configuration, ring-resonator with different round-trip length is established according to the requirement with the minimum round-trip length equals to the length of the RPG. The length of the RPG is considered as minimum feature size of the ring-resonator, and any maximum round-trip length is possible with the RPG by arranging a similar type photonic processing cores in a systematic way.

The change in resonance condition due the variation in the field coupling voltage is analyzed by varying the field-coupling voltage V_{dc}. The performance of the configured ring-resonator is analyzed for the wavelength range of 1545 to 1560 nm, which are depicted in Fig. 6, Fig. 7, and Fig. 8 for $V_{dc} = 0.914$ V,

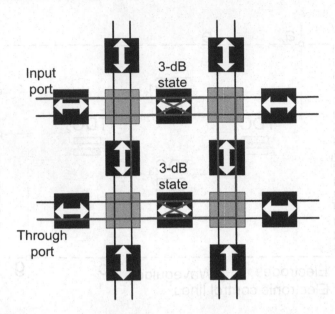

Fig. 5. The schematic representation of ring-resonator (RR) using photonic processing core. The highlighted line shows the configured path of the ring-resonator.

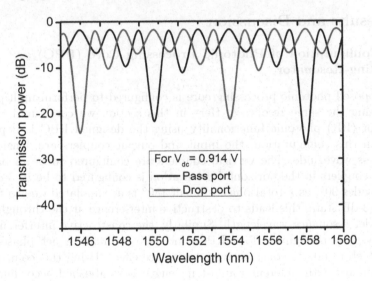

Fig. 6. The transmission characteristics of the ring-resonator configured in the proposed PPC for the field coupling voltage of $V_{dc} = 0.914\,\text{V}$.

0.915 V, and 0.916 V respectively. The overall performance is illustrated in Fig. 9, which includes through/pass port drop-port power levels for three different field-coupling voltages. From the Fig. 9, it is clear that, fluctuations in field-coupling voltage resulted in variation in pass- and drop-port intensities, and not altered

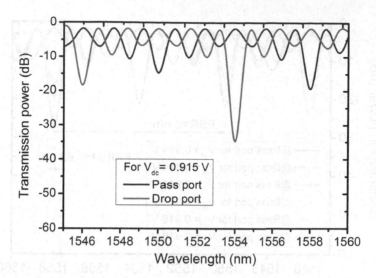

Fig. 7. The transmission characteristics of the ring-resonator configured in the proposed PPC for the field coupling voltage of $V_{dc} = 0.915$ V.

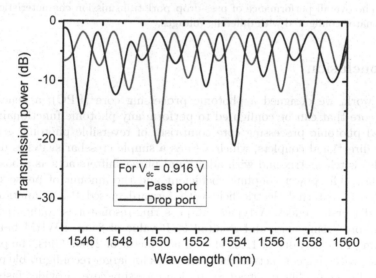

Fig. 8. The transmission characteristics of the ring-resonator configured in the proposed PPC for the field coupling voltage of $V_{dc} = 0.916$ V.

the resonance conditions and FSR value. The configured ring-resonator resulted a FSR value of 8 nm and FWHM bandwidth of 0.63 nm, the Finesse value of 12.6984, and Q-factor value of 2460, which are measured from the configured ring-resonator based on the proposed photonic processing core [25].

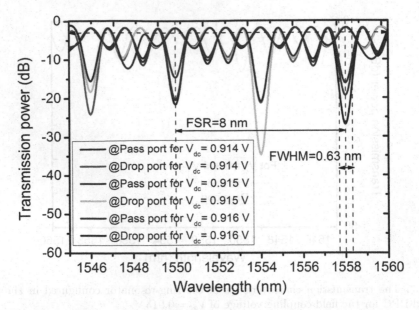

Fig. 9. The overall performance of pass-drop port transmission characteristics of the ring-resonator configured with different voltages.

4 Conclusion

In this work, we designed a photonic processing core (PPC), a generic processing core that can be configured to perform any photonic functionality. The proposed photonic processing core comprises of reversible photonic gates and tunable directional couplers, which acts as a simple crossbar switches in reconfigurable switch matrix and with additional phase shifters acts as a basic functional unit. The power coupling coefficient and the amount of phase-shift are controlled by external electric field with forward biased P-i-N junction based plasma dispersion effect. A typical all-pass ring-resonator is configured in the photonic processing core, and resulted FSR value of 8 nm, FWHM bandwidth of 0.63 nm, Finesse value of 12.6984, and a Q-factor of 2460. Thus, the proposed photonic processing core acts as the basic block for larger reconfigurable photonic integrated circuits. The designed photonic processing core, provides faster operation and reduced power consumption compared to the electronic counter part. Due to the reduced foot-print, the proposed silicon photonic processing core is suitable for large-scaled reconfigurable photonic integrated circuit applications.

Acknowledgment. The authors would like to acknowledge the Science and Engineering Research Board (SERB), Department of Science and Technology (DST), Govt. of India for the financial support (Ref. No.: CRG/2018/001788). The authors also wish to acknowledge SASTRA Deemed University for the research assistantship and the Optiwave Systems Inc for the OptiBPM software package. We gratefully acknowledge the review and recommendations by Dr. Arunachalam V, HOD, Department of Micro and Nanoelectronics, School of Electronics Engineering, VIT University on an earlier version of the manuscript.

References

1. Perez, D., Gasulla, I., Capmany, J.: Field-programmable photonic arrays. Opt. Express **26**(21), 27265 (2018)
2. Akiyama, S., Usuki, T.: High-speed and efficient silicon modulator based on forward-biased pin diodes. Front. Phys. **2**, 1–7 (2014)
3. Tu, X., Song, C., Huang, T., Chen, Z., Fu, H.: State of the art and perspectives on silicon photonic switches. Micromachines **10**, 51 (2019)
4. Perez, D., Gutierrez, A.M., Sanchez, E., Dasmahapatra, P., Capmany, J.: Dual-drive directional couplers for programmable integrated photonics. In: IEEE Photonics Society Summer Topical Meeting Series (SUM), Ft. Lauderdale, FL, USA, pp. 1–2 (2019)
5. Yariv, A.: Coupled-mode theory for guided-wave optics. IEEE J. Quantum Electron. **9**(9), 919–933 (1973)
6. Huang, W.-P.: Coupled-mode theory for optical waveguides: an overview. JOSA A **11**(3), 963–983 (1994)
7. Meerasha, M.A., Meetei, T.S., Madhupriya, G., Rajan, I.R., Varadharajaperumal, M., Pandiyan, K.: The design and analysis of a CMOS-compatible silicon photonic ON–OFF switch based on a mode-coupling mechanism. J. Comput. Electron. **19**(4), 1651–1659 (2020). https://doi.org/10.1007/s10825-020-01550-1
8. Bogaerts, W., Pérez, D., Capmany, J., et al.: Programmable photonic circuits. Nature **586**, 207–216 (2020)
9. Lee, B.G., Dupuis, N.: Silicon photonic switch fabrics: technology and architecture. J. Lightwave Technol. **37**(1), 6–20 (2018)
10. Miller, D.A.B.: Perfect optics with imperfect components. Optica **2**(8), 747–750 (2015)
11. Capmany, J., Perez, D.: Reversible gates for programmable photonics. In: 2019 IEEE Photonics Society Summer Topical Meeting Series (SUM). IEEE (2019)
12. Chung, Y., Dagli, N.: An assessment of finite difference beam propagation method. IEEE J. Quantum Electron. **26**(8), 1335–1339 (1990)
13. Pérez, D., Gasulla, I., Mahapatra, P.D., Capmany, J.: Principles, fundamentals, and applications of programmable integrated photonics. Adv. Opt. Photon. **12**, 709–786 (2020)
14. Lopez, D.P.: Programmable integrated silicon photonics waveguide meshes: optimized designs and control algorithms. IEEE J. Sel. Top. Quantum Electron. **26**(2) (2020)
15. Meerasha, M.A., Pandiyan, K.: Photonic configurable logic block for digital photonic integrated circuits. Electron. Lett. **56**(21), 1130–1133 (2020)
16. Cheng, Q., et al.: Photonic switching in high performance datacenters. Opt. Express **26**(12), 16022–16043 (2018)

17. Soref, R.: Tutorial: integrated-photonic switching structures. APL Photonics **3**(2), 021101 (2018)
18. Tu, X., et al.: State of the art and perspectives on silicon photonic switches. Micromachines **10**(1), 51 (2019)
19. Nedeljkovic, M., Soref, R., Mashanovich, G.Z.: Free-carrier electrorefraction and electroabsorption modulation predictions for silicon over the 1–14-μm infrared wavelength range. IEEE Photonics J. **3**(6), 1171–1180 (2011)
20. Khan, M.U., Xing, Y., Ye, Y., Bogaerts, W.: Photonic integrated circuit design in a foundry+fabless ecosystem. IEEE J. Sel. Top. Quantum Electron. **25**(5) (2019)
21. Bogaerts, W., Chrostowski, L.: Silicon photonics circuit design: methods, tools and challenges. Laser Photonics Rev. **12**(4), 1700237 (2018)
22. Chrostowski, L., Hochberg, M.: Silicon Photonics Design: From Devices to Systems. Cambridge University Press, Cambridge (2015)
23. Faralli, S., et al.: Dynamic switching of a packaged photonic integrated network-on-chip using an FPGA controller. Opt. Lett. **43**(21), 5471–5474 (2018)
24. Gupta, R.K., Chandran, S., Das, B.K.: Wavelength-independent directional couplers for integrated silicon photonics. J. Lightwave Technol. **35**(22), 4916–4923 (2017)
25. Bogaerts, W., et al.: Silicon microring resonators. Laser Photonics Rev. **6**(1), 47–73 (2012)

Author Index

Printed in the United States
by Baker & Taylor Publisher Services